GUINNESS
BOOK OF
WORLD
RECORDS
1983

EEREST WALL: The northwest face of Half Dome in Yosemite, Calif, is 2,200 ft high and nowhere departs more than 7 degrees m the vertical. It took 3 men 5 days to complete the first climb in July 1957. (Photo by Philip Goodliff.)

THE SPACE AGE: When the first Guinness Book was published in 1955, no artificial satellite had yet orbited the Earth and no man had rocketed into space. The space age is not yet 30 years old, but manned and unmanned spacecraft have provided photos from distances approaching 1 billion miles, offering a wholly new perspective of our solar system.

Human achievement literally reached a new high in 1969 when Apollo II astronauts Armstrong and Aldrin landed on the moon, where they snapped this

INTO SPACE AND BACK TO EARTH: Rockets provide the lift needed by the "Columbia" space shuttle to shoot it out of its gantry at the Kennedy Space Center in Cape Canaveral, Florida. The "Columbia" on its various trips carried scientific instruments and even insects (at the suggestion of a teenager). It tested temperatures, ways of handling cargo at space stations, made biological experiments, checked stresses and took infrared photos.

The first authenticated space walk was by Astronaut Ed White (left) who floated for 21 min high over the earth while tethered to the Gemini IV capsule in 1965.

photo (top, far right) of the barren lunar terrain. Planetary research was later taken up by unmanned probes. Viking I landed on Mars in 1976 and took this computer-enhanced photograph, with a 10-min exposure, of a Martian sunset (bottom right) over the Plain of Chryse. The blue to red color variation is explained by a combination of scattering and absorption of sunlight by atmospheric particles. In 1980, Voyager I flew past Saturn (middle right) and sent back this computer composite of photos taken with various filters. It shows subtleties of the rings not visible to the human eye. (All photos courtesy of NASA.)

(Ralph Helfer.)

OLDEST ELEPHANT (above): "Modoc," a female Asiatic elephant, is regarded by some authorities as the oldest non-human land mammal who ever lived. She died at the reported age of 78 in 1974 in Santa Clara, Calif. **MOST VENOMOUS FISH** (left): If you can look long enough at this picture, a face will emerge. This stonefish is thoroughly camouflaged from its enemies as it lies on the bottom in tropical waters of the Indo-Pacific Ocean. Contact with the fins is likely to be fatal.

TOP SHOW DOG (right): Ch. Chik T'Sun of Caversham, a Pekingese from Marietta, Georgia, won 127 awards as "Best in Show" between 1957 and 1960. CHAMPION TURKEY PLUCKER (right, below): Vincent Pilkington of Ireland shows how he set a record of 100 birds killed and plucked in just over 7½ hours, including one in 2 min 44 sec.

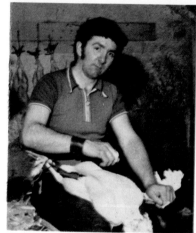

RARE DOG (above): The Shar-Pei or Chinese fighting dog not only has these folds as a baby (shown here) but keeps them as it grows up. Fewer than 200 are known to exist. (Photo from the Walter Skinners.) TALLEST DOG (right): Standing 40½ in high, the Great Dane "Shamgret Danzas" went to Leeds Castle in Kent, England, to appear on TV with his master, G. Comley. He weighs 224 lbs. (Photo by David F. Hoy.)

SLOWEST MOVING LAND MAMMAL (above): The three-toed sloth, or ai, averages only 6–8 ft per min (0.068–0.098 mph) on the ground, making it about twice as fast as the fastest snail (0.03 mph) but only about half as fast as the giant tortoise (0.17 mph). The sloth doubles its speed swinging in the trees, where it can cover 15 ft per min. (Photo by Günter Ziesler.)

SMALLEST HORSE (below): An eyeball-to-eyeball confrontation between a Falabella of Argentina, the most miniature of all horses, and a rooster. These horses, which stand between 15 and 30 in high at the shoulder, were named for their breeder, Julio Falabella, who spent 45 years crossing and recrossing undersized English thoroughbreds with Shetland ponies. Julio Falabella was also the owner of "Firpon," the tallest horse ever documented (see page 61). (Photo by Lynn Kirkman.)

MOST MASSIVE LIVING THING (above): Known as the "General Sherman," this California big tree, a resident of Sequoia National Park, stands 280 ft tall with a girth of 79.8 ft. The 2,145-ton tree theoretically contains the equivalent of 5 billion matches. (Photo, GAF Corporation.)

LARGEST PINNIPED: This specimen of southern elephant seal, who weighs 6,500 lb and is 18 ft 4 in from head to tail, is far from the biggest (9,000 lb).

FRUIT BAT (below) can hear 7½ times better than humans. (Photo by Heather Angel.) LARGEST PINEAPPLE (below, right) weighs 17 lb.

TOP OF THE ROPEWAY (above): This statue called "Christ of the Andes" stands at the summit of the highest aerial cable car ride in the world. The tramway rises from Mérida City, Venezuela (5,879 ft above sea level) to Pico Espejo (15,629 ft), a rise of 10,250 ft. (Photo by Marvin Reiter.)

TOP OF THE WATERFALLS (left): Looking down from a plane at Angel Falls in Venezuela (3,212-ft drop), the steepest cataract in the world, one can see the flow that climbers encounter when they try to descend from the summit in "rappelling." (Photo by David F. Hoy.)

LONGEST ROLLER COASTER: "The Beast" near Cincinnati is 7,400 ft long. (Rick Norton/King's Island photo.) LARGEST VALVE (left): 32 ft in diameter, this is used for engine testing. (Axel Johnson Corp photo.) LARGEST SOLAR ENERGY PLANT (below): Solar One in California consists of 1,818 mirrors this big. (Photo by Franklin Berger.)

TORNADO: Most of these storms wreak great havoc, but this one in 1977 over NW Australia hardly caused any damage as it passed mainly over open fields. (Photo by J. May and C. Crane.)

HIGHEST PRICED PAINTING (above) was Turner's "Juliet and Her Nurse" (see them in lower right corner?) painted in Venice in 1836 and sold for $6,400,000 at Sotheby's auction in N.Y. in 1980.

LARGEST BUILDING CONSTRUCTED OUT OF WATER: The 1,800-ton Ice Palace (below) was built 75 ft 5 in high, entirely with snow and ice by 800 people and 50 bulldozers in Japan in 1980–81.

THE GREAT RED WAY: NYC's Avenue of the Americas was paved with this bright red, star-spangled carpet for the benefit performance of the "Night of 100 Stars" held at Radio City Music Hall on Valentine's Day 1982. Allied Corp contributed the nylon carpet, installing approximately 1,000 feet (52,225 sq ft) in just a few hours. Thousands of ticket holders and close to 300 world-famous entertainers paraded on the carpet after the show on their way to the Actors' Fund Ball at the Hilton nearly three city blocks away.

MOST MATCHBOX LABELS (below): This Japanese phillumenist collected 577,087 different pieces.

MOST CAPACIOUS HOTEL LOBBY (top picture): The Grand Hotel in Taipei, Taiwan, has a floor area measuring 154 x 114 ft (or more than two-fifths of an acre). The decorative ceiling is 31½ ft high. EIFFEL TOWER CLIMBER (left) Jean-Claude Droyer, with the assistance of one man but without mechanical help, climbed the 984 ft to the top of the tower in 2 hrs 18 min 15 sec. (Photo by David F. Hoy.) TREE-EATER (above) Jay Gwaltney ate an 11-ft-tall birch sapling in 89 hrs to win a $10,000 first prize given by a Chicago radio station for doing "the most outrageous thing." (Photo from WKQX.)

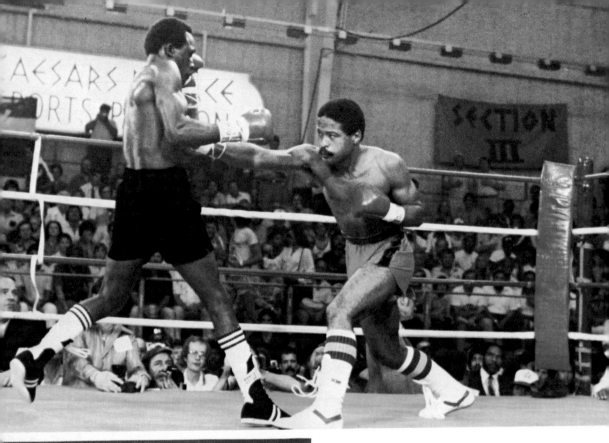

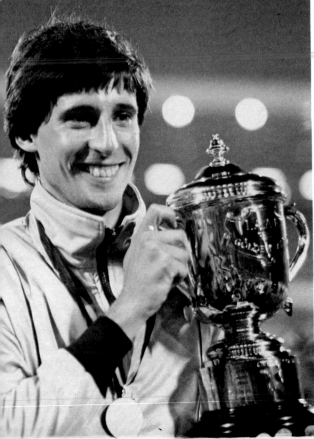

YOUNGEST CHAMPION (above): Wilfredo Benitez of Puerto Rico (on the right) captured the WBA light-welterweight (a.k.a. super-lightweight) title when he was just 17½ years old, the youngest age ever for a world boxing champion, beating Antonio Cervantes on March 6, 1976. Moving up into the heavier weight divisions, Benitez has also won the WBC welterweight title (upsetting Carlos Palomino in 1979) and the WBC light-middleweight title (with a devastating 12th-round KO of Maurice Hope in 1981), making him the youngest of the few fighters who have won championships in three weight divisions. Benitez is known for his uncanny ring intelligence and his dislike of training. (Photo courtesy of Big Fights, Inc.)

TRACK STAR (left): Sebastian Coe happily displays the Golden Mile trophy, just one of the many awards and honors won by the British runner. Although Coe and rival countryman Steve Ovett rarely meet head-to-head in a race, they have been swapping world records back and forth in the middle-distance events (from 800 meters to the mile). During the summer of 1981 they set 3 records for the mile run in 10 days, an unprecedented flurry of record-breaking for that event, culminating in Coe's 3-min-47.33-sec mile in Brussels. (Photo by All-Sport.)

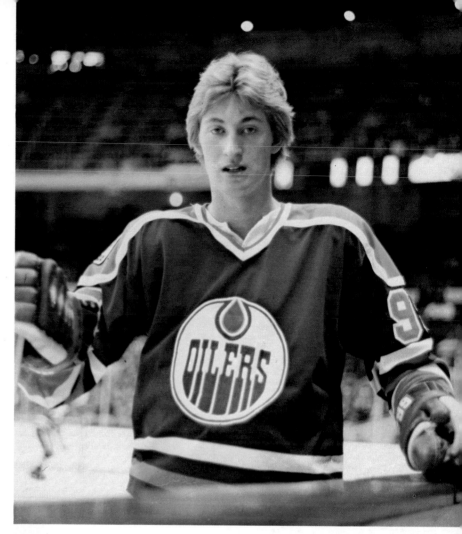

HOCKEY WIZARD (above): Edmonton Oiler superstar Wayne Gretzky astounded hockey fans in Canada and the US by shattering all NHL season scoring records in 1981–82. The 21-year-old center from Brantford, Ontario, scored 92 goals (breaking Phil Esposito's record of 76) and notched 120 assists for a total of 212 points and an astonishing average of 2.65 points per game. Gretzky is neither the fastest nor strongest player on his team; his scoring magic is attributed to both his sense of where everyone is on the rink and his sixth sense of where everyone (and the puck) is going to be. After the 1981 Canada Cup series, the Soviet coach remarked that Gretzky was the smartest player that he had ever seen. (Steve Babineau.)

SAMURAI OF SWAT (left): Using a batting style reminiscent of the New York Giants' baseball great Mel Ott, slugger Sadaharu Oh whacked 868 home runs during his 21-year career with the Yomiuri Giants of Japan's Central League. American baseball experts describe the Japanese leagues as superior to the best minor leagues (Triple A), but not as good as the major leagues—where the career home run record is 755 by Hank Aaron. Oh, who played first base and wore uniform no. 1, was the Central League MVP nine times and he batted .301 lifetime. During his reign, the Giants won 12 Japan series titles. Oh was the highest-paid athlete in Asia, in keeping with Ralph Kiner's dictum, "Home run hitters drive bigger cars."

HIGHEST MPG OF STREET-LEGAL CAR (above): The "California Commuter" uses 75% diesel fuel and 25% sunflower oil to get 156.33 miles per gallon on long runs. Here it is on an L.A. freeway. (Photo by Franklin Berger.)

FASTEST DIESEL CAR (below): The Mercedes C 111/3 has attained 203.3 mph in road tests.

FASTEST HUMAN-POWERED VEHICLE (above): David Grylls can go almost a mile a minute in his "Vector."

GUINNESS
1983 BOOK OF WORLD RECORDS

Editors and Compilers
NORRIS McWHIRTER
(ROSS McWHIRTER 1955-1975)

EDITORIAL STAFF
In England:
PETER MATTHEWS, Sports Editor
MOIRA F. STOWE, Assistant General Editor

In America:
DAVID A. BOEHM, Editor-in-Chief
STEPHEN TOPPING, Senior Editor and
Sports Editor
CYD SMITH, Assistant Editor

Sterling Publishing Co., Inc. New York

FOREWORD

When my great, great, great grandfather acquired the brewery in Dublin in 1759 he could not have foreseen that his own brewery would one day be setting world records. Still less, it could not have occurred to him that his Guinness brewing company would one day create and publish a Guinness Record Book.

Both these things have happened. The brewery grew as the reputation of its principal product grew, spreading first across Ireland, then across the Irish Sea to England and finally around the world. The dark, creamy brew was originally known as Guinness's Extra Stout Porter; later it became Guinness Extra Stout, Guinness Stout, or often nowadays just plain Guinness. Though it may have been known by different names, the essential recipe and the quality has not changed, which is possibly why Guinness can now be bought and enjoyed in 141 countries around the world. That may be a record in itself, I do not know; what we do know is that the Dublin Brewery in the 1920's was the largest in the world and although the brewery has since been overtaken in sheer size, we note with some pride that there are now Guinness breweries in England, Nigeria, Malaysia, Cameroon, Ghana and Jamaica.

It is 223 years since the first Guinness Stout was created by my ancestor. The Record Book is a youngster by comparison; it has just passed its 28th birthday. We have often said we brought out the Book to provide a means of settling peacefully arguments about record performances. It must have settled a few arguments in its time because it is now published in twenty-three languages and in all versions has now passed the 48 million mark. There are some records there too.

We are all proud of our Book. Every new edition brings something fresh, something especially interesting. Every new edition brings me pleasure and I hope it does the same for every one of its readers.

Iveagh

September 15, 1982   [BENJAMIN GUINNESS]

EARL OF IVEAGH, Chairman
Arthur Guinness, Son & Co (Dublin) Ltd

PREFACE

This 21st US edition has been brought up to date and provided with new illustrations. About a quarter of the many thousands of records listed have to be changed from one edition to the next.

In this edition we are again obliged to revise our own entry which records the fact that the global sale of this book in 23 languages has now become the highest of any copyright book, fiction or nonfiction.

We wish to thank correspondents from the many countries of the world for raising and settling various editorial points. Strenuous efforts have been made to improve the value of the material presented and this policy will be continued in future editions.

NORRIS D. MCWHIRTER
General Editor

Guinness Superlatives, Ltd
2 Cecil Court, London Road,
Enfield, Middlesex, England.
01-441-367-4567   Cable: Mostest
Telex 851 23573

World rights reserved
Revised American Edition © 1982, 1981, 1980, 1979, 1978, 1977, 1976, 1975, 1974, 1973, 1972, 1971, 1970, 1969, 1968, 1966, 1965, 1964, 1963, 1962 by Sterling Publishing Co., Inc. Two Park Avenue, New York, N.Y. 10016. © 1960 by Guinness Superlatives Ltd.
Library of Congress Catalog Card No.: 64-4984
ISBN 0-8069-0224-8 Trade
0225-6 Library

CONTENTS

IS IT A RECORD?

From the Editors of *Guinness*

Categories

We are *likely* to publish only those records which improve upon previously published records or which are newly significant in having become the subject of widespread and, preferably, worldwide competition. Records in our sense essentially have to be both measureable and comparable to other performances in the same category.

It should be stressed that unique occurrences, interesting peculiarities and the collecting of everyday objects, are not themselves necessarily records. Records which are *qualified* or limited in some way— for example, by age, handicap, day of the week, etc.—cannot be accommodated in a reference work so general as the *Guinness Book of World Records.*

We do not publish records in gratuitously hazardous categories, such as the lowest starting height for a handcuffed, free-fall parachute jump, or the thinnest burning rope suspending a man in a straitjacket from a helicopter. World records claimed on TV specials are not always set according to Guinness rules. Certain innately dangerous but historically significant activities, such as tightrope walking, are included but are best left to professionals. Other categories which have reached the limits of safety, such as sword swallowing and Volkswagen stuffing, have been retired and either are so marked or have been deleted. No further claims will be considered for publication.

We reserve the right to determine in our sole discretion the record to be published and the use of the name of the record holder for purposes of inclusion in the book.

Rules and Procedures

A record attempt should compete *exactly* with the record in the book and the conditions under which it was set. Where there is doubt about the rules, it is recommended that the strictest interpretation be adopted. Contact with the Guinness Superlatives office in England (address on page 2) for clarification should be made well in advance of a planned attempt.

If there is a recognized world or national governing body for an activity, that body should be consulted for rules and one of its rep-

resentatives, whenever possible, should be involved in officiating. For any attempt, expert officiating by impartial witnesses is desirable.

In marathon events, five-minute rest intervals are permitted, but only AFTER each *completed* hour, except for a few "non-stop" categories in which minimal intervals may be taken only for purposes other than for resting. These rest breaks are optional and may be accumulated (for example, 3 hours of activity earns 15 minutes of rest time, etc.). Violation of the rest-interval rules will disqualify an attempt. The accepted record will be the gross time (that is, the total elapsed time, including rest intervals, from start to finish). However, unused accumulated rest break time cannot be added to the final figure.

In recent years there has been a marked increase in efforts to establish records for sheer endurance in many activities. In the very nature of record-breaking, the duration of such "marathons" will tend to be pushed to greater and greater extremes, and it should be stressed that marathon attempts are not without possible dangers. Those responsible for marathon events would be well counseled to seek medical advice before, and surveillance during, marathons which involve extended periods with little or no sleep.

Documentation and Verification

■ We do *not* normally supply personnel to monitor, invigilate or observe record attempts, but reserve the right to do so. In any case, the burden of proof rests with the claimant. No particular form is required, and no entry fee is payable. Guidelines for documentation are provided below. We cannot accept as accurate any claim that is insufficiently documented.

■ Claimants should obtain independent corroboration in the form of local or national newspaper, radio or TV coverage. Newspaper clippings must be annotated with the name of the newspaper, its place of publication and the date of the issue in which the article appeared. When possible, the name of the reporter and black-and-white and/or color action photographs should also be supplied. Videotapes and audio cassettes should not be sent, but held in reserve in the

event further documentation is requested.

■ Claimants should send signed authentication by independent, impartial adult witnesses or representatives of organizations of standing in their community. Where applicable, a signed document showing ratification by a governing body should be supplied (see above). A claim is naturally enhanced by a witness with a high degree of expertise in the area of endeavor.

■ Signed log books should show there has been unremitting surveillance in the case of endurance events. These log books must include, in chronological order, the times of activity and the times and durations of all rest breaks taken. The log books must be legible and readily decipherable. They must include signatures of witnesses with times of entering and leaving (at least two *independent* witnesses must be on hand at all times). Where applicable, scoresheets must be kept to demonstrate a satisfactory rate of play.

All submissions become the property of the publishers. The publishers will consider, but not guarantee, the return of material, only if a self-addressed stamped envelope or wrapper is supplied *with sufficient postage.*

Revisions

Notwithstanding the best efforts of the editors, errors in the book, while rare, may occur. In the event of such errors, the sole responsibility of the publishers will be to correct such errors in subsequent editions of the book.

If there are discrepancies between entries in one edition and another, it may be generally assumed that the *later* entry is the product of the more up-to-date research.

Editorial Offices

Please consult the book before phoning or writing the editorial offices, which are primarily concerned with maintaining and improving the quality of each succeeding edition. We do not offer advice on choosing a record for anyone to attempt breaking. Also, we are unable to perform the function of a free general information bureau for quiz competitions and the like.

Chapter 1

The Human Being

1. DIMENSIONS

Tallest Giants

The true height of human giants is frequently obscured by exaggeration and commercial dishonesty. The only really admissible evidence on the actual height of giants is that collected in the last 100 years under impartial medical supervision. Unfortunately, medical papers themselves are not guiltless in including fanciful, as opposed to measured, heights.

The assertion that Goliath of Gath (c. 1060 BC) stood 6 cubits and a span (9 ft 6½ in) suggests a confusion of units or some over-enthusiastic exaggeration by the Hebrew chroniclers. The Hebrew historian Flavius Josephus (b 37 or 38 AD, d after 93 AD) and some of the manuscripts of the Septuagint (the earliest Greek translation of the Old Testament) attribute to Goliath the wholly credible height of 4 Greek cubits and a span (6 ft 10 in).

Extreme medieval data, taken from bone measurements, invariably refer to specimens of extinct whale, giant cave bear, mastodon, woolly rhinoceros or other prehistoric non-human remains.

An extreme case of exaggeration concerned Siah Khan ibn Kashmir Khan (b 1913) of Bushehr (Bushire), Iran. Prof D. H. Fuchs showed photographs of him at a meeting of the Society of Physicians in Vienna, Austria, in Jan 1935 claiming that he was 10 ft 6 in tall. Later, when Siah Khan entered the Imperial Hospital in Teheran for an operation, it was revealed that his actual height was 7 ft 2.6 in, a full meter (39.4 in) less.

The tallest recorded "true" (non-pathological) giant was Angus MacAskill (1825–63), born on the island of Berneray, in the Sound of Harris, in the Western Isles, Scotland. He stood 7 ft 9 in tall and died in St Ann's, on Cape Breton Island, Nova Scotia, Canada.

Modern opinion is that the tallest recorded man of whom there is irrefutable evidence was the pre-acromegalic giant Robert Pershing Wadlow, born at 6:30 a.m. in Alton, Ill, on Feb 22, 1918. He was born to Mrs Addie Mae Wadlow (1896–1980) and weighed

(his autograph)

TALLEST MAN WHO EVER LIVED: Robert Wadlow, then only 7 ft 5 in at age 14, towered over his brothers.

5

8½ lb. His abnormal growth started at the age of 2, following a double hernia operation.

Dr C. M. Charles, Associate Professor of Anatomy at Washington University School of Medicine, in St Louis, and Dr Cyril MacBryde measured him at 8 ft 11.1 in, on June 27, 1940. He died 18 days later, at 1:30 a.m. on July 15, 1940, in Manistee, Mich, as a result of cellulitis (inflammation of cellular tissue) of the right ankle aggravated by a brace, which had

TALLEST MAN: Robert Wadlow, now full-grown at 8 ft 11.1 in tall, with his lawyer. His greatest weight was 491 lb, a year before he died at age 22.

been poorly fitted only a week earlier. He was buried in Oakwood Cemetery, Alton, Ill, in a coffin measuring 10 ft 9 in long, 32 in wide, and 30 in deep.

His greatest recorded weight was 491 lb on his 21st birthday. He weighed 439 lb at the time of death. His shoes were size 37AA (18½ in long) and his hands measured 12¾ in from the wrist to the tip of the middle finger. His arm span was 9 ft 5¾ in and he consumed 8,000 calories daily. At the age of 9 he was able to carry his father, Harold F. Wadlow (d Sept 1967), later mayor of Alton, who stood 5 ft 11 in tall and weighed 170 lb, up the stairs of the family home. His last words were, "The doctor says I won't get home for the . . . celebrations" (a reference to his paternal grandparents' golden wedding anniversary).

His height progressed as follows:

Age in Years	Height ft	Height in	Weight in lb	Age in Years	Height ft	Height in	Weight in lb
5	5	4	105	15	7	8	355
8	6	0	169	16	7	10½	374
9	6	2½	180	17	8	0½	315*
10	6	5	210	18	8	3½	—
11	6	7	—	19	8	5½	480
12	6	10½	—	20	8	6¾	—
13	7	1¾	255	21	8	8¼	491
14	7	5	301	22.4†	8	11.1	439

* Following severe influenza and infection of the foot.
† He was still growing during his terminal illness.

The tallest known living human is Muhammad Alam Channa (b 1956), who works as an attendant at the shrine of Lal Shahbaz Qalandar in Pakistan. He began growing abnormally from the age of 12 and reached a height of 7 ft by the age of 20. He is now 8 ft 3 in and weighs more than 397 lb. (See cover.)

The only other men for whom heights of 8 ft or more have been reliably reported are listed on page 9. In seven cases gigantism was followed by acromegaly, a disorder which causes an enlargement of the nose, lips, tongue, lower jaw, hands and feet, due to renewed activity by an already swollen pituitary gland, which is located at the base of the brain.

Giants exhibited in circuses and exhibitions are routinely under contract not to be measured and are, almost traditionally, billed by their promoters at heights up to 18 in in excess of their true heights. Notable examples of such exaggeration were listed in the 1982 *Guinness Book of World Records*. The acromegalic giant Eddie Carmel (b Tel Aviv, Israel, 1938), formerly "The Tallest Man on Earth" of Ringling Bros. and Barnum & Bailey's Circus (1961–8), was allegedly 9 ft 0⅝ in tall (weighing 535 lb), but photographic evidence suggests that his true height was about 7 ft 6⅝ in. He died in NYC on Aug 14, 1972, when his standing height, due to severe kyphoscoliosis (two-dimensional spinal curvature), was *c.* 7 ft.

HEIGHT MADE WADLOW A CELEBRITY: When he visited St Louis in 1939, the crowds found his height of almost 9 feet hard to believe. As a 9-year-old Boy Scout, Robert was a bulwark at leap frogging with his peers.

TALLEST LIVING TWINS (above): Dan and Doug Busch at 6 ft 11 in are overshadowed by a sculpture on the Northern Arizona campus. TALLEST LIVING WOMAN (below): Sandy Allen, 7 ft 7¼ in tall, on her 26th birthday, was given a party by her friends in front of the Guinness Museum in Niagara Falls, Ont, Canada. (Gordon Counsell) HAND of the tallest living man (top right), the Pakistani who is 8 ft 3 in tall, dwarfs that of a normal-sized man. TALLEST WOMAN EVER (right): Zeng Jinlian reached 8 ft 1 in before she died in 1982 at age 17 years 8 months.

TALLEST PEOPLE

	ft	in
John F. Carroll (1932–69) of Buffalo, NY	(a) 8	7¾
John William Rogan (1871–1905) of Gallatin, Tenn	(b) 8	6
Muhammad Alam Channa (b 1956–fl. 1982) of Sehwan Sharif, Pakistan	(c) 8	3
Don Koehler (1925–81) of Denton, Mont, later Chicago	(d) 8	2
Bernard Coyne (1897–1921) of Anthon, Iowa	(e) 8	2
Vainö Myllyrinne (1909–63) of Helsinki, Finland	(f) 8	1.2
Patrick Cotter O'Brien (1760–1806) of Kinsale, County Cork, Ireland	(g) 8	1
"Constantine" (1872–1902) of Reutlingen, W. Germany	(h) 8	0.8
Sulaiman 'Ali Nashnush (b 1943–fl. 1982) of Tripoli, Libya	(i) 8	0.4
Gabriel Estevao Monjane (b 1944–fl. 1982) of Monjacaze, Mozambique	(j) 8	0

(a) Carroll was a victim of severe kypho-scoliosis (two-dimensional spinal curvature). The figure represents his height with assumed normal spinal curvature, calculated from a standing height of 8 ft 0 in, measured Oct 14, 1959. His standing height was 7 ft 8¼ in shortly before his death.
(b) Measured in a sitting position. Unable to stand owing to ankylosis (stiffening of the joints through the formation of adhesions) of the knees and hips.
(c) Started growing abnormally at the age of 10. Has been credited with heights up to 8 ft 6 in.
(d) Spinal curvature reduced his standing height to 7 ft 10 in. He had a twin sister who is 5 ft 9 in tall. His father was 6 ft 2 in tall, his mother 5 ft 10 in.
(e) Eunuchoidal giant ("daddy-longlegs" syndrome). He was rejected by the US Army in 1918 when he stood 7 ft 9 in.
(f) Stood 7 ft 3½ in at the age of 21. Experienced a second phase of growth in his late thirties and may have stood 8 ft 3 in at one time.
(g) Revised height based on skeletal remeasurement in 1975.
(h) Height estimated, as both legs were amputated after they turned gangrenous. He claimed a height of 8 ft 6 in. Eunuchoidal.
(i) Operation in Rome in 1960 to correct abnormal growth was successful.
(j) Measured 7 ft 5 in at age of 16, and 7 ft 10 in Dec 1965. Eunuchoidal. Has not been anthropometrically assessed since joining a Portuguese circus, billed as 8 ft 8⅓ in.

Tallest Twins

The tallest (identical) twins ever recorded were the Knipe brothers (b 1761–fl. 1780) of Magherafelt, near Londonderry, N Ireland, who both measured 7 ft 2 in. The world's tallest living twins (also identical) are Dan and Doug Busch (b Aug 12, 1961) of Flagstaff, Ariz, who both measure 6 ft 11 in.

Tallest Giantess

Giantesses are rarer than giants but their heights are still spectacular. The tallest woman in history was the acromegalic giantess Zeng Jinlian (pronounced San Chung Lin) (b June 26, 1964) of Yujiang village in the Bright Moon Commune, Hunan Province, central China, who was 8 ft 1 in when she died on Feb 13, 1982. She began to grow abnormally from the age of 4 months and stood 5 ft 1½ in before her 4th birthday and 7 ft 1½ in when she was 13. Her hands measured 10 in and her feet 14 in in length. She suffered from both scoliosis and diabetes. Her parents are 5 ft 4½ in and 5 ft 1½ in while her brother was 5 ft 2½ in tall at age 18.

Tallest Living Woman

The tallest living woman is Sandy Allen (b June 18, 1955, in Chicago), who lives now in Niagara Falls, Canada. On July 14, 1977, she measured 7 ft 7¼ in at age 22, when she underwent a pituitary gland operation to inhibit further growth. A 6½-lb baby, her acromegalic growth began soon after birth. She now weighs about 460 lb and takes a size 16EEE shoe.

Tallest Couple

Anna Hanen Swan (1846–88) of Nova Scotia, Canada, was billed at 8 ft 1 in but actually measured 7 ft 5½ in. In London, June 17, 1871, she married Martin van Buren Bates (1845–1919), of Whitesburg, Letcher County, Ky, who stood 7 ft 2½ in, making them the tallest married couple on record.

Shortest Dwarfs

The strictures which apply to giants apply equally to dwarfs, except that exaggeration gives way to understatement. In the same way 9 ft may be regarded as the limit toward which the tallest giants tend, so 23 in must be regarded as the limit toward which the shortest mature dwarfs tend (cf. the average length of new-born babies is 18 to 20 in). In the case of child dwarfs their *ages* are often enhanced by their agents or managers.

There are many forms of human dwarfism, but those suffering from ateleiosis (midgets) are generally the shortest. They have essentially normal proportions but suffer from growth hormone deficiency.

Such dwarfs tended to be even shorter at a time when human stature was generally shorter due to lower nutritional standards.

The shortest mature human of whom there is independent evidence was Pauline Musters ("Princess Pauline"), a Dutch midget. She was born at Ossendrecht Feb 26, 1876, and measured 12 in at birth. At the age of 9 she was 21.65 in tall and weighed only 3 lb 5 oz. She died, at the age of 19, of pneumonia, with meningitis, in New York City on Mar 1, 1895. Although she was billed at 19 in, she had earlier been medically measured and found to be 23.2 in tall. A *post mortem* examination showed her to be exactly 24 in (there was some elongation after death). Her mature weight varied from 7½ lb to 9 lb and her "vital statistics" were 18½–19–17, which suggests she was overweight.

In 1938 a height of 19 in was attributed to Paul Del Rio (b Madrid, Spain, 1920) by *Life Magazine* when he visited Hollywood, but the fact that he created no "fuss" in the film capital and weighed as much as 12 lb suggests he was closer to 26 in tall.

In 1979 a height of 19.68 in and a weight of 4 lb 6 oz were reported for a 9-year-old Greek girl named Stamatoula being cared for at the Lyrion Convent, Athens. The child, believed to be the survivor of twins, is suffering from Seckel's "bird-face" syndrome and growth has allegedly ceased, but in a similar case from Corsica the girl eventually reached a height of 34 in and a weight of 26 lb.

Shortest Male Dwarf

The shortest recorded adult male dwarf was Calvin Phillips, born in Bridgewater, Mass, Jan 14, 1791. He weighed 2 lb at birth and stopped growing at the age of 5. When he was 19 he measured 26½ in tall and weighed 12 lb with his clothes on. He died two years later, in Apr 1812, from progeria, a rare disorder characterized by dwarfism and premature senility.

The most famous midget in history was Charles Sherwood Stratton, *alias* "General Tom Thumb," born Jan 4, 1838. When he came into the clutches of the circus proprietor P. T. Barnum, his birth date was changed to Jan 4, 1832, so that when he was billed as standing 30½ in at the age of 18 he was in fact only 12 years old. He died of apoplexy on July 15, 1883 in his birthplace of Bridgeport, Ct, aged 45 (not 51), and was then 3 ft 4 in tall.

Another celebrated midget was Józef ("Count") Boruwalaski (b Nov 1739) of Poland. He measured only 8 in long at birth, growing to 14 in at the age of one year. He stood 17 in at 6 years, 21 in at 10, 25 in at 15, 35 in at 25 and 39 in at 30. He died near Durham, England, on Sept 5, 1837, aged 97.

William E. Jackson, *alias* "Major Mite," born Oct 2, 1864, in Dunedin, New Zealand, measured 9 in long and weighed 12 oz at birth. In Nov, 1880, he stood 21 in and weighed 9 lb. He died in NYC, on Dec 9, 1900, when he measured 27 in.

The shortest recently living adult human was Nruturam (b May 28, 1929), a rachitic dwarf of Naydwar, India, who measured 28 in, but was reported dead in 1981. Antonio Ferreira (b Arcozelo, Portugal, 1943), an ateliotic dwarf drummer, is reputedly 29½ in tall.

Shortest Twins

The shortest twins ever recorded were the primordial dwarfs Matjus and Bela Matina (b 1903–*fl.* 1935) of Budapest, Hungary, who later became naturalized Americans. They both measured 30 in. The world's shortest living twins are John and Greg Rice (b 1952) of Palm Beach, Fla, who both measure 34 in.

Oldest Dwarf

There are only two centenarian dwarfs on record. The first was Miss Anne Clowes of Matlock, Derbyshire, England, who died Aug 5, 1784, at the age of 103. She was 3 ft 9 in tall and weighed 48 lb. On Apr 6, 1982, Hungarian-born Susanna Bokoyni ("Princess Susanna") of Newton, NJ, celebrated her 103rd birthday. She is 3 ft 4 in tall and weighs 37 lb.

Most Variable Stature

Adam Rainer, born in 1899 in Graz, Austria, measured 3 ft 10.45 in at the age of 21. But then he suddenly started growing at a rapid rate, and by 1931 he had reached 7 ft 1¾ in. He became so weak as a result that he was bedridden for the rest of his life. He measured 7 ft 8 in when he died on March 4, 1950, aged 51, and was the only person in medical history to have been both a giant and a dwarf.

By constant practice in muscular manipulation of the vertebrae, the circus performer Clarence E. Willard (1882–1962) of the US was, at his prime, able to increase his apparent stature from 5 ft 10 in to 6 ft 4 in at will.

Tallest Tribes

The tallest major tribe is the Tutsi (also called Watutsi), Nilotic herdsmen of Rwanda and Burundi, Central Africa, whose young males *average* 5 ft 10¾ in in height.

SHORTEST GIRLS: Princess Pauline (above) weighed 9 lb at her heaviest and reached 23.2 in at age 19. Stamatoula (below), the little Greek girl, photographed at age 9, may never grow taller than 19.68 in. She weighs 4 lb 6 oz. **OLDEST DWARF** (right): Princess Susanna, 103 years old, stands beside her 5-ft-2½-inch roommate.

FAMOUS MIDGET, "General" Tom Thumb (above), who stood 3 ft 4 in at his tallest, posed for this wedding portrait during the time he was in P. T. Barnum's circus.

LIGHTEST HUMAN ADULT (above): Lucia Zarate of Mexico weighed 4.7 lb at age 17. At birth in 1863, she weighed 2½ lbs.

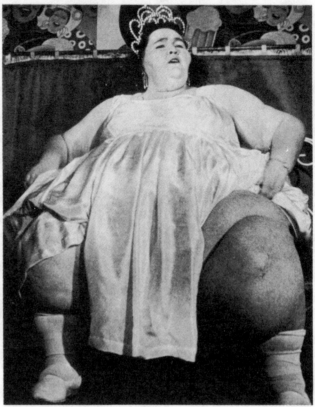

HEAVIEST WOMAN (above): Mrs Percy Pearl Washington could have weighed as much as 880 lb but the scale only registered up to 800 lb. **HEAVIEST TWINS** (below): Billy and Benny McCrary, with 84-in waists, weighed more than 700 lb each when they were tag-team wrestlers.

HEAVIEST MAN PRECISELY WEIGHED (left): Robert Earl Hughes, once weighed at exactly 1069 lb, tipped the scales at 203 lb when he was 6 years old. In this photo he weighed only 700 lb.

Shortest Tribes

The smallest pygmies are the Mbuti, with an average height of 4 ft 6 in for men and 4 ft 5 in for women, with some groups averaging only 4 ft 4 in for men and 4 ft 1 in for women. They live in the forests near the river Ituri in Zaïre, Africa.

WEIGHT

Lightest Humans

The lightest adult human on record was Lucia Zarate (b San Carlos, Mexico, Jan 2, 1863, d Oct 1889), an emaciated ateliotic dwarf of 26½ in who weighed 4.7 lb at the age of 17. She "fattened up" to 13 lb by her 20th birthday. At birth she had weighed 2½ lb.

The thinnest recorded adults of normal height are those suffering from Simmonds' disease (hypophyseal cachexia). Losses up to 65% of the original body weight have been recorded in females, with a "low" of 45 lb in the case of Emma Shaller (b St Louis, Mo, July 8, 1868, d Oct 4, 1890) who stood 5 ft 2 in tall.

Edward C. Hagner (1892–1962), *alias* Eddie Masher, is alleged to have weighed only 48 lb at a height of 5 ft 7 in. He was also known as "the Skeleton Dude." In Aug 1825 the biceps measurement of Claude-Ambroise Seurat (b Apr 10, 1797, d Apr 6, 1826), of Troyes, France, was 4 in and the distance between his back and his chest was less than 3 in. According to one report, he stood 5 ft 7½ in and weighed 78 lb, but in another account was described as 5 ft 4 in and only 36 lb.

It was recorded that the American exhibitionist Rosa Lee Plemons (b 1873) weighed 27 lb at the age of 18. In March 1978 the death was reported of an anorexic 47-year-old woman in Hounslow, England, who scaled only 59 lb at a height of 5 ft 2 in.

In Feb 1981 a weight of 54 lb was recorded for a 31-year-old woman suffering from what is known as the "total allergy syndrome" (aversion to anything that has a synthetic base).

Heaviest Men

The heaviest human in medical history has been Jon Brower Minnoch (b Sept 29, 1941) of Bainbridge Island, Wash, who was carried on planking by a rescue team into University Hospital, Seattle, in March 1978. Dr Robert Schwartz, the endocrinological consultant, estimated by extrapolating his intake and elimination rates that he was "probably more" than 1,400 lb. It took 13 attendants to roll him over in his hospital bed. After nearly 2 years on a 1200-calorie-per-day diet he was discharged at 476 lb. He had to be readmitted in Oct 1981 having reportedly gained 200 lb in 7 days. This former taxicab driver stands 6 ft 1 in tall.

Francis John Lang (b 1934), *alias* Michael Walker of Clinton, Iowa, was attributed a weight of 1187 lb. He could not be admitted for treatment for inflammation of the gall bladder to the Veteran's Administration Hospital, Houston, Tex because of the impossibility of getting him through the doors. He was treated in a trailer in the car park and discharged Jan 5, 1972 unweighed but estimated to be between 900 and 1000 lb. The more precise weight above was claimed for him while he was suffering from drug-induced bulimia, in the summer of 1971 when he was working with the Christian Farms of Killeen, Tex. There is, however, no independent corroboration for the precise upper weight quoted, although photographic evidence suggests the weight was possibly reliable. By Feb 1980 Lang (6 ft 2 in) had reduced to 369 lb.

The highest precisely measured weight for a human is 1069 lb in Feb 1958 for 6-ft-0½-in-tall Robert Earl Hughes (b June 4, 1926), Monticello, Mo. An 11¼-lb baby, he weighed 203 lb at 6 years, 378 lb at 10, 546 lb at 13, 693 lb at 18, 896 lb at 25, and 945 lb at 27. He weighed 1041 lb at the time of his death. His claimed waist of 122 in, his chest of 124 in and his upper arm of 40 in were the greatest on record. Hughes died of uremia (condition caused by retention of urinary matter in the blood) in a trailer at Bremen, Ind, July 10, 1958, aged 32, and was buried in Binville Cemetery, near Mt Sterling, Ill. His coffin, as large as a piano case measuring 7 ft by 4 ft 4 in and weighing more than 1100 lb, had to be lowered by crane. It was once claimed by a commercial interest that Hughes had weighed 1500 lb—a 40% exaggeration.

The only other men for whom weights of 800 lb or more have been reported are listed next:

Mills Darden (1798–1857) US (7ft 6 in)	1,020 lb
John Hanson Craig (1856–94) US (6 ft 5 in)	907 (b)
Arthur Knorr (1914–60) US (6 ft 1 in)	900 (a)
Toubi (b 1946) Cameroon	857½
T. J. Albert (b 1957) St Albans, W Va	856 (c)
T. A. Valenzuela (1895–1937) Mexico (5 ft 11 in)	850

(a) Gained 300 lb in the last 6 months of his life.
(b) Won $1,000 in a "Bonny Baby" contest in New York City in 1858.
(c) A French press report attributed a weight of 1036 lb to him in 1979.

Heaviest Twins

The heaviest were the performers Billy Leon and Benny Loyd McCrary, *alias* Billy and Benny

McGuire (b Dec 7, 1946) of Hendersonville, NC. In Nov, 1978, they were weighed at 743 lb (Billy) and 723 lb (Benny) and had 84-in waists. Billy died of heart failure on July 13, 1979, in Niagara Falls, Canada, after falling from his mini-bike. He was buried in a square coffin with a total weight of over 1000 lb in Hendersonville. A hydraulic lift was needed to lower the coffin to its final resting place. After one 6-week slimming course in a hospital, they emerged weighing 5 lb more each.

Heaviest Women

The heaviest ever recorded was the late Mrs Percy Pearl Washington (b Louisiana, 1926) who died in a hospital in Milwaukee, Wis, Oct 9, 1972. The hospital scales registered only up to 800 lb, but she was believed to weigh about 880 lb. The previous weight record for a woman was set 84 years earlier at 850 lb although a wholly unsubstantiated report exists of a woman, Mrs Ida Maitland (1898–1932) of Springfield, Miss, who reputedly weighed 911 lb.

A more reliable and better documented case was that of Mrs Flora Mae (or May) Jackson (*née* King), a 5-ft-9-in black woman born in 1930 at Shuqualak, Miss. She weighed 10 lb at birth; 267 lb at the age of 11; 621 lb at 25; and 840 lb shortly before her death in Meridian, Miss, on Dec 9, 1965. She was known in show business as "Baby Flo."

Greatest Weight Differential

The greatest recorded for a married couple is 922 lb in the case of Mills Darden (1020 lb) of NC and his wife Mary (98 lb). Despite her diminutiveness, however, Mrs Darden bore her husband at least three (and possibly five) children before her death in 1837.

Slimming

The greatest recorded slimming feat was that of William J. Cobb (b 1926), *alias* "Happy Humphrey," a professional wrestler of Macon, Ga. It was reported in July 1965 that he had reduced from 802 lb to 232 lb, a loss of 570 lb, in 3 years. His waist measurement declined from 101 to 44 in. In Oct 1973, "Happy" was reported back to a normal 650 lb.

The US circus fat lady Mrs Celesta Geyer (b 1901), *alias* Dolly Dimples, reduced from 553 lb to 152 lb 1950–51, a loss of 401 lb in 14 months. Her vital statistics diminished *pari passu* from 79–84–84 to a *svelte* 34–28–36. Her book "How I Lost 400 lb" was not a best seller. In Dec 1967, she was reportedly down to 110 lb.

By July 1979, Jon Brower Minnoch (see page 13) had reduced to 476 lb; if the peak weight quoted for him was authentic, this indicates a weight loss of 924 lb in 16 months.

The speed record for slimming was established by Paul M. Kimelman, 21, of Pittsburgh, Pa, who from Dec 25, 1966, to Aug 1967, went on a crash diet of 300 to 600 calories per day to reduce from 487 lb to 130 lb, a total loss of 357 lb. He has now stabilized at 175 lb. In Feb 1951 Mrs Gertrude Levandowski of Burnips, Mich, successfully underwent a protracted operation for the removal of a cyst which subsequently reduced her weight from 616 lb to 308 lb.

Weight Gaining

A probable record for gaining weight was set by Arthur Knorr (b May 17, 1914), who died July 7, 1960, aged 46, in Reseda, Calif. He gained 300 lb in the last 6 months of his life and weighed 900 lb when he died. Miss Doris James of San Francisco is alleged to have gained 325 lb in the 12 months before her death in Aug 1965, aged 38, at a weight of 675 lb. She was only 5 ft 2 in tall.

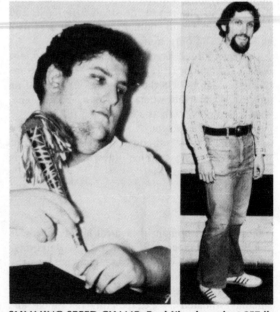

SLIMMING SPEED CHAMP: Paul Kimelman lost 357 lb in 8 months when he was 21. (Left) Before he went on a crash diet he weighed 487 lb. (Right) The slim result— 130 lb. He now remains slim at 175 lb.

BIRTHPLACE OF MAN: Somewhere in the vicinity of this spot in Tanzania, the Leakeys found the remains of the earliest man.

2. ORIGINS OF MAN

Scale of Time

If the age of the earth-moon system (latest estimate at least 4,700 million years) is likened to a single year, Handy Man appeared on the scene at about 8:35 p.m., on Dec 31, Britain's earliest known inhabitants arrived at about 11:32 p.m., the Christian era began about 13 seconds before midnight and the life span of a 117-year-old man (see *Oldest Centenarian*) would be about three-quarters of a second. Present calculations indicate that the sun's increased heat, as it becomes a "red giant," will make life insupportable on earth in about 10,000 million years. Meanwhile there may well be colder epicycles. The period of 1,000 million years is sometimes referred to as an eon.

The earliest known primates appeared in the Paleocene period about 80 million years ago. The earliest known hominoid (man-like) fossil found is the *Oligopithecus savagei,* found in El Faiyum, Egypt, dated to *c.* 33 million years ago.

Earliest Man

The greatest age attributed to fossils of the genus *Homo* is for the remains of 8 adults and 3 children discovered in the summer of 1975 at Laetolil, Tanzania, by Dr Mary Leakey, and dated by the University of Calif at Berkeley to between 3,350,000 and 3,750,000 BC. An arm-bone fragment from Kanapoi has been tentatively regarded as from *Homo* and has been dated from *c.* 4 million years ago.

The most complete of the earliest skeletons of *Homo* is that of "Lucy" (40% complete) found by Dr Donald C. Johanson and named *Australopithecus*

15

OLDEST MAN WHO EVER LIVED: At a verified 117 years on June 29, 1982, Shigechiyo Izumi of Japan is the undisputed record holder. Here, his great-niece-in-law dispenses his favorite drink, Shochu ("firewater"), distilled from black sugar. He drinks ½ pint every night before he goes to sleep at 8, and he wakes at 7 and takes the dog for a walk.

afarensis found in the Afar region of Ethiopia in Nov 1974 dating to 3–4 million years BC.

Parallel tracks of hominid footprints extending over 80 ft were discovered at Laetolil, Tanzania, in 1978, in volcanic ash dating to 3.5 million years ago. The height of the smallest of the seemingly three beings was estimated to be 4 ft 7 in.

The earliest recorded remains of the species *Homo sapiens,* variously dated from 300,000 to 450,000 years ago, in the middle Pleistocene period, were discovered Aug 24, 1965, by Dr László Vértes in a limestone quarry at Vértesszöllös, about 30 miles west of Budapest, Hungary. The remains, designated *Homo sapiens palaeo-hungaricus,* comprised an almost complete occipital bone, part of a skull with an estimated cranial capacity of nearly 1,400 cc (85 cu in).

The earliest evidence of the use of fire by hominids is from a site found in 1978 at Chesowanja, near Lake Baringo, Kenya, dated to 1.42 million years ago.

The earliest evidence for the presence of man in the Americas could date from at least 50,000 BC or "more probably 100,000 BC" according to the late Dr Louis Leakey after the examination of some hearth stones found in the Mojave Desert, Calif, and announced in Oct 1970. The earliest human relic is a skull found in the area of Los Angeles, dated in Dec 1970 to be from 22,000 BC.

3. LONGEVITY

Oldest Centenarian

No single subject is more obscured by vanity, deceit, falsehood and deliberate fraud than the extremes of human longevity. Extreme claims are generally made on behalf of the very aged rather than *by* them.

Many hundreds of claims throughout history have been made for persons living well into their second century and some, insulting to the intelligence, for people living even into their third. The facts are that centenarians surviving beyond their 110th year are of the extremest rarity and the present absolute limit of proven human longevity does not admit of anyone living to celebrate a 118th birthday.

It is highly significant that in Sweden, where alone proper and thorough official investigations follow the death of every allegedly very aged citizen, none has been found to have surpassed 110 years. The most reliably pedigreed large group of people in the world, the British peerage, has, after ten centuries, produced only two peers who reached their 100th birthdays, and only one reached his 101st. However, this is possibly not unconnected with the extreme draftiness of many of their residences and the amount of lead in the game they consume.

Scientific research into extreme old age reveals that the correlation between the claimed density of centenarians in a country and its regional illiteracy is 0.83 ±0.03. In late life, very old people often tend to advance their ages at the rate of about 17 years per decade. This was nicely corroborated by an analysis of the 1901 and 1911 censuses of England and Wales. Early claims must necessarily be without the elementary corroboration of birth dates. England was among the earliest of all countries to introduce local registers (1538) and official birth registration (July 1, 1837), which was made fully compulsory only in 1874. Even in the US, 45% of births occurring between 1890 and 1920 were unregistered.

Charlie Smith of Bartow, Fla obtained a Social Security card in 1955 when claiming to have been born in Liberia on July 4, 1842. The US Dept. of Health, Education and Welfare stated that they were "unable to disclose the type of evidence used" to determine Mr Smith's age because such disclosure "would infringe on the confidentiality of the individual's record." He celebrated what he reckoned to be his 137th birthday on July 4, 1979. However, a reference to the county records at Arcadia, Florida (Book 2, page 392) revealed a marriage contracted at age 35 Jan 8, 1910, and hence an exaggeration of at least 33 years. He died Oct 7, 1979. According to census research by A. Ross Eckler, he was most probably two months short of his 100th birthday.

A claim of a unique 121st birthday in 1981 for Arthur Reed of Oakland, Calif is under investigation. Social Security records, which have not always proved reliable, indicate a birth date of June 28, 1860.

Several celebrated super-centenarians (over 110 years) are believed to have been double lives (father and son, relations with the same names or successive bearers of a title). The most famous example is Christian Jakobsen Drackenberg, allegedly born in Stavanger, Norway, Nov 18, 1626, and died in Aarhus, Denmark, aged seemingly 145 years 326 days on Oct 9, 1772. A number of instances have been commercially sponsored, while a fourth category of recent claims are those made for political ends, such as the 100 citizens of the Russian Soviet Federated Socialist Republic (population about 132,000,000 at mid-1967), claimed in March 1960 to be between 120 and 156. From data on documented centenarians, actuaries have shown that only one 115-year life can be expected in 2,100 million lives (*cf.* world population was estimated to be 4,575 million at mid-1982).

The height of credulity was reached May 5, 1933, when a news agency solemnly filed a story from China with a Peking dateline that Li Chung-yun, the "oldest man on earth," born in 1680, had just died aged 256 years (*sic*). Recently the most extreme case of longevity claimed has been 168 years for Shirali Mislimov of Azerbaijan, USSR, who died Sept 2, 1973 and was reputedly born on March 26, 1805. No interview with this man had ever been permitted to any Western journalist or scientist. He was said to have celebrated the 100th birthday of his third wife, Hartun, in 1966 and that of one of his grandchildren in Aug, 1973. It was reported in 1954 that in the Abkhasian Republic of Georgia, USSR, where aged citizens are invested with an almost saint-like status, 2.58% of the population was aged over 90—some 25 times the proportion in the US.

In the face of authenticated data the claim published in the April, 1961 issue of the Soviet Union's *Vestnik Statistiki* ("Statistical Herald") that there were 224 male and 368 female Soviet citizens aged in excess of 120 recorded at the census of Jan 15, 1959, indicates a reliance on hearsay rather than evidence. Official Soviet insistence in 1961 on the unrivalled longevity of the country's citizenry is curious in view of the fact that the 592 persons in their unique "over 120" category must have spent at least the first 78 years of their prolonged lives under Czarism. It has recently been suggested that the extreme ages claimed by men in Georgia, USSR, are the result of attempts to avoid military service when younger, by assuming the identities of older men.

Dr Zhores A. Medvedev, the exiled Soviet gerontologist, on April 30, 1974, in Washington, DC, referring to the claims of the USSR, stated: "The whole phenomenon looks like a falsification . . . He (Stalin) liked the idea that (other) Georgians lived to be 100 or more . . . Local officials tried hard to find more and more cases for Stalin." He points out that the *average* life span in the regions claiming the highest incidence of centenarians is lower than the

	Years	Days		Born	Died
Japan	117	0	Shigechiyo Izumi	June 29, 1865	fl. June 29, 1982
US (d)	113	273	Fannie Thomas	Apr 24, 1867	Jan 22, 1981
Canada (a)	113	124	Pierre Joubert	July 15, 1701	Nov 16, 1814
Spain (h)	112	228	Josefa Salas Mateo	July 14, 1860	Feb 27, 1973
France	112	66	Augustine Teissier (Sister Julia)	Jan 2, 1869	Mar 9, 1981
UK (c)	112	39	Alice Stevenson	July 10, 1861	Aug 18, 1973
Morocco	112	+	El Hadj Mohammed el Mokri (Grand Vizier)	1844	Sept 16, 1957
Poland	112	+	Rozwlia Mielczarak (Mrs)	1868	Jan 7, 1981
Ireland	111	327	The Hon. Katherine Plunket	Nov 22, 1820	Oct 14, 1932
Australia	111	235	Jane Piercy (Mrs)	Sept 2, 1869	May 3, 1981
S. Africa (b)	111	151	Johanna Booyson	Jan 17, 1857	June 16, 1968
Czechoslovakia	111	+	Marie Bernatkova	Oct 22, 1857	fl. Oct 1968
Channel Islands	110	321	Margaret Ann Neve (née Harvey)	May 18, 1792	Apr 4, 1903
Northern Ireland	110	234	Elizabeth Watkins (Mrs)	Mar 10, 1863	Oct 31, 1973
Yugoslavia	110	150+	Demitrius Philipovitch	Mar 9, 1818	fl. Aug 1928
Netherlands (f)	110	141	Gerada Hurenkamp-Bosgoed	Jan 5, 1870	May 25, 1980
Greece	110	+	Lambrini Tsiatoura (Mrs)	1870	Feb 19, 1981
USSR (i)	110	+	Khasako Dzugayev	Aug 7, 1860	fl. Aug 1970
Norway	109	208	Marie Olsen (Mrs)	May 1, 1850	Nov 24, 1959
Tasmania	109	179	Mary Ann Crow (Mrs)	Feb 2, 1836	July 31, 1945
Italy	109	179	Rosalia Spoto	Aug 25, 1847	Feb 20, 1957
Sweden	109	94	Anna Mathilda Johansson	Nov 21, 1865	Feb 23, 1975
Scotland	109	14	Rachel MacArthur (Mrs)	Nov 26, 1827	Dec 10, 1936
Belgium	108	327	Mathilda Vertommen-Hellemans	Aug 12, 1868	July 4, 1977
Germany (g)	108	128	Luise Schwarz	Sept 27, 1849	Feb 2, 1958
Iceland	108	45	Halldora Bjarndoffir	Oct 14, 1873	Nov 28, 1981
Portugal (e)	108	+	Maria Luisa Jorge	June 7, 1859	fl. July 1967
Finland	107	221	Amalia Wellenius (Mrs)	Aug 6, 1867	Mar 24, 1975
Austria	106	231	Anna Migschitz	Feb 3, 1850	Nov 1, 1956
Malaysia	106	+	Hassan Bin Yusoff	Aug 14, 1865	fl. Jan 1972
Isle of Man	105	221	John Kneen	Nov 12, 1852	June 9, 1958

Note: fl. is the abbreviation for *floruit*, Latin for he (or she) was living at the relevant date.
(a) Mrs Ellen Carroll died in North River, Newfoundland, Canada, Dec 8, 1943, reputedly aged 115 years 49 days.
(b) Mrs Susan Johanna Deporter of Port Elizabeth, South Africa, was reputedly 114 years old when she died Aug 4, 1954. Mrs Sarah Lawrence of Cape Town, South Africa, was reputedly 112 on June 3, 1968.
(c) London-born Miss Isabella Shepheard was allegedly 115 years old when she died at St Asaph, North Wales, Nov 20, 1948, but her actual age was believed to have been 109 years 90 days. Charles Alfred Nuñez Arnold died in Liverpool, England, Nov 15, 1941, reputedly 112 years 66 days (based on a baptismal claim in London on Sept 10, 1829). Mrs Elizabeth Cornish (*née* Veale), who was buried at Stratton, Cornwall, March 10, 1691 or 1692, was reputedly baptized on Oct 16, 1578, 113 years 4 months earlier.
(d) Ex-slave Mrs Martha Graham died in Fayetteville, NC, June 25, 1959, reputedly aged 117 or 118. Census researches by Eckler show that she was seemingly born in Dec 1844, and hence aged 114 years 6 months. Mrs Rena Glover Brailsford died in Summerton, SC, Dec 6, 1977, reputedly aged 118 years. Mrs Rosario Vasquez who died in California on Sept 2, 1980 was reputedly born in Sonora, Mexico, on June 3, 1866, which would make her 114 years 93 days.
(e) Senhora Jesuina da Conçeicão of Lisbon was reputedly 113 years old when she died June 10, 1965.
(f) Thomas Peters was recorded to have been born on Apr 6, 1745 in Leeuwarden and died aged 111 years 354 days on Mar 26, 1857 in Arnhem.
(g) Friedrich Sadowski of Heidelberg reputedly celebrated his 111th birthday Oct 31, 1936. Franz Joseph Eder died in Spitzburg May 3, 1911, allegedly aged 116.
(h) Snr Benita Medrana of Avila died on Jan 28, 1979, allegedly aged 114 years 335 days.
(i) There are allegedly 21,700 centenarians in the USSR compared with 7,000 in the US. Of these, 21,000 are ascribed to the Georgian SSR, or one out of every 232 people. In July 1962 it was reported that 128, mostly male, resided in the one village of Medini.

USSR's average, and that the number of centenarians claimed in the Caucasus has declined rapidly, from 8,000 in 1950 to 4,500 in 1970. Dr I. M. Spector, of the Institute of Traumatology, Kazan, USSR, quoted the maximum life span of man in Apr 1974 as "110–115 years," though Dr Medvedev in Dec 1977, put the *proven* limit in the USSR as low as 108 years.

After 4 years the Andean valley of Vilcabamba in Peru ceased, from Feb 1978, to be the source of highly publicized and uncritical reports about very aged humans. These, it was said, lived up to 25 years beyond the so far acceptable limit of about 115 years.

The discovery by Mazess and Forman was published in March 1978 that inhabitants had been pointing to baptismal entries of their fathers, and even their grandfathers, as their own reduced the age of the valley's oldest man from 140 to 96. The lucrative income from tourism is expected to decline to a similar degree.

The 1900 US Federal census for Crawfish Springs Militia District of Walker County, Ga, records an age of 77 for a Mark Thrash. If the Mark Thrash (reputedly born in Ga in Dec 1822) who died near Chattanooga, Tenn on Dec 17, 1943, was he, and the age attributed being accepted, then he would have survived for 121 years.

The national records in the table on the opposite page can be taken as authentic.

Oldest Authentic Centenarian

The greatest *authenticated* age to which any human has ever lived is a unique 117th birthday in the case of Shigechiyo Izumi of Asan, Tokunoshima Island, Japan. He was born on the island where he lives on June 29, 1865, and recorded as a 6-year-old in Japan's first census of 1871. He watches television and says the best way to a long life is "not to worry" and to leave things to "God, the Sun, and Buddha."

Oldest Mummy

Mummification (from the Persian word *mām*, wax) dates from 2700 BC or the 2nd dynasty of the Egyptian pharaohs. The practice began to decline from *c.* 1000 BC.

OLDEST MOTHER: When she was more than 57 years old, Mrs Ruth Kistler bore daughter Suzan (right). ("Family Doctor" magazine (IPC))

4. REPRODUCTIVITY

Most Children

The greatest officially recorded number of children produced by a mother is 69 by the first of the 2 wives of Feodor Vassilyev (b 1707–*fl.* 1782), a peasant from Shuya, 150 miles east of Moscow. In 27 confinements she gave birth to 16 pairs of twins, 7 sets of triplets and 4 sets of quadruplets. The children, of whom almost all survived to their majority, were born in the period *c.* 1725–1765. At least 67 survived infancy. The case was reported to Moscow by the Monastery of Nikolskiy Feb 27, 1782. Empress Ekaterina II (The Great) (1762–96) was reputed to have evinced wonderment.

Currently the world's most prolific mother is reported to be Leontina Albina (*née* Espinosa) (b 1925) of San Antonio, Chile, who was reported pregnant in Nov 1980 having already produced 44 children. Her husband Gerardo Secundo Albina (variously Alvina) (b 1921) states that they were married in Argentina in 1943 and they had 5 sets of triplets (all boys) before coming to Chile. "Only" 40 (24 boys and 16 girls) survive. Eleven were lost in an earthquake, thus indicating that she had more than the 45 born in Chile.

Oldest Mother

Medical literature contains extreme but unauthenticated cases of septuagenarian mothers such as Mrs Ellen Ellis, aged 72, of Four Crosses, Clwyd, Wales, who allegedly produced a stillborn 13th child May 15, 1776, in her 46th year of marriage. Many cases are cover-ups for illegitimate grandchildren. The oldest recorded mother of whom there is certain evidence is Mrs Ruth Alice Kistler (*née* Taylor), formerly Mrs Shepard, of Portland, Ore. She was born at Wakefield, Mass, June 11, 1899, and gave birth to a daughter, Suzan, in Glendale, Calif, Oct 18, 1956, when her age was 57 years 129 days.

The incidence of quinquagenarian births varies widely, with the highest purported rate being in Albania with nearly 5,500 per million compared with 2 per million in England.

Descendants

In polygamous countries, the number of a person's descendants soon becomes incalculable. The last Sharifian Emperor of Morocco, Moulay Ismail (1672–1727), known as "The Bloodthirsty," was reputed to have fathered a total of 548 sons and 340 daughters.

19

MOST DESCENDANTS: Leaving 582 living children, grandchildren, etc., was the record set by Capt. Wilson Kettle when he died at age 102.

Capt. Wilson Kettle (b 1860) of Grand Bay, Port Aux Basques, Newfoundland, Canada, died Jan 25, 1963, aged 102, leaving 11 children by 2 wives, 65 grandchildren, 201 great-grandchildren, and 305 great-great-grandchildren, a total of 582 living descendants. Mrs Johanna Booyson (see Longevity Table) of Belfast, Transvaal, was estimated to have 600 living descendants in South Africa in Jan 1968.

Most Living Ascendants

Jesse Jones Werkmeister (b Oct 27, 1979) of Tilden, Neb, had a full set of grandparents and great-grandparents, and four great-great-grandparents, making 18 direct ascendants. This was equaled on the birth of Kendel Shenner (b Oct 21, 1980) at Big Beaver, Saskatchewan, Canada.

Multiple Great-Grandparents

While eight 15-year generations are possible in a 105-year life-span for a great-great-great-great-great-grandparent (5 greats), no case of a great-great-great-great-grandparent (4 greats) has yet been recorded.

At least 26 cases of great-great-great-grandparents have been reported in the last 29 years. Of these cases

the youngest person to learn that her great-granddaughter had become a grandmother was Mrs Ann V. Weirick (1888–1978) of Paxtonville, Pa, who received news of her great-great-great-grandson Matthew Stork (b Sept 9, 1976) when aged only 88. She died Jan 6, 1978.

Multiple Births

It was announced by Dr Gennaro Montanino of Rome that he had removed the fetuses of 10 girls and 5 boys from the womb of a 35-year-old housewife July 22, 1971. A fertility drug was responsible for this unique and unsurpassed instance of quindecaplets.

Lightest Twins

The lightest recorded birth weight for surviving twins is 2 lb 3 oz in the case of Mary (16 oz) and Margaret (19 oz) born to Mrs Florence Stimson of Peterborough, England, delivered by Dr Macaulay, Aug 16, 1931.

"Siamese" Twins

Conjoined twins derived this name from the celebrated Chang and Eng Bunker, born at Maklong, Thailand (Siam), May 11, 1811. They were joined by a cartilaginous band at the chest and married in Apr 1843 the Misses Sarah and Adelaide Yates of Wilkes County, NC. They fathered 10 and 12 children respectively. They died within three hours of each other Jan 17, 1874, aged 62.

The earliest successful separation of Siamese twins was performed on xiphopagus twin girls at Mt Sinai Hospital, Cleveland, Ohio, by Dr Jac S. Geller on Dec 14, 1952.

The rarest form of conjoined twins is Dicephales tetrabrachius dipus (two heads, four arms and two legs) of which only three examples are known today. They are the pair Masha and Dasha, born on Jan 4, 1950, in the USSR; an unidentified pair separated in a 10-hour operation June 23, 1977, in Washington, DC; and Fonda Michelle and Shannon Elaine Beaver of Forest City, NC (b Feb 9, 1980).

Oldest Twins

The chances of identical twins both reaching 100 are said to be one in 700 million. The oldest recorded twins were Eli and John Phipps, born Feb 14, 1803, in Affinghton, Virginia. Eli died at the age of 108 years 9 days Feb 23, 1911, in Hennessey, Okla, at

MULTIPLE BIRTHS

Highest number reported at single birth (Decaplets): 10 (2 male, 8 female), Bacacay, Brazil, Apr 22, 1946 (also report from Spain, 1924, and China, May 12, 1936).

Highest number medically recorded (Nonuplets): 9 (5 male, 4 female), to Mrs Geraldine Broderick at Royal Hospital, Sydney, Australia, June 13, 1971. 2 males were stillborn. Richard (12 oz) survived 6 days. 9 (all died), to patient at University of Penn, Philadelphia, May 29, 1972. 9 (all died), reported from Bagerhat, Bangladesh, *c.* May 1977, to 30-year-old mother.

Highest number surviving: 6 out of 6 sextuplets (3 males, 3 females), to Mrs Susan Rosenkowitz (*née* Scoones) at Cape Town, South Africa, Jan 1, 1974. In order of birth they were: David, Nicolette, Jason, Emma, Grant and Elizabeth. They totaled 24 lb 1 oz. 6 out of 6 (4 males, 2 females) to Mrs Rosanna Giannini (b 1952) at Careggi Hospital, Florence, Italy, on Jan 11, 1980. They are Francesco, Fabrizio, Giorgio, Roberto, Letizia and Linda. *Note:* The South African press were unable to verify the birth of 5 babies to Mrs Charmaine Craig (*née* Peterson) in Cape Town on Oct 16, 1980, and a sixth on Nov 8. The reported names were Frank, Salome, John, Andrew, William and belatedly Deborah.

Quintuplets (Heaviest): 25 lb to Mrs Lui Saulien, Chekiang, China, June 7, 1953. 25 lb to Mrs Kamalammal, Pondicherry, India, Dec 30, 1956. (Most sets): No recorded case of more than a single set.

Quadruplets (Heaviest): 22 lb 13 oz to Mrs Ayako Takeda, Tsuchihashi Maternity Hospital, Kagoshima, Japan, Oct 4, 1978 (4 girls). (Most sets): 4, to Mme Feodor Vassilyev (d *ante* 1770), of Shuya, Russia.

Triplets (Heaviest): 26 lb 6 oz (unconfirmed), Iranian case (2 male, 1 female), March 18, 1968. (Most sets): 15, to Maddalena Granata (1839–*fl.* 1886), Nocera Superiore, Italy.

Twins (Heaviest): 27 lb 12 oz (surviving), 14 lb and 13 lb 12 oz, to Mrs J. P. Haskin, Fort Smith, Ark, Feb 20, 1924. The 35 lb 8 oz twins reported in *The Lancet* from Derbyshire, England, Dec 6, 1884, for the Warren Case (2 males) (live-born) is believed to have been a misprint for 25 lb 8 oz. (Most sets): 16, to Mme Vassilyev (see p 19). 15, to Mrs Mary Jonas (d Dec 4, 1899), of Chester, England—all sets were boy and girl. Mrs Barbara Zulu of Barbeton, South Africa, bore 3 sets of girls and 3 mixed sets in 7 years (1967–73).

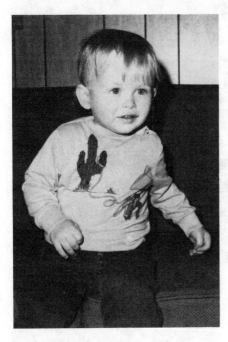

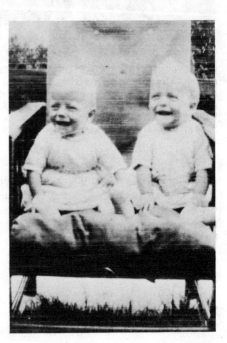

MOST LIVING PARENTS AND GRANDPARENTS (left): Jesse Jones Werkmeister had a total of 18 when he was born in 1979.

LIGHTEST TWINS (right): Weighing a total of only 2 lb 3 oz together at birth, the twin girls born to Mrs Florence Stimson of England set a record in 1931.

HIGHEST NUMBER OF SURVIVING CHILDREN (above): Mrs Susan Rosenkowitz of Cape Town, South Africa, is the proud mother of sextuplets, 3 males, 3 females, who totaled 24 lb 1 oz at birth. NONUPLETS (9 babies) were born to Mrs Geraldine Broderick (right) of Sydney, Australia, but 2 were stillborn.

which time John was still living, in Shenandoah, Iowa. On Jan 14, 1982, identical twin sisters, Lucy Brown Coleman and Elizabeth Brown English of Georgia, beat the odds and celebrated their 100th birthday.

Most Twins, Geographically

In Chungchon, South Korea, it was reported in Sept 1981 that there was unaccountably 38 pairs in only 275 families—the highest ratio ever recorded.

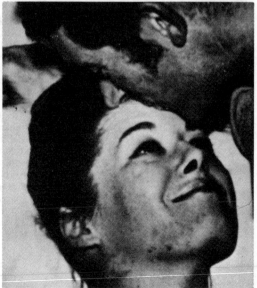

Oldest Triplets

The longest-lived triplets on record were Faith, Hope, and Charity Caughlin, born Mar 27, 1868, in Marlboro, Mass. Mrs (Ellen) Hope Daniels was the first to die, Mar 2, 1962, when 93.

Fastest Triplet Birth

The fastest recorded natural birth of triplets has been 2 minutes in the case of Mrs James E. Duck of Memphis, Tenn (Bradley, Christopher and Carmon) March 21, 1977.

BABIES

Heaviest Babies

The heaviest viable baby on record of normal parentage was a boy of 22 lb 8 oz born to Signora Carmelina Fedele of Aversa, Italy, in Sept 1955.

Mrs Anna Bates, *née* Swan, the 7-ft-5½-in Canadian giantess (see Tallest Couple), gave birth to a boy weighing 23 lb 12 oz (length 30 in) at her home in Seville, Ohio, on Jan 19, 1879, but the baby died less than 24 hours later. Her first child, an 18-lb girl (length 24 in), was stillborn when she was delivered in 1872.

On Jan 9, 1891, Mrs Florentin Ortega of Buenos Aires, Argentina, produced a still-born boy weighing 25 lb.

In May 1939 a deformed baby weighing 29 lb 4 oz was born in a hospital at Effingham, Ill, but died two hours later from respiratory problems.

Most Bouncing Baby

The most bouncing baby on record was probably James Weir (1819–21) whose headstone in the Old

Parish Cemetery, Wishaw, Strathclyde, Scotland, lists him at 112 lb, 3 ft 4 in in height, and 39 in around the waist at the age of 13 months.

Therese Parentean, who died in Rouyn, Quebec, Canada, aged 9, May 11, 1936, weighed 340 lb (*cf.* 378 lb for Robert Earl Hughes at 10 years of age).

Lightest

The lowest birth weight recorded for a surviving infant, of which there is definite evidence, is 10 oz in the case of Marion Chapman, born 6 weeks prematurely on June 5, 1938, in South Shields, northwest England. She was born unattended (length 12¼ in) and was nursed by Dr D. A. Shearer, who fed her hourly for the first 30 hours with brandy, glucose and water through a fountain-pen filler. At three weeks she weighed 1 lb 13 oz and by her first birthday her weight had increased to 13 lb 14 oz. Her weight on her 21st birthday was 106 lb.

The smallest viable baby reported born in the US has been Jacqueline Benson, who was born in Palatine, Ill, Feb 20, 1936, weighing 12 oz.

A weight of 8 oz was reported on March 20, 1938, for a baby born prematurely to Mrs John Womack, after she had been knocked down by a truck in East St Louis, Ill. The baby was taken alive to St Mary's Hospital, but further information is lacking. On Feb 23, 1952, it was reported that a 6 oz baby only 6½ in in length lived for 12 hours in a hospital in Indianapolis. A twin was stillborn.

Longest Pregnancy

Claims up to 413 days have been widely reported, but accurate data are bedevilled by the increasing use of oral contraceptive pills, which can be a cause of amenorrhea. Some women on becoming pregnant erroneously add some preceding periodless months to their pregnancy. In the pre-pill era, English law had accepted pregnancies with extremes of 174 days (1939), and 349 days (1949).

Most Southerly Birth

Emilio Marcos Palma, born Jan 7, 1978, at the Sargento Cabral Base, Antarctica, is the only infant who can claim to be the first born on any continent.

Earliest Test Tube Baby

Louise Brown (5 lb 12 oz) was delivered by Caesarean section from Lesley Brown, 31, in Oldham

Coincidental Birth Dates

The only verified example of a family producing five single children with coincidental birthdays is that of Catherine (1952), Carol (1953), Charles (1956), Claudia (1961) and Cecilia (1966), born to Ralph and Carolyn Cummins of Clintwood, Va, all on Feb 20th.

The random odds against five such births occurring singly on the same date would be 1 to 17,797,577,730—almost 4 times the world's population.

The 3 children of the Henrikson family (above) of Andenes, Norway—Heidi (b 1960); Olav (b 1964) and Lief-Martin (b 1968)—all celebrate their birthday infrequently because these all fall on Leap Year Day—Feb 29.

General Hospital, Lancashire, England, at 11:47 p.m. July 25, 1978. She was externally conceived on Nov 10, 1977.

Most Proximate Births

Gloria Kuehn of Lemay, Mo, gave birth to a daughter, Amy Elizabeth, June 9, 1978, and a son, Gregory Charles, Jan 19, 1979, only 224 days later.

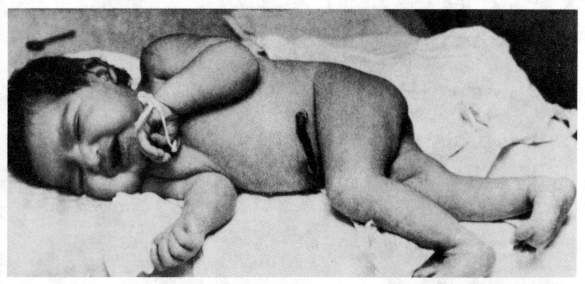

FIRST TEST TUBE BABY: Louise Brown weighed 5 lb 12 oz at birth. She was conceived externally in England in 1977.

5. PHYSIOLOGY AND ANATOMY

Hydrogen (63%) and oxygen (25.5%) are the commonest of the 24 elements in the human body. In 1972, four more trace elements were added—fluorine, silicon, tin and vanadium. The "essentiality" of nickel has not yet been finally pronounced upon.

Longest Bones

Excluding a variable number of sesamoids, there are 206 bones in the human body. The thigh bone or *femur* is the longest. It constitutes usually 27½% of a

SMALLEST BRAIN and SMALLEST WAIST: Writer Anatole France (left) and Ethel Granger (right). His brain weighed 35.8 oz, her waist measured 13 in.

MUSCLE MODEL: When Arnold Schwarzenegger is dressed in street clothes, no one suspects that beneath the surface is "the most perfectly developed man in the history of the world." After being chosen Mr. Universe many times, the Austrian-born model trained to become a Hollywood actor and obtained the hero's role in the popular movie "Conan, the Barbarian." Arnold's chest measures 57 in, his upper arm 22 in around, and he normally weighs 235 lb. ("Conan" photos © Universal Pictures, a division of Universal City Studio, Inc.)

person's stature, and may be expected to be 19¾ in long in a 6-ft-tall man. The longest recorded bone was the *femur* of the German giant Constantine, who died in Mons, Belgium, March 30, 1902, aged 30. It measured 29.9 in. The *femur* of Robert Wadlow, the tallest man ever recorded, measured an estimated 29½ in.

Smallest Bones

The *stapes* or stirrup bone, one of the three auditory ossicles in the middle ear, is the smallest human bone, measuring from 2.6 to 3.4 mm (0.10 to 0.17 in) in length and weighing from 2.0 to 4.3 mg (0.03 to 0.065 of a grain).

Largest Muscles

Muscles normally account for 40% of the body weight and the bulkiest of the 639 muscles in the human body is the *gluteus maximus* or buttock muscle, which extends the thigh.

Smallest Muscles

The smallest muscle is the *stapedius,* which controls the *stapes* (see above), an auditory ossicle in the middle ear, and which is less than 1/20th in in length.

Smallest Waists

Queen Catherine de Medici (1519–89) decreed a standard waist measurement of 13 in for ladies of the French court. This was at a time when females were more diminutive. The smallest recorded waist among women of normal stature in the 20th century is a reputed 13 in in the cases of the French actress Mlle Polaire (1881–1939) and Mrs Ethel Granger (1905–82) of Peterborough, England, who reduced from a natural 22 in over the period 1929–39.

Largest Chest Measurements

The largest chest measurements are among endomorphs (those with a tendency toward globularity). In the extreme case of Robert Earl Hughes of Monticello, Mo (one of the heaviest recorded humans), this was reportedly 124 in, but in the light of his known height and weight a figure of 104 in would be more supportable.

Among muscular subjects (mesomorphs) of normal height *expanded* chest measurements above 56 in

are extremely rare. Vasili Alexeyev (b 1942), the 6-ft-1¼-in Russian super-heavyweight weight-lifting champion, had a 60½-in chest at his top weight of 350 lb.

Arnold Schwarzenegger (b 1948, Graz, Austria), the 6-ft-1-in former Mr Universe and "the most perfectly developed man in the history of the world," had a chest measurement of 57 in at his best body weight of 235 lb.

The powerlifter Gary Aprahamian, the first to achieve a cold (not pumped) biceps measurement over 25 in with 25⅜ in, has a normal chest measurement of 61 in.

Largest Brains

The brain of an average adult male (*i.e.,* 30–59 years) weighs 3 lb 2.2 oz, falling to 2 lb 4.31 oz. The heaviest non-diseased brain on record was that of Ivan Sergeyvich Turgenev (1818–83), the Russian author. His brain weighed 4 lb 6.9 oz, while that of Baron Georges Cuvier (1769–1832), the famous French zoologist, was 4 lb 0.4 oz.

The brain of Oliver Cromwell (1599–1658) reputedly weighed 4 lb 14.8 oz, but the size of his head in portraits and the preserved skull do not support this extreme figure. The brain of Lord Byron, who died in Greece in 1824, aged 36, reportedly weighed 6 Neapolitan pounds (4 lb 3.86 oz), but this figure also included a certain amount of blood. The heaviest brain ever recorded was that of a 50-year-old white male which weighed 4 lb 8.29 oz, reported by Dr Thomas F. Hegert, Chief Medical Examiner for District 9, Florida, Oct 23, 1975. In Jan 1891, the *Edinburgh Medical Journal* reported a case of a 75-year-old man in the Royal Edinburgh Asylum whose brain weighed 4 lb 0.5 oz.

Human brains are getting heavier. Examination of post-mortem records shows that the average male brain weight has increased from 3 lb 0.4 oz in 1860 to 3 lb 2.2 oz today. Women's brains have also put on weight, from 2 lb 11.8 oz to 2 lb 12.6 oz, and in recent years have been growing almost as fast as men's.

Smallest Brain

The non-atrophied brain of the writer Anatole France (1844–1924) weighed only 2 lb 3.8 oz without the membrane, and that of Franz Joseph Gall (1758–1828), a founder of phrenology, 2 lb 10.3 oz. Brains in extreme cases of microcephaly may weigh as little as 10.6 oz (*cf.* 20 oz for the adult male gorilla, and 16–20 oz for other anthropoid apes).

Most Expensive Skull

On Mar 6, 1977, the Royal Swedish Academy of Science paid £5,500 (then $9,350) for the skull of Emanuel Swedenborg (1688–1772), the Swedish philosopher and theologian, at a sale held at Sotheby's, London.

Human Memory

Mehmed Ali Halici of Ankara, Turkey, on Oct 14, 1967, recited 6,666 verses of the Koran from memory in 6 hours. The recitation was followed by six Koran scholars. Rare instances of eidetic memory, the ability to reproject and thus "visually" recall material, are known to science.

Highest I.Q.

People of the very highest measurable intelligence are said to be not especially intuitive or perceptive or free from prejudice. They usually occupy rather undistinguished jobs. Their success in the academic world can be handicapped by often peevish inability to tolerate repetition of what is (to them) obvious.

Comparability between one scale and another and within one scale close to the ceiling of 200 IQ points is impracticable. The most elite ultra-high IQ Society comprises 11 members of the Mega Society for which an IQ of 193 (measured on the widely accepted Binet scale), exhibited in 1 person in about 1,000,000, is requisite.

The two members who have scored 197 are Christopher Phillip Harding (b Keynsham, England, 1944) of Rockhampton, Australia, and Wolfgang Jensen (b Eiserfeld, W Germany, 1962) of Cape Town, South Africa.

The highest I.Q. published for a national population is 106.6 for the Japanese.

Human Computer

The fastest extraction of a 13th root from a 100-digit number is in 1 min 28.8 sec by Willem Klein (b 1914, Netherlands) on Apr 7, 1981 at the National Laboratory for High Energy Physics (KEK), Tsukuba, Japan.

Mrs Shakuntala Devi of India demonstrated the multiplication of two 13-digit numbers, 7,686,369,-774,870 × 2,465,099,745,779, picked at random by the Computer Department of Imperial College, London, on June 18, 1980, in 28 sec. Her correct answer was 18,947,668,177,995,426,462,773,730.

Memorizing Pi

All India Radio broadcast in its *Weekly Roundup* on July 5, 1981, part of a recording made earlier that day by Rajan Srinivasen Mahadevan, 23, in the process of reciting π (Pi) from memory (in English) to 31,811 places in 3 hours 49 min (including 26 min of breaks) at the Lion Seva Mandir, Mangalore. His rate was 156.7 digits per minute.

(Note: It is only the *approximation* of π at 22/7 which recurs after its sixth decimal place and can, of course, be recited *ad nauseam*. The true value is a string of random numbers fiendishly difficult to memorize. The average ability for memorizing random numbers is only 7.)

Longest Necks

The maximum measured extension of the neck by the successive fitting of copper coils, as practiced by the Padaung or Karen people of Burma, is 15¾ in. The neck muscles become so atrophied that the removal of the support of the rings produces asphyxiation.

Most Fingers and Toes

At an inquest held on a baby at Shoreditch, East London, England, on Sept 16, 1921, it was reported that the boy had 14 fingers and 15 toes.

Fewest Toes

The "lobster claw syndrome" exhibited by the two-toed Kalanga people of the Zimbabwe-Botswana border area is hereditary *via* a single mutated gene.

Touch Sensitivity

The extreme sensitivity of the fingers is such that a vibration with a movement of 0.02 of a micron can be detected.

Longest Finger Nails

The longest known set of nails now belongs to the left hand of Shridhar Chillal (b 1937), of Poona, India. The five nails on his left hand, by March 21, 1982, had achieved a measured aggregate length of 116½ in (thumb 29½ in) uncut since 1952. Human nails normally grow from cuticle to cutting length in from 117 to 138 days.

LONGEST NECKS (above): The Padaung women of Burma are much admired for the length of their necks. The copper coils, however, make neck turning difficult and the muscles tend to atrophy. (Planet News) LONGEST FINGER NAILS (right): Shridhar Chillal of India is proud of his left hand with its nails that total 116½ in in length. However, it's a handicap in his job as a photographer, and as for typing, that's impossible. He keeps them covered when he sleeps too. HUMAN COMPUTER (below): Willem Klein does some mathematical computations faster than a machine. He can extract the 13th root of a 100-digit number in less than 1½ min.

LONGEST MOUSTACHE (above):
Between 1949 and 1962, a Brahmin
named Masuriya Din let his moustache grow to a length of 102 in.

LONGEST BEARD (left): Hans
Langseth had this picture of his
17½-foot-long beard taken in
Barney, ND.

LONG HAIR (right): At the 1981
"Olympics of the Longest Hair" in
Paris the easy winner was the
Frenchwoman Marie-Odile Lefebvre. Her hair had the respectable (but not record) length of
72.23 in. With the money she won
she bought herself a hair dryer.

Longest Hair

Swami Pandarasannadhi, the head of the Tiruda-duturai monastery, Tanjore district, Madras, India, was reported in 1949 to have hair 26 ft in length. From photographs it appears that he was afflicted with the disease Plica caudiformis, in which the hair becomes matted and crusted as a result of neglect. The length of the hair of Miss Skuldfrid Sjorgien (b Stockholm) was reported from Toronto, Canada, in 1927 to have attained twice her height at 10 ft 6 in.

Longest Moustache

The longest moustache on record was that of Masuriya Din (b 1908), a Brahmin of the Partabgarh district in Uttar Pradesh, India. It grew to an extended span of 102 in between 1949 and 1962. Karna Ram Bheel (b 1928) was granted permission by a New Delhi prison governor in Feb 1979 to keep his 7-ft-10-in moustache, grown since 1949, during his life sentence.

Longest Beard

The longest beard preserved was that of Hans N. Langseth (1846–1927) of Norway, which measured 17½ ft at the time of his burial in Kensett, Iowa, in 1927 after 15 years residence in the US. The beard was presented to the Smithsonian Institution, Washington, DC in 1967.

The beard of the bearded lady Janice Deveree (b Bracken County, Ky, 1842) was measured at 14 in in 1884.

Most Teeth

Cases of the growth in late life of a third set of teeth have been recorded several times. A reference to an extreme case in France of a fourth dentition known as Lison's case was published in 1896. A triple row of teeth was noted in 1680 by Albertus Hellwigius.

Earliest Dentition

The first deciduous or milk teeth normally appear in infants at 5 to 8 months, these being the mandibular and maxillary first incisors. There are many records of children born with teeth, the most distinguished example being Prince Louis Dieudonné, later Louis XIV of France, who was born with two teeth on Sept 5, 1638. Molars usually appear at 24 months, but in Pindborg's case published in Denmark in 1970, a 6-week premature baby was documented with 8 natal teeth of which 4 were in the molar region.

Most Dedicated Dentist

Brother Giovanni Battista Orsenigo of the Ospedale Fatebenefratelli, Rome, Italy, a religious dentist, conserved all the teeth he extracted in three enormous boxes during the time he exercised his profession from 1868 to 1904. In 1903, the number was counted and found to be 2,000,744 teeth.

Most Valuable Tooth

In 1816 a tooth belonging to Sir Isaac Newton (1643–1727) was sold in London for £730 (now $1,300). It was purchased by a nobleman who had it set in a ring which he wore constantly.

Smallest Visible Object

In Oct 1972, the University of Stuttgart, West Germany reported that their student Frl Veronica Seider (b 1953) possessed a visual acuity 20 times better than average. She could identify people at a distance of more than a mile. The Russians are reputedly working on a new type of lens implant which will give the wearer super-human sight.

Color Sensitivity

The unaided human eye, under the best possible viewing conditions, comparing large areas of color, in good illumination, using both eyes, can distinguish 10,000,000 different color surfaces. The most accurate photo-electric spectrophotometers possess a precision probably only 40% as good as this.

The most extreme form of color blindness, monochromatic vision, is very rare. The highest rate of red-green color blindness exists in Czechoslovakia and the lowest rate among Fijians and Brazilian Indians. About 7.5% of men and 0.1% of women suffer some element of color blindness.

Voice

The highest and lowest recorded notes attained by the human voice before this century were a staccato E in *alt-altissimo* (*e″″*) by Ellen Beach Yaw (US, 1869–1947) in Carnegie Hall, New York City, Jan 19, 1896, and an A, (55 cycles per sec) by Kaspar Foster (1617–73).

Madeleine Marie Robin (1918–60), the French operatic coloratura, could produce and sustain the B flat above high C in the Lucia mad scene in *Lucia di Lammermoor.*

Since 1950 singers have achieved high and low notes far beyond the hitherto accepted extremes. Notes, however, at the bass and treble extremities of the register tend to lack harmonics and are of little musical value.

Fräulein Marita Günther, trained by Alfred Wolfsohn, has covered the range of the piano from the lowest note A͵ to c′ ″ ″. Of this range of 7¼ octaves, 6 octaves are considered to be of musical value.

Roy Hart, also trained by Wolfsohn, has reached notes below the range of the piano. Barry Girard of Canton, Ohio, in May 1975 reached the e (4,340 Hz) above the piano's top note.

The lowest vocal note in the classical repertoire is in Mozart's *Il Seraglio* by Osmin who descends to low D (73.4 cps). J. D. Sumner of Nashville, Tenn, in her album *Blessed Assurance,* reaches the C below low C (32.7 cps). The highest note put into song is G″ ″ first occurring in *Popoli di Tessaglia* by Mozart. Stephan Zucker sang A in *alt-altissimo* for 3.8 sec in the tenor role of Salvini in the world premiere of Bellini's *Adelson e Salvini* in Carnegie Hall, New York City, Sept 12, 1972.

Greatest Range

The normal intelligible outdoor range of the male human voice in still air is 200 yards. The *silbo,* the whistled language of the Spanish-speaking Canary Island of La Gomera, is intelligible across the valleys, under ideal conditions, at 5 miles. There is a recorded case, under freak acoustic conditions, of the human voice being detectable at a distance of 10½ miles across still water at night. It was said that Mills Darden (see *Heaviest Men*) could be heard 6 miles away when he shouted at the top of his voice.

Lowest Detectable Sound

The intensity of noise or sound is measured in terms of pressure. The pressure of the quietest sound that can be detected by a person of normal hearing at the most sensitive frequency of *c.* 2,750 Hz (cycles per sec) is 2×10^{-5} pascal. One tenth of the logarithm to this standard provides a unit termed a decibel (dBA). Prolonged noise above 150 dBA will cause immediate permanent deafness while 200 dBA could be fatal. A noise of 30 dBA is negligible.

Highest Detectable Pitch

The upper limit of hearing by the human ear has been regarded as 20,000 Hz (cycles per sec), although children with asthma can often detect a sound of 30,000 cycles per sec. It was announced in Feb 1964 that experiments in the USSR had conclusively proved that oscillations as high as 200,000 cycles per sec can be heard if the oscillator is pressed against the skull.

Fastest Talker

Extremely few people are able to speak *articulately* at a sustained speed above 300 words per min. The fastest broadcaster has usually been regarded to be Gerry Wilmot (b Oct 6, 1914, Victoria, BC, Canada), the ice hockey commentator in the post World War II period. Raymond Glendenning (1907–74), the BBC horse racing commentator, once spoke 176 words in 30 seconds while reporting a greyhound race. In public life the highest speed recorded is a 327-words-per-min burst in a speech made in Dec 1961, by John Fitzgerald Kennedy (1917–63), then President. Tapes of attempts to recite Hamlet's 262-word soliloquy in under 24 sec (655 wpm) have proved indecipherable. Patricia Keeling-Andrich delivered 403 words from W. S. Gilbert's "The Nightmare" in a test in 60 sec at Chabot College, Hayward, Calif, March 16, 1978.

Shouting

Because of their more optimal frequency, female screams register higher readings on decibel meters than male bellows. The highest scientifically measured emission has been one of 120 dBA on a Bruel & Kjaer Precision Sound Level Meter by Susan Birmingham at Hong Kong Island School Mar 6, 1982.

Rarest Disease

Medical literature periodically records hitherto undescribed diseases. A disease as yet undescribed but predicted by a Norwegian doctor is podocytoma of the kidney—a tumor of the epithelial cells lining the glomerulus of the kidney. The last case of endemic smallpox was recorded in Somalia on Oct 26, 1977.

Kuru, or laughing sickness, afflicts only the Fore tribe of eastern New Guinea and is 100% fatal. This was formally attributed to the cannibalistic practice of eating human brains.

FASTEST TALKER IN PUBLIC LIFE: John F. Kennedy delivered an outburst of 327 words per min in Dec 1961. Here he is addressing the Democratic National Convention of 1956, placing the name of Adlai Stevenson in nomination, and not trying to set a record.

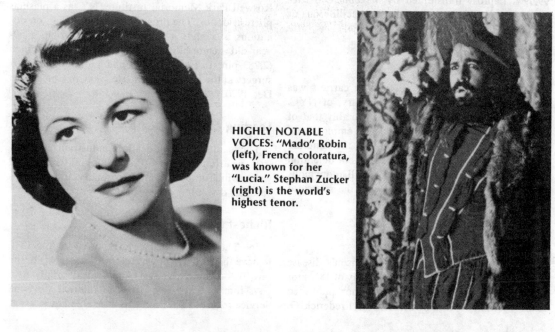

HIGHLY NOTABLE VOICES: "Mado" Robin (left), French coloratura, was known for her "Lucia." Stephan Zucker (right) is the world's highest tenor.

Commonest Diseases

The commonest non-contagious disease is periodontal disease, such as gingivitus, which afflicts some 80% of the US population. In Great Britain 13% of the people have lost all their teeth before reaching 21. During their lifetime few completely escape its effects. Infestation with pinworm (*Enterobius vermicularis*) approaches 100% in some areas of the world.

The commonest contagious illness in the world is coryza (acute nasopharyngitis) or the common cold. The case of the person most resistant to being infected by a cold was reported by the Medical Research Council Common Cold Unit, Salisbury, England, to be J. Brophy, who had only one mild reaction after being exposed 24 times.

Highest Mortality

Rabies in humans has been regarded as uniformly fatal when associated with the hydrophobia symptom. A 25-year-old woman, Candida de Sousa Barbosa of Rio de Janeiro, Brazil, was believed to be the first to survive the disease in Nov 1968, though some sources give priority to Matthew Winkler, 6, on Oct 10, 1970, who was bitten by a rabid bat.

Most and Least Infectious Diseases

The most infectious of all diseases is the pneumonic form of plague, with a mortality rate of 99.99%. Leprosy transmitted by *Mycobacterium leprae* is the least infectious and most bacilliferous of communicable diseases.

Most Notorious Carriers

The most publicized of all typhoid carriers was Mary Mallon, known as Typhoid Mary, of NYC. She was the source of 9 outbreaks, notably that of 1903. Because of her refusal to leave employment, often under assumed names, involving the handling of food, she was placed under permanent detention from 1915 until her death in 1938. A still anonymous dairy farmer from Camden, NY, was the source of 409 cases (40 fatal) in Aug 1909.

Parkinson's Disease

The most protracted case of Parkinson's disease (named after Dr James Parkinson's essay of 1817) for which the earliest treatments were not published until 1946, is 56 years in the case of Frederick G. Humphries of Croydon, London, England, whose symptoms became detectable in 1923.

Most Durable Cancer Patient

The most extreme recorded case of survival from diagnosed cancer is that of Mrs Winona Mildred Melick (*née* Douglass) (b Oct 22, 1876) of Long Beach, Calif. She had four cancer operations, in 1918, 1933, 1966 and 1968, but she died from pneumonia on Dec 28, 1981, just 67 days after her 105th birthday.

Blood Groups

The preponderance of one blood group varies greatly from one locality to another. On a world basis Group O is the most common (46%), but in some areas, for example Norway, Group A predominates.

The rarest blood group on the ABO system, one of 14 systems, is AB, which occurs in less than 3% of the population in the British Isles. The rarest type in the world is a type of Bombay blood (sub-type A-h) found so far only in a Czechoslovak nurse in 1961 and in a brother (Rh positive) and sister (Rh negative) named Jalbert in Mass, reported in Feb 1968. The brother has started a blood bank for himself.

Champion Blood Donor and Greatest User

Since 1966 Allen Doster, a self-employed beautician, has (to Dec 21, 1981) donated 1,414 US pints at Roswell Park Memorial Institute, NY, as a plasmapheresis donor. The present-day normal limit on donations is 5 pints a year. Warren C. Jyrich, a 50-year-old hemophiliac, required 2,400 donor units (2,283 pints) of blood when undergoing open heart surgery at the Michael Reese Hospital, in Chicago, in Dec 1970.

Leading Cause of Death

The leading cause of death in industrialized countries is arteriosclerosis (thickening of the arterial wall), which underlies much coronary and cerebrovascular disease.

Richest Natural Resources

Joe Thomas of Detroit was reported in Aug 1970 to have the highest known count of Anti-Lewis B, the rare blood antibody. A US biological supply firm pays him $1,500 per quart. The Internal Revenue Service regards this income as a taxable liquid asset.

Longest Coma

The longest recorded coma was that of Elaine Esposito (b Dec 3, 1934) of Tarpon Springs, Fla. She never stirred after an appendectomy on Aug 6, 1941, when she was six, in Chicago. She died on Nov 25, 1978, aged 43 years 357 days, having been in a coma for 37 years 111 days. Paul Balay (b 1936) of Lons le Saunier, Dijon, France, has been in a coma since Dec 11, 1955, following a car accident.

Highest Body Temperature

Sustained body temperatures of much over 109 °F are normally incompatible with life, although recoveries after readings of 111 °F have been noted. Marathon runners in hot weather attain 105.8 °F.

In Kalow's case, reported in the British medical magazine *Lancet* (Oct 31, 1970), a woman, following halothane anesthesia, ran a temperature of 112 °F. She recovered after a procainamide infusion.

A temperature of 115 °F was recorded in the case of Christopher Legge in the Hospital for Tropical Diseases, London, England, on Feb 9, 1934. A subsequent examination of the thermometer disclosed a flaw in the bulb, but it is regarded as certain that the patient sustained a temperature of more than 110 °F.

Lowest Body Temperature

There are two recorded cases of patients surviving body temperatures as low as 60.8 °F. Dorothy Mae Stevens (1929–74) was found in an alley in Chicago Feb 1, 1951, and Vickie Mary Davis of Milwaukee, Wis, at age 2 years 1 month was admitted to the Evangelical Hospital, Marshalltown, Iowa, Jan 21, 1956, each with a temperature of 60.8 °F. The little girl had been found unconscious on the floor of an unheated house and the air temperature had dropped to −24 °F. Her temperature returned to normal (98.4 °F) after 12 hours and may have been as low as 59 °F when she was first found. People may die of hypothermia with body temperatures of 95 °F.

Most Alcoholic Person

It is recorded that a hard drinker named Vanhorn (1750–1811), born in London, England, averaged more than four bottles of ruby port per day for 23 years prior to his death at 61. He is believed to have emptied 35,688 bottles.

The youngest recorded death from alcoholic poisoning was that of a 4-year-old boy, Joseph Sweet, in Wolverhampton, England, in 1827, reported in the Stafford Assizes case *R. v. Martin*.

The late Samuel Riley (b 1922) of Sefton Park, Merseyside, England, was found by a disbelieving pathologist to have a level of 1220 mg of alcohol per 100 milliliters in his blood (legal limit for motorists in the UK is 80 mg/100 ml) on March 28, 1979. He had expired in his home and had been an inspector at the plant of a well-known car manufacturer.

Pulse Rate

A normal adult pulse rate is 70–72 beats per min at rest for males, and 78–82 for females. Rates increase to 200 or more during violent exercise or drop to as low as 12 in the extreme case of Dorothy Mae Stevens (see *Lowest Body Temperature*) and Jean Hilliard (b 1962) of Fosston, Minn on Dec 20, 1980.

Fastest Reflexes

The results of experiments published in 1966 have shown that the fastest messages transmitted by the human nervous system travel as fast as 180 mph. With advancing age, impulses are carried 15% slower.

Hiccoughing

The longest recorded attack of hiccoughs is that afflicting Charles Osborne (b 1894) of Anthon, Iowa, from 1922 to date. He contracted it when slaughtering a hog and has hiccoughed about 420 million times in the interim period. He has been unable to find a cure, but has led a reasonably normal life in which he has had two wives and fathered eight children. He does admit, however, that he cannot keep in his false teeth.

Sneezing

The most chronic sneezing fit ever recorded is that of Donna Griffiths (b 1969) of Pershore, England. She started sneezing on Jan 13, 1981, and surpassed the previous duration record of 194 days on July 27, 1981. She sneezed an estimated million times in the first 365 days.

The highest speed at which expelled particles have been measured to travel is 103.6 mph.

Yawning

In Lee's case, reported in 1888, a 15-year-old female patient yawned continuously for a period of five weeks.

Loudest Snore

Research at the Ear, Nose and Throat Department of St. Mary's Hospital, London, published in Nov 1968 shows that a rasping snore can attain a loudness of 69 decibels, as compared to 70 to 90 decibels for a pneumatic drill.

Heart Stoppage

The longest recorded heart stoppage is a minimum of 3 hours 32 min in the case of Miss Jean Jawbone, 20, who was revived by a team of 26, using peritoneal dialysis, in Winnipeg Medical Centre, Manitoba, Canada, Jan 19, 1977.

In Feb 1974 Vegard Slettmoen, 5, fell through the ice on the River Nitselv, Norway. He was found 40 min later, 8 ft down, but was revived in Akerhaus Central Hospital without brain damage.

The longest recorded interval in a post-mortem birth was one of at least 80 min in Magnolia, Miss. Dr Robert E. Drake found Fanella Anderson, aged 25, dead in her home at 11:40 p.m., Oct 15, 1966, and he delivered her of a son weighing 6 lb 4 oz by Caesarean operation in the Beacham Memorial Hospital at 1 a.m. Oct 16, 1966.

Heart Transplants

The first human heart transplant operation was performed on Louis Washkansky, aged 55, at the Groote Schuur Hospital, Cape Town, South Africa, between 1:00 and 6:00 a.m. Dec 3, 1967, by a team of 30 headed by Prof Christiaan N. Barnard (b 1922). The donor was Miss Denise Ann Darvall, aged 25. Washkansky died Dec 21, 1967.

The longest surviving heart transplantee has been Emmanuel Vitria of Marseilles, France, who received a heart transplant Nov 28, 1968, and entered the 14th year of his new life in 1981.

Swallowing

The worst reported case of compulsive swallowing was an insane woman, Mrs H., aged 42, who complained of a "slight abdominal pain." She was found to have 2,533 objects in her stomach, including 947 bent pins. They were removed by Drs Chalk and Foucar in June 1927 at the Ontario Hospital, Canada.

The heaviest object ever extracted from a human stomach was a 5-lb 3-oz ball of hair, from a 20-year-old woman at the South Devon and East Cornwall Hospital, England, March 30, 1895.

Sword "Swallowing"

Edward Benjamin, known as Count Desmond (b July 30, 1941, Binghamton, NY), swallowed thirteen 23-in-long blades to below his xiphisternum and injured himself in the process. *This category has now been retired and no further claims will be entertained.*

Underwater Duration

The record for voluntarily staying underwater is 13 min 42.5 sec by Robert Foster, aged 32, an electronics technician of Richmond, Calif, who stayed under 10 ft of water in the swimming pool of the Bermuda Palms at San Rafael, Calif, on March 15, 1959. He hyperventilated with oxygen for 30 min before his descent. The record without hyperventilation is 6 min 29 sec by Georges Pouliquen in Paris, France, in 1970. It must be stressed that record-breaking of this kind is *extremely* dangerous.

Pill Taking

The highest recorded total of pills swallowed by a patient is 386,436 from June 9, 1967 to Jan 1, 1982, by C. H. A. Kilner (b 1926) of Bindura, Zimbabwe, following a successful pancreas operation.

Most Injections

Mrs Evelyn Ruth Winder (b 1922), a diabetic from Invercargill, New Zealand, injected herself with insulin an estimated 54,920 times over 51 years to May 1982.

Longest Survival in Iron Lung

The longest recorded survival by an iron lung patient is Mrs Laurel Nisbet (b Nov 17, 1912) of La Crescenta, Calif, who has been in an iron lung continuously to date since June 25, 1948.

Longest Operation

The most protracted reported operation for surgical as opposed to medical control purposes was one of 96 hours performed on Mrs Gertrude Levandowski (see *Slimming*), Feb 4–8, 1951. The patient suffered from a weak heart and the surgeons had to exercise the utmost caution during the operation.

The "slowest" operation on record is one on the feet of Mrs Doreen Scott of Derby, England, on Nov 20, 1981. She had been waiting since Mar 10, 1952.

HEART STOPPAGE VICTIM Vegard Slettmoen (above) at age 5 in Norway fell through river ice, remained 8 ft down for 40 min, but was revived without brain damage.

HEART TRANSPLANT PIONEER: Dr Christiaan Barnard (below) in 1967 in Cape Town, South Africa, completed the first of his spectacular operations successfully.

SWORD-SWALLOWER "Count Desmond" swallowed 13 blades 23 in long to set a final record in this category. (Franklin Berger photo)

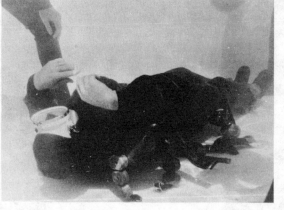

UNDERWATER LONGEST: Robert L. Foster of Calif held his breath for a record 13 min 42½ sec in a swimming pool. Record-breaking of this kind is extremely dangerous.

37

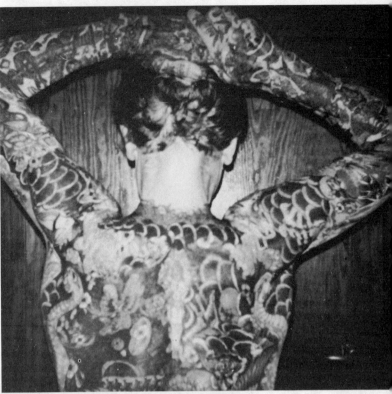

MOST TATTOOS: Rusty Skuse of England (above) is tattooed so that almost all of her body is covered. Her husband, who did the tattooing, says he always had designs on her. Wilfred Hardy (right) also of England, left very little of his body without artistic embellishment. He even has tattoos on his tongue, gums and inner cheeks.

FIRE-EATER: Dangerous as it is for most people, Jean Chapman finds fire no problem for her. She put out 6,607 flaming torches in her mouth in 2 hours in 1982, beating her own record of 4,593 made three years before.

Most Tattoos

The seeming ultimate in being tattooed is represented by Wilfred Hardy of Huthwaite, Nottinghamshire, England. Not content with a perilous approach to within 4% of totality of his outer skin, he has been tattooed on the inside of his cheek, his tongue, gums and eyebrows.

The most decorated woman is Rusty Skuse (*née* Field) (b 1944) of Aldershot, Hampshire, England, who, after 12 years under the needle of her husband, tattoo artist Bill Skuse, has come within 15% of totality.

Fire-Eating

John Zealando (NZ) blew a flame from his mouth to a distance of 24½ ft at the Henderson Square Shopping Centre, Auckland, on Oct 19, 1979. Jack Sholomir of Newport, England, set the formal world record by igniting a bale of straw at a range of 23 feet at Kinnersley, on June 6, 1977.

Reg Morris successively extinguished 7,225 flaming torches in his mouth at the Railway Tavern, Brownhills, England, on Mar 11, 1982. Mrs Jean Chapman successively extinguished 6,607 flaming torches in her mouth in 2 hours (a rate of more than 55 per min) on Feb 13, 1982, in Stoke Poges, Buckinghamshire, England. Fire-eating is potentially a highly dangerous activity.

Fastest Amputation

The shortest time recorded for the amputation of a leg in the pre-anesthetic era was 13 to 15 sec by Napoleon's chief surgeon, Dominique Larrey. There could have been no ligation.

Oldest Subject Operated On

The greatest recorded age at which a person has been subjected to an operation is 111 years 105 days in the case of James Henry Brett, Jr. (b July 25, 1849, d Feb 10, 1961) of Houston, Tex. He underwent a hip operation Nov 7, 1960.

Most Major Operations

Alton Godwin (b Aug 17, 1945) underwent 112 operations between Mar 25, 1980 and Jan 1982 to remove scar tissue from his throat following an oxygen explosion during micro-surgery by laser in the Pittsburgh Eye and Ear Hospital.

Earliest Appendectomy

The earliest recorded successful appendix operation was performed in 1736 by Claudius Amyand (1680–1740). He was Serjeant Surgeon to King George II (reigned 1727–60) of Great Britain.

Earliest Kidney Transplant

R. H. Lawler (b 1895, US) performed the first transplantation of a human kidney in 1950. The longest survival, as between identical twins, has been 20 years.

Laryngectomy

On July 24, 1924, John I. Poole of Plymouth, England, then aged 33, after diagnosis of carcinoma, underwent total laryngectomy in Edinburgh, Scotland. He died on June 19, 1979, after surviving 55 years as a "neck-breather."

Fasting

Most humans experience considerable discomfort after an abstinence from food for even 12 hours, but this often passes off after 24–48 hours. Records claimed without unremitting medical surveillance are of little value.

The longest period for which anyone has gone without solid food is 382 days by Angus Barbieri (b 1940) of Tayport, Fife, Scotland, who lived on tea, coffee, water, soda water and vitamins from June 1965 to July 1966 in Maryfield Hospital, Dundee, Angus, Scotland. His weight declined from 472 lb to 178 lb.

The longest recorded case of survival without food *and* water is 18 days by Andreas Mihavecz, 18, of Bregenz, Austria, who was put in a holding cell April 1, 1979, in a local government building in Höchst, Austria, but was totally forgotten by the police. On April 18, 1979, he was discovered close to death, having had neither food nor water. He had been a passenger in a car crash.

Hunger Strike

The longest recorded hunger strike was one of 94 days by John and Peter Crowley, Thomas Donovan, Michael Burke, Michael O'Reilly, Christopher Upton, John Power, Joseph Kenny and Sean Hennessy in Cork Prison, Ireland, from Aug 11 to Nov 12, 1920. These nine survivors owed their lives to expert medical attention and an appeal by Arthur Griffith.

Isolation

The longest recorded period for which any volunteer has been able to withstand total deprivation of all sensory stimulation (sight, hearing and touch) is 92 hours, recorded in 1962 at Lancaster Moor Hospital, England.

The farthest distance that any human has been isolated from all other humans has been when the lone pilots of the lunar command modules were antipodal to their Apollo missions, two lunar explorers 2,200 miles away.

Longest Dream

Dreaming sleep is characterized by rapid eye movements (known as REM). The longest recorded period of REM is 2 hours 23 min, set by Bill Carskadon on Feb 15, 1967, at the Department of Psychology, University of Illinois, Chicago. His previous sleep had been interrupted.

Sleeplessness

Researches indicate that on the Circadian cycle, for the majority, peak efficiency is attained between 8 p.m. and 9 p.m., and the low comes at 4 a.m.

The longest recorded period for which a person has voluntarily gone without sleep is 449 hours (18 days 17 hours) by Mrs Maureen Weston of Peterborough, England, in a rocking chair marathon from Apr 14 to May 2, 1977. Though she tended to hallucinate toward the end of this surely ill-advised test, surprisingly, she suffered no lasting aftereffects. W. Ananda Upali of Sri Lanka voluntarily went without sleep for 353 hours 10 min (almost 15 days) from Aug 20 to Sept 4, 1979.

Victims of the very rare condition chronic colestites (total insomnia) have been known to go without sleep for many years without suffering any ill effects. The most extreme recorded case is that of Mr Valentine Medina (b Feb 23, 1900) of Cuenca, central Spain, who claims he lost all desire to sleep in 1904 and has not slept since. During the day he works on his farm and at night patrols the village as a watchman. "I've taken sleeping pills until I rattle," he says, "but it does no good."

Motionlessness

The longest that any person has voluntarily remained continuously motionless is 8 hours 33 min by Ms Melody A. Schick at a convention of the National Association of Broadcasters in Las Vegas, Nev, on Apr 15, 1981.

The longest recorded time that anyone was involuntarily made to stand at attention was 53 hours when Staff Sgt. Samuel B. Moody, USAF, was so punished in Narumi prison camp, Nagoya, Japan, in the spring of 1945. He survived to write *Reprieve from Hell*.

Extrasensory Perception

The two most extreme published examples of ESP in scientific literature have been those of the Reiss case of a 26-year-old female at Hunter College, NY, in 1936 and of Pavel Stepánek (Czechoslovakia) in 1967–68. The importance which has been attached to their cases was diminished by subsequent developments. The Reiss subject refused to undergo any further tests under stricter conditions. When Stepánek was retested at Edinburgh University with plastic cards he "failed to display any clairvoyant ability." Much smaller departures from the laws of probability have, however, been displayed in less extreme cases carried out under strict conditions.

g Forces

The acceleration due to gravity (g) is 32 ft 1.05 in per sec per sec at sea level at the Equator. A *sustained* force of 25 g was withstood in a dry capsule during astronautic research by Dr Carter Collins of California.

The highest g force endured was 82.6 g for 0.04 sec on a water-braked rocket sled by Eli L. Beeding, Jr., at Holloman Air Force Base, NM, May 16, 1958. He was put in the hospital for three days.

A man who fell off a 185-ft cliff has survived a *momentary* g force of 209 in decelerating from 68 mph to stationary in 0.015 sec.

In a crash, race car driver David Purley survived a deceleration from 108 mph to zero in 26 in at the Silverstone circuit, Northamptonshire, England, July 13, 1977, which involved a force of 179.8 g. He suffered 29 fractures, 3 dislocations and 6 heart stoppages.

The land divers of Pentecost Island, New Hebrides, dive from 70-ft-high platforms with liana vines attached to their ankles. The resulting jerk can transmit a momentary force in excess of 100 g.

Highest Temperature Endured

The highest dry-air temperature endured by naked men in US Air Force experiments in 1960 was 400°F and for heavily clothed men 500°F. (*Steaks require only 325°F.*) Temperatures of 284°F have been found quite bearable in sauna baths.

MOTIONLESSNESS: The record keeps passing back and forth between Melody Schick (above) and William Fuqua (above right). As we go to press, Melody has the record at 8½ hours with no rest breaks while remaining continuously motionless. Bill has an unverified claim of 10 hours set in May 1982, being investigated, and Melody is set to try to beat that. (See "Newly Verified Records" for the last word.) (Photo of Melody Schick by Bob Halvorsen)

The highest temperature recorded by a pyrometer for the coals in any fire-walk is 1,494°F by "Komar" (Vernon E. Craig) of Wooster, Ohio, at the International Festival of Yoga and Esoteric Sciences, Maidenhead, England, on Aug 14, 1976.

Electric Shock

Excluding lightning bolts, the highest reported voltage electric shock survived was one of 230,000 volts by Brian Latasa, 17, on the tower of an ultra-high-voltage power line in Griffith Park, Los Angeles, Nov 9, 1967. Highly insulated individuals have touched 1,200,000-volt cables in barehand live cable work without harm.

g FORCE SURVIVAL: David Purley is shown here seated on the wreckage of the race car he was driving at 108 mph when he crashed, stopping in a distance of 26 inches. Seriously injured, but lucky to be alive, he survived a force of nearly 180 g.

"COOLEST" MAMMAL: The spiny anteater (above), from Australia and New Guinea, has the lowest blood temperature of any mammal. This one is a baby.

MOST VALUABLE MARINE ANIMAL (below): "Orky," the killer whale at Marineland of the Pacific, Palos Verde, Calif, is worth at least $250,000.

TALLEST ANIMAL (above): George, the tallest giraffe in captivity, along with his friends, licked the telephone wires that ran past his pen, disrupting the system.

VALUABLE ANIMALS: The giant panda (below) cost the San Diego Zoo $250,000 in 1971 for a fertile pair from China.

Chapter 2

The Animal & Plant Kingdoms

ANIMAL KINGDOM (*ANIMALIA*)

Largest and Heaviest Animal

The largest and heaviest animal is the blue or sulphur-bottom whale (*Balaenoptera musculus*), also called Sibbald's rorqual. The largest accurately measured specimen on record was a female landed at the Cia Argentina de Pesca shore station, South Georgia, Falkland Islands, in the South Atlantic, *c.* 1904–20 which measured 110 ft 2½ in in length. Another female measuring 90 ft 6 in, caught in the South Atlantic Ocean by the Soviet *Slava* whaling fleet on Mar 20, 1947, weighed 209 tons.

The blue whale's whistle, which has been measured up to 188 decibels, is the loudest sound emitted by any living source and is detectable 530 miles distant.

Longest Animal

The longest animal ever recorded is the ribbon worm *Lineus longissimus*, also known as the "bootlace worm," which is found in the shallow coastal waters of the North Sea. In 1864 a specimen measuring more than 180 ft was washed ashore at St. Andrews, Fifeshire, Scotland, after a storm.

Tallest Animal

The tallest living animal is the giraffe (*Giraffa camelopardalis*), which is now found only in the dry savannah and semi-desert areas of Africa south of the Sahara. The tallest ever recorded was a Masai bull (*G. camelopardalis tippelskirchi*) named "George," received at Chester Zoo, England, Jan 8, 1959 from Kenya. His "horns" *almost* touched the roof of the 20-ft-high Giraffe House when he was 9 years old. George died July 22, 1969. Less credible heights of up to 23 ft between taxidermist's pegs have been claimed for bulls shot in the field.

Longest-Lived Animal

Few non-bacterial creatures live longer than humans. It would appear that tortoises are the longest-lived such animals. The greatest authentic age recorded for a tortoise is 152-plus years for a male Marion's tortoise (*Testudo sumeirii*), brought from the Seychelles Islands in the Indian Ocean to Mauritius in 1766 by the Chevalier de Fresne, who presented it to the Port Louis army garrison. This specimen (it went blind in 1908) was accidentally killed in 1918. When the famous Royal Tongan tortoise "Tu'malilia" (believed to be a specimen of *Testudo radiata*) died May 19, 1966, it was reputed to be over 200 years old, having been presented to the then King of Tonga by Captain James Cook (1728–79) Oct 22, 1773, but this record may well have been compiled from two (or more) overlapping residents.

Most Valuable Animals

The most valuable animals in cash terms are race horses. It was announced in Oct 1980 that "Easy Jet," a quarterhorse, had been syndicated for $30 million. (See *Horse Racing.*) The most valuable zoo exhibit is the giant panda (*Ailuropoda melanoleuca*) for which the San Diego Zoological Gardens offered $250,000 in 1971 for a fertile pair. The most valuable marine exhibit is the killer whale (*Orcinus orca*) named "Orky" at Marineland of the Pacific, Palos Verdes, Calif. He has grown to 14,000 lb since 1964 and his value is at least $250,000.

Note: For more information about animals, see "Animal Facts and Feats: One of the Guinness Family of Books." This work treats the dimensions and performances of the Classes of the Animal Kingdom in greater detail, giving also sources and authorities for much of the material in this chapter.

Fastest Flying Animal

The fastest-moving animal is the peregrine falcon (*Falco peregrinus*), which has been timed electronically at 217 mph in Germany while making a stoop at a 45-degree angle of descent. In a vertical fall of 5,000 ft, it has been calculated a stooping peregrine in display could probably reach 230–240 mph, but it usually strikes its prey at about half this velocity. The fastest bird in level flight is the large white-throated spinetail swift (*Hirundapus caudacutus*) of Asia. In 1942, air speeds up to 106.25 mph were recorded for this species in the USSR (*cf.* 60 mph for the peregrine). This bird has a blood temperature of 112.5 °F.

Commonest Animal

It is estimated that man shares the earth with 3×10^{33} (3 followed by 33 zeros) other living things. The number of nematode sea-worms has been estimated at 4×10^{25}.

Largest Concentration of Animal Life

The largest concentration of animals ever recorded was an enormous swarm of krill (*Euphausia superba*) estimated to weigh 10 million tons tracked by American scientists off Antarctica in Mar 1981. The swarm was so dense it equaled about one-seventh of the world's yearly catch of fish and shellfish.

Rarest Animal

The best claimants to the title of the rarest land animal are those species which are known only from a single (holotype) specimen. One of these is the Fontoynont's hedgehog-tenrec *Dasogale fontoynonti,* a placental mammal, which is known only from the specimen collected in eastern Madagascar (Malagasy Republic) and now preserved in the Paris (France) Museum of Natural History.

Among subspecies of mammals, the Javan tiger (*Panthera tigris sondaica*) was reduced to 4 specimens by 1980, all of them in the Meru Betiri reserve in eastern Java, but none has been sighted since. The Arabian oryx (*Oryx leucoryx*) has not been reported in the wild since 3 were killed and 4 captured in South Oman in 1972. In Feb 1982 thirteen oryx from the herd at the San Diego Zoo plus 2 calves born in Oman were waiting to be released into the open desert. In 1979 scientists uncovered the first evidence that the Bali leopard (*Panthera pandus balica*) still existed on the island.

Greatest Size Difference Between Sexes

The largest female deep-sea angler fish of the species *Ceratias holboelki* on record weighed half a million times as much as the smallest known parasitic male.

Longest Gestation

The viviparous amphibian Alpine black salamander (*Salamandra atra*) can have a gestation period of up to 38 months at altitudes above 4,600 ft in the Swiss Alps, but this drops to 24–26 months at lower altitudes.

Fastest and Slowest Growth

The fastest growth in the animal kingdom is that of the blue whale calf. A barely visible ovum weighing a fraction of a milligram (0.000035 of an ounce) grows to a weight of *c.* 29 tons in 22¾ months, made up of 10¾ months gestation and the first 12 months of life. This is equivalent to an increase of 30,000 million fold.

The slowest growth in the animal kingdom is that of the deep-sea clam (*Tindaria callistiformis*) of the North Atlantic, which takes an estimated 100 years to reach a length of 0.31 in (8 mm).

Blood Temperatures

The highest mammalian blood temperature is that of the domestic goat (*Capra hircus*) with an average of 103.8 °F and a normal range of from 101.7° to 105.3 °F. The lowest mammalian blood temperature is that of the spiny anteater (*Tachyglossus aculeatus*), a monotreme found in Australia and New Guinea, with a normal range of 72° to 87 °F. The blood temperature of the golden hamster (*Mesocricetus auratus*) sometimes falls as low as 38.3 °F during hibernation, and an extreme figure of 29.6 °F has been reported for a pipistrelle bat (*Pipistrellus pipistrellus*) during a cooling experiment.

Largest Egg

The largest egg of any living animal is that of the whale shark (*Rhiniodon typus*). One egg case measuring 12 in by 5.5 in by 3.5 in was picked up by the shrimp trawler "Doris" June 29, 1953 at a depth of 186 ft in the Gulf of Mexico, 130 miles south of Port Isabel, Tex. The egg contained a perfect embryo of a whale shark 13.78 in long.

Heaviest Brain

The sperm whale (*Physeter macrocephalus*) has the heaviest brain of all living animals. The brain of a 49-ft-long bull processed aboard the Japanese factory ship *Nissin Maru No. 1* in the Antarctic Dec 11, 1949 weighed 9.2 kg (20.24 lb), compared to 6.9 kg (15.38 lb) for a 90-ft blue whale. The heaviest brain recorded for an elephant was an exceptional 16.5 lb in the case of a 2.17-ton Asiatic cow. The normal brain weight for an adult African bull is 9¼–12 lb.

Largest Eye

The giant squid *Architeuthis sp.* has the largest eye of any living animal. The ocular diameter may exceed 15 in, compared to less than 12 in for a 33⅓-rpm long-playing record.

Most Prodigious Eater

The most phenomenal eating machine in nature is the larva of the Polyphemus moth (*Antheraea polyphemus*) of North America which, in the first 48 hours of its life, consumes an amount equal to 86,000 times its own birthweight. In human terms, this would be equivalent to a 7-lb baby taking in 301 tons of nourishment.

Most Acute Sense of Smell

The most acute sense of smell exhibited in nature is that of the male emperor moth (*Eudia pavonia*), which, according to German experiments in 1961, can detect the sex attractant of the virgin female at the almost unbelievable range of 6.8 miles upwind. This scent has been identified as one of the higher alcohols ($C_{16}H_{29}OH$) of which the female carries less than 0.0001 mg.

Highest g Force

The highest g force encountered in nature is the 400 g *averaged* by the click beetle (*Athous haemorrhoidalis*), a common British species, when jackknifing into the air to escape predators. One example measuring 0.47 in in length and weighing 0.00014 oz which jumped to a height of 11¾ in was calculated to have "endured" a peak brain deceleration of 2,300 g at the end of the movement.

1. MAMMALS (*MAMMALIA*)

Largest and Heaviest Animal

The blue whale (see details on page 43) holds the record. The tongue and heart of the 209-ton female taken by the *Slava* whaling fleet in the South Atlantic Ocean on March 20, 1947, weighed 4.73 tons and 1,540 lb respectively.

Blue whales inhabit the colder seas and migrate to warmer waters in winter for breeding. Observations made in the Antarctic in 1947–8 showed that a blue whale can maintain speeds of 20 knots (23 mph) for 10 minutes when frightened. This means a 90-ft blue whale traveling at 20 knots would develop 520 hp. Newborn calves measure 21–28.5 ft long and weigh up to 3.3 tons.

It has been estimated that there were between 21,000 and 23,000 blue whales living throughout the oceans in 1981. The species has been protected *de jure* since 1967 although non-member countries of the International Whaling Commission (*e.g.* Panama and Taiwan) are not bound by this agreement.

Deepest Dive

The greatest *recorded* depth to which a whale has dived is 620 fathoms (3,720 ft) by a 47-ft bull sperm whale (*Physeter macrocephalus*) found with his jaw entangled with a submarine cable running between Santa Elena, Ecuador, and Chorillos, Peru, Oct 14, 1955. At this depth he withstood a pressure of 1,680 lb per sq in of body surface.

On Aug 25, 1969, a sperm whale was killed 100 miles south of Durban, South Africa, after it had surfaced from a dive lasting 1 hour 52 min, and inside its stomach were found two small sharks which had been swallowed about an hour earlier. These were later identified as *Scymnodon sp.*, a species found only on the sea floor. At this point from land the depth of water is in excess of 1,646 fathoms (10,476 ft) for a radius of 30–40 miles, which now suggests that the sperm whale sometimes may descend to a depth of over 10,000 ft when seeking food.

Ambergris

The heaviest piece of ambergris (a fatty deposit in the intestine of the sperm whale) on record weighed 1,003 lb and was recovered from a sperm whale (*Physeter macrocephalus*) Dec 3, 1912 by a Norwegian whaling company in Australian waters. The lump was sold in London for £23,000 (then $111,780).

Largest Animal on Land

The largest living land animal is the African bush elephant (*Loxodonta africana*). The average adult bull stands 10 ft 6 in at the shoulder and weighs 6½ tons. The largest specimen ever recorded, and the largest land animal of modern times, was a bull shot 25 miles north-northeast of Mucusso, southern Angola, Nov 7, 1974. Lying on its side this elephant measured 13 ft 8 in in a projected line from the highest point of the shoulder to the base of the forefoot, indicating that its standing height must have been about 13 ft. Other measurements included an overall length of 35 ft (tip of extended trunk to tip of extended tail) and a forefoot circumference of 5 ft 11 in. The weight was computed to be 26,998 lb (see also *Shooting,* Chapter 12).

Smallest Mammals

The smallest recorded mammal is the endangered Kitti's hog-nosed bat (*Craseonycteris thonglongyai*) or bumblebee bat, which is now restricted to one cave near the forestry station at Ban Sai Yoke on the Kwae Noi River, Kanchanaburi, Thailand. Mature specimens of both sexes have a wing span of about 6.29 in and weigh between 0.062 and 0.071 oz.

The smallest totally marine mammal in terms of weight is probably Commerson's dolphin (*Cephalorhynchus commersoni*) also known as Le Jacobite, which is found in the waters off the southern tip of South America. In one series of six adult specimens the weights ranged from 50.7 lb to 77.1 lb. The sea otter (*Enhydra lutris*) of the north Pacific is of comparable size, weighing from 55 to 81.4 lb, but this species sometimes comes ashore during storms.

Fastest Land Animal

The fastest of all land animals over a short distance (*i.e.* up to 600 yd) is the cheetah or hunting leopard (*Acinonyx jubatus*) of the open plains of East Africa, Iran, Turkmenia and Afghanistan, with a probable maximum speed of 60–63 mph over suitably level ground. Speeds of 71, 84 and even 90 mph have been claimed for this animal, but these figures must be considered exaggerated. Tests in London in 1937 showed that on an oval greyhound track over 345 yd a female cheetah's average speed over three runs was 43.4 mph (compared with 43.26 mph for the fastest race horse), but this specimen was not running at its best and had great difficulty negotiating curves.

The fastest land animal over a sustained distance (*i.e.* 1,000 yd or more) is the pronghorn antelope (*Antilocapra americana*) of the western US. Specimens have been observed to travel at 35 mph for 4 miles, at 42 mph for 1 mile and 55 mph for half a mile.

Slowest Land Mammal

The slowest moving land mammal is the ai or three-toed sloth (*Bradypus tridactylus*) of tropical America. The average ground speed is 6–8 ft per min (0.068 to 0.098 mph), but in the trees it can "accelerate" to 15 ft per min (0.170 mph). (Compare these figures with the 0.03 mph of the common garden snail and the 0.17 mph of the giant tortoise.)

Longest-Lived Mammal

No other mammal can match the proven age of 117 years attained by man (*Homo sapiens*). It is probable that the closest approach is among blue and fin whales (*Balaenoptera musculus* and *B. physalas*). Studies of the annual growth layers or laminations found in the wax-like plug deposited in the outer ear of these whales indicate a maximum life span of 90–100 years.

The longest-lived land mammal, excluding man, is the Asiatic elephant (*Elephas maximus*). The greatest age that has been verified with absolute certainty is 78 years in the case of a cow elephant named "Modoc," who died at Santa Clara, Calif, on July 17, 1975. She was imported into the US from Germany in 1898 at the age of 2.

Highest-Living Mammal

The highest-living wild mammal in the world is probably the yak (*Bos grunniens*), of Tibet and the Szechwanese Alps, China, which occasionally, when foraging, climbs to an altitude of 20,000 ft. The Bharal (*Pseudois nayaur*) and the Pika or Mouse hare (*Ochotona thibetana*) may also reach this height in the Himalayas. In 1890, the tracks of an elephant were found at 15,000 ft on Mt Kilimanjaro, Tanzania.

FASTEST and SLOWEST MAMMALS: The cheetah (above) has been clocked at over 60 mph, a figure 353 times faster than the top speed attained by the three-toed sloth (right).

RARE AND SMALL (above): The endangered hog-nosed bat rivals Savi's pygmy shrew (see Smallest Insectivore) for the title of world's smallest mammal. LARGEST LITTER (right): 32 babies in a record single birth will call this common tenrec "Mother." HIGH-LIVER (below): The yak of Tibet and China may climb, while foraging, to an altitude of 20,000 ft.

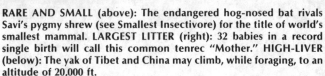

LARGE BUT GENTLE: While the Kodiak bear of Alaska is the largest living carnivorous land animal, often weighing more than 1,000 lb, this 360-lb specimen seems right at home in Minnesota. (Courtesy, Hamm's) RECORD LITTER OF 8 TIGER CUBS (below): The Indian tigress "Baghdad" gave birth to the only recorded tiger octuplets, seven of whom proudly posed for this family portrait when they were half-grown.

Largest Herds

The largest herds on record were those of the South African springbok (*Antidorcas marsupialis*) during migration in the 19th century. In 1849, Sir John Fraser of Bloemfontein observed a herd that took three days to pass through the settlement of Beaufort West, Cape Province. Another herd seen in the same province in 1888 was estimated to contain 100 million head, although 10 million is probably a more realistic figure. A herd estimated to be 15 miles wide and more than 100 miles long was reported from Karree Kloof, Orange River, South Africa, in July 1896.

The largest concentration of wild mammals found living anywhere in the world today is that of the Brazilian free-tailed bat (*Tadarida brasiliensis*) in Bracken Cave, San Antonio, Tex, where up to 20 million animals assemble after migration.

Longest and Shortest Gestation Periods

The longest of all mammalian gestation periods is that of the Asiatic elephant (*Elephas maximus*), with an average of 609 days (or just over 20 months) and a maximum of 760 days, more than 2½ times that of a human.

The gestation period of the American opossum (*Didelphis marsupialis*), also called the Virginian opossum, is normally 12 to 13 days, but it may be as short as 8 days.

The gestation periods of the rare water opossum or Yapok (*Chironectes minimus*) of Central and northern South America (average 12–13 days) and the Eastern native cat (*Dasyurus viverrinus*) of Australia (average 12 days) may also be as short as 8 days.

Largest Litter

The greatest recorded number of young born to a wild mammal at a single birth is 32 (not all of which survived), in the case of the common tenrec (*Centetes ecaudatus*), found in Madagascar and the Comoro Islands. The average litter is 12 to 16.

In March 1961 a litter of 32 was also reported for a house mouse (*Mus musculus*) at the Roswell Park Memorial Institute in Buffalo, NY (average litter size 13–21). (See Chapter 9, prolificacy records—pigs.)

Youngest Breeder

The streaked tenrec (*Hemicentetes semispinosus*) of Madagascar is weaned after only 5 days, and females are capable of breeding 3–4 weeks after birth.

Largest Carnivore

The largest living terrestrial carnivore is the Kodiak bear (*Ursus arctos middendorffi*), which is found on Kodiak Island and the adjacent Afognak and Shuyak islands in the Gulf of Alaska. The average adult male has a nose-to-tail length of 8 ft (tail about 4 in), stands 52 in at the shoulder and weighs 1,050–1,175 lb.

In 1894 a weight of 1,656 lb was recorded for a male shot at English Bay, Kodiak Island, whose *stretched* skin measured 13 ft 6 in from the tip of the nose to the root of the tail. This weight was exceeded by a "cage-fat" male in the Cheyenne Mountain Zoological Park, Colorado Springs, which scaled 1,670 lb at the time of its death Sept 22, 1955.

Weights in excess of 1,600 lb have also been reported for the male polar bear (*Ursus maritimus*), which has an average nose-to-tail length of 7¾ ft and weighs 850–900 lb. In 1960 a polar bear allegedly weighing 2,210 lb before skinning was shot at the polar entrance to Kotzebue Sound, northwest Alaska. The mounted specimen has a standing height of 11 ft 1½ in.

Smallest Carnivore

The smallest living carnivore is the least weasel (*Mustela rixosa*), also called the dwarf weasel, which is circumpolar in distribution. Four races are recognized, the smallest of which is the *M. r. pygmaea* of Siberia. Mature specimens have an overall length (including tail) of 6.96–8.14 in and weigh between 1¼ and 2½ oz.

Largest Marine Carnivore

The largest toothed mammal ever recorded is the sperm whale (*Physeter macrocephalus*), also called the cachalot. The average adult bull is 47 ft long and weighs about 37 tons. The largest specimen ever to be measured accurately was a bull 67 ft 11 in long captured off the Kurile Islands, in the northwest Pacific, by a USSR whaling fleet in the summer of 1950.

Largest Feline

The largest member of the cat family (Felidae) is the long-furred Siberian tiger (*Panthera tigris altaica*), also known as the Amur or Manchurian tiger. Adult males average 10 ft 4 in in length (nose to tip of extended tail), stand 39–42 in at the shoulder, and weigh about 585 lb. A male weighing 846.5 lb was shot in the Sikhote Alin Mountains, Maritime Territory, USSR in 1950. In Nov 1967 an 857-lb Indian tiger (*Panthera tigris tigris*) was shot in northern Uttar Pradesh by David H. Hasinger of Philadelphia. It measured 10 ft 7 in long (between taxidermist's pegs), or 11 ft 1 in over the curves, compared with 9 ft 3 in and 420 lb for the average adult male. It is now on display in the US Museum of Natural History, Smithsonian Institution, Washington, DC.

The average adult African lion (*Pantheria leo*) measures 9 ft overall, stands 36–38 in at the shoulder and weighs 400–410 lb. The heaviest wild specimen on record was one weighing 690 lb shot by Mr Lennox Anderson just outside Hectorspruit in the eastern Transvaal, South Africa in 1936. In July 1970 a weight of 826 lb was reported for a black-maned lion named "Simba" (b Dublin Zoo, 1959) at Colchester Zoo, Essex, England. He died on Jan 16, 1973, at Knaresborough Zoo, North Yorkshire, England, where his stuffed body is currently on display.

Smallest Feline

The smallest member of the cat family is the rusty-spotted cat (*Felis rubiginosa*) of southern India and Sri Lanka. The average adult male has an overall length of 25–28 in (tail 9–10 in) and weighs about 3 lb.

Largest Pinniped (Seal, Sea Lion, Walrus)

The largest of the 32 known species of pinnipeds is the southern elephant seal (*Mirounga leonina*) which inhabits the sub-Antarctic islands. Adult bulls average 16½ ft in length (tip of inflated snout to the extremities of the outstretched tail flippers), 12 ft in maximum body girth and weigh 5,000 lb. The largest accurately measured specimen on record was a bull killed in Possession Bay, South Georgia, Falkland Islands, South Atlantic, Feb 28, 1913, which measured *c.* 22½ ft in length or 21 ft 4 in after flensing and probably weighed 9,000 lb. There are old records of bulls measuring 25, 30 and even 35 ft, but these figures must be considered exaggerated.

Smallest Pinniped

The smallest pinniped is the Baykal seal (*Pusa sibirica*) of Lake Baykal, USSR, and the ringed seal (*Pusa hispida*) of the Arctic. Adult specimens measure up to 5 ft 6 in and weigh up to 280 lb.

Fastest and Deepest Pinnipeds

The highest speed measured for a pinniped is 25 mph for a California sea lion (*Zalophus californianus*). The deepest dive recorded for a pinniped is 1,968 ft for a bull Weddell seal (*Leptonychotes weddelli*) in McMurdo Sound, Antarctica, in March 1966. At this depth, the seal withstood a pressure of 875 lb per sq in of body area.

The exceptionally large eyes of the southern elephant seal (see above) point to a deep-diving ability, and unconfirmed measurements down to 2,000 ft have been claimed.

Most Abundant Pinniped

The most abundant species of pinniped is the crabeater seal (*Lobodon carcinophagus*) of Antarctica. In 1978 the total population was believed to be nearly 15 million.

Longest-Lived Pinniped

A female gray seal (*Halichoerus grypus*) shot at Shunni Wick in the Shetland Islands, Scotland, Apr 23, 1969 was believed to be at least 46 years old, based on a count of dental annuli.

Rarest Pinniped

In 1976 a single specimen of the Caribbean or West Indian monk seal (*Monachus tropicalis*) was sighted between Punta Gorda, Belize, and Livingston, Guatemala.

Largest Bat

The only flying mammals are bats (order Chiroptera), of which there are about 1,000 living species. The bat with the greatest wing span is the Bismarck flying fox (*Pteropus neohibernicus*) of the Bismarck Archipelago and New Guinea. One specimen preserved in the American Museum of Natural History has a wing spread of 5 ft 5 in, but some unmeasured bats probably reach 6 ft.

Smallest Bat

The smallest species of bat is the rare Kitti's hog-nosed or bumblebee bat (see page 46).

Fastest Bat

Because of great practical difficulties, few data on bat speeds have been published. The greatest velocity attributed to a bat is 32 mph in the case of a Brazilian free-tailed bat (*Tadarida brasiliensis*), but this

SANTA VISITS SEAL in Stuttgart (Germany) zoo. This bull elephant seal represents the largest species of pinniped. The biggest specimen, which was killed in the Falkland Islands in 1913, measured 22½ ft long and weighed 9,000 lb. (Keystone)

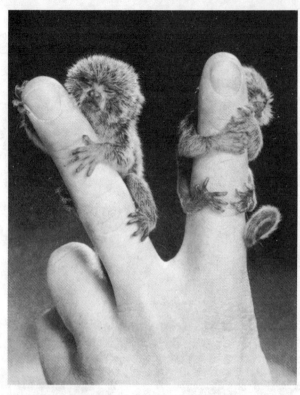

SMALLEST MONKEYS (above): The pygmy marmo-
sets of South America are half tail and can easily be
carried around. HEAVIEST GORILLA in captivity
today is Zaak (right), a resident of the Kobe Oji Zoo
in Japan, who weighs 628 lb.

OLDEST MONKEY: The ca-
puchin (above) lived to 46
years 11 months in Indiana,
but Guas (left, with arrow)
was not only the OLDEST
ORANGUTAN, 59, but also
the oldest non-human pri-
mate of all time. (Zoological
Society of Philadelphia)

may have been wind-assisted. In one American experiment using an artificial mine tunnel and 17 different kinds of bat, only four of them managed to exceed 13 mph in level flight.

Rarest Bat

At least three species of bat are known only from the holotype specimen. They are: the small-toothed fruit bat (*Neopteryx frosti*) from Tamalanti, West Celebes (1938/39); *Paracoelops megalotis* from Vinh, Vietnam (1945); and *Latidens salimalii* from the High Wavy Mountains, southern India (1948).

Longest-Lived Bat

The greatest age reliably reported for a bat is 31 years 5 months for an Indian flying fox (*Pteropus giganteus*) which died at London Zoo on Jan 11, 1979.

Smallest Living Primate

The smallest known primate is the rare pen-tailed shrew (*Ptilocercus lowii*) of Malaysia, Sumatra and Borneo. Adult specimens have a total body length of 9–13 in, a head and body length of 3.9–5.5 in, a tail of 5.1–7.5 in and weigh 1.23–1.76 oz. The pygmy marmoset (*Cebuella pygmae*) of the Upper Amazon Basin and the lesser mouse lemur (*Microcebus murinus*) of Madagascar are also of comparable length but heavier, adults weighing 1.76–2.64 oz and 1.58–2.82 oz respectively.

Largest Living Primates

The largest living primate is the mountain gorilla (*Gorilla gorilla beringei*) of the volcanic mountain ranges of W Rwanda, SW Uganda and E Zaire. The average adult male stands 5 ft 9 in tall (including crest) and weighs about 430 lb. The greatest height (top of crest to heel) recorded for a gorilla is 6 ft 4¾ in for a male collected by a German expedition at Alimbongo, N Kivu, Zaire on May 16, 1938.

The heaviest gorilla ever kept in captivity was a male of the mountain race named "N'gagi," who died in the San Diego Zoo, Calif, on Jan 12, 1944, aged 18 years. He scaled 683 lb at his heaviest in 1943, and weighed 636 lb at the time of his death. He was 5 ft 7¾ in tall and boasted a record chest measurement of 78 in.

The heaviest gorilla living in captivity today is a western lowland (*Gorilla g. gorilla*) male called "Zaak," who was received at the Kobe Oji Zoo, Japan, in Dec 1962. He tipped the scales at 628 lb in June 1976, but has not been weighed since.

Longest-Lived Primate

The greatest irrefutable age reported for a primate (excluding humans) is *c.* 59 years in the case of a male orangutan (*Pongo pygmaeus*) named "Guas," who was received by the Philadelphia Zoo May 1, 1931, when he was at least 13 years old, and died Feb 9, 1977.

The oldest living non-human primate is a male chimpanzee (*Pan troglodytes*) named "Jimmy" at the Seneca Zoo, Rochester, NY, who was still alive in Feb 1982 aged 51 years 8 months.

Rarest Primate

The rarest primate is the hairy-eared lemur (*Allocebus trichotis*) of Madagascar, which was known, until fairly recently, only from a holotype specimen and three skins. However, in 1966 a live one was found on the east coast near Mananara.

Primate Strength

"Boma," a 165-lb male chimpanzee at the Bronx Zoo, NYC, in 1924 recorded a right-handed pull (feet braced) of 847 lb on a dynamometer (compare with 210 lb for a man of the same weight). On another occasion an adult female chimpanzee named "Suzette" (estimated weight 135 lb) at the same zoo registered a right-handed pull of 1,260 lb while in a rage. A record of a 100-lb chimpanzee achieving a two-handed dead lift of 600 lb with ease suggests that a male gorilla could, with training, raise 1,800 lb!

Largest and Smallest Monkeys

The only species of monkey reliably credited with weights of more than 100 lb is the mandrill (*Mandrillus sphinx*) of equatorial West Africa. The greatest reliable weight recorded is 119 lb for a male, but an unconfirmed weight of 130 lb has been reported. Adult females are about half the size of males.

The smallest monkey is the pygmy marmoset (*Cebuella pygmaea*) of the Upper Amazon Basin.

Oldest Monkey

The greatest reliable age recorded for a monkey is 46 years 11 months for a white-throated capuchin (*Cebus capucinus*) which died in the Evansville Zoo, Indiana, on Apr 12, 1976.

BETTER HEARING THAN MAN'S: Both the fruit bat (left) and the dolphin can hear frequencies 7½ times higher than humans.

Highest Detectable Pitch

Because of their ultrasonic echolocation, bats have the most acute hearing of any land animal. Vampire bats (*Desmodontidae*) and fruit bats (*Pteropodidae*) can hear frequencies as high as 150,000 cycles per sec (150 kHz). Compare this with 20 kHz for the adult human limit but 153 kHz for the bottle-nosed dolphin (*Tursiopis truncatus*).

Rarest Rodent

The rarest is believed to be the James Island rice rat (*Oryzomys swarthi*), also called Swarth's rat. Four specimens were collected on this island in the Galápagos group in the eastern Pacific Ocean in 1906, and it was not heard of again until Jan 1966 when a recent skull was found.

Fastest Breeding Rodent

The female meadow vole (*Microtus agrestis*), found in Britain, can reproduce from the age of 25 days and have up to 17 litters of 6–8 young in a year.

Longest-Lived Rodent

The greatest reliable age reported for a rodent is 27 years 3 months for a Sumatran crested porcupine (*Hystrix brachyura*) which died in the National Zoological Park, Washington, DC, on Jan 12, 1965.

Largest Rodent

The largest rodent is the capybara (*Hydrochoerus hydrochaeris*), also called the carpincho or water hog (see page 56), found in tropical South America. Mature specimens have a head and body length of 3¼–4½ ft and weigh up to 174 lb. In Britain, the largest rodent, the coypu (*Myocaster coypus*) or nutria

was introduced from Argentina by fur breeders in 1929. Three years later, the first escapes were recorded and by 1960 at least 200,000 coypus were living in East Anglia. About 80% were killed by the winter of 1963 and a government campaign of extermination has reduced the population to *c.* 8,000 animals. Adult males measure 30–36 in and weigh up to 28 lb in the wild state.

Smallest Rodent

The smallest known rodent is the northern pygmy mouse (*Baiomys taglore*) of central Mexico, southern Ariz and Tex, which measures up to 4.3 in in total length and weighs 0.24–0.28 oz.

Largest Antelope

The largest of all antelopes is the rare giant eland (*Tragelaphus derbianus*) of West and Central Africa, which may surpass 2,000 lb. The common eland (*T. oryx*) of East and South Africa has the same shoulder height of up to 70 in, but is not quite so massive, although there is one record of a 65-in bull being shot in Nyasaland (now Malawi) *c.* 1937 which weighed 2,078 lb.

Smallest Antelope

The smallest known antelope is the royal antelope (*Neotragus pygmaeus*) of West Africa. Mature specimens measure only 10–12 in at the shoulder, and weigh only 7–8 lb, which is the size of a large brown hare. Salt's dik-dik (*Madoqua saltina*) of NE Ethiopia and Somalia weighs only 5–6 lb when adult, but stands about 14 in at the withers.

Rarest Antelope

The rarest antelope is the Arabian oryx (*Oryx leucoryx*) (see *Rarest Animal*).

Oldest Antelope

The greatest reliable age recorded for an antelope is 25 years 4 months for an addax (*Addax nasomaculatus*) which died in the Brookfield Zoo, Chicago, on Oct 15, 1960.

Largest Deer

The largest deer is the Alaskan moose (*Alces alces gigas*). A bull standing 7 ft 8 in at the withers and

DEER AND ANTELOPES

1. SMALLEST RUMINANT: Frank Buck, well-known animal collector, holds a chevrotain in the palm of his hand.

2. LARGEST DEER: The largest measured Alaskan bull moose (not this one) stood 7 ft 8 in high at the withers and weighed 1,800 lb. These antlers don't compare with the record span of 78½ in.

3. SMALLEST ANTELOPES: About the size of a hare, this royal antelope weighs no more than 8 lb.

4. LARGEST ANTELOPES: The giant elands of Africa are rare. They weigh a ton and more.

LONG TUSKS: When Ahmed (above) was alive he was reputed to hold the record, but his tusks were measured at "only" 9 ft 9 in and 9 ft 4 in after his death. When a tree prevented his raising his head, he had to walk backwards to avoid getting his tusks stuck in the ground. His tusks weighed 296 lb together. The HEAVIEST TUSKS (right) came from Kenya and are now in the British Museum. They weigh a total of 465 lb, and the longer of the two is 10 ft 5½ in long.

LARGEST RODENT (left): The capybara of South America is also called the water hog because it is as big as a hog. It weighs up to 174 lb.

weighing 1,800 lb was shot in Sept 1897 in the Yukon Territory, Canada. Unconfirmed measurements of up to 8½ ft at the withers and 2,600 lb have been claimed. The record antler span is 78½ in.

Smallest Deer

The smallest true deer (family Cervidae) is the northern pudu (*Pudu mephistophiles*) of Ecuador and Colombia. Mature specimens measure 13–14 in at the shoulder and weigh 16–18 lb. The smallest ruminant is the lesser Malay chevrotain (*Tragulus javanicus*) of SE Asia, Sumatra and Borneo. Adult specimens measure 8–10 in at the shoulder and weigh 6–7 lb.

Rarest Deer

The rarest deer is Fea's muntjac (*Muntiacus feae*), which until recently was known only from two specimens collected on the borders of Burma and Thailand. In Dec 1979 a female was received at the Bangkok Zoo.

Oldest Deer

The greatest reliable age recorded for a deer is 26 years 8 months for a red deer (*Cervus elaphus scoticus*), which died in the Milwaukee Zoo, Wis,. on June 28, 1954.

Largest Insectivore (Insect-Eating Mammal)

The largest insectivore is the moon rat (*Echinosorex gymnurus*), also known as Raffles' gymnure, found in Burma, Thailand, Malaysia, Sumatra and Borneo. Mature specimens have a head and body length of 10.43–17.52 in, a tail measuring 7.87–8.26 in, and weight up to 3.08 lb. Although the much larger anteaters (family Tachyglossidae and Myrmecophagidae) feed on termites and other soft-bodied insects, they are not insectivores, but belong to the orders Monotremata and Edentata ("without teeth").

Smallest Insectivore

The smallest insectivore is Savi's white-toothed pygmy shrew (*Suncus etruscus*), also called the Etruscan shrew, which is found along the coast of the northern Mediterranean and southwards to Cape Province, South Africa. Mature specimens have a head and body length of 1.32–2.04 in, a tail length of 0.94–1.14 in, and weight of between 0.052 and 0.09 oz.

Longest-Lived Insectivore

The greatest reliable age recorded for an insectivore is 15+ years for a lesser hedgehog-tenrec (*Echinops telefairi*), which was born in the Amsterdam Zoo, Netherlands, in 1966 and was later sent to Jersey Zoo. It was still alive in Mar 1982.

Longest Tusks

The longest recorded elephant tusks (excluding prehistoric examples) are a pair from Zaïre preserved in the National Collection of Heads and Horns, kept by the New York Zoological Society, Bronx Park. The right tusk measures 11 ft 5½ in along the outside curve and the left measures 11 ft. Their combined weight is 293 lb. A single tusk of 11 ft 6 in has been reported, but details are lacking.

Heaviest Tusks

The heaviest recorded tusks are a pair in the British Museum (Natural History), London, which were collected from an aged bull shot by an Arab with a muzzle-loading gun at the foot of Mt Kilimanjaro, Kenya, in 1897. They weigh 240 lb (length 10 ft 2½ in) and 225 lb (length 10 ft 5½ in) respectively, giving a combined weight of 465 lb.

The greatest weight ever recorded for one elephant tusk is 258 lb for a specimen collected in Benin (formerly Dahomey), West Africa, and exhibited at the Paris Exposition in 1900.

Longest Horns

The longest recorded animal horn was one measuring 81¼ in on the outside curve, with a circumference of 18¼ in, found on a specimen of domestic Ankole cattle (*Bos taurus*) near Lake Ngami, Botswana.

The largest head (horns measured from tip to tip along the outside curve across the forehead) is one of 13 ft 11 in on a wild buffalo (*Bubalus bubalus*) shot in India in 1955. The maximum for a Texas longhorn steer is 9 ft 9 in tip to tip.

The longest recorded anterior horn for a rhinoceros is one of 62¼ in found on a female southern race white rhinoceros (*Ceratotheriam simum simum*) shot in South Africa *c.* 1848. The interior horn measured 22¼ in. There is also an unconfirmed record of an anterior horn measuring 81 in.

Largest Marsupial

The largest of all marsupials is the red kangaroo (*Macropus rufus*) of southern and eastern Australia. Adult males or "boomers" stand up to 7 ft tall, weigh up to 175 lb and measure up to 8 ft 11 in in a straight line from the nose to the tip of the extended tail.

Smallest Marsupial

The smallest known marsupial is the very rare Ingram's planigale (*Planigale ingrami*), a flat-skulled mouse found only in northwestern Australia. Adult males have a head and body length of 1.77 in, a tail length of 2 in and weight of about 0.14 oz.

Longest-Lived Marsupial

The greatest reliable age recorded for a marsupial is 26 years 0 months 22 days for a common wombat (*Vombatus ursinus*) which died in London Zoo Apr 20, 1906.

Highest and Longest Marsupial Jump

The greatest measured height cleared by a hunted kangaroo is 10 ft 6 in over a pile of timber. The longest recorded leap was reported in Jan 1951 when, in the course of a chase, a female red kangaroo (*Macropus rufus*) made a series of bounds which included one of 42 ft. There is an unconfirmed report of a great gray kangaroo (*Macropus canguru*) jumping 44 ft 8½ in on the flat.

Rarest Marsupial

The rarest marsupial is probably the thylacine (*Thylacinus cynocephalus*), also known as the "Tasmanian wolf," the largest of the carnivorous marsupials, which reportedly became extinct some time in the late 1930's. The last captive specimen died in the Beaumaris Zoo, Hobart, Tasmania, on Sept 7, 1936. However, in 1961 two fishermen at Sandy Cape, western Tasmania, accidentally killed a young male that was trying to eat their bait. The carcass was stolen but positive identification was made from hair and blood samples. In Dec 1966 the traces of a thylacine lair in which a female and pups had been living were found at Whyte River, near Mawbanna. Since then there have been a number of sightings, but most of these referred to greyhounds.

Most Valuable Furs

The highest-priced animal pelts are those of the sea otter (*Enhydra lutris*), also known as the Kamchatka beaver, which fetched up to $2,700 each before their 55-year-long protection started in 1912. The protection ended in 1967, and at the first legal auction of sea otter pelts in Seattle, Wash, Jan 31, 1968, Neiman-Marcus, the famous Dallas department store, paid $9,200 each for four pelts from Alaska.

In May 1970 a Kojah (mink-sable cross) coat costing $125,000 was sold by Neiman-Marcus to Welsh actor Richard Burton for his then wife, Elizabeth Taylor.

DOMESTICATED ANIMALS

Horse Population

The world's horse population is estimated to be 75 million.

Oldest Horse and Pony

The greatest reliable age recorded for a horse is 62 years in the case of "Old Billy" (foaled 1760), believed to be a cross between a Cleveland and an Eastern blood, who was bred by Edward Robinson of Wild Grave Farm in Woolston, Lancashire, England. In 1762 or 1763 he was sold to the Mersey and Irwell Navigation Company and remained with them in a working capacity, marshalling and towing barges, until 1819 when he was retired to a farm, where he died Nov 27, 1822. The skull of this horse is preserved in the Manchester Museum, and his stuffed head is now on display in the Bedford Museum.

The greatest reliable age recorded for a pony is 54 years for a stallion owned by a farmer in central France which was still alive in 1919.

The greatest age recorded for a thoroughbred racehorse is 42 years in the case of the bay gelding "Tango Duke" (foaled 1935), owned by Mrs Carmen J. Koper of Barongarook, Victoria, Australia. The horse died Jan 25, 1978.

Largest Horse

The heaviest horse ever recorded was "Brooklyn Supreme," a purebred Belgian stallion (foaled Apr 12, 1928) owned by Ralph Fogleman of Callender,

RAREST MARSUPIAL (above): The carnivorous "Tasmanian wolf" is very possibly extinct since the 1960's, when the last male to be positively identified was accidentally killed.

JUMPERS: The red kangaroo (above), known as "Big Red" to Australians, is the largest living marsupial. This photo shows the heavy musculature that allowed one to leap 42 ft in one bound when chased. The Himalayan ibex (left) escapes from hunters by leaping criss-cross down sheer cliffs, momentarily touching its hoofs down on rocky ledges. Movies of the ibex can be seen at the various Guinness Museums.

HEAVIEST HORSE (below): "Brooklyn Supreme," a Belgian stallion, weighed 3,200 lb in 1948 and, at 6 ft 6 in at the withers, towered over his owner, Ralph Fogleman.

TALLEST and STRONGEST HORSES: Firpon (left, above), a Percheron-Shire cross stood 7 ft 1 in high (21.1 hands) at the withers. A team of 2 Clydesdale horses (right, above) hauled these 50 logs, weighing 96,000 lb, 275 yd across snow in 1893 in Mich. The horses themselves weighed a total of 3,500 lb.

SMALLEST HORSE: The Falabella, an Argentine breed named for its developer, is hardly any bigger than a cockerel rooster and weighs 40–80 lb.

Iowa, which was reported to weigh slightly in excess of 3,200 lb shortly before his death Sept 6, 1948, aged 20. He stood 19.2 hands (6 ft 6 in).

In Apr 1973 the Belgian mare "Wilma du Bos" (foaled July 15, 1966), owned by Mrs Virgie Arden of Reno, Nev was reported to weigh slightly in excess of 3,200 lb when in foal and being shipped from Antwerp. The mare stood 18.2 hands (6 ft 2 in) and normally weighed about 2,400 lb.

Tallest Horse

The tallest horse ever documented was the Percheron-Shire cross "Firpon" (foaled 1959) owned by Julio Falabella which stood 21.1 hands (7 ft 1 in) and weighed 2,976 lb. He died on Recco de Roca Ranch in Argentina, March 14, 1972. A height of 21.1 hands was also claimed for the Clydesdale gelding "Big Jim" (foaled 1950), bred by Lyall M. Anderson of West Broomley, Montrose, Scotland. "Big Jim" died in St Louis, Mo, in 1957.

A claim of 21.2 hands (7 ft 1½ in) was made in 1908 for "Morocco" of Allentown, Pa, weighing 2,835 lb.

Smallest Horse

The smallest breed of horse is the Falabella, bred by Julio Falabella (see *Tallest Horse*), developed over a period of 45 years by crossing and recrossing a small group of undersized English thoroughbreds with Shetland ponies. Adult specimens range from 15–30 in at the shoulder and weigh 40–80 lb. Foals standing 3 hands (12 in) have been recorded twice by Norman J. Mitchell of Glenorie, NSW, Australia, in the cases of "Tung Dynasty" (Feb 8, 1978) and "Quicksilver" (1975).

The upper accepted limit for the American Miniature Horse Breeders Association is 34 in.

Strongest Horses

The greatest load hauled by a pair of Clydesdale draught horses was 48 short tons (96,000 lb), equal to 50 pine logs (or 36,055 board-feet of lumber) hauled on a sledge litter 275 yd *pulled across snow* on the Nester Estate at Ewen, Mich, Feb 26, 1893. The two horses had a combined weight of 3,500 lb.

A pair of shire geldings owned by Liverpool Corporation registered a much more impressive *maximum* pull equivalent to a starting load of 56 tons on a dynamometer at the British Empire Exhibition at Wembley, London, Sept 4, 1924.

Dog Population

In 1981 there were an estimated 41 million dogs in the US.

Oldest Dogs

Authentic records of dogs living over 20 years are rare, but even 34 years has been accepted by one authority. The greatest reliable age recorded for a dog is 29 years 5 months for a Queensland "heeler" named "Bluey," owned by Les Hall of Rochester, Vic, Australia. The dog was obtained as a puppy in 1910 and worked among cattle and sheep for nearly 20 years. He was put to sleep Nov 14, 1939.

Most Popular Dog Breed

The breed with the most American Kennel Club new registrations for the year 1981 was the poodle, with 93,050, compared to 95,250 new poodles in 1980. Cocker spaniels moved into second place in 1981 with 83,504 new registrations, beating new Doberman Pinschers who slipped to third with 77,387. The earliest dog show was held in The Town Hall, Newcastle upon Tyne, England, June 28–29, 1859, with 23 pointers and 27 setters.

Rarest Dog

The rarest breed of dog is the Tahltan bear dog, which was formerly used by the Tahltan Indians of western Canada for hunting big game. Only 5 known examples of this hound still survive, and 4 of these are spayed bitches, which means the Tahltan has now reached the point of no return unless a breeding pair can be found. The solitary male, "Iskut" (whelped Mar 14, 1967), is owned by Mrs Winnie Acheson of Arlin, British Columbia, where 3 of the bitches also live.

Tallest Dogs

The tallest breeds of dog are the Great Dane and the Irish wolfhound, both of which can exceed 39 in at the shoulder. The extreme recorded example is the Great Dane "Shamgret Danzas" (whelped in 1975), owned by Mrs G. Comley of Milton Keynes, Buckinghamshire, England, which stands 40½ in and weighs 224 lb. The Irish wolfhound "Broadbridge Michael" (whelped in 1920), owned by Mrs Mary Beynon of Sutton-at-Hone, Kent, England, stood 39½ in at the age of two years.

Largest Dog

The heaviest breed of domestic dog (*Canis familiaris*) is the St Bernard. The heaviest example is "Benedictine," owned by Thomas and Ann Irwin of Grand Rapids, Mich. He was whelped Dec 17, 1970 and weighed 305 lb in May 1978 (height 39 in at shoulder). He has not been weighed since.

Smallest Dogs

The smallest breeds of dog are the Yorkshire terrier, the Chihuahua and the toy poodle, *miniature* versions of which have been known to weigh less than 16 oz when adult. In Apr 1971 a weight of 10 oz was reliably reported for an adult Yorkshire terrier named "Sylvia," owned by Mrs Connie Hutchins of Walthamstow, Greater London, England.

Dog Strength and Endurance

The greatest load shifted by a dog was 6,400½ lb of railroad steel pulled by a 176-lb St Bernard named "Ryettes Brandy Bear," at Bothell, Wash, July 21, 1978. The 4-year-old dog, owned by Douglas Alexander of Monroe, Wash, pulled the weight on a four-wheeled carrier across a cement surface for a distance of 15 ft in less than 90 sec.

The strongest dog in the world in terms of most proportionate weight hauled is "Barbara-Allen's Dark Hans," a 97-lb Newfoundland, who pulled 5,045½ lb (= 52 lb per lb bodyweight) across a cement surface at Bothell, Wash, July 20, 1979. The dog, owned by Miss Terri Dickinson of Kenmore, Wash, was only 12 months old when he made the attempt.

In the annual 1,100-mile dog sled race from Anchorage to Nome, Alaska, the record time is 12 days 7 hours 45 min by Rick Swenson's team of dogs in the 1981 race. Swenson mushed his team to an unprecedented 4th win in 1982.

Largest Litter

The largest recorded litter of puppies is one of 23 thrown on June 9, 1944, by "Lena," a foxhound bitch owned by Commander W. N. Ely of Ambler, Pa. On Feb 6–7, 1975, "Careless Ann," a St Bernard bitch owned by Robert and Alice Rodden of Lebanon, Mo, produced a litter of 23, of which 14 survived.

Most Prolific Dog

The dog who has sired the greatest recorded number of puppies was the greyhound "Low Pressure" nicknamed "Timmy," whelped in Sept 1957 and owned by Mrs Bruna Amhurst of Regent's Park, London. From Dec 1961 until he died in Nov 1969, he had fathered 2,414 registered puppies, with at least 600 others unregistered.

Most Valuable Dogs

Mrs Judith Thurlow of Great Ashfield, Suffolk, England, turned down an offer of £14,000 ($35,000) in June 1972 for her racing greyhound "Super Rory" (b Oct 1970). Show dogs have also fetched extremely high prices. In July 1976 Mrs Eiselle Banks of Rayleigh, Essex, England, turned down an American offer of $20,000 for her international champion Lowchen "Cluneen Adam Adamant" (b Aug 13, 1969). On June 27, 1972, August Belmont of Easton, Md, paid $22,000 for his Labrador retriever puppy, "Wanapum Lucky YoYo," bred by Eddie DeWitt of Redmond, Wash. This is the highest price *actually paid* for a dog.

Police Dogs

The top police dog is "Trep" of the Dade County Crime Force, Fla, who has sniffed out $63 million worth of narcotics. In a school demonstration looking for 10 hidden packets, Trep once found 11.

In Jan 1977 a "contract" worth $10,000 was put out on the life of a very successful drug-sniffing police dog named "Sergeant Blitz" by the underworld in Savannah, Ga. Shortly afterwards, an 8-ft-high concrete wall was built around the dog's kennel as a precautionary measure.

"General," a US Army dog, "arrested" 220 narcotics offenders between Apr 1974 and Mar 1976.

Guide Dog

The longest reported period of *active service* for a guide dog is 13 years 2 months, in the case of a Labrador retriever bitch named "Polly" (whelped Oct 10, 1956), owned by Rose Resnick of San Rafael, Calif. The dog was put to sleep Dec 15, 1971.

"Top Dog"

The greatest altitude attained by a mammal other than man is 1,050 miles by the Samoyed husky bitch fired as a passenger in *Sputnik II* Nov 3, 1957. The dog was variously named "Kudryavka" (feminine form of Curly), "Limonchik" (diminutive of lemon), "Malyshka," "Zhuchka" or by the Russian breed name for husky "Laika."

LARGEST LITTERS: "Careless Ann" (above), a St Bernard, tied the record of 23 puppies, held by "Lena" (below), a foxhound, but only 14 of Ann's survived.

HIGHEST-FLYING DOG: "Laika," a Samoyed husky, reached an altitude of 1,050 miles up when "Sputnik II" was launched by rocket in 1957.

LARGEST DOG: The St Bernard as a species is the biggest breed, and the heaviest example is "Benedictine" (right), who weighs 305 lb and stands 39 in at the shoulder. His son is at his feet. These dogs are owned by Mr & Mrs Irwin of Grand Rapids, Mich. (Schwarzwald Hof Kennels)

DOG LEAPERS: "Young Sabre" (above), a German shepherd belonging to the RAF, scaled a ribbed wall 11 ft 8 in high in England in 1981. "Max of Pangoula," another German shepherd, vaulted over a smooth wooden wall 11 ft 5⅛ in high at a prison's dog training school in Zimbabwe in 1980.

HEAVIEST CAT (top right): Norris McWhirter, author of the "Guinness Book," checks for himself the weight of 43 lb claimed for "Tiger," a long-haired part-Persian. The cat was 37 in long, with a 33-in waist and a 12½-in neck. He had to be put to sleep in 1980.

Top Show Dog

The record number of "Best in Show" awards won by any dog in all-breed shows is 127, compiled from Jan 1957 to Feb 1960 by the Pekingese International Champion "Chik T'Sun of Caversham," owned by Mr and Mrs Charles C. Venable of Marietta, Ga.

Highest and Longest Dog Jumps

The canine "high jump" record for a leap and a scramble over a smooth wooden wall (without any ribs or other aids) is held by a German shepherd called "Max of Pangoula." He scaled an 11-ft-5⅛-in wall at Chikurubi prison's dog training school near Salisbury, Zimbabwe on Mar 18, 1980. His trainer was Chief Prison Officer Alec Mann.

Another German shepherd dog, "Young Sabre," handled by Cpl David Smith, scaled a ribbed wall with regulation shallow slats to a height of 11 ft 8 in at RAF Newton, Nottinghamshire, England, on July 17, 1981.

The longest recorded canine long jump was one of 30 ft by a greyhound named "Bang," made in jumping a gate in coursing a hare at Brecon Lodge, Gloucestershire, England, in 1849.

Greatest Dog Funeral

The greatest dog funeral on record was for the mongrel "Lazaras," belonging to the eccentric, Emperor Norton I of the US, Protector of Mexico, held in San Francisco in 1862, which was attended by an estimated 10,000 people.

Top Dog Trainer

The most successful dog trainer—and the fastest—is Mrs Barbara Woodhouse of Rickmansworth, Hertfordshire, England, who has trained 17,136 dogs to obey the basic commands during the period from 1951 to Mar 25, 1982. Her record for a single day is 80 dogs in June 1973 in Denver, Colo.

Dog Tracking

The greatest tracking feat on record was performed by the Doberman "Sauer" trained by Detective-Sergeant Herbert Kruger. In 1925 he tracked a stock thief 100 miles across the Great Karroo, South Africa, by scent alone.

In 1923 a collie named "Bobbie," lost by his owners while they were on vacation in Wolcott, Ind, turned up at the family home in Silverton, Ore, 6 months later, after having covered a distance of close to 2,000 miles. The dog, later identified by people who had cared for him along the route, had apparently wandered back through Ill, Iowa, Neb, and Colo, before crossing the Rocky Mts in the depths of winter, then continuing through Wyo and Idaho.

Cat Population

The cat population in the US of 23 million is the largest in the world.

Oldest Cats

Cats are generally longer-lived animals than dogs. Information on this subject is often obscured by two or more cats bearing the same nickname in succession. The oldest cat ever recorded was probably the tabby "Puss," owned by Mrs T. Holway of Clayhidon, Devon, England, who celebrated his 36th birthday on Nov 28, 1939 and died the next day. A more recent and better documented case was that of the female tabby "Ma," owned by Mrs Alice St George Moore, of Drewsteignton, Devon, England. She was put to sleep Nov 5, 1957, aged 34.

Largest Cat Litter

The largest litter ever recorded was one of 19 kittens (4 stillborn) delivered by Caesarean section to "Tarawood Antigone," a 4-year-old brown Burmese, on Aug 7, 1970. Her owner, Mrs Valerie Gane of Kingham, Oxfordshire, England, reported that the litter was the result of mismating with a half-Siamese. Of the 15 survivors, 14 were male.

The largest live litter of which all survived was one of 14 kittens born in Dec 1974 to the Persian cat "Bluebell," owned by Mrs Elenore Dawson of Wellington, Cape Province, South Africa.

Most Prolific Cat

A cat named "Dusty," aged 17, living in Bonham, Tex, gave birth to her 420th kitten June 12, 1952.

Heaviest Cat

The heaviest domestic cat (*Felis catus*) on record was a long-haired part-Persian named "Tiger," owned by Mrs Phyllis Dacey of Billericay, Essex, England. During the 2-year period ending Sept 1979, he scaled a constant 42–43 lb (neck 12½ in, waist 33 in, length 37 in) but after receiving treatment for a hormone imbalance, he started to lose weight rapidly. When he was put to sleep on Aug 27, 1980 as a result of kidney trouble, he was down to 18 lb.

Smallest Cats

Because of the reproduction problems involved, there is no recognized smallest breed of cat. Adult weights of under 3 lb, however, have been reliably reported in cases of feline dwarfism (average weight 9–11 lb).

Richest Cats

Dr William Grier of San Diego, Calif, died in June 1963 leaving his entire estate of $415,000 to his two 15-year-old cats, "Hellcat" and "Brownie." When the cats died in 1965 the money went to George Washington University, Washington, DC.

Most Valuable Cat

In 1967 Miss Elspeth Sellar of Grafham, England, turned down an offer of 2,000 guineas (then $5,880) from an American breeder for her 2-year-old champion copper-eyed white Persian tom, "Coylum Marcus" (b March 28, 1965, d Apr 14, 1978).

Mousing Champion

The greatest mouser on record was a tabby named "Mickey," owned by Shepherd & Sons Ltd of Burscough, Lancashire, England, which killed more than 22,000 mice during 23 years with the firm. He died in Nov 1968.

Best Climbing Cat

On Feb 28, 1980 a female cat climbed 70 ft up the sheer outside wall of a 5-story apartment house in Bradford, Yorkshire, England, and took refuge in a roof space. She had been frightened by a dog.

Rabbits

The largest breed of domestic rabbit (*Oryctolagus cuniculus*) is the British giant. Adult specimens average 18–20 lb but weights up to 30 lb have been reliably reported for bucks. In Apr 1980 a 5-month-old female French lop weighing 26.45 lb was exhibited at the Reus Fair in northeastern Spain.

The heaviest recorded wild rabbit (average weight 3½ lb) is one of 7 lb 1½ oz accidentally killed by Paul Short while he was driving near Grantham, England, on Sept 20, 1981. An unconfirmed weight of 35 lb was reported for the New Zealand white "Snowy" from Uxbridge, England, in Sept 1981.

The smallest breeds of domestic rabbit are the Netherlands dwarf and the Polish, both of which reach a maximum of 2¼ lb at maturity.

The most prolific domestic breeds are the New Zealand white and the Californian. Does produce 5–6 litters a year, each containing 8–12 young (compare with 5 litters and 3–7 young for the wild rabbit).

Hares

In Nov 1956 a brown hare (*Lepus europaeus*), weighing a record 15 lb 1 oz, was shot near Welford, Northamptonshire, England. The average adult weight is 8 lb.

LARGEST PET LITTERS

Animal	Number	Breed	Owner
Cat (1970)	15†	Burmese Siamese	Mrs Valerie Gane, Kingham, Oxfordshire, Eng
Dog (1944)	23	Foxhound	Cdr W. N. Ely, Ambler, Pa
(1975)	23	St Bernard	R. and A. Rodden, Lebanon, Mo
Rabbit (1978)	24	New Zealand White	Joseph Filek, Sydney, Cape Breton, Nova Scotia, Canada
Guinea Pig (1972)	12		Laboratory Specimen
Hamster (1974)	26*	Golden Hamster	L. and S. Miller, Baton Rouge, La
Mouse (1961)	32	House Mouse	Laboratory Specimen (US).
Gerbil (1979)	11		Steve Austin, Addington, Surrey, Eng
(1980)	11		Heather James, High Wycombe, Bucks, Eng

† 4 stillborn
* 18 killed by mother

CAGED PET LONGEVITY TABLE

The greatest recorded ages for commonly kept pets are as follows:

	Years	Months	
Rabbit (*Oryctolagus cuniculus*)	18*		European rabbit. Died 1977
Guinea Pig (*Cavia porcellus*)	14	10½	"Snowball," Nottinghamshire, Eng. Died 1979
Gerbil (*Gerbillus gerbillus*)	8+		"Sahara," *fl.* 1981 (owner, Aaron Milstone), Lathrap Village, Mich.
House Mouse (*Mus musculus*)	6	6	"Dixie" (owner, A. Newton), Sheffield, Eng. Died Apr 25, 1981
Rat (*Rattus sp.*)	5	8	Philadelphia. Died 1924

* 18 years also reported for a doe still living in 1947.

Note: A report of 10 years 2 months for a hamster has been published but details are lacking.

2. BIRDS (*AVES*)

Largest Bird

The largest living bird is the North African ostrich (*Struthio camelus camelus*) which is found in reduced numbers south of the Atlas Mountains from Upper Senegal and Niger across to the Sudan and central Ethiopia. Male examples of this flightless or ratite subspecies have been recorded up to 9 ft in height and 345 lb in weight.

The heaviest flying bird, or carinate, is the Kori bustard or paauw (*Otis kori*) of East and South Africa. Weights up to 40 lb have been reliably reported for cock birds shot in South Africa. The mute swan (*Cygnus olor*) which is resident in Britain can also reach 40 lb on occasion, and there is a record from Poland of a cob weighing 49.5 lb which could not fly.

The heaviest bird of prey is the Andean condor (*Vultur gryphus*), which averages 20–25 lb as an adult. An unconfirmed weight of 31 lb has been claimed for a California condor (*Gymnogyps californianus*) (average weight 20 lb) now preserved in the California Academy of Sciences, Los Angeles.

Fastest-Flying Bird

The fastest-flying bird in level flight is the large white-throated spine-tailed swift (*Hirundapus caudacutus*). For details see page 44.

The bird which presents the hunter with the greatest difficulty is the red-breasted merganser (*Mergus serrator*). On May 29, 1960 a specimen flushed from the Kukpuk River, Cape Thompson, northern Alaska, by a light aircraft recorded an air speed of 80 mph in level flight for nearly 13 sec before turning aside.

Fastest and Slowest Wing Beat

The fastest recorded wing beat of any bird is that of the horned sungem (*Heliactin cornuta*) of tropical South America with a rate of 90 beats per sec.

Large vultures (family Vulturidae) sometimes exhibit a flapping rate as low as one beat per sec. Condors can cruise on thermals for 60 miles without beating their wings.

Longest Bird Flights

The greatest distance covered by a ringed bird during migration is 12,000 miles by an Arctic tern (*Sterna paradisaea*), which was banded as a nestling July 5, 1955 in the Kandalaksha Sanctuary on the White Sea coast of the USSR, north of Archangel, and was captured alive by a fisherman 8 miles south of Fremantle, W Australia, May 16, 1956.

Highest-Flying

The highest acceptable altitude recorded for a bird is 27,000 ft for 30 whooper swans (*Cygnus olor*) flying in from Iceland to the UK. They were spotted by an airline pilot over the Outer Hebrides on Dec 9, 1967, and the height was also confirmed by air traffic control in Northern Ireland after the swans had been picked up on radar.

Highest g Force in Bird World

Recent American scientific experiments have revealed that the beak of the red-headed woodpecker (*Melanerpes erythrocephalus*) hits the bark of a tree with an impact velocity of 1,300 mph. This means that when the head snaps back the brain is subject to a deceleration of about 1,000 g.

Most Airborne Birds

The most airborne of all land birds is the common swift (*Apus apus*) which remains aloft for at least 2–3 years, but the sooty tern (*Sterna fuscata*) is the most aerial of all birds. It remains continuously aloft for three or four years after leaving the nesting grounds before it returns to the breeding grounds.

Rarest Bird

Because of the practical difficulties involved in assessing bird populations in the wild, it is virtually impossible to establish the identity of the rarest living bird. The strongest contenders, however, must be the Kauai Ooaa (*Moho braccatus*) of Kauai, Hawaii, of which only a single pair survived in 1980, and the yellow-fronted gardener bowerbird (*Amblyornis flavifrons*), unsighted since 1895, until a single male was observed in Papua New Guinea in 1981.

Longest-Lived Bird

The greatest irrefutable age reported for any bird is 72 years in the case of a male Andean condor (*Vultur gryphus*) named "Kuzya," which died in Moskovskii Zoologicheskeii Park, Moscow, in 1964. This bird had been received there as an adult in 1892. Other records which are regarded as *probably* reliable include 73 years (1818–91) for a greater sulphur-crested cockatoo (*Cacatua galerita*), 72 years (1797–1869) for an African gray parrot (*Psittacus erithacus*), 70 years (1770–1840) for a mute swan (*Cygnus olor*), and 69 years for a raven (*Corvus corax*). In 1972 a southern ostrich (*Struthio camelus australis*) aged 62 years 3 months was killed in the Ostrich Abattoir at Oudtshoorn, Cape Province, South Africa.

"Jimmy," a red and green Amazon parrot owned by Mrs Bella Ludford of Liverpool, England, was allegedly hatched in captivity on Dec 3, 1870, and lived 104 years in his original brass cage. He died Jan 5, 1975.

Largest Wing Span

The wandering albatross (*Diomedea exulans*) of the southern oceans has the largest wing span of any living bird, adult males averaging 10 ft 4 in with wings tightly stretched. The largest recorded specimen was a male measuring 11 ft 11 in caught by members of the Antarctic research ship USNS *Eltanin* in the Tasman Sea on Sept 18, 1965.

The only other bird reliably credited with a wing spread in excess of 11 ft is the vulture-like marabou stork (*Leptoptilus crumeniferus*) of Africa. In the 1930's an extreme measurement of 13 ft 4 in was reported for a male shot in Central Africa, but this species rarely exceeds 9 ft.

Fastest Swimming and Deepest Diving Birds

The fastest swimmer is the gentoo penguin (*Pygoscelis papua*). In Jan 1913 a small group was timed at 22.3 mph underwater near the Bay of Isles, South Georgia, Falkland Islands. This is a respectable flying speed for some birds.

The deepest diver is the emperor penguin (*Aptenodytes forsteri*) of the Antarctic which can reach a depth of 870 ft and remain submerged for as long as 18 min.

Birds with Most Acute Vision

Birds of prey (Falconiformes) have the keenest eyesight in the avian world. Their visual acuity is at least 8–10 times stronger than that of human vision. The golden eagle (*Aquila chrysaetos*) can detect an 18-in-long hare at a range of 2,150 yd (possibly even 2 miles), in good light and against a contrasting background, and a peregrine falcon (*Falco peregrinus*) can detect a pigeon at a range of over 3,500 ft.

Incubation

The longest incubation period is that of the wandering albatross (*Diomedea exulans*), with a normal range of 75–82 days. There is one case of an egg of the mallee fowl (*Leipoa ocellata*) of Australia taking 90 days to hatch. Its normal incubation period is 62 days. The shortest incubation period is the 10 days of the great spotted woodpecker (*Dendrocopus major*) and the black-billed cuckoo (*Coccyzus erythropthalmus*). The idlest of cock birds are hummingbirds (family Trochilidae), eider ducks (*Somateria mollissima*) and golden pheasants (*Chrysolophus pictus*), among whom the hen bird does 100% of the incubation, whereas the female common kiwi (*Apteryx australis*) leaves this entirely to the male for 75–80 days.

Largest Nests

The largest bird's nest on record is one 9½ ft wide and 20 ft deep built by a pair of bald eagles (*Haliaeetus leucocephalus*) and possibly their successors

Inset shows an Andean condor in flight. (Hans Dossenbach/Ardea)

HEAVIEST BIRD OF PREY: The Andean condor (above) weighs a maximum of 26 lb 8 oz and this specimen named "Friedrich" has a near-record wing spread of over 10 ft. The RECORD WING SPAN is held by the wandering albatross with a spread of 11 ft 11 in. The specimen shown here (left), caught in South Georgia of the Falkland Islands group, had a wing span of 11 ft 4 in.

69

MOST ABUNDANT SPECIES (above): About 10 billion red-billed queleas, shown alone and in a more social situation, inhabit sub-Saharan Africa.

SMALLEST BIRD (right): The bee hummingbird (in proportion here) is so tiny, it is smaller than an ostrich's eye.

EGGS (below): The man is holding the huge egg of an elephant bird, which is smaller than the record largest egg of the ostrich (center). The ostrich's is so big—6–8 in long and 4–6 in in diameter—and with so strong a shell, it can support the weight of a 280-lb man. It is 352 times as heavy (at 3¾ lb) as the smallest egg, that of the hummingbird (in hand). The flightless Kiwi bird of New Zealand (right) lays the biggest egg in proportion to its size.

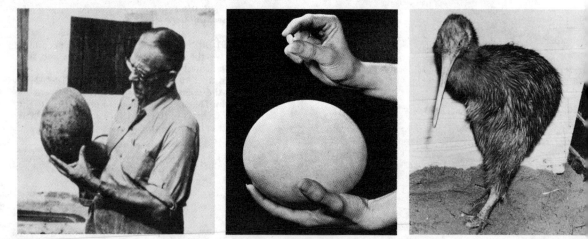

near St Petersburg, Fla, reported in 1963 and estimated to weigh more than 2 tons. The golden eagle (*Aquila chrysaetos*) also constructs huge nests, and one 15 ft deep was reported from Scotland in 1954. It had been in use for 45 years. The incubation mounds built by the mallee fowl (*Leipoa ocellata*) of Australia are much larger, having been measured up to 15 ft in height and 35 ft across, and it has been calculated that the nest site may involve mounding 300 cu yd of matter weighing 330 tons.

Smallest Bird

The smallest bird is the bee hummingbird (*Mellisuga helenae*) found in Cuba and the Isle of Pines. Adult males (females are slightly larger) measure 2.24 in in total length, half of which is taken up by the bill and tail. It weighs 0.056 oz, which means it is lighter than a privet-hawk moth (0.084 oz).

The smallest bird of prey is the 1.23-oz white fronted falconet of northwestern Borneo (*Microhierax latifrons*), which is about the size of a sparrow.

The smallest sea bird is the least storm petrel (*Halocyptena microsoma*), which breeds on many of the small islands in the Gulf of Calif, Mexico. Adult specimens average 5½ in in total length.

Most Abundant Birds

The most abundant species of wild bird is the red-billed quelea (*Quelea quelea*) of the drier parts of Africa south of the Sahara with a population estimated at 10,000 million of which a tenth are destroyed each year by pest control units.

The most abundant domesticated bird is the chicken, the domesticated form of the wild red jungle fowl (*Gallus gallus*) of Southeast Asia. In 1974 there were believed to be about 4,000 million chickens in the world, or about one chicken for every member of the human race.

The most abundant sea bird is probably Wilson's storm-petrel (*Oceanites oceanicus*) of the Antarctic. No population estimates have been published, but the number must run into the hundreds of millions.

Largest Bird Eggs

Of living birds, the one producing the largest egg is the ostrich (*Struthio camelus*). The average egg weighs 3.63–3.88 lb, measures 6–8 in in length, 4–6 in in diameter and requires about 40 min for boiling. The shell, though 1/16th in thick, can support the weight of a 280-lb man.

Smallest Bird Eggs

The smallest egg laid by any bird is that of the Vervain hummingbird (*Mellisuga minima*) of Jamaica. Two specimens measuring less than 0.39 in in length weighed 0.0128 oz and 0.0132 oz respectively. The egg of the smallest bird, the bee hummingbird, weighs 0.0176 oz.

Longest and Most Feathers

The longest feathers grown by any bird are those of the cock long-tailed fowls, or onagadori (a strain of *Gallus gallus*), which have been bred in southwestern Japan since the mid-17th century. In 1973 a tail covert measuring 34 ft 9½ in was reported by Masasha Kubota of Kochi, Shikoku. The two central pairs of tail feathers of the flying Reeve's pheasant (*Syrmaticus reevesi*) of north and west China can exceed 8 ft.

In a series of "feather counts" on various species of birds, a whistling swan (*Cygnus columbianus*) was found to have 25,216 feathers, 20,177 of which were on the head and neck. The ruby-throated hummingbird (*Archilochus colubris*) has only 940, although hummingbirds have more feathers per area of body surface than any other living bird.

Champion Bird-Watcher

The world's leading bird-watcher is Norman Chesterfield (b Mar 8, 1913) of Wheatley, Ont, Canada. By Jan 1982 he had logged 5,556 of the 8,733 known species.

DOMESTICATED BIRDS

Heaviest Chicken

The heaviest breed of chicken is one called the white sully developed by Grant Sullens of West Point, Calif, over a period of 7 years. One monstrous rooster named "Weirdo" reportedly weighed 22 lb in Jan 1973, and was so ferocious that he crippled a dog which came too close and killed two cats.

Chicken Flying

The record distance flown by a chicken is 310 ft 6 in by *"Shorisha"* (means champion) owned by Morimitzu Neura at Hammatzu, Japan Mar 8, 1981. Hens are better flyers than cocks.

DOMESTICATED BIRDS: Norris McWhirter (upper left) checks the scales at an auction in London in 1980 at which a 78-lb-11¼-oz turkey was sold for $4,400. (Left) "George," a domestic gander, lived for 49 years 8 months though the average age for a goose is 25 years. (Above) "Prudle," a male talking gray parrot, has a 1,000-word vocabulary and was unbeaten in competition for 12 years. Mrs Lyn Logue of London is the proud owner.

Heaviest Turkey

The greatest dressed weight recorded for a turkey (*Meleagris gallopavo*) is 78 lb 11¼ oz for a stag reared by Leacroft Turkeys, Ltd of Barwell, England. It won the annual heaviest turkey competition held at the Savoy Hotel, London, Dec 8, 1980.

Most Expensive Turkey

The highest price reached at auction (auctioneer Bernard Cribbins) for a turkey was £2200 ($4,400) paid by Peter Lane, managing director of W. Fenn, Covent Garden (London) poulterers, for the 78 lb 11¼ oz stag (see above).

Most Talkative Bird

The world's most talkative bird is a male African gray parrot (*Psittacus erythacus*) named "Prudle," owned by Mrs Lyn Logue of Golders Green, London, England, which won the "best talking parrot-like bird" title at the National Cage and Aviary Bird Show in London for 12 consecutive years (1965–76) before retiring undefeated. Prudle, who has a vocabulary of nearly 1,000 words, was taken from a nest in a tree about to be felled at Jinja, Uganda, in 1958.

Longest-Lived Domestic Birds

The longest-lived domesticated bird (excluding the ostrich) is the domestic goose which normally lives about 25 years. A gander named "George," owned by Mrs Florence Hull of Lancashire, England, died on Dec 16, 1976, aged 49 years 8 months. He was hatched in Apr 1927. The longest-lived small cage bird is the canary (*Serinus canaria*). The oldest example on record was a 34-year-old cock bird named "Joey," owned by Mrs K. Ross of Hull, England. The bird was purchased in Calabar, Nigeria, in 1941, and died Apr 8, 1975.

The oldest budgerigar (*Melopsittacus undulatus*) (also called parakeet) on record was a hen bird named "Charlie," owned by Miss J. Dinsey of Stonebridge, London, England, which lived for 29 years 2 months, and died June 20, 1977.

LARGEST REPTILES: This 19-ft-6-in estuarine crocodile, killed in New Guinea, was only 10 in shorter than the "official" record holder. (From "To Catch a Crocodile," published by Angus & Robertson)

3. REPTILES (*REPTILIA*)

(Crocodiles, snakes, turtles, tortoises and lizards)

Largest and Heaviest Reptiles

The largest reptile in the world is the estuarine or salt-water crocodile (*Crocodylus porosus*) of Southeast Asia, northern Australia, New Guinea, Malay Archipelago and the Solomon Islands. Adult males average 14–16 ft in length and scale 900–1,150 lb. In 1823 a notorious man-eater allegedly 27 ft in length and weighing an estimated 4,400 lb was shot at Jala Jala on Luzon Island in the Philippines after terrorizing the neighborhood for many years, but the dimensions of the skull suggest this crocodile must have measured about 20 ft. It is now preserved in the Museum of Comparative Zoology at Harvard University, Cambridge, Mass.

The holder of the "official" record is a 20-ft-4-in male which drowned after getting entangled in a fisherman's net at Obo on the Fly River, Papua New Guinea in 1979.

In July 1957 an unconfirmed (but probably reliable) length of 28 ft 4 in was reported for an estuarine crocodile shot by Mrs Kris Pawlowski on MacArthur Bank in the Norman River, northwestern Queensland, Australia.

Largest Lizards

The largest of all lizards is the Komodo monitor or Ora (*Varanus komodoensis*), a dragon-like reptile found on the Indonesian islands of Komodo, Rintja, Padar and Flores. Adult males average 8 ft in length and weigh 175–200 lb. Lengths up to 23 ft (*sic*) have

LARGEST OF ALL LIZARDS: The Komodo monitor of Indonesia can exceed 300 lb. (K. W. Fink/Ardea)

been quoted for this species, but the largest specimen to be accurately measured was a male presented to an American zoologist in 1928 by the Sultan of Bima which taped 10 ft 0.8 in. In 1937 this animal was put on display in the St Louis Zoological Gardens for a short period. It then measured 10 ft 2 in in length and weighed 365 lb.

The longest lizard in the world is the slender Salvadori dragon (*Varanus salvadori*) of New Guinea. One of 18 ft was reported by "Operation Drake" in Dec 1979.

Oldest Lizard

The greatest age recorded for a lizard is more than 54 years for a male slow worm (*Anguis fragilis*) kept

in the Zoological Museum in Copenhagen, Denmark, from 1892 until 1946.

Longest-Lived Chelonians

Tortoises are the longest-lived of all vertebrates. (See *Longest-Lived Animal*.) Other reliable records over 100 years include a common box tortoise (*Testudo carolina*) of 138 years and a European pond tortoise (*Emys orbicularis*) of 120+ years. The greatest proven age of a continuously observed tortoise is 116+ years for a Mediterranean spur-thighed tortoise (*Testudo graeca*) which died in Paignton Zoo, Devon, England, in 1957.

Largest Chelonians

The largest living chelonian is the Pacific leatherback turtle (*Dermochelys coriacea schlegelii*). The average adult measures 6–7 ft in overall length (length of carapace 4–5 ft) and weighs up to 1,000 lb. The greatest weight reliably recorded is 1,908 lb for a male captured off Monterey, Calif on Aug 29, 1961. Its length was 8 ft 4 in overall.

OLDEST CROCODILIAN: This female American alligator lived for 66 years. Brought to the Adelaide Zoo in Australia in 1914 as a 2-year-old it lived in captivity until 1978.

The largest living tortoise is *Geochelone* (*Testudo*) *gigantea* of the Indian Ocean islands of Aldabra, Mauritius, and the Seychelles (introduced 1874). Adult males in the wild sometimes exceed 450 lb in weight, but much heavier captive specimens have been recorded. One male preserved in the Rothschild Museum at Tring, Herts, Eng weighed 593 lb when alive.

Slowest-Moving Chelonians

In a recent "speed" test carried out in the Seychelles, in the Indian Ocean, a male giant tortoise (*Geochelone gigantea*) could only cover 5 yd in 43.5 sec (0.23 mph) despite the enticement of a female tortoise. The National Tortoise Championship held at Tickhill, South Yorkshire, England, has the animals going up a 1:12 grade and the meet record is 18 ft in 43.7 sec by "Charlie."

SPEEDIEST REPTILE (above): The six-lined race runner reached 18 mph in racing a car. HEAVIEST CHELONIAN (right) is the Pacific leatherback turtle, which averages 1,000 lb and is 7 ft long. The specimen shown here, caught in 1970 off Mozambique, East Africa, weighed 1,322 lb.

Rarest Reptile

A new species of crested iguana (*Brachophylus vitiensis*) was discovered on Yadua Tabu, Fiji Islands, in Jan 1979.

Fastest Reptile

The highest speed measured for any reptile on land is 18 mph by a six-lined race runner (*Cnemidophorus sexlineatus*) pursued by a car near McCormick, SC, in 1941. The highest speed claimed for any reptile in water is 22 mph by a frightened Pacific leatherback turtle (see *Largest Chelonians*).

Smallest Reptiles

The smallest known species of reptile is believed to be *Sphaerodactylus parthenopion,* a tiny gecko found only on the island of Virgin Gorda, one of the British Virgin Islands in the Caribbean. It is known only from 15 specimens, including some gravid females, found between Aug 10 and 16, 1964. The three largest females measured 0.71 in from snout to vent, with a tail of approximately the same length.

It is possible that another gecko, *Sphaerodactylus elasmorhynchus,* may be even smaller. The only specimen ever discovered was an apparently mature female, with a snout-vent length of 0.67 in and a tail of the same length, found March 15, 1966 among the roots of a tree in the western part of the Massif de la Hotte in Haiti.

A species of dwarf chameleon, *Evoluticauda tuberculata,* found in Madagascar, and known only from a single specimen, has a snout-vent length of 0.71 in and a tail length of 0.55 in. Chameleons, however, are more bulky than geckos, and it is not yet known if this specimen was fully grown.

Shortest Snakes

The shortest known snake is the thread snake *Leptotyphlops bilineata,* found on the Caribbean islands of Martinique, Barbados and St Lucia. It has a maximum recorded length of 4.7 in.

The shortest venomous snake is the striped dwarf garter snake (*Elaps dorsalis*) of South Africa. Adults average 6 in in length.

Heaviest Snakes

The heaviest snake is the anaconda (*Eunectes murinus*), which is nearly twice as heavy as a reticulated python of the same length. The specimen shot in Brazil *c.* 1960 (see below) was not weighed, but based on its maximum bodily girth of 44 in, it must have weighed nearly 500 lb.

The heaviest venomous snake is the eastern diamondback rattlesnake (*Crotalus adamanteus*), found in the southeastern US. One specimen measuring 7 ft 9 in in length weighed 34 lb. Less reliable weights up

OLDEST AND SMALLEST SNAKES: "Popeye" (left) lived for more than 40 years in the Philadelphia Zoo before he had to be euthanased. The thread snake (right) is being compared to a 25-cent-size coin of Somalia.

to 40 lb and lengths up to 8 ft 9 in have been reported.

A posthumous weight of 28 lb was reported for a king cobra (*Ophiophagus hannah*) 14 ft 5 in long at the New York Zoological Park (Bronx Zoo) in Feb 1973.

Longest Snakes

The longest of all snakes (average adult length) is the reticulated python (*Python reticulatus*) of Southeast Asia, Indonesia and the Philippines, which regularly exceeds 20 ft. In 1912 a specimen measuring exactly 32 ft 9½ in was shot near a mining camp on the north coast of Celebes in the Malay archipelago.

Lengths of 37½ ft, 42 ft and even 45 ft have been claimed for the anaconda (*Eunectes murinus*) of tropical South America, but these extreme measurements were probably based on stretched skins. The greatest authenticated length recorded for an anaconda is 27 ft 9 in for a female killed in Brazil *c.* 1960.

The longest (and heaviest) snake ever held in captivity was a female reticulated python (*Python reticulatus*) named "Colossus" who died in Highland Park Zoo, Mifflin, Pa on Apr 15, 1963. She measured 28 ft 6 in and scaled 320 lb at her heaviest.

The longest venomous snake in the world is the king cobra (*Ophiophagus hannah*), also called the hamadryad, of Southeast Asia and the Philippines. A specimen collected near Port Dickson in Malaya in April 1937 grew to 18 ft 9 in in the London Zoo. It was destroyed at the outbreak of war in 1939.

Oldest Snake

The greatest irrefutable age recorded for a snake is 40 years 3 months and 14 days in the case of a common Boa (*Boa constrictor constrictor*) at Philadelphia Zoological Gardens. Named "Popeye," he was purchased from a London dealer in Dec 1936, and he was euthanased (his life was humanely ended) on Apr 15, 1977 because of medical problems associated with advanced age.

Fastest-Moving Land Snake

The fastest-moving land snake is probably the slender black mamba (*Dendroaspis polylepis*). On Apr 23, 1906 an angry black mamba was timed at a speed of 7 mph over a measured distance of 47 yd near Mbuyuni on the Serengeti Plains, Tanzania. Stories that black mambas can overtake galloping horses (maximum speed 43.26 mph) are wild exaggerations, though a speed of 15 mph may be possible for short bursts over level ground.

Most Venomous Snakes

The most venomous snake is the sea snake *Hydrophis belcheri* which has a venom 100 times as toxic as that of the Australian taipan (*Oxyuranus scutellatus*). *The snake abounds around Ashmore Reef in the Timor Sea, off the coast of northwestern Australia.*

*The m*ost venomous land snake is the small scaled or fierce snake (*Parademansia microlepidotus*) of southwestern Queensland and northeastern South Australia and Tasmania. One specimen yielded 0.00385 oz of venom after milking, a quantity sufficient to kill at least 125,000 mice. Until 1976, this 6-ft-6-in-long snake was regarded as a western form of the taipan, but its venom differs significantly from the latter.

It is estimated that between 30,000 and 40,000 people (excluding Chinese and Russians) die from snakebite each year, 75% of them in densely populated India. Burma has the highest mortality rate with 15.4 deaths per 100,000 population per annum.

Longest Fangs

The longest fangs of any snake are those of the Gaboon viper (*Bitis gabonica*), of tropical Africa. In a 6-ft-long specimen, the fangs measured 1.96 in. A Gaboon viper bit itself to death on Feb 12, 1963 in the Philadelphia Zoological Gardens. Keepers found the dead snake with its fangs deeply embedded in its own back.

②

①

PYTHONS: 1. A 25-ft reticulated python is being force-fed at the NY Zoological Park. 2. This reticulated python has just swallowed a large bush pig. 3. Python skins 22 ft long are hanging up to dry in a London warehouse.

③

PYTHONS:
4. "Susie," a 22-ft-long python, is alive and having a good time in India.

④

77

LARGEST FROG (left): The Goliath frog of West Africa (shown with a falcon for size comparison) can be over 32 in long and weigh up to 7¼ lb. LARGEST AMPHIBIAN (right above): The Chinese giant salamander, which lives in cold mountain streams, can grow to a length of 6 feet and weigh almost 150 lb.

LARGEST and SMALLEST TOADS: The South American marine toad (left) can weigh up to 2 lb 11¼ oz. The tiniest (above) measures less than one inch.

4. AMPHIBIANS (*AMPHIBIA*)

(Salamanders, toads, frogs, newts, caecilians, etc.)

Largest Amphibian

The largest species of amphibian is the Chinese giant salamander (*Andrias davidianus*), which lives in the cold mountain streams and marshy areas of northeastern, central and southern China. The average adult measures 3 ft 9 in in total length and weighs 55–66 lb. One huge individual collected in Hunan Province in southern China measured 5 ft 11 in in total length and weighed 143 lb. The much rarer Japanese giant salamander (*Andrias japonicus*) is slightly smaller, but one captive specimen weighed 88 lb when alive and 100 lb after death, the body having absorbed water from the aquarium.

Largest Newt

The largest newt is the pleurodele or ribbed newt (*Pleurodeles waltl*), found in Morocco and on the Iberian Peninsula. Specimens measuring up to 15.74 in in total length and weighing over 1 lb have been reliably reported.

Largest Frog

The largest known frog is the rare Goliath frog (*Rana goliath*) of Cameroon and Equatorial Guinea. A female weighing 7 lb 4.5 oz was caught in the River Mbia, Equatorial Guinea, on Aug 23, 1960. It had a snout-vent length of 13.38 in and measured 32.08 in overall with legs extended.

Largest Tree Frog

The largest species of tree frog is *Hyla vasta*, found only on the island of Hispaniola (Haiti and the Dominican Republic) in the West Indies. The average snout-vent length is about 3.54 in, but a female collected from the San Juan River, Dominican Republic, in March 1928 measured 5.63 in.

Largest Toad

The largest toad is probably the marine toad (*Bufo marinus*) of tropical South America. An enormous female collected on Nov 24, 1965 at Miraflores Vaupes, Colombia, and later exhibited in the reptile house at the Bronx Zoo, New York City, had a snout-vent length of 9.37 in, and weighed 2 lb 11¼ oz at the time of its death in 1967.

Smallest Amphibian

The smallest species of amphibian is believed to be the arrow-poison frog *Sminthillus limbatus,* found only in Cuba. Fully-grown specimens have a snout-vent length of 0.44–0.48 in.

Smallest Newt

The smallest newt is believed to be the striped newt (*Notophthalmus perstriatus*) of the southeastern US. Adult specimens average 2.01 in in total length.

Smallest Tree Frog

The smallest tree frog is the least tree frog (*Hyla ocularis*), found in the southeastern US. It has a maximum snout-vent length of 0.62 in.

Smallest Toad

The smallest toad is the sub-species *Bufo taitanus beiranus,* first discovered *c.* 1906 near Beira, Mozambique, East Africa. Adult specimens have a maximum recorded snout-vent length of 0.94 in.

Smallest Salamander

The smallest species of salamander is the pygmy salamander (*Desmognathus wrighti*), which is found only in Tenn, NC, and Va. Adult specimens measure 1.45–2.0 in in total length.

Longest-Lived Amphibian

The greatest authentic age recorded for an amphibian is about 55 years for a male Japanese giant salamander (*Andrias japonicus*) which died in the aquarium at Amsterdam Zoological Gardens June 3, 1881. It was brought to Holland in 1829, at which time it was estimated to be 3 years old.

Highest and Lowest

The greatest altitude at which an amphibian has been found is 26,246 ft in the Himalayas for a common toad (*Bufo vulgaris*). This species has also been found at a depth of 1,115 ft in a coal mine.

Most Poisonous Venom

The most active known venom is the batrachotoxin derived from the skin secretions of the golden arrow-poison frog (*Phyllobates terribilis*) of western Colombia, America, which is at least 20 times more toxic than that of any other known arrow-poison frog. An average adult specimen contains enough poison (0.038 oz) to kill 2,200 people.

Longest Frog Jump

The record for three consecutive leaps is 33 ft 5½ in by a female South African sharp-nosed frog (*Rana oxyrhyncha*) named "Santjie" at a frog derby held at Lurula Natal Spa, Paulpietersburg, Natal, Africa May 21, 1977. At the annual Calaveras County Jumping Frog Jubilee at Angels Camp, Calif, in 1975, another specimen "Ex Lax" made a *single* leap of 17 ft 6¾ in for its owner Bill Moniz.

5. FISHES (AGNATHA, GNATHOSTOMATA)

Largest Freshwater Fishes

The largest fish which spends its whole life in fresh or brackish water is the rare Pa Beuk or Pla Buk (*Pangasianodon gigas*), a giant catfish found in the Mekong River of Laos and Thailand. Adult males average 8 ft in length and weigh about 360 lb. This size was exceeded by the European catfish or wels (*Silurus glanis*) in earlier times (in the 19th century lengths of up to 15 ft and weights up to 720 lb were reported for Russian specimens), but today anything over 6 ft and 200 lb is considered large. The arapaima (*Arapaima glanis*), also called the pirarucu, found in the Amazon and other South American rivers and often claimed to be the largest freshwater fish, averages 6½ ft and 150 lb. The largest "authentically recorded" measured 8 ft 1½ in and weighed 325 lb. It was caught in the Rio Negro, Brazil, in 1836. In Sept 1978 a Nile perch (*Lates niloticus*) weighing 416 lb was netted in the eastern part of Lake Victoria, Kenya.

Largest Sea Fishes

The largest fish is the rare, plankton-feeding whale shark (*Rhiniodon typus*) which is found in the warmer areas of the Atlantic, Pacific and Indian Oceans. It is not, however, the largest marine animal, since it is smaller than the larger species of whales (mammals). A whale shark measuring 60 ft 9 in long and weighing an estimated 90,000 lb was caught in a bamboo fish-trap at Koh Chik, in the Gulf of Siam, in 1919.

The largest carnivorous fish (excluding plankton-eaters) is the great white shark (*Carcharodon car-*

charias), also called "the man-eater," which ranges from the tropics to temperate-zone waters. In June 1930 a specimen measuring 37 ft in length was reportedly trapped in a herring weir at the White Head Island, New Brunswick, Canada, but this measurement is unconfirmed. In June 1978 a great white shark measuring 29 ft 6 in in length was killed after a fierce battle by fishermen at San Miguel in the Azores. It weighed more than 10,000 lb.

The longest of the bony or "true" fishes (Pisces) is the Russian sturgeon (*Acipenser huso*), also called the Beluga, which is found in the temperate areas of the Adriatic, Black and Caspian Seas, but enters large rivers like the Volga and the Danube for spawning. Lengths up to 26 ft 3 in have been reliably reported, and a gravid female taken in the estuary of the Volga in 1827 weighed 3,250 lb.

The heaviest bony fish in the world is the ocean sunfish (*Mola mola*), which is found in all tropical, sub-tropical and temperate waters. On Sept 18, 1908 a huge specimen was accidentally struck by the SS *Fiona* off Bird Island about 40 miles from Sydney, NSW, Australia, and towed to Port Jackson. It measured 14 ft between the anal and dorsal fins and weighed 5,017 lb.

Smallest Sea Fishes

The shortest recorded marine fish—and the shortest known vertebrate—is the dwarf goby (*Trimmatom nanus*) of the Chagos Archipelago, central Indian Ocean. In one series of 92 specimens collected by the 1978–9 Joint Services Chagos Research Expedition of the British Armed Forces, the adult males averaged 0.338 in in length and the adult females 0.350 in. The lightest of all vertebrates and the smallest catch possible for any fisherman is the dwarf goby (*Schindleria praematurus*) from Samoa which measures 0.47–0.74 in. Mature specimens have been known to weigh only 2 mg, which is equivalent to 17,750 to the oz.

The smallest known shark is the long-faced dwarf shark (*Squaliolus laticaudus*) of the western Pacific which does not exceed 5.9 in.

Smallest Freshwater Fish

The shortest and lightest freshwater fish species is the dwarf pygmy goby (*Pandaka pygmaea*), a colorless and nearly transparent species found in streams and lakes on Luzon, the Philippines. Adult males measure only 0.28–0.38 in long and weigh only 4–5 mg (0.00014–0.00017 oz).

LARGEST CARNIVOROUS FISH: The enormous bulk of the great white shark is apparent in this photo (above) of the largest ever recorded—29 ft 6 in. It was harpooned by Azorean fishermen in June 1978, and its jaws (right) makes the movie-made monster seem tame by comparison. (Below) This pair of dugongs—the mermaids of legend—was captured in the Red Sea. It's hard to believe that sailors ever thought these fish looked like maidens.

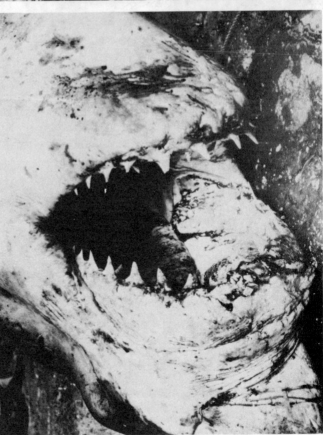

FAST FISH (above): Measurements are difficult to secure but the striped marlin with a top speed of 35 mph is certainly among the speediest. Claims of 68 mph have been cited for the sailfish. WALKING CATFISH (left): Not only can some species walk but others (from Africa) carry an electric discharge of about 350 volts at 1 amp. LARGEST SEA FISH (left, below): This whale shark weighed 90,000 lb and was 60 ft 9 in long. (Associated Press). LARGEST FRESHWATER FISH (below): This giant catfish from Europe weighed 565 lb and measured 11 ft long.

Fastest Fishes

The cosmopolitan sailfish (*Istiophorus platypterus*) is generally considered to be the fastest species of fish, although the practical difficulties of measurement make data extremely difficult to secure. A figure of 68.1 mph (100 yd in 3 sec) has been cited for one off Fla. The swordfish (*Xiphias gladius*) has also been credited with very high speeds, but the evidence is based mainly on bills that have been found deeply embedded in ships' timbers. A speed of 50 knots (57.6 mph) has been calculated from a penetration of 22 in by a bill into a piece of timber, but 30–35 knots (35–40 mph) is the most conceded by some experts. A wahoo (*Acanthocybium solandri*) 43 in in length is capable of attaining a speed of 47.8 mph. A large bluefin tuna (*Tunnus thynnus*) is capable of even higher speeds, but has not been clocked above 43.4 mph in a 20-sec dash.

The four-winged flying fish (*Cypselurus heterurs*) may also exceed 40 mph during its rapid rush to the surface before take-off (the average speed in the air is about 35 mph). Record flights of 90 sec, 36 ft in altitude and 3,640 ft in length have been recorded in the tropical Atlantic.

Longest-Lived Fishes

Aquaria are of too recent origin to be able to establish with certainty which species of fish can fairly be regarded as the longest-lived. Early indications are that it is the lake sturgeon (*Acipenser fulvescens*) of North America. In one study of the growth rings (annuli) of 966 specimens caught in the Lake Winnebago, Wis region, 1951–54, the oldest sturgeon was found to be a male, 6 ft 7 in long, which gave a reading of 82 years and was still growing. In July 1974 a figure of 228 years (*sic*) was attributed by growth ring count to a female Koi fish, a form of fancy carp, named "Hanako" living in a pond in Higashi Shirakawa, Gifu Prefecture, Japan, but the greatest authoritatively accepted age for this species is "more than 50 years."

The death of an 88-year-old female European eel (*Anguilla anguilla*) named "Putte" in the aquarium at Halsingborg Museum, Sweden was reported in 1948. She was allegedly born in the Sargasso Sea of the North Atlantic in 1860, and was caught in a river as a 3-year-old elver (young eel).

Oldest Goldfish

Goldfish (*Carassius auratus*) have been reported to live for over 40 years in China. A specimen named "Fred," owned by A. R. Wilson of Worthing, Sussex, England, died on Aug 1, 1980, aged 41 years.

Shortest-Lived Fishes

The shortest-lived fishes are probably certain species of the sub-order Cyprinodontei (killifish) found in Africa and South America which normally live about 8 months in the wild.

Most Abundant Fish

The most abundant species is probably the 3-in-long deep-sea bristlemouth (*Cyclothone elongata*) which has a worldwide distribution.

Deepest Fish

The greatest depth from which a fish has been recovered is 27,230 ft in the Puerto Rico Trough (27,488 ft) in the Atlantic by Dr Gilbert L. Voss of the US research vessel *John Elliott*. The fish was a 6½-in-long *Bassogigas profundissimus* taken in Apr 1970 and was only the fifth such brotulid ever caught.

Dr Jacques Piccard and Lieutenant Don Walsh, US Navy, reported they saw a sole-like fish about 1 ft long (tentatively identified as *Chascanopsetta lugubris*) from the bathyscaphe *Trieste* at a depth of 35,802 ft in the Challenger Deep (Marianas Trench) in the western Pacific Jan 24, 1960. This sighting, however, has been questioned by some authorities, who still regard the brotulids of the genus *Bassogigas* as the deepest-living vertebrates.

Most Venomous Fish

The most venomous fish are the stonefish (Synanceidae) of the tropical waters of the Indo-Pacific, and in particular *Synanceja horrida* which has the largest venom glands of any known fish. Direct contact with the spines of its fins, which contain a strong neurotoxic poison, often proves fatal.

Most Valuable Fish

Benihana, a Japanese ranchu or lion-head goldfish, winner of the Japanese, British and North American triple crown, was valued in July 1980 at $10,000.

Dr Takayaki Hosogi, the owner of "Fujitavo," a 7-year-old, 35-in-long carp which won the All-Japan Koi Championship Mar 1, 1982, refused an offer of $125,000.

Most and Least Fish Eggs

The ocean sunfish (*Mola mola*) produces up to 300 million eggs, each of them measuring about 0.05 in in diameter. The egg yield of the tooth carp *Jordanella floridae* of Florida is only about 20 over a period of several days.

Most Electric Fish

The most powerful electric fish is the electric eel (*Electrophorus electricus*), which is found in the rivers of Brazil, Colombia, Venezuela and Peru. An average-sized specimen can discharge 400 volts at 1 ampere, but measurements up to 650 volts have been recorded.

6. STARFISHES (*ASTEROIDEA*)

Largest and Heaviest Starfishes

The largest of the 1,600 known species of starfish in terms of total arm span is the very fragile brisingid *Midgardia xandaros*. A specimen collected by the Texas A & M University research vessel *Alaminos* in the southern part of the Gulf of Mexico in the late summer of 1968 measured 54.33 in from tip to tip but the diameter of its disc was only 1.02 in. Its dry weight was only 2.46 oz. The heaviest species of starfish is the five-armed *Thromidia catalai* of the Western Pacific. One specimen, collected off Ilot Amedee, New Caledonia, Sept 14, 1969, and later deposited in the Noumea Aquarium, weighed an estimated 13.2 lb with a total arm span of 24.8 in.

Smallest Starfish

The smallest known starfish is *Marginaster capreensis* found deep in the Mediterranean, which is not known to exceed a diameter of 0.78 in.

Deepest Starfish

The greatest depth from which a starfish has been recovered is 24,881 ft for a specimen of *Porcellanaster ivanovi*, collected by the Russian research ship *Vityaz* in the Marianas Trench, in the Western Pacific in about 1962.

HEAVIEST STARFISH: Appropriately named the rhinoceros starfish, this weighed 13 lb.

7. ARACHNIDS (*ARACHNIDA*)

Largest and Heaviest Spiders

The largest known spiders are the exceptionally bulky theraphosid spiders of the genera *Lasiodora* and *Grammostola* of Brazil, both of which have been credited with leg spans in excess of 10 in. One female *Lasiodora klugi* collected at Manaos, Brazil, in 1945, measured 9½ in across the legs and weighed almost 3 oz.

Smallest Spider

The smallest known spider is *Patu marplesi* (family Symphytognathidae) of Western Samoa. The type specimen (a male found in moss at *c.* 2,000-ft altitude near Malolelei, Upolu, in Jan 1956) measures 0.016 in overall—half the size of a printed period (.).

Largest and Smallest Webs

The largest webs are the aerial ones spun by the tropical orb weavers of the genus *Nephila*, which have been measured up to 18 ft 9¾ in in circumference.

The smallest webs are spun by spiders like *Glyphesis cottonae*, etc. which are about the size of a small postage stamp.

Most Venomous Spiders

The most venomous spiders are the Brazilian wandering spiders of the genus Phoneutria and particularly *P. fera*, which has the most active neurotoxic

BIGGER BUT NOT HEAVIER: The starfish on the right was found by a Russian expedition in 1970 in the flooded crater of a volcano in the Kurile Islands of Siberia just north of Japan.

STRONGEST SPIDER BITE: The frightening-looking tarantula is not, however, the most venomous.

venom of any living spider. These large and highly aggressive creatures frequently enter human dwellings and hide in clothing and shoes. When disturbed, they bite furiously several times, and hundreds of accidents involving these species are reported annually. Fortunately an effective antivenin is available, and when deaths do occur they are usually of children under 7.

Fastest Spider

The highest speed measured for a spider on a level surface is 1.73 ft per sec (1.17 mph) in the case of a specimen of *Tegenaria atrica*. This is 33 times its body length per sec (compare with the human record of 5½ times its body length per sec).

Rarest Spider

The most elusive of all spiders are the rare trap-door spiders of the genus *Liphistius* which are found in Southeast Asia.

Longest-Lived Spider

The longest-lived of all spiders are the primitive *Mygalomorphae* (tarantulas and allied species). One mature female tarantula, collected at Mazatlan, Mexico, in 1935 and estimated to be 12 years old at the time, was kept in a laboratory for 16 years, making a total of 28 years.

SMALLEST CRAB: The tiny parasitic pea crab, which may have a shell diameter of only ¼ inch, lives in the cavities of bivalve mollusks. (Heather Angel)

8. CRUSTACEANS

(Crabs, lobsters, shrimps, prawns, crayfish, barnacles, water fleas, fish lice, wood lice, sand hoppers and krill, etc.)

Largest Crustacean

The largest of all crustaceans (although not the heaviest) is the sanschouo or giant spider crab (*Macrocheira kaempferi*), also called the stilt crab, which is found in deep waters off the southeastern coast of Japan. Mature specimens usually have a 12–14-in-wide body and a claw span of 8–9 ft, but unconfirmed measurements up to 19 ft have been reported. A specimen with a claw span of 12 ft 1½ in weighed 41 lb.

Largest Lobster

The largest species of lobster, and the heaviest of all crustaceans, is the American or North Atlantic lobster (*Homarus americanus*). The largest lobster, a specimen weighing 44 lb 6 oz measuring 3 ft 6 in from the end of the tail-fan to the tip of the largest claw, was caught off Nova Scotia, Canada, on Feb 11, 1977. It was later sold to Steve Karathanos, owner of a Bayville, NY restaurant.

Smallest Crustaceans

The smallest known crustaceans are water fleas of the genus *Alonella,* which may measure less than 0.0098 in long. They are found in British waters.

The smallest known lobster is the Cape lobster (*Homarus capensis*) of South Africa which measures 3.9–4.7 in in total length.

The smallest crabs in the world are the aptly named pea crabs (family Pinnotheridae). Some species have a shell diameter of only 0.25 in, including *Pinnotheres pisum*.

Longest-Lived Crustacean

The longest-lived of all crustaceans is the American lobster (*Homarus americanus*). Very large specimens may be as much as 50 years old.

Deepest and Highest Crustaceans

The greatest depth from which a crustacean has been recovered is 34,450 ft for *live* amphipods from the Challenger Deep, Marianas Trench, W Pacific by the US research vessel *Thomas Washington* in Nov 1980. Amphipods and isopods have also been collected at a height of 13,300 ft in the Ecuadorean Andes.

9. INSECTS

Heaviest Insects

The heaviest insects are the Goliath beetles (family Scarabaeidae) of equatorial Africa. The largest members of the group are *Goliathus regius* and *Goliathus goliathus* (*giganteus*). In one series of fully-grown males the weight ranged from 2.5–3.5 oz.

Longest Insect

The longest insect in the world is the giant stick-insect *Pharnacia serratipes* of Indonesia, females of which have been measured up to 13 in in body length. The longest beetles known (excluding antennae) are the Hercules beetles (*Dynastes hercules* and *D. Neptunus*) of Central and South America, which have been measured up to 7.48 in, and 7.08 in, respectively. More than half the length, however, is taken up by the prothoracic horn.

Smallest Insects

The smallest insects recorded so far are the "hairy-winged" beetles of the family Ptiliidae (= Trichopterygidae) and the "battledore-wing fairy

LOCUST SWARM (above): The largest swarm, which was seen crossing the Red Sea in 1889, consisted of about 250 billion insects, covered 2,000 sq mi. (Crown copyright) The inset shows a desert locust that lost its way and was found in London, England. (Press Association)

flies" (parasitic wasps) of the family Myrmaridae. They measure only 0.008 in in length, and the fairy flies have a wing span of only 0.04 in. This makes them smaller than some of the protozoa (single-celled animals).

The male bloodsucking banded louse (*Enderleinellus zonatus*), ungorged, and the parasitic wasp *Caraphractus cinctus* may each weigh as little as 0.005 mg, or 5,670,000 to an oz. The eggs of the latter each weigh 0.0002 mg or 141,750,000 to an oz.

Commonest Insect

The most numerous of all insects are the spring-tails (order Collembola), which have a very wide geographical range. It has been calculated that the top 9 in of soil in one acre of grassland contains 230 million springtails or more than 5,000 per sq ft.

MAMMOTH MOTH (above): This rare great owlet moth reputedly had a wing expanse of over 14 in, but the specimen was somehow mislaid.
HEAVIEST INSECT (left): The Goliath beetle (next to a lady bug) weighs as much as 3½ oz and measures 4¾ in.

Fastest-Flying Insects

Experiments have proved that a widely publicized claim by an American entomologist in 1926 that the deer bot-fly (*Cephenemyia pratti*) could attain a speed of 818 mph was wildly exaggerated. If true, it would have generated a supersonic "pop." Acceptable modern experiments have now established that the highest maintainable air speed of any insect, including the deer bot-fly, is 24 mph, rising to a maximum of 36 mph for short bursts. A relay of bees (maximum speed 11 mph) would use only a gallon of nectar in cruising 4 million miles at 7 mph.

Longest-Lived Insects

The longest-lived insects are the splendor beetles (*Buprestidae*), some of which remain in the larvae stage for more than 30 years. Queen termites (*Isoptera*), previously thought to live 50 years or more, are now known to have a maximum life of about 15 years.

Loudest Insects

The loudest of all insects is the male cicada (family Cicadidae). At 7,400 pulses per min its tymbal (sound) organs produce a noise (officially described by the US Dept of Agriculture as "Tsh-ee-EEEE-e-ou") detectable over a quarter of a mile distance.

Southernmost Insect

The farthest south at which any insect has been found is 77°S (900 miles from the South Pole) in the case of a springtail (order Collembola).

Largest Locust Swarm

The greatest swarm of desert locusts (*Schistocera gregaria*) ever recorded was one covering an estimated 2,000 sq mi, observed crossing the Red Sea in 1889. Such a swarm must have contained about 250 billion insects weighing about 550,000 tons.

Fastest Wing Beat

The fastest wing beat per min of any insect under natural conditions is 62,760 by a tiny midge of the genus *Forcipomyia*. In experiments with truncated wings at a temperature of 98.6°F, the rate increased to 133,080 beats per min. The muscular contraction-expansion cycle in 0.00045 or 1/2,218th sec represents the fastest muscle movement ever measured.

Slowest Wing Beat

The slowest wing beat of any insect is 300 per min by the swallowtail butterfly (*Papilio machaon*). Most butterflies beat their wings at a rate of 460–636 per min.

Honey from a Hive

The greatest amount of wild honey ever extracted from a single hive is 404 lb, recorded by Ormond R. Aebi of Santa Cruz, Calif, Aug 29, 1974.

Largest Flea

The largest known flea is *Hystrichopsylla schefferi schefferi*, described from a single specimen taken from the nest of a mountain beaver (*Aplodontea rufa*) at Puyallup, Wash in 1913.

Flea Jumps

The champion jumper among fleas is the common flea (*Pulex irritans*). In one American experiment carried out in 1910 a specimen allowed to leap at will performed a long jump of 13 in and a high jump of 7¾ in. In jumping 130 times its own height a flea subjects itself to a force of 200 g. Siphonapterologists recognize 1,830 varieties.

The common flea's prowess as a long jumper and high jumper when compared to humans' becomes even more striking. If a human could jump like a flea the world and Olympic high jump record would be 853 ft, equivalent to jumping from street level up to the 70th floor of the Empire State Building in NYC.

Largest Butterflies and Moths (Order Lepidoptera)

The largest known butterfly is the Queen Alexandra birdwing (*Ornithoptera alexandrae*) of New Guinea. Females may have a wing span exceeding 11.02 in and weigh over 0.176 oz.

The largest moth (though not the heaviest) is the Hercules moth (*Coscinoscera hercules*) of tropical Australia and New Guinea. A wing area of up to 40.8 sq in and a wing span of 11 in have been recorded. In 1948 an unconfirmed measurement of 14.17 in was reported for a female captured near the post office at the coastal town of Innisfail, Queensland, Australia. The rare owlet moth (*Thysania agrippina*) of Brazil has been measured up to 11.81 in in wing span, and the Philippine atlas moth (*Attacus crameri caesar*) up to 11.02 in, but both these species are lighter than *C. hercules*.

Smallest Butterfly

The smallest of the estimated 140,000 known species of Lepidoptera are the moths *Johanssonia acetosae* (*Stainton*), found in Great Britain, and *Stigmella ridiculosa* from the Canary Islands, which have a wing span of 0.08 in and a similar body length. The smallest known butterfly is the dwarf blue (*Brephidium barberae*) from South Africa. It is 0.55 in from wing tip to wing tip.

10. CENTIPEDES (*CHILOPODA*)

Longest and Shortest

The longest recorded species of centipede is a large variant of the widely distributed *Scolopendra morsitans,* found on the Andaman Islands, Bay of Bengal, India. Specimens have been measured up to 13 in in length and 1½ in in breadth. The shortest recorded centipede is an unidentified species which measures only 0.19 in.

Most Legs

The centipede with the greatest number of legs is *Himantarum gabrielis* of southern Europe which has 171–177 pairs when adult.

Fastest

The fastest centipede is probably *Scutigera coleoptrata* of southern Europe which can travel at a rate of 19.68 in per sec or 1.1 mph.

11. MILLIPEDES (*DIPLOPODA*)

Longest and Shortest

The longest species of millipede known are the *Graphidostreptus gigas* of Africa and *Scaphistostreptus seychellarum* of the Seychelles Islands in the Indian Ocean, both of which have been measured up to 11.02 in in length and 0.78 in in diameter. The shortest millipede in the world is the British species *Polyxenus lagurus,* which measures 0.082–0.15 in in length.

Most Legs

The greatest number of legs reported for a millipede is 355 pairs (710 legs) for an unidentified South African species.

CENTIPEDE (right): This insect can have 177 pairs of legs.

12. SEGMENTED WORMS (ANNELIDA)

Longest and Shortest Earthworms

The longest known species of giant earthworm is *Microchaetus rappi* (= *M. microchaetus*) of South Africa. An average-sized specimen measures 4 ft 6 in in length (25½ in when contracted), but much larger examples have been reliably reported. In *c.* 1937 a giant earthworm measuring 22 ft in length when naturally extended and 0.78 in in diameter was collected in the Transvaal, and in Nov 1967 another specimen measuring 11 ft in length and 21 ft when naturally extended was found reaching over the national road (width 19 ft 8½ in) near Debe Nek, eastern Cape Province, South Africa.

The shortest segmented worm known is *Chaetogaster annandalei,* which measures less than 0.019 in in length.

13. MOLLUSKS

(Squids, octopuses, snails, shellfish, etc.)

Largest Squid

The largest known invertebrate is the Atlantic giant squid *Architeuthis dux*. On Nov 2, 1878 a specimen measuring 55 ft in total length (head and body 20 ft, tentacles 35 ft) was killed after it ran aground in Thimble Tickle Bay, Newfoundland, Canada. It weighed an estimated 4,400 lb. In Oct 1887 another giant squid (*Architeuthis longimanus*) measuring 57 ft in total length was washed up in Lyall Bay, NZ, but 49 ft of this was tentacle.

Largest Octopus

The largest octopus known to science is *Octopus apollyon* of the coastal waters of the N Pacific which regularly exceeds 12 ft in radial spread and 55 lb in weight. One huge individual caught single-handed by skin diver Donald E. Hagen in Lower Hoods Canal, Puget Sound, Wash, on Feb 18, 1973, had a relaxed radial spread of 23 ft and weighed 118 lb 10 oz. In Nov 1896 the remains of an unknown animal weighing an estimated 6–7 tons were found on a beach near St Augustine, Fla. Tissue samples were later sent to the US National Museum in Wash, DC, and in 1970 they were *positively* identified as belonging to a giant form of octopus (*Octopus giganteus*). Some experts, however, do not agree with this assessment because there was no evidence of tentacles or a

beak and believe the decomposing carcass was more probably that of a large whale or shark.

Longest-Lived Mollusk

The longest-lived mollusk is the quahog (*Venus mercenaria*), a thick-shelled clam found in the North Atlantic. Recent research in America involving the study of microscopic rings laid down annually on the tooth holding the shells together indicates that this species sometimes lives for 150 years.

Largest Bivalve Shells

The largest of all existing bivalve shells is the marine giant clam *Tridacna gigas*, found on the Indo-Pacific coral reefs. A specimen measuring 43 in by 29 in and weighing 579½ lb was collected from the Great Barrier Reef of Australia in 1917, and is now preserved in the American Museum of Natural History, NYC. Another lighter specimen was measured at 53.9 in overall.

Most Expensive Shell

A sum of $10,000 was refused by Philip Clover of Glen Ellen, Calif for a cone shell *Conus servus* in 1978.

Largest Gastropods

The largest known gastropod is the trumpet or baler conch (*Syrinx aruanus*) of Australia. One outsized specimen collected off W Australia in 1979 and now owned by Don Pisor of San Diego, Calif, measures 30.39 in in length and has a maximum girth of 39.37 in. It weighed nearly 40 lb when alive.

The largest known land gastropod is the African giant snail (*Achatina* sp.). An outsized specimen "Gee Geronimo" found by Christopher Hudson (1955–79) of Hove, E Sussex, England, measured 15½ in from snout to tail (shell length 10¾ in) in Dec 1978 and weighed exactly 2 lb. The snail was collected in Sierra Leone in June 1976 where shell lengths up to 14 in have been reliably reported.

Snail Speed

The fastest-moving species of land snail is probably the common garden snail (*Helix aspersa*). According to tests carried out in the US absolute top speed for this snail is 0.0313 mph (or 55 yd per hour) while some species are at full stretch at 0.00036 mph (or 23 in per hour). The snail-racing equivalent of the 4-minute mile is 24 in in 3 min, which would result in a 7,920-min or 5½-day mile.

LARGEST OCTOPUS KNOWN TO SCIENCE (above) comes from the coastal waters of the North Pacific and regularly exceeds 12 ft in radial spread, 55 lb in weight. GIANT EARTHWORM (right): This one from Gippsland, Victoria, Australia, measured 13 ft long when naturally extended. GIANT SQUID (below): This 405-lb specimen (not nearly the largest) was taken from the stomach of a sperm whale caught in the Azores.

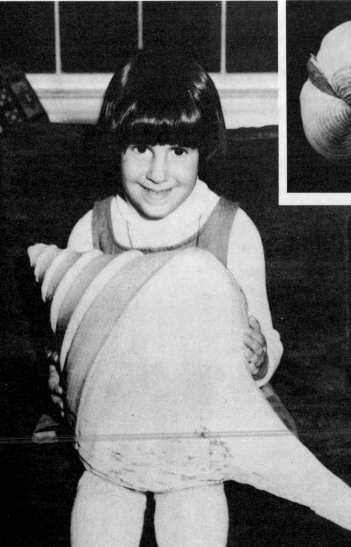

MOLLUSKS (left): The trumpet conch is the largest known gastropod. This specimen weighed 35 lb when alive. (Above): The quahog clam of the North Atlantic holds the mollusk longevity record. This species may live for 150 years. (Heather Angel) (Below): The giant land snail *Achatina* with a more usual-sized relative.

14. RIBBON WORMS (NEMERTINA)

Longest Worm

The longest of the 550 recorded species of ribbon worms, also called nemertines (or nemerteans), is the "boot-lace worm" (*Lineus longissimus*), found in the shallow waters of the North Sea. A specimen washed ashore at St Andrews, Fife, Scotland, in 1864, after a severe storm, measured more than 180 ft in length, making it easily the longest recorded worm of any variety.

15. JELLYFISHES (SCYPHOZOA)

Largest and Smallest

The largest jellyfish is the cnidarian Arctic giant jellyfish (*Cyanea capillata arctica*) of the northwestern Atlantic. One specimen washed up in Massachusetts Bay had a bell diameter of 7 ft 6 in and tentacles stretching 120 ft.

Some true jellyfishes have a bell diameter of less than 0.78 of an inch.

Most Venomous

The most venomous cnidarian is the Australian sea wasp (*Chironex fleckeri*), which carries a neurotoxic venom similar in strength to that found in the Asiatic cobra. These box jellyfish have caused the deaths of at least 66 people off the coast of Queensland, Australia since 1880. Victims die within 1–3 min if medical aid is not available. A most effective defense is wearing ladies' panty hose, outsize versions of which are now worn by Queensland life savers at surf carnivals.

16. SPONGES (PORIFERA)

Largest and Smallest

The largest sponge is the barrel-shaped loggerhead sponge (*Spheciospongia vesparium*), found off the islands of the West Indies and off Fla. Single individuals measure up to 3½ ft high and 3 ft in diameter. Neptune's cup or goblet (*Poterion patera*) of Indonesia grows up to 4 ft in height, but it is a less bulky animal. In 1909, a wool sponge (*Hippospongia canaliculatta*) measuring 6 ft in circumference was collected off the Bahama Islands. When first taken from the water it weighed between 80 and 90 lb, but after it had been dried and relieved of all excrescences it scaled 12 lb. (This sponge is now preserved in the US National Museum, Washington, DC.)

The smallest known sponge is the widely distributed *Leucosolenia blanca*, which measures 0.11 in in height when fully grown.

Deepest Sponges

Sponges have been taken from depths of up to 18,500 ft.

17. EXTINCT ANIMALS

Longest Dinosaur

The longest dinosaur so far recorded is Diplodocus ("double-beam"), an attenuated titanosaurid which ranged over western North America about 150 million years ago. A composite reconstruction in the Carnegie Museum of Natural History, Pittsburgh, measures 87 ft 6 in in total length—head and neck 22 ft; body 15 ft; tail 50 ft 6 in—and has a mounted height of 11 ft 9 in at the pelvis (the highest point on the body).

Heaviest

The heaviest land vertebrates of all time were the massive brachiosaurids ("arm lizards") of the late Jurassic period (135–165 million years ago) of East Africa, the Sahara, Portugal and the southwestern US. A complete skeleton excavated by a German expedition at the famous Tendaguru site, southern Tanganyika (Tanzania), 1909–11, and now mounted in the Humboldt Museum for Naturkunde, East Berlin, measures 74 ft 6 in in total length (height at shoulder 21 ft) and has a raised head height of 39 ft. *Brachiosaurus brancai*, as it was named, weighed a computed 86 tons in life.

In the summer of 1972 the remains of another enormous brachiosaurid new to science were discovered in the Dry Mesa Quarry on the Oncompahgre Plateau, western Colorado. From the evidence of the bones already collected, including 8-ft-long matching shoulder blades, "Supersaurus," as it has been nicknamed, is about 22 per cent larger than Brachiosaurus: this presupposes an overall length of about 90 ft, a shoulder height of 26 ft and a raised head height of nearly 50 ft if it is built on the same anatomical lines. The weight of such an animal, based on the cube of the fossil dimensions, would be about 152 tons. In 1979 another shoulder blade measuring 8 ft 10 in in length was discovered in the same quarry.

Largest Land Predator

The largest of the flesh-eating dinosaurs was probably the 7½-ton *Tyrannosaurus rex* (king "tyrant lizard"), which stalked about 75 million years ago over what are now Montana and Wyoming. No complete skeleton of this dinosaur has ever been discovered, but a composite individual has a bipedal height of 18 ft, and measures 40 ft in overall length. *Tarbosaurus efremovi*, its Mongolian counterpart, was also about the same size (total length 42 ft), but although it had a longer skull than Tyrannosaurus its head was less massive and it may have lost out in terms of overall bulk.

The body of a huge *Antrodemus* (= Allosaurus) with a much heavier body in proportion to its height than Tyrannosaurids, was excavated near Kenton, Okla in 1934. This carnosaur had a bipedal height of 16 ft and measured 42 ft in overall length.

Most Brainless

The *Stegosaurus* ("plated reptile"), which measured up to 30 ft in length, had a walnut-sized brain weighing only 2½ oz. It represented 0.004 of 1% of its body weight of 1¾ tons compared with 0.074 of 1% for an elephant and 1.88% for a human. It roamed widely across the Northern Hemisphere about 150 million years ago.

Largest Dinosaur Eggs

The largest dinosaur eggs are those of *Hypselosaurus priscus sauropod* which lived about 80 million years ago. Some specimens found in Oct 1961 in the valley of the Durance, near Aix-en-Provence, southern France, would have had, uncrushed, a length of 12 in and a diameter of 10 in.

Largest Flying Creature

The largest flying creature was the pterosaur *Quetzalcoatlus northropi* which glided over what is now Texas about 65 million years ago. Partial remains discovered in Big Bend National Park, Tex, in 1971, indicate that this reptile must have had a wing span of 36-39 ft and weighed about 190 lb.

Largest Bird

The largest prehistoric bird was the flightless *Dromornis stirtoni,* a huge emu-like creature which lived in central Australia 11 million years ago. Fossil leg bones found near Alice Springs in 1974 indicate that the bird must have stood about 10 ft in height and weighed about 1,100 lb. The giant moa *Dinornis maximus* of New Zealand, was even taller, attaining a height of over 12 ft, but probably only weighed about 500 lb.

The largest known flying bird was the giant teratorn *Argentavis magnificens* which lived in Argentina about 6 million years ago. Fossil remains discovered at a site 100 miles west of Buenos Aires in 1979 indicate that this gigantic vulture had a wing span of 23–25 ft and weighed about 265 lb.

Largest Mammals

The largest land mammal ever recorded was *Baluchitherium* (= Indricotherium, Pristinotherium and Benaratherium), a long-necked hornless rhinoceros which roamed across western Asia and Europe (Yugoslavia) about 35 million years ago. A restoration in the American Museum of Natural History, NYC, measures 17 ft 9 in to the top of the shoulder hump and 37 ft in total length, and this particular specimen must have weighed about 33 tons in the flesh. The bones of this gigantic browser were first discovered in the Bugti Hills in east Baluchistan, Pakistan, in 1907–08.

The largest marine mammal was the serpentine *Basilosaurus* (*Zeuglodon*) *cetoides,* which swam in the seas over what are now Arkansas and Alabama 50 million years ago. It measured up to 70 ft in length.

Largest Marine Reptile

The largest marine reptile ever recorded was *Stretosaurus macromerus,* a short-necked pliosaur from the Kimmeridge Clay of Cambridgeshire and Oxfordshire, Eng. A mandible found at Cumnor, and now in the University Museum, Oxford, has a restored length of over 9 ft 10 in, and must have belonged to a reptile measuring at least 46 ft in total length. *Kronosaurus queenslandicus,* another pliosaur, was also of comparable size, and a complete skeleton in the Museum of Comparative Zoology at Harvard University, Cambridge, Mass, measures 42 ft in total length.

Largest Mammoth

The largest prehistoric elephant was the steppe mammoth *Mammuthus trogontherii* (*Parelephas*), which roamed over what is now central Europe a million years ago. A fragmentary skeleton found in Mosbach, West Germany, indicates a shoulder height of 14 ft 9 in.

PLANT KINGDOM (*PLANTAE*)

Oldest Living Thing

"King Clone," the oldest known clone of the creosote plant (*Larria tridentata*) found in southwestern Calif, was estimated in Feb 1980 by Prof Frank C. Vasek to be 11,700 years old.

Earliest Fossil of a Flower

The oldest fossil of a flowering plant with palmlike imprints was found in Colorado in 1953 and dated about 65 million years old.

Largest Forest

The largest afforested areas are the vast coniferous forests of the northern USSR, lying mainly between latitude 55°N. and the Arctic Circle. The total wooded areas amount to 2,700 million acres (25% of the world's forests), of which 38% is Siberian larch. The USSR is 34% afforested.

Rarest Plants

Plants thought to be extinct are rediscovered each year and there are thus many plants of which specimens are known in but a single locality. The small pink blossoms of *Presidio manzanita* survive in a single specimen reported in June 1978 at an undisclosed site in Calif.

BLOOMS

Largest Blooms

The mottled orange-brown and white parasitic stinking corpse lily (*Rafflesia arnoldi*) has the largest of all blooms. These attach themselves to the cissus vines of the jungle in southeast Asia. They measure up to 3 ft across and ¾ in thick, and attain a weight of 15 lb.

The spathe and spadix of the less massive green and purple flower of *Amorphophallies titanum* of Sumatra may attain a length of 5 ft.

Largest Inflorescence

The largest known inflorescence is that of *Puya raimondii,* a rare Bolivian plant with an erect panicle (diameter 8 ft) which emerges to a height of 35 ft. Each of these bears up to 8,000 white blooms. In 1974 the flower-spike of an agave in Berkeley, Calif was measured to be 52 ft long. (See also *Slowest-Flowering Plant.*)

Largest Blossoming Plant

The largest blossoming plant is the giant Chinese wisteria at Sierra Madre, Calif. It was planted in 1892 and now has branches 500 ft long. It covers nearly an acre, weighs 252 tons and has an estimated 1,500,000 blossoms during its blossoming period of five weeks, when up to 30,000 people pay admission to visit. In Nov 1974 it was reported that a passion plant, owned by Dennis and Patti Carlson of Blaine, Minn, and fed with a hormone, had grown to a length of 600 ft.

Smallest Plants

The smallest flowering plant is the floating aquatic duckweed *Wolffia punctata* which has fronds only 1/35 in in length. The "flower" of a single stamen (male) or single pistil (female) is only 1/80th × 1/160th of an inch. The smallest plant is a unicellular alga and is classified under *Protista* (page 105).

Most Valuable Flower

The $10,000 prize offered by the Burpee Co. in 1954 for producing the first all-white marigold was won on Aug 12, 1975 by Alice Vonk of Sully, Iowa.

Plants at Highest Altitude

The greatest certain altitude at which any flowering plants have been found is 21,000 ft on Kamet (25,447 ft), India, by N. D. Jayal in 1955. They were *Ermania himalayensis* and *Ranunculus lobatus.*

Fastest Growth

The case of a *Hesperogucca whipplei* of the family Liliaceae growing 12 ft in 14 days was reported from Treco Abbey, Isles of Scilly, England, in July 1978.

Slowest-Flowering Plant

The slowest-flowering of all plants is the rare *Puya raimondii,* the largest of all herbs, discovered in Bolivia in 1870. The panicle emerges after about 150 years of the plant's life. It then dies. (See also above under *Largest Inflorescence.*)

Some agaves, erroneously called century plants, first flower after 40 years.

Note: US records on pages 98 and 101 were gathered with the assistance of Grace's Gardens, Hackettstown, NJ.

FRUITS & VEGETABLES

Most and Least Nutritive Fruits. An analysis of the 38 commonly eaten raw (as opposed to dried) fruits shows that the one with the highest calorific value is the avocado (*Persea americana*) with 741 calories per edible lb. That with the lowest value is cucumber with 73 calories per lb. Avocados probably originated in Central and South America and also contain vitamins A, C, and E and 2.2% protein.

Apple. An apple weighing 3 lb 1 oz was reported by V. Loveridge of Ross-on-Wye, England in 1965. In 1981, James Shipaila of Grand Rapids, Mich, reported an apple with a circumference of 16⅝ in.

Artichoke. An 8-lb artichoke was grown in 1964 at Tollerton, N. Yorkshire, England, by A. R. Lawson.

Broccoli. A head of broccoli weighing 28 lb 14¾ oz was grown in 1964 by J. T. Cooke of Huntington, W. Sussex, England.

Cabbage. In 1865 William Collingwood of The Stalwell, County Durham, England, grew a red cabbage with a circumference of 259 in. It reputedly weighed 123 lb.

Carrot. A carrot weighing 15 lb 7 oz was grown by Miss I. G. Scott of Nelson, NZ, in Oct 1978.

Cauliflower. A record cauliflower weighing 52 lb 11½ oz was also grown by Mr Cooke (see *Broccoli*) in 1966.

Celery. A 35-lb bunch was reported grown by C. Bowcock of Willaston, England in 1973.

Collard. A 35-ft-tall, 59¼-in-wide collard was grown by Bobby Rackley of Rocky Mount, NC, in 1980.

Cucumber. Nadine Williams of Knott, Tex, grew a 17-lb-4-oz cucumber in 1981. A Vietnamese variety 6 ft long was reported by L. Szabo of Debrecen, Hungary in Sept 1976.

Eggplant. A 3-lb eggplant was reported by Mrs L. J. Hampton of Hope, Ark, in 1981.

Garlic. In 1980, Howard Trivelpeice of Eureka, Calif, grew an elephant garlic weighing 2 lb 15¾ oz with a 16-in circumference.

Gourd. A record gourd 82 in long was grown by Mark and Randy Ohlin of Poland, Ohio, in 1979. A gourd weighing 196 lb was reported from J. Leathes of Herringfleet Hall, Suffolk, England in 1846.

Grapefruit. A 3-lb-8-oz grapefruit was grown in 1977 by A. J. Frost of Wellington, Bedfordshire, England.

Kohlrabi. A kohlrabi weighing 36 lb was grown in 1979 by Emil Krejci of Mt Clemens, Mich.

Lemon. Mrs D. G. Knutzen of Whittier, Calif, reported in Jan 1977 a lemon with a circumference of 28¾ in, weighing 6 lb 4 oz.

Lettuce. A head of 25 lb was grown by C. Bowcock of Willaston, England in 1974.

Lima Bean. One bean pod measuring 14 in in length was grown by Norma McCoy of Hubert, NC, in 1979.

Melons. A watermelon weighing 200 lb was reported by Grace's Gardens in Apr 1980. The growers were Ivan and Lloyd Bright of Hope, Ark. The largest cantaloupe reported was one of 51 lb 8 oz grown by Gene Daughtridge of Rocky Mount, NC, in 1981.

Mushrooms. A specimen of the edible *Termitomyces titanicus* found near Kitwe, Zambia, on Dec 18, 1978, measured 26 in in diameter and weighed 5.5 lb. A mushroom weighing 18 lb 10 oz was reported from Whidbey Island, Wash, in Sept 1968.

Okra Stalk. An okra stalk 17 ft tall was grown in 1979 by P. C. Cain of Kosciusko, Miss.

Onion. An onion weighing 7 lb 6 oz was reported grown by S. C. Hill of Galashiels, Scotland, in 1981.

Orange. The heaviest orange is one weighing 5 lb 3 oz exhibited in Nelspruit, South Africa on June 19, 1981. The size of a human head, it was stolen.

Parsnip. A parsnip 60 in long was reported by M. Zaninovich of Waneroo, Western Australia. The heaviest was 10 lb 8½ oz grown by C. Moore of Peacehaven, W. Sussex, England in 1980.

Peanut. Ed Weeks of Tarboro, NC, grew a peanut 3½ in long in 1978.

Pear. A pear weighing 3.09 lb was harvested on May 10, 1979 by K. and R. Yeomans, Armidale, NSW, Australia.

Pepper. A NuMex Big Jim pepper 13½ in long was grown by June Rutherford of Hatch, NM, in 1975. A sweet pepper plant owned by Ralph Savarese of Pascagoula, Miss grew to be 56 in tall, yielding 53 peppers, in 1978.

Pineapple. A pineapple weighing 17 lb was picked by H. Retief in Malindi, Kenya, in 1978.

Potato. A potato weighing 18 lb 4 oz was reported dug up by Thomas Seddal in his garden in Chester, England, on Feb 17, 1795. A yield was reported of 515 lb from a 2½-lb parent seed by C. Bowcock of Willaston, England, planted in 1977.

Radishes. A radish weighing 25 lb was grown by Glen Tucker of Stanbury, South Australia, in Aug 1974, and another of 25 lb by Herbert Breslow of Ruskin, Fla, in 1977.

Squash. A squash weighing 513 lb was grown by Harold Fulp, Jr., at Ninevah, Ind, in 1977. Mike Jovanovich of LaPonte, Ind grew 1,851 lb of squash from one seed in 1979.

Strawberry. One berry weighing 2⅜ oz was grown by Lester Slate of Dover-Foxcroft, Maine. A plant weighing 7¼ oz was reported by E. Oxley of Walton-on-the-Naze, England, in 1972.

VEGETABLES:
1. Pepper 13½ in long.
2. Cucumber weighing
   17 lb 4 oz.
3. Gourd 82 in long.
4. Peanut 3½ in long.
5. Cantaloupe weighing
   51½ lb.
6. Watermelon weighing
   200 lb.
FRUIT:
7. Lemon measuring 28¾ in
   around and weighing
   6 lb 4 oz.

99

VEGETABLE:
1. Eggplant of 3 lb.

FLOWERS:
2. Sunflower 23 ft 6½ in high.
3. Cactus. Saguaro type 52½ ft high (note girl standing at foot). (Marvin Frost)
4. Stinking corpse lily has largest blooms—3 ft across.
5. Most expensive orchid, sold for $6,000 in 1906.

SEED:
6. Largest comes from Seychelles Islands and weighs 40 lb.

Sugar Beet. A 45½-lb sugar beet was grown by the Bob Meyer Farms in Brawley, Calif, in 1974.

Tomato. A 6-lb-8-oz tomato was grown by Clarence Dailey of Monona, Wis, in Aug 1976. A 45-ft-9½-in-long plant was grown in 1981 at the Chosen Hill School in Gloucester, England.

Turnip. A turnip weighing 73 lb was reported in Dec 1768. In modern times the record is 35 lb 4 oz for a turnip grown by C. W. Butler of Nafferton, Humberside, England. A purple top turnip of 30 lb was grown by Denverd Fleming of Phil Campbell, Ala, in 1979.

Zucchini. A zucchini weighing 19.14 lb was grown in 1979 by Douglas Andre of Millington, Mich.

GARDEN FLOWERS & PLANTS

Aspidistra. The aspidistra (*Aspidistra elatior*) was introduced as a parlor palm to Britain from Japan and China in 1822. The biggest aspidistra in the world is one 51¾ in tall, grown by Cliff W. Evans at Kiora, Moruya, NSW, Australia, and measured in Dec 1977.

Begonia. A begonia plant 3 ft 8 in tall was grown by Ellen Cassidy of Richmond, British Columbia, Canada in 1979.

Cactus. The largest of all cacti is the saguaro (*Cereus giganteus* or *Carnegiea gigantea*), found in Ariz, southeastern Calif, and Sonora, Mexico. The green fluted column is surmounted by candelabra-like branches rising to a height of 52 ft 6 in in the case of a specimen measured in the boundary of the Saguaro National Monument, Ariz. They have waxy white blooms which are followed by edible crimson fruit. An armless cactus 78 ft in height was measured in 1978 by Hube Yates in Cave Creek, Ariz.

Fourteen-Leafed Clover. A fourteen-leafed white clover (*Trifolium repens*) grown on one petiole was found by Randy Farland near Sioux Falls, SD, June 16, 1975.

Dahlia. A 10-ft-6½-in dahlia was grown by Michael Power of Waterford, Ireland, in 1981.

Gladiolus. A gladiolus 8 ft 4 in high was grown in 1981 by A. Breed of Melrose, Scotland.

Hollyhock. The tallest reported hollyhock (*Althaea rosea*) is one of 24 ft 3 in grown by W. P. Walshe of Eastbourne, E. Sussex, England in 1961.

Petunia. A petunia plant 8 ft 4 in high was grown by G. A. Warner of Fife, Scotland in 1978.

Philodendron. A philodendron 552 ft long (as of mid-April 1982) now grows in the home of Mr M. J. Linhart in Thornton, England.

Rhododendron. The largest species of rhododendron is the scarlet *Rhododendron arboreum,* examples of which reach a height of 60 ft at Mangalbaré, Nepal. The cross section of the trunk of a *Rhododendron giganteum,* from Yunnan, China, reputedly 90 ft high, is preserved at Inverewe Garden, Highland, Scotland.

Rose Tree. A "Lady Banks" rose tree at Tombstone, Ariz, has a trunk 40 in thick, stands 9 ft high and covers an area of 5,380 sq ft, supported by 68 posts and several thousand feet of iron piping. This enables people to be seated under the arbor. The original cutting came from Scotland in 1884.

Sunflower. The record height of 23 ft 6½ in was reached by a sunflower grown by Frank Killand of Exeter, England in 1976. Beverly Arthur of Union City, Ohio, reported a sunflower with a 17-in diameter across the head in 1981.

Most Spreading Plant. The greatest area covered by a single clonal growth is that of the wild box huckleberry (*Gaylussacia brachyera*), a mat-forming evergreen shrub first reported in 1796. A colony covering 8 acres was discovered in 1845 near New Bloomfield, Pa. Another colony, covering about 100 acres, was "discovered" on July 18, 1920, near the Juniata River in Pa. It has been estimated that this colony began 13,000 years ago.

Weeds. The most intransigent weed is the mat-forming water weed *Salvinia auriculata,* found in Africa. It was detected on the filling of Kariba Lake, in May 1959 and within 11 months had choked an area of 77 sq mi, rising by 1963 to 387 sq mi. The worst land weeds are regarded as purple nut sedge, Bermuda grass, barnyard grass, jungle rice, goose grass, Johnson grass, Guinea grass, cogon grass and lantana.

Hedges. The tallest hedge is the Meikleour beech hedge in Perthshire, Scotland. It was planted in 1746 and has now attained a trimmed height of 85 ft. It is 600 yd long, and some of its trees now exceed 100 ft.

The tallest yew hedge is in Earl Bathurst's Park, Gloucestershire, England. It was planted in 1720, runs for 170 yd, reaches 36 ft in height and 15 ft in thickness, and takes 20 man-days to trim.

The tallest box hedge, 35 ft in height, is at Birr Castle, Offaly, Ireland, and dates from the 18th century.

Vines. The largest recorded grape vine was one planted in 1842 at Carpinteria, Calif. By 1900 it was yielding more than 9 tons of grapes in some years, and averaging 7 tons per year. It died in 1920.

Deepest and Densest Roots

The greatest reported depth to which roots have penetrated is a calculated 400 ft in the case of a wild fig tree at Echo Caves, near Ohrigstad, East Transvaal, South Africa. A single winter rye plant (*Secale cereale*) has been shown to produce 387 miles of roots in 1.83 cu ft of earth.

Largest Leaves

The largest leaves of any plant belong to the raffia palm (*Raphia ruffia*) of the Mascarene Islands in the Indian Ocean, and the Amazonian bamboo palm (*R. toedigera*) of South America, whose leaf blades may measure up to 65 ft in length with petioles up to 13 ft.

The largest undivided leaf is that of *Alocasia macrorrhiza,* found in Sabah, East Malaysia. One found in 1966 measured 9 ft 11 in long and 6 ft 3½ in wide, and had an area of 34.2 sq ft on one side.

Daisy Chain

The longest daisy chain made in 7 hours was one of 4,529 ft 6 in at the Museum of Childhood, Sudbury, England, on June 6, 1981. The team is limited to 16.

Wreath

The largest wreath was constructed by the Geneva Kiwanis Club, NY, during Nov 1981. It measured 54 ft 6½ in in diameter and weighed 4 tons.

Seaweed

Claims made that seaweed off Tierra del Fuego, South America, grows to 600 and even 1,000 ft in length have gained currency. More recent and more reliable records indicate that the longest species of seaweed is the Pacific giant kelp (*Macrocystis pyrifera*), which does not exceed 196 ft in length. It can grow 18 in in a day.

TREES

Oldest Tree

The oldest recorded tree was a bristlecone pine (*Pinus longaeva*) designated WPN-114, which grew at 10,750 ft above sea level on the northeast face of the Wheeler Ridge of the Sierra Nevadas, Calif. During studies in 1963 and 1964 it was found to be about 4,900 years old, but was cut down with a chain saw. The oldest known *living* tree is the bristlecone pine named *Methuselah* at 10,000 ft on the Calif side of the White Mts, with a confirmed age of 4,600 years. In March 1974 it was reported that this tree produced 48 live seedlings. Dendrochronologists estimate the *potential* life span of a bristlecone pine at nearly 5,500 years, but that of a "big tree" (*Sequoiadendron giganteum*) at perhaps 6,000 years. No single cell lives more than 30 years. A report in March 1976 stated that some enormous specimens of Japanese cedar (*Cryptomeria japonica*) had been dated by carbon-14 to 5200 BC. The great ages attributed to the Canary Islands dragon tree (*Dracaena draco*) are discounted by botanists.

Earliest Species of Tree

The earliest species of tree still surviving is the maidenhair tree (*Ginkgo biloba*) of China, which first appeared about 160 million years ago, during the Jurassic era. It was "re-discovered" by Kaempfer (Netherlands) in 1690, and reached England *c.* 1754. It has been grown in Japan since *c.* 1100 where it was known as *ginkyo* (silver apricot) and now called *icho.*

Most Massive Tree

The most massive living thing on earth is a California "big tree" (*Sequoiadendron giganteum*) named the "General Sherman," standing 280 ft tall, in Sequoia National Park, Calif. In 1980, it had a true girth of 79.8 ft (at 5 ft above the ground). The "General Sherman" has been estimated to contain the equivalent of 600,120 board ft of timber, sufficient to make 5,000 million matches. The foliage is bluegreen, and the red-brown tan bark may be up to 24 in thick in parts. In 1968 the official published figure for its estimated weight was 2,145 tons.

The seed of a "big tree" weighs only 1/6,000th oz. Its growth to maturity may therefore represent an increase in weight of 250,000 million fold.

The tree canopy covering the greatest area is the great banyan *Ficus bengalensis* in the Indian Botanical Garden, Calcutta with some 1,000 subsidiary trunks formed from aerial roots. It covers overall some 4 acres and is believed to date from *c.* 1770.

Tallest Trees

The tallest known species of tree is the coast redwood (*Sequoia sempervirens*), growing indigenously near the coast of Calif north of Monterey to the Oreg border. The tallest measured example is the "Tallest Tree" in Redwood Creek Grove, Humboldt County, Calif, discovered by Dr Paul A. Zahl in 1963 to be 367.8 ft with dead top and re-estimated at 366.2 ft in

OLDEST TREES: Bristlecone pines (right) can live for 4,900 years in Calif. The maidenhair (ginkgo or ginkyo) tree (above) is the earliest species still surviving, after 160 million years.

1970. It has a girth of 43 ft 11 in. The "Tallest Tree" is dying back slowly. Several trees with healthy growing tips are 360+ ft in groves by Bull Creek near Weott, Calif.

The tallest non-sequoia is a Douglas fir at Quinault Lake Park Trail, Wash, of *c.* 310 ft. The tallest broadleaf tree is a *Eucalyptus regnans* (mountain ash) growing in the Styx Valley, Tasmania, and measured at 325 ft.

The identity of the tallest tree of all time has never been satisfactorily resolved. A claim as high as 525 ft has been made (subsequently reduced on re-measurement, in May 1889 to 220 ft). The now accepted view is that the maximum height recorded by a qualified surveyor was 375 ft for the Cornthwaite Tree (*Eucalyptus regnans* formerly *E. amygdalina*) in Thorpdale, Gippsland, Victoria, Australia, measured in 1880. Claims for a Douglas fir (*Pseudotsuga taxifolia*) felled by George Carey in 1895 in British Columbia with a height of 417 ft and a 77-ft circumfer-

ence have been obscured, though not necessarily invalidated by a falsified photograph.

Trees of Greatest Girth

The Santa Maria del Tule tree, in the state of Oaxaca, in Mexico, is a 160-foot-tall Montezuma cypress (*Taxodium mucronatum*) with a girth of 125 ft at a height of 5 ft above the ground. A figure of 167 ft in circumference was reported for the pollarded European chestnut (*Castanea sativa*) known as the "Tree of the 100 Horses" on the edge of Mt Etna, Sicily, Italy, in 1972.

Most Leaves

Little work has been done on the laborious task of establishing which species has the most leaves. A large oak has perhaps 250,000, but a cypress may have some 45–50 million leaf scales.

103

Fastest-Growing Tree

Discounting bamboo, which is not botanically classified as a tree, but as woody grass, the fastest rate of growth recorded is 35 ft 3 in in 13 months by an *Albizzia falcata* planted on June 17, 1974, in Sabah, Malaysia. The youngest recorded age for a tree to reach 100 ft is 64 months for one of the species planted on Feb 24, 1975, also in Sabah.

Slowest-Growing Trees

The speed of growth of trees depends largely upon conditions, although some species, such as box and yew, are always slow-growing. The extreme is represented by a specimen of Sitka spruce which required 98 years to grow to 11 in tall, with a diameter of less than 1 in, on the Arctic tree-line. The growing of miniature trees or *bonsai* is an Oriental cult mentioned as early as *c.* 1320.

Tallest Christmas Tree

The tallest cut Christmas tree was a 221-ft Douglas fir erected at Northgate Shopping Center, Seattle, Wash, in Dec 1950.

Remotest Tree

The tree most distant from any other is believed to be one at an oasis in the Ténéré Desert, Niger Republic. There were no other trees within 31 miles. In Feb 1960 it survived being rammed by a truck being backed up by a French driver. The tree was transplanted and is now in the Museum of Niamey, Niger.

Most Expensive Tree

The highest price ever paid for a tree is $51,000 for a single Starkspur golden delicious apple tree from near Yakima, Wash, bought by a nursery in Missouri in 1959.

Heaviest and Lightest Woods

The heaviest of all woods is black ironwood (*Olea laurifolia*), also called South African ironwood, with a specific gravity of up to 1.49, and weighing up to 93 lb per cu ft.

The lightest wood is *Aeschynomene hispida,* found

in Cuba, which has a specific gravity of 0.044 and a weight of only 2¾ lb per cu ft. The wood of the balsa tree (*Ochroma pyramidale*) is of very variable density—between 2½ and 24 lb per cu ft. The density of cork is 15 lb per cu ft.

Seeds

The largest seed is that of the double coconut or Coco de Mer (*Lodoicea seychellarum*), the single-seeded fruit of which may weigh 40 lb. This grows only in the Seychelles Islands in the Indian Ocean. The smallest seeds are those of epiphytic orchids, at 35 million to the oz (*cf.* grass pollens at up to 6,000 million grains per oz). A single plant of the American ragweed can generate 8,000 million pollen grains in 5 hours.

The most protracted claim for the viability of seeds is that made for the Arctic lupin (*Lupinus arcticus*) found in frozen silt at Miller Creek in the Yukon, Canada, in July 1954 by Harold Schmidt. The seeds were germinated in 1966 and dated by the radio-carbon method of associated material to at least 8,000 BC and more probably to 13,000 BC.

Largest Orchids

The largest of all orchids is *Grammatophyllum speciosum,* native to Malaysia. Specimens up to 25 ft high have been recorded. The largest orchid flower is that of *Phragmipedium caudatum,* found in tropical areas of America. Its petals grow up to 18 in long, giving it a maximum outstretched diameter of 3 ft. The flower is, however, much less bulky than that of the stinking corpse lily (see *Largest Blooms*).

Tallest and Smallest Orchids

The tallest free-standing orchid is *Grammatophyllum speciosum* (see above). *Galeola foliata* may attain 45 ft on decaying rainforest trees in Queensland, Australia. The smallest orchid is *Bulbophyllum minutissimum,* found in Australia. Claims have also been made for *Notylia norae,* found in Venezuela. The smallest orchid flowers are less than 0.04 in long, borne by *Stella graminea.*

Highest-Priced Orchid

The highest price ever paid for an orchid is £1,207.50 (then $6,000), paid by Baron Schröder to Sanders of St Albans for an *Odontoglossum crispum* (variety *pittianum*) at an auction by Protheroe & Morris of Bow Lane, London, England, on March 22, 1906. A cymbidium orchid called "Rosanna Pinkie" was sold in the US for $4,500 in 1952.

Tallest and Fastest-Growing Bamboo

The tallest recorded bamboo was a thorny bamboo culm (*Bambusa arundinacea*) felled at Pattazhi, Travancore, India, in Nov 1904, which measured 121½ ft. Some species of the 45 genera of bamboo have attained growth rates of up to 36 in per day (0.00002 mph), on their way to reaching a height of 100 ft in less than 3 months.

Mosses

The smallest of mosses is the pygmy moss (*Ephemerum*), and the longest is the brook moss (*Fontinalis*), which forms streamers up to 3 ft long in flowing water.

Largest and Smallest Ferns

The largest of all the more than 6,000 species of fern is the tree-fern (*Alsophila excelsa*) of Norfolk Island, in the South Pacific, which attains a height of up to 60 ft. The smallest are *Hecistopteris pumila*, found in Central America, and *Azolla caroliniana*, which is native to the US.

Grasses

The world's commonest grass is *Cynodon ductylon* or Bermuda grass. The "Callie" hybrid, selected in 1966, grows as much as 6 in a day and stolons reach 18 ft in length.

KINGDOM PROTISTA

Protista were first discovered in 1676 by Anton van Leeuwenhoek (1632–1723), a Dutch microscopist. Among Protista are characteristics common to both plants and animals. The more plant-like are termed Protophyta (protophytes), including unicellular algae, and the more animal-like are placed in the phylum Protozoa (protozoans) which includes amoebas and flagellates.

The largest protozoans which are known to have existed were the now extinct Nummulites, which each had a diameter of 0.95 in. The largest existing protozoan is *Pelomyxa palustris,* which may attain a length of up to 0.6 in. The smallest of all protophytes is the marine microflagellate alga *Micromonas pusilla,* with a diameter of less than 2 microns or 0.00008 in.

The protozoan *Monas stigmatica* has been measured to move a distance equivalent to 40 times its own length in a sec. No human can cover even seven times his own length in a sec.

The protozoan *Glaucoma,* which reproduces by binary fission, divides as frequently as every 3 hours. Thus in the course of a day it could become a "six greats grandparent" and the progenitor of 510 descendants.

KINGDOM FUNGI

Fungi were once classified in the subkingdom Protophyta of the kingdom Protista.

Matthew Fogarty of Ayton, Berwickshire, England, found the largest recorded puffball (*Lycoperdon gigantea*), 64 in in circumference and 16¼ in high, on Mar 9, 1980.

A specimen also of 64 in in circumference was recorded in NY State in 1877.

A 72-lb example of the edible mushroom *Polyporus frondosus* was reported by Joseph Opple near Solon, Ohio, in Sept 1976.

The largest officially recorded tree fungus was a specimen of *Oxyporus* (*Fomes*) *nobilissimus,* measuring 56 in by 37 in and weighing at least 300 lb found by J. Hisey in Wash State in 1946.

Most Poisonous Toadstool

The yellowish-olive death cup (*Amanita phalloides*) is regarded as the world's most poisonous fungus. From 6 to 15 hours after tasting, the effects are vomiting, delirium, collapse and death. Among its victims was Cardinal Giulio de' Medici, Pope Clement VII (1478–1534).

KINGDOM PROCARYOTA

Earliest Life Form

In June 1980 Prof J. William Schopf announced the discovery of 5 microbial life forms in rock dated to 3,500 million years old in the "North Pole" region of northern W Australia.

Largest and Smallest Bacteria

Anton van Leeuwenhoek (1632–1723) was the first to observe bacteria, in 1675. The largest of the bacteria is the sulphur bacterium *Beggiatoa mirabilis,* which is from 16 to 45 microns in width and which may form filaments several millimeters long.

The smallest of all free-living organisms are the pleuro-pneumonia-like organisms (PPLO) of the *Mycoplasma.* One of these, *Mycoplasma laidlawii,* first discovered in sewage in 1936, has a diameter during the early part of its life of only 100 millimicrons, or 0.000004 in. Examples of the strain known as H.39 have a maximum diameter of 300 millimicrons and weigh an estimated 1.0×10^{-16} of a gram. A blue whale at 177 tons would weigh 1.77×10^{23} or 177,000 quintillion times as much.

Fastest Bacteria

The rod-shaped bacillus *Bdellovibrio bacteriovoras,* by means of a polar flagellum rotating 100 times/sec, can move 50 times its own length of 2 μm per second. This would be the equivalent of a human sprinter reaching 200 mph.

Highest Bacteria

In Apr 1967 the US National Aeronautics and Space Administration (NASA) reported that bacteria had recently been discovered at an altitude of 135,000 ft (25.26 miles).

Longest-Lived Bacteria

The oldest deposits from which living bacteria are claimed to have been extracted are salt layers near Irkutsk, USSR, dating from about 600 million years ago. The discovery was not accepted internationally. The US Dry Valley Drilling Project in Antarctica claimed resuscitated rod-shaped bacteria from caves up to a million years old.

Toughest Bacteria

The bacterium *Micrococcus radiodurans* can withstand atomic radiation of 6,500,000 röntgens or 10,000 times greater than radiation that is fatal to the average man.

Largest and Smallest Viruses

Dmitriy Ivanovsky (1864–1920) first reported filterable objects in 1892, but Martinus Willem Beijerink (1851–1931) first confirmed the nature of viruses in 1898. These are now defined as aggregates of two or more types of chemical (including either DNA or RNA) which are infectious and potentially pathogenic. The longest known is the rod-shaped *Citrus tristeza* virus with particles measuring 200 × 10 nm (1 nanometer = 1×10^{-9}m).

The smallest known viruses are the nucleoprotein plant viruses such as the satellite of tobacco *necrosis virus* with spherical particles 17 nm in diameter. A putative new infectious sub-microscopic organism but without nucleic acid, named a "prion," was announced from the Univ of Calif in Feb 1982.

PARKS, ZOOS, AQUARIA AND OCEANARIA

Largest Park

The largest park is the Wood Buffalo National Park in Alberta, Canada (established 1922), which has an area of 11,172,000 acres (17,560 sq mi).

Largest Game Reserve

It has been estimated that throughout the world there are some 500 zoos with an estimated annual attendance of 330 million. The largest zoological preserve in the world is the Etosha Reserve, Namibia (South-West Africa), with an area which has grown since 1907 to 38,427 sq mi. (It is thus larger than Ireland.)

Oldest Zoo

The oldest known zoo is that at Schönbrunn, Vienna, Austria, built in 1752 by the Holy Roman Emperor Franz I for his wife Maria Theresa. The oldest privately owned zoo in the world is that of the Zoological Society of London, founded in 1826. Its collection is housed partly in Regent's Park, London (36 acres), and partly at Whipsnade Park, Bedford-shire (541 acres, opened 1931). At the stocktaking on Jan 1, 1982, it was found to house 10,696 specimens—2,168 mammals, 2,163 birds, 417 reptiles and amphibians, an estimated 1,498 fish, and an estimated total of 4,450 invertebrates. Locusts, bees and ants are excluded from this figure.

The earliest known collection of animals (not a public zoo) was that set up by Shulgi, a 3rd dynasty ruler of Ur in 2094–2047 BC at Puzurish in southeast Iraq.

Largest Aquarium

The largest, as opposed to fish farm, is the John G. Shedd Aquarium, 12th St and Lake Shore Drive, Chicago, completed in Nov 1929 at a cost of $3,250,000. The total capacity of its display tanks is 450,000 gallons, with reservoir tanks holding 2 million gallons. Exhibited are 5,500 specimens from 350 species. Most of these specimens are collected by the Aquarium collecting boat based in Miami, Fla, and are shipped by air to Chicago. The record attendances are 78,658 in a day on May 21, 1931, and 4,689,730 visitors in the single year of 1931.

Oceanaria

The first oceanarium, opened in 1938, is Marineland of Florida located 18 miles south of St Augustine. Up to 7 million gallons of sea water are pumped daily through two major tanks, one rectangular (100 ft long by 40 ft wide by 18 ft deep) containing 450,000 gallons and one circular (233 ft in circumference and 12 ft deep) containing 400,000 gallons. The tanks are seascaped, including coral reefs and even a shipwreck.

The largest salt water tank is that at Hanna-Barbera's Marineland of the Pacific located on the Palos Verdes Peninsula, Calif. It is 251½ ft in circumference and 22 ft deep, with a capacity of 640,000 gallons. The total capacity of the whole oceanarium is 2,500,000 gallons. Their killer whale "Orky" at 14,000 lb is the largest in captivity.

Chapter 3

The Natural World

1. NATURAL PHENOMENA

EARTHQUAKES

It is estimated that each year there are some 500,000 detectable seismic or micro-seismic disturbances of which 100,000 can be felt and 1,000 cause damage. (Note: Seismologists record all earthquake dates with the year first, based *not* on local time but on Greenwich Mean Time.)

Kanamori Scale Magnitudes M_s	Gutenberg-Richter Scale Magnitude M_w	PROGRESSIVE LIST OF STRONGEST INSTRUMENTALLY RECORDED EARTHQUAKES	
8.8	8.6	Colombia coast	1906 Jan 31
(8.6)	8.6	Assam, India	1950 Aug 15
(9.0)	(8¼)	Kamchatka, USSR	1952 Nov
(9.1)	(8.3)	Andreanol, Aleutian Is., US	1957
(9.5)	(8.3)	Lebu, Chile	1960 May 22

Where $M_s = \frac{2}{3} (\log_{10}E\text{-}11.8)$
and $M_w = \frac{2}{3} [\log_{10} (2E \times 10^4) - 10.7]$
Where E = energy released in dyne/cm

Greatest Earthquake

An inherent limitation in the widely used Gutenberg-Richter scale (published in 1954) precludes its usefulness when extended to the relative strengths of the strongest earthquakes ever recorded. Its use of surface-wave magnitudes, based on amplitudes of waves of a period of 20 sec, results in the "damping" of any increase in amplitude where fault ruptures break over a length much above 37 miles. These however provenly may reach a length of 500–600 miles. This "overload" or "saturation effect" has re-

sulted in the adoption since 1977 of the Kanamori scale for comparing the most massive earthquakes. Magnitudes are there defined in terms of energy release using the concept of the seismic moment, devised by K-Aki in 1966. Thus the most massive instrumentally recorded earthquake has been the cataclysmic Lebu shock south of Concepción, Chile on 1960 May 22 estimated at 10^{26} ergs. While this uniquely rates a magnitude of 9.5 on the Kanamori scale, it ranks in only equal 4th place (with the 1922 Chilean earthquake) at Magnitude 8.3 on the Gutenberg-Richter scale. For the removal of doubt the progressive records on the two scales are presented in the adjacent table.

Worst Death Toll

The greatest loss of life occurred in the earthquake in the Shensi, Shansi and Honan provinces of China, of 1556 Feb 2 (New Style) (Jan 23 Old Style), when an estimated 830,000 people were killed. The highest death toll in modern times has been in the Tangshan earthquake (magnitude 8.2) in eastern China on 1976 July 27 (local time was 3:00 a.m. on July 28). A first figure published Jan 4, 1977 revealed 655,237 killed, later adjusted to 750,000. On Nov 22, 1979, the New China News Agency unaccountably reduced the death toll to 242,000. The site of the city was still a prohibited area 5½ years later in Jan 1982. The greatest material damage was in the earthquake on the Kwanto plain, Japan, at 11:58 a.m. of 1923 Sept 1 (magnitude 8.2, epicenter in Latitude 35°15′N., Longitude 139°30′E.). In Sagami Bay, the sea bottom in one area sank 1,310 ft. The official total of persons killed and missing in this earthquake, called the *Shinsai* or Great 'Quake, and the resultant fires was 142,807. In Tokyo and Yokohama 575,000 dwellings were destroyed. The cost of the damage was estimated at $2,800 million. It has however been estimated that a 7.5-magnitude shock (G-R scale) 30 miles north of Los Angeles would result in damage estimated at $70 billion.

VOLCANOES

The total number of known active volcanoes is 850 of which many are submarine. The greatest concentration is in Indonesia, where 77 of its 167 volcanoes have erupted within historic times. The name "volcano" was first applied to the now dormant Vulcano Island in the Aeolian group in the Mediterranean, and that name derives from Vulcan, Roman god of destructive fire.

Highest Volcanoes

The highest extinct volcano in the world is Cerro Aconcagua (Stone Sentinel), 22,834 ft high, on the Argentine side of the Andes. It was first climbed on Jan 14, 1897 by Mathias Zurbriggen, and was the highest mountain climbed anywhere until June 12, 1907.

The highest dormant volcano is Volcán Llullaillaco (22,057 ft), on the frontier between Chile and Argentina.

The highest volcano regarded as active is Volcán Antofalla (21,162 ft) in Argentina, though a more

LARGEST VOLCANO CRATER: Mt Aso in Japan has a crater with axes of 17 miles and 10 miles, and a 71-mile circumference.

definite claim is made for Volcán Guayatiri or Guallatiri (19,882 ft), in Chile, which erupted in 1959.

Longest Lava Flow

The longest lava flow, known as *pahoehoe* (twisted cord-like solidifications), is that from the eruption of Laki in southeast Iceland, which flowed 40½–43½ miles. The largest known prehistoric flow is the Roza basalt flow in North America, *c.* 15 million years ago, which had an unsurpassed length (300 miles), area (15,400 sq mi) and volume (300 cu mi).

Largest Crater

The world's largest *caldera* or volcano crater is that of Mt Aso (5,223 ft) in Kyushu, Japan, which measures 17 miles north to south, 10 miles east to west and 71 miles in circumference.

AFTER THE BLOW-OFF OF MT ST HELENS: The largest volcanic eruption in US history occurred on May 18, 1980, when the top of the volcano 50 miles northeast of the city of Portland, Ore, blasted with a force 500 times greater than the atomic bomb that fell on Hiroshima, Japan. Ash and steam caused the sun to be blotted out. The dust became a thick sludge that clogged sewers and chimneys. Motorists were stopped in their tracks when ash-clogged air filters stalled engines. This weary motorist has decided to use a snow shovel. The 250-mph avalanche triggered by the Mt St Helens eruption was estimated to have contained 96 billion cu ft of matter. (Jim Shelton/AP Laserphoto)

Greatest Eruption

The total volume of matter discharged in the eruption of Tambora, a volcano on the island of Sumbawa, in Indonesia, Apr 5–7, 1815, has been estimated as 36.4 cu mi. The energy of this eruption, which lowered the height of the island from 13,450 ft to 9,350 ft, was 8.4×10^{26} ergs. The volcano thus lost 4,100 ft in height and a crater 7 mi in diameter was formed. This compares with a probable 15 cu mi ejected by Santoríni and 4.3 cu mi ejected by Krakatoa. The internal pressure causing the Tambora eruption has been estimated at 46,500,000 lb per sq in.

The ejecta in the Taupo eruption in New Zealand c. AD 130 has been estimated at 33,000 million *tons* of pumice moving at one time at 400 mph. It flattened 6,180 sq mi (over 26 times the devastated area of Mt St Helens). Less than 20% of the 15.4×10^9 tons of pumice ejected in this most violent of all documented volcanic events fell within 125 miles of the vent.

Greatest Explosion

The greatest explosion (possibly since Santoríni in the Aegean Sea c. 1470 BC) occurred c. 10:00 a.m. (local time), or 3:00 a.m. G.M.T., on Aug 27, 1883 with an eruption of Krakatoa, an island (then 18 sq mi) in the Sunda Strait between Sumatra and Java, in Indonesia. A total of 163 villages were wiped out, and 36,380 people killed by the wave it caused. Rocks were thrown 34 miles high, and dust fell 10 days later at a distance of 3,313 miles. The explosion was recorded 4 hours later on the island of Rodrigues, 2,968 miles away, as "the roar of heavy guns" and was heard over 1/13th part of the surface of the globe. This explosion has been estimated to have had about 26 times the power of the greatest H-bomb test detonation, but was still only a fifth of the size of the Santoríni cataclysm.

GEYSERS

Tallest Geyser

The Waimangu ("black water" in the Maori language) geyser, in New Zealand, erupted to a height in excess of 1,500 ft in 1904, but has not been active since it erupted violently at 6:20 a.m. Apr 1, 1917, killing 4 people.

Currently the world's tallest active geyser is the US National Park Service Steamboat Geyser, in Yellowstone National Park, Wyo, which erupted at intervals ranging from 5 days to 10 months between 1962 and 1969 to a height of 250–380 ft. The *Geysir* ("gusher") near Mt Hekla in south-central Iceland, from which all others have been named, spurts, on occasion, to 180 ft, while the adjacent Strokkur, reactivated by drilling in 1963, spurts at 10–15 min intervals.

Greatest Geyser Discharge

The greatest measured water discharge from a geyser has been 990,000 gallons by the Giant Geyser in Yellowstone National Park, Wyo, which has been dormant since 1955.

2. STRUCTURE AND DIMENSIONS

The earth is not a true sphere, but flattened at the poles and hence an oblate spheroid. The polar diameter of the earth (7,899.806 miles) is 26.575 miles less than the equatorial diameter (7,926.381 miles). The earth has a pear-shaped asymmetry with the north polar radius being 148 ft longer than the south polar radius. There is also a slight ellipticity of the equator since its long axis (about Longitude 37° W.) is 522 ft greater than the short axis. The greatest departures from the reference ellipsoid are a protuberance of 240 ft in the area of Papua New Guinea, and a depression of 344 ft south of Sri Lanka (Ceylon) in the Indian Ocean.

The greatest circumference of the earth—at the equator—is calculated as 24,901.46 miles, compared with 24,859.73 miles at the meridian. The area of the surface is estimated to be 196,937,400 sq mi. The period of axial rotation, *i.e.* the true sidereal day, is 23 hours 56 min 4.0996 sec, mean time.

Earth's Structure

The mass of the earth is 6,585,600,000,000,000,000,000 tons and its density is 5.515 times that of water. The volume is an estimated 259,875,300,000 cu mi. The earth picks up cosmic dust but estimates

TALLEST GEYSER: Waimangu in New Zealand peaked at 1,500 ft up in 1904.

vary widely with 30,000 metric tons a day being the upper limit. Modern theory is that the earth has an outer shell or lithosphere 50 miles thick, then an outer and inner rock layer or mantle extending 1,745 miles deep, beneath which there is an iron-rich core of radius measuring 2,164 miles. If the iron-rich core theory is correct, iron would be the most abundant element in the earth. At the center of the core the estimated density is 13.09 g/cm^3; the temperature 4,000–4,500°C and the pressure 23,600 tons f/sq in.

OCEANS

Largest Ocean

The area of the earth covered by the sea is estimated to be 139,670,000 sq mi, or 70.92% of the total surface. The mean depth of the hydrosphere was at one time estimated to be 12,450 ft, but recent surveys suggest a lower estimate of 11,660 ft. The total weight of the water is estimated as 1.45×10^{18} tons, or 0.022% of the earth's total weight. The volume of the oceans is estimated to be 308,400,000 cu mi, compared with 8,400,000 cu mi of fresh water.

The largest ocean is the Pacific. Excluding adjacent seas, it represents 46% of the world's oceans and is 64,190,000 sq mi in area. From Guayaquil, Ecuador, on the east, to Bangkok, Thailand, on the west, the Pacific could be said to stretch 10,905 miles in the shortest straight navigable line.

Longest Voyage Possible

The longest possible great circle sea voyage is one of 19,860 miles from a point 150 miles west of Karachi, Pakistan, to a point 200 miles north of Uka' Kamchatka, USSR, *via* the Mozambique Channel, Drake Passage, and Bering Sea.

Remotest Spot in the Ocean

The world's most distant point from land is a spot in the South Pacific, approximately 48°30'S., 125°30'W., which is about 1,660 miles from the nearest points of land, namely Pitcairn Island, Ducie Island and Cape Dart, Antarctica. Centered on this spot, therefore, is a circle of water with an area of about 8,657,000 sq mi—about 7,000 sq mi larger than the USSR, the world's largest country.

Sea Temperature

The temperature of the water at the surface of the sea varies from 28.5°F in the White Sea to 96°F in the shallow areas of the Persian Gulf in summer. The normal Red Sea temperature is 71.6°F. Ice-focused solar rays have been known to heat lake water to nearly 80°F. The highest temperature recorded in the ocean is 662°F measured by the research submersible *Alvin* at Lat. 21°N on the East Pacific Rise in Nov 1979, emanating from a sea-floor geothermal spring at a depth of 8,530 ft.

Deepest Depths in the Ocean

The deepest part of the ocean was first pinpointed in 1951 by the British survey ship *Challenger* in the Marianas Trench in the Pacific Ocean. The depth was measured by sounding and by echo-sounder and published as 5,960 fathoms (35,760 ft). Subsequent visits to this same Challenger Deep have resulted in less reliable claims by echo-sounder only, culminat-

ing in one of 36,198 ft or 6.85 mi by the USSR's research ship *Vityaz* in March 1959. On Jan 23, 1960 the US Navy bathyscaphe *Trieste* descended to the bottom there, but the depth calibrations (made for fresh rather than salt water) yielded a figure 60 ft deeper than the 1951 survey (35,820 ft). A metal object, say a pound-ball of steel, dropped into water above this trench would take nearly 63 minutes to fall to the sea bed 6.85 miles below, where the hydrostatic pressure is 17,040 lb/sq in.

The average depth of the Pacific is 13,740 ft.

Largest Sea

The largest of the seas (as opposed to oceans) is the South China Sea, with an area of 1,148,500 sq mi. The Malayan Sea comprising the waters between the Indian Ocean and the South Pacific, south of the Chinese mainland, covering 3,144,000 sq mi, is not now an entity accepted by the International Hydrographic Bureau.

Largest Gulf

The largest gulf in the world is the Gulf of Mexico, with an area of 580,000 sq mi and a shoreline of 3,100 miles from Cape Sable, Fla, to Cabo Catoche, Mexico.

Largest Bay

The largest bay measured by shoreline length is Hudson Bay in northern Canada with a shoreline of 7,623 miles and an area of 317,500 sq mi. The area of the Bay of Bengal however is bigger—839,000 sq mi.

Highest Sea-Mountain

The highest known submarine mountain or sea-mountain was one discovered in 1953 near the Tonga Trench between Samoa and New Zealand. It rises 28,500 ft from the sea bed, with its summit 1,200 ft below the surface.

Greatest Tides

The greatest tides in the world occur in the Bay of Fundy, which separates the peninsula of Nova Scotia from Maine and the Canadian province of New Brunswick. Burncoat Head in the Minas Basin, Nova Scotia, has the greatest mean spring range with 47.5 ft, and an extreme range of 53.5 ft.

GREATEST TIDES: A ship docked in the Bay of Fundy dramatically illustrates the 50-ft difference between high and low tide. (Nova Scotia Information Service)

Extreme tides are due to lunar and solar gravitational forces affected by their perigee, perihelion, and conjunctions. Barometric and wind effects can superimpose an added "surge" element. Coastal and sea-floor configurations can accentuate these forces.

Greatest and Strongest Currents

The greatest current in the oceans of the world is the Antarctic Circumpolar Current or West Wind Drift Current, which was measured in 1969 in the Drake Passage between South America and Antarctica, to be flowing at a rate of 9,500 million cu ft per sec—nearly three times that of the Gulf Stream. Its width ranges from 185 to 1,240 miles and has a proven surface flow rate of 4/10ths of a knot.

The world's strongest currents are the Nakwakto Rapids, Slingsby Channel, British Columbia, Canada (Lat. 51°05′N., Long. 127°30′W.) where the flow rate may reach 16.0 knots (18.4 mph).

Highest Waves

The highest officially recorded sea wave was measured by Lt Frederic Margraff, USN from the USS *Ramapo* proceeding from Manila, Philippines, to San

TALLEST ICEBERG: Sighted off Greenland in 1958 was this gigantic 550-ft-high ice float. (US Coast Guard)

Diego, Calif, on the night of Feb 6–7, 1933 during a 68-knot (78.3 mph) hurricane. The wave was computed to be 112 ft from trough to crest.

The highest instrumentally measured wave was one calculated to be exactly 86 ft high, recorded by the British ship *Weather Reporter* in the North Atlantic on Dec 30, 1972 in Lat. 59°N., Long. 19°W.

It has been calculated on the statistics of the Stationary Random Theory that one wave in more than 300,000 may exceed the average by a factor of 4.

On July 9, 1958 a landslip caused a wave to wash 1,740 ft high along the fjord-like shore of Lituya Bay, Alaska.

"Tidal Wave"

The highest recorded seismic sea wave, or *tsunami,* (often mistakenly called a "tidal wave") was one of an estimated 278 ft, which appeared off Ishigaki Island, Ryukyu Chain, Apr 24, 1971. It tossed an 850-ton block of coral more than 1.3 miles. *Tsunami* (a Japanese word meaning: *tsu,* overflowing; *nami,* a wave) have been observed to travel at 490 mph. Between 479 BC and 1977 there were at least 500 instances of *tsunami,* of which 270 were destructive.

Icebergs

The largest iceberg on record was an Antarctic tabular iceberg of over 12,000 sq mi (208 miles long and 60 miles wide) sighted 150 miles west of Scott Island, in the South Pacific Ocean, by the USS *Glacier* Nov 12, 1956. This iceberg was thus larger than Belgium.

The 200-ft-thick Arctic ice island T.1 (140 sq mi), discovered in 1946, was tracked for 17 years.

The tallest iceberg measured was one of 550 ft reported off western Greenland by the USCG icebreaker *East Wind* in 1958.

The most southerly Arctic iceberg was sighted in the Atlantic by a USN weather patrol at Lat. 28°44′N., Long. 48°42′W., in Apr 1935.

The most northerly Antarctic iceberg was a remnant sighted in the Atlantic by the ship *Dochra* at Lat. 26°30′S., Long. 25°40′W., Apr 30, 1894.

Straits

The longest straits in the world are the Tatarskiy Proliv or Tartar Straits between Sakhalin Island and the USSR mainland, running 497 miles from the Sea of Japan to Sakhalinsky Zaliv. This distance is marginally longer than the Malacca Straits, which extend 485 miles.

The broadest named straits are the Davis Straits between Greenland and Baffin Island, which at one point narrow to 210 miles. The Drake Passage between the Diego Ramírez Islands, Chile, and the South Shetland Islands, is 710 miles across.

The narrowest navigable straits are those between the Aegean island of Euboea and the mainland of Greece. The gap is only 45 yd wide at Khalkis. The Seil Sound, Strathclyde, Scotland, narrows to a point only 20 ft wide where a bridge joins the island of Seil to the mainland and is thus said by the islanders to span the Atlantic.

LAND

There is satisfactory evidence that at one time the earth's land surface comprised a single primeval continent of 80 million sq mi, now termed Pangaea, and that this split about 190 million years ago, during the Jurassic period, into two super-continents, termed Laurasia (Eurasia, Greenland and North America) and Gondwanaland (comprising Africa, Arabia, India, South America, Oceania and Antarctica), named after Gondwana, India, which itself split 120 million years ago. The South Pole was apparently in the area of the Sahara as recently as the Ordovician period of *c.* 450 million years ago.

Rocks

The age of the earth is generally considered to be within the range 4,600 ± 100 million years, by analogy with directly measured ages of meteorites and of the moon. However, no rocks of this great age have yet been found on the earth, since geological processes have presumably destroyed the earliest record.

The greatest reported age for any scientifically dated rock is 3,800 ± 100 million years for granite gneiss rock found near Granite Falls in the Minnesota River valley, as measured by the lead-isotope and rubidium-uranium methods by the US Geological Survey, and announced on Jan 26, 1975. These metamorphic samples compare with the Amitsoq gneiss from Godthaab, Greenland, which is unreservedly accepted to be between 3,700 and 3,750 million years old.

The largest exposed isolated monolith is the 1,237-ft-high Mt Augustus (3,627 ft above sea level), discovered June 3, 1858 about 200 miles east of Carnarvon, Western Australia. It is an up-faulted monoclinal gritty conglomerate 5 miles long and 2 miles across and thus twice the size of the celebrated monolithic arkose Ayer's Rock (1,100 ft), 250 miles southwest of Alice Springs, in Northern Territory, Australia.

Largest and Smallest Continents

Only 29.08%, or an estimated 57,270,000 sq mi, of the earth's surface is land, with a mean height of 2,480 ft above sea level. The Eurasian land mass taken alone is the largest with an area (including islands) of 20,733,000 sq mi. However, if the Afro-Eurasian land mass, which is separated artificially only by the Suez Canal, is taken as a unit it covers an area of 32,233,000 sq mi or 56.2% of the earth's land mass.

The smallest is the Australian mainland, with an area of about 2,941,526 sq mi, which, together with Tasmania, New Zealand, New Guinea and the Pacific Islands, is described as Oceania.

Land Remotest from the Sea

There is an as yet unpinpointed spot in the Dzoosotoyn Elisen (desert), in northern Xinjiang Uygur Zizhiqu (Sin Kiang), China's most northwesterly province, that is more than 1,500 miles from the open sea in any direction. The nearest large city to this point is Urumqi (Urumchi) to its south.

Largest Peninsula

The world's largest peninsula is Arabia, with an area of about 1,250,000 sq mi.

Largest Islands

Discounting Australia, which is usually regarded as a continental land mass, the largest island is Greenland (renamed Kalaatdlit Nunaat, May 1, 1979), with an area of about 840,000 sq mi. There is some evidence that Greenland is in fact several islands overlaid by an ice-cap without which it would have an area of 650,000 sq mi.

The largest island surrounded by fresh water is the Ilha de Marajó (13,500 sq mi), in the mouth of the Amazon River, Brazil. The largest inland island (*i.e.* land surrounded by rivers) is Ilha do Bananal, Brazil (7,000 sq mi).

The largest island in a lake is Manitoulin Island (1,068 sq mi) in the Canadian (Ontario) section of Lake Huron. The island itself has a lake of 41.09 sq mi on it, called Manitou Lake, which is the world's largest lake within a lake, and in that lake are a number of islands.

Newest Island

The world's newest island, Lateiki, which appeared in the South Pacific after a volcanic eruption, was annexed by Tonga in June 1979.

Remotest Islands

The remotest island in the world is Bouvet Øya (formerly Liverpool Island), discovered in the South Atlantic by J. B. C. Bouvet de Lozier Jan 1, 1739 and first landed on by Capt George Norris on Dec 16, 1825. Its position is 54°26′S., 3°24′E. This uninhabited Norwegian dependency is about 1,050 miles from the nearest land—the uninhabited Queen Maud Land coast of eastern Antarctica.

The remotest inhabited island in the world is Tristan da Cunha, discovered in the South Atlantic by Tristão da Cunha, a Portuguese admiral, in Mar 1506. It has an area of 38 sq mi (habitable area 12 sq mi) and was annexed by the United Kingdom Aug 14, 1816. After evacuation in 1961 (due to volcanic activity), 198 islanders returned in Nov 1963. The nearest inhabited land is the island of St Helena, 1,320 miles to the northeast. The nearest continent, Africa, is 1,700 miles away.

Greatest Archipelago

The greatest archipelago is the 3,500-mile-long crescent of over 13,000 islands that form Indonesia.

Largest Atolls

The largest atoll is Kwajalein in the Marshall Islands, in the central Pacific. Its slender 176-mile-long coral reef encloses a lagoon of 1,100 sq mi.

The atoll with the largest land area is Christmas Atoll, in the Line Islands, in the central Pacific Ocean. It has an area of 248 sq mi. Its principal settlement, London, is only 2½ miles distant from Paris, its other settlement.

Highest Rock Pinnacle

The highest rock pinnacle is Ball's Pyramid near Lord Howe Island in the Pacific, which is 1,843 ft high, but has a base axis of only 220 yd. It was first scaled in 1965.

Longest Reef

The longest reef is the Great Barrier Reef off Queensland, northeastern Australia, which is 1,260 statute miles in length. Between 1959 and 1971 a large section between Cooktown and Townsville was destroyed by the proliferation of the Crown of Thorns starfish (*Acanthaster planci*).

HIGHEST MOUNTAIN: A team of Chinese scientists braves the intense cold and steep slopes of Mt Everest, 29,028 ft high.

Highest Mountains

An eastern Himalayan peak of 29,028 ft above sea level on the Tibet-Nepal border (in an area first designated Chu-mu-lang-ma on a map of 1717) was discovered to be the world's highest mountain in 1852 by the Survey Department of the Government of India, from theodolite readings taken in 1849 and 1850. In 1860 its height was computed to be 29,002 ft. On July 25, 1973, the Chinese announced a height of 8,848.1 m or 29,029 ft 3 in. In practice the altitude can only be justified as 29,028 ± 25 ft. The 5½-mile-high peak was named Mt Everest after Sir George Everest (1790–1866), formerly Surveyor-General of India. Other names for Everest are Sagarmatha (Nepalese), Qomolongma (Chinese) and Mi-ti Gu-ti Cha-pu Long-na (Tibetan). After a total loss of 11 lives since the first reconnaissance in 1921, Everest was finally conquered at 11:30 a.m. May 29, 1953. (For details of ascents, see *Mountaineering*.)

SUMMIT FARTHEST FROM EARTH'S CORE: The peak of Mt Chimborazo in the Andes rises 20,561 ft above sea level, but its equatorial location makes it farther from the center of the earth than the top of the taller Mt Everest.

The mountain whose summit is farthest from the earth's center is the Andean peak of Chimborazo (20,561 ft), 98 miles south of the equator in Ecuador. Its summit is 7,057 ft further from the earth's center than the summit of Mt Everest. The highest mountain on the equator is Volcán Cayambe (19,285 ft), Ecuador, at Longitude 77° 58′ W.

The highest insular mountain in the world is the unsurveyed Ngga Pula, formerly Mt Sukarno, formerly Carstensz Pyramide, in Irian Jaya, Indonesia. According to cross-checked altimeter estimates, it is 16,500 ft high.

The highest unclimbed mountain is now only the 31st highest—Zemu Gap Peak (25,526 ft) in the Sikkim Himalayas.

The world's tallest mountain measured from its submarine base (3,280 fathoms) in the Hawaiian Trough to peak is Mauna Kea (Mountain White) on the island of Hawaii, with a combined height of 33,476 ft, of which 13,796 ft are above sea level. Another mountain whose dimensions, but not height, exceed those of Mt Everest is the Hawaiian peak of Mauna Loa (Mountain Long) at 13,680 ft. The axes of its el-liptical base, 16,322 ft below sea level, have been estimated at 74 mi and 53 mi. It should be noted that Cerro Aconcagua (22,834 ft) is more than 38,800 ft above the 16,000-ft-deep Pacific abyssal plain or 42,834 ft above the Peru-Chile Trench, which is 180 mi distant in the South Pacific.

Steepest Mountain Slope

Mount Rakaposhi (25,498 ft) rises 19,652 ft from the Hunza Valley, Pakistan, with an overall gradient of 31° over a distance of 32,808 ft.

Greatest Mountain Ranges

The greatest land mountain range is the Himalaya-Karakoram, which contains 96 of the world's 109 peaks of over 24,000 ft. The greatest of all mountain ranges is, however, the submarine Indian-East Pacific Oceans Cordillera, extending 19,200 miles from the Gulf of Aden to the Gulf of California by way of the seabed between Australia and Antarctica, with an average height of 8,000 ft above the base ocean depth.

Longest Lines of Sight

Alaska's Mt McKinley (20,320 ft) has been sighted from Mt Sanford (16,237 ft) 230 mi away. McKinley, so named in 1896, was called Denali (Great One) in the Athabascan language. Vatnajokull (6,952 ft) on the eastern coast of Iceland, has been seen by refracted light from the Faeroe Islands 340 mi distant across the Norwegian Sea.

Greatest Plateau

The most extensive high plateau is the Tibetan Plateau in Central Asia. The average altitude is 16,000 ft and the area is 77,000 sq mi.

Sheerest Wall

The 3,200-ft-wide northwest face of Half Dome, Yosemite, Calif, is 2,200 ft high, but nowhere departs more than 7° from the vertical. It was first climbed (Class VI) in 5 days in July 1957 by Royal Robbins, Jerry Gallwas, and Mike Sherrick.

Highest Halites

Along the northern shores of the Gulf of Mexico for 725 miles there exist 330 subterranean "mountains" of salt, some of which rise more than 60,000 ft from bedrock and appear as the low salt domes first discovered in 1862.

Lowest Official Hill

The official map of Seria, Bounei (on the island of Borneo) shows a hillock named Bukit Thompson on the Padang Golf Course at 15 ft.

Sand Dunes

The highest measured sand dunes are those in the Saharan sand sea of Isaouane-n-Tifernine of east central Algeria at Lat. 26° 42′ N., Long. 6° 43′ E. They have a wave-length of nearly 3 miles and attain a height of 1,410 ft.

Deepest and Largest Depressions

The deepest depression so far discovered is beneath the Hollick-Kenyon Plateau in Marie Byrd Land, Antarctica, where, at a point 5,900 ft above sea level, the ice depth is 14,000 ft, hence indicating a bedrock depression 8,100 ft below sea level.

The deepest exposed depression on land is the shore surrounding the Dead Sea, 1,291 ft below sea level. The deepest point on the bed of this lake is 2,600 ft below the Mediterranean. The deepest part of the bed of Lake Baykal in Siberia, USSR, is 4,872 ft below sea level.

The greatest submarine depression is a large area of the floor of the northwest Pacific which has an average depth of 15,000 ft.

The largest exposed depression in the world is the Caspian Sea basin in the Azerbaydzhani, Russian, Kazakh, and Turkmen republics of the USSR and northern Iran. It is more than 200,000 sq mi, of which 143,550 sq mi is lake area. The preponderant land area of the depression is the Prikaspiyskaya Nizmennost', lying around the northern third of the lake and stretching inland for a distance of up to 280 miles.

Longest and Shortest Rivers

The two longest rivers are the Amazon (*Amazonas*), flowing into the South Atlantic, and the Nile (*Bahr-el-Nil*) flowing into the Mediterranean. Which is the longer is more a matter of definition than of simple measurement.

The true source of the Amazon was discovered in 1953 to be a stream named Huarco, rising near the summit of Cerro Huagra (17,188 ft) in Peru. This stream progressively becomes the Toro, then the Santiago, then the Apurímac, which in turn is known as the Ene, and then the Tambo before its confluence with the Amazon prime tributary, the Ucayali. The length of the Amazon from this source to the South Atlantic *via* the Canal do Norte was measured in 1969 to be 4,007 miles (usually quoted to the rounded-off figure of 4,000 miles).

If, however, a vessel navigating downriver turns to the south of Ilha de Marajó through the straits of Breves and Boiuci into the Pará, the total length of the waterway becomes 4,195 miles. The Pará is not, however, a tributary of the Amazon, being hydrologically part of the basin of the Tocantins.

The length of the Nile watercourse, as surveyed by M Devroey (Belgium) before the loss of a few miles of meanders due to the formation of Lake Nasser, behind the Aswan High Dam, was 4,145 miles. This course is the hydrologically acceptable one from the source in Burundi of the Luvironza branch of the Kagera feeder of the Victoria Nyanza *via* the White Nile (*Bahr-el-Jebel*) to the delta.

The world's shortest named river is the D River, Lincoln City, Ore, which connects Devil's Lake to the Pacific Ocean and is 440 ft long at low tide.

Greatest Flow

The greatest flow of any river is that of the Amazon, which discharges an average of 4,200,000 cu ft of water per sec into the Atlantic Ocean, rising to more than 7 million "cusecs" in full flood. The lowest 900 miles of the Amazon average 300 ft in depth.

Largest Basin and Longest Tributaries

The largest river basin is that drained by the Amazon (4,007 miles). It covers about 2,720,000 sq mi, has about 15,000 tributaries and sub-tributaries, of which four are more than 1,000 miles long. This includes the longest of all tributaries, the Madeira with a length of 2,100 miles, which is surpassed by only 14 rivers in the whole world.

The longest sub-tributary is the Pilcomayo (1,000 miles long) in South America. It is a tributary of the Paraguay River (1,500 miles long), which is itself a tributary of the Paraná (2,500 miles).

Submarine and Subterranean Rivers

In 1952 a submarine river 250 miles wide, known as the Cromwell Current, was discovered flowing eastward 300 ft below the surface of the Pacific for 3,500 miles along the equator. Its volume is 1,000 times that of the Mississippi.

In Aug 1958 a crypto-river was tracked by radioisotopes flowing under the Nile, with a mean annual flow six times greater—500,000 million cu meters (20 million million cu ft).

Greatest River Bores

The bore on the Ch'ient'ang'kian (Hang-chou-fe) in eastern China is the most remarkable in the world. At spring tides, the wave attains a height of up to 25 ft and a speed of 13 knots. It is heard advancing at a range of 14 miles.

The bore on the Hooghly branch of the Ganges travels for 70 miles at more than 15 knots. The annual downstream flood wave on the Mekong River of Southeast Asia sometimes reaches a height of 46 ft. The greatest volume of any tidal bore is that of the Canal do Norte (10 miles wide) in the mouth of the Amazon.

Longest Estuary

The longest estuary is that of the often-frozen Ob', in the northern USSR, at 550 miles. It is up to 50 miles wide.

Largest Delta

The largest delta is that created by the Ganga (Ganges) and Brahmaputra in Bangladesh (formerly East Pakistan) and West Bengal, India. It covers an area of 30,000 sq mi.

Longest Fjords

The longest "fjord" is the Nordvest Fjord arm of the Scoresby Sund in eastern Greenland, which extends inland 195 miles from the sea. The longest of Norwegian fjords is the Sogne Fjord, which extends 113.7 miles inland from Sygnefest to the head of the Lusterfjord arm at Skjolden. It averages barely 3 miles in width and has a deepest point of 4,085 ft. If measured from Huglo along the Bømlafjord to the head of the Sørfjord arm at Odda, the Hardangerfjorden can also be said to extend 113.7 miles. The longest Danish fjord is Limfjorden (100 miles long).

Longest and Fastest-Moving Glaciers

It is estimated that 6,020,000 sq mi, or about 10.4% of the earth's land surface, is permanently glaciated. The longest glacier known is the Lambert Glacier, discovered by an Australian aircraft crew in Australian Antarctic Territory in 1956–57. It is up to 40 miles wide and, with its upper section known as the Mellor Glacier, it measures at least 250 miles in length. With the Fisher Glacier limb, the Lambert forms a continuous ice passage about 320 miles long. The longest Himalayan glacier is the Siachen (47 miles) in the Karakoram range, though the Hispar and Biafo combine to form an ice passage 76 miles long.

The fastest-moving glacier is the Quarayaq in Greenland which flows 65–80 ft per day.

Largest Glacial Pothole

The largest known glacial pothole is one 30 ft in diameter and 50 ft deep near Bloomingdale, Ontario, Canada.

Greatest Avalanches

The greatest avalanches, though rarely observed, occur in the Himalayas, but no estimate of their volume has been published. It was estimated that 3½ million cu meters (120 million cu ft) of snow fell in an avalanche in the Italian Alps in 1885. (See also *Disasters.*)

Highest Waterfall

The highest waterfall (as opposed to a vaporized "Bridal Veil") is the Salto Angel (Angel Falls), in Venezuela, on a branch of the Carrao River, an upper tributary of the Caroní, with a total drop of 3,212 ft and the longest single drop 2,648 ft. It was re-discovered in 1935 by a US pilot named Jimmy Angel (d Dec 8, 1956). He later crashed nearby on Oct 9, 1937. The fall, known by the Indians as Cherun-Meru, was first reported by Ernesto Sanchez La Cruz in 1910. On July 26, 1981, Jim Bridwell and John N. Long (both US) rappelled or abseiled a record 1,800 ft down the face of the precipice adjacent to Angel Falls.

Greatest Waterfall Flow

On the basis of the average annual flow, the greatest waterfall is the Guairá (374 ft high), known also as the Salto dos Sete Quedas, on the Alto Paraná River between Brazil and Paraguay. Although attaining an average height of only 110 ft, its estimated annual average flow over the lip (5,300 yd wide) is 470,000 cu ft per sec. It has a peak flow of 1,750,000 cu ft per sec. The amount of water this represents can be imagined by supposing it was pouring into the dome of the Capitol in Washington, DC— it would fill it completely in 3/5ths of a sec.

The seven cataracts of Boyoma (formerly Stanley) Falls in the Congo (Zaïre) have an average annual flow of 600,000 cu ft per sec.

It has been calculated that, when some 5½ million years ago the Mediterranean basins began to be filled from the Atlantic through the Straits of Gibraltar, a waterfall was formed 26 times greater than the Guairá and perhaps 2,625 ft high.

Widest Waterfalls

The widest waterfalls are Khône Falls (50–70 ft high) in Laos, with a width of 6.7 miles and a flood flow of 1,500,000 cu ft per sec.

Largest Lagoon

The largest lagoon in the world is Lagoa dos Patos in southernmost Brazil. It is 158 miles long and extends over 4,110 sq mi.

Underground Lake

Reputedly the largest underground lake is the Lost Sea, which lies 300 ft underground in the Craighead Caverns, Sweetwater, Tenn. Discovered in 1905, it covers an area of 4½ acres.

Largest Lakes

The largest inland sea or lake is the Kaspiskoye More (Caspian Sea) between southern USSR and Iran. It is 760 miles long and its total area is 143,550 sq mi. Of the total area, 55,280 sq mi (38.6%) are in Iran, where the lake is named the Darya-ye-Khazar. Its maximum depth is 3,360 ft and its surface is 93 ft below sea level. Its estimated volume is 21,500 cu mi of saline water. Its surface has varied between 105 ft below sea level (11th century) and 72 ft (early 19th century). The USSR government plans to reverse the flow of the upper Pechora River from flowing north to the Barents Sea by blasting a 70-mile-long canal with nuclear explosives into the south-flowing Kolva River so that *via* the Kama and Volga rivers the Caspian will be replenished.

The fresh-water lake with the greatest surface area is Lake Superior, one of the Great Lakes. The total area is about 31,800 sq mi, of which 20,700 sq mi are in the US (Minn, Wis and Mich) and 11,100 sq mi in Ontario, Canada. It is 600 ft above sea level. The fresh-water lake with the greatest volume is Baykal (see below) with an estimated volume of 5,520 cu mi.

Highest Lake

The highest steam-navigated lake is Lago Titicaca (maximum depth 1,214 ft), with an area of about 3,200 sq mi (1,850 sq mi in Peru, 1,350 sq mi in Bolivia), in South America. It is 130 miles long and is situated at 12,506 ft above sea level.

There is an unnamed glacial lake near Mt Everest at 19,300 ft. Tibet's largest lake, Nam Tso (772 sq mi), lies at an elevation of 15,060 ft.

Deepest Lake

The deepest lake is Ozero (Lake) Baykal in central Siberia, USSR. It is 385 miles long and between 20 and 46 miles wide. In 1957 the lake's Olkhon Crevice was measured to be 6,365 ft deep and hence 4,872 ft below sea level.

Natural Bridge (Arch)

The longest natural bridge in the world is the Landscape Arch in the Arches National Park 25 miles north of Moab, Utah. This natural sandstone arch spans 291 ft and is set about 100 ft above the canyon floor. In one place erosion has narrowed its section to 6 ft.

Larger in mass, however, is the Rainbow Bridge, Utah, discovered on Aug 14, 1909, which has a span of 278 ft but is over 22 ft wide.

"LOST SEA" (above): This 4½-acre underground lake in Tennessee was not discovered until 1905. It is 300 ft below the earth's surface, in Craighead Caverns.

HIGHEST WATERFALL (right): Angel Falls in Venezuela has a single drop of 2,648 ft, and a total fall of 3,212 ft (compared to 167 ft for the American Niagara Falls). Note the airplane passing in front of Angel Falls. There are other immensely high waterfalls in the area which are still unnamed.

LARGEST AND DEEPEST LAKE: Baykal (below) in central Siberia is the freshwater lake with the greatest depth and volume—it is 6,365 ft deep and contains some 5,520 cu mi of water.

(Ruth Robertson)

121

LONGEST NATURAL BRIDGE (above): Landscape Arch near Moab, Utah, spans 291 ft. Its size can be judged by the man in the lower left corner of the picture. (National Park Service)

LARGEST RIVER: The source of the Amazon is in the jungles of Brazil and Peru. (K. W. Emmermacher, Lima)

HIGHEST LAKE (below): Titicaca in South America is high in the Andes between Peru and Bolivia, at 12,500 ft above sea level. Balsa boats, built by the natives, sail on this lake.

The highest natural arch is the sandstone arch 25 miles west-northwest of K'ashih, Sinkiang, China, estimated in 1947 to be nearly 1,000 ft tall, with a span of about 150 ft.

Longest and Largest Cave and Cavern

The most extensive cave system is under the Mammoth Cave National Park, Ky, first discovered in 1799. On Sept 9, 1972 an exploration group led by Dr John P. Wilcox completed a connection, pioneered by Mrs Patricia Crowther, on Aug 30, between the Flint Ridge Cave system and the Mammoth Cave system, so making a combined system with a total mapped passageway length of 224.7 miles.

The largest cave chamber is the Sarawak Chamber, Lobang Nasip Bagus, in the Gunung Mulu National Park, Sarawak, discovered and surveyed by the 1980 British-Malayasian Mulu Expedition. Its length is 2300 ft; its average width is 980 ft and it is nowhere less than 230 ft high. Yankee Stadium would fit into one end.

DEEPEST CAVES BY COUNTRIES
These depths are subject to continuous revisions.

Depth in Ft

4888	Gouffre Jean Bernard	France
4390	Sima de Las Puertas de Illamina	Spain
4199	Snezhnaya, Caucasus	USSR
4068	Sistema Huautla	Mexico
3855	Mammuthöhle	Austria
3117	Antro di Corchia	Italy
2821	Reseau de Siebenhengste	Switzerland
2625	Anou Boussouil	Algeria
2569	Jaskini Snieznej, Tatras	Poland
2510	Brezno pri Gamsovi Glavici	Yugoslavia
2464	Ghar Parau, Zagros	Iran
2296	Kef Toghobeit	Morocco

Tallest Stalagmite

The tallest known stalagmite is La Grande Stalagmite in the Aven Armand cave, Lozère, France, which has attained a height of 98 ft from the cave floor. It was found in Sept 1897.

Longest Stalactite

The longest known stalactite is a wall-supported column extending 195 ft from roof to floor in the Cueva de Nerja, near Málaga, Spain. Probably the longest free-hanging stalactite is one of 23 ft in the Poll an Ionain cave in County Clare, Ireland.

The tallest cave column is the 106-ft-tall Bicentennial Column in Ogle Cave in Carlsbad Cavern National Park, NM.

Largest and Deepest Gorges

The largest land gorge is the Grand Canyon on the Colorado River in north-central Ariz. It extends from Marble Gorge to the Grand Wash Cliffs, over a distance of 217 miles, varies in width from 4 to 13 miles and is up to 5,300 ft deep.

The submarine Labrador Basin Canyon is c. 2,150 miles long.

The deepest canyon in low relief territory is Hell's Canyon, dividing Oregon and Idaho. It plunges 7,900 ft from the Devil Mountain down to the Snake River.

A stretch of the Kali River in central Nepal flows 18,000 ft below its flanking summits of the Dhaulagiri and Annapurna groups.

The deepest submarine canyon yet discovered is one 25 miles south of Esperance, Western Australia, which is 6,000 ft deep and 20 miles wide.

Largest Desert

Nearly an eighth of the world's land surface is arid with an annual rainfall of less than 9.8 in. The Sa-

LONGEST STALACTITE (below): The steepest column—195 ft—is in the Cueva de Nerja near Málaga, Spain.

123

hara in North Africa is the largest in the world. At its greatest length, it is 3,200 miles from east to west. From north to south it is between 800 and 1,400 miles. The area covered by the desert is about 3,250,000 sq mi. The land level varies from 436 ft below sea level in the Qattara Depression, Egypt, to the mountain Emi Koussi (11,204 ft) in Chad. The diurnal temperature range in the western Sahara may be more than 80 °F.

Largest Swamp

The largest tract of swamp is in the basin of the Pripet or Pripyat River—a tributary of the Dnieper in the USSR. These swamps cover an estimated area of 18,125 sq mi.

Sea Cliffs

The highest sea cliffs yet pinpointed anywhere in the world are those on the north coast of east Molokai, Hawaii, near Umilehi Point, which descend 3,300 ft to the sea at an average gradient of more than 55°.

3. WEATHER*

The meteorological records given here necessarily relate largely to the last 140 to 160 years, since data before that time are both sparse and often unreliable. Reliable registering thermometers were introduced as recently as c. 1820.

It is believed that 1.2 million years ago the world's air temperature averaged 95 °F.

The longest continuous observations have been maintained at the Radcliffe Observatory, Oxford, England, since 1815.

Upper Atmosphere

The lowest temperature ever recorded in the atmosphere is −225.4 °F at an altitude of about 50 to 60 miles, during noctilucent cloud research above Kronogård, Sweden, July 27–Aug 7, 1963.

A jet stream moving at 408 mph at 154,200 ft (29.2 miles) was recorded by Skua rocket above South Uist, Outer Hebrides, Scotland, on Dec 13, 1967.

---

* For more specialized weather records, see "Weather Facts and Feats," a Guinness Superlatives Book, published in 1980 by Sterling.

Most Equable Temperature

The location with the most equable recorded temperature over a short period is Garapan, on Saipan, in the Mariana Islands, Pacific Ocean. During the nine years 1927–35, inclusive, the lowest temperature recorded was 67.3 °F Jan 30, 1934, and the highest was 88.5 °F Sept 9, 1931, giving an extreme range of 21.2 °F. Between 1911–66 the Brazilian offshore island of Fernando de Noronha had a minimum temperature of 65.5 °F Nov 17, 1913, and a maximum of 89.6 °F March 2, 1965, an extreme range of 24.1 °F.

Greatest Temperature Ranges

The highest *shade* temperature ever recorded was 136.4 °F at Al' Aziziyah (El Azizia), Libya, on Sept 13, 1922.

The lowest *screen* temperature ever recorded was −126.9 °F at Vostok (11,220 ft above sea level), Antarctica on Aug 24, 1960. The coldest permanently inhabited place is the Siberian village of Oymyakon (pop. 600) in the USSR, where the temperature reached −96 °F in 1964.

The greatest temperature variation recorded in a day is 100 °F (a fall from 44 °F to −56 °F) at Browning, Mont, Jan 23–24, 1916. The most freakish rise was 49 °F in 2 min at Spearfish, SD, from −4 °F at 7:30 a.m. to 45 °F at 7:32 a.m. Jan 22, 1943.

The greatest recorded temperature ranges in the world are around the Siberian "cold pole" in the eastern USSR. Temperatures in Verkhoyansk (67°33′N, 133°23′E) have ranged 192 °F from −94 °F (unofficial) to 98 °F.

Humidity and Discomfort

Human discomfort depends not merely on temperature but on the combination of temperature, humidity, radiation and wind speed. The US Weather Service uses a Temperature-Humidity Index, which equals two-fifths of the sum of the dry and wet bulb thermometer readings plus 15. When the THI in still air reaches 75, at least half of the people will be uncomfortable while at 79 few, if any, will be comfortable. A THI reading of 98.2 has been recorded twice in Death Valley, Calif—on July 27, 1966 (119 °F, 31% humidity) and on Aug 12, 1970 (117 °F, 37% humidity). A person driving at 45 mph in a car without a windshield in a temperature of −45 °F would, by the chill factor, experience the equivalent of −125 °F, which is within 2 °F of the world record.

WEATHER

1. **MOST RAINY DAYS:** Mt Waialeale on Kauai, Hawaii, is the wettest place on earth—350 days and 451 in of rain per year. (Alex Hansen)

2. **FLEW THROUGH EYE OF A SUPER-TYPHOON:** The crew of the US Air Weather Service plane back from recording the lowest barometric pressure—870 millibars—ever measured, in 1979. (USAF)

3. **HOTTEST PLACE:** Dallol, Ethiopia, has an average (mean) temperature of 94°F on a year-round basis.

4. **HOTTEST IN SHADE:** The highest temperature ever recorded was 136.4°F at this spot in Libya in 1922.

5. **HOTTEST STREAK:** Death Valley, Calif had 43 consecutive days of 120°F heat in 1917.

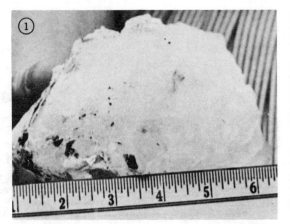

WEATHER:

1. LARGEST HAILSTONE: This 1.67-lb iced stone measured 17½ in in circumference. It fell in Coffeyville, Kans in 1970.

2. LOWEST TEMPERATURE: A temperature of −126.9°F was recorded at Vostok Station, a Soviet research outpost in Antarctica. (Novosti Press Agency)

3. POLE OF COLD STATION: Polus Nedostupnosti, where Soviet researchers conduct experiments in temperatures that average −72°F annually.

4. WINDIEST PLACE: The Commonwealth Bay Station in the Antarctic on the George V Coast where gales of 200 mph are measured. (Dept of Supply, UK)

Thickest Ice

The greatest recorded thickness of ice on the earth's surface is 2.97 miles (15,670 ft) measured by radio echo soundings from a US Antarctic Research aircraft at 69° 9′ 38″ S 135° 20′ 25″ E in Wilkes Land on Jan 4, 1975.

Deepest Permafrost

The deepest recorded permafrost is more than 4,500 ft, reported from the upper reaches of the Viluy River, Siberia, USSR, in Feb 1982.

Lightning

The visible length of lightning strokes varies greatly. In mountainous regions, when clouds are very low, the flash may be less than 300 ft long. In flat country with very high clouds, a cloud-to-earth flash may measure 4 miles, though in the most extreme cases such flashes have been measured at 20 miles.

The speed of a lightning discharge varies from 100 to 1,000 miles per sec for the downward leader track, and reaches up to 87,000 miles per sec (nearly half the speed of light) for the powerful return stroke.

Every few million strokes there is a giant discharge, in which the cloud-to-earth and the return lightning strokes flash from and to the top of the thunder clouds.

Waterspouts

The highest waterspout of which there is reliable record was one observed May 16, 1898, off Eden, NSW Australia. A theodolite reading from the shore gave its height as 5,014 ft. It was about 10 ft in diameter.

Most Intense Rainfall

Difficulties attend rainfall readings for very short periods but the figure of 1.50 in in 1 min at Barst, Guadeloupe, Nov 26, 1970, is regarded as the most intense recorded in modern times. The cloudburst of "near two foot in less than a quarter of half an hour" at Oxford, England, on the afternoon of May 31 (Old Style), 1682, is regarded as unacademically recorded.

Cloud Extremes

The highest standard cloud form is cirrus, averaging 27,000 ft and above, but the rare nacreous or mother-of-pearl formation sometimes reaches nearly 80,000 ft. The lowest is stratus, below 3,500 ft. The cloud form with the greatest vertical range is cumulonimbus, which has been observed to reach a height of nearly 68,000 ft in the tropics.

Mirages

The largest mirage on record was that sighted in the Arctic at 83° N., 103° W. by Donald B. MacMillan in 1913. This type of mirage, known as the Fata Morgana, appeared as the same "hills, valleys, snow-capped peaks extending through at least 120 degrees of the horizon" that Peary had misidentified as Crocker Land 6 years earlier.

On July 17, 1939, a mirage of Snaefell Jokull glacier (4,715 ft) on Iceland was seen from the sea at a distance of 335–350 miles.

Longest-Lasting Rainbow

A rainbow lasting for over 3 hours was reported from North Wales on Aug 14, 1979.

OTHER WEATHER RECORDS

Hottest Place (Annual mean): Dallol, Ethiopia, 94°F, 1960–66.
In Death Valley, Calif, 120°F or more were recorded on 43 consecutive days, July 6–Aug 17, 1917. At Marble Bar, W Australia (maximums 121°F) maximum over 100°F for 160 consecutive days Oct 31, 1923–Apr 7, 1924.

Coldest Place (Extrapolated annual mean): Polus Nedostupnosti, Pole of Cold (78°S., 96°E.), Antarctica, −72°F (16°F lower than Pole). (Coldest measured mean): Plateau Station, Antarctica −70°F.

Greatest Rainfall (24 hours): 73.62 in, Cilaos, La Réunion, Indian Ocean, March 15–16, 1952. (Calendar month): 366.14 in, Cherrapunji, Meghalaya, India, July, 1861. (12 months): 1,041.78 in, Cherrapunji, Meghalaya, Aug 1, 1860–July 31, 1861.

Greatest Snowfall (24 hours): 76 in, Silver Lake, Colo, Apr 14–15; 1921. (12 months): 1,224.5 in, Paradise, Mt Rainier, Wash, Feb 19, 1971–Feb 18, 1972. (Single): 189 in, Mt Shasta Ski Bowl, Calif. (Greatest depth): 25 ft 5 in at Paradise, Mt Rainier, Wash, Apr 1972.

Maximum Sunshine (Year): 97% (over 4,300 hours), eastern Sahara. 768 consecutive days, Feb 9, 1967–March 17, 1969, St Petersburg, Fla.

Minimum Sunshine: Nil at North Pole—for winter stretches of 186 days.

LIGHTNING SPEED: Flashes travel from 100 to 1,000 miles per sec downward and can reach up to 87,000 miles per sec upward.

Barometric Pressure (Highest): 1,083.8 mb (32 in), Agata, Siberia, USSR, (alt. 862 ft) Dec 31, 1968. (Lowest): 870 mb (25.69 in), 300 miles west of Guam in the Pacific Ocean on Oct 12, 1979 by the US Air Weather Service. The USS *Repose,* a hospital ship, recorded 856 mb (25.55 in) in the eye of a typhoon off Okinawa on Sept 16, 1945.

Highest Surface Wind-speed: 231 mph, Mt Washington (6,288 ft), NH, Apr 12, 1934. 280 mph in a tornado at Wichita Falls, Tex, Apr 2, 1958.

Thunder Days (Year): 322 days, Bogor (formerly Buitenzorg), Java, Indonesia (average, 1916–19). Between Lat 35° N and 35° S there are some 3,200 thunderstorms each 12 nighttime hours, some of which can be heard at a range of 18 miles.

Wettest Place (Annual mean): Mt Waialeale (5,148 ft), Kauai, Hawaii, 451 in (average, 1920–72). In 1948, max 621 in.

Driest Place (Annual mean): Calama, in the Desierto de Atacama, near Calama, Chile. None.

Longest Drought: *c.* 400 years to 1971, Desierto de Atacama, near Calama, Chile.

Most Rainy Days (Year): Mt Waialeale, Kauai, Hawaii, up to 350 days per year.

Largest Hailstones: 1.67 lb (7½ in diameter, 17½ in circumference), Coffeyville, Kans, Sept 3, 1970. An ice block of coalesced hailstones 35–70 oz reported at Manchester, Eng, Apr 2, 1973. The *Canton Evening News* (Ohio) reported on Apr 14, 1981 that 5 were killed and

225 injured recently by a hailstorm with stones weighing up to 30 lb.

Longest Sea Level Fogs (Visibility less than 1,000 yd): Fogs persist for weeks on the Grand Banks, Newfoundland, Canada, and the average is more than 120 days per year.

Windiest Place: The Commonwealth Bay, George V Coast, Antarctica, where gales reach 200 mph.

Chapter 4
The Universe & Space

Light-Year

That distance traveled by light (speed 186,282.397 miles per sec, or 670,616,629.4 mph, *in vacuo*) in one tropical (or solar) year (365.24219878 mean solar days at Jan 0, 12 hours Ephemeris time in 1900 AD) and is 5,878,499,814,000 miles. The unit was first used in March 1888.

Magnitude

A measure of stellar brightness such that the light of a star of any magnitude bears a ratio of 2.511886 to that of a star of the next magnitude. Thus a fifth magnitude star is 2.511886 times as bright, while one of the first magnitude is exactly 100 (or 2.511886^5) times as bright, as a sixth magnitude star. In the case of such exceptionally bright bodies as Sirius, Venus, the moon (magnitude −11.2) or the sun (magnitude −26.7), the magnitude is expressed as a minus quantity.

Proper Motion

That component of a star's motion in space which, at right angles to the line of sight, constitutes an apparent change of position of the star in the celestial sphere.

The universe is the entirety of space, matter and antimatter. An appreciation of its magnitude is best grasped by working outward from the earth, through the solar system and our own Milky Way galaxy, to the remotest extra-galactic nebulae and quasars.

Meteor Shower

Meteoroids are mostly of cometary or asteroidal origin. A meteor is the light phenomenon caused by entry of a meteoroid into earth's atmosphere. The greatest meteor "shower" on record occurred on the night of Nov 16–17, 1966, when the Leonid meteors (which recur every 33¼ years) were visible between western North America and eastern USSR. It was calculated that meteors passed over Arizona at a rate of 2,300 per min for a period of 20 min from 5 a.m. Nov 17, 1966.

Oldest and Largest Meteorites

It was reported in Aug 1978 that dust grains in the Murchison meteorite which fell in Australia in Sept 1969 predate the formation of the solar system.

When a meteoroid penetrates to the earth's surface, the remnant is described as a meteorite. This occurs about 150 times per year over the whole land surface of the earth. The largest known meteorite is one found in 1920 at Hoba West, near Grootfontein in southwest Africa. This is a block of about 9 ft long by 8 ft broad, weighing 132,000 lb.

The largest meteorite exhibited by any museum is the "Tent" meteorite, weighing 68,085 lb, found in 1897 near Cape York, on the west coast of Green-

LARGEST STONY METEORITE: The Jilin, which hit China in 1976, weighed 3,902 lb and was part of a shower.

"Astronomy Facts and Feats" by Patrick Moore, a Guinness Superlatives Book (Sterling), contains more information on the subjects covered in this chapter.

land, by the expedition of Commander (later Rear-Admiral) Robert Edwin Peary (1856–1920). It was known to the Eskimos as the Abnighito and is now exhibited in the Hayden Planetarium in NYC.

The largest piece of stony meteorite recovered is a piece of 3,902 lb which was part of a shower that struck Jilin (formerly Kirin), China, March 8, 1976. The oldest dated meteorites are from the Allende Fall over Chihuahua, Mexico, Feb 8, 1969, dating back 4,610 million years.

There was a mysterious explosion of 12½ megatons at Lat. 60° 55′ N., Long. 101° 57′ E., in the basin of the Podkamennaya Tunguska River, 40 miles north of Vanavar, in Siberia, USSR at 00 hrs 17 min 11 sec UT June 30, 1908. The cause was variously attributed to a meteorite (1927), a comet (1930), a nuclear explosion (1961) and to antimatter (1965). This devastated an area of about 1,500 sq mi, and the shock was felt more than 600 miles away. The theory is now favored that this was the terminal flare of stony debris from a comet, possibly Encke's Comet, at an altitude of less than 20,000 ft. A similar event may have occurred over the Isle of Axeholm, Lincolnshire, England, a few thousand years before.

Largest Craters

It has been estimated that some 2,000 asteroid-earth collisions have occurred in the last 600 million years. A total of 96 collision sites or astroblemes have been recognized. A crater 150 miles across and a half mile deep has been postulated in Wilkes Land, Antarctica, since 1962. It would have been caused by a 14,560 million-ton meteorite striking at 44,000 mph. In Dec 1970 USSR scientists reported an astrobleme in the basin of the Popigai River with a 60-mile diameter and a maximum depth of 1,300 ft. There is a possible crater-like formation or astrobleme 275 miles in diameter on the eastern shore of Hudson Bay, where the Nastapoka Islands are just off the coast.

The largest proven crater is the Coon Butte or Barringer Crater, discovered in 1891 near Canyon Diablo, Winslow, northern Ariz. It is 4,150 ft in diameter and now about 575 ft deep, with a parapet rising 130–155 ft above the surrounding plain. It has been estimated that an iron-nickel mass with a diameter of 200–260 ft, and weighing about 2,240,000 tons, gouged this crater c. 25,000 BC.

Evidence was published in 1963 discounting a meteoric origin for the crypto-volcanic Vredefort Ring (diameter 26 miles) to the southwest of Johannesburg, South Africa, but this claim has now been reasserted.

The New Quebec (formerly the Chubb) "Crater," first sighted June 20, 1943, in northern Ungava, Canada, is 1,325 ft deep and measures 6.8 miles around its rim.

Fireball

The brightest fireball ever recorded photographically was one observed over Sumava, Czechoslovakia, Dec 4, 1974, by Dr Zdeněk Ceplecha, which had a momentary magnitude of −22, or 10,000 times brighter than a full moon.

Tektites

The largest tektite of which details have been published was one of 7.04 lb found in 1932 at Muong Nong, Saravane Province, Laos, and now in the Paris Museum.

Aurorae

Polar lights, known since 1560 as Aurora Borealis or Northern Lights in the northern hemisphere and since 1773 as Aurora Australis in the southern hemisphere, are caused by electrical solar discharges in the upper atmosphere and occur most frequently in high latitudes. Aurorae are visible at some time on *every* clear dark night in the polar areas within 20° latitude of the magnetic poles.

The extreme height of aurorae has been measured at 620 miles, while the lowest may descend to 45 miles.

Reliable figures exist only from 1952. Extreme cases of displays in very low latitudes were those reported at Cuzco, Peru (Aug 2, 1744); Honolulu, Hawaii (Sept 1, 1859); and, questionably, Singapore (Sept 25, 1909).

THE MOON

The earth's closest neighbor in space and only natural satellite is the moon, at a mean distance of 238,855 statute miles center to center or 233,812 miles surface to surface. In the present century the closest approach (smallest perigee) was 216,398 miles surface-to-surface or 221,441 miles center-to-center on Jan 4, 1912, and the farthest distance (largest apogee) will be 247,675 miles surface-to-surface or 252,718 miles center-to-center on Mar 2, 1984. It has a diameter of 2,159.3 miles and a mass of 7.23×10^{19} long tons with a mean density of 3.34. The average orbital speed is 2,287 mph.

LARGEST PROVEN CRATER ON EARTH (above): The Coon Butte or Barringer Crater near Winslow, Ariz is almost a mile wide and 575 ft deep. It was gouged out of the desert in about 25,000 BC. (Photo Reportage, Ltd)

FAMOUS FOOTSTEP (right): The first step onto the moon left this print in the dust. Neil Armstrong, astronaut, had a quote prepared: "That's one small step for a man, one giant leap for mankind." (NASA)

CRATERS ON THE FAR SIDE OF THE MOON (below): Never seen on earth, the hidden side was first photographed by a Soviet space probe in 1959.

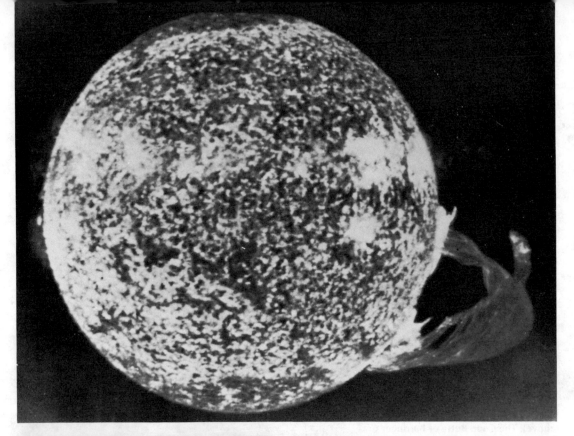

SOLAR ERUPTION (above): This flare on the surface of the sun spanned more than 365,000 miles. It occurred on Dec 19, 1973, and was the largest prominence ever observed.

HALLEY'S COMET (left) is due to be sighted from earth in Dec 1984. This will be its 33rd sighting on earth. The first appearance was in 467 BC. Edmund Halley (below) was the first to correctly predict its return—Christmas Day, 1758, some 16 years after his death. (Photo from NASA)

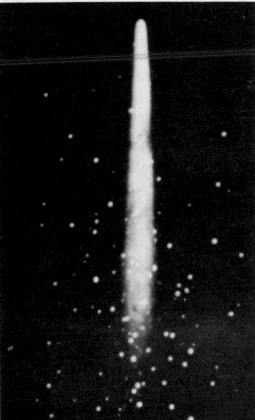

The first direct hit on the moon was achieved at 2 min 24 sec after midnight (Moscow time) Sept 14, 1959, by the Soviet space probe *Lunik II* near the *Mare Serenitatis*. The first photographic images of the hidden side were collected by the USSR's *Lunik III* from 6:30 a.m. Oct 7, 1959, from a range of up to 43,750 miles, and transmitted to the earth from a distance of 292,000 miles. The first "soft" landing was made by the USSR's *Luna IX* in the area of the Ocean of Storms Feb 3, 1966.

Largest and Deepest Craters

Only 59% of the moon's surface is directly visible from the earth because it is in "captured rotation," *i.e.,* the period of rotation is equal to the period of orbit. The largest wholly visible crater is the walled plain Bailly, toward the moon's South Pole, which is 183 miles across, with walls rising to 14,000 ft. Partly on the averted side, the Orientale Basin measures more than 600 miles in diameter.

The deepest crater is the moon's Newton crater, with a floor estimated to be between 23,000 and 29,000 ft below its rim and 14,000 ft below the level of the plain outside. The brightest directly visible spot on the moon is *Aristarchus.*

Highest Moon Mountains

As there is no sea level on the moon, the heights of lunar mountains can be measured only in relation to an adopted reference sphere with a radius of 1,079.943 miles. Thus the greatest elevation attained on this basis by any of the 12 US astronauts has been 25,688 ft, on the Descartes Highlands, by Capt John Watts Young, USN, and Major Charles M. Duke, Jr, Apr 27, 1972.

"Blue Moon"

Owing to sulphur particles in the upper atmosphere from a forest fire covering 250,000 acres between Mile 103 and Mile 119 on the Alaska Highway in northern British Columbia, Canada, the moon took on a bluish color, as seen from Great Britain, on the night of Sept 26, 1950. The moon appeared green after the Krakatoa eruption of Aug 27, 1883 (see *Volcanoes*) and in Stockholm for 3 min Jan 17, 1884.

Moon Samples

The age attributed to the oldest of the moon material brought back to earth by the *Apollo* program crews has been soil dated to 4,720 million years.

Temperature Extremes on the Moon

When the sun is overhead, the temperature on the lunar equator reaches 243 °F (31 °F above the boiling point of water). By sunset the temperature is 58 °F, but after nightfall it sinks to −261 °F.

THE SUN

The earth's 66,620 mph orbit of 584,017,800 miles around the sun is elliptical; hence our distance from the sun varies. The orbital speed varies between 65,520 mph (minimum) and 67,750 mph. The average distance of the sun is 1.000000230 astronomical units or 92,955,829 miles. The closest approach (perihelion) is 91,402,000 miles, and the farthest departure (aphelion) is 94,510,000 miles. The solar system is revolving around the center of the Milky Way once in each 225 million years at a speed of 481,000 mph and has a velocity of 42,500 mph relative to stars in our immediate region such as Vega, toward which it is moving.

Sun's Temperature and Dimensions

The sun has an internal temperature of about 16,000,000K (K stands for the Kelvin absolute scale of temperatures), a core pressure of 560 million tons per sq in (7.7 PPa) and uses up nearly 4½ million tons of hydrogen per sec, thus providing a luminosity of 3×10^{27} candlepower, with an intensity of 1½ million candles per sq in. The sun has the stellar classification of a "yellow dwarf" and, although its density is only 1.407 times that of water, its mass is 332,946 times as much as that of the earth. It has a mean diameter of 865,270 miles. The sun with a mass of 2.096×10^{27} tons represents more than 99% of the total mass of the solar system.

Largest and Most Frequent Sunspots

To be visible to the *protected* naked eye, a sunspot must cover about one two-thousandth part of the sun's disc and thus have an area of about 500 million sq mi. The largest recorded sunspot occurred in the sun's southern hemisphere on Apr 8, 1947. Its area was about 7,000 million sq mi, with an extreme longitude of 187,000 miles and an extreme latitude of 90,000 miles. Sunspots appear darker because they are more than 1,500 °C cooler than the rest of the sun's surface temperature of 5,525 °C. The largest observed solar prominence was one protruding 365,000 miles, photographed on Dec 19, 1973 during the third and final Skylab mission.

In Oct 1957 a smoothed sunspot count showed 263, the highest recorded index since records started in 1755 (*cf.* previous record of 239 in May 1778). In 1943 a sunspot lasted for 200 days from June to Dec.

Earliest Recorded Eclipses

The earliest extrapolated eclipses that have been identified are 1361 BC (lunar) and Oct 2136 BC (solar). For the Middle East only, lunar eclipses have been extrapolated to 3450 BC and solar eclipses to 4200 BC.

TOTAL ECLIPSE: The sun covered by the moon is the most spectacular natural phenomenon.

Longest Eclipse Duration

The maximum possible duration of an eclipse of the sun is 7 min 31 sec. The longest actually *measured* was June 20, 1955 (7 min 8 sec), seen from the Philippines. That of July 16, 2186 in the mid-Atlantic should last 7 min 29 sec. This will be the longest for 1,469 years. Durations can be extended by observers being airborne, as on June 30, 1973 when an eclipse was "extended" to 72 min for observers aboard a *Concorde* jet. An annular eclipse may last for 12 min 24 sec. The longest totality of any lunar eclipse is 104 min. This has occurred many times.

Most and Least Frequent Eclipses

The highest number of eclipses possible in a year is seven, as in 1935, when there were five solar and two lunar eclipses; or four solar and three lunar eclipses, as will occur in 1982. The lowest possible number in a year is two, both of which must be solar, as in 1944 and 1969.

Earliest Recorded Comets

The earliest records of comets date from the 7th century BC. The speeds of the estimated 2,000,000 comets vary from 700 mph in outer space to 1,250,000 mph when near the sun.

The successive appearances of Halley's Comet have been traced back to 467 BC. It was first depicted in the Nuremberg Chronicle of 684 AD. The first prediction of its return by Edmund Halley (1656–1742) proved true on Christmas Day, 1758, 16 years after his death. Its next perihelion should be at 9:30 p.m. Greenwich Mean Time Feb 9, 1986, exactly 75.81 years after the last, which was Apr 19, 1910. *The 33rd sighting may occur as early as Dec 1984.*

Closest Comet Approach

On July 1, 1770 Lexell's Comet, traveling at a speed of 23.9 miles per sec (relative to the sun), came within 745,000 miles of the earth. However, the earth is believed to have passed through the tail of Halley's Comet, most recently on May 19, 1910.

Largest Comets

Comets are so tenuous that it has been estimated that even the head of one rarely contains solid matter much greater than 0.6 mile in diameter. The tails, as in the case of the brightest of all, the Great Comet of 1843, may trail for 205 million miles. The head of Holmes Comet of 1892 once measured 1½ million miles in diameter.

Comet Bennett which appeared in Jan 1970 was found to be enveloped in a hydrogen cloud measuring some 8 million miles long.

Shortest and Longest Comet Period

Of all the recorded periodic comets (these are members of the solar system), the one which most frequently returns is Encke's Comet, first identified in 1786. Its period of 1,206 days (3.3 years) is the shortest established. Not one of its 51 returns (to the end of 1977) has been missed by astronomers. Now increasingly faint, it is expected to "die" by Feb 1994. The most frequently observed comets are Schwassmann-Wachmann I, Kopff and Oterma, which can be observed every year between Mars and Jupiter.

At the other extreme is Delavan's Comet of 1914, whose path has not been accurately determined. It is not expected to return for perhaps 24 million years.

PLANETS

Planets (including the earth) are bodies within the solar system which revolve around the sun in definite orbits.

Largest, Fastest and Hottest Planets

Jupiter, with an equatorial diameter of 88,846 miles and a polar diameter of 83,082 miles, is the largest of the nine major planets, with a mass 317.83 times and a volume 1,321.4 times that of the earth. It also has the shortest period of rotation, with a "day" of only 9 hours 50 min 30.003 sec in its equatorial zone.

Mercury, which orbits the sun at an average distance of 35,983,100 miles, has a period of revolution of 87.9686 days, so giving the highest average speed in orbit of 107,030 mph.

A surface temperature of 864°F has been estimated from measurements made from Venus by the USSR probes *Venera 7* and US *Pioneer* Cytherean surface probes. Venus has a canyon 4 miles deep and 250 miles long, 1,000 miles south of the Venusian equator.

Smallest and Coldest Planets

The smallest and coldest planets, Pluto and its partner Charon (announced on June 22, 1978), have an estimated surface temperature of −360°F (100°F above absolute zero). Their mean distance from the sun is 3,674,488,000 miles and their period of revolution is 248.54 years. Pluto's diameter is about 1,880 miles and it has a mass about 1/500th that of the earth. Pluto was first recorded by Clyde William Tombaugh (b Feb 4, 1906) at Lowell Observatory, Flagstaff, Ariz Feb 18, 1930 from photographs taken on Jan 23 and 29, and announced on March 13. Because of its orbital eccentricity, Pluto will be closer to the sun than Neptune between Jan 23, 1979 and March 15, 1999.

Nearest Planet to Earth

The fellow planet closest to the earth is Venus, which is, at times, about 25,700,000 miles inside the earth's orbit, compared with Mars' closest approach of 34,600,000 miles outside the earth's orbit. Mars, known since 1965 to be cratered, has temperatures ranging from 85°F to −190°F.

Planet Features

By far the highest and most spectacular surface feature is Olympus Mons (formerly Nix Olympica) in the Tharsis region of Mars, with a diameter of 310–370 miles and a height of 75,450–95,150 ft above the surrounding plain.

Viewed from earth, by far the brightest of the five

SIGHTING MARS: This global mosaic, made from more than 1,500 computer-corrected TV pictures taken by Mariner IX in 1971 and 1972, showed the North Pole ice cap and proved the existence of many craters but no canals. (NASA)

planets visible to the naked eye is Venus, with a maximum magnitude of −4.4. The faintest is Pluto, with a magnitude of 15. Uranus at magnitude 5.5 is only marginally visible.

Earth is the densest planet with an average figure of 5.515 times that of water, while Saturn has an average density only about one-eighth of this value or 0.687 times that of water.

The planet with the longest "day" or period of rotation is Venus, which spins on its axis once every 243.16 days, so its "day" is longer than its "year" (224.7007 days). The shortest "day" is that of Jupiter (see *Largest Planet*).

The most dramatic recorded conjunction (coming together) of the seven principal members of the solar system besides the earth (sun, moon, Mercury, Venus, Mars, Jupiter and Saturn) occurred on Feb 5, 1962, when 16° covered all seven during an eclipse. It is possible that the seven-fold conjunction of Sept 1186 spanned only 12°. The next notable conjunction will take place May 5, 2000.

Largest Asteroids

In the belt which lies between Mars and Jupiter, there are some 45,000 (only 2,614 numbered as of Apr 1982) minor planets or asteroids which are, for the most part, too small to yield to diameter measurement. The largest and first discovered (by G. Piazzi at Palermo, Sicily, Jan 1, 1801) of these is

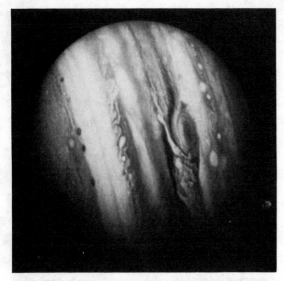

LARGEST PLANET: Jupiter, with an equatorial diameter of 88,846 miles and a volume 1,321.4 times that of the earth, is the largest planet in the solar system. Visible at the lower right is Ganymede, the largest and heaviest satellite in the solar system. This photo was taken by Voyager 1 on Jan 24, 1979, from more than 25 million miles away. (NASA)

Ceres, with a diameter of 637 miles. The only one visible to the naked eye is asteroid 4 *Vesta* (diameter 345 miles), discovered March 29, 1807 by Dr Heinrich Wilhelm Olbers (1758–1840), a German amateur astronomer. The closest measured approach to the earth by an asteroid was 485,000 miles, in the case of *Hermes* on Oct 30, 1937 (asteroid now lost).

The most distant detected is 2060 *Chiron,* found between Saturn and Uranus Oct 18–19, 1977, by Charles Kowal from the Hale Observatory, Calif.

Largest and Smallest Satellites

The largest and heaviest satellite is *Ganymede* (Jupiter III) which is 2.02 times heavier than our moon and has a diameter of 3,270 miles.

The smallest satellite is *Leda* (Jupiter XIII) with a diameter of less than 9 miles.

Most Satellites

Of the nine major planets, all but Venus and Mercury have known natural satellites. The planet with the most is Saturn with at least 21 satellites. The earth and Pluto are the only planets with a single satellite. The distance of the solar system's known satellites from their parent planets varies from the 5,827

miles of *Phobos* from the center of Mars to the 14,730,000 miles of Jupiter's outer satellite *Sinope* (Jupiter IX). The solar system has a total of at least 48 satellites.

STARS

Largest and Most Massive Stars

The most massive star is the faint-blue R 136a in the Tarantula Nebula (or 30 Doradus), an appendage of the Lesser Magellanic Cloud, announced on Jan 19, 1981 and believed to be of 3,500 solar masses and 150,000 light-years distant. Betelgeux (at top left in the constellation Orion) has a diameter of more than 250 million miles, and in 1978 was found to be surrounded by a tenuous "shell" of potassium of 1.6 million million miles (11,000 astronomical units). The light from Betelgeux which reaches the earth today left the star in 1460 AD.

Smallest Stars

The least massive stars known are the two components of the binary star *Wolf 424,* a faint star in the constellation Virgo. Each of the two stars has only 0.06 solar masses.

Farthest Star

The solar system, with its sun, nine principal planets, 43 satellites, asteroids and comets, was estimated in 1921 to be about 32,000 light-years from the center of the lens-shaped Milky Way galaxy (diameter 100,000 light-years) of about 100,000 million stars. The most distant star in our galaxy was therefore estimated to be about 80,000 light-years distant.

A recalibration published in 1980, however, indicates that our galaxy has a diameter of *c.* 70,000 light-years only, with the most distant star less than 60,000 light-years away.

Nearest Stars

Excepting the special case of our own sun, the nearest star is the very faint *Proxima Centauri,* which is 4.22 light-years (24,800,000 million miles) away. The nearest star visible to the naked eye is the southern hemisphere star *Alpha Centauri,* or *Rigel Kentaurus* (4.35 light-years), with a magnitude of −0.29. By 11,800 AD, the nearest star will be Barnard's Star (see *Stellar Planets*) at a distance of 3.75 light-years.

Brightest Star

Sirius A (*Alpha Canis Majoris*), also known as the Dog Star, is apparently the brightest star of the 5,776 stars visible in the heavens, with an apparent magnitude of −1.46. It is in the constellation *Canis Major* and is visible in the winter months of the northern hemisphere, being due south at midnight on the last day of the year. The Sirius system is 8.64 light-years distant and has a luminosity 26 times as much as that of the sun. It has a diameter of 1,450,000 miles and a mass of 4.704×10^{27} (4,704 septillion) tons. The faint white dwarf companion star Sirius B has a diameter of only 6,000 miles but is 350,000 times heavier than the earth.

Most and Least Luminous Stars

If all stars could be viewed at the same distance, the most luminous would be the apparently faint variable *S. Doradûs,* in the Greater Magellanic Cloud (*Nebecula Major*), which can be nearly one million times brighter than the sun, and has an absolute magnitude of −8.9. The variable *η Carinae* in *c.* 1840 was perhaps 4 million times more luminous than the sun. The faintest star detected visually is a very red star, known as LP 425–140, which is 23.5 light-years distant, with about one-millionth of the sun's brightness.

Longest Name for a Star

The longest name for any star is *Shurnarkabtisha-shutu,* which is Arabic for "under the southern horn of the bull."

Constellations

The largest of the 89 constellations is *Hydra* (the Sea Serpent) which covers 1,302.844 sq degrees or 6.3% of the hemisphere and contains at least 68 stars visible to the naked eye (to 5.5 mag.). The constellation *Centaurus* (Centaur), ranking ninth in area, embraces, however, at least 94 such stars. The smallest constellation is *Crux Australis* (Southern Cross) with an area of 68.477 sq degrees compared with the 41,252.96 sq degrees of the whole sky.

Brightest Super-Nova

Super-novae, or temporary "stars" which flare and then fade, occur perhaps five times in 1,000 years in our galaxy. The brightest "star" ever seen by historic man is believed to be the super-nova SN 1006 in Apr 1006 near *Lupus β* which flared for 2 years and attained a magnitude of −9 to −10. It is now believed to be the radio source G.327.6 + 14.5, nearly 3,000 light-years distant.

Stellar Planets

Planetary companions, with a mass of less than 7% of their parent star, have been reported for 61 *Cygni* (1942), *Lalande 21185* (1960), *Krüger 60, Ci 2354, BD + 20° 2465* and one of the two components of 70 *Ophiuchi.*

A planet with 6 times the mass of Jupiter, 750 million miles from *Epsilon Eridani,* was reported by Peter van de Kamp in Jan 1973.

In Aug 1975, van de Kamp reported that Barnard's Star (Munich 15040) possibly had two planets equivalent in mass to Jupiter and Saturn.

Listening operations ("Project Ozma") on *Tau Ceti* and *Epsilon Eridani* were maintained from Apr 4, 1960 to March 1961, using an 85-ft radio telescope at Deer Creek Valley, Green Bank, W Va. The apparatus was probably insufficiently sensitive for any signal from a distance of 10.7 light-years to be received. Monitoring has been conducted from Gorkiy, USSR, since 1969.

Black Holes

The first tentative identification of a Black Hole was announced in Dec 1972 in the binary-star X-ray source Cygnus X-1. This is a small, dark companion of some 10 solar masses, from which the escape velocity tends to c (the velocity of light). The critical size has been estimated to be as low as a diameter of 3.67 miles. In early 1978 supermassive Black Holes were suggested with a mass of 100 million suns— 2×10^{35} metric tons.

THE UNIVERSE

Outside the Milky Way galaxy, which is part of the so-called Local Group of galaxies moving toward the Virgo cluster 50 million light-years distant, at a speed estimated to be between 450,000 and 1,100,000 mph, there exist 10,000 million other galaxies. These range in size up to the largest known object in the universe, the radio galaxy 3C-345, announced from Effelsberg, near Bonn, West Germany in March 1980, which is 78 million light-years across. It is estimated to be 5,000 million light-years distant.

Farthest Visible Object

The remotest heavenly body visible to the naked eye is the Great Galaxy in *Andromeda* (Mag. 3.47) known as Messier 31. This is a rotating nebula of spiral form, its distance from the earth about 2,120,000 light-years, or about 12,500,000,000,000,000,000 miles, and it is moving toward us.

It is just possible, however, that, under ideal seeing conditions, Messier 33, the Spiral in Triangulum (Mag. 5.79), can be glimpsed by the naked eye of keen-sighted people at a distance of 2,360,000 light-years.

"Quasars"

In Nov 1962 the existence of quasi-stellar radio sources ("quasars" or QSO's) was established by Maarten Schmidt with 3C-273 with a red shift of $z = 0.158$. Quasars have immensely high luminosity for bodies so distant and of such small diameter. In Apr 1975 it was announced that 3C–279 had a measured luminosity of 2.75×10^{14} times that of the sun. The first double quasar (0957 + 56) among the 1,500 known was announced in May 1980.

"Pulsars"

The earliest observation of a pulsating radio source of "pulsar" CP 1919 by Dr Jocelyn Bell Burnell was announced from the Mullard Radio Astronomy Observatory, Cambridgeshire, England, on Feb 29, 1968. The 100th was announced from Jodrell Bank, England in June 1973. The fastest so far discovered is NP 0532 in the Crab Nebula with a pulse period of 33 milliseconds. It is now accepted that pulsars are rotating neutron stars with an inner core density of 74,400 million metric tons per cu in.

Remotest Object

The interpretation of very large red shifts exhibited by quasars remains controversial. The record value of $z = 3.78$ for Quasar PKS 2000-330 has been interpreted as indicating proximity to the maximum presently acceptable distance (the observable horizon) of 16,500 million light-years or 9.7×10^{21} miles. The most distant known galaxy 3C-427, which has a red shift of 1.175, was announced in Mar 1981. The 3° background radiation or primordial hiss discovered in 1965 by Arno Penzias and Robert Wilson of Bell Laboratories appears to be moving at a velocity of 99.9998% of the speed of light.

Age of the Universe

For the age of the universe a consistent value of 14½ ± 2 eons or gigayears (an eon or gigayear being 1 billion years) is obtained from cosmochronology (Schramm 1978) and nucleochronology (Winters and Macklin 1982). A reliable value cannot be estimated from the Hubble ratio method since reported values vary between 40 and 110 km/s/Mpc, equivalent to a universe age of between 8 and 25 eons. The value of 14½ eons is equivalent to a Hubble ration of 60 km/s/Mpc.

ROCKETRY AND MISSILES

War rockets, propelled by a charcoal-saltpeter-sulphur gunpowder, were described by Tsen Kung Liang of China in 1042. These early rockets became known in Europe by 1258.

The first launching of a liquid-fueled rocket (patented July 14, 1914) was by Dr Robert Hutchings Goddard (1882–1945) (US) at Auburn, Mass March 16, 1926, when his rocket reached an altitude of 41 ft and traveled a distance of 184 ft. The USSR's earliest rocket was the semi-liquid-fueled GIRD-IX tested Aug 17, 1933.

Longest Ranges

On March 16, 1962 Nikita Khrushchev, then Prime Minister of the USSR, claimed in Moscow that the USSR possessed a "global rocket" with a range of about 19,000 miles (more than half the earth's circumference), capable of hitting any target in the world from either direction.

Most Powerful Rocket

It has been suggested that the USSR lunar booster which blew up at Tyuratam in the summer (July ?) of 1969 had a thrust of 10–14 million lb. There is some evidence of a launch of a USSR "G" class lunar booster, larger than Saturn V, May 11, 1973.

The most powerful rocket that has been publicized is the Saturn V, used for the Project Apollo and Skylab programs, on which development began in Jan 1962 at the John F. Kennedy Space Center, Merritt Island, Fla. The rocket is 363 ft 8 in tall, with a payload of over 82 tons in the case of *Skylab I*, and gulps 15 tons of propellant per sec for 2½ min. Stage I (S-IC) is 138 ft tall and powered by five Rocketdyne F-1 engines, using liquid oxygen (LOX) and kero-

ROCKETRY

1. Dr. Robert Goddard and his invention, the liquid-fueled rocket. He blazed the trail for the space age when he launched this rocket on Mar 16, 1926.

2. The age of space travel began on Apr 12, 1961, when the USSR shot off the Vostok 1 with a man aboard.

3. The man was Yuriy Gagarin. Since then he was awarded all these medals.

4. Today's powerful Saturn V rockets are many times bigger and more powerful than Goddard ever conceived. Note the size of the man in the circle in this NASA photo fron Cape Canaveral.

sene, each delivering 1,514,000 lb thrust. Stage II (S-II) is powered by 5 LOX and liquid hydrogen Rocketdyne J-2 engines with a total thrust of 1,141,453 lb, while Stage III (designated S-IVB) is powered by a single 228,290-lb-thrust J-2 engine. The whole assembly generates 175,600,000 hp and weighs up to 7,600,000 lb when fully loaded, as in the case of *Apollo XVII*. Saturn V was first launched Nov 9, 1967 from Cape Canaveral (then Kennedy), Fla.

Highest Velocity Space Vehicles

The first space vehicle to achieve the Third Cosmic velocity sufficient to break out of the solar system was *Pioneer 10*. The Atlas SLV-3C launcher with a modified Centaur D second stage and a Thiokol Te-364-4 third stage left the earth at an unprecedented 32,114 mph March 2, 1972. The highest recorded velocity of any space vehicle has been 149,125 mph by the US-German solar probe *Helios B* launched Jan 15, 1976. By March 1983 *Pioneer 10* will cross the orbit of Neptune 2,845 million miles distant.

Highest Payload

Skylab I (launched May 14, 1973) fell on its 34,981st orbit of the earth over the Western Australian coast on July 11, 1979, thus leaving *Salyut 6* as the heaviest object in space. Large pieces of *Skylab I* were found 7.45 miles south of Rawlinna and sold to a Hong Kong syndicate. The piece which most worried keraunothnetophobes was a 5,175-lb airlock shroud.

Ion Rockets

Speeds of up to 100,000 mph are envisaged for rockets powered by an ion discharge. An ion thruster has been maintained for 9,715 hours (or 404 days 19 hours) at the Lewis Research Center in Cleveland, Ohio. Ion rockets were first used in flight by NASA's SERT I rocket, launched on July 20, 1964.

SPACE FLIGHT

See Chapter 11 for human achievements in space.
The physical laws controlling the flight of artificial satellites were first propounded by Sir Isaac Newton (1642–1727) in his *Philosophiae Naturalis Principia Mathematica* ('Mathematical Principles of Natural Philosophy'), begun in March 1686 and first published in the summer of 1687.

The first artificial satellite was successfully put into orbit at an altitude of 142/588 miles and a velocity of more than 17,750 mph from Tyuratam, a site located 170 miles east of the Aral Sea, on the night of Oct 4, 1957. This spherical satellite, *Sputnik* ("Fellow Traveler") 1, officially designated "Satellite 1957 Alpha 2," weighed 184.3 lb, with a diameter of 22.8 in, and its lifetime is believed to have been 92 days, ending on Jan 4, 1958. It was designed under the direction of Dr Sergey Pavlovich Korolyov (1907–66).

Largest Space Object

The heaviest object orbited is the *Apollo XV* (spacecraft plus third stage) which, prior to translunar injection in parking orbit, weighed 155.9 tons. The 442-lb US R.A.E. (radio astronomy explorer) B, or *Explorer 49,* launched on June 10, 1973, has antennae 1,500 ft from tip to tip.

Earliest Successful Manned Satellites

The first successful manned space flight began at 9:07 a.m. (Moscow time), or 6:07 a.m. G.M.T., Apr 12, 1961. Flight Major (later Colonel) Yuriy Alekseyevich Gagarin (b March 9, 1934) completed a single orbit of the earth in 89.34 min in the USSR's space vehicle *Vostok* ("East") 1 (10,416 lb). The take-off was from Tyuratam in Kazakhstan, and the landing was 108 min later near the village of Smelovka, near Engels, in the Saratov region of the USSR. The maximum speed was 17,560 mph and the maximum altitude 203.2 miles in a flight of 25,394.5 miles. Major Gagarin, invested a Hero of the Soviet Union and awarded the Order of Lenin and the Gold Star Medal, was killed in a jet plane crash near Moscow on March 27, 1968.

First Fatality in Space Flight

Col. Vladimir Mikhailovich Komarov (b March 16, 1927) was launched in *Soyuz* ("Union") 1 at 00:35 a.m. G.M.T. Apr 23, 1967. The spacecraft was in orbit for about 25½ hours before crashing on the final descent due to parachute failure. Komarov was thus the first man indisputably known to have died during space flight.

First Extra-Terrestrial Vehicles

The first wheeled vehicle landed on the moon was the Soviet *Lunokhod I* which began its earth-controlled travels on Nov 17, 1970. It moved a total of 6.54 miles on gradients up to 30° in the Mare Imbrium and did not become non-functioning until Oct 4, 1971.

The lunar speed and distance record was set by the *Apollo XVI* Rover with 11.2 mph and 22.4 miles.

Most Expensive Project

The total cost of the US manned space program up to and including the lunar mission of *Apollo XVII* has been estimated at $25,541,400,000. The cost of the USSR space program from 1958 to Sept 1973 has been estimated to have cost $45,000 million. The cost of the NASA Shuttle program was $9.9 billion to the launch of *Columbia* on Apr 12, 1981.

Closest Approach to the Sun

The research spacecraft *Helios B* approached within 27 million miles of the sun on Apr 16, 1976. It was carrying both US and West German instrumentation.

THE ELEMENTS

There are 94 known naturally occurring elements comprising, at ordinary temperatures, two liquids, 11 gases, 72 metals and 9 other solids. To date the discovery of a further 13 transuranic elements (Elements 95 to 107) has been claimed of which 9 are undisputed.

Category	Name	Symbol	Discovery of Element	Record
Commonest (lithosphere)	Oxygen	O	1771 Scheele (Germ-Swed)	46.60% by weight
Commonest (atmosphere)	Nitrogen	N	1772 Rutherford (GB)	78.09% by volume
Commonest (extra-terrestrial)	Hydrogen	H	1776 Cavendish (GB)	90% of all matter
Rarest (of the 94)	Astatine	At	1940 Corson (US) *et al.*	1/100th oz in earth's crust
Lightest	Hydrogen	H	1776 Cavendish (GB)	0.005612 lb/ft^3
Lightest (Metal)	Lithium	Li	1817 Arfwedson (Swed)	33.30 lb/ft^3
Densest[1]	Osmium	Os	1804 Tennant (GB)	1410 lb/ft^3
Heaviest (Gas)	Radon	Rn	1900 Dorn (Germ)	0.6274 lb/ft^3 at $0\,°C$
Newest[2]	Unnilseptium	Uns	1976 Oganesyan *et al.* (USSR)	highest atomic number (element 107)
Purest	Helium	^{4}He	1868 Lockyer (GB) and Jannsen (France)	2 parts in 10^{15} (1978)
Hardest	Carbon	C	— prehistoric	Diamond allotrope, Knoop value 8400
Most Expensive	Californium	Cf	1950 Seaborg (US) *et al.*	Sold in 1970 for $10 per μg
Most Stable[3]	Tellurium	^{128}Te	1782 von Reichenstein (Austro Hung)	Half-life of 1.5×10^{24} years
Least Stable	Lithium (isotope 5)	Li 5	1817 Arfwedson (Swed)	Lifetime of 4.4×10^{-22} sec.
Most Isotopes	Caesium	Cs	1860 Bunsen & Kirchoff (Germ)	35
	Xenon	Xe	1898 Ramsay and Travers (GB)	35
Least Isotopes	Hydrogen	H	1776 Cavendish (GB)	3 (confirmed)
Most Ductile	Gold	Au	*ante* 3000 BC	1 oz drawn to 43 miles
Highest Tensile Strength	Boron	B	1808 Gay-Lussac and Thenard (France)	3.9×10^6 lb f/in^2
Lowest Melting/Boiling Point[4]	Helium	^{4}He	1895 Ramsay (GB)	$-272.375\,°C$ under pressure 24.985 atm and $-268.928\,°C$
Highest Melting/Boiling Point	Tungsten	W	1783 J. J. & F. d'Elhuyar (Spain)	$3422\,°C$ and $5730\,°C$
Largest Expansion (negative)	Plutonium	Pu	1940 Seaborg (US) *et al.*	-5.8×10^{-5} cm/cm/deg C between 450–480 °C (Delta prime allotrope, disc. 1953)
Lowest Expansion (positive)	Carbon (diamond)	C	— prehistoric	1.0×10^{-6} cm/cm/deg C (at 20 °C)
Highest Expansion (metal)	Caesium	Cs	1860 Bunsen & Kirchoff (Germ)	9.7×10^{-5} cm/cm/deg C (at 20 °C)
Highest Expansion (solid)	Neon	Ne	1898 Ramsay and Travers (GB)	1.94×10^{-3} cm/cm/deg C at 248.59 °C
Most Toxic	Radium	^{224}Ra	1898 The Curies and Bemont (France)	naturally occurring isotope 17,000 × more toxic than plutonium 239

[1] Work published by Robert H. Crabtree (Yale University) in 1978 that while the specific gravity of Osmium is 22.59 ± 0.02 that of Iridium is 22.57 ± 0.01 i.e. the difference is smaller than the experimental error involved.
[2] Provisional IUPAC name. Evidence alleging the existence of Elements 116, 124 and 126 published on June 17, 1976 subsequently was declared to have been misconceived. Unnilhexium (Unh) or element 106 was identified by Ghiorso (US) *et al.* on Sept 9, 1974.
[3] Double beta decay estimate. Alpha particle record is Samarium 148 at 8×10^{15} years and Beta particle record is Cadmium 113 at 9×10^{15} years.
[4] Monatomic hydrogen H is expected to be a non-liquifiable superfluid gas.

For table of the 107 elements, chemical compounds and atomic tables, see the *Guinness Book of Essential Facts* (Sterling, 1979)

Chapter 5

The Scientific World

ELEMENTS

All known matter in, on, and beyond the earth is made up of chemical elements. It is estimated that there are 10^{87} electrons in the known universe. The total of naturally occurring elements so far detected is 94, comprising, at ordinary temperature, 2 liquids, 11 gases and 81 solids. The so-called "fourth state" of matter is plasma, when negatively charged electrons and positively charged ions are in flux.

Lightest and Heaviest Sub-Nuclear Particles

By Aug 1980 the existence of 24 "stable particles, 42 meson resonance triplets and 54 baryon resonance multiplets" was accepted, representing the possible eventual discovery of 224 particles and an equal number of anti-particles. The heaviest "stable" particle fully accepted is the charmed lambda baryon, symbol Λ_c^+, of mass 2273 ± 6 MeV and a lifetime of 7×10^{-13} seconds, first identified in Mar 1975 at the Brookhaven National Laboratory, New Upton, Long Island, NY. The heaviest particle known is the upsilon triple prime meson, symbol Υ''', of mass 10550 MeV, which consists of a bottom or beauty quark and its anti-quark, and which was first identified in April 1980 by two groups using the Cornell electron storage ring facilities at Cornell University, Ithaca, NY.

Sub-atomic concepts require that the masses of the graviton, photon, and neutrino should all be zero. Based on the sensitivities of various cosmological theories, upper limits for the masses of these particles are 7.6×10^{-67}g. for the graviton; 3.0×10^{-53}g. for the photon and 1.4×10^{-32}g. for the neutrino (cf. 9.10953×10^{-28}g. for the mass of an electron). The neutrino, so named by Enrico Fermi (1901–54), was postulated in 1931 by Wolfgang Pauli and discovered by Frederick Reines in 1956.

Newest Particle

In July–Aug 1980 two groups using the SPEAR electron storage ring facilities at the Stanford Linear Accelerator Center, Stanford University, Calif, announced the discovery of the charmed eta meson, symbol η_c, of mass 2980 MeV, which is the lowest ground-state of the combination of a charmed quark and its anti-quark.

Most and Least Stable Particles

In 1974 the proton was measured to be stable against decay for a lifetime in excess of 2×10^{30} years. Theoretical predictions under the "grand unified theory" suggest the lifetime of a proton may be less than 1×10^{34} years! The least stable or shortest-lived nuclear particles discovered are the four baryon resonances N (2600), N (3030), Δ (2850) and Δ (3230), all 1.6×10^{-24} sec.

Most Absorbent Substance

The US Dept of Agriculture Research Service announced on Aug 18, 1974 that "H-span" or Super Slurper, composed of one half starch derivative and one fourth each of acrylamide and acrylic acid, can, when treated with iron, retain water 1,300 times its own weight.

Smelliest Substance

The most evil-smelling substance, of the 17,000 smells so far classified, must be a matter of opinion, but ethyl mercaptan (C_2H_5SH) and butyl seleno-mercaptan (C_4H_9SeH) are powerful claimants, each with a smell reminiscent of a combination of rotting cabbage, garlic, onions and sewer gas.

Most Expensive Perfume

The retail prices of the most expensive perfumes tend to be fixed at public relations rather than economic levels. The most expensive fragrant ingredient in perfume is pure French middle note jasmine essence at $6,960 per kilo or $197 per oz. The key ingredient is muscone, a macrocyclic ketone, from natural musk oil, which in 1980 sold for $34,500 per kilo

CHEMICAL COMPOUNDS

It has been estimated that there are 4,040,000 described chemical compounds of which 63,000 are in common use (1978).

Most Refractory	Tantalum Carbide $TaC_{0.88}$	Melts at 4010° ± 75 deg C
Most Refractory (plastics)	Modified polymides	900 °F for short periods
Lowest Expansion	Invar metal (Ni-Fe alloy with C and Mn)	1.3×10^{-7} cm/cm/deg C at 20°C
Highest Tensile Strength	Sapphire whisker Al_2O_3	6×10^6 lb/in^2
Highest Tensile Strength (plastics)	Polyvinyl alcoholic fibres	1.4×10^5 lb f/in^2
Most Magnetic	Cobalt-copper-samarium Co_3Cu_2Sm	10,500 oersted coercive force
Least Magnetic alloy	Copper nickel alloy CuNi	963 parts Cu to 37 parts Ni
Most Pungent	Vanillaldehyde	Detectable at 2×10^{-8} mg/litre
Sweetest[1]	Talin from arils of katemfe (Thaumatococcus daniellii) discovered in W. Africa	6150 × as sweet as 1% sucrose
Bitterest	Bitrex or Benzyl diethyl ammonium benzoate	200 × as bitter as quinine sulphate
Most Acidic[2]	Perchloric acid ($HClO_4$)	pH value of normal solution tends to 0.
Most Alkaline	Caustic soda (NaOH) and potash (KOH) and tetramethylammonium hydroxide ($N(CH_3)_4OH$)	
Highest Specific Impulse	Hydrogen with liquid fluorine	447 lb f/sec/lb
Most Poisonous	Thiopentone (a barbiturate)	Intracardiac injection will kill in 1 to 2 sec
Highest Ductility in tension (max. superplasticity)	Pb38 Sn62	49½ times pre-stressed length by Ahmed and Langdon, Univ of S California, 1977

[1] Found in 1839, reported in 1852 but the protein thaumatin not isolated until 1972.
[2] The most powerful acid, assessed on its power as a hydrogen-ion donor, is a solution of antimony pentafluoride in fluorosulphonic acid—SbF_5 + FSO_3H. Concentrated hydrochloric acid HCL, an aqueous solution has a pH value tending to −1.

---

or $977.50 per oz. The most expensive perfume in the world is *De Berens No. 1* retailing at about $150 per ⅓ oz, depending on the international currency exchange rate.

Most Prescribed Drug

The top-selling prescription drug in the world is the anti-ulcer drug Tagamet which is marketed by Smithkline-Beckman of Philadelphia. The sales in 1981 were estimated at $800 million.

Most Potent Poison

The rickettsial disease, Q-fever, can be instituted by a *single* organism but is only fatal in 1 in 1,000

SWEETEST SUBSTANCE: Seeds from katemfe, the plants that exude the sweetest known substance—much sweeter than sugar.

cases. About 10 organisms of *Francisella tularenesis* (formerly known as *Pasteurella tularenesis*) can institute tularemia, variously called alkali disease, Francis disease or deerfly fever, and this is fatal in upwards of 10 cases in 1,000.

Most Powerful Nerve Gas

In the early 1950's, substances known as V-agents, notably VX, 300 times more toxic than phosgene ($COCl_2$) used in World War I, were developed at the Chemical Defence Experimental Establishment, Porton Down, Wiltshire, England. V-agents are lethal if 0.4 milligrams are inhaled by an adult. Patents were applied for in 1962 and published in Feb 1974.

Most Powerful Drugs

The most powerful commonly available drug is d-Lysergic Acid Diethylamide tartrate (LSD-25, $C_{20}H_{25}N_3O$) first produced in 1938 for common cold research and as a hallucinogen by Dr Albert Hoffmann (Swiss) Apr 16–19, 1943.

The most potent analgesic drug is the morphine-like R33799, confirmed in 1978 to have almost 12,000 times the potency of morphine.

Interferon was reportedly available for $10 per millionth of a microgram.

DRINK

Most Alcoholic Liquor

The strength of liquor is gauged by degrees proof. In the US, proof is double the actual percentage of alcohol (C_2H_5OH) by volume at 60°F (15.6°C) in a liquor. Pure or absolute alcohol is thus 200 proof. A "hangover" is due to toxic congenerics such as amyl alcohol ($C_5H_{11}OH$).

During independence (1918–40) the Estonian Liquor Monopoly marketed 196 proof potato alcohol. In 31 US states *Everclear* (190 proof or 95% alcohol) is marketed by the American Distilling Co, "primarily as a base for homemade cordials."

Strongest and Weakest Beer

The strongest and most expensive beer is Samichlaus Bier brewed by Brauerai Hürlimann of Zurich, Switzerland, which retails for $10 per pint. It is 13.94% alcohol by volume at room temperature with an original gravity of 1107.6°.

The weakest liquid ever marketed as beer was a sweet ersatz beer which was brewed in Germany by Sunner, Colne-Kalk, in 1918. It had an original gravity of 1000.96°, with less than 0.2% alcohol.

Liqueurs

The most expensive liqueur in France is *Eau de vie de pêche,* sold for 190 francs ($27.75) a bottle at Fauchon in Paris.

The most expensive bottle of spirits sold at auction was a magnum of *Grande Armée Fine Champagne Cognac* 1811 at Christie's of London on Nov 13, 1978, for £780 ($1,560). *Cognac Chaterau la faut* (1865) retails for 2800 francs ($410) a bottle at Fauchon in Paris.

Most Expensive Wine

Record prices paid for single bottles *usually* arise when two or more self-promoters are seeking publicity. They bear little relation to the market value.

The highest price paid for any bottle (meaning a container as opposed to a measure) of wine is $31,000 for a bottle of 1822 Château Lafite, bought by John Grisanti at the Heublein auction in San Francisco on May 28, 1980, conducted by Michael Broabent of Christie's. The US record is $2,000 a bottle ($24,000 a case) of Napamedoc Cabernet, vintage 1979, by Robert Mondavi Winery on June 21, 1981.

Oldest Vintage Wine

The oldest datable wine has been an amphora salvaged and drunk by Capt Jacques Cousteau from the wreck of a Greek trader sunk in the Mediterranean *c.* 230 BC. Wine jars recovered from the Pompeii eruption of 79 AD were found labelled VESUVINUM—the oldest known trademark. A bottle of 1748 Rudesheimer Rosewein was auctioned at Christie's of London, for £260 ($570) Dec 6, 1979.

Greatest Wine Auction and Tasting

The largest single sale of wine was conducted by Christie's of London, July 10–11, 1974 at Quaglino's Ballroom when 2,325 lots containing 432,000 bottles realized £962,190 (then $2,309,256).

The largest wine tasting ever reported was that staged by the Wine Institute at St Francis Hotel, San Francisco, July 17, 1980, with 125 pourers, 90 openers and a consumption of 3,000 bottles.

Largest and Smallest Bottles

The largest bottles normally used in the wine and spirit trade are the Jeroboam (equal to 4 bottles of champagne or, rarely, of brandy, and from 5 to 6½ bottles of claret, depending on whether the bottle was blown or molded) and the double magnum (equal, since *c.* 1934, to 4 bottles of claret or, more rarely, red burgundy). A complete set of champagne bottles would consist of the ¼ bottle, ½ bottle, bottle, magnum, Jeroboam, Rehoboam, Methuselah, Salmanazer, Balthazar and the Nebuchadnezzar, which has a capacity of 16 liters (33.8 pints), and is equivalent to 20 bottles.

In May 1958 a 5-ft-tall sherry bottle with a capacity of 20½ Imperial gallons (24.6 US gallons) was blown in Stoke-on-Trent, Staffordshire, England. This bottle, with the capacity of 131 normal bottles, was named an "Adelaide."

The smallest bottles of liquor now sold are White Horse bottles of Scotch whisky containing 1.3 millilitres (about 4/100ths of an ounce) for about 41 cents per bottle in "cases" of 12.

Largest Collections

The largest reported collection of unduplicated miniature bottles is one of 14,806 as of May 28, 1982, by Douglas Tavener of Chippenham, England.

The largest recorded collection of distilled spirits or liquors in any bar is 1,203 unduplicated labels collected by Ian Boasman at Bistro French, Church Street, Preston, England, audited in Apr 1982.

The greatest collection of whisky bottles is one of 3,100 unduplicated labels assembled by Signor Edward Giaccone at his Whiskyteca, Salo, Lake Garda, Italy.

Champagne Cork Flight

The longest distance for a champagne cork to fly from an untreated and unheated bottle 4 ft from level ground is 104 ft 6 in by George Thorward at Los Gatos, Calif, Dec 9, 1979.

TELESCOPES

Earliest Telescope

Although there is evidence that early Arabian scientists understood something of the magnifying power of lenses, the first known use of lenses to form a telescope has been attributed to Roger Bacon (c. 1214–92) in England. The prototype of modern refracting telescopes was completed by Johannes Lippershey for the Netherlands government on Oct 2, 1608.

Largest Reflector

The largest telescope is the alt-azimuth mounted, 236.2-inch telescope sited on Mt Semirodriki, near Zelenchukskaya in the Caucasus Mts, USSR, at an altitude of 6,830 ft. Work on the mirror, weighing 78 tons, was not completed until the summer of 1974. Regular observations were begun on Feb 7, 1976, after 16 years' work. The weight of the 138-ft-high assembly is 946 tons. Being the most powerful of all telescopes, its range, which includes the location of objects down to the 25th magnitude, represents the limits of the observable universe. Its light-gathering power would enable it to detect the light from a candle at a distance of 15,000 miles.

A design for a 500-ton 393.7-in reflector comprising 36 independently controlled fitting hexagonal mirrors was adopted in Oct 1980. If sited on Mauna Kea, Hawaii it would be expected to cost $50 million and be completed by 1989. The design of a 984-in composite hexagonal reflector was announced by the USSR in Aug 1979.

Note: The attachment of an electronic charge-coupled-device (CCD) increases the "light-grasp" of a telescope by a factor up to 100 fold. Thus a 200-in telescope becomes the equivalent of a 2000-in telescope.

Largest Refractor

The largest refracting (*i.e.* magnification by lenses) telescope in the world is the 62-ft-long, 40-in telescope completed in 1897 at the Yerkes Observatory, Williams Bay, Wis, belonging to the University of Chicago. In 1900, a 49.2-in refractor 180 ft in length was built for the Paris Exposition, but its optical performance was too poor to justify attempts to use it.

Oldest and Highest Observatories

The oldest astronomical observatory building extant is the Chomsong-dae in Kyongju, South Korea, which was built in 632 AD.

The highest-altitude observatory in the world is the University of Denver's High Altitude Observatory at an altitude of 14,100 ft, opened in 1973, on Mt Evans, Colo. The principal instrument is a 24-in Ealing Beck reflecting telescope.

Largest Radio-Telescope

The largest radio-telescope installation is the US National Science Foundation VLA (Very Large Array). It is Y-shaped with each arm 13 miles long with 27 mobile antennae (each 82 ft in diameter) on rails. It is 50 miles west of Socorro in the Plains of San Augustin, NM and was dedicated on Oct 10, 1980 at a cost of $78 million.

A computer-linked very long base-line array of 82-ft radio telescopes stretched over 2,600 miles on Lat 49.3°N has been planned by the Canadian Astronomical Society.

Largest Dish Telescopes

Radio waves of extraterrestrial origin were first detected by Karl Jansky of Bell Telephone Laboratories, Holmdel, NJ, using a 100-ft-long shortwave rotatable antenna in 1932. The largest trainable dish-type radio-telescope is the 328-ft-diameter, 3,360-ton assembly at the Max Planck Institute for Radio Astronomy of Bonn in the Effelsberger Valley, W Germany; it became operative in May 1971. The cost of the installation, begun in Nov 1967, was DM36,920,000 ($14,760,000).

The world's largest dish-type radio-telescope is the partially-steerable ionospheric assembly built over a natural bowl at Arecibo, Puerto Rico, completed in Nov 1963 at a cost of about $9 million. It has a diameter of 1,000 ft and the dish covers 18½ acres. Its sensitivity was raised by a factor of 1,000 and its range to the edge of the observable universe at some 15,000 million light-years by the fitting of new aluminum plates at a cost of $8,800,000. Rededication was on Nov 16, 1974.

The RATAN-600 radio-telescope completed in the northern Caucasus, USSR, in 1976 has 895 metal mirror panels mounted in a circle 1,890 ft across.

Solar Telescope

The world's largest solar telescope is the 480-ft-long McMath telescope at Kitt Peak National Observatory near Tucson, Ariz. It has a focal length of 300 ft and an 80-in heliostat mirror. It was completed in 1962 and produces an image measuring 33 in in diameter.

Planetaria

The ancestor of the planetarium is the rotatable Gottorp Globe, built by Andreas Busch in Denmark between 1654 and 1664 to the orders of Olearius, court mathematician to Duke Frederick III of Holstein. It is 34.6 ft in circumference, weighs 4 tons and is now preserved in Leningrad, USSR. The stars were painted on the inside.

The earliest optical installation was not until 1923 in the Deutsches Museum, Munich, by Zeiss of Jena, Germany.

The world's largest planetarium, with a diameter of 82½ ft, is in Moscow.

OBSERVATORIES: (Left) The oldest observatory building extant is this one in South Korea, which was built in 632 AD. (Below) The highest-altitude observatory—14,100 ft up—rises above the clouds on Mt Evans, Colo. It belongs to the University of Denver and houses a 24-in reflecting telescope. (Denver Research Institute)

SOLAR TELESCOPE: (Left) The McMath, the world's largest, is at Kitt Peak National Observatory, near Tucson, Ariz. Completed in 1962, it produces an image 33 in across. (© Alex Hansen)

VLA (right) stands for Very Large Array. This installation near Socorro, NM, is the world's largest radio telescope. It has 27 mobile railed antennae and each arm is 13 miles long.

LARGEST OPTICAL TELESCOPE (below): This reflector has a 78-ton mirror and took the Russians 16 years to complete before observations began in 1976 in the Caucasus Mts.
(Novosti)

PRECIOUS STONE RECORDS

The carat was standardized at 205 mg (0.007054 oz) in 1877. The metric carat of 200 mg was introduced in 1914.

Largest	*Largest Cut Stone*	*Other Records*
Diamond (pure crystallized carbon) 3,106 metric carats (over 1¼ lb)—*The Cullinan,* found by Mr Gray, Jan 25, 1905, in the Premier Mine, Pretoria, South Africa	530.2 metric carats. 74 facets. Cleaved from *The Cullinan* in 1908 in Amsterdam by Jak Asscher and polished by Henri Koe. Known as *The Star of Africa* No. 1 and now in the British Royal Sceptre. The *Cullinan II* is 317.40 carats. Third on the list of the 55 diamonds of more than 100 carats is the Great Mogul of 280 old carats lost in the sack of Delhi in 1739 and arguably the most valuable object ever lost.	The rarest color for diamond is blood red. The largest example is a flawless 5.05-carat stone from South Africa now in a private collection in the US. The diamond per carat record price of $113,000 was set by the 41.3-carat "Polar Star" bought in Geneva for $4.6 million Nov 21, 1980.
Emerald (green beryl) [$Be_3Al_2(SiO_3)_6$]	11,130-carat crystal from Stretensk, Ural Mts, USSR in 1834. Now in the Mineralogical Museum, Moscow.	An 18.35-carat ring was sold for $520,000 at Sotheby Parke Bernet, NYC, in Apr 1977. The Swiss customs at Geneva confirmed on Apr 16, 1972 the existence of a hexagonal emerald of about 20,000 carats, thus possibly worth more than $100 million. An 86,136 carat piece was found in Carnaiba, Bahia, Brazil, in Aug 1974. Carved in Hong Kong by Richard Chan, it is now appraised by Gleim Jewelers of Palo Alto, Calif, at $1,292,000.
Sapphire (corundum, any color but red) (Al_2O_3) 2,302-carat stone found at Anakie, Queensland, Australia, in *c.* 1935, now a 1,318-carat head of President Abraham Lincoln (1809–65)	1,444-carat black star stone carved from a 2,097-carat stone in 1953–55 into a bust of Pres-Gen Dwight David Eisenhower (1890–1969).	*Note:* The sapphire head and bust are in the custody of the Kazanjian Foundation of Los Angeles. Auction record for a single stone was set by a step-cut sapphire of 66.03 carats at £579,300 (about $1,332,400) from the Rockefeller Collection at Sotheby's Zurich May 9, 1980.
Ruby (red corundum) (Al_2O_3) 3,421-carat broken stone reported found in July 1961 (largest piece 750 carats)	1,184-carat natural gem stone of Burmese origin. The largest star ruby is the 138.72-carat Rosser Reeves stone on display at the Smithsonian in Washington, DC	A world record carat price of $100,639 was set at Christie's sale in Geneva in Nov 1979 for a 4.12-carat cabochon-shaped ruby.

GEMS

Largest Gems

The largest recorded crystal of gem quality was a 520,000-carat (229-lb) aquamarine ($Al_2Be_3[Si_6O_{18}]$) found near Marambaia, Brazil in 1910. It yielded over 200,000 carats of gem quality cut stones.

Most Precious Gems

Rubies have been the world's most precious gems since 1955 when the value of rubies rose due to a drying up of supplies from Ceylon and Burma. A flawless natural ruby of good color was by 1969 selling for up to $10,000 per carat—more valuable than emerald, diamond or sapphire. In Nov 1979 a record carat price of $100,369 for a 4.12-carat cabochon-shaped ruby was set at Christie's sale in Geneva.

The ability to produce very large corundum prisms of 12 in or over in length in the laboratory for use in lasers seems to have little bearing on the market for natural gems.

Hardest Gems

The hardest of all gems, and hardest known naturally occurring substance, is diamond, which is, chemically, pure carbon. Diamond has 50 times the indentation hardness of the next hardest mineral, corundum (Al_2O_3). Hardnesses are compared on Mohs' scale, on which talc is 1, a fingernail is 2½, window glass 5, topaz 8, corundum 9, and diamond 10. Diamonds average 7,000 on the Knoop scale,

RECORDS FOR OTHER PRECIOUS MATERIALS

Largest	Where Found	Notes on Present Location, etc.
Pearl (Molluscan consecretion) 14 lb 1 oz 9½ in long × 5½ in in diameter—*Pearl of Lao-tze*	At Palawan, Philippines, May 7, 1934, in shell of giant clam	The property since 1936 of Wilburn Dowell Cobb, until his death, valued at $4,080,000 in July 1971, sold on May 15, 1980 at auction in San Francisco by his estate for $200,000 to Peter Hoffmann, jeweler of Beverley Hills, Calif
Opal (SiO_2 NH_2O) 220 troy oz (yellow-orange)	Andamooka, South Australia	The Andamooka specimen (34,215 carats) which was unearthed by a bulldozer, is in two filling pieces, making a block 11 × 10 × 5 in. Owned by the Palgrave Corp since Sept 1969, displayed in Sydney and valued in excess of $1 million
Rock Crystal (Quartz) (SiO_2) Ball: 106¾ lb 12⅞ in in diameter, the *Warner* sphere	Burma (originally a 1,000-lb piece)	US National Museum, Washington, DC
Topaz $Al_2SiO_4(F,OH)_2$ "Brazilian Princess" 21,327 carats, 221 facets (light blue)	Light blue, from Brazil	Exhibited by Smithsonian Institution, Nov 1978. Valued at $1,066,350, or $50 a carat. Cut from a 79-lb crystal. World's largest faceted stone
Amber (coniferous fossil resin) 33 lb 10 oz	Reputedly from Burma, acquired in 1860	Bought by John Charles Bowing (d 1893) for £300 in Canton, China. Natural History Museum, London, since 1940
Turquoise monolith $[CuAl_6(PO_4)_4(OH)_8 4H_2O]$ 218 lb	Riverside County, Calif Jan 17, 1975	Found by Chester Jastromb and Kenneth Casper. Original weight was probably c. 250 lb
Nephrite Jade $Ca_2(Mgte)_5(Si_4O_{11})_2(OH)_2$ Boulder of 143 tons (315,315 lb)	Reported in China, Sept 17, 1978	Jadeite can be virtually any color except red or blue
Marble (Metamorphosed $CaCO_3$) 100.8 tons (single slab)	Quarried at Yule, Colo	A piece of over 50 tons was dressed from this slab for the coping stone of the Tomb of the Unknown Soldier in Arlington National Cemetery, Va
Nuggets—Gold (Au) 7,560 oz (472½ lb) (reef gold) *Holtermann Nugget*	Beyers & Holtermann Star of Hope Gold Mining Co, Hill End, NSW, Australia Oct 19, 1872	The purest large nugget was the *Welcome Stranger,* found at Moliagul Victoria, Australia, which yielded 2,248 troy oz of pure gold from 2,280¼ oz
Silver (Ag) 2,750 lb troy	Sonora, Mexico	Appropriated by the Spanish Government before 1821

with a peak value of 8,400. This index represents a micro-indentation index based on kilograms per one hundredth of a square millimeter ($kg/[mm^2]^{-2}$).

Rarest Gem Mineral

Painite ($CaZrB[Al_9O_{18}]$) is the rarest. It was discovered by A.C.D. Pain near Mogok, Burma, in 1951. Deep red crystals of 1.31 and 2.12 grams are in the British Museum, Natural History, London, and a third of 0.34 grams at the Gemological Institute of America.

Smallest Brilliant Cut Diamond

A 57-facet diamond of 0.0012 of a carat (0.24 milligrams) by A. Van Moppes & Zoon (Diamant) BV of Amsterdam was certified on Jan 26, 1949.

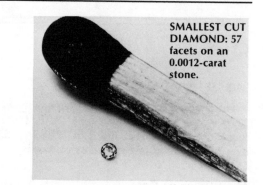

SMALLEST CUT DIAMOND: 57 facets on an 0.0012-carat stone.

Densest Gem Mineral

The densest of all gem minerals is stibiotantalite $[(SbO)_2 (Ta,Nb)_2O_6]$, a rare brownish-yellow mineral found in San Diego County, Calif with a density of 7.46 grams per cc. The alloy platiniridium has a density of more than 22.0.

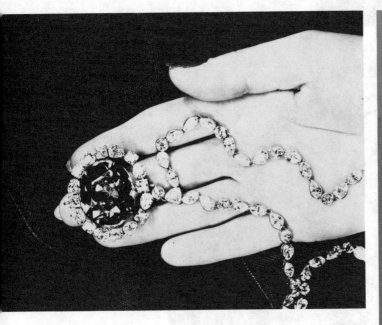

HOPE DIAMOND (above): The world's largest blue diamond, on exhibit in the Smithsonian Institution, Washington, DC, weighs 44.4 carats, but is reputed to carry a curse with it. The BRITISH ROYAL SCEPTRE (right) on exhibit in the Tower of London features the Star of Africa No. 1 with 74 facets, cut from the famous Cullinan diamond. LARGEST RUBY (below): Owned by Rosser Reeves, well-known NY advertising man, this 138.72-carat star ruby, named for its owner, was donated to the Smithsonian where it is also on exhibit.

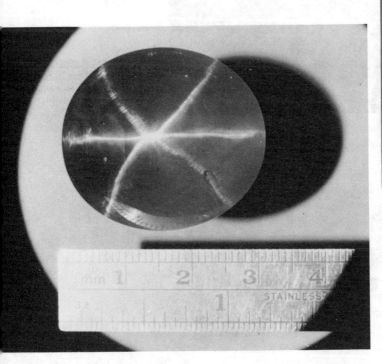

(Eljay Photo Service/K. Davidson)

(Dane Penland/Smithsonian Institution)

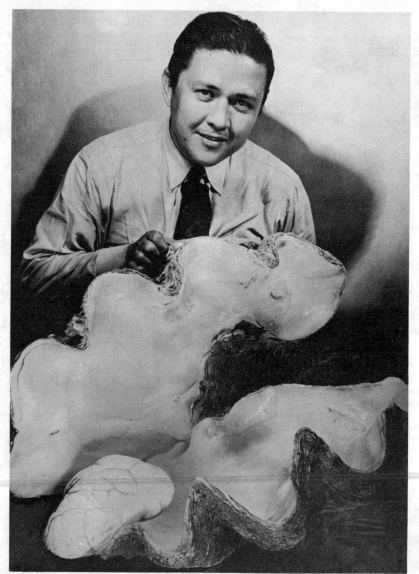

LARGEST PEARL: Wilburn Cobb, owner of this 14-lb baroque pearl from a Philippine giant clam, showed how it was formed in its shell. Cobb valued it at $4,080,000 but it was sold upon his death for $200,000 in 1980. The latest appraisal was $32,600,000 in 1981. (Photo courtesy of Frank Forster)

RAREST GEM (below): Painite, named for its discoverer, A. C. D. Pain, is deep red, and was first found in Burma in 1951.

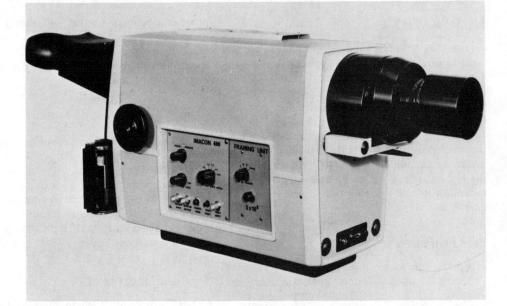

PHOTOGRAPHY

Earliest Cameras

The earliest photograph was taken in the summer of 1826 by Joseph Nicéphore Niepce (1765–1833), a French physician and scientist. It showed the courtyard of his country house at Gras, near St Loup-de-Varennes. It probably took 8 hours to expose and was taken on a bitumen-coated polished pewter plate measuring 7¾ in by 6½ in.

One of the earliest photographs taken was one of a diamond-paned window in Lacock Abbey, Wiltshire, England, taken in Aug 1835 by William Henry Fox Talbot (1800–1877), the inventor of the negative-positive process.

Largest and Smallest Cameras

The largest camera ever built is the 30¼-ton Rolls-Royce camera built for Product Support (Graphics) Ltd of Derby, England, completed in 1959. It measures 8 ft 10 in high, 8 ft 3 in wide and 35 ft long. The lens is a 63″ f/15 Cooke Apochromatic. Its value after improvements in 1971 was in excess of $240,000.

Apart from cameras built for intra-cardiac surgery and espionage, the smallest camera that has been marketed is the circular Japanese "Petal" camera with a diameter of 1.14 in and a thickness of 0.65 in. It has a focal length of 0.47 in. The BBC-TV program *Record Breakers* showed prints from this camera Dec 3, 1974.

Most Expensive Cameras

The most expensive complete range of camera equipment is that of Nikon of Tokyo, Japan who marketed a range of 9 cameras with 74 lenses and 490 accessories in 1982. The total cost of the range would exceed $140,000.

The highest auction price for an antique camera was £21,000 ($42,000) for a J. B. Dancer stereo camera patented in 1856 and sold at Christie's, London, on Oct 12, 1977.

Fastest Camera

In 1972, Prof Basoff of the USSR Academy of Sciences published a paper describing an experimental camera with a time resolution of 5×10^{-13} of a second or ½ a picosecond. The fastest production camera in the world is the Imacon 675 manufactured by John Hadland (P.I.) Ltd of Bovingdon, England, which is capable of taking pictures at a rate of 600 million pictures per sec. Uses include laser, ballistic, detonic, plasma and corona research.

First Aerial Photography

The earliest aerial photograph was taken in 1858 by Gaspard Félix Tournachon (1820–1910), *alias* Nadar, from a balloon near Villacoublay, on the outskirts of Paris, France.

NUMERATION

In dealing with large numbers, scientists use the notation of 10 raised to various powers, to eliminate a profusion of zeros. Example: 19,160,000,000,000 miles would be written 1.916×10^{13} miles. A very small number is treated similarly—for example, 0.0000154324 of a gram would be written 1.54324×10^{-5} gram (g). Of the prefixes used before numbers the smallest is "atto-," from the Danish *atten* for 18, indicating a quintillionth part (10^{-18}) of the unit, and the highest is "exa-" (Greek, *hexa*=six), symbol E, indicating 10^{18} or six groups of 3 zeros meaning a quintillion fold.

Prime Numbers

A prime number is any positive integer (excluding 1) having no integral factors other than itself and unity, *e.g.* 2, 3, 5, 7, or 11. The lowest prime number is 2. The highest known prime number is $2^{44497} - 1$ (a number of 13,395 digits), discovered Apr 8, 1979, after a 2-month-long run on a Cray One Computer at the University of Calif's Lawrence Livermore Laboratory by Harry Nelson, 47, and David Slowinski, 25.

Perfect Numbers

A number is said to be perfect if it is equal to the sum of its divisors other than itself, *e.g.* 1+2+4+7+14=28. The lowest perfect number is 6 (1+2+3). The highest known, and the 26th so far discovered, is $(2^{44497} - 1) \times 2^{44496}$. It is a consequence of the highest known prime (see above).

Highest Numbers

The highest lexicographically accepted named number in the system of successive powers of ten is the centillion, which is 10 raised to the power 600 in the British system, or 10^{303} in the US system. The highest named number outside the decimal notation is the Buddhist *asankhyeya,* which is equal to 10^{140} or 100 quinto-quadragintillions.

The number 10^{100} (10 duotrigintillion) is designated a Googol, a term devised by Dr Edward Kasner of the US (d 1955). Ten raised to the power of a Googol is described as a Googolplex. Some conception of the magnitude of such numbers can be gained when it is said that the number of electrons in some models of the observable universe probably does not exceed 10^{87}.

The highest number ever used in a mathematical proof is a bounding value published in 1977 and known as Graham's number. It concerns bichromatic hypercubes and is inexpressible without the special "arrow" notation, devised by Knuth in 1976, extended to 64 layers.

Earliest Measures

The earliest known measure of weight is the *beqa* of the Amratian period of Egyptian civilization *c.* 3800 BC found at Naqada, Egypt. The weights are cylindrical with rounded ends from 188.7 to 211.2 grams (6.65–7.45 oz). The unit of length used by the megalithic tomb-builders in Britain *c.* 2200 BC appears to have been 2.72 ± 0.003 ft. This was deduced by Prof Alexander Thom (b 1894) in 1966.

Smallest Linear Unit

The shortest unit of length is the atto-meter, which is 1.0×10^{-16} of a centimeter.

Most Accurate and Inaccurate Versions of "Pi"

The greatest number of decimal places to which *pi* (π) has been calculated is 2 million by Dr Kazunori Miyoshi (b Oct 15, 1946) using a FACOM M200 computer in 137.3 hours at the University of Tsukuba, Japan, June 18–July 10, 1981. The published value to two million places was 3.141592653589793 ... (omitting the next 1,999,975 places) ... 1457297909. The publication of this has been described as the world's most boring 800-page book.

In 1897, the General Assembly of Indiana enacted in House Bill No. 246 that *pi* was *de jure* 4, for the most inaccurate version.

Longest Roman Numeral

The date requiring the most Roman tellers is 1888, with 13, namely MDCCCLXXXVIII. It was used on the entrance to the High Court of New South Wales (Australia) completed in that year, so drawing the comment that the building would become equally famous for the length of its sentences.

Longest Slide Rule

The longest slide rule is one 323 ft 9.5 in in length completed on Nov 11, 1979 by Greg Maggs and Robert Kolstad at the University of Illinois College of Law Building in Champaign, Ill.

Rubik Cubism

An early Rubik's cube speed contest (with standard dislocation and inspection time) held in Munich, W Germany, Mar 13, 1981, resulted in a 38.0-sec tie between Ronald Brinkman and Jury Fröschl. In 1975 Ernö Rubik (Hungary) patented the device which has 43,252,003,274,489,856,000 possible combinations.

Longest and Shortest Time Measure

The longest measure of time is the *kalpa* in Hindu chronology. It is equivalent to 4,320 million years. In astronomy a cosmic year is the period of rotation of the sun around the center of the Milky Way galaxy, *i.e.* about 225,000,000 years. In the Late Cretaceous Period of *c.* 85 million years ago, the earth rotated faster so resulting in 370.3 days per year, while in Cambrian times, some 600 million years ago, there is evidence that the year contained 425 days.

Owing to variations in the length of a day, which is estimated to be increasing irregularly at the average rate of about a millisecond per century, due to the

SLIDE RULE: Laid out at the University of Illinois Law Building, an instrument 323 ft long needs a long straight path—about the length of a football field.

moon's tidal drag, the second has been redefined. Instead of being 1/86,400th part of a mean solar day, it is now reckoned as 1/31,556,925.9747th part of the solar (or tropical) year at 1900 AD, Jan 0 at 12 hours, Ephemeris time. In 1958 the second of Ephemeris time was computed to be equivalent to 9,192,631,770 ± 20 cycles of the radiation corresponding to the transition of a cesium 133 atom when unperturbed by exterior fields. The greatest diurnal change recorded has been 10 milliseconds on Aug 8, 1972, due to the most violent solar storm recorded in 370 years of observation. The shortest blip of light is one of 0.2 of a picosecond (0.2×10^{-12} of a sec) produced by the Center of Laser Studies, University of Southern Calif, in Aug 1978. Light travels 0.0023 in in that period of time.

PHYSICAL EXTREMES (TERRESTRIAL)

Highest Temperatures

The highest man-made temperatures yet attained are those produced in the center of a thermonuclear fusion bomb, which are of the order of 300 million-400 million °C. Of controllable temperatures, the highest effective laboratory figure reported is 67 million °C at the University of Rochester's Laser Energetics Laboratory on May 22, 1979. Prior to 1963, a figure of 3,000 million °C was reportedly achieved in the USSR with Ogra injection-mirror equipment.

Lowest Temperatures

The lowest temperature reached is 5×10^{-8} Kelvins above absolute zero attained in a 2-stage nuclear demagnetization cryostat at the Helsinki University of Technology, Otaniema, Finland by the team of Prof Olli V. Lounasmaa (b 1920) and announced in March 1979. Absolute or thermodynamic temperatures are defined in terms of ratios rather than as differences reckoned from the unattainable absolute zero, which on the Kelvin scale is −273.15 °C or −459.67 °F.

The lowest equilibrium temperature ever attained is 0.0003 °K by nuclear refrigeration in a 3-lb copper specimen by Prof Lounasmaa and his team at the Helsinki University of Technology (see above), Apr 17, 1974.

Highest Pressures

The highest sustained laboratory pressures yet reported are of 1.72 megabars (12,300 tons force per sq in) achieved in the giant hydraulic diamond-faced press at the Carnegie Institution's Geophysical Laboratory in Washington, DC, reported in June 1978. This laboratory announced solid hydrogen achieved at 57 kilobars pressure on March 2, 1979. If created, metallic hydrogen is expected to be silvery white but soft, with a density of 1.1 g/cc. The pressure required for this transition is estimated by H. K. Mao and P. M. Bell to be 1 megabar at 25°C. Using dynamic methods and impact speeds of up to 18,000 mph, momentary pressures of 75 million atmospheres (548,000 tons per sq in) were reported from the US in 1958.

Highest Vacuum

The highest or "hardest" vacuums obtained in scientific research are of the order of 10^{-14} torr, achieved at the IBM Thomas J. Watson Research Center, Yorktown Heights, NY in Oct 1976 in a cryogenic system with temperatures down to −269°C (−452°F). This is equivalent to depopulating baseball-sized molecules from 1 yard apart to 50 miles apart.

Fastest Centrifuge

Ultra-centrifuges were invented by Theodor Svedberg (b Aug 30, 1884) (Sweden) in 1923.

The highest man-made rotary speed ever achieved and the fastest speed of any earth-bound object is 4,500 mph by a swirling tapered 6-in carbon fiber rod in a vacuum at Birmingham University, England, reported Jan 24, 1975.

Loudest Noise

The loudest noise created in a laboratory is 210 decibels or 400,000 acoustic watts reported by NASA in Oct 1965. The noise came from a 48-ft steel and concrete horn at Huntsville, Ala. Holes can be bored in solid material by this means.

Quietest Place

The "dead room," measuring 35 ft by 28 ft, in the Bell Telephone System Laboratory at Murray Hill, NJ is the most anechoic room in the world, eliminating 99.98% of reflected sound.

Highest Note

The highest note yet attained is 60,000 megahertz (60 GHz) (60,000 million vibrations per sec), gen-

erated by a laser beam striking a sapphire crystal at MIT, Cambridge, Mass, in Sept 1964.

Highest Measured Frequency

The highest frequency ever directly measured is a visible yellow light at $5.20206528 \times 10^{14}$ hertz (c. 520 terahertz or million million cycles per second) in Feb 1979 by the US National Bureau of Standards Boulder Laboratories and the Natural Research Council Laboratory in Ottawa, Canada.

Finest Balance

The most accurate balance is the Sartorius Model 4108, manufactured in Göttingen, W Germany, which can weigh objects of up to 0.5 grams (about .018 oz) to an accuracy of 0.01 μg or 0.00000001 g, which is equivalent to little more than one-sixtieth of the weight of the ink on a period dot (.).

Hottest Flame

The hottest flame that can be produced is from carbon subnitride (C_4N_2) which at one atmosphere pressure is calculated to reach 5,261 K.

Lowest Viscosity

The California Institute of Technology announced on Dec 1, 1957, that there was no measurable viscosity, i.e. perfect flow, in liquid helium II, which exists only at temperatures close to absolute zero (−273.15°C or −459.67°F).

Lowest Friction

The lowest coefficient of static and dynamic friction of any solid is 0.02, in the case of polytetrafluoroethylene ($[C_2F_4]_n$), called PTFE—equivalent to wet ice on wet ice. It was first manufactured in quantity by E. I. du Pont de Nemours & Co Inc in 1943, and is marketed as Teflon.

In the centrifuge at the University of Virginia a 30-lb rotor magnetically supported has been spun at 1,000 revolutions per sec in a vacuum of 10^{-6} mm of mercury pressure. It loses only one revolution per sec per day, thus spinning for years.

Most Powerful Electric Current

The most powerful electric current generated is that from the Zeus capacitor at the Los Alamos Scientific Laboratory, NM. If fired simultaneously the

QUIETEST PLACE ON EARTH: These photos of the "dead room" at the Bell Lab in NJ show experiments in sound taking place.

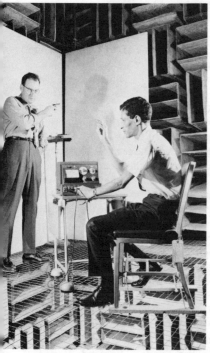

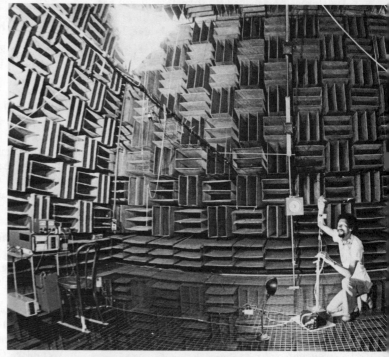

The room is "anechoic," that is, 99.9% of all sound is absorbed, rather than reflected as is usually the case. The floor is a suspended wire grid and does not mirror the walls, as it might seem. The men above are shooting off a pistol to measure the decibels it registers with echo control as if they were one mile up in the earth's atmosphere. The "split" head in the photo to the right is being tested to see how much music it absorbs when a recording is played, so that concert hall acoustics can be improved.

4,032 capacitors would produce for a few microseconds twice as much current as that generated elsewhere on earth.

Highest Voltage

The highest potential difference ever obtained in a laboratory has been 32 ± 1.5 million volts by the National Electrostatics Corporation at Oak Ridge, Tenn, on May 17, 1979.

Strongest and Weakest Magnetic Fields

The strongest magnetic field strength achieved has been one of 301 kilogauss at the Francis Bitter National Magnet Laboratory at MIT, Cambridge, Mass, by Mathias J. Leupold and Robert J. Weggel, announced in July 1977. The outer magnet is of superconducting niobium-titanium.

The weakest magnetic field ever measured is one of 8×10^{-11} gauss in the heavily shielded room at the same laboratory. It is used for research by Dr David Cohen into the very weak magnetic fields generated in the heart and brain.

Heaviest Magnet

The heaviest magnet is one measuring 196 ft in diameter, with a weight of 40,000 tons, for the 10 GeV synchrophasotron in the Joint Institute for Nuclear Research at Dubna, near Moscow. Intermagnetics General Corporation announced in 1975 plans for a 180-kG vanadium-gallium magnet.

Most Powerful Microscope

The most powerful microscope was announced by Dr Lawrence Bartell and Charles Ritz of the University of Michigan in July 1974 with an image magnification of 260 million fold. It uses an optical laser to decode holograms produced with 40 Kev radiation and has produced photographs of electron clouds of atoms of neon and argon.

Sharpest Objects and Smallest Tubes

The sharpest objects yet made are glass micropipette tubes used in intracellular work on living cells. Techniques developed and applied by Prof Kenneth T. Brown and Dale G. Flaming of the Dept of Physiology, Univ of Calif, San Francisco, achieved by 1977 beveled tips with an outer diameter of 0.02 μm and 0.01 μm inner diameter. The latter is smaller than the smallest known nickel tubing by a factor of 340 and is 6,500 times thinner than human hair.

Finest Cut

Biological specimens embedded in epoxy resin can be sectioned by a glass knife microtome to a thickness of 1/875,000th in or 2.9×10^{-5} mm under ideal conditions.

Most Durable Light

The average bulb lasts for 750 to 1,000 hours. There is some evidence that a carbon filament bulb burning in the Fire Department, Livermore, Alameda County, Calif has been burning since 1901.

Brightest Light

The brightest steady artificial light sources are laser beams, with an intensity exceeding the sun's 1,500,000 candles per sq in by a factor of well in excess of 1,000.

In May 1969 the USSR Academy of Sciences announced blast waves traveling through a luminous plasma of inert gases heated to 90,000 K. The flareup for up to 3 microseconds shone at 50,000 times the brightness of the sun, *viz.* 75 billion candles per sq in. Of continuously burning sources, the most powerful is a 200-kilowatt high pressure xenon arc lamp of 600,000 candle-power, reported from the USSR in 1965.

The synchrotron radiation from a 4 in $\times$ ½ in slit in the SPEAR high energy physics plant at the end of the 2-mile-long Stanford Linear Accelerator, Calif has been described as the world's most powerful light beam.

The most powerful searchlight ever developed was one produced during the 1939–45 war by the General Electric Company Ltd at the Hirst Research Centre in Wembley, Greater London, England. It had a consumption of 600 kW and gave an arc luminance of 300,000 candles per sq in and a maximum beam intensity of 2,700 million candles from its parabolic mirror (diameter 10 ft).

Most Powerful Laser Beams

The first illumination of another celestial body was achieved May 9, 1962, when a beam of light was successfully reflected from the moon by the use of a maser (microwave amplification by stimulated emission of radiation) or laser (light amplification by stimulated emission of radiation) attached to a 48-in telescope at MIT, Cambridge, Mass. The spot was estimated to be 4 miles in diameter on the moon. The device was propounded in 1958 by Dr Charles Hard

Townes (b US 1915) of Bell Telephone Laboratories. A maser light flash is focused into a liquid nitrogen-cooled ruby crystal. Its chromium atoms are excited into a high-energy state in which they emit a red light which is allowed to escape only in the direction desired. Such a flash for 1/5,000th sec can bore a hole through a diamond by vaporization at 10,000 °C, produced by 2×10^{23} photons.

The "Shiva" laser was reported at the Lawrence Livermore Laboratory, Calif to be concentrating 2.6×10^{13} watts into a pinhead-sized target for 9.5×10^{-11} sec in a test on May 18, 1978.

Most Powerful Particle Accelerator

The 6,562-ft diameter proton synchrotron at the Fermi National Accelerator Laboratory near Batavia, Ill, is the highest-energy atom-smasher in the world. An energy of 500 billion (5×10^{11}) electron volts was attained on May 14, 1976. Work on doubling the energy to nearly 1 Tera electron volts or 1,000 GeV was begun in July 1979. This involves 1,000 superconducting magnets maintained at a temperature of −452 °F by means of the world's largest helium liquefying plant, which produces 1,170 gallons per hour and began operating Apr 18, 1980.

The $76,800,000 CERN intersecting storage rings (ISR) project near Geneva, Switzerland, started on Jan 27, 1971, using two 28 GeV proton beams and is designed to yield the equivalent of 1,700 GeV or 1.7 TeV (1.7 million million electron volts) in its center of mass experiments.

The aim of CERN to collide beams of protons and antiprotons in their Super Proton Synchrotron (SPS) at 270 GeV × 2 = 540 GeV was achieved at 4:55 a.m. on July 10, 1981. This is the equivalent of striking a fixed target with protons at 150 TeV or 150,000 GeV.

Highest Velocity

The highest velocity at which any solid visible object has been projected is 350,000 mph in the case of a plastic disc at the Naval Research Laboratory, Wash DC, reported in Aug 1980.

Wind Tunnels

The largest wind tunnel is a low-speed tunnel with a closed test section measuring 40 × 80 ft, built in 1944, at Ames Research Center, Moffett Field, Calif. The tunnel encloses 900 tons of air and cost approximately $7 million. The maximum volume of air that can be moved is 60 million cu ft per min. On July 30, 1974, NASA announced an intention to increase it in size to 80 × 120 ft for 345-mph speeds with a 135,000 hp system.

The most powerful is the 216,000-hp installation at the Arnold Engineering Test Center at Tullahoma, Tenn, opened in Sept 1956. The highest Mach number attained with air is Mach 27 at the plant of the Boeing Company, Seattle, Wash. For periods of microseconds, shock Mach numbers of the order of 30 (22,830 mph) have been attained in impulse tubes at Cornell University, Ithaca, NY.

Largest Bubble Chamber

The largest bubble chamber is the $7 million installation completed in Oct 1973, at Weston, Ill. It is 15 ft in diameter and contains 7,259 gallons of liquid hydrogen at a temperature of −247 °C (−412.6 °F) with a superconducting magnet of 30,000 gauss.

Most Accurate Physical Device

The accuracy of the caesium beam frequency standard approaches 8 parts in 10^{14} compared to 2 parts in 10^{13} for the methane-stabilized helium-neon laser and 6 parts in 10^{13} for the hydrogen maser.

Smallest Hole

Inco Nickel Company was reported in Aug 1977 to have produced a hole with a diameter of a ten millionth of an inch (0.000004 mm), or one thousand times smaller than the width of a human hair.

A hole of 40 Å was shown visually using a JEM 100C electron microscope and quantel electronics devices at the Dept of Metallurgy, Oxford, England on Oct 28, 1979. To find such a hole is equivalent to finding a pinhead in a haystack measuring 1.2 miles × 1.2 miles.

Chapter 6

The Arts & Entertainment

1. PAINTING*

Earliest Art

Evidence of Paleolithic art was first found in 1834 at Chaffaud Vienne, France, by Brouillet when he recognized an engraving of two deer on a piece of flat bone from the cave, dating to *c.* 20,000 BC. The number of stratigraphically dated cave art is limited. The oldest known dated examples come from La Ferrassie, near Les Eyzies in the Périgord, France, in layers dated to *c.* 25,000 BC. Blocks of stone were found with engraved animals and female symbols; some of the blocks also had symbols painted in red ochre. Pieces of ochre with ground facets have been found at Lake Mungo, NSW, Australia, in a context *ante* 30,000 BC but there is no evidence whether these were used for body-painting or art.

Largest Paintings

Panorama of the Mississippi, completed by John Banvard (1815–91) in 1846, showing the river scene for 1,200 miles in a strip probably 5,000 ft long and 12 ft wide, was the largest painting in the world, with an area of more than 1.3 acres. The painting is believed to have been destroyed when the rolls of canvas, stored in a barn at Cold Spring Harbor, NY, caught fire shortly before Banvard's death May 16, 1891.

The largest painting now in existence is probably *The Battle of Gettysburg,* completed in 1883, after 2½ years of work, by Paul Philippoteaux (France) and 16 assistants. The painting is 410 ft long, 70 ft high and weighs 11,792 lb. It depicts the climax of the Battle of Gettysburg, in south-central Pa, July 3, 1863. In 1964, the painting was bought by Joe King

of Winston-Salem, NC, after being stored by E. W. McConnell in a Chicago warehouse since 1933.

The largest "Old Master" is *Il Paradiso,* painted between 1587 and 1590 by Jacopo Robusti, *alias* Tintoretto (1518–94), and his son Domenico on Wall "E" of the Sala del Maggior Consiglio in the Palazzo Ducale (Doge's Palace) in Venice, Italy. The work is 72 ft 2 in long and 22 ft 11½ in high and contains more than 100 human figures.

Most Valuable Painting

The "Mona Lisa" (*La Gioconda*) by Leonardo da Vinci (1452–1519) in the Louvre, Paris, was assessed for insurance purposes at the highest figure ever at $100 million for its move for exhibition in Washington, DC and NYC from Dec 14, 1962, to March 12, 1963. However, insurance was not concluded because the cost of the closest security precautions was less than that of the premiums. It was painted in *c.* 1503–07 and measures 30.5 × 20.9 in. It is believed to portray Mona (short for Madonna) Lisa Gherardini, the wife of Francesco del Giocondo of Florence. The husband is said to have disliked it and refused to pay for it. Francis I, King of France, in 1517 bought the painting for his bathroom for 4,000 gold florins or 492 oz of gold (in mid-1981 equivalent to more than $500,000).

Highest Auction Prices

The highest price ever bid in a public auction for any painting was $6,400,000 for *Juliet and Her Nurse,* painted by Joseph Mallard William Turner (1775–1851) in Venice in 1836, and sold May 30, 1980 at Sotheby Parke Bernet, NYC, to an undisclosed collector, possibly "a woman in white from Argentina," on behalf of the Whitney Museum, NYC. The previous owner was 82-year-old Flora

---

* For further details on art, see "Art Facts and Feats," A Guinness Superlatives Book (Sterling)

HIGHEST PRICED PAINTINGS—PROGRESSIVE RECORDS

Price	Painter, title, sold by and sold to	Date
$32,500	Antonio Correggio's *The Magdalen Reading* (in fact spurious) to Elector Friedrich Augustus II of Saxony.	1746
$42,500	Raphael's *The Sistine Madonna* to Elector Friedrich Augustus II of Saxony.	1759
$80,000	Van Eyck's *Adoration of the Lamb*, 6 outer panels of Ghent altarpiece by Edward Solby to the Government of Prussia.	1821
$123,000*	Murillo's *The Immaculate Conception* by estate of Marshall Soult to the Louvre (against Czar Nicholas I) in Paris.	1852
$350,000	Raphael's *Ansidei Madonna* by the 8th Duke of Marlborough to the National Gallery, London.	1885
$500,000	Raphael's *The Colonna Altarpiece* by Sedelmeyer to J. Pierpont Morgan.	1901
$514,400	Van Dyck's *Elena Grimaldi-Cattaneo* (portrait) by Knoedler to Peter Widener (1834–1915).	1906
$514,400	Rembrandt's *The Mill* by 6th Marquess of Lansdowne to Peter Widener.	1911
$582,500	Raphael's smaller *Panshanger Madonna* by Joseph (later Baron) Duveen (1869–1939) to Peter Widener.	1913
$1,572,000	Leonardo da Vinci's *Benois Madonna* to Czar Nicholas II in Paris.	1914
$2,300,000*	Rembrandt's *Aristotle Contemplating Bust of Homer* by Mr/Mrs Alfred Erickson to Metropolitan Museum of Art.	1961
$5,000,000–$6,000,000	Leonardo da Vinci's *Ginevra de' Benci* by Prince Franz Josef II of Liechtenstein to National Gallery, Washington.	1967
$5,544,000*	Velázquez's *Portrait of Juan de Pareja,* sometimes known as *The Slave of Velázquez* by the Earl of Radnor (UK) to Wildenstein Gallery, NY.	1970
$6,400,000*	Turner's *Juliet and Her Nurse* by Whitney Museum to an anonymous buyer.	1980

* Indicates price at auction, otherwise prices were by private treaty.

Whitney Miller who said, "I'm staggered." With the 10% Sotheby buyer's fee, the total amounted to $7,040,000. The 3 ft × 4 ft canvas had been in Mrs Miller's family since 1901 and had not been on public view until 1966.

The highest price ever paid for a painting by a female artist is $775,000 at Christie's, NYC, May 19, 1982, for *La Lisense* by Mary Cassatt (US) (b Pittsburgh 1844–d 1926). She worked mainly in Paris.

Highest Price Paid by Private Treaty

It was announced on Nov 12, 1980 that the National Gallery, London had acquired Albrecht Altdorfer's *Christ Taking Leave of His Mother,* valued by Christie's at "about £6 million" (more than $12 million), from the trustees of the Wernher collection at Luton Hoo, Bedfordshire, England.

Miniature Portrait

The highest price ever paid for a portrait miniature is $172,500 by an anonymous buyer at a sale held by Sotheby's, London, Mar 24, 1980, for a miniature of Jane Broughton, age 21, painted on vellum by Nicholas Hilliard (1547–1619) in 1574. The painted surface measures 1.65 in diameter.

Living Artist

The highest price paid for paintings in the lifetime of the artist is $1,950,000 paid for the two canvases *Two Brothers* (1905) and *Seated Harlequin* (1922) by Pablo Diego José Francisco de Paula Juan Nepomuceno Crispin Crispiano de la Santisima Trinidad Ruiz y Picasso (1881–1973), born in Spain. This was paid by the Basle City government to the Staechelin Foundation to enable the Basle Museum of Arts to

PICASSO, unlike most artists, received sizable fees during his lifetime for his work. This painting, "Mère et enfant de profil," sold for $532,000, but his world record was $1,950,000 for two canvases.

161

retain the painting after an offer of $2,560,000 had been received from the US in Dec 1967.

The highest price at auction for a work by a now living artist is £360,000 ($774,000) at Christie's, London, on Mar 30, 1981, for Salvador Dali's *Le Sommeil.*

Modern Painting

The record for a 20th century painting was set at $5.3 million at Sotheby Parke Bernet, NYC on May 21, 1981 by Picasso's 1901 *Self Portrait: Yo Picasso* sold to an anonymous dealer.

The 19th century record is $5,200,000 for Van Gogh's *Le Jardin du Poète, Arles,* sold by Christie's in NYC on May 13, 1980.

Highest Price Drawing

The highest price ever attached to any drawing was £804,361 ($2,252,210) for the cartoon *The Virgin and Child with St. John the Baptist and St. Anne,* measuring 54½ in × 39¼ in, drawn in Milan, probably in 1499–1500, by Leonardo da Vinci (1452–1519). The National Gallery (London) retained possession in 1962, after three US bids of over $4 million were reputedly made for the cartoon.

Youngest Exhibitor

Lewis Melville "Gino" Lyons (b Apr 30, 1962) painted his *Trees and Monkeys* on June 4, 1965, submitted it to the Royal Academy of Arts, England, on March 17, 1967, for its Annual Summer Exhibition, and it was exhibited on Apr 29, 1967.

Most Repetitious Painter

Antonio Bin of Paris has painted the *Mona Lisa* on some 300 occasions. These copies sell for up to $2,250 each.

Most Prolific Painters

Picasso was the most prolific of all painters. During a career that lasted for 78 years, it has been estimated that he produced about 13,500 paintings or designs, 100,000 prints or engravings, 34,000 book illustrations, and 300 sculptures and ceramics plus drawings and tapestries. His lifetime work has been valued at well over $1 billion. The Museum of Modern Art in NYC gave over its entire museum to a one-man show of Picasso's work, May–Sept 1980.

Morris Katz (b 1932) of Greenwich Village, NYC, is the most prolific painter of saleable portraits in the world. His total sold, as of Apr 21, 1982, was 110,600. Described as the "King of Shlock Art," who paints with palette knife and crushed pads of toilet paper, he sells his paintings "cheap and often." He also set a speed record—painting a 20 x 24 canvas in 2 min 57 sec at the Empire State Building Observatory on June 8, 1982.

Most Prolific Portrait Painter

John A. Wismont, Jr (b NYC, Sept 20, 1941), formerly of Disneyland, Anaheim, California, painted 45,423 watercolor paintings in his career (up to 1978) including 9,853 in 1976.

Finest Brush

The finest standard brush sold is the 000 in Series 7 by Winsor and Newton, known as the "triple goose." It is made of 150–200 Kolinsky sable hairs weighing 0.000529 oz.

Oldest and Largest Museums

The oldest museum in the world is the Ashmolean Museum in Oxford, England, built in 1679.

The largest museum is the American Museum of Natural History between 77th and 81st Sts on Central Park West, NYC. Founded in 1874, it comprises 19 interconnected buildings with 23 acres of floor space.

Largest Galleries

The world's largest art gallery is the Winter Palace and the neighboring Hermitage in Leningrad, USSR. One has to walk 15 miles to visit each of the 322 galleries, which house nearly 3 million works of art and objects of archeological interest.

The largest modern art museum is the Georges Pompidou National Center for Art and Culture opened in Paris in 1977 with a floor space of 183,000 sq ft.

Largest Poster

The largest recorded poster is a greeting card measuring 53 ft 3 in × 166 ft delivered to Spalding College Center, Louisville, Ky, on its 60th anniversary on Oct 3, 1980 bearing a "Happy Birthday" inscription and the college's pelican mascot.

(above)
LARGEST POSTER: Containing 8,839½ sq ft, this birthday card commemorating Spalding College's 60th anniversary was unveiled on the campus in Louisville, Ky, on Oct 3, 1980.

(Left)
PICASSO was the world's most prolific painter, with more than 150,000 works of art to his credit. "Femme Assise" (see the woman's face?), painted in 1909, is a prime example of his style of cubism.

MOST PROLIFIC LIVING PAINTER (below): Morris Katz of NYC's Greenwich Village, "the King of Shlock Art" (self-styled), uses crushed toilet paper and a palette knife to create paintings like this in record time of less than 3 min. Some of his 110,600 output took longer—just a little.

163

MUSEUMS today may not look like museums—this one at first sight looks like a steamship. It is the modern art museum in Paris called "the Pompidou." Opened in 1977 in the midst of controversy, it also contains, besides its exhibit area, a library and a restaurant in its 183,000 sq ft of floor space. (French Govt Tourist Office)

MOST MASSIVE MOBILE (left): Alexander Calder's "White Cascade" can be seen in a bank in Philadelphia. (Edw. J. Bonner)

LARGEST MOSAIC (right): The four walls of the library of the University of Mexico tell the history of Mexico.

Earliest Mural

The earliest known murals on man-made walls are those at Çatal Hüyük in southern Anatolia, Turkey, dating from *c.* 5850 BC.

Largest Mural

The largest logo and mural painting is the American Revolution Bicentennial symbol on the curved roof of the Arizona Veterans Memorial Coliseum, Phoenix, Ariz. It occupies 110,000 sq ft, or more than 2½ acres. It was painted over in 1977. After being outlined with the aid of a computer, it took 45 man-days, under the supervision of its designer John M. Glitsos, to apply the necessary 870 gallons of patriotic red, white and blue paint Aug 18–26, 1973.

A ground mural, measuring 1,400 ft long by 100 ft wide, named *Yellow Brick Road—Leisure Time*, painted on a disused runway near the Tamiami Stadium, South Dade, Fla, was completed March 18, 1976.

Largest Mosaic

The largest mosaic is on the walls of the central library of the Universidad Nacional Autónoma de México, Mexico City. There are four walls, the two largest measuring 12,949 sq ft each, representing the pre-Hispanic past.

2. SCULPTURES

Earliest Sculptures

The earliest known examples of sculpture are the so-called Venus figurines from Aurignacian sites, dating to *c.* 25,000–22,000 BC, *e.g.* the famous Venus of Willendorf from Austria and the Venus of Brassempouy (Landes, France). A piece of ox rib found in 1973 at Pech de l'Aze, Dordogne, France, in an early Middle Paleolithic layer of the Riss glaciation *c.* 105,000 BC appears to have several intentionally engraved lines on one side. A churingo or curved ivory plaque rubbed with red ochre from the Middle Paleolithic Mousterian site at Tata, Hungary, has been dated to 100,000 BC by the thorium/uranium method.

Largest Sculptures

The largest sculptures are the mounted figures of Jefferson Davis (1808–89), Gen Robert Edward Lee (1807–70) and Gen Thomas Jonathan ("Stonewall") Jackson (1824–63), covering 1.33 acres on the face of Stone Mountain, near Atlanta, Ga. They are 90 ft high. Roy Faulkner was on the mountain face for 8 years 174 days with a thermo-jet torch, working with the sculptor Walker Kirtland Hancock and other helpers from Sept 12, 1963 to March 3, 1972.

When completed the world's largest sculpture will be that of the Indian chief Tashunca-Uitco (*c.* 1849–77) known as Crazy Horse, of the Oglala tribe of the Dakota or Nadowessioux (Sioux) group. The sculpture was begun on June 3, 1948 near Mount Rushmore, SD. A projected 561 ft high and 641 ft long, it has required blasting 7 million tons of stone and is the life work of one man, Korczak Ziolkowski. The horse's nostril will be 50 ft deep and 35 ft across.

Most Expensive Sculptures

The highest price ever paid for a sculpture is $3,900,000 paid by private treaty in London in early 1977 by J. Paul Getty's Museum in Calif for the 4th-century BC bronze statue of a youth attributed to the school of Lysippus. It was found by fishermen on the seabed off Faro, Italy in 1963. The $46-million museum with 38 galleries, opened in Malibu in Jan 1974, has a $1,400 million endowment.

The highest price paid for the work of a living sculptor is $1,265,000 given at Sotheby Parke Bernet Galleries, NYC, May 21, 1982, for the 75-in-long elmwood *Reclining Figure* by Henry Moore (b Castleford, W Yorkshire, England, July 30, 1898).

Ground and Hill Figures

In the Nazca Desert south of Lima, Peru there are straight lines (one more than 7 miles long), geometric shapes and plants and animals drawn on the ground sometime between 100 BC and 700 AD for an uncertain but probably religious, astronomical or even economic purpose by a not precisely identified civilization. They were first detected from the air *c.* 1928 and can only be recognized as artwork from the air.

In Aug 1968 a 330-ft-tall figure was found on a hill above Tarapacá, Chile.

Most Massive Mobile

The most massive mobile is *White Cascade* weighing more than 8 tons and measuring 100 ft from top to bottom installed on May 24–25, 1976 at the Federal Reserve Bank of Philadelphia. It was designed by Alexander Calder (d 1976), whose first mobiles were exhibited in Paris in 1932.

3. LANGUAGE AND LITERATURE

Earliest Language

Anthropologists have evidence that the truncated pharynx of Neanderthal man precluded his speaking anything akin to a modern language any more than an ape or a modern baby. Cro-Magnon man of 40,000 BC had however developed an efficient vocal tract. Clay tablets of the neolithic Danubian culture discovered in Dec, 1966, at Tartaria, Moros River, Rumania have been dated to the fifth or fourth millennium BC. The tablets bear symbols of bows and arrows, gates and combs. Writing tablets bearing an early form of the Elamite language dating from 3500 BC were found in southeastern Iran in 1970. Tokens or tallies from Tepe Asiab and Ganji-I-Dareh Tepe in Iran have however been dated to 8500 BC.

Oldest Language

The written language with the longest continuous history is Egyptian from the earliest hieroglyphic inscriptions on the palette of Narmer, dated to *c.* 3100 BC to Coptic used in churches at the present day, more than 5,000 years later. Hieroglyphs were used until 394 AD, and thus may be overtaken by Chinese characters as the most durable script in the 21st century.

OLDEST LANGUAGE: Written Egyptian began with the first pharaoh, Narmer, c. 3100 BC, and this palette commemorates his victories. Hieroglyphs were used until 394 AD.

Oldest Words in English

Some as yet unpublished research indicates some words of a pre-Indo-European substrate survive in English, including apple (apal), bad (bad), gold (gol), and tin (tin).

Commonest Language

Today's world total of languages and dialects still spoken is about 5,000 of which some 845 come from India. The language spoken by more people than any other is Northern Chinese, or Mandarin, by an estimated 68% of the population, hence 675 million people in 1981. The so-called national language (*Guóyǔ*) is a standardized form of Northern Chinese (*Běifānghuà*) as spoken in the Peking area. This was alphabetized into *zhùyīn fùhào* of 37 letters in 1918. In 1958 the *pinyin* system, which is a phonetic pronunciation guide, was introduced. The next most commonly spoken language and the most widespread is English, by an estimated 400 million in mid-1981. English is spoken by 10% or more of the population in 37 sovereign countries.

Rarest Language

Languages, in which no one can converse because there is only one speaker left alive are themselves dwindling in number. Eyak is still spoken in southeastern Alaska by 2 aged sisters if they meet. "Rosa," the last pure-blooded Yaghan, from Tierra del Fuego, was said in Feb 1982 to be very weak and 88 years old.

Most Complex Language

The following extremes of complexity have been noted: Chippewa, the North American Indian language of Minnesota, has the most verb forms with up to 6,000; Tillamook, the North American Indian language of Oregon, has the most prefixes with 30; Tabassaran, a language in Daghestan, USSR, uses the most noun cases with 35; the Eskimo language uses 63 forms of the present tense and simple nouns have as many as 252 inflections.

In Chinese, the 40-volume *Chung-wen Ta Tz'u-tien* Dictionary lists 49,905 characters. The fourth tone of "i" has 84 meanings, varying as widely as "dress," "hiccough" and "licentious." The written language provides 92 different characters for "i⁴." The most complex written character in Chinese is that representing *xie* which has 64 strokes and means "talkative." The most complex in current use is *yu,* which consists of 32 strokes and means to urge or implore.

Rarest and Commonest Sounds

The rarest speech sound is probably the sound written *ř* in Czech which occurs in very few languages and is the last sound mastered by Czech children. In the southern Bushman language !xo, there is a click, articulated with both lips, which is written ⊙. The *l* sound in the Arabic word *Allah,* in some contexts, is pronounced uniquely in that language. The commonest sound is the vowel *a* (as in English "father"); no language is known to be without it.

Most and Least Irregular Verbs

Esperanto was first published by its inventor, Dr Ludwig Zamenhof (1859–1917), of Warsaw, in 1887 without irregular verbs and is now estimated from textbook sales to have a million speakers. The even earlier language Volapuk, invented by Johann Martin Schleyer (1831–1912) also has absolutely regular configuration. Standard Swahili, though designed to be strictly regular, has 3 irregular imperatives. According to *The Morphology and Syntax of Present-day English* by Prof Olu Tomori, English has 283 irregular verbs. This total, however, includes at least 30 which have been added merely with a prefix.

Largest Vocabulary

The English language contains about 490,000 words, plus another 300,000 technical terms, the most in any language, but it is doubtful if any individual uses more than 60,000. Those in Great Britain who have undergone a full 16 years of education use perhaps 5,000 words in speech and up to 10,000 words in written communications. The members of the International Society for Philosophical Enquiry (no admission for IQ's below 148) have an average vocabulary of 36,250 words.

Smallest Literature

Of written languages, that with the smallest literature is Tyrrhenian, also known as Lemnian, once spoken on the island of Lemnon and believed to be related to Etruscan. The only surviving fragment is a 10-line inscription from the 6th century BC.

Greatest Linguist

If the yardstick of ability to speak with fluency and reasonable accuracy is adhered to, it is doubtful whether any human could maintain fluency in more than 20–25 languages concurrently or achieve fluency in more than 40 in a lifetime.

The most multilingual living person in the world is Georges Henri Schmidt (b Strasbourg, France, Dec 28, 1914), who served as Chief of the UN Terminology Section 1965–71. In the 1975 edition of *Who's Who in the United Nations* he listed "only" 19 languages because he was then unable to find the time to "revive" his former fluency in 12 others.

Historically, the greatest linguists have been proclaimed as Cardinal Mezzofanti (fluent in 26 or 27), Prof Rask (1787–1832), Sir John Bowring (1792–1872), and Dr Harold Williams of New Zealand (1876–1928), who had been fluent in 28 languages.

Oldest Alphabet

The development of the use of an alphabet in place of pictograms occurred in the Sinaitic world between 1700 and 1500 BC. This western Semitic language developed the consonantal system based on phonetic and syllabic principles.

The oldest letter is "O," unchanged in shape since its adoption in the Phoenician alphabet *c.* 1300 BC. The newest letters added to the English alphabet are "j" and "v," which are of post-Shakespearean use, *c.* 1630. Formerly they were used only as variants of "i" and "u." There are now some 65 alphabets in use.

Longest and Shortest Alphabets

The language with most letters is Cambodian with 72 (including useless ones). Rotokas, spoken in the center of Bougainville Island in the South Pacific, has least with 11 (just a, b, e, g, i, k, o, p, ř, t and u).

Most and Least Consonants and Vowels

The language with the most distinct consonantal sounds is the Caucasian language Ubyx, with 85, and that with the least is Rotokas with only 6 consonants. The language with the most vowels is Sedang, a central Vietnamese language with 55 distinguishable vowel sounds. The language with the least (2 vowels) is the Caucasian language Abkhazian. The record in written English for consecutive vowels is 6 in the musical term *euouae.* The Estonian word Jäääärne, meaning "the edge of the ice," has the same 4 consecutively. Voiauai, a language in Pará state, Brazil, consists solely of 7 vowels. The English word "latch-string" has 6 consecutive consonants, but the German word Angstschweiss has 8.

Largest Letters

The largest permanent letters in the world are the giant 600-ft letters spelling READYMIX on the ground in the Nullarbor near East Balladonia, W Australia. This was constructed in Dec 1971.

Smallest Letters

The 16 letters MOLECULAR DEVICES have been etched into a salt crystal by an electron beam so that the strokes were only 2 to 3 mm wide—the width of 20 hydrogen atoms. This was done by Michael Isaacson at Cornell University in Feb 1982.

Longest Words

The longest word ever to appear in literature occurs in *The Ecclesiazusae*, a comedy by Aristophanes (448–380 BC). In the Greek it is 170 letters long but transliterates into 182 letters in English, thus: lopadotemachoselachogaleokranioleipsanodrimhy-potrimmatosilphioparaomelitokatakechymenokich-lepikossyphophattoperisteralektryonoptekephalliok-igklopeleiolagoiosiraiobaphetraganopterygon. The term describes a fricassee of 17 sweet and sour ingredients, including mullet, brains, honey, vinegar, pickles, marrow (the vegetable) and ouzo (a Greek drink laced with anisette).

A compound word of 195 Sanskrit characters (which transliterates into 428 letters in the Roman alphabet) describing the region near Kanci, Tamil Nadu, India, appears in a 16th century work by Tirumalāmbā, queen of Vijayanagara.

The longest word in the Oxford English Dictionary is floccipaucinihilipilification (alternatively spelt in hyphenated form with "n" in seventh place), with 29 letters, meaning "the action of estimating as worthless," first used in 1741, and later by Sir Walter Scott (1771–1832). Webster's Third International Dictionary lists among its 450,000 entries pneumon-oultramicroscopicsilicovolcanoconiosises (45 letters), the plural of a lung disease contracted by some miners.

The nonce word used by Dr Edward Strother (1675–1737) to describe the spa waters at Bristol was aequeosalinocalcinoceraceoaluminosocupreovi-triolic (52 letters).

The longest regularly formed English word is praetertranssubstantiationalistically (37 letters), used by Mark McShane in his novel *Untimely Ripped,* published in 1963. The medical term hepaticocho-langiocholecystenterostomies (39 letters) refers to the surgical creations of new communications between gall bladders and hepatic ducts and between intestines and gall bladders. The longest in common use are disproportionableness and incomprehensibilities (21 letters). Interdenominationalism (22 letters) is found in Webster's and hence perhaps interdenom-inationalistically (28 letters) is permissible.

Longest Palindromic Words

The longest known palindromic word (same spelling backwards as forwards) is *saippuakivikauppias* (19 letters), the Finnish word for a dealer in lye. The longest in the English language is *redivider* (9 letters). The 9-letter word, *Malayalam,* is a proper noun given to the language of the Malayali people in Kerala, southern India, while *Kanakanak* near Dellingham, Alaska, is a 9-letter palandromic place name. The 9-letter word ROTAVATOR is a registered trademark belonging to Howard Machinery Ltd, of England. The contrived chemical term *detartrated* has 11 letters. In American English the word *releveler* is also a 9-letter palindrome, though in England it is spelled *releveller* and hence is not palindromic.

Some baptismal fonts in Greece and Turkey bear the circular 25-letter inscription NIΨON ANOMH-MATA MH MONAN OΨIN meaning "wash (my) sins not only (my) face."

The longest palindromic composition devised is one of 40,000 words completed by Edward Benbow of Bewdley, England, in Jan 1981. It begins, "Anon, now, even odder, I have made lines . . ." and hence predictably ends, ". . . Senile dam Eva, Hired Don. Eve won, Nona."

Most Meanings

The most overworked word in English is the word "set" which has 58 noun uses, 126 verbal uses and 10 as a participial adjective.

Most Succinct Word

The most challenging word for any lexicographer to define briefly is the Fuegian (southernmost Argentina and Chile) word *mamihlapinatapei* meaning "looking at each other hoping that either will offer to do something which both parties desire but are unwilling to do."

Commonest Words and Letters

In written English, the most frequently used words are in order: the, of, and, to, a, in, that, is, I, it, for *and* as. The most used in conversation is I. The commonest letter is "e" and the commonest initial letter is "T."

Most Homophones

The most homophonous sounds in English are *air* and *sol* which, according to the researches of Dora Newhouse of Los Angeles, both have 38 homophones. The homophone with the most variant spellings is *air,* with Aire, are, Ayer, ayr, Ayre, ear, e'er, Eire, ere, err, Eyre, and heir.

Most Accents

Accents were introduced in French in the reign of Louis XIII (1601–43). The word with most accents is *hétérogénéité,* meaning heterogeneity. An atoll in the Pacific Ocean 320 miles east southeast of Tahiti is named Héréhérétué.

Shortest Holoalphabetic Sentence

The contrived headline describing the escape from shipboard confinement of a wryneck bird from the valley kibbutz (designated by the Hebrew letter "qoph") might read, "Cwm Krutza qoph jynx fled brigs," representing the ultimate in 26-letter sentences containing all 26 letters. This was devised by Greg and Peter Maggs of Urbana, Ill, with the aid of 3 computers.

Worst Tongue-Twisters

The most difficult tongue-twister is deemed by Ken Parkin of Teesside, England, to be "The sixth sick sheik's sixth sheep's sick"—especially when spoken quickly.

Longest Abbreviation

The longest known abbreviation of a name is S.K.O.M.K.H.P.K.J.C.D.P.W.B., the initials of the Syarikat Kerjasama Orang-orang Melayu Kerajaan Hilir Perak Kerana Jimat Cermat Dan Pinjam-meminjam Wang Berhad. This is the Malay name for The Cooperative Company of the Lower State of Perak Government's Malay People for Money Savings and Loans Ltd in Teluk Anson, Perak, West Malaysia (formerly called Malaya). The abbreviation for this abbreviation is Skomk.

The 55-letter full name of Los Angeles (El Pueblo de Nuestra Señora la Reina de los Angeles de Porciuncula) is abbreviated to LA, or 3.63% of its length.

Longest Acronym

The longest acronym is NIIOMTPIABOPARM-BETZHELBETRABSBOMONIMONIMONKON-OTDTEKHSTROMONT with 56 letters (54 in Cyrillic) in the *Concise Dictionary of Soviet Terminology* meaning: The laboratory for shuttering, reinforcement, concrete and ferro-concrete operations for composite-monolithic and monolithic constructions of the Department of the Technology of Building—assembly operations of the Scientific Research Institute of the Organization for building mechanization and technical aid of the Academy of Building and Architecture of the USSR.

Longest Anagrams

The longest non-scientific English words which can form anagrams are the 18-letter transpositions "conservationalists" and "conversationalists." The longest scientific transposals are cholecystoduodenostomy/duodenocholecystostomy and hydropneumopericardium/pneumohydropericardium, each of 22 letters.

Longest Scientific Name

The longest scientific name is that of protein resulting from a fusion of β galactosidase and the repressor of β-galactosidase, published in Oct 1978. It consists of 4,059 letters in its abbreviated code form and more than 8,000 letters in its full form. The first nine letters are "Methionyl. . . ." It is anticipated the decoding of biological macromolecules will eventually produce even larger names.

Longest Sentence in Literature

A sentence of 1,300 words appears in *Absalom, Absalom!* by William Faulkner, and one of 3,153 words with 86 semi-colons and 390 commas occurs in the *History of the Church of God* by Sylvester Hassell of Wilson, NC, *c.* 1884. The first 40,000 words of the *Gates of Paradise* by George Andrzeyevski appear to lack any punctuation. Some authors such as James Joyce (1882–1941) appear to eschew punctuation altogether.

LONGEST PLACE NAME IN USE is this 57-letter Maori name for a hill in New Zealand. In 1959 the first letter in the third line was changed from "A" to "O".

The longest sentence recorded ever to have gotten past the editor of a major newspaper is one of 1,286 words in *The New York Times* by Herbert Stein in the issue of Feb 13, 1981.

The Report of the President of Columbia University, 1942–43, contained a sentence of 4,284 words.

Longest Place Names

The official name for Bangkok, capital of Thailand, is Krungthep Mahanakhon. The full name is however: Krungthep Mahanakhon Bovorn Ratanakosin Mahintharayutthaya Mahadilok pop Noparatratchathani Burirom Udomratchanivetmahasathan Amornpiman Avatarnsathit Sakkathattiyavisnukarmprasit (167 letters) which, in the most scholarly transliteration, emerges with 175 letters.

The longest place name now in use is Taumatawhakatangihangakoauauotamatea (turipukakapikimaungahoronuku) pokaiwhenuakitanatahu, the unofficial 85-letter version of the name of a hill (1,002 ft above sea level) in the Southern Hawke's Bay district of North Island, New Zealand. This Maori name means "the hill whereon was played the flute of Tamatea, circumnavigator of lands, for his lady love." The official version has 57 letters (1 to 36 and 65 to 85).

Ijouaououene, a mountain in Morocco, has 8 consecutive vowel letters as rendered by the French.

Shortest Place Names

The shortest place names in the world are the French village of Y (population 143), so named since 1241, the Danish village Å on the island Fyn, the Norwegian village of Å (pronounced "Aw"), the Swedish place Å in Vikholandet, U in the Caroline

Islands of the Pacific, and the Japanese town of Sosei which is alternatively called Aioi or O. There was once a 6 in West Virginia. Today in the US, there are 7 two-lettered place names, including Ed and Uz, both in Kentucky.

Most Spellings

The spelling of the Dutch town of Leeuwarden has been recorded in 225 versions since AD 1046. The Leicestershire village of Shepshed is recorded in 49 spellings since the Scepesvesde of the Doomsday Book in 1086.

Earliest and Longest Personal Names

The earliest personal name which has survived is seemingly that of a predynastic king of Upper Egypt *ante* 3050 BC, who is indicated by the hieroglyphic sign for a scorpion. It has been suggested that the name should be read as Sekhen. The earliest known name of any resident of Britain is Divitiacus, King of the Suessiones, the Gaulish ruler of the Kent area *c.* 75 BC under the name Prydhain.

The longest name used by anyone is Adolph Blaine Charles David Earl Frederick Gerald Hubert Irvin John Kenneth Lloyd Martin Nero Oliver Paul Quincy Randolph Sherman Thomas Uncas Victor William Xerxes Yancy Zeus Wolfeschlegelsteinhausenbergerdorff, Senior, who was born at Bergedorf, near Hamburg, Germany, Feb 29, 1904. On printed forms, he uses only his eighth and second Christian names and his shortened surname, which actually has 550 more letters. He lives in Philadelphia, and has recently shortened his surname to Wolfe+585, Senior.

The longest Christian or given name on record is one of 210 letters, Kapiolani Malamalama O Hawaii Nei Ku'uipo O Keali'i Inu Lama O Kapa'akea He Makua O Kawika Kealoha Pumehana O Kaila A Mumi A Konia Lapa Vila Nui Ma Lamalama O Kou La Hanau O Oe U'ilana Ku'u Lei Ku'u Milimili E Aloha No Ko Makou Ia Ka Pua Lilia Ke Kuini Lapa Vila, in the case of Lily K. Kahumoka, born on June 24, 1981, in Charleston, SC.

Shortest Personal Name

The commonest single-letter surname is O, prevalent in Korea, but with 52 examples in US phone books (1973–81) and 12 in Belgium. This name causes the most distress to those concerned with the prevention of cruelty to computers. Every other letter, except Q, has been traced in US phone books (used as a surname) by A. Ross Eckler. There are two one-letter Burmese names: E (calm), pronounced "aye," and U (egg), pronounced "oo." U used before the name means "uncle."

Most Christian Names

The great-great-grandson of Carlos III of Spain, Don Alfonso de Borbón y Borbón (1866–1934), had 89 Christian names, of which several were lengthened by hyphenation.

Commonest Family Names

The commonest family name in the world is the Chinese name Chang which is borne, according to estimates, by between 9.7% and 12.1% of the Chinese population, so indicating even on the lower estimate that there are at least some 75 million Changs—more than the entire population of all but 7 of the 164 other sovereign countries of the world.

The commonest surname in the English-speaking world is Smith. There are 659,050 nationally insured Smiths in Great Britain, of whom 10,102 are plain John Smith, and another 19,502 are John plus one or more given-name Smiths. Including uninsured persons, there are over 800,000 Smiths in England and Wales alone. There were an estimated 2,382,509 Smiths in the US in 1973.

There are, however, estimated to be 1,600,000 persons in Britain with M', Mc or Mac (Gaelic "son of") as part of their surnames. The commonest of these is Macdonald which accounts for about 55,000 of the Scottish population.

Commonest Christian Names

In UK birth registrations in 1980, the most favored first name for boys whose family name is Smith (9,135 entries) was Matthew, with a small lead over David and Paul (followed by Stephen and Daniel). Among the girls Emma was well ahead of Claire, Sarah, Kelly and Rebecca. (This survey was carried out by C. V. Appleton.) In the US, David has been tops over Michael and Bruce, and generally it is a close race with Barbara probably winning out over Carol and Joy/Joyce. Up until at least 1925 in both countries William and John were first and second.

Most Versions of a Family Name

Edward A. Nedelcov of Regina, Saskatchewan, Canada, has collected 779 versions of the spelling of his family name since Jan 1960. Mzilikazi of Zulu-land (b c. 1795) had his name chronicled in 325 spellings, according to researches by Dr R. Kent Rasmussen.

Most Contrived Name

In the US, the determination to derive commercial or other benefit from being the last listing in the local telephone book has resulted in self-given names starting with up to 9 z's—the extreme example being Mr Zachary Zzzzzzzzzzra in the San Francisco book. Last in the book for North Hollywood, LA, however, is Mr B. Zzzzygot.

Oldest Text

The oldest known written text is the pictographic expression of Sumerian speech, dating from c. 3500 BC. The Samarian papyri, written in Aramaic, found 8½ miles north of Jericho, are dated 375–335 BC.

Oldest Printed Work

The oldest surviving printed work is a Korean scroll or *sutra,* printed from wooden blocks found in the foundations of the Pulguk Sa pagoda, Kyongju, Korea, Oct 14, 1966. It has been dated no later than 704 AD. It was claimed in Nov 1973 that a 28-page book of Tang dynasty poems at Yonsei University, Korea, was printed from metal type c. 1160.

Oldest Mechanically Printed Book

It is generally accepted that the earliest mechanically printed full-length book was a "42-line" Gutenberg Bible, printed at Mainz, Germany, c. 1454 by Johann Henne zum Gensfleisch zur Laden, called "zu Gutenberg" (c. 1398–c. 1468). Work on watermarks published in 1967 indicates a copy of a surviving printed "Donatus" Latin grammar was made from paper made in c. 1450. The earliest exactly dated printed work is the Psalter completed Aug 14, 1457, by Johann Fust (c. 1400–1466) and Peter Schöffer (1425–1502), who had been Gutenberg's chief assistant. The earliest printing by William Caxton, though undated, would appear to be *The Recuyel of the Historyes of Troye* in late 1473 to spring 1474.

Manuscripts

The highest value ever paid for a complete manuscript is £2.2 million (about $4½ million) by Armand

Hammer paid at Christie's, London on Dec 12, 1980 for Leonardo da Vinci's 36-page Codex Leicester manuscript compiled in about 1507. It was sold by the Holkham estate.

Largest Publication

The largest publication in the world is the 1,112-volume set of *British Parliamentary Papers* of 1800–1900 published by the Irish University Press in 1968–1972. A complete set weighs 3.64 tons, costs $69,000 and would take 6 years to read at 10 hours per day. The production and binding involved the death of 34,000 Indian goats and $39,000 worth of gold ingots. The total print run was 500 sets.

Largest Book

The largest book in the world is the *Super Book* measuring 9 ft × 10 ft 2⅛ in, weighing 557 lb, consisting of 300 pages published in Denver, Colo in 1976.

Smallest Book

The smallest marketed bound printed book with cursive material is one of 20 pages measuring 1/18 × 1/18 of an inch comprising the children's story "Ari" (The Ant) made by Asao Hoshio in Tokyo, Japan, and published in 200 copies in June 1980.

Most Expensive Book

The highest price ever paid for a printed book is $2,400,000 for one of the only 21 known complete copies of the Gutenberg Bible, printed in Mainz, (West) Germany, in *c.* 1454. It was bought from the Carl and Lily Pforzheimer Foundation by the University of Texas in a sale arranged by Quaritch of London in NYC, June 9, 1978.

Highest-Priced Printed Document

The highest price ever paid for a broadsheet was $404,000 for one of the 16 known copies of *The Declaration of Independence,* printed in Philadelphia in 1776 by Samuel T. Freeman & Co, and sold to a Texan in May 1969.

Highest-Priced Atlas

The highest price paid for an atlas is $697,000 for a 16th century Mercator atlas of Europe sold at auction at Sotheby's, London, March 13, 1979.

Post Cards

The top-selling post card of all time was said to be a drawing by Donald McGill (1875–1962) with the caption: He: "Do you like Kipling?" She: "I don't know, you naughty boy, I've never kippled." It sold about 6 million. Between 1904 and his death, McGill sold more than 350 million cards to users and deltiologists (picture post card collectors).

Longest Novel

The longest important novel ever published is *Les hommes de bonne volonté* by Louis Henri Jean Farigoule (1885–1972), *alias* Jules Romains, of France, in 27 volumes in 1932–46. The English version, *Men of Good Will,* was published in 14 volumes in 1933–46 as a "novel-cycle." The 4,959-page edition published by Peter Davies Ltd has an estimated 2,070,000 words, excluding a 100-page index. The novel *Tokuga-Wa Ieyasu* by Sohachi Yamaoka has been serialized in Japanese daily newspapers since 1951. Now completed, it will require nearly 40 volumes in book form.

Earliest and Largest Encyclopaediae

The earliest known encyclopaedia was compiled in Athens by Speusippus (*post* 408–*c.* 338 BC) in *c.* 370 BC. He was a nephew of Plato. The largest encyclopaedia ever compiled was the *Great Standard Encyclopaedia* of Yung-lo ta tien of 22,937 manuscript books (370 still survive); written by 2,000 Chinese scholars in 1403–08.

Most Comprehensive Encyclopaedia

The most comprehensive academic encyclopaedia is the *Encyclopaedia Britannica,* first published in Edinburgh, Scotland, in Dec 1768–1771. A group of booksellers in the US acquired reprint rights in 1898 and complete ownership in 1899. In 1943, the *Britannica* was given to the University of Chicago. The current 30-volume 15th edition contains 33,141 pages and 43 million words from 4,277 contributors. It is now edited in Chicago and in London.

Longest Index

The Ninth Collective Index of *Chemical Abstracts,* completed on Aug 23, 1978, contains 20,550,000 entries in 95,882 pages in 57 volumes, and weighs 251 lb.

LARGEST BOOK (above): Titled "Super Book,"
this 300-page, 557-lb volume, published in
Denver, Colo, measures 9 ft by more than 10 ft.
TOP-SELLING POST CARD (left): About 6 million people liked this joke so much they sent
copies of this card to friends. LARGEST INDEX
(below): This 10-ft-high stack of volumes contains 95,882 pages with more than 20½ million
entries indexing chemical abstracts.

"Do you like Kipling?"
"I don't know, you naughty boy,
I've never kippled!"

TOP-SELLING AUTHORS AND AUTHORESSES (reading clockwise): The MOST PROLIFIC NOVELIST was Kathleen Lindsay
(above) of South Africa who wrote 904 novels, using 6 pen
names, 2 of them masculine. (Argus So. African Newspapers Ltd.)
Today's BEST-SELLING AUTHORESS is Barbara Cartland (center,
above) with 300 million copies sold of her 344 light romances.
Agatha Christie (right, above), whose 87 novels also sold 300
million copies, was published in 103 languages. The YOUNGEST
AUTHORESS to be commercially published is Dorothy Straight
(right) who was 4 years old in 1962 when she wrote her book,
"How the World Began," which was published in the US in 1964.
(Pantheon Books) Surpassing all writers, however, was Mao Tse-
Tung (right, below), whose "Quotations" was distributed or sold
in a quantity estimated at 800 million copies. Possession of a
copy was virtually mandatory for each Chinese adult between
1966 and 1971. Jacqueline Susann (center, below) has the HIGH-
EST SALES FOR A SINGLE NOVEL, "Valley of the Dolls," which
has sold more than 25 million copies since 1966. John Creasey
(left, below) is the FASTEST NOVELIST. Not only did he write 22
novels one year and 564 in 42 years, but he once wrote 2 books in
one week with a half-day off. He used his own name and 13
pseudonyms.

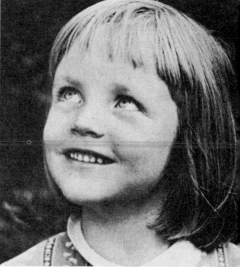

Most Prolific Writers

The most prolific writer for whom a word count has been published was Charles Hamilton, *alias* Frank Richards (1875–1961), the Englishman who created Billy Bunter. At the height of his career in 1908 he wrote the whole of the boys' comics *Gem* (founded 1907) and *Magnet* (1908–1940) and most of two others, totaling 80,000 words a week. His lifetime output has been put at 100 million words. He enjoyed the advantages of electric light rather than candlelight, and of being unmarried.

The champion of the goose-quill era was Józef Ignacy Kraszewski (1812–1887) of Poland, who produced more than 600 volumes of novels and historical works.

Soho Tokutomi (1863–1957) wrote the history *Kinsei Nippon Kokuminshi* in 100 volumes of 429,425 pages and 19,452,952 letters in 35 years.

The greatest number of novels published by any author is 904 by Kathleen Lindsay (Mrs Mary Faulkner) (1903–1973) of Somerset West, Cape Province, South Africa. She wrote under six pen names, two of them masculine. The most prolific living novelist is Lauran Paine of California, who has had 856 works published under 71 pen names.

After receiving a probable record 743 rejection slips, the British novelist John Creasey (1908–73), under his own name and 13 *noms de plume,* had 564 books totaling more than 40 million words published from 1932 to his death on June 9, 1973.

Enid Mary Blyton (Mrs Darrell Waters) (1898–1968) (UK), completed 600 titles of children's stories, many of them brief, with 59 in the single year 1955. They have been translated into a record 128 languages.

Highest Printings

The world's most widely distributed book is the Bible, portions of which have been translated into 1,735 languages. It has been estimated that between 1815 and 1975 some 2,500 million Bibles were printed, of which 1,500 million were handled by Bible Societies. The total distribution of Bibles by the United Bible Societies (covering 150 countries) in the year 1981 was 10,441,456.

It has been reported that 800 million copies of the red-covered booklet *Quotations from the Works of Mao Tse-tung* were sold or distributed between June 1966, when possession became virtually mandatory in China, and Sept 1971, when their promoter, Marshal Lin Piao, died in an air crash.

The total disposal through non-commercial chan-

nels by Jehovah's Witnesses of the 192-page hardbound book *The Truth That Leads to Eternal Life* published by the Watchtower Bible and Tract Society of Brooklyn, NYC, on May 8, 1968, reached 102,137,804 in 116 languages by Apr 1, 1982.

Some 75 million copies of *The American Spelling Book* by Noah Webster were distributed with Federal funds.

Top-Selling Authors

The all-time sales estimate of books by Erle Stanley Gardner (1889–1970) (US) to Jan 1, 1981, is 314,833,102 copies in 37 languages. The top-selling woman writer has been Dame Agatha Christie (*née* Agatha Mary Clarissa Miller), later Lady Mallowan (formerly Mrs Archibald Christie) (1890–1976). Her 87 crime novels have sold an estimated 300 million copies in 103 languages. *Sleeping Murder* was published posthumously in 1977.

Currently the top-selling authoress is Barbara Cartland (Mrs McCorquodale) with global sales nearing 300 million copies for 344 titles in 17 languages. In 1977, 1980 and 1981 she published 24 titles in the calendar year.

It was announced on March 13, 1953, that 672,058,000 copies of the works of Marshal Josef Vissarionovich Dzhugashvili, also known as Stalin (1879–1953), had been sold or distributed in 101 languages.

Oldest Authoress

The oldest authoress was Mrs Alice Pollock (*née* Wykeham-Martin) (1868–1971) of Haslemere, Surrey, England, whose book *Portrait of My Victorian Youth* (Johnson Publications) was published in March 1971 when she was aged 102 years 8 months.

Youngest Author

The youngest recorded commercially published author is Dorothy Straight (b May 25, 1958) of Washington, DC, who wrote *How the World Began* in 1962, aged 4. It was published in Aug 1964 by Pantheon Books.

Highest-Paid Writer

In 1958, a Mrs Deborah Schneider of Minneapolis wrote 25 words to complete a sentence in a competition for the best blurb for Plymouth cars. She won from about 1,400,000 entrants the prize of $500 every month for life. On normal life expectations she would collect $12,000 per word. No known anthology includes Mrs Schneider's deathless prose.

Greatest Advance

The greatest advance royalty paid for any book is $3,208,875 by Bantam Books Inc. for the novel *Princess Daisy,* by Judith Krantz, in an auction in NYC on Sept 5, 1979.

Best Sellers

It is believed that the 1879 edition of *The McGuffey Reader,* compiled by Henry Vail and published for school distribution in the US by Van Antwerp Bragg and Co, sold 60 million copies in the pre-copyright era.

The authors who have written what is now the all-time copyrighted best seller as well as the world's fastest-selling title are Norris Dewar McWhirter (b Aug 12, 1925) and his twin brother Alan Ross McWhirter (killed Nov 27, 1975), editors and compilers of the *Guinness Book of World Records,* first published from 107 Fleet Street, London, England, in Oct 1955. To mid-1982, global sales in 21 languages are estimated at over 45 million copies, increasing by some 60,000 per week.

The novel with the highest sales has been *Valley of the Dolls* (first published March 1966) by Jacqueline Susann (Mrs Irving Mansfield) (1921–74) with a world-wide total of 25,412,000 to May 1, 1982. In the first 6 months Bantam sold 6.8 million.

Slowest Seller

The accolade for the world's slowest-selling book (known in publishing as slooow-sellers) probably belongs to David Wilkins' Translation of the New Testament from Coptic into Latin, published by Oxford University Press in 1716 with 500 copies. Selling an average of one each 139 days, it remained in print for 191 years.

Fastest Publishing

The fastest time in which a book has been published is 46½ hours from receipt of manuscript to finished copies in the case of *Miracle on Ice* by the staff of *The New York Times* on Feb 27–28–29, 1980. The 96-page story of the US Olympic gold medal ice hockey team was published by Bantam Books Inc.

Most Rejections

The greatest recorded number of publishers' rejections for a manuscript is 137 for *One Man Versus the Establishment* by William E. E. Owens of Street, Somerset, England.

Largest Dictionary

The largest English language dictionary is the 12-volume Royal quarto *The Oxford English Dictionary* of 15,487 pages published between 1884 and 1928 with a first supplement of 963 pages in 1933 and a further 4-volume supplement, edited by R. W. Burchfield, in which the third and fourth volumes have yet to appear. The work contains 414,825 word listings, 1,827,306 illustrative quotations and reputedly 227,779,589 letters and figures, 63.8 times more than the Bible. The greatest outside contributor has been Marghanita Laski with 175,000 since 1958.

Deutsches Wörterbuch started by Jacob and Wilhelm Grimm in 1854 was completed in 34,519 pages and 33 volumes in 1971. Today's price is DM4,920.30 (now $2,000).

The New Grove Dictionary of Music and Musicians (Editor: Stanley Sadie) published in 20 volumes by Macmillan's in Feb 1981 contains over 22 million words and 4,500 illustrations and is the largest specialist dictionary yet published.

Oldest Bible

Biblical texts in Hebrew are known to have become stabilized as early as 70 AD. The oldest leather and papyrus Dead Sea Scrolls date from *c.* 250 BC. The oldest known Bible is the *Codex Vaticanus,* written in Greek *ante*-350 AD, and preserved in the Vatican Museum, Rome.

The earliest complete Bible *printed* in English was edited by Miles Coverdale (*c.* 1488–1569), while living in Antwerp, and printed in 1535. The New Testament in English, however, had been printed by William Tyndale in Cologne and in Worms, Germany, in 1525.

Largest Printers

The largest printers in the world are R. R. Donnelley & Co of Chicago. The company, founded in 1864, has plants in 15 main centers, and has turned out $957 million worth of work per year. More than 67,000 tons of inks and 1,344,000 tons of paper and board are consumed every year.

The largest printer under one roof is the US Government Printing Office in Washington, DC, founded in 1860. The Superintendent of Documents has been selling over $50 million worth of US governmental publications every year and has maintained an inventory of nearly 20,000 titles in print. However, the current administration has ordered a cutback in printing of books and pamphlets with public appeal, and is planning to offer government-created material to private publishers.

Longest-Lived Comic Strip

The most durable newspaper comic strip has been the Katzenjammer Kids (Hans and Fritz) created by Rudolph Dirks, first published in the *New York Journal* on Dec 12, 1897, and carried on by his son.

The earliest strip was *The Yellow Kid* which first appeared in the *New York Journal* on Oct 18, 1896. The most widely syndicated is *Blondie,* which appears in 1,800 newspapers in 55 countries, in 15 languages, with a readership of an estimated 150 million daily.

Most Widely Syndicated Cartoonist

Ranan R. Lurie (b May 26, 1932) is the most widely syndicated cartoonist in the world. His work is published in 45 countries.

Earliest Autograph

The earliest surviving signature known is that of the French king Clotaire I (Le Vieux) of Soissons (558–561) born *c.* 497. A signum exists for William I (the Conqueror) *c.* 1070.

Most Expensive Autographs

The highest price ever paid on the open market for a single letter is $100,000 paid on Oct 18, 1979 at a Charles Hamilton Auction in NYC for a brief receipt signed by Button Gwinnett (1732–77), one of the three men from Georgia and the 56 signatories to the Declaration of Independence on July 4, 1776.

An expense account by Paul Revere, dated Jan 3, 1774 and signed by John Hancock, was auctioned for $70,000 at Sotheby Parke Bernet, NYC, April 26, 1978.

The highest price paid for a signed autograph letter of a living person is $12,500 at the Hamilton Galleries on Jan 22, 1981, for a letter from President Ronald Reagan praising Frank Sinatra.

Most Valuable Autographs

Only one example of the signature of Christopher Marlowe (1565–93) is known. It is in the Kent County Archives, England, on a will of 1583. It is estimated that a seventh Shakespearean signature would realize at least $2 million at auction.

Most Autographs

Dong Kingman, well-known Chinese-American watercolor artist, signed personally 10,000 each of 12 of his lithographed paintings (making 120,000 in all) in Hong Kong in 12 days of continuous sitting, May 8–19, 1980, for Rocky Aoki's *Benihana Collection.*

MOST AUTOGRAPHS: Dong Kingman

Bond Signing

The greatest feat of autographing was performed by Arne Aaaser of Den Norske Creditbank, Oslo, Norway. He signed 20.000 bonds in 16 hours 2 min 50 sec, March 4–5, 1982.

Poets Laureate

The youngest Poet Laureate was Laurence Eusden (1688–1730), who at the age of 30 years 3 months on Dec 24, 1718, was appointed. The greatest age at which a poet has succeeded is 73 in the case of William Wordsworth (1770–1850) on Apr 6, 1843. The longest-lived Laureate was John Masefield, who died on May 12, 1967, aged 88 years 345 days. The longest which any poet has worn the laurel is 41 years 322 days, in the case of Alfred (later the 1st Lord) Tennyson (1809–92), who was appointed Nov 19, 1850, and died in office Oct 6, 1892.

Longest Poem

The lengthiest poem ever published has been the Kirghiz folk epic *Manas,* which appeared in printed form in 1958, but which has never been translated into English. It runs to "more than 500,000 lines." Short translated passages appear in *The Elek Book of Oriental Verse.*

The longest poem ever written in the English language appears to be one on the life of King Alfred by John Fitchett (1766–1838) of Liverpool, England, which ran to 129,807 lines and took 40 years to write. His editor, Robert Riscoe, added the concluding 2,585 lines.

Roger Brien's (b Montreal, 1910) *Prométhée—dialogue des vivants et des morts* runs to 456,047 lines written in 1964–81. Brien has written another 497,000 lines of French poetry in over 90 published works.

Most Successful Poem

The most translated poem is believed to be "If" by Joseph Rudyard Kipling (1865–1936), first published in 1910. It has appeared in 27 languages and according to Kipling was "anthologized to weariness."

Longest Letter

The longest personal letter based on word count is one of 1,113,747 words written in 8 months ending in May 1976 by Jacqueline Jones of Lindale, Texas, to her sister Mrs Jean Stewart of Springfield, Me.

Letters to the Editor

The *Upper Dauphin Sentinel,* Pa, published a letter of 23,513 words over 8 issues from Aug to Nov 1979, written by John Sultzbaugh of nearby Lykens, Pa.

The shortest literary correspondence on record was that between Victor Marie Hugo (1802–85) and his publisher, Hurst and Blackett, in 1862. The author was on holiday and anxious to know how his new novel *Les Misérables* was selling. He wrote "?". The reply was "!".

Most Durable Pen Pals

The longest sustained correspondence on record is one of 74 years between Mrs E. Darlington of Marple, Cheshire, England and Mrs Gertrude Walker of Hawthorn, South Australia, which started Jan 5, 1906.

Most Personal Mail

The highest confirmed count of letters received by any private citizen in a year is 900,000 letters by baseball star Henry Aaron, reported by the US Postal Department in June 1974 the year that he surpassed Babe Ruth's career home run record. About a third of them were letters of hate.

Longest Diary

The diary of Edward Robb Ellis (b 1911) of NYC, begun in 1927 after 55 years, is estimated to run to 15 million words. Mrs P. Joyce Evans (b May 6, 1890) of Swansea, Glamorgan, South Wales, completed the first 75 years of her diary in 1981.

Largest Libraries

The largest library is the Library of Congress (founded Apr 24, 1800), on Capitol Hill, Washington, DC. By 1981, it contained 78,641,212 items, including 19,578,334 books and pamphlets. With the James Madison Memorial Extension, which was dedicated in Apr 1980, the buildings contain 64.6 acres of floor space and 532 miles of book shelves.

The largest non-statutory library is the New York Public Library (founded 1895) on Fifth Avenue, NYC, with a floor area of 525,276 sq ft and 88 miles of shelving. Including 82 branch libraries, its collection embraces 10,205,469 volumes, 11,816,587 manuscripts, and 346,358 maps.

Overdue Books

The most overdue book taken out by a known borrower was a book on febrile diseases (London, 1805, by Dr J. Currie) checked out in 1823 from the University of Cincinnati Medical Library and reported returned Dec 7, 1968, by the borrower's great-grandson Richard Dodd. The fine was calculated as $2,264, but waived.

Oldest Newspapers

The oldest existing newspaper in the world is the Swedish official journal *Post och Inrikes Tidningar,* founded in 1645. It is published by the Royal Swedish Academy of Letters. The oldest existing commercial newspaper is the *Haarlems Dagblad/Oprechte Haarlemsche Courant,* published in Haarlem, in the Netherlands. The *Courant* was first issued as the *Weeckelycke Courante van Europa* on Jan 8, 1656, and a copy of issue No. 1 survives.

Most Newspapers

The US had 1,745 English-language daily newspapers on Oct 1, 1980. They had a combined net paid circulation of 62,201,840 copies per day. The peak year for US newspapers was 1910 when there were 2,202. The leading newspaper readers in the world are the people of Sweden, where 554 newspapers are sold per each 1,000 persons.

Largest Newspaper Issue

The most massive single issue of a newspaper was *The New York Times* of Sunday, Oct 17, 1965. It comprised 15 sections with a total of 946 pages, including about 1,200,000 lines of advertising. Each copy weighed 7½ lb and sold for 50 cents locally.

Highest Newspaper Circulation

The first newspaper to achieve a circulation of 1 million was *Le Petit Journal,* published in Paris, France, which reached this figure in 1886 when selling at 5 centimes.

The highest circulation for any newspaper is that for the *Yomiuri Shimbun* (founded 1874) of Japan which reached 13,872,893 copies on Apr 1, 1982. This has been achieved by totaling the figures for editions published in various centers with a morning circulation of 8,914,473 and an evening circulation of 4,958,420.

The newspaper which achieves the closest to a saturation circulation is *The Sunday Post,* established in Glasgow in 1914. In 1981 its estimated readership in Scotland of 2,790,000 represented 69 per cent of the entire population aged 15 and older.

Oldest Periodical

The oldest continuing periodical in the world is *Philosophical Transactions of the Royal Society,* published in London, which first appeared on Mar 6, 1665.

Largest Circulation Periodicals

The largest circulation of any weekly periodical is that of *TV Guide,* which, in 1974, became the first magazine in history to sell a billion copies in a year. The weekly average for July to Dec 1981, was 17,670,543.

In its 41 basic international editions the *Reader's Digest* (established Feb 1922) circulates 31,145,000 copies monthly, in 17 languages, including a US edition of more than 17,750,000 copies.

Parade, the syndicated Sunday newspaper color magazine supplement, is distributed with 137 newspapers every Sunday, yielding a circulation of 21,920,842 (Mar 1982).

Advertising Rates

The highest price ever for a single page of advertising is $199,040 for a four-color back cover of *Parade* in Mar 1982 (circulation see above). The record for a four-color inside page is $194,062 in *Parade* (in Mar 1982). The advertising revenue from the Oct 1978 US edition of *Reader's Digest* was a peak $10,393,200.

The highest expenditure ever incurred on a single advertisement in a periodical is $3,200,000 by Gulf and Western Industries for insertions in the Feb 5, 1979 *Time* magazine (US and selected overseas editions).

The world's highest newspaper advertising rate is 23,190,000 yen ($96,625) for a full page in the morning edition and 16,800,000 yen ($70,000) for the evening edition of the *Yomiuri Shimbun* of Tokyo (Apr 1982), at the rate of 240 yen to the dollar.

Most Durable Advertiser

The Jos Neel Co, a clothing store in Macon, Ga (founded 1880) has run an ad in the *Macon Telegraph* every day in the upper left hand corner of page 2 since Feb 22, 1889 or 33,362 times to May 1982.

Most Misprints

The record for misprints in *The Times* (London) was set on Aug 22, 1978, when on page 19 there were 97 in 5½ single column inches. The passage concerned "Pop" (Pope) Paul VI.

Crossword Puzzles

The earliest crossword was one with 32 clues invented by Arthur Wynne (b Liverpool, England) and published in the *New York World* on Dec 21, 1913.

The largest crossword ever published is one compiled by Stephen Robinson of Coventry, England, published by Onsworld Ltd of Stamford, England, on Oct 22, 1979. It contains 6,257 clues across and 6,051 down and covers 18½ sq ft.

Christmas Cards

The greatest number of personal Christmas cards sent out is believed to be 62,824 by Werner Erhard of San Francisco, founder of est, in Dec 1975.

Oldest Map

The oldest known map of any kind is a clay tablet depicting the Euphrates River flowing through northern Mesopotamia (Iraq), dated *c.* 3800 BC. The earliest printed map in the world dates from Isidore of Seville's *Etymologiarum* of 1472.

4. MUSIC*

Earliest Notation and Instruments

The earliest surviving musical notation dates from *c.* 1800 BC. A heptonic scale deciphered from a clay tablet by Dr Duchesne-Guillemin in 1966–67 was found at a site in Nippur, Sumer, now Iraq. Also dated *c.* 1800 BC is an Assyrian love song to a Ugaritic god, reconstructed for an 11-string lyre from a tablet of notation and lyric at the University of California, Berkeley, March 6, 1974. Musical history is, however, able to be traced back to the 3rd millennium BC when the yellow bell (*huang chung*) had a recognized standard musical tone in Chinese temple music. Whistles and flutes made from perforated phalange bones have been found at Upper Paleolithic sites of the Aurignacian Period (*c.* 25,000–22,000 BC), *e.g.* at Istallóskö, Hungary, and in Molodova, USSR.

Earliest Piano

The earliest pianoforte in existence is one built in Florence, Italy, in 1720, by Bartolommeo Cristofori (1655–1731) of Padua, and now preserved in the Metropolitan Museum of Art, NYC.

Grandest Piano

The grandest grand piano built was one weighing 1⅓ tons and measuring 11 ft 8 in long, made by Chas. H. Challen & Son Ltd of London in 1935. The longest bass string measured 9 ft 11 in and the tensile stress on the 726-lb frame was 33.6 tons.

Most Expensive Piano

The highest price ever paid for a piano is $390,000 for a Steinway grand of *c.* 1888 sold at Sotheby Parke Bernet, NYC on March 26, 1980 for the Martin Beck Theatre and bought by a non-pianist.

* "Music Facts and Feats," A Guinness Superlatives Book (Sterling) can be referred to for a more detailed treatment of musical facts and records.

EARLIEST PIANO: Built in 1720 in Florence, Italy, this pianoforte is preserved now in NYC. (Metropolitan Museum of Art)

ALPHORN (left, above): Built in 1976 from a single spruce log originally for a Swiss cheese company, this has now been extended to almost 60 ft long. Here it is being blown in the German Alps for a Guinness TV show. (David A. Boehm) **LARGEST DOUBLE BASS (right, above):** Built in 1924 in NJ, this 14-ft-tall instrument had leathern strings. The builder said the Archangel Gabriel ordered it.

MUSICAL INSTRUMENTS (reading clockwise): 1. The world's tallest electric guitar, 10 ft 1 in high, weighing 300 lb, was built in San Francisco (Edmund Shea) 2. This 1-in-long playable violin topped the record that stood since 1976. 3. The largest brass instrument, a tuba, is 7½ ft tall and uses 39 ft of tubing. (Europix) 4. Stan Harper is playing the world's largest harmonica, the Hohner 48-chord which has 354 separate holes. 5. Underwater violinist Mark Gottlieb, with his sister Karen at the organ, performed in a pool for 2 Guinness TV shows. 6. The largest non-electric guitar stands 8 ft 10 in tall. Many of these instruments are on display in the various Guinness Museums. (See last page of book for museum information.)

Organs

The largest and loudest musical instrument ever constructed and now only partly functional is the Auditorium Organ in Atlantic City, NJ. Completed in 1930, this heroic instrument has two consoles (one with seven manuals and another movable one with five), 1,477 stop controls and 33,112 pipes ranging in tone from 3/16 in to the 64-ft tone. It is powered with blower motors of 365 horsepower, cost $500,000 and has the volume of 25 brass bands, with a range of 7 octaves.

The largest church organ is in Passau Cathedral, Germany. It was completed in 1928 by D. F. Steinmeyer & Co. It has 16,000 pipes and five manuals.

The most versatile electric organ is the 8-manual Kawai T50 built in Japan in 1977 to mark the company's golden jubilee.

The chapel organ at the US Military Academy at West Point, NY, has, since 1911, been expanded from 2,406 to 18,200 pipes.

The loudest organ stop in the world is the Ophicleide stop of the Grand Great in the Solo Organ in the Atlantic City Auditorium (see above). It is operated by a pressure of 100 in of water (3½ lb per sq in) and has a pure trumpet note of earsplitting volume, more than 6 times the volume of the loudest locomotive whistles.

Most Durable Organist

The longest recorded reign as an organist has been 81 years in the case of Charles Bridgeman (1779–1873) of All Saints Parish Church, Hertford, England, who was appointed in 1792 and was still playing in 1873. The year in which he reached his crescendo was not recorded.

Double Bass

The largest double bass ever constructed was 14 ft tall, built in 1924 in Ironia, NJ by Arthur K. Ferris, allegedly on orders from the Archangel Gabriel. It weighed 1,300 lb with a sound box 8 ft across, and had leathern strings totaling 104 ft. Its low notes could be felt rather than heard.

Five members of "Bass Ten" from Bournemouth, Dorset, England, bowed and 5-fingered a double bass simultaneously in a rendition of Monti's *Czardas* on Oct 25, 1981.

Most Valuable Cello

The highest price paid at auction for a violoncello is $290,000 at Sotheby's, London on Nov 8, 1978 for a Stradivari made in Cremona, Italy in 1710.

Most Valuable Violin

The highest price ever paid at auction for a violin is $297,250 for one of the "Hubermann" *ex* Kreisler Stradivari dated 1733 at Sotheby's, London, on May 3, 1979. Some 700 of the 1,116 violins by Stradivarius (1644–1737) have survived. His inlaid "Hellier" violin was sold by private treaty in the US in March 1979, for a reported $400,000.

Underwater Violinist

The pioneer violinist to surmount the problems of playing the violin under water has been Mark Gottlieb. Submerged in the Evergreen State College swimming pool in Olympia, Wash, in Mar 1975, he gave his first submarine rendition of Handel's "Water Music." His most intractable problem was his underwater *détaché*. On Oct 7, 1979, the first underwater quartet performed in the *Challenge the Guinness* TV show on Channel 7 in Tokyo, Japan.

Most Durable Fiddlers

Rolland S. Tapley retired as a violinist from the Boston Symphony Orchestra after playing for a reputedly unrivaled 58 years from Feb 1920 to Aug 27, 1978. Otto E. Funk, 62, walked 4,165 miles from NYC to San Francisco, playing his Hopf violin every step of the way westward. He arrived June 16, 1929, after 183 days on the road.

Stringed Instrument

The largest moveable stringed instrument ever constructed was a pantaleon with 270 strings stretched over 50 sq ft, used by George Noel in 1767. The greatest number of musicians required to operate a single instrument was the 6 needed to play the gigantic orchestrion, known as the Appolonican, built in 1816 and played until 1840.

Largest and Most Expensive Guitars

The largest and presumably also the loudest playable guitar is an electric guitar 10 ft 1 in tall and in excess of 300 lb in weight built by Sparkling Ragtime Productions of San Francisco and the Guild of American Luthiers, Tacoma, Wash, in Dec 1980.

The most expensive standard-sized guitar is the German chittara battente, built by Jacob Stadler (dated 1624), which sold for £10,500 ($25,200) at Christie's, London, June 12, 1974.

The largest non-electric guitar was made by the Harmony Co of Chicago and stands 8 ft 10 in tall, weighs 80 lb and has a volume of 16,000 cu in (cf, the standard 1,024 cu in). Examples are exhibited in the Guinness Museums in NYC and San Francisco.

Brass Instrument

The largest recorded brass instrument is a tuba standing 7½ ft tall, with 39 ft of tubing and a bell 3 ft 4 in across. This contrabass tuba was constructed for a world tour by the band of John Philip Sousa (1854–1932), the "march king," c. 1896–98, and is still in use. This instrument is now owned by a circus promoter in South Africa.

Longest Alphorn

The longest alphorn has been extended to 59 ft 9½ in long. It was originally built from a single spruce log for a cheese company in Switzerland in 1976. It was demonstrated by Herr Lamy for the David Frost-Guinness TV show on June 28, 1981.

Largest Drum

The largest drum ever constructed was one 12 ft in diameter weighing 600 lb for the Boston World Peace Jubilee of 1872.

Easiest and Most Difficult Instruments

The American Music Conference announced in Sept 1977 that the easiest instrument is the ukelele and the most difficult are the French horn and the oboe. The latter has been described as "the ill wood-wind that no one blows good."

Largest Orchestras

The most massive orchestra ever assembled was one of 20,100 at the Ullevaal Stadium, Oslo, June 28, 1964, made up of Norges Musikkorps Forbund bands from all over Norway.

On June 17, 1872, Johann Strauss the Younger (1825–99) conducted an orchestra of 987 instruments supported by a choir of 20,000, at the World Peace Jubilee in Boston, Mass. There were 400 first violinists.

Marching Bands

The largest on record was one of 2,512 musicians and 494 baton twirlers, flag bearers and directors who played and marched in Minneapolis, Minn, on Oct 12, 1981.

The longest recorded musical march by a marching band is one of 37.9 miles from Lillehammer to Hamar, Norway, in 15 hours when, on May 10, 1980, 26 of 35 members of the Trondheim Brass Band survived the playing of 135 marches.

Greatest Classical Concert Attendance

The greatest attendance at any classical concert was an estimated 400,000 for a presentation by the Boston Pops Orchestra, conducted by Arthur Fiedler (b Dec 17, 1894, d July 10, 1979) at the Hatch Memorial Shell, Boston, Mass on July 4, 1976. At the 1978 concert the 83-year-old conductor was presented with a testimonial bearing a record 500,000 signatures.

Pop Festival Attendance

The greatest claimed attendance was 600,000 for a rock festival ("Summer Jam") at Watkins Glen, NY July 29, 1973. Of those attending, about 150,000 actually paid for admission. There were 12 "sound towers." The attendance at the third Pop Festival at East Afton Farm, Freshwater, Isle of Wight, England, on Aug 30, 1970, was claimed by its promoters, Fiery Creations, to be 400,000.

One-Man Concert Attendance

The largest live audience ever attracted by a solo performer is 400,000 estimated to have heard Elton John in Central Park, NYC, free, in Oct 1980. Some 175,000 in the Maracaña Stadium, Rio de Janeiro, Brazil paid to hear Frank Sinatra (b 1915) sing on Jan 26, 1980.

Highest and Lowest Notes

The extremes of orchestral instruments (excluding the organ) range between a handbell tuned to g‴‴ or 6,272 cycles per sec, and the sub-contrabass clarinet, which can reach C͵ or 16.4 cycles per sec. The highest note on a standard pianoforte is C‴‴, 4,186 cycles per sec, which is also the violinist's limit. In 1873, a sub double bassoon able to reach B͵͵# or 14.6 cycles per sec was constructed, but no surviving specimen is known. The extremes for the organ are g‴‴‴ (the sixth G above middle C) (12,544 cycles per sec) and C͵͵ (8.12 cycles per sec) obtainable from ¾-in and 64-ft pipes, respectively.

LARGEST MARCHING BAND (left): With 2,512 musicians and 494 baton twirlers, flag bearers and directors, Minneapolis set a record in Oct 1981. Of HIGHEST-PAID SINGERS, Jenny Lind, the "Swedish Nightingale," (above) was one whose concerts could bring in up to $653 for a seat in 1850 when the dollar was worth 15 times as much as in 1982. (Radio Times Hulton) Frank Sinatra (below) drew 175,000 people to his ONE-MAN CONCERT in Brazil in Jan 1980.

MUSIC WORLD LUMIN-
ARIES (reading counter-
clockwise): Enrico Caruso,
dressed in his role of Pagliacci (1) (© A. Dupont) was
the richest opera singer
(2) (Radio Times Hulton) in the
1920's and his recordings of
"Vesti la Giubba" were the
first to sell a total of one
million. (3) Liberace earns
$2 million each season.
(4) Composer Havergal
Brian wrote a symphony
that requires 800 per-
formers, including 4 brass
bands. (5) Gustav Mahler
composed the longest classical symphony—it takes 1
hour 40 min. (Radio Times Hulton) (6) The largest opera
house is the Metropolitan in
NYC, with 3,800 seats.

Most Prolific Composers

The most prolific composer of all time was probably Georg Philipp Telemann (1681–1767) of Germany. He composed 12 complete sets of services (one cantata every Sunday) for a year, 78 services for special occasions, 40 operas, 600 to 700 orchestral suites, 44 Passions, plus concertos and chamber music.

The most prolific symphonist was Johann Melchior Molter (c. 1695–1765) of Germany, who wrote 165. Joseph Haydn (1732–1809) of Austria wrote 104 numbered symphonies, some of which are regularly played today.

Most Rapid Composer

Among classical composers the most rapid was Wolfgang Amadeus Mozart (1756–91) of Austria, who wrote c. 1,000 operas, operettas, symphonies, violin sonatas, divertimenti, serenades, motets, concertos for piano and many other instruments, string quartets, other chamber music, masses and litanies, of which only 70 were published before he died, aged 35. His opera *The Clemency of Titus* (1791) was written in 18 days and three symphonic masterpieces, *Symphony No. 39 in E flat major, Symphony in G minor* and the *"Jupiter" Symphony in C,* were reputedly written in the space of 42 days in 1788. His overture to *Don Giovanni* was written in full score at one sitting in Prague in 1787 and finished on the day of its opening performance.

Longest Silence

The most protracted silence in modern sheet music is one entitled *4 minutes 33 seconds* in a totally silent *opus* by John Cage (US). Commenting on this trend among young composers, Igor Fyodorovich Stravinsky (1882–1971) said that he looked forward to their subsequent compositions being "works of major length."

Longest Symphony

The longest of all single classical symphonies is the orchestral *Symphony No. 3 in D minor* by Gustav Mahler (1860–1911) of Austria. This work, composed in 1896, requires a contralto, a women's and a boys' choir, in addition to a full orchestra. A full performance requires 1 hour 40 min, of which the first movement alone takes between 30 and 36 min.

The *Symphony No. 2* (the Gothic, now renumbered as *No. 1),* composed in 1919–22 by Havergal Brian (1876–1972) was played by over 800 performers (4 brass bands) in the Victoria Hall, Hanley, Staffordshire, England on May 21, 1978, conducted by Trevor Stokes. A recent broadcast required 1 hour 45½ min. Brian wrote an even vaster work based on Shelley's *Prometheus Unbound* lasting 4 hours 11 min but the full score has been missing since 1961.

The symphony *Victory at Sea* written by Richard Rodgers and arranged by Robert Russell Bennett for NBC-TV in 1952 lasted 13 hours.

Longest Piano Composition

The longest continuous non-repetitious piece for piano ever specifically composed for the piano has been "The Well-Tuned Piano" by La Monte Young first presented by the Dia Art Foundation at the Concert Hall, Harrison St, NYC on Feb 28, 1980. The piece lasted 4 hours 12 min 10 sec.

Highest-Paid Pianist

The highest-paid classical concert pianist was Ignace Jan Paderewski (1860–1941), Prime Minister of Poland (1919–21), who accumulated a fortune estimated at $5 million of which $500,000 was earned in a single season in 1922–23. The *nouveau riche* wife of a US industrialist once required him to play in her house behind a curtain.

Liberace (b May 16, 1917 West Allis, Wis) has earned more than $2 million per 26-week season with a peak of $138,000 for a single night's performance at Madison Square Garden, NYC, in 1954. His full name is Wladziu Valentino Liberace.

Greatest Span

Pianist Sergei Vassilievitch Rachmaninov (1873–1943) had a span of 12 white notes and could play a left-hand chord of C, E flat, G, C, G.

Worst Singer

While no agreement exists as to the identity of history's greatest singer, there is unanimity on the worst. The excursions of the soprano Florence Foster Jenkins (1868–1944) into lieder and even high coloratura culminated on Oct 25, 1944 in her sell-out concert at Carnegie Hall, NYC. The diva's (already high) high F was said to have been made higher in 1943 by a crash in a taxi. It is one of the tragedies of musicology that Madame Jenkins' *Clavelitos,* accompanied by Cosme McMoon, was never recorded for posterity. Eight of her other "renderings" were, however.

Highest-Paid Singers

Of great fortunes earned by singers, the highest on record are those of Enrico Caruso (1873–1921), the Italian tenor, whose estate was about $9 million, and the Italian-Spanish coloratura soprano Amelita Galli-Curci (1889–1963), who received about $3 million. In 1850, up to $653 was paid for a single seat at the concerts given in the US by Johanna ("Jenny") Maria Lind (1820–87), later Mrs Otto Goldschmidt, the "Swedish Nightingale." She had a range of nearly three octaves, of which the middle register is still regarded as unrivaled.

The tenor "Count" John Francis McCormack (1884–1945) of Ireland gave up to 10 concerts to capacity audiences in a single season in Carnegie Hall, NYC.

Longest Opera

The longest of commonly performed operas is *Die Meistersinger von Nürnberg* by Wilhelm Richard Wagner (1813–83) of Germany. A normal uncut performance of this opera as performed by the Sadler's Wells company between Aug 24 and Sept 19, 1968 entailed 5 hours 15 min of music. *The Heretics* by Gabriel von Wayditch, a Hungarian-American, is orchestrated for 110 pieces and lasts 8½ hours.

Shortest Opera

The shortest opera published, *The Deliverance of Theseus* by Darius Milhaud (b Sept 1892), first performed in 1928, lasts for 7 min 27 sec.

Longest Aria

The longest single aria, in the sense of an operatic solo, is Brünnhilde's immolation scene in Wagner's *Götterdämmerung*. A well-known recording has been precisely timed at 14 min 46 sec.

Opera Houses

The largest is the Metropolitan Opera House, Lincoln Center, NYC, completed in Sept 1966, at a cost of $45,700,000. It has a capacity of 3,800 seats in an auditorium 451 ft deep. The stage is 234 ft in width and 146 ft deep. The tallest opera house is one housed in a 42-story building on Wacker Drive in Chicago.

The Teatro della Scala (La Scala) in Milan, Italy, shares with the Bolshoi Theatre in Moscow, the distinction of having the greatest number of tiers. Each

has 6 with the topmost being nicknamed the *Galiorka* by Russians.

Youngest and Oldest Opera Singers

The youngest opera singer in the world has been Jeanette Gloria (Ginetta) La Bianca, (b Buffalo, NY May 12, 1934) who made her official debut as Rosina in *The Barber of Seville* at the Teatro dell'Opera, Rome, May 8, 1950, aged 15 years 361 days, but who appeared as Gilda in *Rigoletto* at Velletri, Italy, 45 days earlier. Miss La Bianca was taught by Lucia Carlino and managed by Angelo Carlino.

The tenor Giovanni Martinelli sang Emperor Altoum in *Turandot* in Seattle, Wash Feb 4, 1967, when aged 81.

Longest Operatic Encore

The longest listed in the *Concise Oxford Dictionary of Opera* was of the entire opera of Cimarosa's called *Il Matrimonio Segreto* at its premiere in 1792. This was at the command of Austro-Hungarian Emperor Leopold II (1790–92).

Oldest Bell

The oldest bell is the tintinnabulum found in the Babylonian Palace of Nimrod in 1849 by Mr (later Sir) Austen Henry Layard (1817–94). It dates from *c.* 1100 BC. The oldest known tower bell is one in Pisa, Italy dated MCVI (1106).

Largest Carillon

The largest carillon (minimum of 23 bells) is the Laura Spelman Rockefeller Memorial carillon in Riverside Church, NYC. It has 74 bells weighing 112 tons. The bourdon, giving the note lower C, weighs 40,926 lb. This 20.5-ton bell, cast in England, with a diameter of 10 ft 2 in, is the largest *tuned* bell.

Heaviest Bell

The heaviest bell is the Tsar Kolokol, cast on Nov 25, 1735 in Moscow. It weighs 216 tons, measures 19 ft 4¼ in in diameter, is 19 ft 3 in high, and its greatest thickness is 24 in. The bell is cracked, and a fragment, weighing about 12 tons, is broken from it. The bell has stood on a platform in the Kremlin, in Moscow, since 1836.

The heaviest bell in use is the Mingun bell, weighing 101.4 tons, in Mandalay, Burma, which is struck by a teak boom from the outside. It has a diameter of 16 ft 8½ in at the lip.

HEAVIEST BELL IN USE TODAY: In Mandalay, Burma, this bell weighing more than 100 tons is struck from the outside with a boom of teak wood.

The heaviest swinging bell in the world is the Petersglocke in the southwest tower of Cologne Cathedral, Germany, cast in 1923, with a diameter of 11 ft 1¾ in, weighing 28.4 tons.

Bell Ringing

Eight bells have been rung to their full "extent" (40,320 unrepeated changes of Plain Bob Major) only once without relays. This took place in a bell foundry at Loughborough, Leicestershire, England, beginning at 6:52 a.m. on July 27, 1963 and ending at 12:50 a.m. on July 28, after 17 hours 58 min. The peal was composed by Kenneth Lewis of Altrincham, Cheshire, and the 8 ringers were conducted by Robert B. Smith, aged 25, of Marple, Cheshire. Theoretically it would take 37 years 355 days to ring 12 bells (maximus) to their full extent of 479,001,600 changes.

Oldest Songs

The oldest known song is the *shaduf* chant, which has been sung since time immemorial by irrigation workers on the man-powered pivoted-rod bucket raisers of the Nile water mills (or *saqiyas*) in Egypt. The oldest known harmonized music performed today is the English song *Sumer is icumen in* which dates from *c.* 1240.

Top Songs of All Time

The most frequently sung songs in English are *Happy Birthday to You* (based on the original *Good Morning to All,* by Mildred and Patty S. Hill of New York, published in 1935 and in copyright until 2010); *For He's a Jolly Good Fellow* (originally the French *Malbrouk*), known at least as early as 1781, and *Auld Lang Syne* (originally the Strathspey *I fee'd a Lad at Michaelmas*), some words of which were written by Robert Burns (1759–96). *Happy Birthday* was sung in space by the Apollo IX astronauts March 8, 1969.

Top Selling Sheet Music

Sales of three non-copyright pieces are known to have exceeded 20 million copies, namely *The Old Folks at Home* by Stephen Foster (1855), *Listen to*

MOST SUCCESSFUL SONG WRITER: Paul McCartney (right) is joined by his wife, Linda, and Norris McWhirter, Guinness editor-in-chief, for the presentation of the first ever rhodium disc, honoring the ex-Beatle's triple listing in the Guinness Book.

the *Mocking Bird* (1855) and *The Blue Danube* (1867). Of copyright material, the two top-sellers are *Let Me Call You Sweetheart* (1910, by Whitson and Friedman) and *Till We Meet Again* (1918, by Egan and Whiting), each with some 6 million by 1967. Other huge sellers have been *St Louis Blues, Stardust* and *Tea for Two.*

Most Successful Song Writer

In terms of sales of single records, the most successful of all song writers has been Paul McCartney, formerly of the Beatles and now of Wings. Between 1962 and Jan 1, 1978 he wrote jointly or solo 43 songs which sold one million or more records. He was the recipient in Oct 1979 in London of the first Guinness Award as the most honored composer and performer in music.

National Anthems

The oldest national anthem is the *Kimigayo* of Japan, in which the words date from the 9th century.

The anthem of Greece constitutes the first four verses of the Solomos poem, which has 158 verses. The shortest anthems are those of Japan, Jordan and San Marino, each with only four lines. Of the 23 wordless national anthems, the oldest is that of Spain, dating from 1770.

Longest Rendering of an Anthem

"God Save the King" was played non-stop 16 or 17 times by a German military band on the platform of Rathenau Railway Station, Brandenburg, on the morning of Feb 9, 1909. The reason was that King Edward VII was struggling inside the train to get into his German Field-Marshal uniform before he could emerge.

Earliest Hymns

The music and parts of the text of a hymn in the *Oxyrhynchus Papyri* from the 2nd century are the earliest known hymnody. More than 950,000 Christian hymns are in existence. The earliest exactly datable hymn is the *Heyr Rimna Smiour* (Hear, the maker of heaven) from 1208 by the Icelandic bard and chieftain Kolbeinn Tumason (1173–1208).

Longest and Shortest Hymns

The longest hymn is *Hora novissima tempora pessima sunt; vigilemus* by Bernard of Cluny (12th century), which runs to 2,966 lines. In English the longest is *The Sands of Time Are Sinking* by Mrs Anne Ross Cousin, *née* Cundell (1824–1906), which is in full 152 lines, though only 32 lines in the Methodist Hymn Book. The shortest hymn is the single verse in Long Metre *Be Present at Our Table, Lord,* anonymous but attributed to "J. Leland."

Most Prolific Hymnists

Mrs Frances Jane Van Alstyne, *née* Crosby (US) (1820–1915), wrote more than 8,500 hymns although she had been blinded at the age of 6 weeks. She is reputed to have knocked off one hymn in 15 minutes. Charles Wesley (1707–88) wrote about 6,000 hymns. In the seventh (1950) edition of *Hymns Ancient and Modern* the works of John Mason Neale (1818–66) appear 56 times.

5. THEATRE

LARGEST THEATRE built for theatricals: The Perth Entertainment Centre in Western Australia seats 8,003 people and boasts a stage area of 12,000 sq ft.

Theatre as we know it has its origins in Greek drama performed in honor of a god, usually Dionysus. The earliest amphitheatres date from the 5th century BC. The largest of all known is one at Megalopolis in central Greece, where the auditorium reached a height of 75 ft and had a capacity of 17,000. The first stone-built theatre in Rome (erected in 55 BC) could accommodate 40,000 spectators.

Oldest Theatre

The oldest indoor theatre is the Teatro Olimpico in Vicenza, Italy. Designed in the Roman style by Andrea di Pietro, *alias* Palladio (1508–80), it was begun three months before his death and finished in 1582 by his pupil Vincenzo Scamozzi (1552–1616). It is preserved today in its original form.

Largest and Smallest Theatres

The largest building used for theatre is the National People's Congress Building (*Ren min da hui tang*) on the west side of Tian An Men Square, Peking, China. It was completed in 1959 and covers an area of 12.9 acres. The theatre seats 10,000 and is only occasionally used as such, as in 1964 for the play "The East Is Red."

The highest capacity purpose-built theatre is the Perth Entertainment Centre in Western Australia, completed at a cost in Australian dollars of $8.3 million in Nov 1976, with a capacity of 8,003 seats. The stage area is 12,000 sq ft.

The smallest regularly operated professional theatre is the Piccolo in Juliusstrasse, Hamburg, W Germany. It was founded in 1970 and has a maximum capacity of 30 seats.

Largest Amphitheatre

The largest amphitheatre ever built is the Flavian amphitheatre or Colosseum of Rome, Italy, completed in 80 AD. Covering 5 acres and with a capacity of 87,000, it has a maximum length of 612 ft and maximum width of 515 ft.

Largest Stage

The largest stage is in the Ziegfeld Room, Reno, Nev with a 176-ft passerelle, 3 main elevators capable of lifting 1,200 show girls, two 62½-ft-circumference turntables and 800 spotlights.

Longest Runs

The longest continuous run of any show is of *The Mousetrap* by Agatha Christie (Lady Mallowan) (1890–1976). This thriller opened at the Ambassadors Theatre (capacity 453), London, Nov 25, 1952 and moved after 8,862 performances "down the road" to St Martin's Theatre, London, March 25, 1974. The 30th Anniversary performance on Nov 25, 1982 will be the 12,481st.

The Vicksburg Theatre Guild of Vicksburg, Miss, have been playing the melodrama *Gold in the Hills* by J. Frank Davis discontinuously but every season since 1936.

The greatest number of performances of any theatrical presentation is 39,521 (to Jan 27, 1982) in the case of *The Golden Horseshoe Revue*—a show staged at Disneyland Park, Anaheim, Calif. The show was first put on on July 16, 1955 and has been seen by 16 million people. The three main performers nowadays, Dick Hardwick (formerly Wally Boag), Fulton Burley, and Betty Taylor, play as many as five houses a day in a routine lasting 45 min.

The long-run record for any "Broadway" show was set on Dec 8, 1979 when the musical *Grease* was performed for the 3,243rd time, beating the record of *Fiddler on the Roof*. After opening at the Eden Theatre on Feb 14, 1972, *Grease* moved to the Royale Theatre on Nov 27, 1972, where it finally closed on Apr 13, 1980, after a total of 3,388 performances. The book, music and lyrics were written by Jim Jacobs (b Chicago, 1942) and Warren Casey (b Yonkers, NY, 1935). Profits of $4 million have accrued to the producers Kenneth Waissman and his wife Maxine Fox from the gross $70 million in the US alone including motion picture profits.

The broadway record for the longest run of a drama (rather than a musical) is 3,224 performances (including benefits, etc.) by *Life With Father,* written by Howard Lindsay and Russel Crouse. The play opened at the Empire Theatre on Nov 8, 1939, and closed July 12, 1947, at the Alvin Theatre.

The record for a musical in London is just short of the Broadway record—3,357 performances without a break by *Jesus Christ Superstar,* Aug 8, 1972–Aug 23, 1980.

The off-Broadway musical show *The Fantasticks* by Tom Jones and Harvey Schmidt achieved its 9,149th performance as it entered its 23rd year at the Sullivan Street Playhouse, Greenwich Village, NYC, May 2, 1982. It has been played in a record 4,500 productions in 57 countries.

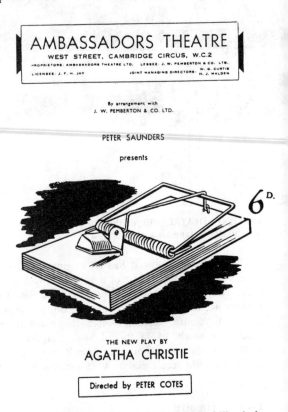

LONGEST-RUNNING PLAY: Original playbill of the play that has been running continuously for 30 years in London. (Raymond Mander-Joe Mitchenson Theatre Collection)

LONGEST-RUNNING "BROADWAY" SHOW: "Grease" was performed on the NY stage 3,388 times by Apr 13, 1980, even while the movie "Grease" was competing with it. In the scene shown here the group includes Jeff Conaway, Marilu Henner, Judy Kaye and John Travolta, who went on to further fame. (Betty Hunt Associates) The Guinness Book recognized the record by sending its representative, Geri Martin (inset), to present a certificate to producer Kenneth Waissman.

LONGEST-RUNNING "OFF-BROADWAY" MUSICAL (left, above): "The Fantasticks" has been performed for more than 23 years in NYC, and has also been played in 57 foreign countries. **LONGEST PERFORMING CAREER** (center, above): Charlie Revel of Barcelona, Spain, made his stage debut in 1899 and now at the age of 85 he is still performing in Europe. He received a medal from the King of Sweden in 1980. (Eliel Ahnemark) **LONGEST RUN FOR A ONE-MAN SHOW** (right, above): Victor Borge played 849 times in 27 months in NYC.

MOST MEDIA AWARDS FOR AN ACTRESS (above): Rita Moreno, seen here talking to her friend, Kermit, has won an Oscar, a Tony, a Grammy and an Emmy for her performances in movies, theatre, on records and on television.

CONSISTENT ACTRESS: Marian Seldes appeared in all 1,793 performances during the 4½-year Broadway run of the comedy-thriller "Deathtrap." She also played in all 32 pre-opening performances—25 "out-of-town" (Boston) and 7 previews. Despite suffering five murderous "husbands," Seldes found time to write a book and to teach classes at Juilliard.

MODERN CLASSIC: "The Front Page" (below) has been revived on the Broadway stage and elsewhere more frequently than any other play since the 1920's. It satirizes newspaper offices and reporters.

One-Man Shows

The longest run of one-man shows is 849 by Victor Borge (b Copenhagen Jan 3, 1909) in his *Comedy in Music* from Oct 2, 1953, to Jan 21, 1956, at the Golden Theater, NYC.

The world aggregate record for one-man shows is 1,700 performances of *Brief Lives* by Roy Dotrice (b Guernsey, England, May 26, 1923) including 400 straight at the Mayfair Theatre, London, ending July 20, 1974. He was on stage for more than 2½ hours per performance of this 17th century monologue, and required 3 hours for makeup and 1 hour for removal, thus aggregating 40 weeks in the chair as well.

Youngest Broadway Producer

Margo Feiden (Margo Eden) (b NY, Dec 2, 1944) produced the musical *Peter Pan*, which opened Apr 3, 1961, when she was 16 years 5 months old. She wrote *Out Brief Candle*, which opened Aug 18, 1962, and is now a leading art dealer.

Longest Play

The longest recorded theatrical production has been *The Warp* by Neil Oram, directed by Ken Campbell, a 10-part play cycle played at the Institute of Contemporary Art, the Mall, London, Jan 18–20, 1979. Russell Denton was on stage for all but 5 min of the 18 hours 5 min. The three intermissions totaled 3 hours 10 min.

Most Durable Leading Actress

Dame Anna Neagle (b Oct 20, 1904) played the lead in *Charlie Girl* at the Adelphi Theatre, London, England, for 2,062 of 2,202 performances between Dec 15, 1965 and March 27, 1971. She played the same rôle a further 327 times in 327 performances in Australasia.

Marian Seldes did not miss a single performance in Ira Levin's long-running Broadway hit *Deathtrap* from the show's opening on Feb 26, 1978, to its close on June 13, 1982. She portrayed the character Myra Bruhl in 1,793 consecutive performances.

Frances Etheridge has played Lizzie, the housekeeper, in *Gold in the Hills* (see *Longest Runs*) more than 660 times in 46 years since 1936.

Most Ardent Theatregoers

The highest precisely recorded number of paid theatre attendances is 3,522 shows in 29 years from Mar 28, 1953 to Mar 28, 1982, by John Iles of Salisbury, Wiltshire, England. He estimates that he has traveled 142,969 miles and seen 170,697 performers, spending 9,167 hours inside theatres.

It has been estimated by the press that H. Howard Hughes (b 1904) of Fort Worth, Tex, had seen 4,160 shows in the period 1956–1976.

Edward Sutro (1900–78) in England saw 3,000 first-night productions from 1916 to 1956, and possibly more than 5,000 in his 60 years of theatre-going.

Shakespeare

The first all-amateur company to have staged all 37 of Shakespeare's plays was The Southsea Shakespeare Actors, Hampshire, England, when in Oct 1966, they presented *Cymbeline*. The amateur director throughout was K. Edmonds Gateloy.

The longest play is *Hamlet*, with 4,042 lines and 29,551 words, 1,242 words longer than *Richard III*. Of Shakespeare's 1,277 speaking parts, the longest is the title role in *Hamlet* with 11,610 words.

Versatility in Show Business Awards

Rita Moreno (b Dec 11, 1931, Rosa Dolores Alverio in Puerto Rico, now Mrs Leonard Gordon) is the only female entertainer to win awards in 4 media: an Oscar for *West Side Story* (1962); a Grammy for *Electric Company Album* (1972); a regular Tony for *The Ritz* (1975); and an Emmy for *The Muppet Show* (1977) and *The Rockford Files* (1978).

Barbra Streisand (b Apr 24, 1942 in Brooklyn, NYC) received Oscar, Grammy and Emmy awards in addition to a special "Star of the Decade" Tony award.

Ice Shows

Holiday on Ice Productions Inc, founded by Morris Chalfen in 1945, stages the world's most costly live entertainment with its seven productions playing simultaneously in several of 75 countries drawing 20 million spectators paying $40 million in a year. The total number of skaters and other personnel exceeds 900.

Shortest Criticism

The shortest dramatic criticism in theatrical history was that attributed to Wolcott Gibbs (1902–58), writing about the farce *Wham!* He wrote the single word "Ouch!"

MAN OF 2,000 DISGUISES: Jan Leighton as

Henry Kissinger ①
Sherlock Holmes ②
Popeye ③
Groucho Marx ④

General MacArthur ⑤
Albert Einstein ⑥
Napoleon ⑦
Jan Leighton undisguised ⑧

Most Rôles

The greatest recorded number of theatrical, film and television rôles is 2,018 from 1951 to May 24, 1982 by Jan Leighton (US). (*See above.*)

Cabaret

The highest paid entertainer is Wayne Newton (b 1942) who is paid up to $250,000 per performance in Las Vegas hotels by the Summa Corporation.

Longest Chorus Line

63 "Atomic Girls" of the Shochiku Revue danced in line in the Ko Kusai Theatre, Tokyo, in the revue's 49th season in 1980. They danced a 4½-min routine.

Shortest Runs

The shortest run on record was that of *The Intimate Revue* at the Duchess Theatre, London, March 11, 1930. Anything which could go wrong did. With scene changes taking up to 20 minutes apiece, the management scrapped seven scenes to get the finale on before midnight. The run was described as "half a performance."

A number of Broadway productions open and close the same night. There were 11 such "turkeys" in the 1978–79 season.

The largest loss incurred was probably the estimated $2 million on *Frankenstein* which opened and closed on Broadway Jan 4, 1981.

Lowest Attendance

The first recorded one-man audience occurred at the Oldham Grange Arts Centre, Lancashire, England, on Oct 23, 1980, when Ronald Bradbury made theatrical history by sitting through *Oh Mistress Mine* as the sole spectator, while the show went on.

Fashion Shows

The most prolific producer and most durable commentator of fashion shows is Adalene Ross of San Francisco, with over 4,692 in both categories to mid-1982. The largest audience for a fashion show was as many as 40,000 at Shea Stadium, NYC, on July 31, 1982, when baseball fans and invitees saw Jordache's new fashions worn by live models, whose parading was additionally observed on an 864-sq-ft specially-installed screen in center field.

6. RADIO BROADCASTING

The earliest description of a radio transmission system was written by Dr Mahlon Loomis (b Fulton County, NY, July 21, 1826, d 1886) on July 21, 1864, and demonstrated between two kites at Bear's Den, Loudoun County, Va, in Oct 1866. He received US Patent No. 129971, entitled Improvement in Telegraphing, on July 20, 1872.

Earliest Patent

The first patent for a system of communication by means of electro-magnetic waves, numbered No. 12039, was granted June 2, 1896, to the Italian-Irish Marchese, Guglielmo Marconi (1874–1937). A public demonstration of wireless transmission of speech was given in the town square of Murray, Ky, in 1892 by Nathan B. Stubblefield. He died, destitute, March 28, 1928. The first permanent wireless installation was at The Needles on the Isle of Wight, Hampshire, England, by Marconi's Wireless Telegraph Co, Ltd, in Nov 1896.

Earliest Broadcast

The first advertised broadcast was made on Dec 24, 1906, by Canadian-born Prof Reginald Aubrey Fessenden (1868–1932) from the 420-ft mast of the National Electric Signaling Company at Brant Rock, Mass. The transmission included Handel's *Largo*. Fessenden had achieved the broadcast of speech as early as Nov 1900, but this was highly distorted.

Transatlantic Transmissions

The earliest transatlantic wireless signals (the letter S in Morse Code) were received by Marconi, George Stephen Kemp and Percy Paget from a 10-kilowatt station at Poldhu, Cornwall, England, at Signal Hill, St John's, Newfoundland, Canada, at 12:30 p.m. Dec 12, 1901. Human speech was first heard across the Atlantic in Nov 1915, when a transmission from the US Navy station at Arlington, Va, was received by US radio-telephone engineers up on the Eiffel Tower, Paris.

Earliest Radio-Microphone

The first radio-microphone, which was in essence also the first "bug," was devised by Reg Moores (GB) in 1947, and first used on 76 MHz in the ice

show *Aladdin* at Brighton Sports Stadium, England, in Sept 1949.

Most Radio Stations

The country with the greatest number of radio broadcasting stations is the US. As of Feb 1982, there were 9,317 authorized stations, of which 4,641 were AM and 4,676 FM.

Longest Radio Broadcast

The longest continuous radio broadcast (excluding disc-jockeying) has been one of 373 hours 35 min by Bruce "Spanky" Smith of KCRJ-FM96 Radio, Arizona. *No further claims for this category will be entertained.*

Highest Radio Listener Response

The highest recorded response to a radio show occurred Nov 27, 1974, when on a 5-hour talk show on WCAU, Philadelphia, Howard Sheldon, the astrologist, registered a total of 388,299 calls on the "Bill Corsair Show."

INVENTOR OF RADIO: Guglielmo Marconi first patented a radio on June 2, 1896, and he received the first wireless signal from across the Atlantic in 1901.

7. TELEVISION

The invention of television, the instantaneous viewing of distant objects by electrical transmissions, was not an act but a process of successive and interdependent discoveries. The first commercial cathode ray tube was introduced in 1897 by Karl Ferdinand Braun (1850–1918), but was not linked to "electric vision" until 1907 by Boris Rosing of Russia in St Petersburg (now Leningrad). A. A. Campbell Swinton (GB 1863–1930) published the fundamentals of television transmission June 18, 1908 in a brief letter to *Nature* entitled "Distant Electric Vision." The earliest public demonstration of television was given on Jan 27, 1926, by John Logie Baird (1888–1946) of Scotland, using a development of the mechanical scanning system suggested by Paul Nipkov in 1884. He had achieved the transmission of a Maltese Cross over 10 ft in Hastings, East Sussex, England, in Feb 1924, and the first facial image (of William Taynton, 15) on Oct 30, 1925. Taynton had to be bribed with 2 shillings sixpence. A patent application for the Iconoscope had been filed Dec 29, 1923, by Dr Vladimir Kosma Zworykin (born in Russia 1889, became a US citizen in 1924). It was not issued until Dec 20, 1938. The patent application filed on Jan 7, 1927, by Philo Taylor Farnsworth (US) was, however, granted on Aug 26, 1930. Farnsworth succeeded with a low-definition image at 202 Green Street, Los Angeles, in Nov 1927.

Video Tape Recording

Alexander M. Poniatoff first demonstrated video tape recording, known as Ampex (his initials plus "ex" for excellence) in 1956.

The earliest demonstration of a home video recorder was on June 24, 1963, at the BBC News Studio at Alexandra Palace, London, of the Telcan developed by Norman Rutherford and Michael Turner of the Nottingham Electronic Valve Co.

Earliest Service

The first high-definition (*i.e.* 405 lines) television broadcasting service was opened from Alexandra Palace, London, Nov 2, 1936, when there were about 100 sets in the UK. A television station in Berlin, Germany, began low-definition (180 line) transmission March 22, 1935. The transmitter burned out in Aug 1935.

Most Transmitters and Sets

The Dec 1983 projection for US TV households is 84,800,000, with 32.2 million on cable TV, 17.8 million on pay TV, 25 million on subscription satellite TV, and 3.4 million having video disc or video cassette. The number of homes with color sets reached 66,250,000 (85%) by Jan 1981.

Television Viewing

In July 1978 it was estimated that the *average* American child, by his or her 18th birthday, has watched the equivalent of 710 solid days (17,040 hours) of TV, seen more than 350,000 commercials and more than 15,000 TV murders. There are 571 TV sets per 1,000 people in the US compared with 348 in Sweden and 330 in Britain.

Iceland has a TV-free day on Thursday to reduce disruption of family life. Otherwise transmissions are normally limited to between 8 and 11 p.m. July 1982 was declared a TV-free month. Upper Volta had only one set for each 1,000 inhabitants by 1974.

Transatlantic Transmissions

The earliest transatlantic satellite transmission was achieved at 1 a.m. July 11, 1962, *via* the active satellite *Telstar I* from Andover, Me, to Pleumeur Bodou, France. The picture was of Frederick R. Kappell, chairman of the American Telephone and Telegraph Company, which owned the satellite. The first "live" broadcast was made July 23, 1962, and the first woman to appear was the *haute couturière* Ginette Spanier, directrice of Balmain, Paris, the next day. On Feb 9, 1928, the image of John Logie Baird (see above) and a Mrs Howe was transmitted from Station 2KZ at Coulsdon, Surrey, England, to Station 2CVJ, Hartsdale, NY.

Greatest TV Audience

The greatest number of viewers for a televised event is an estimated 1,000 million for the live and recorded transmissions of the XXth and XXIst Olympic Games in Munich and Montreal in 1972 and 1976. The estimate for the papal visit to Ireland by Pope John Paul II on Sept 29, 1979 was also 1,000 million.

LARGEST TV PRODUCTION: BBC and Time-Life, between 1978 and 1984, will have spent a minimum of $14 million for the production of the 37 plays of Shakespeare. The scenes (top to bottom, left to right) are from "Julius Caesar," "Romeo and Juliet," "As You Like It," "Measure for Measure," and "Richard II" (with Derek Jacobi in the title role).

199

TELEVISION "INVENTOR" John Logie Baird of Scotland gave the first public demonstration of TV in 1926. Working with others, Baird developed systems that led to the marvels on our home screens today. In the photo above, Baird is seated before one of his early transmitters which required powerful illumination.

PERFORMERS WHO HAVE MADE THE MOST OUT OF TELEVISION: (Left below) Jerry Lewis, whose telethon over the 1981 Labor Day weekend made a record $31,498,772 for the Muscular Dystrophy Association. Johnny Carson (center) is paid $5 million annually for "Tonight," his show, now down to one hour, on which he appears 4 times weekly, making him the highest paid performer on the air. Barbara Walters (right) is the highest paid news and current affairs interviewer at about $1 million a year.

The program which attracted the highest viewership was the episode of *Dallas* transmitted by CBS on Nov 21, 1980 to 53.3% of all households in the US. It was estimated that 83 million people in 41.4 million homes watched—for a record 76% of all viewing at that hour.

Largest TV Prizes

On July 24, 1975, WABC-TV, NYC transmitted the first televised Grand Tier draw of the State Lottery in which the winner took the grand prize of $1 million.

Mary Buchanan, 15, won a prize of $25,000 for 40 years (total $1 million) on WKRQ Cincinnati on Nov 21, 1980.

Largest Contracts

The highest rate for any TV contract ever signed was one for $7 million for 7 hours of transmission with NBC by Marie Osmond, announced on Mar 9, 1981. This includes talent and production costs.

Currently, television's highest-paid performer is Johnny Carson (b Oct 23, 1925), the host of the *Tonight* show. His current five-year NBC contract reportedly calls for annual payments of some $5 million for his one-hour evening show on which he appears 4 times weekly.

The highest-paid current affairs or news performer is Barbara Walters, who signed a 5-year contract with ABC Apr 21, 1976 for about $1 million per year.

Alan Alda, star of M*A*S*H receives a record $225,000 per episode, thereby totaling $5,400,000 for 24 episodes per year.

Peter Falk (b Sept 16, 1927), the disarmingly persistent detective, Columbo, was paid from $300,000 to $350,000 per single episode for his series of 6, so totaling $1,950,000 in 1976.

Carroll O'Connor, star of *Archie Bunker's Place*, contracted for payments of $200,000 for each of the 1980 season's 24 half-hour episodes.

Commercial Payments

In 1977, James Coburn of Beverly Hills, Calif was reputedly paid $500,000 for uttering two words on a series of Schlitz beer commercials. The words "Schlitz Light" were thus priced at a quarter of a million dollars per syllable.

Brooke Shields (b May 31, 1965) was reportedly paid $250,000 for one minute of film by a Japanese TV commercial film maker in 1979.

Faye Dunaway was reported in May 1979 to have been paid $900,000 for uttering 6 words for a Japanese department store TV commercial.

The same Brooke Bond chimpanzee commercial first transmitted on Nov 21, 1971 in England has been repeated 1,687 more times up to Oct 1979.

Most Takes for a TV Commercial

The highest number of "takes" for a TV commercial was 28 by Pat Coombs, the comedienne, who in 1973 supported Dick Emery on BBC-TV. Her explanation was: "Every time we came to the punch line I just could not remember the name of the product."

Largest Production

The BBC production of the 37 plays of Shakespeare in 1978–84 will cost a minimum of $14 million. The series was conceived by its producer, Cedric Messina.

Most Successful Telethon

The Jerry Lewis Labor Day 1981 Telethon raised $31,498,772 in pledges for the Muscular Dystrophy Association.

Longest Program

The longest pre-scheduled telecast on record was one of 163 hours 18 min by GTV 9 of Melbourne, Australia, covering the Apollo XI moon mission July 19–26, 1969. The longest continuous TV transmission under a single director was the Avro Television Production *Open het Dorpe* transmitted in the Netherlands Nov 26–27, 1962 for 23 hours 20 min under the direction of Theo Ordeman.

Most Durable TV Show

The most durable is NBC's *Meet the Press*, first transmitted Nov 6, 1947 and weekly since Sept 12, 1948. It was originated by Lawrence E. Spivak, who until 1975 appeared weekly as either moderator or panel member. Mike Douglas on Dec 11, 1980 presented his 4,754th version of his show which started in 1960.

Greatest Sale

The greatest number of episodes of any TV program ever sold was 1,144 episodes of *Coronation Street* to CBKST, Saskatoon, Saskatchewan, Canada, by Granada Television, May 31, 1971. This constituted 20 days 15 hours 44 min of continuous viewing. A further 728 episodes (Jan 1974–Jan 1981) were sold to CBC (Canadian Broadcasting Company) in 1982.

Highest TV Advertising Rates

The highest TV advertising rate has been $345,000 per 30 sec for CBS network prime time during the transmission of Super Bowl XVI, Jan 24, 1982.

Thinnest Set

The Sony FD 200, weighing 8.4 oz, marketed in Feb 1982, is only 0.12 in thick. The 250-line picture is on a 0.19-in screen (measured diagonally).

Most Prolific Producer

The most prolific TV producer is Aaron Spelling (b 1928) who, in 25 years from 1956 to 1981, produced 1,100 episodes totaling 1,457½ hours of air time. His output included *Starsky and Hutch* (89 episodes) and *Charlie's Angels* (109 episodes).

Most Prolific Scriptwriter

The most prolific television writer is the Rt. Hon. Lord Willis (b Jan 13, 1918), known as Ted Willis, who in the period 1949–82 has created 25 series, 25 stage plays, and 24 feature films. He had 21 plays produced. His total output since 1942 can be estimated at 17 million words.

8. MOTION PICTURES*

The earliest motion pictures ever taken were by Louis Aimé Augustin Le Prince (1842?–90). He reportedly achieved dim moving outlines on a white-washed wall at the Institute for the Deaf, Washington Heights, NYC, as early as 1885. The earliest surviving film is from his camera patented in Britain taken in early Oct 1888 of the garden of his father-in-law Joseph Whitley in Rounday, Leeds, South Yorkshire, at 10 to 12 frames per sec.

The first commercial presentation of motion pictures was at Holland Bros Kinetoscope Parlor at 1155 Broadway, NYC, on Apr 14, 1894. Viewers could see 5 films for 25 cents or 10 for 50 cents from a double row of Kinetoscopes developed by William Kennedy Laurie Dickson (1860–1935), assistant to Thomas Alva Edison (1847–1931).

The earliest publicly-presented film on a screen was *La Sortie des Ouvriers de l'Usine Lumière* probably shot in Aug or Sept 1894 in Lyon, France. It was exhibited at 44 Rue de Rennes, Paris, on Mar 22, 1895, by the Lumière brothers, Auguste Marie Louis Nicholas (1862–1954) and Louis Jean (1864–1948).

Earliest Sound Movie ("Talkie")

The earliest sound-on-film motion picture was achieved by Eugene Augustin Lauste (b Paris, Jan 17, 1857) who patented his process Aug 11, 1906 and produced a workable system using a string galvanometer in 1910 at Benedict Road, Stockwell, London. Dr Lee de Forest (1873–1961) was responsible for the screening of the first sound picture before a paying audience at the Rialto Theater, NYC, Apr 15, 1923. The first all-talking picture was Warner Bros' *Lights of New York,* shown at the Strand Theatre, NYC, July 6, 1928.

Movie-Going

The people of the Philippines (population 48.4 million) go to the movies more often than those of any other country in the world, with an average of 19.06 attendances per person per year (1979–80). The Soviet Union claims to have the most movie theatres in the world, with 163,400 in 1974, but this includes buildings equipped with 16-mm projectors. The US has 16,965 actual movie theatres (1979).

San Marino has more seats for watching films per total population than any other country, with one cinema for each 1,512 inhabitants. The least number are in Saudi Arabia (population 8.4 million) which has no movie theatres.

Largest Movie Theatres

The largest is the Radio City Music Hall, NYC, opened on Dec 27, 1932, with 5,945 seats (now 5,882). The Roxy, opened in NYC on March 11,

---

* For more records and greater details on this subject, see *Movie Facts and Feats, A Guinness Record Book* by Patrick Robertson (1980, Sterling).

MOST OSCARS IN STARRING ROLES (below): Katharine Hepburn added a fourth Oscar to her collection in 1982. Scenes are (top to bottom) from "Morning Glory," "Guess Who's Coming to Dinner" with Spencer Tracy, "The Lion in Winter" with Peter O'Toole, and "On Golden Pond."

MOST AWARDS FROM THE ACADEMY (above): Walt Disney is holding only 4 of the 20 Oscars he was awarded. (© Walt Disney Productions)

HISTORICAL CHARACTER MOST OFTEN REPRESENTED IN MOVIES: Napoleon holds the record, having been played in at least 163 films to 1982. One of the most famous Napoleons was Marlon Brando's portrayal (shown here) in "Desirée" in 1954.

WORLD'S MOST BEAUTIFUL WOMAN? Hollywood gave this appellation to Greta Garbo, but who would have believed it when she appeared in 1921 as a 16-year-old in this film (above) in her native Sweden. By 1927, after she had become a big star, she liked to be serenaded by a 3-piece female group with a violin, cello, and vocalist—"to get in the mood."

MOST OSCAR NOMINATIONS (above): Tied with Spencer Tracy with 9, Sir Laurence Olivier won only one Best Actor award—for his "Hamlet" (shown here) in 1948. Olivier actually failed his first screen test, to play opposite Greta Garbo in 1933.

FIRST MOVIE BIOGRAPHY OF A FILM STAR (left) was a film called "The Life Story of Charles Chaplin," produced in 1926 by an Englishman named Chick Wango in an attempt to cash in on the "little tramp's" popularity. It was never released because of the threat of legal action. Chaplin had already had such successes as "The Gold Rush" in which he ate his boots (made of licorice) when starving.

1927, had 6,214 seats (later 5,869) but was closed March 29, 1960.

Cineplex, opened at the Toronto Eaton Centre, Canada, on Apr 19, 1979, has 18 separate theatres with an aggregate capacity of 1,700.

The largest drive-in cinema is Loew's Open Air at Lynn, Mass, with a capacity for 5,000 cars.

Oldest Movie Theatre

The earliest structure designed and used exclusively for exhibiting projected films is believed to be one erected at the Atlanta Show, Ga in Oct 1895, to exhibit C. F. Jenkins' phantoscope.

Biggest Screen

The permanently installed cinema screen with the largest area is one 100 ft 6 in × 75 ft, installed in the Imax Theatre, Parques Interama S.A., Buenos Aires, Argentina, in Dec 1981. It was made by Harkness Screens Ltd of Hertfordshire, England.

A temporary screen 297 × 33 ft was used at the 1937 Paris Exposition.

Most and Least Expensive Films

The highest ever budgeted film has been *Star Trek* which received its world premiere in Washington, DC on Dec 6, 1979. Paramount stated that the cost of this space epic directed by Robert Wise and produced by Gene Roddenberry, was $46 million. A figure of $60 million has been attributed to *Superman II* but never substantiated.

The least expensive film was Cecil Hepworth's highly successful release of *Rescued by Rover* in 1905 in England which cost $37.40.

Film Rights

The highest price ever paid for film rights is $9,500,000 announced on Jan 20, 1978 by Columbia for *Annie,* the Broadway musical by Charles Strouse, based on the comic strip *Little Orphan Annie.*

Highest Box Office Gross

The film which has had the highest world gross earnings is *Star Wars,* written and directed by George Lucas and produced by Gary Kurtz which from May 25, 1977 to Dec 1979 grossed $267 million.

Superman II grossed $5.06 million in a single day in 1,395 North American movie theatres on June 20, 1981.

HIGHEST GROSS: "Star Wars" still has not been beaten in worldwide sales, although "Superman II" had a bigger single day, and others had big opening weeks. Here are two of the robot stars.

Longest Film

The longest film ever premiered was the 48-hour-long *The Longest Most Meaningless Movie in the World* in 1970. It was British-made and later cut to 90 min.

Highest Earnings by an Actor

The highest rate of pay in cinema history was set by Marlon Brando (b Apr 3, 1924) for his brief part in *Superman.* He received in excess of $2,500,000, but the final amount will depend on box office percentages.

Burt Reynolds (b Nov 2, 1936) was reported in July 1980 to have received $238,095 per day from 20th Century Fox for his part in *Cannonball Run.*

Dar Robinson was paid $100,000 for the 1,100-ft-high leap he made from the CN Tower in Toronto in Nov 1979 for *High Point.* His parachute opened at only 300 ft above the ground.

Most Portrayed Character

The character most frequently recurring on the screen is Sherlock Holmes, created by Sir Arthur Conan Doyle (1859–1930). Sixty-one actors portrayed Holmes in 175 films between 1900 and 1980.

Most Prolific Director

Allan Dwan (1895–1981), the Canadian-born pioneer, directed, from 1909 to the early 1960's, more than 400 films.

Largest Studios

The largest complex of film studios are those of Universal Studios at Universal City, Los Angeles. The back lot contains 561 buildings. There are 34 sound stages.

Largest Loss

It was reported on Nov 20, 1980 that United Artists had withdrawn its 4-hour-long *Heaven's Gate* because its total cost including distribution and studio overheads had reached $57,000,000. It was reissued in May 1981 in shorter form, but further losses (amount unannounced) were incurred.

MOST PORTRAYED CHARACTER on screen: Sixty-one actors played Sherlock Holmes in 175 films, 1900–80. Here Basil Rathbone is the master detective. (The Cinema Bookshop)

Most Oscars

Walter (Walt) Elias Disney (1901–66) won more "Oscars"—the awards of the Academy of Motion Picture Arts and Sciences, instituted on May 16, 1929, for 1927–28—than any other person. The physical count comprises 20 statuettes and nine other plaques and certificates, including posthumous awards.

The only performer to win four Oscars for her starring rôles has been Katharine Hepburn (b Nov 9, 1909), in *Morning Glory* (1933), *Guess Who's Coming to Dinner* (1967), *The Lion in Winter* (1968) and *On Golden Pond* (1981). She was nominated 13 times. Three of her Oscars are on display at the Guinness World Records Exhibit Hall in the Empire State Building in NYC.

Only 4 actors have won 2 Oscars in starring roles—Fredric March in 1932, 1946; Spencer Tracy in 1937, 1938; Gary Cooper in 1941, 1952; and Marlon Brando in 1954, 1972.

The youngest person ever to win an Oscar was Shirley Temple (b Apr 23, 1928) with her 1934 award at age 6, and the oldest is George Burns (b Jan 20, 1896) at age 80 for *The Sunshine Boys* in 1976.

The films with most awards have been *Ben Hur* (1959) with 11, followed by *Gone with the Wind* (1939) and *West Side Story* (1961), both with 10. The film with the highest number of nominations was *All About Eve* (1950) with 14. It won 6.

Oscars are named after Oscar Pierce of Texas. When the figurines were first delivered to the executive offices of the Academy of Motion Picture Arts and Sciences, the Executive Secretary exclaimed, "Why, they look just like my Uncle Oscar." And the name stuck.

9. PHONOGRAPH

The phonograph was first *conceived* by Charles Cros (1842–88), a French poet and scientist who described his idea in sealed papers deposited in the French Academy of Sciences Apr 30, 1877. The first practical device was realized by Thomas Alva Edison (1847–1931), who gained his first patent Feb 19, 1878 for a machine constructed by his mechanic, John Kruesi. It was first demonstrated on Dec 7, 1877, and patented on Feb 19, 1878.

The first practical hand-cranked, wax-coated-cylinder phonograph was manufactured in the US by Chichester Bell and Charles Sumner Tainter in 1886. The forerunner of the modern disc phonograph was patented in 1887 by Emile Berliner (1851–1929), a German immigrant to the US. Although a toy machine based on his principle was produced in Germany in 1889, the gramophone was not a serious commercial competitor to the cylinder phonograph until 1896.

Pre-recorded tapes were first marketed by Recording Associates in NYC in 1950.

The country with the greatest number of record players is the US with a total in excess of 75,000,000. A total of more than half a billion dollars is spent annually on 500,000 juke boxes in the US.

Sales in the US of discs and tapes reached a record $4,100 million in 1978, which includes sales of 273 million stereo LP's, 190 million singles and 127.8 million stereo tapes. In Sweden disc and tape sales were a record $17.95 per capita in 1976.

Oldest Records

The oldest records in the BBC library are white wax cylinders dating from 1888. The earliest commercial disc recording was manufactured in 1895. The BBC library, the world's largest, contains over 1 million records, including 5,250 with no known matrix.

The earliest jazz record made was *Indiana* and *The Dark Town Strutters Ball*, recorded for the Columbia label in NYC on or about Jan 30, 1917 by the Original Dixieland Jazz Band, led by Dominick (Nick) James La Rocca (1889–1961). This was released May 31, 1917. The first jazz record to be released was the ODJB's *Livery Stable Blues* (recorded Feb 24), backed by *The Dixie Jass Band One-Step* (recorded Feb 26), released by Victor on March 7, 1917.

Smallest Record

The smallest functional record is one 1⅜ inches in diameter of *God Save the King* of which 250 were made by HMV Record Co in 1924.

Most Successful Solo Recording Artists

On June 9, 1960 the Hollywood Chamber of Commerce presented Harry Lillis (*alias* Bing) Crosby, Jr (1904–77) with a platinum disc to commemorate the alleged sale of 200 million from 2,600 singles and 125 albums he had recorded. On Sept 15, 1970 he received a second platinum disc when Decca Records claimed a sale of 300,650,000 discs.

Crosby's first commercial recording was *I've Got the Girl* recorded on Oct 18, 1926 (master number W142785 [Take 3] issued on the Columbia label), and his first million-seller was *Sweet Leilani* in 1937. No independently audited figures of his global lifetime sales from his royalty reports have ever been published, and experts regard figures so high as this, before the industry became highly developed, as exaggerated.

Similarly no independently audited figures have been published for Elvis Aaron Presley (b Tupelo, Miss, 1935, d 1977). In view of Presley's worldwide tally of over 170 major hits on singles and over 80 top-selling albums from 1956 and continuing after his death, it may be assumed that it was he who succeeded Crosby as the top-selling solo artist of his time.

Most Successful Group

The singers with the greatest sales of any group have been The Beatles. This group from Liverpool,

SMALLEST RECORD RECORD: Only 1⅜ in in diameter, this is functional—one of 250 made in Britain in 1924, recording "God Save the King."

England, comprised George Harrison (b Feb 25, 1943), John Ono (formerly John Winston) Lennon (b Oct 9, 1940; d Dec 8, 1980), James Paul McCartney (b June 18, 1942) and Richard Starkey, *alias* Ringo Starr (b July 7, 1940). The all-time Beatles sales by the end of 1978 have been estimated at 100 million singles and 100 million albums. All 4 ex-Beatles sold several million further records as solo artists.

Since the break-up of the Beatles in 1970, it is estimated that the most successful group in the world in terms of record sales is the Swedish foursome ABBA (Agnetha Faltskog, Bjorn Ulvaeus, Benny Andersson and Anni-Frid Lyngstad).

Earliest Golden Disc

The first recorded piece eventually to aggregate a total sale of a million copies was a performance by Enrico Caruso (b Naples, Italy, 1873, d 1921) of the aria *Vesti la giubba* (*On with the Motley*) from the opera *I Pagliacci* by Ruggiero Leoncavallo (1858–1919), the earliest version of which was recorded on Nov 12, 1902.

The first single recording to surpass the million mark was Alma Gluck's rendition of *Carry Me Back to Old Virginny* on the Red Seal Victor label on a 12-in single-faced (later backed) record (No. 74420).

The first actual golden disc was one sprayed by RCA Victor for presentation to Glenn Miller (1904–44) for his *Chattanooga Choo Choo* on Feb 10, 1942.

Most Golden Discs

The only *audited* measure of million-selling singles and 500,000-selling albums within the US is certification by the Recording Industry Association of America introduced Mar 14, 1958. Out of the 2,954 RIAA gold-record awards made to Jan 1, 1982, the most have gone to The Beatles with 42 (plus one with Billy Preston) as a group. Paul McCartney has an additional 21 awards outside the group with Wings.

The most awards to an individual is 38 to Elvis Presley, spanning 1958 to Jan 1, 1982. Globally, however, Presley's total of million-selling singles has been authoritatively put at "approaching 80."

Most-Recorded Songs

Two songs have each been recorded over 1,000 times—*Yesterday* by Paul McCartney and John Lennon, with 1,186 versions between 1965 and Jan 1, 1973, and *Tie a Yellow Ribbon Round the Old Oak Tree*, written by Irwin Levine and L. Russell Brown, with more than 1,000 versions recorded from 1973 to Jan 1, 1979.

Biggest Sellers

The greatest seller of any record to date is *White Christmas* by Irving Berlin (b Israel Bailin, at Tyumen, Russia, May 11, 1888), with 25 million for the Crosby single (recorded May 29, 1942) and more than 100 million in other versions.

The highest claim for any "pop" record is an unaudited 25 million for *Rock Around the Clock*, copyrighted in 1953 by the late Max Friedman and James E. Myers, under the name of Jimmy De Knight, and recorded Apr 12, 1954 by Bill Haley and the Comets.

The best-selling album of all time is the double album (4 sides) of the soundtrack of the film *Saturday Night Fever*, with 25 million copies sold worldwide by May 1, 1979. The majority of the songs were written by the Bee Gees, comprising the three Gibb brothers, Barry Alan (b Isle of Man, Sept 6, 1946) and the twins Robin and Maurice (b Dec 22, 1949).

The first classical long-player to sell a million was a performance featuring the pianist Harvey Lavan (Van) Cliburn, Jr (b Kilgore, Tex, July 12, 1934) of the *Piano Concerto No. 1* by Pyotr Ilyich Tchaikovsky (1840–93) of Russia. This recording was made in 1958 and sales reached 1 million by 1961, 2 million by 1965 and about 2,500,000 by Jan 1970.

Fastest Seller

The fastest-selling record of all time is *John Fitzgerald Kennedy—A Memorial Album* (Premium Albums), an LP recorded on Nov 22, 1963, the day of Mr Kennedy's assassination, which sold 4 million copies at 99 cents in six days (Dec 7–12, 1963), thus ironically beating the previous speed record set by the humorous LP record *The First Family* about the Kennedys in 1962–63.

Best-Seller Chart Records

Singles record charts were first published by *Billboard* on July 20, 1940, when the No. 1 record was *I'll Never Smile Again* by Tommy Dorsey (b Nov 19, 1905, d Nov 26, 1956). Three discs have stayed at the top for a record 13 consecutive weeks—*Frenesi* by Artie Shaw from Dec 1940; *I've Heard that Song Before* by Harry James from Feb 1943; and *Goodnight Irene* by Gordon Jenkins and the Weavers from Aug 1950. *I Go Crazy* by Paul Davis stayed on the chart for 40 consecutive weeks from Aug 1977. The Beatles

RECORD SETTERS:
First Bing Crosby (above) was the undisputed champion singer on discs when, in 1960, his records had sold 200 million. By 1970, his total had reached 300 million. Following close behind in the solo singer race was Elvis Presley (top right) with 170 singles and 80 albums, all hits. Along came the Beatles (center) to lead the groups with sales of 100 million singles and 100 million albums to the end of 1978. After the Beatles break-up in 1970, the most successful group has been the ABBA foursome (right) from Sweden. (© Rex Features) Sales figures in the recording industry are difficult to verify.

STILL THE ROCK LEADER: Sales of the rendition of "Rock Around the Clock" by Bill Haley and the Comets (above) made in 1954 has topped the 25 million mark. (London Features Intl) LOUDEST POP GROUP is the distinction won by The Who (right), who have assaulted the eardrums of multitudes at 120 decibels.

have had the most No. 1 records (20) and Elvis Presley has had the most hit singles on the *Billboard Hot 100*—97 from 1956 to May 1981.

Billboard first published an album chart on March 15, 1945, when the No. 1 record was *King Cole Trio* featuring Nat "King" Cole (b March 17, 1919, d Feb 15, 1965). *South Pacific* was No. 1 for 69 weeks (nonconsecutive) from May 1949. *Johnny's Greatest Hits* by Johnny Mathis stayed on the chart for 490 weeks (over 9 years) from Apr 1958. The Beatles had the most No. 1 recordings (15) and Presley the most hit albums (81 from 1956 to May 1981).

Most Recordings

Miss Lata Mangeshker (b 1928) has reportedly recorded between 1948 and 1974 not less than 25,000 solo, duet and chorus-backed songs in 20 Indian languages. She frequently has 5 sessions in a day and has "backed" 1,800 films to 1974. Mohammed Rafi (d Aug 1, 1980) claimed to have recorded 28,000 songs in 11 Indian languages between 1944 and Apr 1980.

Advance Sales

The greatest advance sale was 2,100,000 for *Can't Buy Me Love* by The Beatles, released in the US on March 16, 1964.

Loudest Pop Group

The amplification for *The Who* concert at Charlton Athletic Football Ground, London, England, May 31, 1976, provided by a Tasco PA system, had a total power of 76,000 watts from eighty 800 W Crown DC 300 A amplifiers and twenty 600 W Phase Linear 200's. The readings at 50 m (164 ft) from the front of the sound system were 120 decibels. *Exposure to such noise levels is known to cause PSH—Permanent Shift of Hearing or partial deafness.*

Chapter 7
The World's Structures

For more records and greater details on this subject, see *Towers, Bridges and Other Structures* (Sterling), one of the Guinness Family of Books.

EARLIEST STRUCTURES

The earliest known human structure is a rough circle of loosely piled lava blocks found in 1960 on the lowest cultural level at the Lower Paleolithic site at Olduvai Gorge in Tanzania. The structure was associated with artifacts and bones and may represent a work-floor, dating to *circa* 1,750,000 BC.

The earliest evidence of *buildings* yet discovered is that of 21 huts with hearths of pebble-lined pits and delimited by stake holes, found in Oct 1965 at the Terra Amata site in Nice, France, thought to belong to the Acheulián culture of 120,000 years ago. Excavation carried out between June 28 and July 5, 1966 revealed one hut with palisaded walls having axes of 49 and 20 ft.

The oldest free-standing structures are now believed to be the megalithic temples at Mgarr and Skorba in Malta and Ggantija in Gozo, dating from *c.* 3250 BC.

The remains of a stone tower 20 ft high built into the walls of Jericho have been excavated, and dated to 5000 BC.

1. BUILDINGS FOR WORKING

Largest Industrial Building

The largest industrial plant in the world is the Nizhnig Tagil Railroad Car and Tank Plant, USSR, which has 204.3 acres of floor space. It has an annual capacity to produce 2,500 T-72 tanks.

Largest Commercial Buildings

The greatest ground area covered by any building under one roof is the auction building of the cooperative VBA (Verenigde Bloemenveilingen Aalsmeer), which measures 884.8 yd × 410.1 yd with a floor surface of 74.94 acres. The first section of this site of the world's largest flower auction at Aalsmeer, Netherlands, was completed in Feb 1972.

The building with the largest cubic capacity is the Boeing Company's main assembly plant at Everett, Wash, completed in 1968. The building, constructed for the manufacture of Boeing 747 jet airliners, has a maximum height of 115 ft and has a capacity of 200 million cu ft.

Largest Scientific Building

The most capacious scientific building is the Vehicle Assembly Building (VAB) at Complex 39, the selected site for the final assembly and launching of the Apollo moon spacecraft on the Saturn V rocket, at the John F. Kennedy Space Center (KSC) on Merritt Island near Cape Canaveral, Fla. It is a steel-framed building measuring 716 ft in length, 518 ft in width and 525 ft in height. The building contains four bays, each with its own door 460 ft high. Construction began in Apr 1963 by the Ursum Consortium. Its floor area is 343,500 sq ft (7.87 acres) and its capacity is 129,482,000 cu ft. The building was "topped out" on Apr 14, 1965 at a cost of $108,700,000.

Largest Administrative Building

The largest ground area covered by any office building is that of the Pentagon, in Arlington, Va. Built to house the US Defense Department's offices, it was completed Jan 15, 1943 and cost about $83 million. Each of the outermost sides of the Pentagon is 921 ft long and the perimeter of the building is about 1,500 yd. The 5 stories of the building enclose a floor area of 6½ million sq ft. During the day 29,000 people work in the building. The telephone system of the building has more than 44,000 telephones connected by 160,000 miles of cable and its 220 staff members handle 280,000 calls a day. Two restaurants, 6 cafeterias and 10 snack bars and a staff of 675 form the catering department of the building. The corridors measure 17 miles in length and there are 7,748 windows to be cleaned.

211

Largest Office Buildings

The largest office buildings with the largest rentable space are the twin towers comprising the World Trade Center in NYC, with a total of 4,370,000 sq ft (100.32 acres) in each. The taller tower (Tower Two) is 1,362 ft 3¼ in high. The tip of the TV antenna on Tower One is 1,710 ft above street level.

Tallest Buildings

The *tallest* office building is the Sears Tower, the national headquarters of Sears Roebuck & Co on Wacker Drive, Chicago, with 110 stories, rising to 1,454 ft and completed in 1974. Its *gross* area is 4,400,000 sq ft (101.0 acres). It was "topped out" on May 4, 1973, surpassing the World Trade Center in New York in height, at 2:35 p.m. Mar 6, 1973 with the first steel column reaching to the 104th story. The addition of two TV antennae brought the total height to 1,559 ft. The building's population is 16,700, served by 103 elevators and 18 escalators. It has 16,000 windows.

In Asia, where buildings must be constructed to be earthquake-proof, the tallest building is the 60-story "Sunshine 60" in Ikebukuro, Tokyo, Japan, completed in 1978 to a height of 787.4 ft. It has the world's fastest elevators, which go 2,000 ft/min.

The tallest office block in Britain is also the tallest cantilevered building in the world. The National Westminster tower block in London, completed in 1979 at a cost of £72 million ($165 million) has 49 stories and 3 basement levels, serviced by 21 elevators, and is 600 ft 4 in tall.

England may soon have a 139-story office building to be 1,825 ft tall. The Mersyside County Council unveiled highly tentative plans on Nov 9, 1979 for a £500 million ($1,075,000,000) project.

Largest Embassy

The largest embassy is the USSR embassy on Bei Xiao Jie, Peking, China, in the northeastern corner of the walled city. The whole 45-acre area of the old Orthodox Church mission (established 1728), now known as the *Bei guan,* was handed over to the USSR in 1949.

Largest Garages and Parking Lots

The largest garage (as opposed to parking lot) is at O'Hare Airport, Chicago, with 6 levels and a capacity for 9,250 cars. It is operated by Allright Auto Parks, Inc, the world's largest parking company.

The largest private garage ever built was one for 100 cars at the Long Island, NY, mansion of William Kissam Vanderbilt (1849–1920).

The parking lots at Giants Stadium, East Rutherford, NJ, have a capacity for 26,000 automobiles and 500 buses.

Largest Hangars

The largest hangar is the Goodyear Airship hangar at Akron, O, which measures 1,175 ft long, 325 ft wide and 200 ft high. It covers 364,000 sq ft (8.35 acres) and has a capacity of 55 million cu ft.

The largest single fixed-wing aircraft hangar is the Lockheed-Georgia engineering test center at Marietta, Ga measuring 630 ft × 480 ft (6.94 acres) completed in 1967. The maintenance hangar at the Frankfurt/Main Airport, W Germany, covers slightly less area but has a frontage of 902 ft. The cable-supported roof has a span of 426.5 ft.

Delta Air Lines' jet base, on a 140-acre site at Hartsfield International Airport, Atlanta, Ga has 36 acres under its roof.

Air-Supported Structure

The largest air-supported roof is the roof of the 80,600-capacity octagonal Pontiac Silverdome Stadium, Mich measuring 522 ft wide and 722 ft long. The air pressure is 5 lb per sq in, supporting the 10-acre translucent fiberglass roofing. The structural engineers were Geiger-Berger Associates of NYC. The largest standard-size air hall is one in Lima, Ohio, which is 860 ft long, 140 ft wide and 65 ft high made by Irvin Industries of Stamford, Conn.

Tallest Chimneys and Cooling Towers

The tallest chimney is the $5½ million International Nickel Company's stack, 1,245 ft 8 in tall, at Copper Cliff, Sudbury, Ontario, Canada, completed in 1970. It was built by Canadian Kellogg Ltd and the diameter tapers from 116.4 ft at the base to 51.8 ft at the top. It weighs 42,998 tons and became operational in 1971.

The world's most massive chimney rises 1,148 ft at Puentes, Spain, built by the M. W. Kellogg Co. It contains 20,600 cu yd of concrete and 2,900,000 lb of steel and has an internal volume of 6,700,000 cu ft.

The largest cooling tower is adjacent to the nuclear power plant at Uentrop, W Germany, completed in 1976, which is 590 ft tall.

LARGEST OFFICE BUILDINGS: The Sears Tower (above) dominates the Chicago skyline with its 110 stories and a height of 1,454 ft (1,559 ft counting TV towers). The twin towers of the World Trade Center (right) dominate the NYC skyline, but are 100 ft shorter. In gross area the Sears Tower contains 4,400,000 sq ft compared to the World Trade Center's total of 8,740,000 sq ft.

LARGEST AIR-SUPPORTED ROOF: The octagonal Pontiac Silverdome Stadium in Mich has its roof held up by 5 lb of air pressure per sq in.

213

LARGEST CASTLE AND PALACE: The largest inhabited castle is Windsor (top photo), the British royal residence near London. The aerial view shows that it is a waisted parallelogram. The largest palace is the Imperial Palace in Peking, which has been converted into a museum. Called "The Forbidden City," it actually consists of 17 palace buildings and 5 halls.

Wooden Buildings

The oldest extant wooden buildings are those comprising the Pagoda, Chumanar Gate, and the Temple of Horyu (Horyu-ji), at Nara, Japan, built between 670 and 715 AD. The nearby Daibutsuden, built in 1704–11, once measured 285.4 ft long, 167.3 ft wide and 153.3 ft tall. The present dimensions are 188 ft × 165.3 ft × 159.4 ft.

The largest timber buildings are the two US Navy airship hangars built in 1942–43 at Tillamook, Ore. Now used as a saw mill by the Louisiana-Pacific Corporation, they measure 1,000 ft long, 170 ft high at the crown and 296 ft wide at the base. They are worth $6 million.

Largest Sewage Works

The largest single sewage works is the West-Southwest Treatment Plant, opened in 1940 on a site of 501 acres in Chicago. It serves an area containing 2,940,000 people. It treated an average of more than 835 million gallons of wastes per day in 1973. The capacity of its sedimentation and aeration tanks is 1,600,000 cu yd.

Grain Elevator

The largest single-unit grain elevator is that operated by the C-G-F Grain Company at Wichita, Kans. Consisting of a triple row of storage tanks, 123 on each side of the central loading tower or "head house," the unit is 2,717 ft long and 100 ft wide. Each tank is 120 ft high, with an inside diameter of 30 ft, giving a total storage capacity of 20 million bushels of wheat. The largest collection of elevators is at Thunder Bay, Ontario, Canada, on Lake Superior, with a total capacity of 103.9 million bushels.

2. BUILDINGS FOR LIVING

Castles and Forts

Fortifications existed in all the great early civilizations, including that of ancient Egypt from 3000 BC. Fortified castles in the more accepted sense only existed much later. The oldest in the world is that at Gomdan, Yemen, which originally had 20 stories and dates from before 100 AD.

The largest inhabited castle is the British Royal residence of Windsor Castle, Berkshire. It is primarily of 12th-century construction and is in the form of a waisted parallelogram, 1,890 ft × 540 ft. The total area of Dover Castle (England), however, covers 34 acres with a width of 1,100 ft and a curtain wall of 1,800 ft, or, if underground works are taken in, 2,300 ft.

The largest ancient castle is Hradcany Castle, Prague, Czechoslovakia, built in the 9th century. It is a very oblong, irregular polygon with an axis of 1,870 ft and an average traverse diameter of 420 ft, with a surface area of 18 acres.

The walls of Babylon, north of Al Hillah, Iraq, built in 600 BC were up to 85 ft in thickness.

Largest Palaces

The largest palace is the Imperial Palace (*Gu gong*) in the center of Peking (*Bei jing*, northern capital), China, which covers a rectangle 1,050 yd × 820 yd, an area of 177.9 acres. The outline survives from the construction of the third Ming emperor Yung-lo of 1402–24, but due to constant rearrangements most of the intramural buildings are 18th century. These consist of 5 halls and 17 palaces of which the last occupied by the last Empress was the Palace of Accumulated Elegance (*Chu xia gong*) until 1924.

The largest residential palace is the Vatican Palace, in the Vatican City, an enclave in Rome, Italy. Covering an area of 13½ acres, it has 1,400 rooms, chapels and halls, of which the oldest date from the 15th century.

The world's largest moats are those which surround the Imperial Palace in Peking. From plans drawn by French sources they appear to measure 54 yd wide and have a total length of 3,600 yd. The city's moats total 23½ miles in all.

Tallest Apartment Buildings

The tallest block of apartments in the world is Lake Point Towers of 70 stories, 645 ft high in Chicago.

Largest Hotels

The hotel with the most rooms is the 12-story Hotel Rossiya in Moscow, with 3,200 rooms providing accommodation for 6,000 guests, opened in 1967. It would thus require more than 8½ years to spend one night in each room. In addition, there is a 21-story "Presidential" tower in the central courtyard. The hotel employs about 3,000 people and has 93 elevators. The ballroom is reputed to be the world's largest. Muscovites are not permitted as residents while foreigners are charged 16 times more than the very low rate charged to officials of the USSR. The Izmailovo Hotel complex, opened July 1980 for the XXIInd Olympic Games in Moscow, was designed to accommodate 9,500 people.

The largest commercial hotel building in the world is the Waldorf-Astoria, opened on Oct 1, 1931 on Park Avenue, between 49th and 50th Streets, NYC. It occupies a complete block of 81,337 sq ft (1.87 acres) and reaches a maximum height of 625 ft 7 in. The Waldorf-Astoria has 47 stories and 1,852 guest rooms, maintains the largest hotel radio receiving system in the world and has an electricity bill of about $2 million a year. The Waldorf can accommodate 10,000 people at one time, with a staff of 1,700. Its restaurants have catered for parties up to 6,000 at a time. The coffee-makers' daily output reaches 1,000 gallons. The hotel has housed six heads of state simultaneously.

Tallest Hotels

The tallest hotel, measured from the street level of its main entrance to the top, is the 723-ft-tall 70-story Peachtree Center Plaza Hotel in Atlanta, Ga, opened in Jan 1976. The $50 million, 1,100-room hotel was designed by architect John Portman, is operated by Western International Hotels, and owned by Portman Properties. Their Detroit Plaza Hotel in Detroit is taller when measured from its back entrance to the top. This hotel, opened in early 1977, is 748 ft tall starting from its lower street level. Designed by the same architect as the Peachtree, it is operated also by Western International Hotels, and contains 1,400 rooms.

Ground was broken in June 1980 for the building of a $235 million Raffles City hotel project in Singapore, which will be 70 stories and 754 ft high at its central tower.

Largest Lobby

The world's largest hotel lobby is that of The Grand Hotel Taipei, Taiwan, completed on Oct 10, 1973. It measures 154 × 114 ft and is 31½ ft high.

Most Expensive Hotel Suite

The costliest hotel accommodation is the Royale Suite of the Hotel Nova-Park Elysées in Paris which rents for 35,000 francs (1982 = c. $5,500) per day. On three complete floors, it consists of 7 rooms with 7 bathrooms, 3 terraces, and a conference room! It has

a private telex machine plus 6 telephone lines. Designed for political figures (Jimmy Carter was one of the first occupants), the windows in the suite are made of bullet-proof glass and an anti-bugging device adds to the security. There is a back door and a private elevator direct to the garage for fast escapes. The suite covers 431.5 sq meters (4,644 sq ft) and has a private kitchen with adjoining suites for bodyguards (Carter had 16). The TV has 24-hour news and stock reports running along with entertainment programs, as do all the rooms in the hotel. The bathtubs in the suite are large enough for 2, and have jacuzzi spouts and a water thermostat. A limousine is provided by the hotel to take guests to and from the airports. Occupants of the suite, like all the guests in the hotel, have access to a "fitness club" with gym equipment, sauna bath, swimming pool, disco, nightclub, garden restaurant, and 3 other restaurants indoors, as well as secretarial services.

Spas

The largest spa measured by number of available hotel rooms is Vichy, Allier, France, with 14,000 rooms. Spas are named after the watering place called Spa in the Liège province of Belgium where hydropathy was developed from 1626. The highest French spa is Barèges, Hautes-Pyrénées, at 4,068 ft above sea level.

Barracks

The oldest purpose-built barracks are believed to be Collins Barracks, formerly the Royal Barracks, Dublin, Ireland, completed in 1704 and still in use.

Habitations at Highest Altitude

The highest inhabited buildings are those in the Indian–Tibet border fort of Bāsisi at c. 19,700 ft. In Apr 1961, however, a 3-room dwelling was discovered at 21,650 ft on Cerro Llullaillaco (22,058 ft), on the Argentine–Chile border, believed to date from the late pre-Columbian period c. 1480. An unnamed settlement on the T'e-li-mo trail in southern Tibet is at an apparent altitude of 19,800 ft.

Largest House

The largest private house in the world is 250-room Biltmore House in Asheville, NC. It is owned by George and William Cecil, grandsons of George

TALLEST HOTEL (right): The cylindrical 70-story Peachtree Center Plaza Hotel in Atlanta, Ga, with 1,100 rooms, cost $50 million. It stands 723 ft tall (compared to 1,250 ft for the Empire State Building).

MOST EXPENSIVE SUITE (below): The office and one of the bedrooms of the Royale Suite, which rents for about $5,500 per day, at the new Hotel Nova-Park Elysées in Paris. Intended for politicians who need protection, the suite has bullet-proof windows and an escape elevator, an anti-bugging device, private telex, and adjoining suites for bodyguards. Jimmy Carter slept here (1982).

LARGEST PRIVATE HOME (left): With 250 rooms, Biltmore House near Asheville, NC, had 119,000 acres when it was built (1890–95), and now with only 12,000 acres is valued at $55 million.

LARGEST INDOOR STADIUM (right): The 13-acre Superdome in New Orleans, LA, has seats for 97,365 conventioneers and a record roof that has a span of 680 ft in diameter. **LARGEST STADIUM** of any type (below): Strahov Stadium in Prague, Czechoslovakia, has space for 240,000 spectators and a field big enough for up to 40,000 gymnasts.

Washington Vanderbilt II (1862–1914). The house was built between 1890 and 1895 on an estate of 119,000 acres, at a cost of $4,100,000, and is now valued at $55 million with 12,000 acres.

The most expensive private house ever built is the Hearst Ranch at San Simeon, Calif. It was built 1922–39 for William Randolph Hearst (1863–1951), at a total cost of more than $30 million. It has more than 100 rooms, a 104-ft-long heated swimming pool, an 83-ft-long assembly hall and a garage for 25 limousines. The house would require 60 servants to maintain it.

Most Expensive Homes

The highest asking price for any private house is $16.5 million in July 1980 for the late Conrad Hilton's (1888–1979) Casa Encantada built in 1938 in an 8½-acre estate in Bel-Air, Los Angeles. It has 64 rooms and 26 bathrooms and 23,000 sq ft of living space. The Hilton attorney reportedly discouraged viewing by anyone less than a demi centi-millionaire.

The most expensive penthouse apartment is a 4-story penthouse at the top of Galleria International on East 57th Street, NYC. With 4 main bedrooms, a 22-ft swimming pool, library, sauna and several solariums, it was on the market in March 1976 for $3,500,000.

Smallest Residence

The British naval veteran Alexander Wortley (1900–80) lived his last 20 years in a green painted box in the garden of David Moreau in Langley Park, Buckinghamshire, England. It measured 5 × 4 × 3 ft with an extension for his feet—small enough to keep women out. He paid no rent or taxes and did not believe in insurance, pensions or governments.

3. BUILDINGS FOR ENTERTAINMENT

Largest Circus

The largest permanent circus is Circus Circus, Las Vegas, Nev, opened Oct 18, 1968 at a cost of $15 million. It covers an area of 129,000 sq ft capped by a 90-ft-high tent-shaped flexiglass roof. (Circus Stunt records are in Chapter 11.)

The largest traveling circus is the Circus Vargas in the US which can accommodate 5,000 people under its Big Top.

Largest Stadiums

The largest stadium is the Strahov Stadium in Praha (Prague), Czechoslovakia. It was completed in 1934 and can easily accommodate 240,000 spectators for mass displays of up to 40,000 Sokol gymnasts.

The largest football (soccer) stadium is the Maracaña Municipal Stadium in Rio de Janeiro, Brazil, which has a normal capacity of 205,000, of whom 155,000 may be seated. A crowd of 199,854 was accommodated for the World Cup final between Brazil and Uruguay on July 16, 1950. A dry moat, 7 ft wide and over 5 ft deep, protects players from spectators and *vice versa.*

The largest covered stadium in the world is the Azteca Stadium, Mexico City, opened in 1968, which has a capacity of 107,000, of whom nearly all are under cover.

Largest One-Piece Roof

The transparent acrylic glass "tent" roof over the Munich Olympic Stadium, W Germany, measures 914,940 sq ft in area. It rests on a steel net supported by masts. The roof of longest span is the 680-ft diameter of the Louisiana Superdome (see photo). The major axis of the elliptical Texas Stadium, Irving, Tex, completed in 1971 is, however, 784 ft 4 in.

Largest Indoor Arena

The largest indoor stadium is the 13-acre $173-million 273-ft-tall Superdome in New Orleans, La, completed in May 1975. Its maximum seating capacity for conventions is 97,365 or 76,791 for football. Box suites rent for $35,000, excluding the price of admission. A gondola with six 312-in TV screens produces instant replay.

Night Clubs

The oldest night club (*boîte de nuit*) is "Le Bal des Anglais" at 6 Rue des Anglais, Paris 5, France. It was founded in 1843 but closed *c.* 1960.

The largest night club in the world is Gilley's Club (formerly Shelly's) built in 1955 and extended in 1971 on Spencer Highway, Pasadena, Tex. It has a seating capacity of 6,000 under one roof covering 4 acres.

In the more classical sense the largest night club is "The Mikado" in the Akasaka district of Tokyo, Japan, with a seating capacity of 2,000. It is "manned" by 1,250 hostesses. Binoculars are essential to an appreciation of the floor show.

The lowest night club is the "Minus 206" in Tiberias, Israel, on the shores of the Sea of Galilee. It is 676 ft below sea level. An alternative candidate is "Outer Limits," opposite the Cow Palace, San Francisco, which was raided for the 151st time on Aug 1, 1971. It has been called both "The Most Busted Joint" and "The Slowest to Get the Message."

Largest Amusement Park

The largest amusement resort is Disney World on 27,443 acres of Orange and Osceola Counties, 20 miles southwest of Orlando in central Florida. It was opened on Oct 1, 1971. This $400 million investment attracted 10,700,000 visitors in its first year.

The most attended resort in the world is Disneyland, Anaheim, Calif (opened 1955) where the total number of visitors reached 213,840,692 on Apr 27, 1982. The greatest attendance on one day was 82,516 on Aug 16, 1969.

Fairs

The earliest major international fair was the Great Exhibition of 1851 in the Crystal Palace, Hyde Park, London, which in 141 days attracted 6,039,195 admissions.

The largest International Fair site was that for the St Louis-Louisiana Purchase Exposition, which covered 1,271.76 acres. It also staged the 1904 Olympic Games and drew an attendance of 19,694,855.

The record attendance for any fair was 64,218,770 for Expo '70 held on an 815-acre site at Osaka, Japan, from March to Sept 13, 1970. It made a profit of 19,439,402,017 yen (over $45 million).

Ferris Wheel

The original Ferris Wheel, named after its constructor, George W. Ferris (1859–96), was erected in 1893 at the Midway, Chicago, at a cost of $385,000. The wheel was 250 ft in diameter, 790 ft in circumference, weighed 1,198 tons, and carried 36 cars each seating 60 people, making a total of 2,160 passengers. The structure was removed in 1904 to St Louis, and was eventually sold as scrap for $1,800.

In 1897, a Ferris Wheel with a diameter of 300 ft was erected for the Earl's Court Exhibition, London. It had 10 1st-class and 30 2nd-class cars.

The largest wheel now operating is at Kobe Portopialand, Japan, with a height of 208 ft 4 in. It was constructed by Hankyu Railway Corporation of Osaka, Japan, and completed in Mar 1981.

Roller Coasters

The maximum speeds claimed for roller coasters have in the past been exaggerated for commercial reasons. The twin-track, triple-helix American Eagle at Marriott's Great America, Gurnee, Ill, opened on May 23, 1981, has a vertical drop of 147.4 ft on which a speed of 66.31 mph is reportedly reached. The longest roller coaster in the world is *The Beast* at King's Island near Cincinnati, Ohio. Rigorous scientific tests at the base of its 141-ft-high drop returned a speed of 64.77 mph on Apr 5, 1980. It probably achieves higher speeds when in regular use during the warmer summer months. The total track length of 7,400 ft incorporates 800 ft of tunnels, a 540-degree helix and a second drop of 135 ft. The wooded site covers 35 acres.

The tallest is the 193-ft-high Tojoko Land Loop Coaster in Hyogo, Japan, opened on Aug 4, 1979.

Longest Slide

The longest slide in the world is the Bromley Alpine Slide on Route 11 in Peru, Vt. This has a length of 4,600 ft (0.87 mile) and a vertical drop of 820 ft.

Largest Pleasure Beach

The largest pleasure beach is Virginia Beach, Va. It has 28 miles of beach front on the Atlantic and 10 miles of estuary frontage. The area which embraces 255 sq mi, contains 134 hotels and motels.

Pleasure Piers

The Old Pier at Weymouth, Dorset, England dates back to 1812. The longest pleasure pier is Southend Pier at Southend-on-Sea in Essex, England. It is 1.34 miles in length, and was first opened in Aug 1889, with final extensions made in 1929. In 1949–50, the pier had 5,750,000 visitors. The pier railway was closed in Oct 1978. The resort with the most piers is Atlantic City, NJ with 6 pre-war and 5 currently.

Bars

The largest beer-selling establishment is the Mathäser, Bayerstrasse 5, Munich, W Germany, where the daily sale reaches 100,800 pints. It was established in 1829, was demolished in World War II, rebuilt by 1955, and now seats 5,500 people. Consumption at the Dube beer halls in the Bantu township of Soweto, Johannesburg, South Africa, may, however, be higher on some Saturdays when the average of 7,160 gallons (57,280 pints) is far exceeded.

HIGHEST ROLLER COASTER (right): The twin-track, triple-helix American Eagle in Gurnee, Ill, attains a reported peak speed of 66.31 mph on a 147.4-ft drop. LARGEST AMUSEMENT PARK is Disney World (below) in central Florida, which can count on about 10–12 million visitors a year. This is Cinderella's Castle. LONGEST SLIDE (lower right): The Bromley Alpine Slide in Peru, Vt, is seven-eighths of a mile long and drops 820 ft vertically.

LONGEST BRIDGE SPAN: The 4,626-ft span over the Humber Estuary in western England is so great that it requires the tops of bridge towers to be slightly out of vertical parallel because of the curvature of the earth.

The longest bar with beer pumps was built in 1938 at the Working Men's Club, Mildura, Victoria, Australia. It has a counter 298 ft in length, served by 27 pumps. Temporary bars have been erected of greater length. The Falstaff Brewing Corp put up a temporary bar 336 ft 5 in in length on Wharf St., St Louis, on June 22, 1970.

The bar at Erickson's on Burnside Street, Portland, Ore in its heyday (1883–1920) ran continuously around and across the main saloon, measuring 684 ft. The chief bouncer, Edward "Spider" Johnson, had a chief assistant named "Jumbo" Reilly who weighed 320 pounds and was said to resemble "an ill-natured orangutan." Beer was 5 cents for 16 fluid ounces.

Wine Cellar

The largest wine cellars are at Paarl, those of the Ko-operative Wijnbouwers Vereeniging (K.W.V.), near Capetown, in the center of the wine district of South Africa. They cover an area of 25 acres and have a capacity of 36 million gallons.

The largest wooden wine cask is the Heidelberg Tun completed in 1751 in the cellar of the Friedrichsbau Heidelberg, W Germany. Its capacity is 1,855 hectolitres (48,985 US gallons).

Ballroom

The largest dance floor, 256 ft long, is one used for championships at Earl's Court Exhibition Hall, Kensington, London.

4. TOWERS AND MASTS

Tallest Structure

The tallest structure is the guyed Warszawa Radio mast at Konstantynow 60 miles northwest of Warsaw, Poland, which is 2,120 ft 8 in tall, or more than four-tenths of a mile. The mast was completed July 18, 1974 and put into operation July 22, 1974. Work began on the tubular steel construction, with its 15 steel guy ropes, in 1970. It was designed by Jan Polak and weighs 615 tons. The mast is so high that anyone falling off the top would reach terminal velocity, and hence cease to be accelerating, before hitting the ground. It recaptured for Europe a record held in the US since the Chrysler Building surpassed the Eiffel Tower in 1929.

Tallest Tower

The tallest self-supporting tower (as opposed to a guyed mast) is the $44 million CN Tower in Metro Centre, Toronto, Canada. It rises to 1,822 ft 1 in. Excavation began Feb 12, 1973, for the 145,000-ton structure of reinforced, lost-tensioned concrete, and it was "topped out" Apr 2, 1975. A 416-seat restaurant revolves in the 7-floor Sky Pod at 1,140 ft, from which the visibility extends to hills 74½ miles distant. Lightning strikes the top about 200 times (in 30 storms) each year.

The tallest tower built before the era of television

masts is the Tour Eiffel (Eiffel Tower), in Paris, designed by Alexandre Gustave Eiffel (1832–1923) for the Paris exhibition and completed on March 31, 1889. It was 985 ft 11 in tall, now extended by a TV antenna to 1,052 ft 4 in, and weighs 8,091 tons. The maximum sway in high winds is 5 in. The whole iron edifice, which has 1,792 steps, took 2 years, 2 months, and 2 days to build and cost 7,799,401 francs 31 centimes.

5. BRIDGES

Arch construction was probably understood by the Sumerians as early as 3200 BC and a reference exists to a Nile bridge in 2650 BC. The oldest surviving datable bridge in the world is the slab stone single-arch bridge over the River Meles in Smyrna (now Izmir), Turkey, which dates from c. 850 BC.

Longest Suspension Bridge

The longest bridge span is the main span of the Humber Estuary Bridge in England, at 4,626 ft. Work began on July 27, 1972. The towers are 533 ft 1⅜ in tall from datum and are 1⅜ inches out of parallel, to allow for the curvature of the earth. Including the Hessle and Barton side spans, the bridge stretches 1.37 miles. On March 22, 1980 an accident occurred with the slinging of the decking. The bridge was structurally completed on July 18, 1980 at a cost of £91 million (about $185 million) and was opened by HM the Queen on July 17, 1981. Tolls range between $2 for cars and $15 for heavy vehicles.

The Mackinac Straits Bridge between Mackinaw City and St Ignace, Mich is the longest suspension bridge measured between anchorages (1.58 miles) and has an overall length, including viaducts of the bridge proper measured between abutment faces, of 3.63 miles. It was opened in Nov 1957 (dedicated June 28, 1958) at a cost of $100 million and has a main span of 3,800 ft.

The double-deck road-railroad Akashi-Kaikyo suspension bridge linking Honshu and Shikoku, Japan, is planned to be completed in 1988. The main span will be 5,840 ft in length with an overall suspended length with side spans totaling 11,680 ft. Work began in Oct 1978, and the eventual cost is expected to exceed 1 trillion yen ($4,500 million).

Plans for a Messina Bridge linking Sicily with the Italian mainland are dependent on Common Market budgets. One preliminary study calls for towers 1,000 ft high and a span exceeding 1.86 miles. The total cost has been estimated to exceed $4,000 million.

Longest Cantilever Bridge

The Québec Bridge (Pont de Québec) over the St Lawrence River in Canada has the longest cantilever span—1,800 ft between the piers and 3,239 ft overall. It carries a railroad track and two roadways. Begun in 1899, it was finally opened to traffic Dec 3, 1917, at a cost of Can. $22,500,000 and 87 lives.

Longest Steel Arch Bridge

The longest steel arch bridge is the New River Gorge bridge near Fayetteville, W Va, completed in 1977, with a span of 1,700 ft.

Widest Bridges

The widest long-span bridge is the 1,650-ft-long Sydney Harbour Bridge, Australia, which is 160 ft wide. It carries 2 electric overhead railroad tracks, 8 lanes of roadway and a cycleway and footway. It was officially opened March 19, 1932.

The Crawford Street Bridge in Providence, RI, has a width of 1,147 ft. The River Roch is bridged for a distance of 1,460 ft where the culvert passes through the center of Rochdale, Greater Manchester, England, and this is sometimes claimed to be a breadth.

Railroad Bridges

The longest railroad bridge in the world is the Huey P. Long Bridge, Metairie, La, with a railroad section 22,996 ft (4.35 miles) long. It was completed Dec 16, 1935, with a longest span of 790 ft.

The Yangtse River Bridge completed in 1968 in Nanking, China, is the longest combined highway and railroad bridge. The rail deck is 4.20 miles and the road deck an additional 2.85 miles.

Floating Bridge

The longest floating bridge is the Second Lake Washington Bridge in Seattle, Wash. Its total length is 12,596 ft and its floating section measures 7,518 ft (1.42 miles). It was built at a cost of $15 million, and completed in Aug 1963.

Highest Bridges

The highest bridge is the suspension bridge over the Royal Gorge of the Arkansas River in Colorado. It is 1,053 ft above the water level. It has a main span of 880 ft and was constructed in 6 months, ending on

Dec 6, 1929. The highest railroad bridge in the world is at Fades, outside Clermont-Ferrand, France. It was built 1901–09 with a span of 472 ft and is 435 ft above the River Sioule.

Covered Bridge

The longest covered bridge is that at Hartland, New Brunswick, Canada, measuring 1,282 ft overall, completed in 1899.

Longest Bridging

The world's longest bridging is the Second Lake Pontchartrain Causeway, opened March 23, 1969, joining Lewisburg and Metairie, La. Its length is 126,055 ft (23.87 miles). It cost $29,900,000 and is 228 ft longer than the adjoining First Causeway completed in 1956.

The longest railroad viaduct in the world is the rock-filled Great Salt Lake railroad trestle, carrying the Southern Pacific Railroad 11.85 miles across the Great Salt Lake, Utah. It was opened as a pile and trestle bridge March 8, 1904, and converted to rock fill in 1955–1960.

The longest stone arch bridging in the world is the 3,810-ft-long Rockville Bridge north of Harrisburg, Pa with 48 spans containing 219,520 tons of stone and completed in 1901.

Longest Aqueducts

The greatest of ancient aqueducts was the Aqueduct of Carthage in Tunisia, which ran 87.6 miles from the springs of Zaghouan to Djebel Djougar. It was built by the Romans during the reign of Publius Aelius Hadrianus (117–138 AD). By 1895, 344 arches still survived. Its original capacity has been calculated at 8,400,000 gallons per day. The triple-tiered aqueduct Pont du Gard, built in 19 AD near Nîmes, France, is 160 ft high. The tallest of the 14 arches of the Aguas Livres Aqueduct, built in Lisbon, Portugal, in 1784, is 213 ft 3 in.

The longest aqueduct, in the modern sense of a water conduit as opposed to an irrigation canal, is the California State Water Project aqueduct, completed in 1974 to a length of 826 miles, of which 385 miles is canalized.

6. CANALS

Relics of the oldest canals in the world, dated by archeologists to c. 4000 BC were discovered near Mandali, Iraq, early in 1968.

Longest Canals

The longest canalized system is the Volga-Baltic Canal opened in Apr 1965. It runs 1,850 miles from Astrakhan up the Volga, via Kuybyshev, Gorkiy and Lake Ladoga, to Leningrad, USSR. The longest canal of the ancient world was the Grand Canal of China from Peking to Hangchow. It was begun in 540 BC and not completed until 1327 AD by which time it extended for 1,107 miles. The estimated work force c. 600 AD reached 5 million on the Pien section. By 1950 the silt had piled up to the point that it was, in no place, more than 6 ft deep. It is now, however, opened up and plied by ships of up to 2,240 tons.

The Beloye More (White Sea) Baltic Canal from Belomorsk to Povenets in the USSR is 141 miles long with 19 locks. It was completed with the use of forced labor in 1933 and cannot accommodate ships of more than 16 ft in draft.

The longest big ship canal is the Suez Canal, linking the Red and Mediterranean Seas, opened Nov 16, 1869, but inoperative from June 1967 to June 1975. The canal was planned by the French diplomat Ferdinand de Lesseps (1805–1894) and work began Apr 25, 1859. It is 100.6 miles in length from Port Said lighthouse to Suez Roads, 197 ft wide. The work force was 8,213 men and 368 camels. The largest vessel to transit has been S.S. *British Progress,* a VLCC (Very Large Crude Carrier) of 228,569 tons dwt (length 1,081.5 ft; beam 159.7 ft at a maximum draft 84 ft). This was southbound in ballast on July 5, 1976.

Busiest Canal

The busiest big ship canal is the Panama, first transited on Aug 15, 1914. In 1974, there were a record 14,304 ocean-going transits. The largest liner to transit is *Queen Elizabeth 2* (66,851 gross tons) in Jan 1980, for a toll of $89,154.62. The ships with the greatest beam to transit have been the *Acadia Forest* and the *Atlantic Forest,* each of 106.9 ft. The lowest toll was 36 cents for the swimmer Richard Halliburton in 1928. The fastest transit was 2 hours 41 min by the US Navy hydrofoil *Pegasus* on June 20, 1979.

Seaway

The longest artificial seaway is the St Lawrence Seaway (189 miles long) along the NY State-Ontario border from Montreal to Lake Ontario, which enables 80% of all ocean-going ships, and bulk carriers with a capacity of 29,000 tons, to sail 2,342 miles

LONGEST AND HIGHEST AQUEDUCTS: The Romans were famous for the building of aqueducts as their cities were dependent on a steady supply of water. In Carthage (now Tunisia) the Romans built an aqueduct 87.6 miles long. The triple-tiered aqueduct Port du Gard near Nîmes, France (right), built in 19 AD, is the highest in the ancient world—160 ft high.

from the North Atlantic, up the St Lawrence Estuary and across the Great Lakes to Duluth, Minn, on Lake Superior (602 ft above sea level). The project cost $470 million and was opened Apr 25, 1959.

Irrigation Canal

The longest irrigation canal is the Karakumskiy Kanal, stretching 528 miles from Haun-Khan to Ashkhabad, Turkmenistan, USSR. In Sept 1971 the navigable length was reported to have reached 280 miles. The length of the $925 million project will eventually reach 930 miles.

Largest and Deepest Locks

The largest single lock connects the Schelde with the Kanaaldok system at Zandvliet, west of Antwerp, Belgium. It is 1,640 ft long and 187 ft wide and is an entrance to an impounded sheet of water 11.2 miles long.

The deepest lock is the John Day Dam lock on the Columbia River, Ore and Wash, completed in 1963. It can raise or lower barges 113 ft and is served by a 1,100-ton gate.

Highest Lock Elevator

The highest lock elevator overcomes a head of 225 ft at Ronquieres on the Charleroi-Brussels Canal, Belgium. The two 236-wheeled caissons, each able to carry 1,510 tons, take 22 minutes to cover the 4,698-ft-long ramp.

Largest Canal Cut

The Gaillard Cut (known as the "Ditch") on the Panama Canal is 270 ft deep between Gold Hill and Contractor's Hill with a bottom width of 500 ft. In one day in 1911 as many as 333 dirt trains each carrying 400 tons left this site. The total amount of earth excavated for the whole Panama Canal was 666,194,450 sq yd to Oct 1, 1979. This total will be raised by the further widening of the Gaillard Cut.

7. DAMS

The earliest known dams were those uncovered by the British School of Archeology in Jerusalem in 1974 at Jawa in Jordan. These stone-faced earth dams are dated to *c.* 3200 BC.

Most Massive Dam

Measured by volume, the largest dam is the 98-ft-high New Cornelia Tailings earthfill dam near Ajo, Ariz with a volume of 274,026,000 cu yd, completed in 1973 to a length of 6.74 miles. The Guri dam across the Caroni River in Venezuela will eventually have a volume of 363,394,000 sq yd.

Largest Concrete Dam

The largest concrete dam, and the largest concrete structure, is the Grand Coulee Dam on the Columbia River, Wash. Work was begun in 1933, it began operating on March 22, 1941, and was completed in 1942, at a cost of $56 million. It has a crest length of 4,173 ft and is 550 ft high. It contains 10,585,000 cu yd of concrete, and weighs about 21,600,000 tons. The hydroelectric power plant (now being extended) will have a capacity of 9,780,000 kW.

Longest River Dam and Sea Dam

The longest river dam is the 62-ft-high Kiev dam on the Dnieper River, USSR, which was completed

in 1964 to a length of 33.6 miles. The Yacyreta-Apipe dam across the Paraná on the Paraguay–Argentina borders will extend for 43.24 miles. In the early 17th century, an impounding dam of moderate height was built in Lake Hungtze, Kiangsu, China, to a reputed length of 62 miles.

The longest sea dam is the Afsluitdijk stretching 20.195 miles across the mouth of the Zuider Zee in two sections of 1.553 miles (mainland of North Holland to the Isle of Wieringen) and 18.641 miles (Wieringen to Friesland). It has a sea-level width of 293 ft and a height of 24 ft 7 in.

Highest Dam

The highest dam is the Grand Dixence in Switzerland, completed in Sept 1961 at a cost of $372 million. It is 935 ft from base to rim, 2,296 ft long and the total volume of concrete in the dam is 7,792,000 cu yd.

The Rogunsky earthfill dam in the USSR will have a final height of 1,066 ft across the Vakhsh River, Tadjikistan, with a crest length of only 2,165 ft.

Strongest Structure

The world's strongest structure will be the 793-ft-high Sayano-Shusenskaya dam on the Yenisey River, USSR. Under construction, it is designed to bear a load of 20,160,000 tons from a fully-filled reservoir of 41,000 million cu yd capacity.

Largest Reservoirs and Man-Made Lake

The most voluminous man-made reservoir is Bratsk reservoir on the Angara River, USSR, with a volume of 137,214,000 acre-ft. The dam was completed in 1964.

The largest artificial lake measured by surface area is Lake Volta, Ghana, formed by the Akosombo dam, completed in 1965. By 1969, the lake had filled an area of 3,275 sq mi with a shoreline 4,500 miles in length.

The completion in 1954 of the Owen Falls Dam near Jinja, Uganda, across the northern exit of the White Nile River from the lake Victoria Nyanza, marginally raised the level of that *natural* lake by adding 166 million acre-feet, and technically turned it into a reservoir with a surface area of 17,169,920 acres (26,828 sq mi).

Largest Polder

The largest of the five great polders in the old Zuider Zee, Netherlands, will be the 149,000-acre (232.8 sq mi) Markerwaard. Work on the 66-mile-long surrounding dyke was begun in 1957. The water area remaining after the erection of the 1927–32 dam (20 miles in length) is called IJssel Meer, which will have a final area of 487.5 sq mi.

Largest Levees

The most massive levees ever carried out are the Mississippi levees begun in 1717 and vastly augmented by the US Government after the disastrous floods of 1927. These extend for 1,732 miles along the main river from Cape Girardeau, Mo, to the Gulf of Mexico and comprise more than 1,000 million cu yd of earthworks. Levees on the tributaries comprise an additional 2,000 miles. The 650-mile segment from Pine Bluff, Ark, to Venice, La, is continuous.

8. TUNNELS

Longest Tunnel

The longest tunnel of any kind is the NYC-W Delaware water supply tunnel begun in 1937 and completed in 1944. It has a diameter of 13 ft 6 in and runs for 105 miles from the Rondout Reservoir in the Catskill Mountains into the Hillview Reservoir, on the border line of NYC and Yonkers.

Bridge-Tunnel

The longest bridge-tunnel system is the Chesapeake Bay Bridge-Tunnel, extending 17.65 miles from eastern shore of Virginia to Virginia Beach, Va. It cost $200 million, took 42 months to complete, and opened on Apr 15, 1964. The longest bridged section is Trestle C (4.56 miles long) and the longest tunnel is the Thimble Shoal Channel Tunnel (1.09 miles).

Canal-Tunnel

The longest canal-tunnel is that on the Rove Canal between the port of Marseilles, France and the Rhône River, built in 1912–27. It is 4.53 miles long, 72 ft wide and 50 ft high, involving 2,250,000 cu yd of excavation.

Subway Tunnel

The longest continuous vehicular tunnel is the Moscow Metro underground railroad line from Belyaevo to Medvedkovo. It runs 19.07 mi and was completed in 1978–79.

Railroad Tunnel

The longest main-line rail tunnel is the 13-mile-1,397-yd Oshimizu Tunnel (Daishimizu) on the Tokyo-Niigata Joetsu line in central Honshu, Japan, under the Tanigawa Mt, which was holed through on Jan 25, 1979. The cost of the whole project will reach $6,300 million. There have been 13 fatalities in 7 years.

Sub-Aqueous Tunnel

The longest sub-aqueous railroad tunnel will be the Seikan Rail Tunnel (33.49 miles), 787 ft beneath the sea bed of the Tsugaru Strait between Tappi Saki, Honshu, and Fukushima, Hokkaido, Japan. Once due to be completed by March 1979 at a cost of $552 million, major flooding on May 6, 1976, has put back completion beyond 1982. Tests started on the sub-aqueous section (14.5 miles) in 1963 and construction began in June 1972.

Currently the world's longest sub-aqueous rail tunnel is the Shin Kanmon Tunnel, completed in May 1974 which runs 11.61 miles from Honshu to Kyushu, Japan.

Road Tunnel

The longest road tunnel is the 10.14-mile-long two-lane St Gotthard Road Tunnel from Goschenen to Airolo, Switzerland, opened to traffic on Sept 5, 1980. Nineteen lives were lost during the construction, which cost almost $400 million since autumn 1969.

The largest-diameter road tunnel was blasted through Yerba Buena Island in San Francisco Bay. It is 76 ft wide, 58 ft high and 540 ft long. More than 72 million vehicles pass through on its two decks every year.

Irrigation, Hydroelectric and Sewerage Tunnels

The longest irrigation tunnel is the 51.5-mile-long Orange-Fish Rivers Tunnel, South Africa, begun in 1967, at an estimated cost of $150 million. The boring was completed in Apr 1973. The lining to a minimum thickness of 9 in will give a completed diameter of 17 ft 6 in.

The Majes project in Peru involves 60.9 miles of tunnels for hydroelectric and water supply purposes. The dam is at 13,780 ft altitude.

The Chicago TARP (Tunnels and Reservoir Plan) involves 120 miles of sewerage tunneling.

Tunneling

The 7-day record for rapid tunneling was set in the McDowell Tunnel Extension, Charleston, SC, when 2,063 ft was achieved in 7 consecutive 16-hour periods, Mar 30–Apr 5, 1982, by the Mole Construction Co of Cleveland, Ohio, on an 8½-ft-diameter heading through marl.

9. SPECIALIZED STRUCTURES

Advertising Signs

The largest neon advertising sign was owned by the Atlantic Coast Line Railroad Co at Port Tampa, Fla. It measured 387 ft 6 in long and 76 ft high, weighed 196 tons and contained about 4,200 ft of red neon tubing. It was demolished on Feb 19, 1970.

Broadway's largest billboard has been 11,426 sq ft in area—equivalent to 107 ft × 107 ft. Broadway's largest working sign in Times Square, NYC, in 1966, showed two 42½-ft-tall "bottles" of Haig Scotch Whisky and an 80-ft-long "bottle" of Gordon's Gin being "poured" into a frosted glass.

LARGEST ADVERTISING SIGN: The Eiffel Tower (left) in Paris from 1925–36 carried a 6-color sign that could be seen 24 miles away.

The largest advertising sign ever erected was the electric Citroën sign on the Eiffel Tower, Paris. It was switched on on July 4, 1925 and could be seen 24 miles away. It was in six colors with 250,000 lamps and 56 miles of electric cables. The letter "N" which terminated the name "Citroën" between the second and third levels measured 68 ft 5 in in height. The whole apparatus was taken down after 11 years in 1936.

Radio CFMI spelt out its call sign in 400 ft letters on Grouse Mountain, Vancouver, BC, Canada on Feb 14, 1980 with 450 flares visible from more than 42 miles distant.

The most massive working sign today is reputed to be outside the Circus Circus Hotel, Reno, Nev, named Topsy the Clown. It is 127 ft tall and weighs over 40 tons with 1.4 miles of neon tubing. The clown's smile measures 14 ft across.

The highest advertising signs are the four Bank of Montreal logos atop the 72-story 935-ft-tall First Canadian Place building in Toronto. Each sign, built by Claude Neon Industries Ltd measures 20 ft × 22 ft, and was lifted into place by helicopter.

Largest Bonfire

A bonfire, octagonal in shape and 120 ft high with a base circumference of 155 ft, tapering to 20 ft at the summit, was built at Whitehaven, Cumbria, England, in 1902 in celebration of the Coronation of Edward VII. It used 896 tons of wood and 1,000 Imperial gallons of petroleum and tar, each.

Longest Breakwater

The longest breakwater protects the port of Galveston, Texas. The granite South Breakwater is 6.74 miles long.

Lighthouses

The lighthouse with the most powerful light is Créac'h d'Ouessant lighthouse, established in 1638 and last altered in 1939 on l'Île d'Ouessant, Finisterre, Brittany, France. It is 163 ft tall and, in times of fog, has a luminous intensity of 500 million candelas.

The lights with the greatest visible range are those 1,092 ft above the ground on the Empire State Building, NYC. Each of the four-arc mercury bulbs has a rated candlepower of 450 million, visible 80 miles away on the ground and 300 miles away from aircraft. They were switched on on March 31, 1956.

The tallest lighthouse is the steel tower 348 ft tall near Yamashita Park in Yokohama, Japan. It has a power of 600,000 candles and a visibility range of 20 miles.

Cemetery

The world's largest cemetery is one in Leningrad, USSR, which contains over 500,000 of the 1,300,000 victims of the German army's siege of 1941–42.

The world's largest crematorium is at the Nikolo-Arkhangelskoye Cemetery, East Moscow, completed in March 1972. It has 7 twin furnaces and several Halls of Farewell for atheists.

Tallest Columns

The tallest columns (as opposed to obelisks) are the 36 fluted pillars of Vermont marble in the colonnade of the Education Building, Albany, NY. Each one measures 90 ft tall and 6½ ft in base diameter.

The tallest load-bearing stone columns are those measuring 69 ft in the Hall of Columns of the Temple of Amun at Karnak, opposite Thebes on the Nile, the ancient capital of Upper Egypt. They were built in the 19th dynasty in the reign of Rameses II in c. 1270 BC.

Largest Dome

The world's largest dome is the Louisiana Superdome in New Orleans. It has an outside diameter of 680 ft. (For more details, see *Largest Indoor Arena.*) The largest dome of ancient architecture is that of the Pantheon, built in Rome in 112 AD, with a diameter of 142½ ft.

Doors

The largest doors are the 4 in the Vehicle Assembly Building near Cape Canaveral, Fla with a height of 460 ft. (See *Largest Scientific Buildings.*)

The world's heaviest door is that leading to the laser target room at Lawrence Livermore National Laboratory, Calif. It weighs 360 tons, is up to 8 ft thick and was installed by Overly.

Largest Drydock

The largest drydock is that at Koyagi, Nagasaki, Japan completed in 1972. It measures 3,248 × 328 ft with a maximum shipbuilding capacity of 1 million tons deadweight.

Largest Earthworks

The largest earthworks carried out prior to the mechanical era were the Linear Earth Boundaries of the Benin Empire in the Bendel State of Nigeria. These were first reported in 1900 and partially surveyed in 1967. In Apr 1973 it was estimated by Patrick Darling that the total length of the earthworks was probably between 4,000 and 8,000 miles, with the total amount of earth moved estimated at from 500 to 600 million cu yd.

Longest Fence

The longest fence is the dingo-proof fence enclosing the main sheep areas of Australia. The wire fence is 6 ft high, goes 1 ft underground, and stretches for 3,437 miles, more than the distance from Seattle to NY. The Queensland State Government discontinued full maintenance in 1982.

TALLEST FLAGPOLE: Chula Vista, Calif.

Tallest Flagpole

The tallest flagpole ever erected was outside the Oregon Building at the 1915 Panama-Pacific International Exposition in San Francisco. Trimmed from a Douglas fir, it stood 299 ft 7 in in height. The tallest unsupported flagpole is a metal pole standing 191.94 ft high (plus about 12½ ft below ground) and weighing 20,000 lb. The pole was erected on June 27, 1981, at Chula Vista, Calif, and flies the American flag 24 hours a day. The concept was carried through by Jerry Leaf.

Tallest Fountain

The tallest fountain is at Fountain Hills, Ariz built at a cost of $1½ million for McCulloch Properties Inc. At full pressure of 375 lb/sq in and at a rate of

7,000 gallons/min, the 560-ft column of water weighs more than 9 tons. The nozzle speed achieved by the three 600 hp pumps is 146.7 mph.

Largest Garbage Dump

Reclamation Plant No. 1, Fresh Kills, Staten Island, NY, opened in March 1974, is the world's largest sanitary landfill. In its first 4 months, 500,000 tons of refuse from NYC was dumped on the site by 700 barges.

Largest Revolving Globe

The largest revolving globe is the 24-ton sphere (27 ft 11 in in diameter) behind the Coleman Map Building, Babson College, Wellesley, Mass, completed at a cost of $200,000 in 1956.

Longest Jetty

The longest deep-water jetty is the Quai Hermann du Pasquier at Le Havre, France with a length of 5,000 ft. Part of an enclosed basin, it has a constant depth of water of 32 ft on both sides.

Largest Kitchen

The largest kitchen ever set up has been the Indian Government field kitchen set up in Apr 1973 at Ahmadnagar, Maharashtra, in the famine area. The kitchen daily provided 1.2 million subsistence meals.

Tallest Lampposts

The tallest lighting columns ever erected are steel standards of 164 ft 0½ in, first put up on Dec 1, 1981, at Ware, England, by Concrete Utilities Ltd. The company has exported 4 to the United Arab Emirates.

Largest Building Demolished by Explosives

The largest was the 21-story Traymore Hotel, Atlantic City, NJ on May 26, 1972. The 600-room hotel had a cubic capacity of 6,495,500 cu ft. Controlled Demolition Inc of Towson, Md did the job.

The tallest chimney ever demolished by explosives was the Matla Power Station chimney, Kriel, South Africa, on July 19, 1981. It stood 902 ft high and was brought down by the Stanton (Steeplejack) Co Ltd of Manchester, England.

The greatest recorded simultaneous smokestack demolition was when 18 were felled at the London Brick Company Coronation Works at Bedfordshire, England, on Nov 30, 1980 when Mrs Wyn Witherall fired the 100 lb of explosives laid by T. W. Robinson & Co.

Largest Maze

The largest maze is at Longleat, near Warminster, Wiltshire, England, with 1.61 miles of paths flanked by 16,180 yew trees. It was opened on June 6, 1978.

Tallest Menhir

The tallest menhir found is the 425-ton Grand Menhir Brisé, now in 5 pieces, which originally stood 69 ft high at Locmariaquer, Brittany, France.

Tallest Monuments

The tallest monument is the stainless steel Gateway to the West Arch in St Louis, completed Oct 28, 1965, to commemorate the westward expansion after the Louisiana Purchase of 1803. It is a sweeping arch, spanning 630 ft and rising to a height of 630 ft, which cost $29 million. It was designed in 1947 by Eero Saarinen (d 1961).

The tallest monumental column commemorates the battle of San Jacinto (Apr 21, 1836), on the bank of the San Jacinto River near Houston, Tex. General Sam Houston (1793–1863) and his force of 743 Texan troops killed 630 Mexicans (out of a total force of 1,600) and captured 700 others, with the loss of 9 men killed and 30 wounded. Constructed in 1936–39, at a cost of $1½ million, the tapering column is 570 ft tall, 47 ft square at the base, and 30 ft square at the observation tower, which is surmounted by a star weighing 220 tons. It is built of concrete, faced with buff limestone, and weighs 35,150 tons.

Largest Prehistoric Monuments

The largest megalithic prehistoric monuments are the 28½-acre earthworks and stone circles of Avebury, Wiltshire, England rediscovered in 1646. The earliest calibrated date in the area of this neolithic site is c. 4200 BC. The whole work is 1,200 ft in diameter with a 40-ft ditch around the perimeter and required an estimated 15 million man-hours of work. The largest trilithons exist at Stonehenge, to the south of Salisbury Plain, Wiltshire, with single sarsen blocks weighing over 50 tons and requiring over 550

HOTEL BEING DEMOLISHED: The 600-room Traymore in Atlantic City, NJ, was torn down in 1972 to make way for a casino.

men to drag them up a 9° gradient. The earliest stage in the construction of the ditch has been dated to 2180 BC ± 105. Whether Stonehenge was a lunar calendar, a temple, or an eclipse-predictor remains debatable.

Naturist Resorts

The oldest naturist resort (the term "nudist camp" is deplored by naturists) is Der Freilichtpark, Klingberg, W Germany, established in 1903. The largest is the Beau Valley Country Club, Warmbaths, South Africa, extending over 988 acres with up to 20,000 visitors a year. However, 100,000 people visit the smaller Centre Helio-Marin at Cap d'Agde, southern France, which covers 222 acres.

Obelisks

The longest an obelisk has remained *in situ* is that still at Heliopolis, near Cairo, Egypt, erected by Senusret I *c.* 1750 BC.

The largest standing obelisk is the Egyptian obelisk brought from Egypt to the Hippodrome of Constantinople in Istanbul, Turkey in 390 AD. It stands 190.2 ft tall. Cleopatra's Needle on the Embankment, London, which is 68 ft 5½ in tall and weighs 208.7 tons, was towed up the Thames from Egypt on Jan 21, 1878 and positioned on Sept 13.

Longest Pier

The longest pier is the Dammam Pier, Saudi Arabia, on the Persian Gulf. A rock-filled causeway 4.84 miles long joins the steel trestle pier 1.80 miles long, which joins the Main Pier (744 ft long), giving an overall length of 6.79 miles. The work was begun in July 1948 and completed March 15, 1950.

Largest and Oldest Pyramids

The largest pyramid, and the largest monument ever constructed, is the Quetzalcóatl at Cholula de Rivadabia, 63 miles southeast of Mexico City. It is 177 ft tall and its base covers an area of nearly 45 acres. Its total volume has been estimated at 4.3 million cu yd, compared with 3,360,000 cu yd for the Pyramid of Cheops (see page 232). The pyramid-building era here was between the 2nd and 6th centuries AD.

The oldest known pyramid is the Djoser step pyramid at Saqqâra, Egypt, constructed to a height of 204 ft, originally with a Tura limestone casing, *c.* 2650 BC. The largest known single block came from

231

the Third Pyramid of Mycerinus and weighs 319.2 tons. The oldest New World pyramid is that on the island of La Venta in southeastern Mexico built by the Olmec people *c.* 800 BC. It is 100 ft tall with a base diameter of 420 ft.

Tallest Scaffolding

The greatest scaffolding structure ever erected was one 486 ft high, using 152 miles of tubing, for the reconstruction of Guy's Hospital, London, in 1971.

Largest Scarecrow

Blackmore village, Essex, England, built the world's most scaring scarecrow in Sept 1981 to a height of 14 ft with arms 8 ft wide.

Seven Wonders of the World

The Seven Wonders of the World were first designated by Antipater of Sidon in the 2nd century BC. They included the Pyramids of Giza, built by three Fourth Dynasty Egyptian Pharaohs, Khwfw (Khufu or Cheops), Kha-f-Ra (Khafre, Khefren or Chephren) and Menkaure (Mycerinus) near El Giza (El Gizeh), southwest of El Qahira (Cairo) in Egypt. The Great Pyramid ("Horizon of Khufu") was finished *c.* 2580 BC. Its original height was 480 ft 11 in (now, since loss of its topmost stones and the pyramidion, reduced to 449 ft 6 in) with a base line 756 ft long thus covering slightly more than 13 acres. It has been estimated that a permanent work force of 4,000 required 30 years to maneuver into position the 2,300,000 limestone blocks averaging 2¾ tons each, totaling about 7,225,000 tons and a volume of 90,700,000 cu ft. A cost estimate published in Dec 1974 indicates that today it would require 405 men working 6 years at a cost of $1,130 million.

Of the other 6 wonders, only fragments remain of the Temple of Artemis (Diana) of the Ephesians, built *c.* 350 BC at Ephesus, Turkey (destroyed by the Goths in 262 AD), and of the Tomb of King Mausolus of Caria, built at Halicarnassus, now Bodrum, Turkey, *c.* 325 BC. No trace remains of the Hanging Gardens of Semiramis, at Babylon, Iraq (*c.* 600 BC); the 40-ft-tall marble, gold and ivory statue of Zeus (Jupiter) by Phidias (5th century BC) at Olympia, Greece (lost in a fire at Istanbul); the 117-ft-tall statue by Chares of Lindus of the figure of the god Helios (Apollo), called the Colossus of Rhodes (sculptured 292–280 BC, destroyed by an earthquake in 224 BC); or the 400-ft-tall lighthouse built by Sos-tratus of Cnidus *c.* 270 BC as a pyramid-shaped tower of white marble (destroyed by an earthquake in 1375 AD) on the island of Pharos (Greek, *pharos*=lighthouse), off the coast of El Iskandarya (Alexandria), Egypt.

Largest Snow Construction

The world's largest snow construction is the Ice Palace built in the winter of 1980–81 using nearly 1,800 tons of snow, at Tokamachi City, Niigata prefecture, Japan. The overall height was 75 ft 5 in and a total of 800 people and 50 bulldozers were used in the construction.

Longest Stairs

The longest is the service staircase for the Niesenbahn funicular which rises to 7,759 ft near Spiez, Switzerland. It has 11,674 steps and a banister. The T'ai Chan temple stairs of 6,600 stone-cut steps in the Shantung Mts, China, ascend 4,700 ft in 5 miles.

The longest spiral staircase is one 1,103 ft deep with 1,520 steps, installed in the Mapco-White County Coal Mine, Carmi, Ill, by Systems Control Inc in 1981.

Tallest Statue

The tallest full-figure statue is that of the "Motherland," an enormous prestressed concrete female figure on Mamayev Hill, outside Volgograd, USSR, designed in 1967 by Yevgenyi Vuchetich, to commemorate victory in the Battle of Stalingrad (1942–43). The statue from its base to the tip of a sword clenched in her right hand measures 270 ft.

The Indian Rope Trick statue by Calle Örnemark near Jonkoping, Sweden, measures 337 ft from the feet of the *fakir* to the top of the rope 9.8 in in diameter. Its total weight is 159 tons.

Largest Tent

The largest tent ever erected was one covering an area of 188,368 sq ft (4.32 acres) put up by the firm of Deuter from Augsburg, W Germany, for the 1958 "Welcome Expo" in Brussels, Belgium.

Largest Tidal River Barrier

The largest tidal river barrier is the Thames Barrier at Woolwich, London, with 9 piers and 10 gates. There are 6 rising sector gates 200 ft 1½ in wide and 4

LONGEST WALL: The Chinese themselves marvel at the Great Wall, as much as Western visitors do. At this point the wall is 30 ft high and 25 ft across, with 40-ft-high guard towers. It is estimated that it took 300,000 laborers to build the full length of the wall—2,150 miles plus 1,780 miles of branches and spurs—in the early 3rd century BC. (Japan Air Lines)

falling radial gates 103 ft 4 in wide. The site was chosen in 1971. Costs to the end of 1982 were £400 million ($720 million).

Largest Tomb

The largest tomb is that of Emperor Nintoku (d *c.* 428 AD) south of Osaka, Japan. It measures 1,594 ft long × 1,000 ft wide × 150 ft high.

Tallest Totem Pole

The tallest totem pole is 173 ft tall raised on June 6, 1973 at Alert Bay, British Columbia, Canada. It tells the story of the Kwakiutl and took 36 man-weeks to carve.

Longest Wall

The Great Wall of China, completed during the Ch'in dynasty, reign of Shih Huang-ti (246–210 BC), has a main-line length of 2,150 miles with a further 1,780 miles of branches and spurs, with a height of from 15 to 39 ft and up to 32 ft thick. It runs from Shanhaikuan, on the Gulf of Pohai, to Yümên-kuan and Yang-kuan and was kept in repair up to the 16th century. Some 32 miles of the Wall have been de-

stroyed since 1966. Part of the Wall was blown up to make way for a dam in July 1979.

Water Flume

The first of the now nearly 250 water flumes was built in Newport Beach, Calif in 1971.

Waterwheel

The largest waterwheel is the Mohammadieh Noria wheel at Hama in Syria, with a diameter of 131 ft. It dates from Roman times.

Largest Vat

The largest vat is named "Strongbow," used by H. P. Bulmer Ltd, a cider company in Hereford, England. It measures 64½ ft in height, 75½ ft in diameter, and has a capacity of 1,956,000 gallons.

Largest Windows

The largest sheet of glass ever manufactured was one of 538.2 sq ft, or 65 ft 7 in × 8 ft 2½ in, exhibited by the Saint Gobain Company in France at the *Journées Internationales de Miroiterie* in March 1958.

233

The largest single windows are those in the Palace of Industry and Technology at Rondpoint de la Défense, Paris, with an extreme width of 715.2 ft and a maximum height of 164 ft.

Ziggurat (Stage or Temple Tower)

The largest surviving ziggurat (from the verb *zaqaru*, Babylonian, to build high) is the Ziggurat of Ur (now Muqqayr, Iraq) with a base 200 ft × 150 ft built to at least 3 stories of which only the first and part of the second now survive to a height of 60 ft. It has been dated between *c.* 2050 BC and *c.* 2800 BC.

10. BORINGS AND MINES

Man's deepest penetration into the earth's crust is a geological exploratory drilling in the Kola peninsula, USSR, which was announced in Nov 1981 to have reached 36,089 ft. Progress once averaging 36 ft per day has understandably greatly slowed as the eventual target of 49,210 ft is neared.

The deepest recorded drilling into the sea bed is by the *Glomar Challenger* of the US Deep Sea Drilling Project to 5,709 ft off northwestern Spain in 1976. The deepest site is now 23,077 ft below the surface on the western wall of the Marianas Trench in May 1978.

Oil Fields

The largest oil field is the Ghawar Field, Saudi Arabia, developed by ARAMCO, which measures 150 miles by 22 miles.

Greatest Gusher

The most prolific wildcat recorded is the 1,160-ft-deep Lucas No. 1, at Spindletop, about 3 miles south of Beaumont, Tex, on Jan 10, 1901. The gusher was heard more than a mile away and yielded 800,000 barrels during the 9 days it was uncapped. The surrounding ground subsequently yielded 142 million barrels.

Greatest Oil Spill

The worst oil spill in history was 260,000 tons of oil from the super-tankers *Atlantic Empress* and *Aegean Captain* when they collided off Tobago on July 19, 1979.

The slick from the Mexican marine blow-out be-

neath the drilling rig *Ixtoc I* in the Bay of Campeche, Gulf of Mexico on June 3, 1979 reached 400 miles by Aug 5, 1979. It eventually was capped on Mar 24, 1980, after a loss of 3 million barrels.

Greatest Flare

The greatest gas fire ever burnt was at Gassi Touil in the Algerian Sahara from noon on Nov 13, 1961 to 9:30 a.m. on Apr 28, 1962. The pillar of flame rose 450 ft and the smoke 600 ft. It was eventually extinguished by Paul Neal ("Red") Adair (b 1932), of Houston, Tex, using 550 lb of dynamite. His fee was understood to be about $1 million.

Oil Platforms

The world's most massive oil platform is the *Stratfjord B* Concrete Gravity-base platform built at Stavanger, Norway, and operated by Mobil Exploration Norway Inc. Tow-out to its permanent field began on Aug 1, 1981, and it was the heaviest object ever moved—899,360 tons ballasted weight. She was towed by 8 tugs with a combined power of 115,000 hp. The height of the concrete structure is 670 ft and the overall height 890 ft. It thus weighs almost three times the weight of each of the towers of the World Trade Center (324,800 tons).

The world's tallest platform is the Block 280 Guyed Tower in 1,000 ft of water in the Gulf of Mexico weighing 43,008 tons or four times the weight of the Eiffel Tower.

Wells

The deepest water well is the Stensvad Water Well 11-W1 7,320 ft deep, drilled by the Great Northern Drilling Co Inc in Rosebud County, Mont in Oct–Nov 1961.

The Thermal Power Co geothermal steam well begun in Sonoma County, Calif in 1955 is now down to 9,029 ft.

Largest Gas Tank

The largest gas holder or tank is that at Fontaine l'Eveque, Belgium, where disused mines have been adapted to store up to 17,650 million cu ft of gas at ordinary pressure. Probably the largest conventional gas tank is that at Wien-Semmering, Vienna, Austria, completed in 1968, with a height of 274 ft 8 in and a capacity of 10.59 million cu ft.

Largest Gas Deposits

The largest gas deposit in the world is at Urengoi, USSR, with an eventual production of 235 billion cu yd per year through 6 pipelines, from a total estimated to be 9 trillion cu yd.

Mines

The earliest known mining operations were in the Ngwenya Hills of the Hhohho District of northwestern Swaziland where hematite (red iron ore) was mined for body paint c. 41,000 BC. The earliest known copper mines were reported in Feb 1977, in the Timna Valley, north of Elath, Israel, tentatively dated *ante* 3000 BC.

The deepest mine is the Western Deep Levels Mine at Carletonville, South Africa. The deepest penetration attained is 12,500 ft in the No. 2 Shaft. At such extreme depths where the rock temperatures reach 131°F, refrigerated ventilation is necessary. Rock bursts due to the pressures on the 2,500-million-year-old rock are a continuous hazard.

Gold Mines

The largest gold-mining area is the Witwatersrand gold field where 38 mines out of 120 are now operative. The field extends 30 miles east and west of Johannesburg, South Africa. Gold was discovered there in 1886 by George Harrison and by 1944 more than 45% of the world's gold was mined there by 320,000 Bantu and 44,000 Europeans. In 1980 almost 51% of the world's supply came from this area whose production reached a peak of 1,103 tons in 1970. These mines have produced 36,000 of the estimated 112,000 tons of gold ever mined.

The largest gold mine in area is East Rand Proprietary Mines Ltd in Boksburg, Transvaal, S Africa, whose 8,785 claims cover 12,100 acres. The largest, by volume extracted, is Randfontein Estates Gold Mine Co Ltd with 170 million cu yd—enough to cover Manhattan Island to a depth of 8 ft. The main tunnels if placed end to end would stretch a distance of 2,600 miles.

The world's most productive gold mine is Maruntau in the Kyzyl Kum desert, USSR, with an estimated output up to 88 tons per year.

The richest gold mine historically has been Crown Mines of Transvaal, S Africa, whose all-time yield is nearly 49.4 million fine oz. The richest in yield in 1979 was W Driefontein with 0.64 troy oz per ton milled, but Vaal Reefs produced the most with 73.8 tons in 1978.

Iron Mines

The largest iron mine is at Lebedinsky, USSR, in the Kursk Magnetic Anomaly which has altogether an estimated 22,400 million tons of rich (45–65%) ore and 11,200,000 million tons of poorer ore in seams up to 2,000 ft thick. The world's greatest reserves are, however, those of Brazil, estimated to total 58,000 million tons, or 35% of the world's total surface stock.

Copper Mines

Historically the world's most productive copper mine has been the Bingham Canyon Mine, Utah, belonging to the Kennecott Copper Corp with over 9 million tons in the 65 years 1904–68. Currently the most productive is the Chuquicamata mine (formerly owned by the Anaconda Company but now nationalized) 150 miles north of Antofagasta, Chile, with more than 330,000 tons.

The Palabora open pit copper mine in northeastern Transvaal, S Africa, started in 1965, yielded a record 573 tons of ore and waste in the 24 hours of Aug 9, 1980.

The largest underground copper mine is the San Manuel Copper Mine in Arizona, owned by the Magma Copper Co with 355.8 miles of underground workings, and an average annual extraction of over 193 million tons of ore.

Silver, Lead and Zinc Mines

The largest lead, zinc and silver mine is the Kidd Creek Mine of Texasgulf Canada Ltd, located at Timmins, Ontario, Canada.

Since 1970, the leading lead mine has been the Viburnum Trend in southeastern Mo with 489,397 tons in 1972, from which is extracted some 10% of the world's output of lead.

The largest zinc smelter is the Cominco Ltd plant at Trail, British Columbia, Canada, which has an annual capacity of 295,000 tons of zinc and 900 tons of cadmium.

Uranium

The largest uranium mine, Rio Tinto Zinc's open cast pit located in Namibia (South-West Africa) went into full production in 1978, and is producing 5,250 tons per day.

Production is expected to start in 1984 on the greater find of at least 275,000 tons of high grade uranium oxide, some 7,875 ft under Mid-west Lake in northern Saskatchewan, Canada.

Coal Mine

The largest open cast mine is the Fortuna-Garsdorf lignite mine near Bergheim, W Germany. Since 1955 the cut has been extended to 2½ × 2 mi and to 820 ft deep.

Tungsten Mine

The largest tungsten mine with published output figures is the Union Carbide mine in Mount Morgan, near Bishop, Calif. Opened in 1937, it has a capacity of 2,200 tons per day and a work force of 420.

Tin Mining

The most productive dredging for tin ever recorded was 882.9 tons of concentrate (76.8% pure tin) by Ayer Hitam No. 2 Dredge at Puchong, Malaysia in the 30 days of Nov 1976 at 237 ft below surface level in a pond lowered 70 ft by pumping.

Platinum

The largest platinum refinery is the Impala plant at Springs Mine, South Africa. Largest producer is the Rustenburg Group, with more than 1 million oz per year.

Largest Quarry

The largest excavation is the Bingham Canyon Copper Mine, 30 miles south of Salt Lake City, Utah. From 1906 to mid-1976 the total excavation has been 3,700 million tons over an area of 2.81 sq mi to a depth of 2,540 ft. *This is seven times the amount of material moved to build the Panama Canal.* Three shifts of 900 men work around the clock with 39 electric shovels, 67 locomotives, 113 dump trucks and 17 drilling machines for the 31.3 tons of explosive used daily. The record extraction in one 24-hour day is 504,167 tons on Oct 13, 1974.

The deepest open pit of the premechanical, pick-and-shovel era is the Kimberley Open Mine in South Africa, which took 43 years (1871 to 1914) to dig to a depth of nearly 1,200 ft, with a diameter of about 1,500 ft and a circumference of nearly a mile, covering an area of 36 acres. Over 3 tons (14,504,566 carats) of diamonds have been extracted from the 23,500,000 tons of earth dug out. The inflow of water has now risen to a depth of 845 ft.

Spoil Dump

The largest artificial spoil dump is the New Cornelia Tailings at Ten Mile Wash, Ariz, with a volume of 274,026,000 cu yd.

Chapter 8

The Mechanical World

1. SHIPS

Aborigines are known to have been able to cross the Torres Strait from New Guinea to Australia, then at least 43½ miles across, as early as 40,000 BC. They are believed to have used double canoes. A 3-ft oar found at Star Carr, North Yorkshire, England, has been dated to c. 7600 BC.

The oldest surviving boat is the 142-ft-long 40-ton Nile boat buried near the Great Pyramid of Khufu, Egypt, c. 2515 BC, and now reassembled.

The oldest shipwreck ever found is one of a Cycladic trading vessel located off the islet of Dhokos, near the Greek island of Hydra reported in May 1975 and dated to 2450 BC ± 250.

Earliest Power Vessels

Propulsion by steam engine was first achieved when in 1783 the Marquis Jouffroy d'Abbans ascended a reach of the Saône River near Lyons, France in the 180-ton paddle steamer *Pyroscaphe.*

The tug *Charlotte Dundas* was the first successful power-driven vessel. She was a stem paddle-wheel steamer built for the Forth and Clyde Canal, Scotland, in 1801–02 by William Symington (1763–1831), using a double-acting condensing engine constructed by James Watt (1736–1819).

The screw propeller was invented and patented by the Kent, England, farmer Sir Francis Pettit Smith (1808–71) in 1836.

Oldest Vessels Afloat

The oldest active steam ship is the *Skibladner,* which has plied Lake Mjøsa, Norway, since 1856. Originally built in Motala, Sweden, she has had two major refittings.

The oldest mechanically propelled boat of certain date is the 48-ton Brestal steam-driven dredger or drag-boat *Bertha* of 50 ft, designed by I. K. Brunel in 1844 and afloat at the Exeter Maritime Museum, Devon, England.

G. H. Pattinson's 40-ft steam launch *Dolly,* raised after 67 years from Ullswater, England in 1962, and now on Lake Windermere, also probably dates from the 1840's.

Earliest Turbine

The first turbine ship was the *Turbinia,* built in 1894, at Wallsend-on-Tyne, England, to the design of Charles Algernon Parsons (1854–1931). The *Turbinia* was 100 ft long and of 44½ tons displacement with machinery consisting of three steam turbines totaling about 2,000 shaft hp. At her first public demonstration in 1897 she reached a speed of 34.5 knots (39.7 mph).

Largest Human-Powered Ships

The largest human-powered ship was the giant Tessarakonteres 3-banked catamaran galley with 4,000 rowers built for Ptolemy IV c. 210 BC in Alexandria, Egypt. It measured 420 ft with up to 8 men to an oar of 38 cubits (57 ft) in length.

The longest canoe is the 117-ft-long, 20-ton Kauri wood Maori war canoe *Nga Toki Matawhaorua,* built with adzes at Kerikeri Inlet, New Zealand in 1940 to hold a crew of 70 or more.

Largest Wooden Ships

The heaviest wooden ship ever built was the *Richelieu,* 333 ft 8 in long and of 8,534 tons, launched in Toulon, France, on Dec 3, 1873. The longest modern wooden ship ever built was the New York-built *Rochambeau* (1867–72), formerly *Dunderberg.* She measured 377 ft 4 in overall. It should be noted that the biblical length of Noah's Ark was 300 cubits or, at 18 in to a cubit, 450 ft (but see *Largest Junks,* next page).

Largest Sailing Ships

The largest sailing vessel ever built was the *France II* (5,806 gross tons), launched at Bordeaux in 1911. The *France II* was a steel-hulled, 5-masted barque (square-rigged on 4 masts and fore and aft rigged on the aftermost mast). Her hull measured 418 ft overall. Although principally designed as a sailing vessel with a stump topgallant rig, she was also fitted with two steam engines. She was wrecked in 1922.

The only 7-masted sailing vessel ever built was the 375.6-ft-long *Thomas W. Lawson* (5,218 gross tons), built at Quincy, Mass in 1902. She was lost in the English Channel on Dec 15, 1907.

Largest Junks

The largest junk on record was the seagoing *Cheng Ho,* flagship of Admiral Cheng Ho's 62 treasure ships, of *c.* 1420, with a displacement of 3,100 tons and a length variously estimated up to 538 ft and believed to have had 9 masts.

A river junk 361 ft long, with treadmill-operated paddle wheels, was recorded in 1161 AD. A floating fortress 600 ft square, built by Wang Chun on the Yangtze, took part in the Chin-Wu river war, *c.* 280 AD. Present-day junks do not, even in the case of the Chiangsu traders, exceed 170 ft in length.

Longest Day's Run Under Sail

The longest day's run claimed by any sailing ship was one of 465 nautical miles (535.45 statute miles) by the clipper *Champion of the Seas* (2,722 registered tons) of the Liverpool Black Ball Line, running before a northwesterly gale in the south Indian Ocean under Capt Alex Newlands. The elapsed time between the fixes was 23 hours 17 min, giving an average of 19.97 knots.

Largest Sails

Sails are known to have been used for marine propulsions since 3500 BC. The largest spars ever carried were those in the British Royal Navy battleship *Temeraire,* completed at Chatham, Kent, on Aug 31, 1877. The fore and main yards measured 115 ft in length. The mainsail contained 5,100 sq ft of canvas, weighing 2 tons, and the total sail area was 25,000 sq ft. This compares with an area of 18,000 sq ft for the parachute spinnaker on Vanderbilt's yacht *Ranger* in 1937.

Fastest Atlantic Crossing

The fastest Atlantic crossing was made by the *United States* (then 51,988, later 38,216, gross tons), former flagship of the United States Lines. On her maiden voyage between July 3 and 7, 1952, from NYC to Le Havre, France and Southampton, England she averaged 35.59 knots, or 40.98 mph, for 3 days 10 hours 40 min (6:36 p.m. GMT July 3, to

5:16 a.m. July 7) on a route of 2,949 nautical miles from the Ambrose Light Vessel, NJ to the Bishop Rock Light, Isles of Scilly, Cornwall, England. During this run, July 6–7, 1952, she steamed the greatest distance ever covered by any ship in a day's run (24 hours)—868 nautical miles, hence averaging 36.17 knots (41.65 mph). The maximum speed attained from her 240,000 shaft hp engines was 38.32 knots (44.12 mph) in trials June 9–10, 1952.

Fastest Pacific Crossing

The fastest crossing of the Pacific Ocean (4,840 nautical miles) was 6 days 1 hour 27 min by the containership *Sea-Land Commerce* (50,315 tons) from Yokohama, Japan to Long Beach, Calif, June 30–July 6, 1973, at an average speed of 33.27 knots (38.31 mph).

Largest Passenger Liner

The largest liner afloat and longest liner ever built is the *Norway* of 70,202.19 gross tons and 1,035 ft 7½ in in length. She was built as the *France* in 1961 and renamed after purchase in June 1979 by Knut Kloster of Norway. Her second maiden voyage was from Southampton on May 7, 1980.

The *Queen Elizabeth 2,* 66,851 gross tons and an overall length of 963 ft, set a "turn-around" record of 8 hours 3 min in NYC on May 17, 1972. In her planned 1983 "Circle Pacific" cruise, the price of her major suites was set at £130,220 ($235,000) each. She was requisitioned as a troopship on May 3, 1982.

The original *Queen Elizabeth,* no longer afloat, was the heaviest ever built with 83,673 gross tons but a length of 1,031 ft, 4 ft shorter than the *Norway.*

Largest Battleships

The largest battleship now is the USS *New Jersey,* with a full-load displacement of 59,000 tons and an overall length of 888 ft. She was the last fire support ship on active service and was decommissioned on Dec 17, 1969. The USS *Iowa* is being reactivated at a cost of $411 million.

The Japanese battleships *Yamato* (completed on Dec 16, 1941 and sunk southwest of Kyushu by US planes on Apr 7, 1945) and *Musashi* (sunk in the Philippine Sea by 11 bombs and 16 torpedoes on Oct 24, 1944) were the largest battleships ever commissioned, each with a full-load displacement of 72,809 tons. With overall length of 863 ft, a beam of 127 ft and a full-load draught of 35½ ft, they mounted nine 18.1-in guns in three triple turrets. Each gun

FASTEST PACIFIC CROSSING (left): The containership "Sea-Land Commerce" made it from Yokohama to Calif in just over 6 days (4,840 nautical miles). 7-MASTED SAILING VESSEL (the only one ever built) was the "Thomas W. Lawson" (right) built in 1902 in Mass. She served only 5 years before being lost at sea in the English Channel.

weighed 181 tons and was 75 ft in length, firing a 3,200-lb projectile.

Largest Aircraft Carriers

The warships with the largest full-load displacement in the world are the US Navy aircraft carriers USS *Nimitz* and *Dwight D. Eisenhower* at 91,400 tons. They are 1,092 ft in length overall and have a speed well in excess of 30 knots with their nuclear-powered 280,000 shaft hp reactors. They have to be refuelled after about 900,000 miles steaming. Their complement is 6,100. The total cost of the *Eisenhower*, commissioned on Oct 18, 1977 exceeded $2 billion excluding the more than 90-plus aircraft carried. The USS *Enterprise* is, however, 1,102 ft long and thus still the longest warship ever built.

Longest, Fastest and Deepest Submarines

The world's largest submarine is the first of the USSR Typhoon class code named Oscar. Its completion at the secret covered shipyard at Severodvinsk in the White Sea was announced by NATO on Sept 23, 1980. It is believed to have a dived displacement of 30,000 tons, measure 590 ft overall and is armed with 24 × SS.N.18 5,200-mile-range ballistic missiles with 1–2 megaton warheads.

The Russian Alfa-Class nuclear-powered submarines have a reported maximum speed of 42 knots (about 48 mph) down to a depth of 3,000 ft.

The two US Navy vessels able to descend 12,000 ft are the 3-man *Trieste II* (DSV 1) of 303 tons, recommissioned in Nov 1973 and the DSV 2 (deep submergence vessel) USS *Alvin*. The *Trieste II* was reconstructed from the record-breaking bathyscaphe *Trieste,* but without the Krupp-built sphere, which enabled it to descend to 35,820 ft.

Fastest Destroyer

The highest speed attained by a destroyer was 45.25 knots (51.84 mph) by the 3,120-ton French destroyer *Le Terrible* in 1935. She was built in Blainville and powered by four Yarrow small-tube boilers and two Rateau geared turbines giving 100,000 shaft hp. She was removed from the active list in 1957.

Largest Hydrofoil

The largest naval hydrofoil is the 212-ft-long *Plainview* (310 tons full load), launched by Lockheed Shipbuilding and Construction Company at Seattle, Wash June 28, 1965. She has a service speed of 50 knots (57 mph).

Three 165-ton Supramar PTS 150 Mk. III hydrofoils, carrying 250 passengers at 40 knots, ply the Malmö-Copenhagen crossing between Sweden and Denmark. They were built by Westermoen Hydrofoil Ltd of Mandal, Norway.

A 500-ton wing ground effect vehicle capable of carrying 900 tons has been reported in the USSR.

Largest Barges

Two RoRo (roll-on roll-off) barges, the *El Rey* and *La Princessa,* of 16,700 tons and 580-ft length each, owned and operated by the Crowley Maritime Corp of San Francisco are currently the largest. They carry up to 376 trailer trucks each with tri-level loading, between Florida and Puerto Rico. The company has on the drawing board plans for 700-ft long barges for 1982.

Largest Tanker

The largest tanker and ship of any kind is the 564,763 tons deadweight *Seawise Giant* completed for C. Y. Tung in Jan 1981. She is 1,504 ft long with a beam of 225 ft 11 in, has a draught of 80 ft 9 in. She was converted by Nippon Kokan by adding a 265-ft-8-in midship section to the 16.47-knot 422,018-dwt tanker *Oppama.*

LARGEST BARGES: These 580-ft-long ships can carry 376 trailer trucks, which roll on and roll off (RoRo). (Aero-Pic)

Largest Cargo Vessel

The largest vessel capable of carrying dry cargo is the Liberian ore/oil carrier *World Gala* of 282,460 dwt with a length of 1,109 ft and beam of 179 ft, owned by Liberian Trident Transports Inc, completed in 1973.

Most Powerful Tugs

The largest and most powerful tugs are the *Wolraad Waltemade* and her sister ship *John Ross* (2,822 grt) rated at 19,200 hp and with a bollard pull of 172.7 tons at 90% of full power. They have an overall length of 310 ft 5 in and a beam of 49 ft 10 in. They were built to handle the largest tankers, and were completed respectively in Apr 1976 (Leith, Scotland) and in Oct 1976 (Durban, South Africa).

Largest Car Ferry

The largest car and passenger ferry is the 30.5-knot, 24,600 grt GTS *Finnjet* which entered service across the Baltic between Helsinki and Travemünde, W Germany May 13, 1977. She can carry 350 cars and 1,532 passengers.

Most Powerful Dredger

The most powerful dredger is the 468.4-ft-long *Prins der Nederlanden* of 10,586 grt. Using two suction tubes, she can dredge 22,400 tons of sand from a depth of 115 ft in less than one hour.

Most Powerful Icebreaker

A 61,000-ton nuclear powered barge-carrying merchantman designed for work along the USSR's Arctic coast was completed in early 1982 and is known to be designed to break ice.

The largest *converted* icebreaker is the 1,007-ft-long SS *Manhattan* (43,000 shp), which was converted by the Humble Oil Co into a 150,000-ton icebreaker with an armored prow 69 ft 2 in long. She made a double voyage through the Northwest Passage in arctic Canada from Aug 24 to Nov 12, 1969. The Northwest Passage was first navigated by Roald Amundsen (Norway) in the sealing sloop *Gjöa* on July 11, 1906.

Most Expensive Yacht

King Khalid's Saudi Arabian 212-ft $10-million royal yacht was upstaged as the most expensive in 1979 by a five-deck 282-footer built by the Benetti Shipyard, Viareggio, Italy for a reputed hull price of $24 million to the order of Adnan Khashoggi. It has a helicopter and 5 speed boats.

Largest Collision

The closest approach to an irresistible force striking an immovable object occurred on Dec 16, 1977, 22 miles off the coast of southern Africa, when the tanker *Venoil* (330,954 dwt) struck her sister ship *Venpet* (330,869 dwt).

Largest Wreck

Energy Determination is the largest ship ever wrecked. Weighing 312,186-dwt this VLCC (Very Large Crude Carrier) blew up and broke in two in the Straits of Hormuz on Dec 12, 1979. Her full value was $58 million.

Greatest Roll

The ultimate in rolling was recorded in heavy seas in the Tasman Sea south of Australia in the Trans-Tasman single-handed race when Bill Belcher's 10-meter (32-ft-9-in) sloop *Josephine II* double rolled through 720° before dumping him on Middleton Reef on Apr 15, 1978.

Southernmost Voyage

The farthest south ever reached by a ship was achieved on Feb 15, 1912, when the *Fram* reached Latitude 78° 41′ S off the Antarctic coast.

Largest Whale Factory

The largest whale factory ship is the USSR's *Sovietskaya Ukraina* (32,034 gross tons), with a summer dwt of 46,000 tons, completed in Oct 1959. She is 714 ft 6 in in length and 84 ft 7 in in the beam.

Deepest Anchorage

The deepest anchorage ever achieved is one of 24,600 ft in the mid-Atlantic Romanche Trench by Capt Jacques-Yves Cousteau's research vessel *Calypso,* with a 5½-mile-long nylon cable, on July 29, 1956.

Largest Crossing-the-Line Ceremony

The largest recorded ceremony on any warship for initiating those who have crossed the equator for the first time occurred aboard the USS *Nimitz* in the South Atlantic in mid-Jan 1980 when 4,421 *Nimitz* polywogs became shellbacks.

2. ROAD VEHICLES*

CARS

Most Cars

In 1979 it was estimated that in the US 143,092,000 drivers drove 159,400,000 vehicles 1,525,000 million miles, or 204.9 miles per week per driver.

Earliest Automobiles

The earliest car of which there is record is a 2-ft-long steam-powered model, constructed by Ferdinand Verbiest (d 1687), a Belgian Jesuit priest, which he described in his *Astronomia Europaea*. His 1668 model was possibly inspired either by Giovanni Branca's description of a steam turbine published in 1629, or by writings on "fire carts" during the Chu dynasty (*c.* 800 BC) in the library of the Emperor K'ang-hsi of China, to whom he was an astronomer during the period *c.* 1665–80.

The earliest mechanically-propelled passenger vehicle was the first of two military steam tractors completed at the Paris Arsenal in 1769 by Nicolas-Joseph

Cugnot (1725–1804). This reached about 2¼ mph. His second, larger tractor, completed in 1771, today survives in the *Conservatoire national des arts et métiers* in Paris.

The first true internal-combustion-engined vehicle was built by a Londoner, Samuel Brown (patented Apr 25, 1826) whose 4-hp 2-cylinder atmospheric-gas 88-liter engined carriage climbed Shooters Hill, Blackheath, Kent, England in May 1826.

Earliest Gasoline-Driven Cars

The first successful gasoline-driven car, the Motorwagen, built by Karl-Friedrich Benz (1844–1929) of Karlsruhe, ran at Mannheim, Germany in late 1885. It was a 560-lb 3-wheeler reaching 8–10 mph. Its single-cylinder 4-stroke chain-drive engine (bore 91.4 mm, stroke 160 mm) delivered 0.85 hp at 200 rpm. It was patented on Jan 29, 1886. Its first 1-km road test was reported in the local newspaper, the *Neue Badische Landeszeitung*, of June 4, 1886, under the news heading "Miscellaneous." Two were built in 1885 of which one has been preserved in "running order" at the Deutsches Museum, Munich.

---

* Automotive records in greater detail may be found in *Car Facts and Feats*, one of the Guinness Family of Books (Sterling).

Earliest Registrations

The world's first plates were probably introduced by the Parisian police in France in 1893. The first American plates were in 1901 in NY. Registration plates were introduced in Britain in 1903. The original A1 plate was secured by the 2nd Earl Russell (1865–1931) for his 12-hp Napier. This plate, willed to Trevor Laker of Leicester, was sold in Aug 1959, for £2,500 (then $7,000) in aid of charity. It was reported in Apr 1973 that a "cherished" number plate changed hands in a private sale for £14,000 (then $35,000). Sir Run Run Shaw, the movie producer, on Dec 9, 1978 bid HK $330,000 (about $66,000) for a "Good Fortune" number plate at a Hong Kong Government charity auction.

Fastest Rocket-Engined Car

The highest speed claimed for any wheeled land vehicle is 739.666 mph or Mach 1.0106 *in a one-way stretch* by the rocket-engined *Budweiser Rocket,* designed by William Fredrick, and driven by Stan Barrett at Edwards Air Force Base, Calif on Dec 17, 1979. The vehicle, owned by Hal Needham, has a 48,000-hp rocket engine with 6,000 lb of extra thrust from a sidewinder missile. The rear wheels (100 lb solid discs) lifted 10 in off the ground above Mach 0.95 acting as 7,500 rpm gyroscopes. However, this published speed of Mach 1.0106 is *not* officially sanctioned by the USAF whose Digital Instrumented Radar was not calibrated or certified. The radar information was *not* generated by the vehicle directly but by an operator aiming the dish by means of a TV screen. Hence, a claim of 6 significant figures appears unjustifiable. (For *official* land speed record, see Chapter 11, *Speed on Land.*)

Fastest Jet-Engined Car

The highest speed attained by any jet-engined car is 613.995 mph over a flying 666.386 yd by the 34-ft-7-in-long, 9,000-lb *Spirit of America—Sonic I,* driven by Norman Craig Breedlove (b Los Angeles, March 23, 1938) on Bonneville Salt Flats, Utah, on Nov 15, 1965. The car was powered by a General Electric J79 GE-3 jet engine, developing 15,000 lb static thrust at sea level.

Fastest Wheel-Driven Cars

The highest speed attained by a (turbine) wheel-driven car is 429.311 mph over a flying 666.386 yd by Donald Malcolm Campbell (1921–67), a British engineer, in the 30-ft-long *Bluebird,* weighing 9,600 lb, on the salt flats at Lake Eyre, South Australia, on July 17, 1964. The car was powered by a Bristol-Siddeley Proteus 705 gas-turbine engine developing 4,500 shp. Its *peak* speed was *c.* 445 mph. It was rebuilt in 1962, after a crash at about 360 mph on Sept 16, 1960.

The highest speed attained by a multi-engined wheel-driven car is 418.504 mph over a flying 666.386 yd by Robert Sherman Summers (b Omaha, Neb, Apr 4, 1937) in *Goldenrod* at Bonneville Salt Flats, Utah, on Nov 12, 1965. The car, measuring 32 ft long and weighing 5,500 lb was powered by four fuel-injected Chrysler Hemi engines (total capacity 27,924 cc) developing 2,400 bhp. The highest speed attained by a single-engined wheel-driven car is 357.391 mph by Bob Herda in *Autolite 999* at Bonneville Salt Flats, Utah, on Nov 2, 1967.

Fastest Diesel-Engined Car

The diesel-engined prototype 230-hp 3-liter Mercedes C 111/3 attained 203.3 mph in tests on the Nardo Circuit, Italy, Oct 5–15, 1978.

Fastest Racing Car

The fastest racing car yet produced was the Porsche 917/30 Can-Am car powered by a 5,374-cc flat 12 turbo-charged engine developing 1,100 bhp. On the Paul Ricard circuit near Toulon, France in Aug 1973 Mark Donohue (US) reached a speed of 257 mph. The two models built took 2.2 sec to go from 0 to 60 mph, 4.3 sec from 0 to 100 mph, and 12.6 sec from 0 to 200 mph. In 1973, the UOP Shadow Can-Am car's 8.1-liter turbo-charged Chevrolet V8 engine developed 1,240 bhp.

Fastest Production Road Model

Various detuned track cars have been licensed for road use but are not purchasable production models. Manufacturers of very fast and very expensive models are understandably reluctant to allow maximum speed tests to be carried out. The fastest current manufacturer's *claim* (as opposed to independent road-tests) for production road cars are 173.6 mph for the DeTomaso Pantera and 173.4 mph for the Lamborghini Countach LP400S. The highest ever *tested* speed is 168 mph for the Aston Martin V8 Vantage by *Motor.* The 0–60 mph acceleration was 5.2 sec.

The highest road-tested acceleration reported is 0–60 mph in 4.2 sec and 0–100 mph in 10.8 sec by the

FASTEST ACCELERATION (right): The A.C. Cobra 1965 could accelerate from 0 to 60 mph in 4.2 sec. **FASTEST JET-ENGINED CAR** (below): The record of 613.995 mph set by the "Spirit of America—Sonic I," in 1965 with Norman Craig Breedlove at the controls still stands. It was once the land speed record.

HIGHEST SPEED ON WHEELS (below): Before the "Budweiser Rocket" set its 739.666 mph one-way record, the driver (Stan Barrett), owner (Hal Needham) and designer (William Fredrick) gathered with General Chuck Yeager and other crew members to look over the vehicle. (Franklin Berger)

MOST MILES ON A GAL-LON (left): 156.33 miles-per-gallon is the record set by this 3-wheeled diesel-powered "California Commuter," on a 263.6-mile trip (averaging 56.3 mph) from Anaheim, Calif to Las Vegas. Here it is on a Los Angeles Freeway. (Franklin Berger)

CHEAPEST CAR (left): There is some uncertainty over whether this 1922 Red Bug Buckboard sold for $150 or $125. It weighed 245 lb.

ICE SLED (below): Rocket-powered, this vehicle streaks across frozen Lake George, NY, at a record 247.93 mph. (Ron Vigneri)

7-liter A. C. Cobra 1965, in Nov 1967 by Roger Bell (*Motor*) and John Bolster (*Autosport*).

Rocket-Powered Ice Sled

The highest speed recorded is 247.93 mph by *Oxygen* driven by Sammy Miller (b Apr 15, 1945) on Lake George, NY, on Feb 15, 1981.

Most Expensive Used Cars

The greatest price paid for a used car is $421,040 for a 1936 Mercedes-Benz Roadster from the M. L. Cohn collection by a telephone bidder in Monaco at Christie's sale Feb 25, 1979 at the Los Angeles Convention Center.

The greatest collection of vintage cars is the William F. Harrah Collection of 1,700, estimated to be worth more than $4 million in Reno, Nev. Mr Harrah was still looking for a Chalmers-Detroit 1909 Tourabout, an Owen car of 1910–12, and a Nevada Truck of 1915 when he died.

Most Expensive Special Cars

The most expensive car ever built is the Presidential 1969 Lincoln Continental Executive delivered to the US Secret Service on Oct 14, 1968. It has an overall length of 21 ft 6.3 in with a 13-ft-4-in wheelbase and, with the addition of 2 tons of armor plate, weighs 12,000 lb. The cost for research, development and manufacture was estimated at $500,000, but it is rented for a mere $5,000 per annum. Even if all four tires were to be shot out it can travel at 50 mph on inner rubber-edged steel discs.

Carriage House Motor Cars Ltd of NYC in March 1978 completed 4 years' work on converting a 1973 Rolls-Royce, including lengthening it by 30 in. The price tag was $500,000.

Most Inexpensive

The cheapest car of all-time was the 1922 Red Bug Buckboard, built by Briggs and Stratton Co of Milwaukee, Wis listed at $150–$125. It had a 62-in wheel base and weighed 245 lb. The early models of the King Midget cars were sold in kit form for self-assembly for as little as $100 as late as 1948.

Longest Production

The longest any car has been in mass production is 44 years (1938 to date), including wartime interruptions, in the case of the Volkswagen "Beetle" series,

originally designed by Ferdinand Porsche. The 20 millionth car came off the final production line in Mexico on May 15, 1981. Residual production continues in South America.

Gasoline Consumption

The world record for fuel economy on a closed circuit course (one of 14.076 miles) was set by Ben Visser (US) in a highly modified 90.8 cu in 1959 Opel CarAvan Station Wagon in the annual Shell Research Laboratory contest at Wood River, Ill, driven by Ben and Carolyn Visser on Oct 2, 1973 with 451.90 ton-miles per gallon and 376.59 miles on one gallon of gasoline. The tire pressure was 200 lb/sq in and the maximum speed was 12 mph.

In Oct 1979 at the International Fuel Saving Competition for cars and special vehicles in Switzerland a 200-cc diesel-engined 3-wheeler driven by Franz Maier of Stuttgart, W Germany covered 1,284.13 km on 1 liter of fuel—equivalent to 3,020.28 miles to the gallon.

Douglas Malewicki drove 263.6 miles from Anaheim, Calif to Las Vegas, Nev, at an average speed of 56.3 mph using only 1.684 gallons of fuel for an mpg of 156.33 in his 3-wheeled 359-cc diesel-powered *California Commuter* road car. The route involved ascents of 7,993 ft.

Largest Engines

The most powerful piston-engine car is "Quad A1." It was designed and built in 1964 by Jim Lytle and was first shown in May 1965 at the Los Angeles Sports Arena. The car features 4 Allison V–12 aircraft engines with a total of 6,840 cu in (112,087 cc) displacement and 12,000 hp. The car has 4-wheel drive, 8 wheels and tires, and dual 6-disc clutch assemblies. The wheelbase is 160 in. It weighs 5,860 lb and has 96 spark plugs and 96 exhaust pipes.

The largest car ever used was the "White Triplex," sponsored by J. H. White of Philadelphia. Completed early in 1928, after 2 years' work, the car weighed about 4½ tons and was powered by three Liberty V12 aircraft engines with a total capacity of 81,188 cc developing 1,500 bhp at 2,000 rpm. It was used to break the world speed record, but crashed at Daytona, Fla on March 13, 1929.

Currently, the most powerful car on the road is the 6-wheeled Jameson-Merlin powered by a 27,000-cc 1,760-hp Rolls-Royce V12 Merlin aero-engine, governed down to a maximum speed of 185 mph. It has a range of 300 miles with tanks of 72-gallon capacity. The vehicle weighs 2.96 tons overall.

Most Durable Car

The highest recorded mileage for a car was 1,184,880 authenticated miles by Aug 1978 for a 1957 Mercedes 180D owned by Robert O'Reilly of Olympia, Wash. Its subsequent fate is unknown.

Largest Cars

Of cars produced for private road use, the largest has been the Bugatti "Royale" Type 41, known as the "Golden Bugatti," of which only 6 (not 7) were made at Molsheim, France by the Italian, Ettore Bugatti, and some survive. First built in 1927, this car has an 8-cylinder engine of 12.7 liter capacity, and measures over 22 ft in length. The hood is over 7 ft long.

Of "altered" cars, the longest is the stretched 1962 Chevrolet Station Wagon owned by the Rev. Gerald R. Manning of Middletown, Va. The finished result is 32 ft 4 in overall and weighs 4,500 lb.

Largest Production-Car Engine

The highest engine capacity of a production car was 13½ liters (824 cu in), in the case of the Pierce-Arrow 6-66 Raceabout of 1912–18, the Peerless 6-60 of 1912–14 and the Fageol of 1918. The largest currently available is the V-8 engine of 500.1 cu in (8,195 cc), developing 235 bhp net, used in the 1972 Cadillac Fleetwood Eldorado.

Fastest Round-the-World Driving

The fastest circumnavigation embracing more than an equator's length of driving (24,901.47 road miles) is one in 74 days 1 hour 11 min by Garry Sowerby (driver) and Ken Langley (navigator) of Canada from Sept 6 to Nov 19, 1980 in a Volvo 245 westwards from Toronto through 4 continents and 23 countries. The distance covered was 26,561.0 miles.

The first recorded round-the-world drive by truck was by Daniele Pellegrini and Cesare Gerolimetto of Italy, in a 122-hp Iveco 75 PC 6-cylinder 4-wheel drive Fiat diesel from Vicenza on Aug 17, 1976, arriving back 2 years 245 days later on Apr 19, 1979. The route took 114,300 miles including 1,500 miles off-road.

Largest Vehicles and Windshield Wipers

The most massive vehicle ever constructed is the Marion 8-caterpillar crawler used for conveying *Saturn V* rockets to their launching pads at the John F. Kennedy Space Center, Cape Canaveral, Fla. It measures 131 ft 4 in by 114 ft and two of them built at the same time cost $12,300,000. The loaded train weight is 9,000 tons. Its windshield wipers with 42-in blades are the world's largest.

The most massive automotive land vehicle is "Big Muskie," the 10,700-ton mechanical shovel built by Bucyrus Erie for the Musk mine. It is 487 ft long, 151 ft wide and 222 ft high with a grab capacity of 325 tons.

The longest vehicle ever built is the Arctic Snow Train now owned by the world-famous wire-walker Steve McPeak (see Chapter 11). This 54-wheeled 572-ft-long vehicle was built by R G Le Tourneau, Inc of Longview, Tex for the US Army. Its gross train weight is 400 tons with a top speed of 20 mph and it was driven by a crew of 6 when used as an "Overland Train" for the military. McPeak repaired it and every punctured tire lone-handed in often sub-zero temperatures in Alaska. It generates 4,680 shp and has a capacity of 7,826 gallons.

Buses

The first municipal motor bus service was inaugurated on Apr 12, 1903, between the Eastbourne railway station and Meads, East Sussex, in England. A steam-powered bus named *Royal Patent* ran between Gloucester and Cheltenham, England, for 4 months in 1831.

The longest regularly scheduled bus route is by "Across Australia Coach Lines," who inaugurated a regularly scheduled service between Perth and Brisbane on Apr 9, 1980. The route is 3,389 miles and takes 75 hours 55 min.

The longest buses are the 12-ton, 76-ft-long articulated buses, with 121 passenger seats and room for an additional 66 "strap-hangers," built by the Wayne Corporation of Richmond, Ind for use in the Middle East.

Largest Ambulance

The largest ambulances are the 59-ft-0½-in-long articulated Alligator Jumbulances Mark VI, VII and VIII, operated by The Across Trust to convey the sick and handicapped on holidays and pilgrimages from Britain to Continental Europe. They are built by Van Hool of Belgium with Fiat engines, cost £176,000 ($316,800) and convey 44 patients and staff.

Largest Dump Truck

The largest dump truck is the Terex Titan 33-19 manufactured by the Terex Division of the General

Motors Corp. It has a loaded weight of 604.7 tons and a capacity of 350 tons. When unloading, its height is 56 ft. The 16-cylinder engine delivers 3,300 hp and the fuel tank holds 1,560 gallons. It went into service in Nov 1974.

Largest Tires

The largest tires are manufactured in Topeka, Kans by the Goodyear Co for giant dump trucks. They are 11 ft 6 in in diameter, weigh 12,500 lb and cost more than $50,000. A tire 17 ft in diameter is believed to be the practical upper limit.

Most Powerful Fire Engine

The most powerful fire appliance is the 860-hp 8-wheel Oshkosh fire truck used for aircraft fires. It can discharge 49,920 gallons of foam through 2 turrets in just 150 sec. It weighs 66 tons.

Most Powerful Wrecker

The most powerful wrecker is the Vance Corp 28-ton 30-ft-long Monster No. 2 stationed at Hammond, Ind. It can lift in excess of 179 tons on its short boom.

Longest Motor Trip

The longest continuous trailer tour was one of 143,716 miles by Harry B. Coleman and Peggy Larson in a Volkswagen Camper from Aug 20, 1976 to Apr 20, 1978 through 113 countries. Saburo Ouchi (b Feb 7, 1942) of Tokyo, Japan, drove 167,770 miles in 91 countries from Dec 2, 1969 to Feb 10, 1978.

LARGEST DUMP TRUCK (above): The Terex Titan, made by a division of General Motors, is the name of this monster that weighs 604.7 tons loaded. It uses the world's largest tires, 11½ ft in diameter, made by Goodyear, costing $50,000 each.

LONGEST VEHICLE ever built (below) is Steve McPeak's Arctic Snow Train. It has 54 wheels, is 572 ft long, and rolls at a top speed of 20 mph.

Largest Earth Mover

The Balderson "Double Dude" plow harnessed to a Caterpillar SXS D9H 820 flywheel hp tractor can cast 14,185 cu yd of earth per hour.

Largest Tractor

The largest tractor is the $325,000, 65-ton Northern Manufacturing Co 8-wheeled 16V-747. It is 14 ft tall and 20 ft 7 in wide with an 848.6-gallon tank. It was launched in Oct 1978.

Largest Load

The greatest weight moved on wheels anywhere in the world is 3,024 tons by Snellen-Vermeer and Sarens de Coster NV over 109 yd in Rotterdam, Netherlands on Oct 4, 1980. The object moved aboard the Heerema barge H-102 was a buoy 270 ft long and 165 ft in circumference. The train weight of the 1,024-wheeled assembly that did the moving was 3,659.6 tons.

The world's record road load is one of a 1,724.8-ton methanol distillation unit at Madinat Al-Jubail Al-Sinaiyah, Saudi Arabia, in Mar 1982 on a rig with a train weight of 2,128 tons. It measures 88.5 ft wide × 91.8 ft long × 131.2 ft high.

Amphibious Vehicle Circumnavigation

The only circumnavigation of the world by an amphibious vehicle was achieved by Ben Carlin (Australia) (d Mar 7, 1981) in an amphibious jeep "Half-Safe." He completed the last leg of the Atlantic crossing (the English Channel) on Aug 24, 1951. He arrived back in Montreal, Canada on May 8, 1958 having completed a circumnavigation of 39,000 miles over land and 9,600 miles by sea and river. He was accompanied on the transatlantic stage by his ex-wife Elinore (US) and on the long transpacific stage (Tokyo to Anchorage) by Broye Lafayette De Mente (b Mo, 1928).

Largest Taxi Fleet

The largest taxi fleet was that of NYC, which amounted to 29,000 cabs in Oct 1929, compared with the present figure of 12,500, plus an equal number of "gypsy" cabs.

The longest fare on record is one of 7,533 miles through 10 countries from Marble Arch, London, England, from Sept 19 to Oct 18, 1981. The trip was sponsored for charity and the driver was Stephen Tillyer.

Driving in Reverse

Charles Creighton (1908–70) and James Hargis of Maplewood, Mo drove their Ford Model A 1929 roadster in reverse from NYC to Los Angeles (3,340 miles), July 26–Aug 13, 1930 *without* stopping the engine once. They arrived back in NY on Sept 5, again in reverse, thus completing 7,180 miles in 42 days.

The highest average speed attained in any non-stop reverse drive exceeding 500 miles was achieved

JEEP THAT CROSSED THE OCEAN: The "Half-Safe," amphibious vehicle that traveled around the world.

by Gerald Hoagland, who drove a 1969 Chevrolet Impala 501 miles non-stop in 17 hours 38 min at Chemung Speed Drome, NY July 9–10, 1976 to average 28.41 mph.

Two-Wheel Driving

The longest recorded distance for driving on 2 wheels by a professional stuntman is 5.6 miles in a Chevrolet Chevette by Joie Chetwood, Jr, on the Indianapolis Speedway on May 13, 1978.

Elastic-Powered Vehicle

The greatest distance achieved by a vehicle run by the power of an unwinding rubber band is 527.4 yd by "Olive-Goo," designed by a Japanese team on Mar 24, 1980 for a Guinness TV show contest. On Mar 27, 1981, it covered 100 meters in 19.34 sec, just about half as fast as the fastest human runner.

Lawn Mowers

The widest gang mower on record is the 5.6-ton 60-ft-wide 27-unit Big Green Machine, used by the sod farmer Jay Edgar Frick of Monroe, Ohio. It mows an acre in 60 sec.

From March 28 to Apr 1, 1959 a Ransome *Matador* motorized mower was driven for 99 hours non-stop over 375 miles from Edinburgh to London.

Longest Skid Marks

The longest recorded skid marks on a public road were 950 ft long, left by a Jaguar car involved in an accident on the M.1 near Luton, Bedfordshire, England June 30, 1960. Evidence given in the High Court case *Hurlock v. Inglis and others* indicated a speed "in excess of 100 mph" before the application of the brakes.

The skid marks made by the jet-powered *Spirit of America,* driven by Craig Breedlove, after the car went out of control at Bonneville Salt Flats, Utah Oct 15, 1964, were nearly 6 miles long.

Longest Tow

The longest tow on record was one of 4,759 miles from Halifax, Nova Scotia to Canada's Pacific coast, when Frank J. Elliott and George A. Scott of Amherst, Nova Scotia persuaded 168 passing motorists in 89 days to tow their Model T Ford (in fact, engineless) to win a $1,000 bet on Oct 15, 1927.

Most Successful Mechanic

Leopold Alfonso Villa (1899–1979) was a racing mechanic, or chief engineer, for Malcolm and Donald Campbell when they set 21 world speed records (10 land, 11 water) from 1924 to 1964.

MOTORCYCLES*

Earliest

The earliest internal-combustion-engined motorized bicycle was a wooden-framed machine built during Oct-Nov 1885 by Gottlieb Daimler (1834–1900) of Germany at Bad Cannstett and first ridden by Wilhelm Maybach (1846–1929). It had a top speed of 12 mph and developed one-half of one hp from its single-cylinder 264-cc 4-stroke engine at 700 rpm. Known as the "Einspur," it was lost in a fire in 1903. The earliest factory which made motorcycles in quantity was opened in 1894 by Heinrich and Wilhelm Hildebrand and Alois Wolfmüller at Munich, Germany. In its first 2 years this factory produced over 1,000 machines, each having a water-cooled 1,488-cc twin-cylinder 4-stroke engine devel-

oping about 2.5 bhp at 600 rpm—the highest capacity motorcycle engine ever put into production.

Most Expensive Motorcycle

A 1912 Henderson Model A was auctioned for $18,000 in June 1980 in the US.

Fastest Road Motorcycle

The highest speed returned in an independent road test for a catalogued road machine is 154.2 mph for a Dunstall Suzuki GS 1000 CS.

Fastest Track Motorcycle

There is no satisfactory answer to the identity of the fastest track machine, other than to say that the

---

* For more details on this subject see *Motorcycling Facts and Feats,* a Guinness Superlatives Book (Sterling).

current Kawasaki, Suzuki and Yamaha machines have all been geared to attain speeds marginally in excess of 186 mph under race conditions.

Most on One Machine

The Magnificent Seven Stunt Team were augmented to 22 riders on Apr 20, 1981, on an adapted Kawasaki Z900 and rode 440 yd at Santa Pod Raceway, Podington, England.

Duration

The longest time a solo motorcycle has been kept in non-stop motion is 500 hours by Owen Fitzgerald, Richard Kennett and Don Mitchell who covered 8,432 miles in Western Australia July 10–31, 1977.

BICYCLES AND UNICYCLES

The first design for a machine propelled by cranks and pedals, with connecting rods, has been attributed to Leonardo da Vinci (1452–1519) or one of his pupils, dated *c.* 1493. The earliest such design actually built was in 1839–40 by Kirkpatrick Macmillan (1810–78) of Dumfries, Scotland. It is now in the Science Museum, London.

Longest Bicycle

The longest true tandem bicycle ever built (*i.e.* without a third stabilizing wheel) is one of 66 ft 11 in for 35 riders built by the Pedaalstompers Westmalle of Belgium. They rode *c.* 195 ft in practice on Apr 20, 1979. The machine weighs 2,425 lb.

Smallest Bicycle

The world's smallest wheeled *rideable* bicycle is one with 2¼-in wheels, weighing 2 lb, built and ridden regularly by Charlie Charles in his act at Circus Circus Hotel, Las Vegas, Nev. Duplicates are on exhibit in various Guinness Museums.

Largest Bicycle

A classic ordinary bicycle with a 64-in-diameter front wheel and a 20-in diameter back wheel was built *c.* 1886 by the Pope Manufacturing Co of Mass. It is now owned by Paul Niquette of Connecticut.

Fastest Cycle Riding

The speed records for human-powered vehicles are 58.64 mph (single rider) by Dave Grylls of the Ontario Speedway, Calif, Oct 27, 1980, and 62.92 mph (multiple riders) by Dave Grylls and Leigh Barczewski also at the Ontario Speedway, Calif, May 4, 1980.

SMALLEST BIKES: Charlie Charles of Las Vegas builds and rides bikes with 2¼-in wheels, like this one.

Underwater Cycling

Thirty-two certified scuba divers in 60 hours, Nov 27–29, 1981, rode a submarine tricycle 64.96 miles on the bottom of Amphi High School pool, Tucson, Ariz, to raise money for a charity.

Unicycle Records

Robert Neil "Bob" McGuinness (b 1951) unicycled 3,976 miles across Canada from Halifax to Vancouver in 79 days, June 6–Aug 24, 1978.

Johnnie Severin of Atwater, Calif set a record for 100 mi in 9 hours 20 min 53 sec Jan 10, 1981.

LONGEST BIKE: 35 riders can sit on this almost 67-ft-long tandem built in Belgium. It weighs 2,425 lb.

Brian Davis, 33, of Tillicoultry, Scotland, rode 901 miles in 19 days 1 hour 45 min, May 16—June 4, 1980, for a place to place record in England.

The sprint record from a standing start over 100 meters is 14.89 sec by Floyd Crandall of Pontiac, Mich in Tokyo, Japan, Mar 24, 1980.

The tallest unicycle ever mastered is one 101 ft 9 in tall ridden by Steve McPeak (with a safety wire or mechanic suspended to an overhead crane) for a distance of 376 ft in Las Vegas Oct 19, 1980. The free-style riding of even taller unicycles (that is, without any safety harness) must inevitably lead to serious injury or fatality.

3. RAILROADS*

Railed trucks were used for mining as early as 1550 at Leberthal, Alsace, near the French-German border, and at the Broseley Colliery, Shropshire, England in Oct 1605, but the first self-propelled locomotive ever built was by Richard Trevithick (1771–1833) for the 3-ft-gauge plateway at Coalbrookdale, Shropshire, in 1803. The first known to have *run* was his second locomotive, at Penydarren, Wales, on Feb 22, 1804.

The earliest established railway to have a steam-powered locomotive was the Middleton Colliery Railway, running between Middleton Colliery and Leeds Bridge, Yorkshire, England.

The first regular steam passenger run was inaugurated over a one-mile section on the 6¼-mile track from Canterbury to Whitstable, Kent, England, on May 3, 1830, hauled by the engine *Invicta*.

The first electric railway was Werner von Siemen's 328-yd oval Berlin electric track opened for the Berlin Trades Exhibition on May 31, 1879.

Fastest Rail Speed

The rail speed record was set by the US Federal Railroad Administration LIMRV (Linear Induction Motor Research Vehicle), built by the Garrett Corp on the 6.2-mile-long Pueblo, Colo test track, when a speed of 254.76 mph was attained on Aug 14, 1974.

The highest speed recorded on any national rail system is 236 mph by the French SNCF high-speed train T6V-PSE on trial near Tonnerre Feb 26, 1981. The TGV (Train às Grande Vitesse), inaugurated on Sept 27, 1981, is in the process of reducing its scheduled time for the Paris–Lyon run of 317 miles from 2 hours 14 min to 2 hours exactly, so averaging 158.5 mph.

Fastest Steam Locomotives

The highest speed ever ratified for a steam locomotive was 126 mph over 440 yd by the LNER 4-6-2 No. 4468 *Mallard* (later numbered 60022), which hauled seven coaches weighing 268.8 tons gross, down Stoke Bank, near Essendine, between Grantham and Peterborough, England, on July 3, 1938. Driver Joseph Duddington was at the controls

* For much greater detail and more records, see *Rail Facts and Feats*, a Guinness Superlatives Book (Sterling). A progressive table of railroad speed records since 1829 appears also in the 1977 edition of the *Guinness Book of World Records*, page 309.

with Fireman Thomas Bray. The engine suffered severe damage. On June 12, 1905, a speed of 127.06 mph was claimed for the the "Pennsylvania Special" near Ada, Ohio, but has never been accepted by leading experts.

Most Powerful Locomotive

The most powerful steam locomotive, measured by tractive effort, was No. 700, a triple-articulated or triplex 2–8–8–8–4 6-cylinder engine which the Baldwin Locomotive Co built in 1916 for the Virginian Railroad. It had a tractive force of 166,300 lb working compound and 199,560 lb working simple.

Probably the heaviest train ever hauled by a single engine was one of 17,100 tons made up of 250 freight cars stretching 1.6 miles by the *Matt H. Shay* (No. 5014), a 2–8–8–8–2 engine which ran on the Erie Railroad from May 1914 until 1929.

Longest Rail Journey

The longest train journey is the 9-day-2-hour "odyssey" from Lisbon, Portugal to Khabarovsk in eastern USSR via Omsk.

Highest Track

The highest standard gauge (4 ft 8½ in) track is on the Peruvian State Railways at La Cima, on the Morococha Branch at 15,806 ft above sea level. The highest point on the main line is 15,688 ft in the Galera tunnel.

Busiest Rail System

The most crowded rail system is the Japanese National Railways, which by 1981 carried 18.7 million passengers daily. Professional pushers are employed in the Tokyo service to squeeze in passengers before the doors can be closed. Among articles reported lost in the crush in 1980 were 543,883 umbrellas, 194,712 eyeglasses and hats, 346,423 clothing items and also 3 person's ashes and 29 Buddhist memorial tablets.

Longest Line

The longest run is one of 5,864½ miles on the Trans-Siberian Line between Moscow and Nakhodka in the Soviet Far East. There are 97 stops on the journey, which takes 8 days 4 hours 25 min. The Baykal-Amur Magistral (BAM) northern line, begun with forced labor in 1938, is expected to be open in 1983, and will cut 310 miles off the route around the southern end of Lake Baykal. A total of 10,000 million cu ft of earth must be removed and 3,700 bridges built in this $14,400 million project.

Steepest Grade

The steepest standard gauge gradient by adhesion is 1:11 between Chedde and Servoz on the meter gauge electric SNCF Chamonix line, France.

Longest Straight Length

The longest straight is on the Commonwealth Railways Trans-Australian line over the Nullarbor Plain from Mile 496 between Nurina and Loongana, Western Australia, to Mile 793 between Ooldea and Watson, South Australia, 297 miles dead straight although not level.

Widest and Narrowest Gauges

The widest gauge in standard use is 5 ft 6 in. This width is used in Spain, India, Pakistan, Bangladesh, Sri Lanka, Argentina and Chile. In 1885, there was a lumber railway in Oregon with a gauge of 8 ft.

The narrowest gauge in use on public rail lines is 1 ft 3 in on the Ravenglass & Eskdale Railway, Cumbria, England (7 miles), and the Romney, Hythe & Dymchurch line in Kent, England (14 miles). "Le Chemin de fer interet locale" between Muir de Bretagne and Caurel, Cote du Nord, France, has a gauge of 12.2 in (31 cm) and runs for 3.1 miles.

Longest Freight Train

The longest and heaviest freight train on record was one 3.5 miles in length, consisting of 450 coal cars with three 3,600-hp diesels pulling, with 5 more pushing on the Iaeger to Williamson, W Va stretch on the Norfolk and Western Railway on Oct 25, 1967. The total weight was more than 44,500 tons.

Greatest Load

The heaviest single pieces of freight ever conveyed by rail are limited by the capacity of the rolling stock. The world's strongest and only rail carrier, with a capacity of 889.7 tons, is the 370.4-ton, 36-axle, 301-ft-10-in-long "Schnabel," built for a US railway by Krupp, W Germany in Mar 1981.

The heaviest load ever moved on rails was the

BUSIEST RAIL SYSTEM: The Japanese National Railways (which includes the Tokyo subway) carries 18.7 million people daily. Their crack train is the Tokkaido Express, shown here passing Mt Fuji.

Church of the Virgin Mary built in 1548 at Most, Czechoslovakia, weighing nearly 12,000 tons, moved in Oct-Nov 1975 because it was in the way of mining for coal deposits. It was moved 800 yd at 0.0013 mph over a period of 4 weeks at a cost of $15,300,000.

Most Countries in 24 Hours

The record number of countries traveled through entirely by train in 24 hours is 10 by W. M. Elbers and R. G. Scholten, July 29–30, 1981. They started in W Germany *via* Netherlands, Belgium, Luxembourg, France, Switzerland, Liechtenstein, Austria, Italy, arriving in Yugoslavia 23 hours 34 min later.

Handpumped Railcars

The fastest time set in the now annual races at Port Moody, BC, Canada, over 300 meters (985 ft) by a 5-man team (1 pusher, 4 pumpers) is 34.08 sec on June 22, 1980.

Largest, Highest and Oldest Stations

The biggest railroad station is Grand Central Terminal, NYC, built 1903–13. It covers 48 acres on 2 levels with 41 tracks on the upper level and 26 on the lower. On average, more than 550 trains and 180,000 people per day use it, with a peak of 252,288 on July 3, 1947.

The highest station is Condor, Bolivia, at 15,705 ft on the meter-gauge Rio Mulato-to-Potosí line.

The oldest station in the world is Liverpool Road Station, Manchester, England, first used in 1830.

Waiting Rooms

The largest waiting rooms are the four in Peking Station, Chang'an Boulevard, Peking, China, opened in Sept 1959, with a total standing capacity of 14,000.

Longest Platform

The longest railroad platform is the Khargpur platform in West Bengal, India, which measures 2,733 ft in length. The State Street Center subway platform in "The Loop," Chicago, measures 3,500 ft in length.

Subways

The earliest (first section opened Jan 10, 1863) and one of the most extensive underground railway or rapid transit systems of the 67 in the world is that of the London Transport Executive, with 260 miles of route, of which 81 miles is bored tunnel and 20 miles is "cut and cover." This whole system is operated by a staff of 11,300 serving 277 stations. The 500 trains comprising 4,353 cars carried 559 million passengers in 1980. The record for a day is 2,073,134 on VE Day, May 8, 1945. The greatest depth is 221 ft. The record for touring all of the 277 stations is 17 hours 37 min by C. M. Mulvany of London on Dec 3, 1981.

The subway with most stations is operated by the NYC Transit Authority (first section opened on Oct 27, 1904) with a total of 231.73 route miles of track and 1,096,006,529 passengers in 1979. The stations are close set and total 462.

253

The busiest subway system is that in Greater Moscow with as many as 6½ million passengers per day. It has 114 stations and 114 miles of track.

Longest Tram Journey

The longest tramway journey now possible is from Krefeld St Tönis to Witten Annen Nord, W Germany. With luck at the 8 interconnections the 65.5-mile trip can be achieved in 5½ hours. By late 1977 there were still some 315 tramway systems surviving, of which the longest is that of Leningrad, USSR, with 2,500 cars on 53 routes.

Oldest Trams

The oldest trams in revenue service in the world are Motor Cars 1 and 2 of the Manx (Isle of Man) Electric Railway, dating from 1893.

Highest Speed Monorail

The highest speed ever attained on rails is 3,090 mph (Mach 4.1) by an unmanned rocket-powered sled on the 6.62-mile-long captive track at the US Air Force Missile Development Center at Holloman, NM, on Feb 19, 1959. The highest speed reached carrying a chimpanzee is 1,295 mph.

The highest speed attained by a tracked hovercraft is 255.3 mph by the jet-powered *L'Aérotrain 02*, invented by Jean Bertin.

An experimental, magnetically levitated Japanese National Railway train on a test track near Miyazaki reached 321 mph on Dec 21, 1979.

Model Railways

The non-stop duration record for a model train (locomotive plus 6 coaches) is 864 hours 30 min from June 1 to July 7, 1978, covering 678 miles, organized by Roy Catton at "Pastimes" Toy Store, Mexborough, S. Yorkshire, England.

The longest recorded run by a model *steam* locomotive is 144 miles in 27 hours 18 min by the 7¼-in gauge "Winifred" built in 1974 by Wilf Grove at Thames Ditton, Surrey, England on Sept 8–9, 1979. "Winifred" works on 80 lb/sq-in pressure and is coal-fired with a 2⅛-in bore cylinder and a 3⅛-in stroke.

The longest train ever operated was one of 750 cars, plus one caboose, pulled by 10 Lionel engines on an 'O' gauge track, by Stewart E. Roberts at the Rickenbacker Air Force Base in Columbus, Ohio July 26, 1980 when it traversed its own length (about 685 ft).

4. AIRCRAFT*

Note: The use of the Mach scale for aircraft speeds was introduced by Prof Ackeret of Zurich, Switzerland. The Mach number is the ratio of the velocity of a moving body to the local velocity of sound. This was first employed by Dr Ernst Mach (1838–1916) of Austria in 1887. Thus Mach 1.0 equals 760.98 mph at sea level at 15° C (59°F) and is assumed, for convenience, to fall to a constant 659.78 mph in the stratosphere, *i.e.* above 11,000 m (36,089 ft).

Earliest Flights

The first controlled and sustained power-driven flight occurred near Kill Devil Hill, Kitty Hawk, NC at 10:35 a.m. on Dec 17, 1903, when Orville Wright (1871–1948) flew the 12-hp chain-driven *Flyer I* at an airspeed of 30 mph, a ground speed of 6.8 mph and an altitude of 8–12 ft for 12 sec, watched by his brother Wilbur (1867–1912), 4 men and a boy. Both

brothers, from Dayton, Ohio, were bachelors because, as Orville put it, they had not the means to "support a wife as well as an airplane." The *Flyer* is now in the National Air and Space Museum of the Smithsonian Institution, Washington, DC.

The first hop by a man-carrying airplane entirely under its own power was made when Clément Ader (1841–1925) of France flew in his *Eole* for about 164 ft at Armainvilliers, France, on Oct 9, 1890. It was powered by a lightweight steam engine of his own design which developed about 20 hp (15 kW).

Richard William Pearce (1877–1953) flew for at least 50 yd along the Main Waitohi Road, South Canterbury, New Zealand, in a self-built petrol-engined monoplane, probably on March 31, 1903.

The earliest "rational design" for a flying machine (according to the British Royal Aeronautical Society) was published by Emanuel Swedenborg (1688–1772) in Sweden in 1717.

---

* For more detail and more records see *Air Facts and Feats,* one of the Guinness Family of Books (Sterling).

FIRST FLIGHT: The Wright brothers, Wilbur and Orville (above), are on the way to making their historic flight dressed in stiff collars and ties. The take-off (below) in 1903 came after a ground speed of 6.8 mph was reached. The plane flew for 12 sec at a height of 8–12 ft. (Air & Space Museum, Washington, both photos) The monument (right) to the Wrights in Dayton, Ohio (their home town), is circled by a gyrocopter. Dr Igor Bensen, the gyrocopter's designer, has made the plans available in kit form for amateur builders.

255

AMERICAN PACESETTER: The first person to fly solo across the Atlantic, Charles A. Lindbergh (left) became an instant hero. He did it in a tiny plane "The Spirit of St. Louis" in 1927 in a 33½-hour ordeal and won $25,000.

AROUND MOST OF THE WORLD: Wiley Post, American (right), flew alone for 15,596 miles in 115½ hours around the world at a latitude so far from the equator that his record could not qualify as a true circumnavigation.

TRIPLANE: The Roe I, built by Elliott Verdon Roe in 1909, was made of wood and covered with brown paper as he could not afford fabric. Roe had many crashes.

Transatlantic Flights

The first crossing of the North Atlantic by air was made by Lt-Cdr (later Rear Admiral) Albert C. Read (1887–1967) and his crew (Stone, Hinton, Rodd, Rhoads and Breese) in an 84-knot Curtiss flying boat NC-4 of the US Navy from Trepassy Harbour, Newfoundland, Canada *via* the Azores, to Lisbon, Portugal, May 16 to 27, 1919. The whole flight of 4,717 miles originating from Rockaway Air Station, Long Island, NY, on May 8, required 53 hours 58 min terminating at Plymouth, England on May 31. The Newfoundland-Azores leg (1,200 miles) took 15 hours 18 min at 81.7 knots.

The first non-stop transatlantic flight was achieved from 4:13 p.m. GMT on June 14, 1919 from Lester's Field, St John's, Newfoundland, 1,960 miles to Derrygimla bog near Clifden, Co Galway, Ireland, at 8:40 a.m. GMT June 15, when the pilot Capt John William Alcock (1892–1919), and Lt Arthur Whitten Brown (1886–1948) flew across in a Vickers *Vimy,* powered by two 360-hp Rolls-Royce *Eagle VII* engines. Both men were given knighthoods on June 21, 1919 when Alcock was 26 years 227 days old, and shared a £10,000 (then $50,000) prize given by a London newspaper.

The 79th man to complete a transatlantic trip but the first to fly alone was Capt (later Col and Brig Gen) Charles A. Lindbergh (1902–74), who took off in his 220-hp Ryan monoplane *Spirit of St Louis* at 12:52 p.m. GMT on May 20, 1927 from Roosevelt Field, Long Island, NY. He landed at 10:21 p.m. GMT on May 21, 1927 at Le Bourget airfield, Paris, France. His flight of 3,610 miles lasted 33 hours 29½ min and he won a prize of $25,000.

The record for the most transatlantic flights is held by Capt John M. Winston, a senior British Airways flight engineer, who flew 1,277 transatlantic flights from May 10, 1947 to Dec 14, 1978—a total of 20,100 hours.

The transatlantic flight speed record is 1 hour 54 min 56.4 sec by Maj James V. Sullivan, 37, and Maj Noel F. Widdifield, 33, flying a Lockheed SR-71A eastwards on Sept 1, 1974. The average speed, slowed by refueling by a KC-135 tanker aircraft, for the NY-London stage of 3,461.53 miles was 1,806.963 mph. The solo record (Gander to Gatwick) is 8 hours 47 min 32 sec by Capt John J. A. Smith in a Rockwell 685 on March 12, 1978.

Transpacific Flight

The first non-stop Pacific flight was by Maj Clyde Pangborn and Hugh Herndon in the Bellanca cabin plane *Miss Veedol* from Sabishiro Beach, Japan, 4,558 miles to Wenatchee, Wash in 41 hours 13 min on Oct 3–5, 1931. (For earliest crossing see 1924 flight below.)

Circumnavigational Flights

A strict circumnavigation of the earth requires passing through two antipodal points and is thus a minimum distance of 24,859.75 miles. (The FAI permits flights which exceed the length of the Tropic of Cancer or Capricorn, namely 22,858.754 miles, to be called round-the-world.)

The earliest such flight (26,345 miles) was made by two US Army Douglas DWC amphibians in 57 "hops." The *Chicago* was piloted by Lt Lowell H. Smith and Lt Leslie P. Arnold and the *New Orleans* was piloted by Lt Erik H. Nelson and Lt John Harding. The planes took off from Seattle, Wash on Apr 6, 1924 and landed back there on Sept 28, 1924.

The earliest solo claim was by Wiley Hardemann Post (1898–1935) (US) in the Lockheed Vega *Winnie Mae,* starting and finishing at Floyd Bennett Field, NYC July 15–22, 1933, in 10 "hops." His distance of 15,596 miles with a flying time of 115 hours 36 min was, however, at too high a latitude to qualify.

The first non-stop round-the-world flight was made by the USAF's Boeing B-50 Superfortress *Lucky Lady II* piloted by Capt James Gallagher from Carswell AFB, Tex in 94 hours 1 min. The aircraft was refueled 4 times on its 23,452-mile flight.

The fastest flight has been a non-stop eastabout flight of 45 hours 19 min by 3 USAF B-52's led by Maj-Gen Archie J. Old, Jr. They covered 24,325 miles on Jan 16–18, 1957, finishing at March AFB, Riverside, Calif having averaged 525 mph with 4 inflight refuelings by KC-97 aerial tankers.

The smallest aircraft to complete a circumnavigation is a 20-ft-11-in single-engined 180-hp Thorp T-18, built in his garage by its pilot Donald P. Taylor of Sage, Calif. His 26,190-mile flight in 37 stages took 176 flying hours, ending in Oshkosh, Wis on Sept 30, 1976.

Jet-Engine Flight

Proposals for jet propulsion date back to 1909, by Capt Marconnet of France and Henri Coanda (1886–1972) of Rumania, and to the turbojet proposals of Maxime Guillaume in 1921. The earliest testbed run was that of the British Power Jets Ltd's experimental WU (Whittle Unit) on Apr 12, 1937, invented by Flying Officer (now Air Commodore

Sir) Frank Whittle (b Coventry, June 1, 1907), who had applied for a patent on jet propulsion in 1930.

The first flight by an airplane powered by a turbo-jet engine was made by the Heinkel He 178, piloted by Flugkapitän Erich Warsitz, at Marienehe, Germany Aug 27, 1939. It was powered by a Heinkel He S3b engine (834-lb st as installed with long tailpipe) designed by Dr Hans von Ohain and first tested in Aug 1937.

Circum-Polar Flight

The first circum-polar flight was flown solo by Capt Elgen M. Long, 44, in a Piper Navajo, Nov 5 to Dec 3, 1971. He covered 38,896 miles in 215 flying hours. The cabin temperature sank to −40°F over Antarctica.

Supersonic Flight

The first supersonic flight was achieved Oct 14, 1947 by Capt (later Brig-Gen) Charles ("Chuck") Elwood Yeager, USAF retired (b Feb 13, 1923), over Edwards Air Force Base, Muroc, Calif in a US Bell XS-1 rocket plane (*Glamorous Glennis*), with Mach 1.015 (670 mph) at an altitude of 42,000 ft.

Solar-Powered Flight

The solar-powered *Solar Challenger,* designed by a team led by Dr Paul MacCready, was flown for the first time entirely under solar power on Nov 20, 1980. On July 7, 1981, piloted by Steve Ptacek (US), the *Solar Challenger* became the first aircraft of this category to achieve a crossing of the English Channel. Taking off from Clergy-Pontaise near Paris, the 180-mile journey to Manston, Kent, England, was completed in 5½ hours. The aircraft had a wingspan of 47 ft.

Largest and Smallest Planes

The aircraft with the largest wing span ever constructed was Howard R. Hughes' H.2 *Hercules* flying boat, built at a cost of $40 million, which rose 70 ft into the air in a test run of 1,000 yd, piloted by Howard Hughes (1905–76), off Long Beach Harbor, Calif on Nov 2, 1947. The 8-engined 213-ton aircraft had a wing span of 319 ft 11 in and a length of 218 ft 8 in, and never flew again. In a brilliant engineering feat she was moved bodily by Goldcoast Corp, aided by the US Navy barge crane YD-171, on Oct 29, 1980, to her final resting place.

The highest recorded gross takeoff weight of any aircraft has been 425 tons in the case of a Boeing 747-200B Jumbo plane during certification tests of its Pratt & Whitney JT9D-7Q engines on May 23, 1979.

The smallest airplane ever flown is the Stits Sky Baby biplane, designed and built by Ray Stits at Riverside, Calif and first flown by Robert H. Starr May 26, 1952. It was 9 ft 10 in long, with a wing span of 7 ft 2 in, and weighed 452 lb empty. Powered by an 85-hp Continental C85 engine, it reaches a top speed of 185 mph.

Heaviest and Fastest Bombers

The heaviest bomber is the 8-jet sweptwing Boeing B-52H *Stratofortress,* which has a maximum takeoff weight of 488,000 lb. It has a wing span of 185 ft and is 157 ft 6¾ in in length, with a speed of over 650 mph. The B-52 can carry 12 SRAM thermonuclear short-range attack missiles or 24 750-lb bombs under its wings and 8 more SRAMs or 84 500-lb bombs in the fuselage.

The 10-engined Convair B-36J, weighing 205 tons, had a greater wing span, at 230 ft, but is no longer in service. It had a top speed of 435 mph.

The fastest operational bombers are the French Dassault Mirage IV, which can fly at Mach 2.2 (1,450 mph) at 36,000 ft; the General Dynamics FB-111A, with a maximum speed of Mach 2.5; and the Soviet swing-wing Tupolev Tu-26 known to NATO as "Backfire," which has an estimated over-target speed of Mach 2.0 to 2.5 and a combat radius of 3,570 miles.

Largest and Fastest Airliners

The highest capacity jet airliner is the Boeing 747 "Jumbo Jet," first flown on Feb 9, 1969. It has a capacity of from 385 to more than 500 passengers with a maximum speed of 602 mph. The Stretched Upper Deck option announced during 1980 allows an extra 32 passengers to be carried. The first of these extended-capacity aircraft are scheduled to enter service in 1983. Its wing span is 195.7 ft and its length, 231.8 ft. It entered service on Jan 22, 1970.

The supersonic BAC/Aerospatiale *Concorde*, first flown on March 2, 1969, with a capacity of 128 passengers, cruises at up to Mach 2.2 (1,450 mph). It flew at Mach 1.05 on Oct 10, 1969, exceeded Mach 2 for the first time on Nov 4, 1970, and became the first supersonic airliner used for passenger service on Jan 21, 1976, when Air France and British Airways opened service simultaneously between, respectively,

FIRST SUPERSONIC FLIGHT was made in 1947 by Capt (later General) Charles Yeager in "Glamorous Glennis," a rocket plane that sped at 670 mph at 42,000 ft.

LARGEST WINGS: Howard Hughes' mammoth flying boat (left), the "Spruce Goose," with wing span of 319 ft 11 in, flew only 1,000 yd in 1947 and never flew again. (Associated Press)

FIRST SUCCESSFUL SOLAR-POWERED PLANE (left, below) Paul MacCready designed this plane which had a takeoff weight of 275 lb when making its first flight under solar battery power on Nov 20, 1980. On July 7, 1981, the plane got international attention when it flew across the English Channel. (Franklin Berger)

SMALLEST PLANE EVER FLOWN: Ray Stits with the "Sky Baby" (below) that he designed. It weighs only 452 lb empty, but can go 185 mph.

SPACE SHUTTLE (above): The $10-billion "Columbia" flew a successful 54½-hour mission before touching down at Rogers Dry Lake, Calif, on its first flight in Apr 1981. (NASA)

FIRST NON-STOP AROUND THE WORLD (above): "Lucky Lady II" needed only 4 refuelings on its 94-hour flight. (John Topham Picture Library) **LARGEST CAPACITY (left):** The "Guppy" holds a cargo of 39,000 cu ft. (Aero Spacelines) The French Dassault Mirage IV (below) is one of the **FASTEST OPERATIONAL BOMBERS** at 1,450 mph at an altitude of 36,000 ft.

Paris—Rio de Janeiro and London—Bahrain. Services between London/NY and Paris/NY began Nov 22, 1977. The NY-London record time is 2 hours 59 min 14 sec (average 1,166.031 mph) set Jan 20, 1980.

Most Capacious Aircraft

The Aero Spacelines Guppy-201 has a cargo hold with a usable volume of 39,000 cu ft and a maximum takeoff weight of 85 tons. Wing span is 156.2 ft, length 143.8 ft and overall height 48.5 ft. The giant Lockheed C-5A Galaxy military transport has a main cargo hold with a usable volume of 34,795 cu ft and a maximum takeoff weight of 384.4 tons. Its wing span is 222.7 ft, length 247.8 ft and overall height 65.1 ft. It has in addition forward and rear upper decks with a combined volume of 8,030 cu ft, which accommodates the flight crew and provides seating for a relief crew and others, totaling 15 forward troops and 75 troops on the rear deck.

Highest Air Speed

The official air speed record is 2,193.167 mph by Capt Eldon W. Joersz and Maj George T. Morgan, Jr, in a Lockheed SR-71A near Beale Air Force Base, Calif on July 28, 1976 over a 10–15-mi course.

The fastest fixed-wing craft was a North American Aviation X-15A-2, which flew for the first time (after modification from X-15A) on June 28, 1964, powered by a liquid oxygen and ammonia rocket propulsion system. Ablative materials on the airframe enabled a temperature of 3,000 °F to be withstood. The landing speed was 210 knots (242 mph) momentarily. The highest speed attained was 4,534 mph (Mach 6.72) when piloted by Maj William J. Knight, USAF (b 1930) on Oct 3, 1967. An earlier version piloted by Joseph A. Walker (1920–66) reached 354,200 ft (67.08 miles) over Edwards Air Force Base, Calif on Aug 22, 1963. The program was suspended after the final flight of Oct 24, 1968.

The US NASA Rockwell International Space Shuttle Orbiter *Columbia* was launched from the Kennedy Space Center, Cape Canaveral, Fla, commanded by Commander John W. Young USN and piloted by Robert L. Crippen on Apr 12, 1981 after the expenditure of $9,900 million since 1972. *Columbia* broke all records for speed by a fixed-wing craft with 16,600 mph at main engine cut-off. After re-entry from 400,000 ft, experiencing temperatures of 3,920 °F, she became the heaviest ever glider at 108 tons with the highest ever landing speed of 216 mph

on Rogers Dry Lake, Calif on Apr 14, 1981. Under a new FAI category P for aerospacecraft, the *Columbia* is holder of the current absolute world records for duration of 54 hours 20 min 52 sec, distance of 937,156 miles, altitude of 169.14 miles and mass lifted to altitude of 212,636.5 lb.

Fastest Jet

The fastest jet aircraft is the USAF Lockheed SR-71 reconnaissance aircraft which first flew on Dec 22, 1964 and attained a speed of 2,193.167 mph July 1976 (see above). It is reportedly capable of attaining an altitude ceiling of close to 100,000 ft. The SR-71 has a wing span of 55.6 ft, a length of 107.4 ft and weighs 170,000 lb at takeoff. Its reported range is 2,982 miles at Mach 3 at 78,750 ft. At least 30 are believed to have been built.

The fastest combat aircraft in service is the USSR Mikoyan MIG-25 fighter (code name "Foxbat"). The reconnaissance "Foxbat-B" has been tracked by radar at about Mach 3.2 (2,110 mph). When armed with 4 large underwing air-to-air missiles known to NATO as "Acrid," the fighter "Foxbat-A" is limited to Mach 2.8 (1,845 mph). The single-seat "Foxbat-A" spans 45 ft 9 in, is 73 ft 2 in long, and has a maximum takeoff weight of 79,800 lb.

Fastest Piston-Engined Aircraft

The fastest speed at which a piston-engined plane has ever been measured was for a cut-down privately owned Hawker *Sea Fury* which attained 520 mph in level flight over Texas in Aug 1966, piloted by Mike Carroll (k 1969) of Los Angeles. The official record is 499.048 mph over Mud Lake, Tonopah, Nev by Steve Hinton in a modified North American P51D *Mustang* powered by a 3,800 hp Rolls-Royce Griffon, over a 1.86-mile course at restricted altitude Aug 14, 1979.

Fastest Propeller-Driven Aircraft

The Soviet Tu-114 turboprop transport is the fastest propeller-driven airplane. It recorded a speed of 545.76 mph carrying heavy payloads over measured circuits. It is developed from the Tupolev Tu-95 bomber, known in the West as the "Bear," and has four 14,795-hp engines. The turboprop powered Republic XF-84H prototype US Navy fighter which flew on July 22, 1955 had a top design speed of 670 mph, but was abandoned.

Largest Aircraft Propeller

The largest aircraft propeller ever used was the 22-ft-7½-in diameter Garuda propeller, fitted to the Linke-Hofmann R II built in Wroclaw, Poland, which flew in 1919. It was driven by four 260-hp Mercedes engines and turned at only 545 rpm.

Greatest Altitude

The official altitude record by an aircraft taking off from the ground under its own power is 123,524 ft (23.39 miles) by Aleksandr Fedotov (USSR) in a Mikoyan E-266M (MIG-25) aircraft, powered by two 30,865-lb thrust turbojet engines on Aug 31, 1977.

The greatest recorded height by any pilot without a pressure cabin or even a pressure suit has been 49,500 ft by British Squadron Leader G. W. H. Reynolds in a Spitfire Mark VC over Libya in 1942.

Flight Duration

The flight duration record is 64 days, 22 hours, 19 min and 5 sec, set by Robert Timm and John Cook in a Cessna 172 "Hacienda." They took off from McCarran Airfield, Las Vegas, Nev just before 3:53 p.m. local time on Dec 4, 1958 and landed at the same airfield just before 2:12 p.m. on Feb 7, 1959. They covered a distance equivalent to 6 times around the world with continued refueling without landing.

The record for duration without refueling is 84 hours 32 min, set by Walter E. Lees and Frederic A. Brossy in a Bellanca monoplane with a 225-hp Packard Diesel engine, at Jacksonville, Fla, May 25–28, 1931.

The longest non-stop flight without refueling was a 12,519-mile flight from Okinawa to Madrid, Spain, by a USAF B-52H in 1962.

Longest and Shortest Scheduled Flights

The longest scheduled non-stop flight is the weekly Pan-Am Sydney-San Francisco non-stop Flight 816 (13 hours 25 min) in a Boeing 747 SP (Special Performance) opened in Dec 1976 over 7,475 statute miles. The longest delivery flight by a commercial jet is 8,936 nautical miles or 10,290 statute miles from Seattle, Wash to Cape Town, South Africa by South African Airway's Boeing 747 SP *Matroosberg*. She made the 17-hour 22½-min flight loaded with 196.5 tons of pre-cooled fuel March 23–29, 1976.

The shortest scheduled flight is made by Loganair between the Orkney Islands (Scotland) of Westray and Papa Westray, which has been flown with twin-engined 10-seat Britten-Norman Islander transports since Sept 1967. Though scheduled for 2 minutes, in favorable wind conditions it is accomplished in 58 sec by Capt Andrew D. Alsop.

Gary W. Rovetto of Island Air on Mar 21 1980 flew on the scheduled flight from Center Island to Decatur Island, Wash in 41 sec.

London–New York for Speed

The record for central London to downtown NYC by helicopter and Concorde is 3 hours 59 min 44 sec and the return in 3 hours 40 min 40 sec, both by David Springbett (GB), on Feb 8 and 9, 1982.

Youngest and Oldest Pilots

The youngest age at which anyone has ever qualified as a military pilot is 15 years 5 months in the case of Sgt Thomas Dobney (b May 6, 1926) of the British Royal Air Force. He had lied about his age (14 years) on induction.

The youngest solo pilot has been Kenny Bennett in an ultra light Quicksilver aircraft on a farm near Alquippa, Pa, 3 days before his 10th birthday, on May 29, 1981.

The oldest pilot is Ed McCarty (b Sept 18, 1885) of Kimberly, Idaho who in 1979 was flying his rebuilt 30-year-old Ercoupe at the age of 94. Glenn E. Messer of Birmingham, Ala has been flying "steady" since May 13, 1911.

Oldest and Youngest Passengers

The oldest person to fly as a passenger was Shigechiyo Izumi (see *Oldest Humans*) when he was 108 in 1973. He flew from Tokunashima, his home island, to Osaka, Japan, and return. Airborne births are reported every year.

Most Flying Hours

Max Conrad (1903–79) (US) logged 52,929 hours 40 min of flight time, a total of more than 6 years airborne, between 1928 and mid-1974. He completed 150 transatlantic crossings in light aircraft.

Most Takeoffs and Landings from Airports

Al Yates and Bob Phoenix of Texas made 193 takeoffs and daylight landings at unduplicated airfields in 14 hours 57 min in a Piper Seminole on June 15, 1979.

Largest Airports

The largest airport is King Abdul-Aziz International Airport near Jeddah, Saudi Arabia, covering an area of 40 sq mi. The Hajj Terminal is now the world's largest roofed structure covering 370 acres.

The present 6 runways and 5 terminal buildings of the Dallas/Fort Worth Airport, Tex are planned to be extended to 9 runways and 13 terminals with 260 gates with an ultimate capacity for 150 million passengers annually.

The largest airport terminal is Hartsfield Atlanta International Airport opened Sept 21, 1980, with floor space covering 50.50 acres. It has 138 gates handling nearly 50 million passengers annually but has a capacity for 75 million.

Highest and Lowest Airports

The highest airport in the world is La Sa (Lhasa) Airport in Tibet at 14,315 ft. The highest landing ever made by a fixed-wing plane was at 19,947 ft on Dhaulagiri, Himalaya, by a Pilatus Porter, named *Yeti*, supplying the 1960 Swiss Expedition. The lowest landing field is El Lisan on the east shore of the Dead Sea, 1,180 ft below sea level, but during World War II BOAC short C-class flying boats operated from the surface of the Dead Sea 1,292 ft below sea level. The lowest international airport is at Rotterdam, Netherlands, at 15 ft below sea level.

Longest Runway

The longest runway is 7 miles in length (of which 15,000 ft is concreted) at Edwards Air Force Base on the bed of Rogers Dry Lake at Muroc, Calif. The whole test center airfield extends over 65 sq mi. In an emergency, an auxiliary 12-mile strip is available along the bed of the Dry Lake.

The longest civil airport runway is one of 16,076 ft (3.04 miles) at Pierre van Ryneveld Airport, Upington, South Africa, constructed in 5 months, Aug 1975–Jan 1976.

Busiest Airport

The busiest airport is the Chicago International Airport, O'Hare Field, with a total of 645,614 movements and 37,992,151 passengers in 1981. This represents a takeoff or landing every 48.8 sec around the clock. Heathrow Airport outside London handles more *international* traffic than any other.

The busiest landing area ever has been Bien Hoa Air Base, South Vietnam, which handled more than

LARGEST AIRPORT: In Texas, Dallas/Fort Worth boasts of a landing field with 6 runways and 5 terminal buildings now, but it is to be extended to serve 150 million passengers a year with 260 gates when completed.

one million takeoffs and landings in 1970. The largest "helipad" was An Khe, South Vietnam.

Airport Distance to City Centers

The airport farthest from the city center it allegedly serves is Viracopos, Brazil, which is 60 miles from São Paulo. The Gibraltar airport is 880 yd from the center.

Fastest Helicopters

Bell Helicopters claimed in June 1980 that their Model 301 (US Army XV-15) tilt-rotor research aircraft attained a true air speed of 346.6 mph in level flight. It is powered by two turbo-shaft engines. The official world speed record for a pure helicopter is 228.9 mph set by Gourguen Karapetyan in a Mil A-10 on a 15–25 km course near Moscow, on Sept 21, 1978.

Largest and Smallest Helicopters

The largest helicopter is the Soviet Mil Mi-12 ("Homer"), also known as the V-12, which set an international record by lifting a payload of 88,636 lb to a height of 7,398 ft Aug 6, 1969. It is powered by four 6,500-hp turboshaft engines, and has a span of 219 ft 10 in over its rotor tips with a fuselage length of 121 ft 4½ in and weighs 115.7 tons.

The Aerospace General Co one-man rocket-assisted mini-copter weighs about 160 lb and can cruise 250 miles at 85 mph.

Highest Helicopters

The altitude record for helicopters is 40,820 ft by an Aerospatiale SA 315 B Lama over France on June 21, 1972. The highest recorded landing has been at 23,000 ft, below the southeast face of Everest, in a rescue sortie in May 1971. The World Trade Center Helipad is 1,385 ft above street level in NYC, on the South Tower.

Autogyros

The autogyro or gyroplane, a rotorcraft with an unpowered rotor turned by the airflow in flight, preceded the practical helicopter with engine-driven rotor. Juan de la Cierva (Spain) made the first successful autogyro flight with his model C.4 (commercially named an *Autogiro*) at Getafe, Spain, on Jan 9, 1923. On Dec 6, 1955, Dr Igor B. Bensen (US) flew his very simple open-seat Gyro-Copter and then made his design available in kit form to amateur builders and pilots.

Wing Cdr Kenneth H. Wallis (GB) holds the straight-line distance record of 543.27 miles, set in his WA-116F autogyro on Sept 28, 1975 (non-stop from Lydd, Kent, England, to Wick, Highland, Scotland). Wallis flew his WA-116 with a 72-hp McCulloch engine to a record altitude of 15,220 ft on May 11, 1968, and to a record speed of 111.2 mph over a 3-km (1.86 mile) straight course on May 12, 1969.

Flying Boats

The fastest flying boat ever built has been the Martin XP6M-1 Seamaster, the US Navy 4-jet-engined minelayer, flown in 1955–59 with a top speed of 646 mph. In Sept 1946, the Martin JRM-2 Mars flying boat set a payload record of 68,327 lb.

The official flying-boat speed record is 566.69 mph, set by Nikolai Andrievsky and a crew of 2 in a Soviet Beriev M-10, powered by 2 AL-7 turbojets, over a 10–15 mile course on Aug 7, 1961. The M-10 holds all 12 records listed for jet-powered flying boats, including an altitude of 49,088 ft set by Georgiy Buryanov and crew over the Sea of Azov Sept 9, 1961.

Human-Powered Flight

The distance record for human-powered flight was set June 12, 1979 by Dr Paul MacCready's man-powered 70-lb aircraft *Gossamer Albatross* with a 96-ft wing span, piloted and pedaled by 136-lb Bryan Allen. The *Albatross* took off from Folkestone,

England and landed at Cap Gris-Nez, France 2 hours 49 min later, a flight spanning 22.26 miles, winning the £100,000 (then $200,000) prize offered by Henry Kremer for the first man-powered crossing of the English Channel.

The 70-lb *Gossamer Condor* (96-ft wing span) designed by Dr Paul MacCready flew the figure-of-8 course between pylons 880 yd apart powered by Bryan Allen at Shafter Airport, Calif on Aug 23, 1977 to win the £50,000 (then $85,000) Kremer prize. The flight lasted 7 min 27.5 sec.

Ballooning

The earliest recorded ascent was by a model hot-air balloon invented by Father Bartolomeu de Gusmão (*né* Lourenço) (b Santos, Brazil, 1685), which was flown indoors at the Casa da India, Terreiro do Paço, Portugal on Aug 8, 1709.

The record distance (great-circle distance between takeoff and first landing point) traveled by a balloon is 5,208.68 miles by the Raven experimental helium-filled balloon *Double Eagle V,* Nov 9–12, 1981, from Nagashima, Japan, to Covello, Calif. The crew for this first manned balloon crossing of the Pacific Ocean was Ben L. Abruzzo, Rocky Aoki, Ron Clark and Larry M. Newman.

The world's distance record for hot-air balloons is 717.52 miles, set by French balloonists Michel Arnould and Hélène Dorigny, Nov 25–26,1981, in the Cameron Type A-530 *Semiramis,* from Ballina, County Mayo, Eire, to St Christophe-en-Boucherie, France. This flight has also been homologated by the FAI as a new world duration record for hot-air balloons of 29 hours 5 min 48 sec, and in addition the *Semiramis* is now the largest hot-air balloon ever built, with a volume of 530,000 cu ft. The FAI endurance and distance record for a gas and hot-air balloon is 96 hours 24 min and 2074.817 miles by *Zanussi* crewed by Donald Allan Cameron (GB) and Major Christopher Davey which failed by only 103 miles to achieve the first balloon crossing of the Atlantic on July 30, 1978.

Highest Manned and Unmanned Balloons

The highest altitude attained by an unmanned balloon was 170,000 ft, by a Winzen Research balloon of 47,800,000 cu ft, launched at Chico, Calif, in Oct 1972.

The greatest altitude reached in a manned balloon is the unofficial 123,800 ft by Nicholas Piantanida (1933–66) of Bricktown, NJ from Sioux Falls, SD on Feb 1, 1966. He landed in a cornfield in Iowa but did not survive.

The official record is 113,740 ft by Cdr Malcolm D. Ross, USNR, and the late Lt-Cdr Victor E. Prather, USN, in an ascent from the deck of USS *Antietam* on May 4, 1961 over the Gulf of Mexico.

The altitude record for a hot-air balloon was set by Julian Nott (GB), who, on Oct 31, 1980, attained an altitude, which has been ratified by the FAI, of 55,137 ft, taking off from Longmont, near Denver, Colo, in the Cameron-built ICI balloon *Innovation.* The record altitude in an open basket is 53,000 ft by Chauncey Dunn (US) on Aug 1, 1979. He wore a pressure suit.

Largest Balloon

The largest balloon built is one with an inflatable volume of 70 million cu ft, by Winzen Research Inc, Minnesota.

Airships

The earliest flight of an airship was by Henri Giffard from Paris in his steam-powered coal-gas 88,300-cu ft 144-ft-long rigid airship Sept 24, 1852.

The largest non-rigid airship ever constructed was the US Navy ZPG 3-W. It had a capacity of 1,516,300 cu ft, was 403.4 ft long and 85.1 ft in diameter, with a crew of 21. It first flew on July 21, 1958, but crashed into the sea in June 1960.

The largest rigid airship was the 236-ton German *Graf Zeppelin II* (LZ130), with a length of 803.8 ft and a capacity of 7,062,100 cu ft. She made her maiden flight on Sept 14, 1938 and in May and August 1939 made radar spying missions in British air space. She was dismantled in April 1940. Her sister ship, the *Hindenburg,* was 5.6 ft longer.

The most people ever carried in an airship were 207 in the US Navy *Akron* in 1931. The transatlantic record is 117 by the German *Hindenburg* in 1937.

The FAI accredited distance record for airships is 3,967.1 miles, set by the German *Graf Zeppelin,* captained by Dr Hugo Eckener between Oct 29 and Nov 1, 1928.

The longest recorded flight by a non-rigid airship (without refueling) is 264 hours 12 min by a US Navy Goodyear-built ZPG-2 class ship (Cdr J. R. Hunt, USN) from the S Weymouth, Mass Naval Air Station March 4, 1957 and landing back at Key West, Fla March 15 after having flown 9,448 miles.

The world duration and distance records for hot-air airships are 1 hour 12 min and 6.61 miles, respectively, held by the Cameron D-38 hot-air airship flown at Bristol, Avon, England, on Aug 26, 1981, by Donald Cameron (UK).

Hovercraft

The first flight by a hovercraft was by the 4½-ton Saunders Roe SR-N1 at Cowes, Isle of Wight, on May 30, 1959. With a 1,500-lb thrust Viper turbojet engine, this craft reached 68 knots in June 1961.

The longest hovercraft journey was one of 5,000 mi through 8 West African countries between Oct 15, 1969 and Jan 3, 1970 by the British Trans-African Hovercraft Expedition.

The largest civil hovercraft is the 342-ton British-built SRN 4 MK III with a capacity of 416 passengers and 60 cars. It is 186 ft in length, powered by 4 Siddeley Marine Proteus engines which give a maximum speed in excess of the permitted operating speed of 65 knots.

The fastest warship is the 78-ft 112-ton US Navy test vehicle SES-100B. She attained 91.9 knots (103.9 mph) on Jan 25, 1980 on the Chesapeake Bay Test Range, Md. A contract for a 3,360-ton Large Surface Effect Ship (LSES) was placed by the US Dept of Defense with Bell Aerospace in Sept 1977 for delivery in mid-1981.

The greatest altitude at which a hovercraft is operating is on Lago Titicaca, Peru, where since 1975 an HM2 Hoverferry is hovering 12,506 ft above sea level.

Model Aircraft

The record for altitude is 26,929 ft by Maynard L. Hill (US) on Sept 6, 1970, using a radio-controlled model. The free-flight speed record is 213.70 mph by V. Goukoune and V. Myakinin (both USSR) with a radio-controlled model at Klementyeva, USSR, on Sept 21, 1971. The record duration flight is one of 32 hours 7 min 40 sec by Eduard Svobodn (Czechoslovakia) flying a radio-controlled glider Aug 23–24, 1980. An indoor model powered by a rubber motor, designed by J. Richmond (US), set a duration record of 52 min 14 sec on Aug 31, 1979.

The smallest model aircraft to fly is one weighing 0.004 oz powered by attaching a horsefly and designed by the insectonaut Don Emmick of Seattle, Wash on July 24, 1979. One flew for 5 min at Kirkland, Wash.

Paper Airplane

The flight duration record for a paper aircraft over level ground is 15.0 sec by William Harlan Pryor in the Municipal Auditorium, Nashville, Tenn, March 26, 1975. A paper plane was reported and witnessed to have flown 1¼ miles after a throw by "Chick" C.

O. Reinhart from a 10th-story office window at 60 Beaver Street, NYC across the East River to Brooklyn, NY in Aug, 1933. It was helped by a thermal updraft from a coffee-roasting plant.

The indoor record with a 12-ft ceiling is 1 min 33 sec set in the Fuji TV studios, Tokyo, Japan on Sept 21, 1980.

An indoor distance record of 155 ft 7 in was recorded by Eugene Sykes at the McChord Air Force Base, Wash, on Feb 4, 1982.

5. POWER PRODUCERS

Earliest and Largest Windmills

The earliest recorded windmills are those used for grinding corn in Iran (Persia) in the 7th century AD. The oldest Dutch mill is the towermill at Zeddam, Gelderland, built c. 1450.

The most powerful wind generator is the 3,000-kW 492-ft-tall turbine, built by Grosse Wind energie-Anlage, which was set up in 1982 on the Friesian coast of W Germany.

A £5.6 million ($12 million) 3,000 kW aerogenerator with 196-ft-10-in blades in Evie, Orkney Islands, is planned for completion in 1982/83.

The largest Dutch windmill is the Dijkpolder, in Maasland, built in 1718. The sails measure 95¾ ft from tip to tip. The tallest windmill in the Netherlands is De Walvisch, in Schiedam, built to a height of 108 ft in 1794.

Atomic Power

The first atomic pile was built in an abandoned squash court at the University of Chicago. It "went critical" at 3:25 p.m. on Dec 2, 1942. The largest atomic or nuclear power station is the Ontario Hydro's Pickering station which in 1973 attained full output of 2,160 MW. The largest single nuclear reactor in the world is the 1,500-MW reactor at the Ignalinskaya station, Lithuania, USSR, assembly of which began in April 1982.

Largest Power Plant

The world's most powerful power station is the Grand Coulee, Wash, with 9.7 million kilowatt hours (ultimately 10,830 MW), which began operating in 1942.

The first generator at the Itaipu on the Paraná River on the Brazil-Paraguay border (with an ultimate power of 12,600,000 kW, from 18 turbines) is expected to turn in 1983.

A 20,000-MW power station project on the Tunguska River, USSR, was announced in Feb 1982.

Largest Generator

Generators in the 2,000,000 kW (or 2,000 MW) range are now in the planning stages both in the UK and the US. The largest under construction is one of 1,300 MW by the Brown Boveri Co of Switzerland for the Tennessee Valley Authority.

Biggest Blackout

The greatest power failure in history struck 7 northeastern US states and Ontario, Canada, Nov 9–10, 1965. About 30 million people in 80,000 sq mi were plunged into darkness. Only two people were killed. In NYC the power failed at 5:27 p.m. on Nov 9, and was not fully restored for 13½ hours. The total losses resulting from another NYC power failure, on July 13, 1977, which lasted as long as 25 hours in some areas, have been estimated at more than $1 billion, including losses due to looting.

Tidal Power Station

The first major tidal power station is the *Usine marèmotrice de la Rance,* officially opened on Nov 26, 1966 at the Rance estuary in the Golfe de St Malo, Brittany, France. Built in 5 years, at a cost of $75,600,000, it has a net annual output of 544 million kW/h. The 880-yd barrage contains 24 turbo-alternators. This harnessing of the tides has imperceptibly slowed the earth's rate of revolution.

Biggest Boiler

The largest boilers ever designed are those ordered in the US from the Babcock & Wilcox Co with a capacity of 1,330 MW, so involving the evaporation of 9,330,000 lb of steam per hour.

Largest Turbines

The largest hydraulic turbines are those rated at 815,000 kW (equivalent to 1.1 million hp), 32 ft in diameter, with a 449-ton runner and a 350-ton shaft,

SOLAR ONE: What looks like a field of mirrors is actually a field of mirrors. To create a solar power plant that yields 10 million watts, 1,818 mirrors had to be strategically placed to reflect the Calif sun. Total cost: $140 million. (Franklin Berger)

installed by Allis-Chalmers at the Grand Coulee "Third Powerplant" in Wash.

The largest reversible pump-turbine is that made by Allis-Chalmers for the Bath County Project, Va. It has a maximum rating of 457 MW as a turbine and maximum operating head of 1,289 ft. The impeller/runner diameter is 20 ft 9 in with a synchronous speed of 257.1 rpm.

Solar Power Plant

The largest solar furnace is the 5 MW Solar Thermal Test Facility at the Sandia Laboratories, Albuquerque, NM, completed in Dec 1977. Sunlight from 222 heliostats is concentrated on a target 114 ft up in the power tower. Work on the $140-million, 1,818-mirror Solar One, near Daggett, Calif, began in Jan 1980 and was completed in mid-1982. The 22 acres of mirror will yield 10 MW.

Longest-Lasting Battery

The zinc foil and sulfur dry pile batteries made by Watlin and Hill of London in 1840 have powered ceaseless tintinnabulation inside a bell jar at the Clarendon Laboratory, Oxford since 1840. The first "perpetual motion" patent filed under the World Patent Cooperation Treaty was No 80/00866 by Edmund and Robert Kraus of Calif.

6. ENGINEERING

The earliest machinery still in use is the *dâlu*—a water-raising instrument known to have been in use in the Sumerian civilization which originated *c.* 3500 BC in Lower Iraq—even earlier than the *Saqiyas* of the Nile.

Largest Blast Furnace

The largest blast furnace is one with an inner volume of 179,040 cu ft and a 48-ft 6½-in diameter hearth at the Oita Works, Kyushu, Japan, completed in Oct 1976, with an annual capacity of 4,905,600 tons.

Highest Cable Cars

The highest and longest aerial ropeway is the Teleférico Mérida (Mérida téléphérique) in Venezuela, from Mérida City (5,379 ft) to the summit of Pico Espejo (15,629 ft), a rise of 10,250 ft. The ropeway is in four sections, involving 3 car changes in the 8-mile ascent in one hour. The fourth span is 10,070 ft in length. The two cars work on the pendulum system—the carrier rope is locked and the cars are hauled by means of three pull ropes powered by a 230-hp motor. They have a maximum capacity of 45 persons and travel at 32 ft per sec (21.8 mph).

The longest single-span ropeway is the 13,500-ft-long span from the Coachella Valley to Mt San Jacinto (10,821 ft), Calif opened Sept 12, 1963.

Largest Cat Cracker

The largest catalytic cracker is the Exxon Co's Bayway Refinery plant at Linden, NJ with a fresh feed rate of 5,040,000 gallons per day.

Longest Conveyor Belt

The longest single-flight conveyor belt is one of 18 miles under construction in W Australia by Cable Belt Ltd of England.

The longest multi-flight conveyor is one of 62 miles between the phosphate mine near Bucraa and the Atlantic port of El Aaiun, Morocco, built by Krupp and completed in 1972. It has 11 flights of between 5.6 and 6.8 miles in length and was driven at 10.06 mph, but has been closed down due to Polisario Front guerilla activity.

Most Powerful Cranes

The most powerful crane is aboard the 60,000-ton 584-ft-long converted tanker *Odin,* owned by Heerema Engineering Service of The Hague, Nether-

lands. On May 26, 1976 she made a test lift of 3,360 tons at a radius maximum of 105 ft in the Calard Canal, Europoort, Holland.

The 92.3-ft-wide Rahco (R. A. Hanson Disc Ltd.) gantry crane at the Grand Coulee Dam Third Powerplant was tested to lift a load of 2,500 tons in 1975. It successfully lowered a 3,944,000-lb generator rotor with an accuracy of 1/32 in.

The tallest mobile crane is the 890-ton Rosenkranz K10001 with a lifting capacity of 1,100 tons and a combined boom and jib height of 663 ft. It is carried on 10 trucks, each limited to 75 ft 8 in and an axle weight of 130 tons. It can lift 33.6 tons to a height of 525 ft.

Dragline Excavators

The Ural Engineering Works at Ordzhonikdze, USSR, completed in March 1962, has a dragline known as the ES-25(100) with a boom of 328 ft and a bucket with a capacity of 31.5 cu yd. The largest walking dragline is the Bucyrus-Erie 4250W with an all-up weight of 13,440 tons and a bucket capacity of 220 cu yd on a 310-ft boom. This, the largest mobile land machine, is now operating on the Central Ohio Coal Co's Muskingum site in Ohio.

Fastest Passenger Elevators

The fastest domestic passenger elevators are the express elevators to the 60th floor of the 787.4-ft-tall "Sunshine 60" building, Ikebukuro, Tokyo, Japan, completed Apr 5, 1978. They were built by Mitsubishi Corp and operate at a speed of 2,000 ft per min, or 22.72 mph.

Much higher speeds are achieved in the winding cages of mine shafts. A hoisting shaft 6,800 ft deep, owned by Western Deep Levels Ltd in South Africa, winds at speeds of up to 40.9 mph (3,595 ft per min). Otitis-media (popping of the ears) presents problems at speeds much above even 10 mph.

First and Longest Escalators

The name "escalator" was registered in the US on May 28, 1900, but the earliest "Inclined Elevator" was installed by Jesse W. Reno on the pier at Coney Island, NYC in 1896.

The longest escalators are on the Leningrad Underground, USSR, at Lenin Square, which have 729 steps and a vertical rise of 195 ft 9½ in.

The longest "moving sidewalks" are those installed in 1970 in the Neue Messe Centre, Düsseldorf, W Germany, which measure 738 ft between comb plates.

Largest Excavator

The largest excavator is the 14,325-ton bucket wheel excavator being assembled at the open cast lignite mine of Hambach, W Germany with a rating of 260,000 cu yd per 20-hour working day. It is 690 ft in length and 269 ft tall. The wheel is 222 ft in circumference with 6.5-cu-yd buckets.

Largest Forging

The largest forging on record is a generator shaft 55 ft long weighing 450,600 lb forged by Bethlehem Steel in Oct 1973 for Japan.

Greatest Lifting Operation

The heaviest lifting operation in engineering history was of the 41,000-ton roof of the Velodrome in Montreal, Canada, in 1975. It was raised by jacks some 4 in to strike its centering.

Largest Oil Tanks

The largest oil tanks ever constructed are the five Aramco 1½ million-barrel capacity storage tanks at Ju'aymah, Saudi Arabia. The tanks are 72 ft tall with a diameter of 386 ft and were completed Mar 1980.

Longest Pipelines

The longest crude oil pipeline is the Interprovincial Pipe Line Co's installation from Edmonton, Alberta, Canada, to Buffalo, NY, a distance of 1,775 miles. Along the length of the pipe 13 pumping stations maintain a flow of 8,280,000 gallons of oil per day.

The eventual length of the Trans-Siberian Pipeline will be 2,319 miles, running from Tuimazy through Omsk and Novosibirsk to Irkutsk. The first 30-mile section was opened in July 1957.

The world's most expensive pipeline is the Alaska pipeline running 798 miles from Prudhoe Bay to Valdez. By completion of the first phase in 1977 it had cost at least $6,000 million. The pipe is 48 in in diameter and will eventually carry up to 2 million barrels of crude oil per day.

The longest submarine pipeline is that of 264 miles for natural gas from the Union Oil Platform to Rayong, Thailand, opened on Sept 12, 1981.

The longest natural gas pipeline is the Trans-Canada Pipeline which by 1974 had 5,654 miles of pipe up to 42 in in diameter. The Tyumen-Chelyabinsk-Moscow-Brandenburg gasline stretches 2,690 miles.

Largest Nuts

The largest nuts ever made weigh 11,713.5 lb each and have an outside diameter of 52 in and a 25-in thread. Known as "Pilgrim Nuts," they are manufactured by Doncasters Moorside Ltd of Oldham, England, for use on the columns of a large forging press. (See photo above.)

Largest Press

The two most powerful production machines are forging presses in the US. The Loewy closed-die forging press, in a plant leased from the US Air Force by the Wyman-Gordon Co at North Grafton, Mass weighs 10,600 tons and stands 114 ft 2 in high, of which 66 ft is sunk below the operating floor. It has a rated capacity of 50,000 tons, and went into operation in Oct 1955. The other similar press is at the plant of the Aluminum Company of America in Cleveland.

Fastest Printer or Typesetting Machine

The fastest printer is the Radiation Inc electro-sensitive system at the Lawrence Radiation Laboratory, Livermore, Calif. Recording of up to 30,000 lines per min each containing 120 alphanumeric characters is attained by controlling electronic pulses through chemically impregnated recording paper which is rapidly moving under closely spaced fixed styli. It can thus print the wordage of the whole Bible (773,692 words) in 65 sec—3,333 times as fast as the world's fastest human typist.

Largest Radar Installations

The largest of the three installations in the US Ballistic Missile Early Warning System is the one near Thule, Greenland 931 miles from the North Pole, completed in 1960 at a cost of $500 million. Its sister stations are at Cape Clear, Alaska, completed in July 1961, and a $115 million installation at Fylingdales Moor, North Yorkshire, England completed in June 1963. The largest scientific radar installation is the 21-acre ground array at Jicamarca, Peru.

Largest Transformer

The largest single-phase transformers are rated at 1,500,000 kV of which 8 are in service with the American Electric Power Service Corporation. Of these, 5 step down from 765 to 345 kV.

Longest and Highest Transmission Lines

The longest span between pylons of any power line is that across the Sogne Fjord, Norway, between Rabnaberg and Fatlaberg. Erected in 1955 by the Whitecross Co Ltd of Warrington, England as part of the high-tension power cable from Refsdal power station at Vik, it has a span of 16,040 ft and a weight of 13 tons. In 1967, two further high-tensile steel/aluminum lines 16,006 ft long, and weighing 37 tons, manufactured by Whitecross and British Insulated Callender's Cables Ltd, were erected here.

The highest power lines are those across the Straits of Messina, with towers of 675 ft (Sicily side) and 735 ft (Calabria) and 11,900 ft apart.

The highest voltages now carried are 1,330,000 volts on the DC Pacific Inter-tie in the US for a distance of 1,224 miles. The Ekibastuz DC transmission lines in Kazakhstan, USSR, are planned to be 1,490 miles long with a 1,500,000-volt capacity.

Largest Valve

The largest valve is the 32-ft diameter 190.4-ton butterfly valve designed by Boving & Co Ltd of London for use at the Arnold Air Force Base engine test facility in Tennessee.

Longest and Strongest Wire Rope

The longest wire rope is the stage winder at No. 9 shaft at Vaal Reefs Gold Mine, South Africa, which measures 9½ miles, installed in July 1979. Each of the two ropes weighs 130 tons.

The thickest ever made are spliced crane strops 11¼ in thick, made of 2,392 individual wires in March 1979 by British Ropes at Willington Quay, Tyneside, England.

CLOCKS

Oldest Clocks

The earliest mechanical clock, that is, one with an escapement, was completed in China in 725 AD by I Hsing and Liang Ling-tsan.

The oldest surviving working clock is the faceless clock dating from 1386, or possibly earlier, at Salisbury Cathedral, Wiltshire, England, which was restored in 1956 having struck the hours for 498 years and ticked more than 500 million times. Earlier dates, ranging back to c. 1335, have been attributed to the weight-driven clock in Wells Cathedral, Somerset, England, but only the iron frame is original. A model of Giovanni de Dondi's heptagonal astronomical clock of 1348–64 was completed in 1962.

Largest Clock

The most massive clock is the Astronomical Clock in the Cathedral of St Pierre, Beauvais, France, constructed between 1865 and 1868. It contains 90,000 parts and measures 40 ft high, 20 ft wide and 9 ft deep. The Su Sung clock, built in China at K'aifeng in 1088–92, had a 22-ton bronze armillary sphere for 1⅔ tons of water. It was removed to Peking in 1126 and was last known to be working in its 40-ft-high tower in 1136.

Public Clocks

The largest four-faced clock is that on the building of the Allen-Bradley Co of Milwaukee, Wis. Each face has a diameter of 40 ft 3½ in with a minute hand 20 ft in overall length.

The tallest four-faced clock is on the Williamsburgh Savings Bank, Brooklyn, NYC. It is 430 ft above street level.

Most Accurate Time Measurer

The most accurate time-keeping devices are the twin atomic hydrogen masers installed in 1964 in the US Naval Research Laboratory, Washington, DC. They are based on the frequency of the hydrogen atom's transition period of 1,420,450,751,694 cycles per sec. This enables an accuracy to within one sec in 1,700,000 years.

Most Accurate Clock

The most accurate and complicated clock in the world is the Olsen clock, installed in the Copenhagen

Town Hall, Denmark. The clock, which has more than 14,000 units, took 10 years to make and the mechanism of the clock functions in 570,000 different ways. The celestial pole motion of the clock will take 25,753 years to complete a full circle, the slowest moving designed mechanism in the world. The clock is accurate to 0.5 sec in 300 years—50 times more accurate than the previous record holder.

Computers

The earliest electronic (valve) computer was Colossus. It was run in 1943 at Bletchley Park, England, to break the German coding machine Enigma. It arose from a concept published in 1936 by Dr Alan Mathison Turing (1912–54). Computers were then greatly advanced by the invention of the point-contact transistor by John Bardeen and Walter Brattain announced in July 1948, and the junction transistor by R. L. Wallace, Morgan Sparks and Dr William Shockley in early 1951. The Microcomputer was invented in 1969–73 by M. E. Hoff Jr of Intel Corporation with the production of the microprocessor silicon chip "4004."

The computer planned to be the world's biggest by a factor of 40 is the $50 million NASF (Numerical Aerodynamic Simulation Facility) at NASA's Ames Research Center, Palo Alto, Calif. The tenders from CDC and Burroughs called for a capacity of 12.8 gigaflops (12,800 million complex calculations per sec).

Most Powerful and Fastest Computers

The world's most powerful and fastest computer is the CRAY-1, designed by Seymour R. Cray of Cray Research Inc, Minneapolis. The clock period is 12.5 nanoseconds and memory ranges up to 1,048,576 64-bit words, resulting in a capacity of 8,388,608 bytes of main memory. It attains speeds of 200 million floating point operations per sec. With 32 CRAY DD-19 disk storage units, it has a storage capacity of 7.7568×10^{10} bits. The cost of a mid-range system was quoted in mid-1979 at $8.8 million.

Control Data Corporation announced the CYBER Model 205-444 system from Arden Hill, Minn, on June 2, 1980, which has a memory of 4 million 64-bit words and cost $16.5 million at delivery in Jan 1981. The CRAY-1/S system, introduced in 1981, has

an additional 8 million words of buffer memory and a storage capacity of 19 gigabytes or 1.55136×10^{11} bits with a system cost of up to $17 million for the maximum configuration.

Oldest Watch

The oldest watch (portable clockwork timekeeper) is one made of iron by Peter Henlein in Nürnberg, Bavaria, Germany, c. 1504, and now in the Memorial Hall, Philadelphia. The earliest wristwatches were those of Jacquet-Droz and Leschot of Geneva, Switzerland, dating from 1790.

Smallest and Thinnest Watch

The smallest watches are produced by Jaeger Le Coultre of Switzerland. Equipped with a 15-jeweled movement, they measure just over ½ in in length and 3/16th in in width. The movement, with its case, weighs under ¼ oz.

The thinnest wristwatch is the Concord Delirium IV which measures 0.039 in (0.98 mm) in thickness and retailed for $16,000 in June 1980 with an 18-carat gold bracelet.

Most Expensive Watches

Excluding watches with jeweled cases, the most expensive standard men's pocket watch is the Swiss *Grande Complication* by Audemars-Piguet, which retailed for $94,000 in May 1982.

The *Kallista* watch with 130 carats of precious stones by Vacheron et Constantin of Geneva, Switzerland was valued in Apr 1981 at $5 million.

The record price for an antique watch is $166,300 paid to Capt Peter Belin, USN by L. C. Mannheimer of Zurich at Sotheby Parke Bernet, NYC on Nov 29, 1979 for a gold studded case watch of c. 1810 made by William Anthony of London.

Largest Sundial

The world's largest sundial is one with a 25-ft gnomon (column) and a readable shadow of 125 ft, installed by Walter R. T. Witschey at the Science Museum of Virginia at Richmond, Va, Mar 12–May 3, 1981. The sun's shadow travels 7 in per min at the equinox.

Chapter 9

The Business World

In this chapter, the pound sterling has been converted, unless otherwise noted, at an average exchange rate of £1 = $2.20 for 1979, $2.30 for 1980, $1.80 for 1981, and at the prevailing exchange rates for earlier and later dates.

1. COMMERCE

Oldest Industry

Agriculture is often described as "the oldest industry in the world," whereas in fact there is no evidence that it was practiced before *c.* 11,000 BC. The oldest known industry is flint knapping, involving the production of chopping tools and hand axes, dating from about 1,750,000 years ago.

Oldest Company

The oldest company is the Faversham Oyster Fishery Co of England, referred to in the Faversham Oyster Fishing Act of 1930 as existing "from time immemorial," *i.e.* in English law from before 1189.

Greatest Assets

The business with the greatest amount in physical assets is the Bell System, which comprises the American Telephone and Telegraph Co, with headquarters at 195 Broadway, NYC, and its subsidiaries. The Bell System's total assets on consolidated balance sheet on Feb 28, 1982 were valued at $138,819 million. The plant involved included more than 142 million telephones. The number of employees is 1,036,000. A total of 20,109 attended the annual meeting in Apr 1961, thereby setting a world record.

The first company to have assets in excess of $1 billion was the US Steel Corp with $1.4 billion at the time of its creation by merger in 1900.

Greatest Sales and Capital

The first company to surpass the $1 billion mark in annual sales was the US Steel Corp in 1917. Now there are over 500 corporations with sales exceeding $2 billion (more than 300 of which are in the US). The list is headed by the Exxon Corp of NY with sales of $108.108 billion in 1981.

Greatest Profit and Loss

The greatest net profit made by any corporation in 12 months is $7,092 million by American Telephone and Telegraph Co, Mar 1, 1981–Feb 28, 1982.

The greatest loss ever recorded by any enterprise in a year was $1,710 million by the Chrysler Corp in 1980.

Biggest Work Force

The greatest payroll of any single civilian organization is that of the USSR National Railway system with a total work force of 2,031,200 in 1976.

Largest Take-Over

The largest corporate cash take-over in commercial history has been the bid of $3,650 million by Shell Oil for the stock of Belridge Oil in 1981.

Largest Merger

The largest signed merger agreement has been that between E. I. DuPont Co and Conoco Inc, at 1 a.m. in Stamford, Conn, on July 6, 1981. DuPont paid an estimated $7.5 billion in cash and stock to Conoco's stockholders.

Largest Write-Off

The largest reduction of assets in the history of private enterprise was the $800 million write-off of Tristar aircraft development costs by Lockheed announced Nov 23, 1974.

Greatest Bankruptcy

William G. Stern (b Hungary, 1936), of Golders Green, north London, England, a US citizen since 1957, who set up Welstar Group Holding Co in the London property market in 1971, was declared bank-

LARGEST AIRPLANE MAKER: The Boeing Co in 1981 had sales of more than $9.7 billion and 96,000 workers. This is part of Boeing's plant in Seattle.

rupt for $229,480,345 in Feb 1979. His application to be discharged on an offer to pay $99,000 over 3 years was rejected by the Appeal Court as "impudent" in March 1982.

Advertising Agency

The largest advertising agency in 1981, as listed in *Advertising Age,* is Dentsu Inc of Japan with estimated total billings of $3,036 million.

Biggest Advertiser

The biggest advertiser is Sears Roebuck and Co with $633 million spent in 1981, excluding its catalogue.

Aircraft Manufacturer

The largest aircraft manufacturer is the Boeing Co of Seattle, Wash. The annual sales totaled $9,788.2 million in 1981, and it had 96,000 employees and assets valued at $6,953.7 million on Jan 1, 1982.

Cessna Aircraft Co of Wichita, Kans had total sales of $1,060,097,000 in 1981. The company has produced more than 171,500 aircraft since Clyde Cessna's first was built in 1911.

Largest Airlines

The largest airline is the USSR State airline "Aeroflot," so named since 1932. This was instituted on Feb 9, 1923, with the title of Civil Air Fleet of the Council of Ministers of the USSR, abbreviated to "Dobrolet." It operates 1,300 aircraft over about 560,000 miles of routes, employs 500,000 people and carried 106 million passengers to 97 countries in 1981. Most luggage is "self-handled," and smoking is allowed only after 4 hours flying.

The commercial airline carrying the greatest number of passengers was Eastern Airlines of Miami, Fla (formed 1928) with 35,515,000 passengers. The company had 37,700 employees and a fleet of 275 jet planes.

Oldest Airlines

The oldest existing national airline is Koninklijke-Luchtvaart-Maatschappij N.V. (KLM) of the Netherlands, which opened its first scheduled service (Amsterdam-London) on May 17, 1920, having been established Oct 7, 1919. One of the original constituents of B.O.A.C., Handley-Page Transport Ltd, was founded in May 1919, and merged into Imperial Airways in 1924. Delag (Deutsche Luftschiffahrt A.G.)

was founded at Frankfurt am Main Nov 16, 1909, and started a scheduled airship service in June 1910. Chalk's International Airline has been flying amphibians between Miami, Fla and the Bahamas since July 1919. Albert "Pappy" Chalk flew from 1911–75.

Aluminum Producer

The largest producer of primary aluminum is the Aluminum Company of America (Alcoa) of Pittsburgh, with its affiliated companies. The company had an output of 1,975,328 tons in 1981.

The Aluminum Company of Canada Ltd owns the largest aluminum smelter in the western world, at Arvida, Quebec, with a capacity of 475,000 tons per year. The parent company Alcan's total sales for the year 1981 were $4,978 million.

Art Auctioneering

The largest and oldest firm of art auctioneers is the Sotheby Parke Bernet Group of London and New York, founded in 1744. Their turnover in 1980–81 was $594,042,400. The highest total for any house sale auction was theirs on May 18–27, 1977, at the 6th Earl of Rosebery's home at Mentmore, Buckinghamshire, England, which reached £6,389,933 ($10,900,000). The government had turned down an offer of £2 million.

The highest total of any sale of fine art is $36 million for a collection ranging from medieval art to impressionist paintings from the estate of Baron Robert von Hirsch, in a 7-day auction conducted by Sotheby's in London from June 19–27, 1978.

Bookstores

The bookshop with the most titles and the longest shelving (30 miles of it) is W. & G. Foyle Ltd of London. First established in 1904 in a small shop in Islington, the company is now at 119–125 Charing Cross Road. On one site, the area is 75,825 sq ft.

The most capacious individual bookstore measured by square footage is Barnes & Noble Bookstore on Fifth Avenue at 18th Street, NYC, with 154,250 sq ft and 12.87 miles of shelving.

The largest second-hand booksellers are Richard Booth (Bookseller) Ltd, Hay-on-Wye, Powys, Wales, with 9.9 miles of shelving and a running stock of 900,000 to 1,100,000 in 30,091 sq ft of selling space.

Breweries

The oldest brewery is the Weihenstephan Brewery near Munich, W Germany, founded in 1040.

The largest single brewer is Anheuser-Busch Inc of St Louis. In 1981 the company sold 54.5 million barrels, the greatest annual volume ever produced by a brewing company. The company's St Louis plant covers 100 acres and after completion of current modernization projects will have an annual capacity in excess of 13 million barrels.

The largest brewery on a single site is Adolph Coors Co of Golden, Colo which sold 13.1 million barrels in 1981.

Arthur Guinness, Son & Co Ltd, founded in 1759, is the largest exporter of beer, ale and stout in the world. Exports of Guinness from the Republic of Ireland in the 52 weeks ending Mar 13, 1982, were 841,609 bulk barrels (1 bulk barrel = 36 Imperial gallons) which is equivalent to 1,331,777 British half-pint glasses per day. The main brewery extends over 56.15 acres at St James's Gate, Dublin, Ireland, the largest in Europe.

Brickworks

The largest brickworks is the London Brick Co plant at Stewartby, Bedfordshire, England. The works, established in 1898, now cover 221 acres and have a production capacity of 13 million bricks and brick equivalent every week.

Car Manufacturer

In 1980, Japan with 11,043,000 vehicles overtook the US as the world's no. 1 motor car manufacturer.

The largest car manufacturer is General Motors Corp of Detroit. During the year 1981, worldwide sales totaled $62,698,500,000. Its assets on Dec 31, 1981, were valued at $13,716,100,000. Its total 1981 payroll was $19,257 million to an average of 741,000 employees. Dividends paid in 1980 were $1,874.1 million.

The largest single automobile plant is the Volkswagenwerk, Wolfsburg, W Germany, with 59,000 employees and a capacity of about 4,000 vehicles daily. The surface area of the factory buildings is 368 acres and that of the whole plant, with 43.5 miles of rail sidings, is 4,895 acres.

Greatest Car Salesman

The all-time record for automobile salesmanship in individual units sold is 1,425 in 1973, by Joe Girard of Detroit, author of "How to Sell Anything to Anybody" and winner of the Number One Car Salesman title every year from 1966 to 1977. His lifetime total of one-at-a-time "belly to belly" selling

FIRST 5 & 10: Frank W. Woolworth got a big start in this shop in Lancaster, Pa.

was 13,001 units sold, all retail. He retired Jan 1, 1978 to teach others his art and to write books on selling.

Chain Store

F. W. Woolworth, which celebrated its centenary year in 1979, now operates the largest chain—6,927 stores worldwide. Frank W. Woolworth, with an idea that he could sell merchandise for a nickel, rented a counter in an already existent Watertown, NY, general store in 1878. Then he opened his first "Five Cent Store" in Utica, NY on Feb 22, 1879. This failed after 6 months. Next he opened a "Five Cent Store" in Lancaster, Pa, which soon became a "5-&-10-Cent" store. This succeeded. The 1981–82 earnings of the company amounted to $82 million.

Chocolate Factory

The largest chocolate and confectionary factory is that built by Hershey Foods Corp of Hershey, Pa in 1903–05. It now has 2 million sq ft of floor space.

Computer Company

The largest computer firm is International Business Machines Corp (IBM) which resisted from 1969 the Justice Dept's largest antitrust suit. This was withdrawn on Jan 8, 1982, as "without merit." In 1981, assets were $29,586 million, with sales of $29,070 million. In Oct 1979 it made the largest public borrowing in corporate history with $1 billion.

Largest Single Department Store

The largest store is R. H. Macy & Co Inc at Broadway and 34th St, NYC. It has a floor space of 50.5 acres, and 12,000 employees who handle 400,000 items. The sales of the company and its subsidiaries totaled $2,656,689,000 in 1981. Mr. Rowland Hussey Macy's sales on his first day at his fancy goods store on 6th Avenue, Oct 27, 1858, were recorded as $11.06.

The department store with the fastest-moving stock is the Marble Arch premier store of Marks & Spencer Ltd at 458 Oxford Street, London. The figure of more than £900 ($1,620) worth of goods per sq ft of selling space (total 90,400 sq ft) per year is believed to be an understatement. The company has 257 branches in the UK and over 6 million sq ft of

LARGE ON CHOCOLATE CANDY: The town of Hershey, Pa, is built around the cocoa factory, founded in 1903.

LARGEST DEPARTMENT STORE: It looks empty now, but when this Marks & Spencer store in London is open, sales are greater per sq ft than anywhere else in the world.

selling space. It now has stores in Continental Europe and Canada.

Distillery

The largest distilling company is The Seagram Company Ltd of Canada. Its sales in the year ending July 31, 1981, totaled $2,772,733,000, of which $2,237,189,000 were from sales by Joseph E. Seagram & Sons Inc in the US. The group employs about 16,000 people, including about 11,000 in the US.

Largest of all Scotch whisky distilleries is Carsebridge at Alloa, Central Region, Scotland, owned by Scottish Grain Distillers Ltd. This distillery is capable of producing more than 9 million gallons of alcohol per year. The largest establishment for blending and bottling Scotch whisky is owned by John Walker & Sons Ltd at Kilmarnock, Strathclyde, where over 3 million bottles are filled each week. "Johnnie Walker" is the world's largest-selling brand of Scotch whisky. The largest malt Scotch whisky distillery is the Tomatin Distillery, Highland, Scotland, established at 1,028 ft above sea level in 1897, with an annual capacity of 5 million proof gallons. The world's largest-selling brand of gin is Gordon's.

Drug Store Chain

The largest chain is that of Boots The Chemists, which has 1,083 retail branches. The firm was founded in England by Jesse Boot (1850–1931), the 1st Baron Trent.

Fisheries

The highest recorded catch of fish was 72,434,000 tons in 1973. Peru had the largest ever national haul with 13,406,000 tons in 1970, comprising mostly anchoveta. The largest net manufactured is one that can fish 8,800,000 cu yd per hour, announced in W Germany in March 1974.

General Merchandise at Retail

The largest general merchandising retailer is Sears Roebuck and Co of Chicago (founded by Richard Warren Sears in the North Redwood railroad station in Minnesota in 1886). Worldwide revenues were $27,357 million in the year ending Dec 31, 1981, when the corporation had 851 retail stores and 1,227 catalogue, retail and telephone sales offices and 1,527 independent catalogue merchants in the US, and total assets valued at $34,509 million.

Grocery Store Chain

The largest grocery chain is Safeway Stores Inc of Oakland, Calif with sales in 1981 amounting to $16,580,318,000 and total current assets valued at $1,464,203,000 as of Jan 2, 1982. The company has 2,477 stores totaling 65,483,000 sq ft. The total payroll covers 157,411 people.

Hotels

The top revenue-earning hotel business is Holiday Inns Inc with 1981 revenues of $4.3 billion from 1,750 hotels (310,000 rooms) in 57 countries at Dec 31, 1981. The business was founded by Charles Kemmons Wilson with his first inn on Summer Avenue in Memphis, Tenn in 1952.

Insurance

The largest life insurance policy ever written was one for $44 million for a Calgary land developer, revealed in Feb 1982 by Transamerica Occidental Life Insurance Co of California. The salesman was local manager Lorenzo F. Reyes.

Linda Mullendore, wife of a murdered Oklahoma rancher, received some $18 million as of Nov 14, 1970, the largest pay-out on a single life. Her husband had paid $300,000 in premiums in 1969.

Insurance Companies and Losses

It was estimated in 1978 that the total premiums paid in the US had surpassed $100 billion or $1,400 per household.

The company with the highest volume of insurance in force is the Prudential Insurance Co of America, Newark, NJ, with $465,175 million as of Dec 31, 1981. The admitted assets are $62,499 million.

The largest single association is the Blue Cross, the medical insurance organization, with a membership of 83,187,312 on Jan 1, 1980. Benefits paid out in 1979 totaled $17,575,807,000.

The largest marine insurance loss ever was the 153,480 grt VLCC (Very Large Crude Carrier) *Energy Determination,* insured at Lloyd's of London and valued at £26.8 million ($59 million), which exploded in the Strait of Hormuz, Dec 12, 1979. The 83,000 grt LNG (Liquid Natural Gas) Carrier *Aquarius,* built in 1977 by General Dynamics Co, is currently insured for $175 million. This vessel is owned by Wilmington Trust Co, Delaware, and chartered to the Burmah Oil Co Ltd.

The largest sum claimed for consequential losses is $1,700 million against owning, operating and building corporations, and Claude Phillips resulting from the 66-million-gallon oil spill from M. T. *Amoco Cadiz* on the Brittany Coast on Mar 16, 1978.

A claim for $300 million was provisionally agreed to by Lloyd's on July 31, 1980 in connection with alleged structural defects in three liquefied natural gas carriers being built for El Paso Natural Gas at Avondale Shipyards, New Orleans, La.

Mineral Water

The world's largest mineral water firm is Source Perrier near Nîmes, France with an annual production of more than 2.1 billion bottles, of which 1.2 billion now come from Perrier and Contrexéville. The French drink 50 liters (106 pints) of mineral water per person per year.

Oil Companies and Refinery

The world's largest oil company is the Exxon Corp (formerly Standard Oil Co), with 180,000 employees and assets valued at $62,931,055,000 on Jan 1, 1982.

The least successful oil company is Magellan Petroleum Corp (founded 1957) which in 1981 marked its 23rd consecutive year without a dividend. The micawberesque shareholders complained that accumulated losses had then reached $15 million.

The world's largest refinery has been the Amerada Hess refinery at St Croix, Virgin Islands, with an annual capacity of 37,475,200 tons.

Paper Mill

The largest paper mill is that established in 1936 by the Union Camp Corp at Savannah, Ga, with an all-time record output in 1980 of 1,038,656 tons.

Pharmaceutical Company

The largest company marketing pharmaceuticals and one of the 3 largest chemical companies is Hoechst of W Germany, with a turnover DM 34,432 million ($13,772.8 million) in 1981.

Photographic Store

The photographic store with the largest selling area is Jessop of Leicester Ltd's Photo Centre,

Hinckley Road, Leicester, England which opened in June 1979 with an area of 27,000 sq ft.

Popcorn Plant

The largest popcorn plant is The House of Clarks Ltd of Dagenham, Barking, England (instituted in 1933), which in 1980–81 produced 60 million packets of popcorn.

Public Relations

The largest public relations firm is Hill and Knowlton Inc of 420 Lexington Avenue, NYC, and sixteen other North American cities. The firm employs a full-time staff of more than 1,000 and also maintains offices in 27 cities overseas.

The world's pioneer public relations publication is *Public Relations News,* founded by Mrs Denny Griswold in 1944. It now has readers in 86 countries.

Publishing

The publishing company generating most net revenue is Time Inc of NYC, with $3,296 million in 1981. The largest educational book publishing concern in the world is the Book Division of McGraw-Hill Inc of NYC, with sales of $377,703,000 in 1981. The company published 1,164 new titles.

Restaurant Chain

The largest restaurant chain is McDonald's Corp in Oakbrook, Ill, founded Apr 15, 1955, in Des Plaines, a suburb of Chicago, by Ray A. Kroc, BH (Bachelor of Hamburgerology). By Jan 1, 1982, the number of restaurants licensed and owned in 29 countries and 3 US territories reached 6,753 with an aggregate output of 40 billion 100% beef hamburgers. Sales systemwide in 1981 were $7,128,602,000.

Shipbuilding

In 1981, there were 16,931,719 tons gross of ships, excluding sailing ships, barges, and vessels of less than 100 tons, completed throughout the world. The figures for Rumania and the People's Republic of China are incomplete. Japan completed 8,399,831 tons gross (49.61% of the world's total).

The leading shipbuilding firm in 1981 was the Mitsubishi Heavy Industries Co of Japan, which launched 29 merchant ships totaling 1,013,318 tons gross.

RESTAURANT SCHOOL: Hamburger U or Moo U in Elk Grove Village, Ill, is owned and operated by McDonald's, the world's largest chain of restaurants, with 6,753 stores. The students (2,000 at a time) learn everything about fast-food cooking, serving and management, so they can get Golden Chef's hats.

Shipping Line

The largest shipping owners and operators are the Exxon Corporation (see *Oil Companies and Refinery*) whose fleets of owned/managed and chartered tankers in 1981 totaled a daily average of 23.47 million deadweight tons.

Shopping Centers

The largest shopping center is the Del Amo Fashion Center, Torrance, Calif, with 2,542,199 sq ft or 58.36 acres under one roof. It was opened in Oct 1981.

The world's first shopping center was Roland Park Shopping Center in Baltimore, Md, built in 1896.

The world's largest wholesale merchandise market is the Dallas Market Center, located on Stemmons Freeway, Dallas, Tex, with more than 7 million sq ft in 6 buildings. The complex covers 135 acres with some 3,200 permanent showrooms displaying merchandise of more than 22,000 manufacturers. The center attracts 600,000 buyers each year to its 30 annual markets and trade shows.

Soft Drink Producer

The world's most profitable soft drink is Coca-Cola with over 250 million sold per day by the end of 1981 in more than 147 countries. "Coke" was invented by Dr John S. Pemberton of Atlanta, Ga in 1886, the company was formed in 1892, and its famous bottle was patented in 1915.

Steel Company

The largest producer of steel has been Nippon Steel of Tokyo, which produced 33,208,000 tons of steel and steel products in 1981. The Fukuyama Works of Nippon Kokan has a capacity of almost 18 million tons per annum. Its work force is 76,000.

Sugar Mill

The highest recorded output for any sugar mill was set in 1966–67 by Ingenio de San Cristobal y Anexas, S.A. of Veracruz, Mexico, with 273,310 tons refined from 3,181,897 metric tons of cane ground.

Tobacco Company

The largest tobacco company is the group of subsidiaries and affiliates of the British-American Tobacco Co Ltd (founded in London in 1902). These subsidiaries and affiliates operate 120 tobacco factories in 52 countries. Consolidated turnover in 1981 was $16,677 million and total assets were $8,978.4 million on Dec 31, 1981. The Group's sales in 1980 topped 560,000 million cigarettes.

The largest cigarette plant is the $300 million Philip Morris plant at Richmond, Va, which opened in Oct 1974. It employs 5,500 people producing 530 million cigarettes a day.

Toy Manufacturer

The largest single toy manufacturer is Mattel Inc of Hawthorne, Calif, founded in 1945. Its total sales in the year ending Jan 30, 1981 were $1,134,252,000 for 3 divisions, of which Mattel Toys is the largest.

Toy Store

The biggest toy store is Hamley's of Regent Street Ltd, founded in London in 1760 in the Holborn area, and moved to Regent Street in 1901. It has selling space of 45,000 sq ft on 6 floors with over 300 employees during the Christmas season. It was taken over by Debenhams on May 12, 1976.

Undertaker (or Mortician)

The world's largest undertaking business is the SCI (Service Corporation International) with 289 funeral homes and 51 cemeteries with associated limousine fleets and flower shops. Their annual revenue in the most recession-proof of industries was $180 million in 1981.

Vintners

The oldest champagne firm is Ruinart Père et Fils, founded in 1729. The oldest cognac firm is Augier Frères & Cie, established in 1643.

LAND

The world's largest landowner is the United States Government, with a holding of 769,863,000 acres (1,203,000 sq mi), which is nearly the area of India, and 12.8 times larger than the UK. The world's largest private landowner is reputed to be International Paper Co, with 9 million acres.

Land Values

Currently the most expensive land is in Kowloon, Hong Kong. In Aug 1981 the Carrian Group bought the 85,000-sq-ft Miramer Hotel site for $473.4 million or $5,569 per sq ft.

The price for a grave site with excellent *Fung Shui* in Hong Kong may cost HK $200,000 (US $33,800) for a 4 × 10 ft plot. The China Square Inch Land Ltd at a charity auction on Dec 2, 1977 sold 1 sq cm (0.155 sq in) of land at Sha Tau Kok for HK $2,000 (the equivalent of US $17,405,833,737 per acre).

The real estate value per square meter of the two topmost French vineyards, the Grande and Petite Cognac vineyards in Bordeaux, has not been recently estimated.

Greatest Land Auction

The greatest auction ever was that at Anchorage, Alaska, on Sept 11, 1969, for 179 tracts of 450,858 acres of the oil-bearing North Slope, Alaska. An all-time record bid of $72,277,133 for a 2,560-acre lease was made by the Amerada Hess Corporation-Getty Oil consortium. The bid indicated a price of $28,233 per acre.

New York Stock Exchange (NYSE) Records

The highest index figure on the Dow Jones average (instituted Oct 1896) of selected industrial stocks at the close of a day's trading was 1,051.70 on Jan 11, 1973, when the average of the daily "highs" of the 30 component stocks was 1,067.20.

The record for a day's trading is 92,881,420 shares on Jan 7, 1981. The old record trading volume in a day on the NYSE of 16,410,030 shares on Oct 29, 1929, the "Black Tuesday" of the famous "crash," was not surpassed until the first 20-million-share day (20,410,000) was achieved on Apr 10, 1968, when the ticker tape fell 47 minutes behind.

The Dow Jones industrial average, which had hit a low of 381.71 on Sept 3, 1929, plunged 30.57 points on Oct 29, 1929, on its way to the Depression's lowest point of 41.22 on July 8, 1932. The largest decline in one day, 38.33 points, occurred on Oct 28, 1929. The total lost in security values from Sept 1, 1929 to June 30, 1932 was $74 billion.

The greatest paper loss in NYSE listed securities in a year was $209,957 million in 1974.

The record-setting daily increase of 28.40 on Oct 30, 1929, was most recently bettered on Nov 1, 1978, when the Dow Jones index increased 35.34 points to 827.79.

The largest transaction on record "share-wise" was on March 14, 1972, for 5,245,000 shares of American Motors at $7.25 each.

The largest stock trade in the history of the NYSE was a 1,874,300-share block of Cutler-Hammer stock at $55 per share in a $103,086,500 transaction on June 12, 1978.

The highest price paid in a transaction for a seat on the NYSE was $625,000 in 1929. The lowest 20th century price was $17,000 in 1942.

The value of stocks listed on the NYSE reached an all-time high on Nov 30, 1980.

Highest and Lowest Rent

The highest rentals in the world for prime sites, according to *World Rental Levels* by Richard Ellis, a London-based real estate and consulting firm, are in Hong Kong at $60.90 per sq ft, just ahead of Manhattan, NYC, at $60 and London at $54.

The rent for a 3-room apartment in the Fuggerei in Augsburg, W Germany, since it was built by Jacob Fugger in 1519, has been 1 Rhine guilder (now DM 1.72 or less than $1) per month. Fugger was the extremely wealthy philanthropist who pioneered social welfare.

FINANCE

The oldest Stock Exchange of the 138 listed in the world is that in Amsterdam, in the Netherlands, founded in 1602.

Highest Value Stock

The highest price quoted was for a share of F. Hoffmann-La Roche of Basel, Switzerland, was 101,000 Swiss Fr (then $38,486) on Apr 23, 1976.

Largest New Issue

The largest security offering in history was one of $1,375 million in American Telephone and Telegraph Co stock in a rights offer on 27,500,000 shares of convertible preferred stock on June 2, 1971.

Largest Equity

The greatest aggregate market value of any corporation is $48 billion, given the closing price of 58⅞ on Dec 31, 1981, for AT&T, multiplied by the 815,107,000 shares outstanding.

Largest Investment House

The largest investment company in the US, and once the world's largest partnership (124 partners before becoming a corporation in 1959), is Merrill Lynch, Pierce, Fenner & Smith, Inc of NYC (founded Jan 6, 1914). Its parent, Merrill Lynch, has assets of $17 billion, 35,000 employees, 540 offices, and 3 million separate accounts.

Largest Bank

The International Bank for Reconstruction and Development (founded Dec 27, 1945), the "World Bank" (a UN specialized agency) at 1818 H Street NW, Wash, DC, has an authorized share capital of $81.1 billion. There were 139 members with a subscribed capital of $36,614 million on June 30, 1981. The International Monetary Fund in Wash, DC, had 145 members with total quotas of SDR60,684.8 million ($67,547.6 million) on March 31, 1982.

The private commercial bank with the greatest deposits is the Bank of America National Trust and Savings Association, of San Francisco, Calif, with $94,369,453,000 on Dec 31, 1981. Its total assets on that date were $121,158,350,000.

The bank with the most branches is The State Bank of India with 8,810 on Jan 1, 1982, with assets of $19,375,200,000.

Largest Bank Building

The tallest bank building is the Bank of Montreal's First Bank Tower, Toronto, which has 72 stories and stands 935 ft high. The largest bank vault, measuring 350 × 100 × 8 ft and weighing 984 tons, is in the Chase Manhattan Building, New York City, completed in May 1961. Its six doors weigh up to 44.7 tons apiece, but each can be closed by the pressure of a forefinger.

CENTER OF FINANCE: The floor of the NY Stock Exchange. This building probably has more telephones per sq ft than any other. (Edward C. Topple/NYSE)

Antique

The largest antique ever sold has been the London Bridge in March 1968. The sale was made by Ivan F. Luckin of the Court of Common Council of the Corporation of London to the McCulloch Oil Corp of Los Angeles for $2,460,000. Over 10,000 tons of facade stonework were reassembled at a cost of $6.9 million at Lake Havasu City, Ariz, and "rededicated" Oct 10, 1971.

Armor

The highest auction price paid for a suit of armor is $752,400 paid on Nov 18, 1981, for the suit ordered by Henry, Prince of Wales, made at Greenwich in 1610–13 by William Pickering for Frederic Ulric, Duke of Brunswick.

The armor of William Somerset, 3rd Earl of Worcester, made at the Royal Workshop, Green-wich, England *c.* 1570, weighed 81 lb 9 oz. If his five bullet-proof exchange elements were substituted the total weight would reach 133 lb 13 oz.

Art Nouveau

The highest auction price paid for any piece of art nouveau is $360,000 for a spider-web leaded glass mosaic and bronze table lamp made by L. C. Tiffany, sold at Christie's, NYC, Apr 8, 1980. (For other artwork, see *Jewels*.)

Beds

In Bruges, Belgium, Philip, Duke of Burgundy, had a bed 12½ ft wide and 19 ft long erected for the perfunctory *coucher officiel* ceremony with Princess Isabella of Portugal in 1430. The largest bed in exis-

LARGEST ANTIQUE EVER SOLD: The nursery rhyme predicted that London Bridge would fall down, but no one ever expected it would be sold—and to Lake Havasu City, Ariz! Yet that is exactly what happened. The bridge was taken apart in London, shipped, and reassembled in 1971. This was the opening day celebration.

LARGEST BLANKET (right): Pieced together from 20,160 knitted squares, this covered 68 × 100 ft.

tencc is the Great Bed of Ware, dating from *c.* 1580, from the Crown Inn, Ware, Hertfordshire, England, now preserved in the Victoria and Albert Museum, London. It is 10 ft 8½ in wide, 11 ft 1 in long and 8 ft 9 in tall.

The heaviest bed is a waterbed 9 ft 7 in wide and 9 ft 10 in long, owned by Milan Vacek of Canyon Country, Calif, since 1977. The thermostatically heated water alone weighs 4,205 lb.

Beer Cans and Coasters

Beer cans date from a test marketing by Krueger Beer of Richmond, Va, in 1935. The largest collection is claimed by John F. Ahrens of Mt Laurel, NJ, with over 13,000 *different* cans. A Rosalie Pilsner can sold for $6,000 in the US in Apr 1981.

The largest collection of beer coasters (or mats) is owned by Leo Pisker of Vienna, who had collected nearly 89,000 different coasters from 146 countries by Apr 1982.

Bird

The highest price ever paid for a stuffed bird is £9,000 ($23,400 at the time). This was on March 4, 1971 in the salesrooms of Sotheby's, London, by the Iceland Natural History Museum for a specimen of the Great Auk (*Alca impennis*) in summer plumage, which was taken in Iceland *c.* 1821. This particular specimen stood 22½ in high. The Great Auk was a flightless North Atlantic seabird, which was finally exterminated in Eldey, Iceland in 1844, becoming extinct through hunting.

Blankets

The largest blanket ever made measured 68 × 100 ft and weighed 600 lb. It was knitted in 20,160 6-in squares in 10 months (Oct 1977–July 1978) by the English *Woman's Weekly* readers for Action Research for The Crippled Child.

The most expensive blanket was a Navajo bayeta serape sold for $59,400 at Sotheby's in May 1981.

Candle

A candle 80 ft high and 8½ ft in diameter was exhibited at the 1897 Stockholm Exhibition by the firm of Lindahls. The overall height was 127 ft.

Carpets and Rugs

The earliest carpet known (and still in existence) is a woolen pile-knotted carpet, red on a white ground, excavated at Pazyryk, USSR in 1947 and dated to the 5th century BC, and now preserved in Leningrad.

Of ancient carpets the largest on record was the gold-enriched silk carpet of Hashim (dated 743 AD) of the Abbasid caliphate in Baghdad, Iraq. It is reputed to have measured 180 × 300 ft.

A 52,225-sq-ft (or 1.23-acre) 28-ton red carpet was laid along the Avenue of the Americas from Radio City Music Hall to the NY Hilton Feb 13, 1982, by the Allied Corp for the "Night of 100 Stars" show in NYC.

BIGGEST RED CARPET (below): More than 100 celebrities came for the "Night of 100 Stars" at the Radio City Music Hall on Feb 14, 1982. They used this 1,000-ft-long carpet to get to the Actors' Fund Ball 3 blocks away.

The most magnificent carpet ever made was the Spring carpet of Khusraw made for the audience hall of the Sassanian palace at Ctesiphon, Iraq. It was about 7,000 sq ft of silk and gold thread, encrusted with emeralds. It was cut up as booty by military looters in 635 AD and from the known realization value of the pieces must have had an original value of some $2,400 million.

In 1946 the Metropolitan Museum of Art, NYC privately paid $1 million for the 26.5 × 13.6 ft Anholt Medallion carpet made in Tabriz or Kashan, Persia, c. 1590. The highest price ever paid at auction for a carpet is $229,900 for a Mamluk carpet 12 ft 5 in × 7 ft 3 in, presumed woven in Cairo c. 1500 and sold at Sotheby's, London March 29, 1978.

The most finely woven carpet known is one with more than 2,490 knots per sq in from a fragment of an Imperial Mughal prayer carpet of the 17th century, now in the Altman collections in the Metropolitan Museum of Art, NYC.

Ceramics

The Greek urn thrown by Euxitheos and painted by Ueuphromios in c. 530 BC was bought by private treaty by the Metropolitan Museum of Art, NYC, for $1.3 million in Aug 1972.

Chair

The world's largest chair is the 2,000-lb, 33-ft-1-in-high, 19-ft-7-in-wide chair constructed by Anniston Steel & Plumbing Co, Inc for Miller's Office Furniture in Anniston, Ala, and completed in May 1981.

The highest price ever paid for a single chair is $85,000 for the John Brown Chippendale mahogany corner chair attributed to John Goddard of Newport, RI, and made c. 1760. This piece was included in the Landsdell K. Christie collection dispersed by Sotheby Parke Bernet, NYC, Oct 21, 1972.

Chandelier

The largest chandelier was built in Murano, Italy in 1953 for the Casino Knokke, Belgium. It measures 26 ft 3 in in circumference and 23 ft in height, and weighs 40.7 tons with 1,896 electric lights.

Cigars

The largest smokeable cigar ever made measures 12½ ft, taking 315 man hours and using 1,503 full to-bacco leaves. It was made by the Cuban-born Garcia brothers of Las Palmas, Canary Islands.

The largest marketed cigar in the world is the 14-in Valdez Emperado by San Andres Cigars.

Joseph Hruby of Lyndhurst, Ohio, has the largest known collection of cigar bands with 165,480 examples, dating from c. 1895.

The most expensive standard cigar in the world is the Montecristo "A," which retails in Great Britain at a suggested £9.75 ($17.50).

Cigarettes

The heaviest smokers in the world are the people of the US where about 665 billion cigarettes (an average of 3,900 per adult) were consumed at a cost of some $15 billion in 1978. The people of China, however, were estimated to consume 725 billion in 1977.

The world's most popular cigarette is "Marlboro," a filter cigarette made by Philip Morris, which sold 234.46 billion units in 1981.

The longest cigarettes ever marketed were "Head Plays," each 11 in long and sold in packets of 5 in the US in about 1930, to save tax. The shortest were "Lilliput" cigarettes, each 1¼ in long and ⅛ in in diameter, made in Great Britain in 1956.

The world's largest collection of cigarettes is that of Robert E. Kaufman, MD, of NYC. In Apr 1982, he had 7,580 different brands of cigarettes with 43 kinds of tips made in 172 countries. The oldest brand represented is "Lone Jack," made in the US c. 1885. Both the longest and shortest are represented.

Cigarette Cards

The earliest known tobacco card is "Vanity Fair" dated 1876 issued by Wm S. Kimball & Co of Rochester, NY. The largest known collection is that of Edward Wharton-Tigar (b 1913) of London with a collection of more than 1 million cigarette and trade cards in about 45,000 sets.

The highest price ever paid for a cigarette card was $3,500 in 1975 for one of the 6 known baseball cards of Honus Wagner. Wagner was a non-smoker.

Cigarette Lighter

The most expensive pocket cigarette lighter is the 18-carat white gold Dunhill Gemline lighter, set with a 2.57-ct VSG-color emerald-cut diamond with an additional 8.37 ct worth of brilliant-cut diamonds of VSH color, which was selling for £32,500 ($58,500) at Dunhill's in St James's London, in 1981.

Cigarette Packs

The earliest surviving cigarette pack is the Finnish "Petit Canon" packet for 25, made by Tollander & Klärich in 1860, from the Ventegodt Collection. The rarest is the Latvian 700-year anniversary (1201–1901) Riga packet, believed to be unique, from the same collection.

The largest verified private collection of packets is one of 60,955, from over 150 countries owned by Vernon Young of Farnham, England.

Cloth

The most expensive of all cloths is Shatoosh (or Shatusa), a brown-gray wool from the throat hair of Indian goats. It is more expensive than vicuña and was sold by Neiman-Marcus of Dallas at $1,000 per yard, but supplies have now dried up. (Also see *Fabrics*.)

Credit Card Collection

The largest collection of valid credit cards, as of May 1, 1982, is one of 1,122, all different, by Walter Cavanagh (b 1943) of Santa Clara, Calif (known as "Mr Plastic Fantastic"). The cost of acquisition was nil, and he keeps them in the world's longest wallet, 250 ft long, weighing 35 lb and worth more than $1.25 million in credit.

Curtain

The largest ever built was the bright orange-red 4½-ton 185-ft-high curtain suspended 1,350 ft above and across the Rifle Gap, Grand Hogback, Colo, by the Bulgarian-born sculptor Christo (*né* Javacheff), 36, on Aug 10, 1971. It blew apart in a 50-mph gust of wind 27 hours later. The total cost of displaying this work of art was $750,000.

The world's largest functional curtain is one 550 ft long × 65 ft high in the Brabazon Hangar at British Aerospace, Filton, Bristol, used to enclose aircraft in the paint-spraying bay. It is electrically drawn.

Dolls

The highest price paid at auction for dolls was £16,000 ($36,800) for a pair of William and Mary painted wooden dolls in original clothes 22 in high at Sotheby's, London, Apr 19, 1974. After an export license was refused, they were purchased, after a public subscription, by the Victoria and Albert Museum, London.

A rag doll 27 ft long and properly proportioned was made at Macy's NY "Clowning Around Day" on Aug 26, 1979 and presented for exhibition to the Guinness Museum in the Empire State Building, NYC.

Dress

The dress with the highest price tag ever exhibited was one designed by Serge Lepage, and exhibited in the Schiaparelli spring/summer collection in Paris on Jan 23, 1977. Called "The Birth of Venus" and studded with 512 diamonds, it carried a record price tag of 7.5 million francs (then $1.5 million).

Emperor Field Marshal Jean-Bédel Bokassa's coronation robe, with a 39-ft-long train, was encrusted with 785,000 pearls and 1,220,000 crystal beads by Guiselin of Paris for $144,500 for use at Bangui, Central African Empire in Dec 1977.

A platinum bikini valued at $9,500 was made by Mappin and Webb Jewelers, London. It was worn by Miss United Kingdom in the 1977 Miss World beauty pageant.

Fabrics

The oldest surviving fabric discovered from Level VI A at Çátal Hüyük, Turkey, has been radio-carbon dated to 5900 BC.

The most expensive fabric obtainable is an evening-wear fabric 37½ in wide, hand embroidered, sequinned and pearl-beaded in a series of designs on pure silk grounds. One design has as many as 29,900 tiny sequins and pearls per sq yd, and is designed by Alan Hershman of London; it cost $522 per meter in Apr 1982. (Also see *Cloth*.)

Fireworks

The largest firework ever produced was *Fat Man II*, made by NY Pyrotechnic Products Inc, fired near Titusville, Fla, Oct 22, 1977. The 720-lb shell was 40½ in in diameter.

Flags

The oldest known flag is one dating to *c.* 500 BC, found in the excavations of the princesses groves in Hunan, Changsha, China. The Friesian flag still flown in the Netherlands dates from the 9th century AD. The study of flags is known as vexillology.

The largest flag made, "The Great American Flag," was displayed in Evansville, Ind on March 22,

1980 (later, in front of the Washington Monument in Washington, DC). It weighs 7.7 tons and measures 411 × 210 ft. The flag now sits in storage, waiting until enough money can be raised for it to be permanently installed on the Verrazano-Narrows Bridge, NYC, where it will be unfurled on appropriate holidays. The project is the brainchild of Len Silverfine, whose previous attempt was a flag nearly as big which was torn apart after a few hours during a test hanging on June 28, 1976.

Floats

The largest float is the 150-ft-long, 22-ft-wide "Agree" Float, bearing 51 All-American Homecoming Queens, used at the Orange Bowl parade, Miami, Fla, Dec 29, 1977.

Furniture

The highest price ever paid for a single piece of furniture is 7,600,000 francs ($1,700,000) by the J. Paul Getty Museum in Malibu, Calif for a 10-ft-high marquetry and ormolu Louis XV corner cabinet made by Dubois, sold at Sotheby Parke Bernet, Monte Carlo, June 25, 1979.

The largest item of furniture is the wooden bench in Green Park, Obiharo, Hokkaido, Japan, which seats 1,282 people and measures 1,321 ft 4 in long. It was completed by a team of 770 on July 19, 1981.

The largest marketed sofa is the King Talmage Sofa, 12 ft 2 in in length, made by Talmageville Furniture manufacturers in California.

Glass

The most priceless example of the art of glassmaking is usually regarded as the Portland Vase which dates from late in the 1st century BC or 1st century AD. It was made in Italy and was in the possession of the Barberini family in Rome from at least 1642. It was eventually bought by the Duchess of Portland in 1792, but smashed while in the British Museum in 1847.

An auction record was set at Sotheby's, London, June 4, 1979, when a Roman cage cup of *c*. 300 AD measuring 7 in in diameter and 4 in in height was sold to Robin Symes for £520,000 ($1,040,000).

The thinnest glass made is 1/85th of an inch thick for digital displays by Nippon Glass Corp.

Gold Plate

The highest auction price for a single piece of gold plate is £66,000 (then $122,000) for an English George III salver, known as "The Rutland Salver,"

LARGEST FLAG: Built to fly on the Verrazano Bridge, this banner temporarily rested on the lawn near the Washington Monument in 1981.

made by Paul Storr of London in 1801, and sold by Sotheby Parke Bernet, London, on May 4, 1978. The salver, which is 12 in in diameter, is engraved with the arms of Manners, Dukes of Rutland and of the 16 towns and cities, the gold Freedom boxes of which were melted down to make the salver.

The gold coffin of the 14th century BC Pharaoh Tutankhamun, discovered by Howard Carter on Feb 16, 1923, in Luxor, western Thebes, Egypt, weighed 243 lb.

Gun

The highest price ever paid for a single gun is £125,000 ($312,500) given by the London dealers, F. Partridge, for a French flintlock fowling piece made for Louis XIII, King of France, *c*. 1615 and attributed to Pierre le Bourgeoys (d 1627) of Lisieux, France. This piece, now in the Metropolitan Museum of Art, NYC, was included in the collection of the late William Goodwin Renwick (US) sold by Sotheby's, London, Nov 21, 1972. (Also see *Pistols*.)

Hat

The highest price ever paid for a hat is 165,570 francs (including tax) ($29,471) by Moët et Chandon, a champagne house, at an auction by Maîtres Liery, Rheims et Laurin, France on Apr 23, 1970, for one last worn by Emperor Napoleon I (1769–1821) on Jan 1, 1815.

Icon

The record price for an icon is $150,000, paid at Christie's, NYC, Apr 17, 1980 for the *Last Judgement* (from the George R. Hann collection, Pittsburgh) made in Novgorod, Russia, in the 16th century.

Jade

The highest price ever paid for an item in jade is 1,250,000 Swiss francs ($390,625) for a necklace set with 31 graduated beads of Imperial green jade. This was sold by Christie's at the Hotel Richmond, Geneva, Switzerland May 9, 1973. The highest price paid for jade objects is HK $1.4 million ($297,000 US) for a pair of 19th century green jadeite table screens 17¼ in in height sold by Sotheby's in Hong Kong Nov 2, 1976.

Jewels

The highest auction price paid for any jewels (or any work of art) is $6½ million approximately (with the buyer's premium, over $7 million) for two pear-shaped diamond drop earrings of 58.6 and 61 carats at Sotheby's, Geneva, Switzerland, Nov 14, 1980. Neither the buyer nor seller was disclosed.

Jig-Saw Puzzles

The largest jig-saw ever made is one 50 ft 9¾ in × 50 ft 5¾ in with 10,201 pieces by Richard & Roger Meade unveiled at East Wilkes High School, NC, July 26, 1980. Gimbels, NYC, sold in 1933 a Ringling Barnum Circus Puzzle 8½ × 13 ft weighing 597 lb with 50,000 pieces made by Eureka Jig Saw Puzzle Co of Philadelphia. The earliest jig-saws were made as "dissected maps" by John Spilsbury (1739–69) in Russell Court off Drury Lane, London, England, *c.* 1762.

Knife

The penknife with the greatest number of blades is the Year Knife made by the cutlers Joseph Rodgers & Sons Ltd, of Sheffield, England, whose trademark was granted in 1682. The knife was built in 1822 with 1,822 blades, and was designed to match the year of the Christian era until 2000 AD, but had to halt at

2,000-YEAR KNIFE was made to hold 2,000 blades, after a short halt at 1,973.

1,973 because there was no more space for blades. Now a way has been found to add blades to 2,000.

Matchbox Labels

Collectors of labels are phillumenists. The oldest match label of accepted provenance is that of Samuel Jones *c.* 1830. The finest collection of trademark labels (excluding any bar or other advertising labels) is some 280,000 pieces collected by Robert Jones of Indianapolis. Under less rigorous standards, the world's foremost phillumenist would be Teiichi Yoshizawa (b 1904) of Chiba, Japan, who since 1924 has amassed 577,087 pieces and advertising labels from over 100 countries.

Nylon

The lowest denier nylon yarn ever produced is the 6 denier used for stockings exhibited at the Nylon Fair in London in Feb 1956. The sheerest stockings normally available are 9 denier. An indication of the thinness is that a hair from the average human head is about 50 denier.

Paperweight

The highest price ever paid for a glass paperweight is £48,000 ($96,000) at Christie's, London, July 10, 1979, for a St Louis 19th century paperweight.

Pens

The most expensive writing pens are the 18-carat pair of pens (one fiber-tipped and one ballpoint) capped by diamonds of 3.88 carats sold by Alfred Dunhill Ltd, London, for £9,943 ($17,900) the pair.

Most Expensive Pipe

A very large meerschaum pipe with a bowl fashioned into a portrayal of Anthony and Cleopatra has been priced at $15,000 by Racine and Laramie of San Diego, Calif, in Feb 1982.

Pistols

The highest price paid for a pair of pistols at auction is the £78,000 ($178,400) given by the London dealer Howard Ricketts at Sotheby Parke Bernet, London on Dec 17, 1974, for a pair of English Royal flintlock holster pistols made c. 1690–1700 by Pierre Monlong. They were sent for sale by Anne, Duchess of Westminster. The highest price paid at auction for a single pistol is £110,000 ($253,000) at Christie's London on July 8, 1980 for a Sadeler wheel-lock holster pistol from Munich dated c. 1600.

Playing Cards

The rarest pack of playing cards is the 17th century "Lives of the Saints," published by the Bowles family and estimated to be worth $4,000. A 7 of diamonds signed by Edward Gibbon (who wrote *The Decline and Fall of the Roman Empire*) as an IOU in 1786 for £320 has been sold for $1,000.

Porcelain and Pottery

The highest auction price for any ceramic or any Chinese work of art is £720,000 ($1,296,000) for a blue and white Ming vase of 1426–35 bought by Hirano of Japan at Sotheby's, London, in Dec 1981.

Post Cards

Deltiology is claimed to be the third largest collecting hobby next only to stamps and coins. Austria issued the first cards in 1869 followed by Britain in 1872. Values tend to be obscured by the philatelic element.

Pot Lid

The highest price paid for a pot lid is $5,940 for a seaweed-patterned "Spanish Lady" lid sold at Phillips, London, on May 19, 1982.

Ropes

The largest rope ever made was a coir fiber launching rope with a circumference of 47 in made in 1858 for the British liner *Great Eastern* by John and Edwin Wright. It consisted of four strands, each of 3,780 yd.

The longest fiber rope ever made without a splice was one of 10,000 fathoms (11.36 miles) of 6½-in circumference manila by Frost Brothers (now British Ropes Ltd) in London in 1874.

Shoes

The most expensive standard shoes obtainable are the mink-lined golf shoes with 18-carat gold embellishments and ruby-tipped gold spikes by Stylo Matchmakers International Ltd of Northampton, England, which retail for $9,320 per pair.

James Smith, founder of James Southall & Co of Norwich, England, introduced sized shoes in 1792.

LARGEST BOOT: This size 141 fits few people, and its weight of 81¾ lb is even too heavy for a giant. But it was simply made for display in 1887, and is now in a museum.

The 1887 Jubilee Boot made for the Newark trades procession, Nottinghamshire, England, is 4 ft 3½ in long and weighs 81¾ lb. It is a size 141, and is owned by Clarks Shoe Museum, Somerset, England.

The largest shoes ever sold, excluding those made for cases of elephantiasis, are a pair of size 42 built for the giant Harley Davidson of Avon Park, Fla. The largest shoes normally available are size 14.

Silver

The highest price ever paid for silver was £612,500 ($1,163,750) for the Duke of Kingston tureens made in 1735 by Meissonier and sold by Christie's, Geneva, Switzerland, Nov 8, 1977.

The largest single pieces of silver are the pair of water jugs of 10,000 troy oz (685.7 lb) made in 1902 for the Maharaja of Jaipur (1861–1922). They are 5 ft tall and have a capacity of 1,800 Imperial gallons (2,162 US gallons).

Snuff Box

The highest price ever paid for a snuff box is 1,540,000 Sw Fr (about $730,000) in a sale at Christie's, Geneva, on May 11, 1982, for a gold snuff box dating from 1760–65 and once owned by Frederick the Great of Prussia. It was purchased by S. J. Phillips, the London dealers, for stock.

Spoons

The highest price paid for a spoon is $23,400 for a Diamond Point spoon of the late 14th century, found by Malcolm Laws in the thatch of a Devon, England, farmhouse in 1972, and sold at Phillips, London, on Jan 22, 1982.

Sword

The highest price recorded for a sword is $145,000 paid for the gold sword of honor presented by the Continental Congress of 1779 to Gen Marie Jean Joseph Lafayette, sold at Sotheby Parke Bernet, NYC, on Nov 20, 1976.

Table

A buffet table 2,692 ft 5 in long with 20,000 dishes was set up by a hotelier in Marienheide, W Germany to feed 10,000 people attending a charitable fund-raising outdoor event on Apr 22, 1978.

Tablecloth

The world's largest tablecloth is one 219 yd long × 2 yd wide double damask, made by John S. Brown & Sons Ltd of Belfast, N Ireland, and shipped to a royal palace in the Middle East. There was also an order for matching napkins for 450 places.

Tapestries

The earliest known examples of tapestry-woven linen are three pieces from the tomb of Thutmose IV, the Egyptian pharaoh, which date from 1483 to 1411 BC.

The highest price paid for a tapestry is £550,000 ($1,155,000) for a Swiss Medieval tapestry frieze in two parts dated 1468–76 at Sotheby's, Geneva, Switzerland, Apr 10, 1981, by the Basle Historische Museum.

The largest single piece of tapestry ever woven is "Christ in His Majesty," measuring 72 × 39 ft, designed by Graham Vivian Sutherland (1903–80), for an altar hanging in Coventry Cathedral, West Midlands, England. It cost $29,400, weighs 4/5 of a ton, and was delivered from Pinton Frères of Felletin, France on March 1, 1962.

The famous Bayeux *Telle du Conquest, dite tapisserie de la reine Mathilde,* a hanging 19½ in wide × 231 ft long depicts events of the period 1064–6 in 72 scenes and was probably worked in Canterbury, Kent, England c. 1086. It was "lost" for 2½ centuries from 1476 until 1724. The Overlord Embroidery of 34 panels each 8 × 3 ft, commissioned by Lord Dulverton (b 1915) from the Royal School of Needlework, London, was completed in 1979 after 100 man-years of work and is 41 ft longer than the Bayeux and has the largest area of any embroidery with 816 sq ft.

An uncompleted 8-in deep, 1,230-ft-long embroidery of scenes from C. S. Lewis's Narnia children's stories has been worked by Mrs Margaret S. Pollard of Truro, Cornwall, England to the order of Michael Maine.

Thimble

The record auction price for a thimble is £8,000 ($18,400) paid by the London dealer Winifred Williams at Christie's, London on Dec 3, 1979 for a Meissen dentil-shaped porcelain piece of c. 1740.

Time Capsule

The largest time capsule is the Tropico Time Tunnel measuring 10,000 cu ft in a cave in Rosamond, Calif, sealed by the Kern Antelope Historical Society on Nov 20, 1966, and intended for opening in the year 2866.

Toy Soldier

The auction record for a toy soldier is $468 for a 3-in British Camel Corps lead soldier of 1910, sold at Phillips of London on Aug 12, 1981.

Typewriters

The first patent for a typewriter was by Henry Mill in 1714, but the earliest known working machine was made by Pellegrine Turri (Italy) in 1808. The highest price paid for an antique machine is £3,000 ($6,450) for an 1886 Daw and Tait machine, auctioned at Sotheby's, London, Dec 12, 1980.

Vase

The Chinese ceramic authority, Chingwah Lee of San Francisco, was reported in Aug 1978 to have appraised a unique 39-in K'ang Hsi 4-sided vase, then in a bank vault in Phoenix, Ariz, at $60 million.

The largest vase on record is one 8 ft high, weighing 650 lb, thrown by Sebastiano Maglio at Haeger Potteries of Dundee, Ill (founded 1872) during Aug 1976.

LARGEST VASE is a modern one standing 8 ft high and weighing 650 lb. It was thrown in Illinois in 1976.

Wreaths

The most expensive wreath on record was that sent to the funeral of President Kennedy in Washington, DC on Nov 25, 1963, by the civic authority of Paris. It was handled by Interflora Inc and cost $1,200. The only rival was a floral tribute sent to the Mayor of Moscow in 1970 by Umberto Formichello, general manager of Interflora, which is never slow to scent an opportunity.

Writing Paper

The most expensive writing paper is that sold by Cartier, Inc, Fifth Avenue, NYC at $10,000 per 100 sheets with envelopes. It is of handmade paper from Finland with deckle edges and a "personalized" portrait watermark. Second thoughts and misspellings can be costly.

3. AGRICULTURE

It has been estimated that only 21% of the world's land surface is cultivatable and that only 7.6% is actually under cultivation. Evidence adduced in 1971 from Nok Nok Tha and Spirit Cave, Thailand, tends to confirm that plant cultivation and animal domestication was part of the Hoabinhian culture c. 11,000 BC. Reindeer may have been domesticated as early as c. 18,000 BC but definite evidence is lacking. Goat was domesticated at Asiab, Iran by c. 8050 BC and dog at Star Carr, North Yorkshire, England by c. 7700 BC: the earliest definite date for sheep is c. 7200 BC at Argissa-Magula, Thessaly, Greece and for pig and cattle c. 7000 BC at the same site. The earliest date for horse is c. 4350 BC from Dereivka, Ukraine, USSR.

Farms

The largest farms are collective farms in the USSR. These have been reduced in number from 235,500 in 1940 to only 18,000 in 1980, and have been increased in size so that units of over 60,000 acres are common.

The pioneer farm of Laucidio Coelho near Campo Grande, Mato Grosso, Brazil, c. 1901 was 3,358 sq mi (2,150,000 acres) with 250,000 head of cattle at the time of his death in 1975.

Largest Wheat Field

The largest single fenced field sown with wheat was one of 35,000 acres, sown in 1951 near Lethbridge, Alberta, Canada.

Largest Hop Field

The largest hop field is one of 1,836 acres near Toppenish, Wash, owned by John I. Haas, Inc, the world's largest hop growers, with hop farms in Calif, Ida, Ore and Wash with a total net area of 4,112 acres.

Largest Vineyard

The largest vineyard extends over the Mediterranean façade between the Rhone and the Pyrénées in the départements (provinces) of Aude, Hérault, Gard and Pyrénées-Orientales. It has an area of 2,075,685 acres of which 52.3% is *monoculture viticole*.

Largest Cattle Station

The largest cattle station is Strangeray Springs, South Australia, extending over 11,594 sq mi or 7,420,160 acres—larger in area than the state of Maryland. Until 1915 the Victoria River Downs Station, Northern Territory, was over three times larger, with an area of 22,400,000 acres (35,000 sq mi).

Largest Sheep Station

The largest sheep station is Commonwealth Hill, in the northwest of South Australia. It grazes between 70,000 and 90,000 sheep, about 700 cattle and 54,000 uninvited kangaroos, in an area of 4,080 sq mi. The largest sheep move on record occurred when 27 horsemen moved a mob of 43,000 sheep 40 miles from Barcaldine to Beaconsfield Station, Queensland, Australia, in 1886.

Multiple Births (Livestock)

A cow named "Lyubik" gave birth to 7 calves at Mogilev, USSR, it was reported on Apr 25, 1964. Two claims of 5 have been recorded, as well as two lifetime records of 30. A Danish black and white bull named "Soender Jylland's Jens" left 220,000 surviving progeny by artificial insemination when put down aged 11 in Copenhagen in Sept 1978.

The highest recorded number of piglets in one litter is 34, thrown June 25–26, 1961, by a sow owned by Aksel Egedee of Denmark. In Feb 1955 a sow in

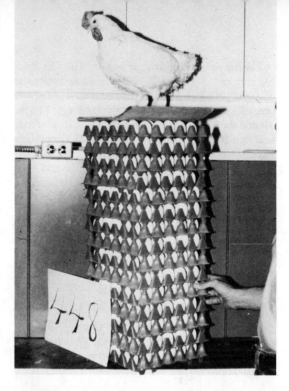

CHAMPION LAYER: This white leghorn broke all records by laying 371 eggs in 364 days in 1979. She went on to lay 448 eggs.

England had a litter of 34, of which 30 were born dead.

A case of 8 lambs at a birth have been reported several times, but none lived. Five cases of sextuplet lambs have been reported since 1977. A case of a sheep living to 26 years was recorded in a flock book in Ireland.

Largest Rice Farm

The largest contiguous wild rice (*Zizania aquatica*) farm is Clearwater Rice Inc at Clearbrook, Minn with 2,000 acres. In 1972 it yielded 262,000 lb.

Largest Chicken Ranch

The largest chicken ranch is the 345-acre "Egg City," in Moorpark, Calif, established by Julius Goldman in 1961. Some 2,220,000 eggs are laid daily by 3 million hens.

Egg-Laying

The highest authenticated rate of egg-laying is by a white leghorn chicken hen, no. 2988 at the College of Agriculture, Univ of Missouri, with 371 eggs in 364 days in an official test, conducted by Prof Harold V. Biellier, ending on Aug 29, 1979.

The heaviest egg *reported* is one of 16 oz with double yolk and double shell, laid by a white leghorn at Vineland, NJ, Feb 25, 1956. The largest *recorded* was one of "nearly 12 oz" for a 5-yolked egg 12¼ in around the long axis and 9 in around the shorter axis laid by a Black Minorca at Mr Stafford's Damsteads Farm, Mellor, Lancashire, England in 1896.

The highest claim for the number of yolks in a chicken's egg is 9 reported by Mrs Diane Hainsworth of Hainsworth Poultry Farms, Mt Morris, NY, in July 1971 and also from a hen in Kirghizia, USSR in Aug 1977.

The white goose "Speckle" owned by Donny Brandenberg of Goshen, Ohio, on May 3, 1977 laid a 24-oz egg measuring 13½ × 9½ in circumferences.

Largest Turkey Farm

The largest turkey farm is that of Bernard Matthews Ltd, centered at Great Witchingham, Norfolk, England, with some 1,800 workers tending 6,400,000 turkeys.

Largest Piggery

The largest piggery is at the Sljeme pig unit in Yugoslavia, which is able to process 300,000 pigs in a year. Even bigger units may exist in Rumania, but details are lacking.

Mushroom Farm

The largest mushroom farm is Butler County Mushroom Farm Inc, founded in 1937 in a disused limestone mine near West Winfield, Pa. It has over 1,000 employees working underground, in a maze of galleries 110 miles long, producing about 45 million lb of mushrooms per year.

Largest Community Garden

The largest recorded community garden project is that operated by the City Beautiful Council, and the Benjamin Wegerzyn Garden Center in Dayton, Ohio. It comprises 1,173 allotments, each of 812¼ sq ft.

Most Disrupted Farm

Farmer Dudley Glanfield, owner of the 650-acre Twelve Oaks Farm, Windlesham, Surrey, England, has since 1956 unsuccessfully fought Compulsory Purchase Orders for the following: a line of Central Electricity Generating Board giant pylons; Southern Electricity Board high and low voltage lines; 3 North Thames Gas mains; 2 South Western Suburban Water mains; 3 Esso Petrol lines; a giant sewer pipeline; GPO telephone lines and 1 mile of M3 highway bisecting the heart of his estate which he has signposted "Grand Central Station—Every Ruddy Thing Passes Through Here."

Crop Yields

A yield of 83.2 cwt/acre of Athene Winter Barley was achieved in 1980 by M. J. Leigh on behalf of R. M. Harris at Watcombe Manor, Watlington, England, from a 30-acre field.

A yield of 352.64 bushels of corn (15½% moisture) from an acre, using De Kalb XL-54, was achieved by Roy Lynn, Jr near Kalamazoo, Mich Sept 30, 1977.

The highest recorded yield for sugar beet is 55.71 tons per acre by Andy Christensen and Jon Giannini in the Salinas Valley, California.

The greatest number of US barrels of potatoes picked in a 9½ hr day is 235 by Walter Sirois (b 1917) of Caribou, Maine, on Sept 30, 1950.

Milk Yields

The highest recorded world lifetime yield of cows' milk is 403,439 lb by the US Holstein cow "Breezewood Patsy Bar Pontiac" (b June 11, 1964) owned by Gelbke Bros. of Vienna, Ohio, to June 22, 1981.

The greatest recorded yield for one lactation (365 days) is 55,661 lb by the Holstein "Beecher Arlinda Ellen" owned by Mr and Mrs Harold L. Beecher of Rochester, Ind in 1975. The highest reported milk yield in a day is 241 lb by "Urbe Blanca" in Cuba on or about Jan 23, 1982.

The record for hand milking was set by Andy Faust at Collinsville, Okla, in 1937 when he achieved 120 gallons in 12 hr.

The highest recorded milk yield for any goat is 7,714 lb in 365 days by "Osory Snow-Goose" owned by Mr and Mrs G. Jameson of Leppington, N.S.W., Australia in 1977. The part Nubian milk goat "Lou" owned by Mrs Jonnie Stinson of Springtown, Tex was lactating for the 5 years up to her death on Nov 15, 1980.

Butter Fat Yield

The world record lifetime yield is 16,370 lb by the US Holstein "Breezewood Patsy Bar Pontiac" in 3,979 days (see above also for milk yield record). Her lactation record for 365 days of 2,230 lb was reported on Oct 8, 1976.

CORN YIELD RECORD HOLDER (left): More than 352 bushels of corn per acre was Roy Lynn, Jr's achievement in 1977. BULL (below): "Joe's Pride" is a mixture of bison, charolais, and Hereford, called a "beefalo." He was sold in 1974 for $2½ million.

Cheese

The most active cheese-eaters are the people of France, with an annual average in 1979 of 38.1 lb per person. The biggest producer is the US with a factory production of 4,773,500,000 lb (2,386,750 tons) in 1980.

The oldest and most primitive cheeses are the Arabian *kishk*, made of the dried curd of goat's milk. There are today 450 named cheeses of 18 major varieties, but many are merely named after different towns and differ only in shape or the method of packing. France has 240 varieties.

The world's most expensive cheese is Le Leruns made from ewe's milk at 90 francs per kilo (about $6 per lb).

The largest cheese ever made was a cheddar of 34,591 lb, made in 43 hours, Jan 20–22, 1964, by the Wisconsin Cheese Foundation for exhibition at the NY World's Fair. It was transported in a specially designed 45-ft-long refrigerated tractor trailer "Cheese-Mobile."

Chicken Plucking

The record time for plucking chickens clean was set in the 1976 championship contest at Masaryktown, Fla, Oct 9, when a team of 4 women (Doreena Cary, Diane Grieb, Kathy Roads and Dorothy McCarthy) plucked 12 birds naked in 32.9 sec.

293

Leaving a single feather produces the cry "Fowl!" Ernest Hausen (1877–1955) of Fort Atkinson, Wisc, died undefeated after 33 years as a champion. On Jan 19, 1939 he was timed for one chicken at 4.4 sec, and reportedly twice did 3.5 sec a few years later.

Turkey Plucking

Vincent Pilkington of Cootehill, County Cavan, Ireland, killed and plucked 100 turkeys in 7 hours 32 min on Dec 15, 1978. His record for a single turkey is 1 min 30 sec on RTE Television in Dublin on Nov 17, 1980.

Sheep Shearing

The highest recorded speed for sheep shearing in a working day was that of John Fagan, who machine-sheared 804 lambs (average 89.3 per hour) in 9 hours at Hantoru Rd, Pio Pio, New Zealand, on Dec 8, 1980. The hand-shearing (solo blade) record for a 9-hour day is 353 lambs by Peter Casserly of Christchurch, New Zealand, Feb 13, 1976.

In a shearing marathon, 4 men machine-sheared 2,519 sheep in 24 hours at Stewarts Trust, Waikia, Southland, New Zealand, on Feb 11, 1982.

Mr Lavor Taylor (b Feb 27, 1896) of Ephraim, Utah claims to have sheared 513,000 sheep to Feb 1982.

Heaviest Cattle and Pigs

Of heavyweight cattle the heaviest on record was a Holstein-Durham cross named "Mount Katahdin" exhibited by A. S. Rand of Maine, 1906–10 and frequently weighed at an even 5,000 lb. He was 6 ft 2 in at the shoulder with a 13 ft girth and died in a barn fire c. 1923.

The largest breed of heavyweight cattle is the Chianini, brought to Italy from the Middle East in pre-Roman times. Mature bulls average 5 ft 8 in at the forequarters and weigh 2,865 lb. In 1955 a bull named "Donetto" tipped the scales at 3,834 lb at the Arezzo show—a world record for a bull of any breed.

The highest recorded birthweight for a calf is 225 lb from a British Friesian cow at Rockhouse Farm, Swansea, Wales, in 1961.

The heaviest hog recorded was the Poland-China hog "Big Bill" of 2,552 lb measuring 9 ft long with a belly on the ground, owned by Burford Butler of Jackson, Tenn, and chloroformed in 1933. He was mounted and displayed by the Wells family in Jackson, Tenn until 1946.

The highest recorded birthweight for a lamb is 38 lb at Clearwater, Sedgwick County, Kansas, in 1975, but neither this lamb nor the ewe survived.

LIVESTOCK RECORDS

Note: Some exceptionally high livestock auction sales are believed to result from collusion.

Bull

The highest price ever paid for a bull is $2,500,000 for the beefalo (a ⅜ bison, ⅜ charolais, ¼ Hereford) "Joe's Pride" sold by D. C. Basolo of Burlingame, Calif to the Beefalo Cattle Co of Canada, of Calgary, Alberta, on Sept 9, 1974.

Cow

The highest price ever paid for a cow is $300,000 for the Holstein-Friesian "Pammies Citation Paula" by Dreamstreet Holsteins Inc, Walton, NY, at the Hilltop Hanover Farm sale Nov 21, 1980.

Sheep

The highest price ever paid for a ram is $A79,000 (about $80,500) by the Gnowangerup Animal Breeding Centre, Western Australia for a Merino ram from the Colinsvale Stud, Mount Bryan, South Australia, at the Royal Adelaide Show on Sept 10, 1981.

The highest price ever paid for wool is $A125 per kg greasy ($58 per lb) for a bale of extra superfine combing Merino fleece from the Launceston, Tasmania sales on Mar 4, 1982. It was sold by E. J. Dowling & Sons of Ross, Tasmania, to Fujii Keori Ltd of Osaka, Japan. This Japanese firm has been top bidder ever since 1972.

Pig

The highest price ever paid for a pig is $42,500 for a Duroc boar named "Glacier," owned by Baize Durocs of Stamford, Tex, by Wilbert & Myron Meinhart of Hudson, Iowa, Feb 24, 1979.

Horse

The highest price for a draught horse is $47,500 paid for the 7-year-old Belgian stallion "Farceur" by E. G. Good at Cedar Falls, Iowa Oct 16, 1917.

Donkey

Perhaps the lowest ever price for livestock was at a sale at Kuruman, Cape Province, South Africa in 1934 where donkeys were sold for less than 4¢ each.

Chapter 10

The Human World

1. POLITICAL AND SOCIAL

The land area of the earth is estimated at about 57,267,400 sq mi (including inland waters), or 29.08% of the world's surface area.

Largest Political Division

The British Commonwealth of Nations, a free association of 45 sovereign independent states and 4 associated states, covers an area of 13,095,000 sq mi with a population which in 1980 surpassed 1,000 million.

COUNTRIES

The world comprises 168 sovereign countries and 47 separately administered non-sovereign territories, making 215. The United Nations, additionally, still list three: East Timor (now incorporated into Indonesia), Western Sahara (now in Morocco) and the uninhabited Canton Island (now in Kiribati). They do not list the *de facto* territories of Taiwan, Mayotte or Spanish North Africa. Neither do they list the three Baltic States of Estonia, Latvia and Lithuania whose forcible incorporation into the USSR in 1940 is not internationally recognized. Six further territories without indigenous populations, namely the four Antarctic dependencies (Australian, British, French and the Ross Dependency of New Zealand) and the two further Australian dependencies of Coral Sea Islands and the Territory of Heard and McDonald Islands, would bring the total to 224.

Largest Country

The country with the greatest area is the Union of Soviet Socialist Republics (the Soviet Union), comprising 15 Union (constituent) Republics with a total area of 8,649,500 sq mi, or 15% of the world's total land area, and a total coastline (including islands) of 66,090 miles. The country measures 5,580 miles from east to west and 2,790 miles from north to south. Its population on Jan 1, 1982 was 268.8 million.

Smallest Country

The smallest independent country is the State of the Vatican City, which was made an enclave within the city of Rome, Feb 11, 1929. The enclave has an area of 108.7 acres (0.17 sq mi).

The maritime sovereign country with the shortest coastline is Monaco with 3.49 miles excluding piers and breakwaters.

The world's smallest republic is Nauru, less than 1 degree south of the equator in the Western Pacific. It became independent on Jan 31, 1968, has an area of 5,263 acres (8.2 sq mi) and a population of 8,000 (latest estimate, mid-1980). Tuvalu, a British dependency in Oceania, has an area of 6,080 acres (9.5 sq mi), but a population of 7,300 (May 1979).

The smallest colony in the world is Gibraltar, with an area of 2½ sq mi. However, Pitcairn Island, the only inhabited (63 people in 1980) island of a group of 4 (total area 18½ sq mi), has an area of 1½ sq mi, or 960 acres.

The official residence, since 1834, of the Grand Master of the Order of the Knights of Malta, totaling 3 acres and comprising the Villa del Priorato di Malta on the lowest of Rome's seven hills (the 151-ft Aventine) retains certain diplomatic privileges as does 68 Via Condotti. The order has accredited representatives to foreign governments. Hence, it is sometimes cited as the smallest "state" in the world.

Flattest and Most Elevated Countries

The country with the lowest highest point is the Republic of the Maldives, which attains 8 ft above sea level. The country with the highest lowest point is Lesotho, a kingdom surrounded by the Republic of South Africa. The egress of the Senqu (Orange) riverbed is 4,530 ft above sea level.

Frontiers

The country with the most land frontiers is China, with 13—Mongolia, USSR, North Korea, Hong Kong, Macau, Vietnam, Laos, Burma, India, Bhutan, Nepal, Pakistan, and Afghanistan. France, if all her *Départements d'outre-mer* are included, may, if her territorial waters are extended, have 20 frontiers.

The longest *continuous* frontier is between Canada and the US, which (including the Great Lakes boundaries) extends for 3,987 miles (excluding 1,538 miles with Alaska).

The frontier which is crossed most frequently is that between the US and Mexico. It extends for 1,933 miles and has more than 120 million crossings every year. The Sino-Soviet frontier, broken by the Sino-Mongolian border, extends for 4,500 miles with no reported figures of crossings.

The "frontier" of the Holy See (Vatican City) in Rome measures 2.53 miles. The land frontier between Gibraltar and Spain at La Linea, closed since 1969, measures 1,672 yd. Zambia, Zimbabwe, Botswana and Namibia (South West Africa) meet at a point.

Most Impenetrable Boundary

The 858-mile-long "Iron Curtain," dividing the Federal Republican (West) and the Democratic Republican (East) parts of Germany, utilizes 2,230,000 land mines and 50,000 miles of barbed wire, in addition to many watchtowers containing detection devices. The whole 270-yd-wide strip occupies 133 sq mi of E German territory and costs an estimated $7 billion to build and maintain. It reduced the westward flow from more than 200,000 in 1961 to 5,761 escapees in 1962 and to only 18 a month in 1980, the year of the 106th fatality among escapees.

Most Densely Populated Places

The most densely populated territory is the Portuguese province of Macau (or Macao), on the southern coast of China. It has an estimated population of 275,000 (mid-1980) in an area of 6.2 sq mi, giving a density of 44,350 per sq mi.

Of territories with an area of more than 400 sq mi, Hong Kong (405 sq mi) contains 5,068,000 people (estimated mid-1980), giving the territory a density of 12,513 per sq mi. Hong Kong is now the most populous of all colonies. The name "Hong Kong" is the transcription of the local pronunciation of the Peking dialect version of Xiang gang (a port for incense). The 1976 by-census showed that the West area of the urban district of Mong Kok on the Kowloon Peninsula had a density of 652,910 people per sq mi. In 1959, at the peak of the housing crisis in Hong Kong, it was reported that in one house designed for 12

POPULATIONS

Estimates of the human population of the world largely hinge on the accuracy of the component figure for the population of the People's Republic of China, which published no census between 1953 (582.6 million) and mid-1979 (958.05 million).

The increase in the world's population is 232,800 per day or 161 per min.

WORLD POPULATION—PROGRESSIVE ESTIMATES

Date	Millions	Date	Millions
10000 BC	c. 5	1940	2,295
1 AD	c. 200	1950	2,513
1000	c. 275	1960	3,049
1250	375	1970	3,704
1500	420	1975	4,033
1650	550–600	1976	4,107
1700	615	1977	4,182
1750	720	1978	4,258
1800	900	1980	4,415
1900	1,625	1981	4,495*
1920	1,862	1982	4,580*
1930	2,070	2000	6,200**

* Provisional estimate for mid-year.
** Some demographers maintain that the figure will (or must) stabilize at 10–15,000 million, but above 8,000 million during the 21st century. The Tsui-Bogue estimate from the University of Chicago for 2000 AD is 5,800 million, compared with the UN low-estimate of 5,855 million, mid-estimate as given and high-estimate of 6,508 million.
Note: The all-time peak annual increase of 2.0% c. 1958–62 had declined to 1.8% by 1980. This however still produces a rising annual increment, now rising from about 85 million to more than 90 million a year in the 1990's.

It is estimated that 75 billion humans have been born and died in the last 600,000 years.

people the number of occupants was 459, including 104 in one room and 4 living on the roof.

The Principality of Monaco, on the south coast of France, has a population of 26,000 (estimated June 30, 1979) in an area of 369.9 acres, giving a density of 37,230 per sq mi. This is being relieved by marine infilling which will increase the area to 447 acres.

Singapore has 2,413,945 (mid-1980) people in an inhabited area of 73 sq mi.

Of countries over 1,000 sq mi, the most densely populated is Bangladesh with a population of 88,656,000 (mid-1980 estimate) living in 55,126 sq mi at a density of 1,608 per sq mi.

The Indonesian island of Java (with an area of 48,763 sq mi) had a population of 94,693,000 (1981 estimate), giving a density of 1,941 per sq mi.

MOST DENSELY POPU-
LATED: Hong Kong
(above) has more than 5
million people crowded
in 405 sq mi, including
one sq mi that contains
652,910 people. (HK Info
Svce) Even more crowded
and not as large in area is
Macao (left), only 40 mi
distant, with 275,000
people packed into 6.2
sq mi.

HIGHEST CAPITAL CITY: La Paz, Bolivia (top left), sits high in the Andes at almost 12,000 ft above sea level, and its airport is another 1,400 ft higher. (© Bell, Howarth, Ltd) OLDEST "CITY" is Jericho (top right) whose walls were featured in song and in the Bible. They have been standing since 7800 BC when the city was inhabited by perhaps 3,000. (J. Allen Cash) OLDEST CAPITAL is Damascus, Syria (right above) which has been continuously inhabited since 2500 BC. SMALLEST AND LEAST POPULOUS INDEPENDENT STATE is Vatican City (bottom right) with just over 100 acres within Rome, 728 population and 0 birth rate.

Most Populous Country

The country with the largest population is China, which in *pinyin* is written Zhogguo. The mid-1979 UN estimate was 958,050,000. The rate of natural increase in the People's Republic of China is now estimated to have been reduced from 2.3% in 1971 to less than 1.2% in 1978, so the 1 billion mark should not now be reached until mid-1983.

Least Populous State

The independent state with the smallest population is the Vatican City or the Holy See (see *Smallest Country*), with 728 inhabitants in mid-1978, and a zero birth rate.

Most Sparsely Populated Territory

Antarctica became permanently occupied by relays of scientists as of Oct 1956. The population varies seasonally and reaches 1,500 at times.

The least populated territory, apart from Antarctica, is Kalaatdlit Nunaat (formerly Greenland), with a population of 50,000 (estimate of mid-1980) in an area of 840,000 sq mi, giving a density of one person to every 16.15 sq mi. Some 84.3% of the island comprises an ice cap.

CITIES

Most Populous City

The most populous "urban agglomeration" in the world is the Tokyo-Yokohama Metropolitan Area, of 1,081 sq mi, containing an estimated 28,043,000 people in 1978. The municipal population of Tokyo in 1980 was 11,357,337. The population of the metropolitan area of Greater Mexico City in 1979 was published as 13,950,364.

Oldest City

The oldest known walled town is Jericho (Ariha), about 5 miles north of the Dead Sea. Radio-carbon dating on specimens from the lowest levels reached by archeologists indicate habitation there by perhaps 3,000 people as early as 7800 BC. The village of Zawi Chemi Shanidar, discovered in 1957 in northern Iraq, has been dated to 8910 BC. The oldest capital city in the world is Dimashq (Damascus), capital of Syria. It has been continuously inhabited since *c.* 2500 BC.

Elevations of Cities, Capitals and Dwellings

The highest capital city, before the domination of Tibet by China, was Lhasa, at an elevation of 12,087 ft above sea level.

La Paz, the administrative and *de facto* capital of Bolivia, stands at an altitude of 11,916 ft above sea level. El Alto airport is at 13,385 ft. The city was founded in 1548 by Capt Alonso de Mendoza on the site of an Indian village named Chuquiapu. It was originally called Ciudad de Nuestra Señora de La Paz (City of Our Lady of Peace), but in 1825 was renamed La Paz de Ayacucho, its present official name. Sucre, the legal capital of Bolivia, stands at 9,301 ft above sea level.

The new town of Wenchuan, founded in 1955 on the Chinghai-Tibet road, north of the Tangla Range, is the highest at 16,732 ft above sea level. The highest dwellings in the world are those at Basisi, India, near the Tibetan border, at *c.* 19,700 ft.

The settlement of Ein Bokek, which has a synagogue, on the shores of the Dead Sea, is the lowest town in the world at 1,299 ft below sea level.

The northernmost capital is Reykjavik, Iceland, at 64° 08′ N. Its population was estimated to be 83,887 in 1978.

Largest Town in Area

The largest town in area is Mount Isa, Queensland, Australia. The area administered by the City Council is 15,822 sq mi.

Most Remote Town from Sea

The town most remote from the sea is Wulumuch'i (Urumchi) formerly Tihwa, Sinkiang, capital of the Uighur Autonomous Region of China, at a distance of about 1,400 miles from the nearest coastline. Its population was estimated to be 320,000 in 1974.

Emigration

More people emigrate from Mexico than from any other country. An estimated 800,000 emigrated illegally into the US in 1976 alone.

Immigration

The country which regularly receives the most legal immigrants is the US with more than 800,000 in 1980. It has been estimated that in the period 1820–1980, the US received more than 50 million *of-*

ficial immigrants. One immigrant in every 24 in the US is, however, an *illegal* immigrant. Another 700,-000 were added in 1980.

Most Patient "Refusnik"

The USSR citizen who has waited longest for an exit visa is Benjamin Boyomolney (b Apr 7, 1946) who first applied in 1966.

Birth Rate

The highest estimated by the UN is 54.6 per 1,000 for Kenya in 1980. The rate for the whole world was 29 per 1,000 in 1978. A world-wide survey published in July 1979 showed only Nepal (44.4) with a still rising birth rate. Excluding Vatican City, where the rate is negligible, the lowest recorded rate is 10.0 for the Federal Republic of (W) Germany for 1980.

Death Rate

The rate for the whole world was 11 per 1,000 in 1978. The highest of the latest available recorded death rates is 25.4 deaths per 1,000 of the population in Yemen (1975–80). The lowest of the latest available recorded rates is 1.9 deaths per 1,000 in Tonga in 1976.

Natural Increase

The rate of natural increase for the whole world is estimated to be 27.5 − 10.7 = 16.8 per 1,000 in 1982. The highest of the latest available recorded rates is 40.4 (54.6 − 14.2) in Kenya in 1980.

The lowest rate of natural increase in any major independent country is W Germany with a negative figure of − 1.5 per 1,000 for 1980 (10.0 births and 11.5 deaths).

Marriage Ages

The country with the lowest average for marriage is India, with 20.0 years for males and 14.5 for females. At the other extreme is Ireland, with 31.4 for males and 26.5 for females. In the People's Republic of China, the *recommended* age for marriage for men has been 28 and for women 25.

Sex Ratio

There were estimated to be 1,003.5 men in the world for every 1,000 women (1975). The country with the largest recorded shortage of males is the USSR, with 1,145.9 females to every 1,000 males (1981 census). The country with the largest recorded woman shortage is Pakistan, with 885 to every 1,000 males in 1972. The figures are, however, probably under-enumerated due to *purdah*, a policy that keeps women from appearing in public.

Divorces

The country with the most divorces is the US with a total of 1,182,000 in 1980—a rate of 48.98% of the current annual total of marriages.

Infant Mortality

Based on deaths before one year of age, the lowest of the latest available recorded rates is 6.7 deaths per 1,000 live births in Sweden in 1980. The world rate in 1978 was 91 per 1,000.

The highest recorded infant mortality rate reported has been 195 to 300 per 1,000 live births for Burma in 1952, and 259 for Zaïre in 1950.

In Ethiopia the infant mortality rate was unofficially estimated to be nearly 550 per 1,000 live births in 1969. Many Third World countries have ceased to make returns.

Life Expectation

There is evidence that life expectation in Britain in the 5th century AD was 33 years for males and 27 years for females. In the decade 1890–1900 the expectation of life among the population of India was 23.7 years. World expectation of life has increased from 47.4 years (1950–55) to 64.5 years (1995–2000).

Based on the latest available data, the highest recorded expectation of life at age 12 months is 73.0 years for males and 79.2 years for females in Iceland (1975–76).

The lowest recorded expectation of life at birth is 27 years for both sexes in the Vallée du Niger area of Mali in 1957 (sample survey, 1957–58). The figure for males in Gabon was 25 years in 1960–61, but 45 for females.

STANDARDS OF LIVING

Housing

For comparison, a dwelling unit is defined as a structurally separated room or rooms occupied by private households of one or more persons and having separate access or a common passageway to the street. The country with the greatest recorded number of private dwelling units is India, which had 100,251,000 occupied in 1972.

Hospitals

The largest hospital is the Pilgrim State Hospital, a mental hospital at West Brentwood, LI, NY, with 3,618 beds. It formerly contained 14,200 beds.

The busiest maternity hospital in the world is the Mama Yemo Hospital in Kinshasha, Zaïre, with 41,930 deliveries in 1976. The record "birthquake" occurred on one day in May 1976 with 175 babies born. It has 559 beds.

The longest stay in a hospital occurred when Martha Nelson was admitted to the Columbus State Institute for the Feeble-Minded in Ohio in 1875, and stayed until she died in Jan 1975, aged 103 years 6 months, in the Orient State Institution, Ohio, spending more than 99 years in institutions.

In mid-1980 the average cost of a day's stay in a Calif hospital was $411, or $2,874 per average stay.

Physicians

The country with the most physicians is the USSR, with 831,300, or one to every 307 persons. China had an estimated 1.4 million paramedical personnel known as "barefoot doctors" by 1981. The country with the lowest recorded proportion is Upper Volta, with 58 physicians (one for every 92,759 people).

Eight sons of John Robertson of Dumbarton, Scotland, graduated as medical doctors between 1892 and 1914. Harry Lewis Lutterloh and Elizabeth Grantham of Chatham County, NC, were the grandparents of 19 medical doctors. From 1850 to 1982 they practiced a total of 704 man-years.

The oldest doctor currently known to be in practice is Dr Gallo Leoz (b Apr 12, 1879). He practices in Madrid, Spain, as an ophthalmologist.

Dentists

The country with the most dentists is the US, where 138,000 were registered members of the American Dental Association in 1980.

Psychiatrists and Psychologists

The country with the most psychiatrists is the US. The registered membership of the American Psychiatric Association (inst. 1894) was 25,440 in 1980. The membership of the American Psychological Association (inst. 1892) was 50,000 in 1980.

GOVERNMENT

Oldest Ruling House

The Emperor of Japan, Hirohito (b Apr 29, 1901), is the 124th in line from the first Emperor, Jimmu Tenno or Zinmu, whose reign was traditionally from 660 to 581 BC, but probably from c. 40 to c. 10 BC. He has been Emperor since Dec 25, 1926.

Longest Reigns

The longest recorded reign of any monarch is that of Pepi II, a Sixth Dynasty Pharaoh of ancient Egypt. His reign began in c. 2310 BC when he was aged 6, and lasted c. 94 years.

Currently the longest reigning monarch in the world is King Sobhuza II (b July 22, 1899), the *Ngwenyama* (Paramount Chief) of Swaziland, who succeeded to the throne on Dec 10, 1899, at the age of 141 days and reigned under the regency of his grandmother Queen Labotsibeni until he assumed full powers on Dec 6, 1921. *Burke's Royal Families of the World* lists 28 wives and 85 children.

The longest reign of any major European monarch was that of King Louis XIV of France, who ascended the throne May 14, 1643, aged 4 years 231 days, and reigned for 72 years 110 days until his death Sept 1, 1715, four days before his 77th birthday.

Grand Duke Karl Friedrich of Baden (1728–1811) ruled from May 12, 1738, for 73 years 29 days.

Musoma Kanijo, chief of the Nzega district of western Tanganyika (now part of Tanzania), reputedly reigned for more than 98 years from 1864, when aged 8, until his death on Feb 2, 1963.

The 6th Japanese Emperor Koo-an traditionally reigned for 102 years (from 392 to 290 BC), but probably his actual reign was from about 110 AD to about 140 AD. The reign of the 11th Emperor Suinin was traditionally from 29 BC to 71 AD (99 years), but probably was from 259 to 291 AD.

Shortest Reign

King Virabahu of the Kalinga Kshatriya dynasty of Ceylon (Sri Lanka) was assassinated a few hours after he was crowned at Polonnaruwa in 1196.

Youngest King and Queen

Twenty-seven of the world's 168 sovereign states are not republics. They are led by 1 Emperor, 13 Kings, 3 Queens, 4 princely rulers, a Sultan, 3 Emirs, a Pope and one elected monarch. Queen Elizabeth II is Head of State of 15 Commonwealth countries. That with the youngest king is Bhutan (in the Himalayas) where King Jigme Singye Wangchuk (b Nov 11, 1955) succeeded to the throne on July 24, 1972, aged 16 years 8 months. The youngest queen is Margrethe II of Denmark (b Apr 16, 1940). Obi Keagboekuzi I of Agbor, Nigeria, the 18th obi since 1270, was born on June 29, 1977, and succeeded his father, the 17th obi, on Oct 31, 1979, aged 2 years 4 months.

Heaviest Monarch

The heaviest monarch is the 6-ft-3-in-tall King Taufa'ahau of Tonga, who in Sept 1976 weighed 462 lb on the only adequate scale in the country (at the airport).

Most Prolific Royalty

The most prolific monogamous "royals" have been Prince Hartmann of Liechtenstein (1613–1686) who had 24 children, of whom 21 were live born, by the Countess Elisabeth zu Salm-Reifterscheidt (1623–1688). HRH Duke Roberto I of Parma also had 24 children, but by two wives.

Oldest Parliament

The earliest known legislative assembly was a bicameral one in Erech, Iraq, c. 2800 BC. The oldest legislative body is the *Alpingi* (Althing) of Iceland, founded in 930 AD. This body, which originally comprised 39 local chieftains was abolished in 1800, but restored by Denmark to a consultative status in 1843 and a legislative status in 1874. The legislative assembly with the oldest continuous history is the Tynwald Court of the Isle of Man, in the Irish Channel, which is believed to have originated more than 1,000 years ago.

Largest Legislature

The largest legislative assembly is the National People's Congress of the People's Republic of China. The Congress which was convened in 1979 had 3,471 members.

Smallest Quorum

The House of Lords has the smallest quorum, expressed as a percentage of eligible voters, of any legislative body in the world, namely less than one-third of 1%. To transact business there must be three peers present, including the Lord Chancellor or his deputy.

Highest-Paid Legislators

The most highly paid of all the world's legislators are US Congressmen, who receive a basic annual salary of $60,622.50 (since Oct 12, 1979). In addition, up to $1,021,167 per year is allowed for office help, with a salary limit of $49,941 for any one staff member per year (limited to 16). Besides, Senators are authorized up to $143,000 per year, depending on the state, for an Official Office Expense Account from which are paid official travel expenses, telegrams, long-distance telephone calls, air-mail postage, stationery, subscriptions to newspapers, and office expenses in the home state. When abroad they have access to "counterpart funds." They also are entitled to very low charges for filming, speech and radio transcriptions, and beauty treatments (females only).

A retiring President electing to also take his Congressional pension (if any) would enjoy a combined pension of $103,500 per annum.

Longest Membership

The longest span as a legislator was 83 years by József Madarász (1814–1915). He first attended the Hungarian Parliament in 1832–36 as *oblegatus absentium* (*i.e.* on behalf of an absent deputy). He was a full member in 1848–50 and from 1861 until his death on Jan 31, 1915.

Filibusters

The longest continuous speech in the history of the US Senate was that of Senator Wayne Morse of Oregon, Apr 24–25, 1953, when he spoke on the Tidelands Oil Bill for 22 hours 26 min without resuming his seat. Senator Strom Thurmond, Democrat (SC), spoke against the Civil Rights Bill for 24 hours 19 min, Aug 28–29, 1957, interrupted only briefly by the swearing-in of a new Senator.

The record for a filibuster in any legislature is 43 hours by Texas State Senator Bill Meier from Euless, who spoke against nondisclosure of industrial accidents in May 1977.

Longest UN Speech

The longest speech made in the UN was one of 4 hours 29 min by the president of Cuba, Fidel Castro Ruz (b Aug 13, 1927) in Aug 1960.

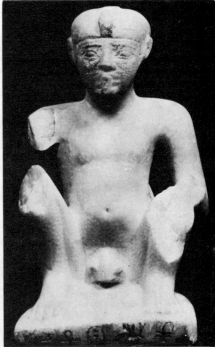

OLDEST PRIME MINISTER (left): The Grand Vizier of Morocco lived to 116 (Muslim) or 112½ (Gregorian) years before he died in 1957. LONGEST REIGN (above): Pepi II of ancient Egypt took over as Pharaoh when he was 6 in 2310 BC and ruled for 94 years. (Mansell)

Oldest Treaty

The world's oldest treaty is the Anglo-Portuguese Treaty of Alliance signed in London over 600 years ago on June 16, 1373. The text was confirmed "with my usual flourish" by John de Banketre, Clerk.

Longest Term of Office

Prof Dr António de Oliveira Salazar (1889–1970) was the President of the Council of Ministers (*i.e.* Prime Minister) of Portugal from July 5, 1932, for 36 years and 84 days until superseded on Sept 27, 1968, eleven days after going into a coma.

Andrei Andrevich Gromyko (b July 6, 1909) has been Minister of Foreign Affairs of the USSR since Feb 15, 1957, having been Deputy Foreign Minister since 1946.

Oldest Prime Minister

The longest-lived prime minister of any country is Christopher Hornsrud, who served as Prime Minister of Norway Jan 28 to Feb 15, 1928 (b Nov 15, 1859, d Dec 13, 1960), aged 101 years 28 days.

Richard Gavin Reid (b Glasgow, Scotland, Jan 17, 1879), Premier of Alberta, Canada, 1934–1935, died Oct. 17, 1980, aged 101 years 274 days.

El Hadji Muhammad el Mokri, Grand Vizier of Morocco, died on Sept 16, 1957, at a reputed age of 116 Muslim (*Hijiri*) years, equivalent to 112.5 Gregorian years.

The oldest age of appointment has been 81 years in the case of Morarji Ranchhodji Desai of India (b Feb 29, 1896) in March 1977.

Largest Elections

The largest elections are those for the 529-seat Indian *Lok Sabha* (House of the People). The incoming Prime Minister, Mrs Indira Gandhi, was better known by her symbol (a cow) than by her name among the 335 million voters.

Closest Elections

The ultimate in close general elections occurred in Zanzibar (now part of Tanzania) on Jan 18, 1961, when the Afro-Shirazi Party won by a single seat,

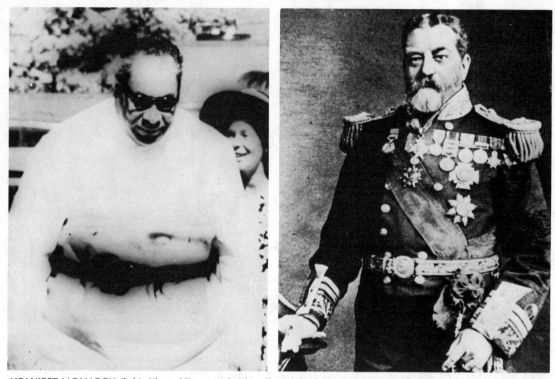

HEAVIEST MONARCH (left): King of Tonga, 6 ft 3 in tall, weighed 462 lb in 1976 on the only adequate scale in the island nation (at the airport). (© Popperfoto) SHORTEST WAR (right): Admiral Rawson of the British Navy won a war against Zanzibar in 1896 after 38 min of bombardment.

after the seat of Chake-Chake on Pemba Island had been gained by a single vote.

The narrowest recorded percentage win in an election would seem to be for the office of Southern District highway commissioner in Mississippi on Aug 7, 1979. Robert E. Joiner was declared winner over W. H. Pyron with 133,587 votes to 133,582. The loser got more than 49.9999% of the votes.

Most One-Sided Election

North Korea recorded a 100% turn-out of electors and a 100% vote for the Workers' Party of Korea in the general election of Oct 8, 1962.

The highest personal majority won by any politician has been 424,545 votes from a total electorate of 625,179 achieved by Ram Bilas Paswan, the Janata candidate for Hajipur in Bihar, India, in Mar 1977.

Most Rigged Election

In the 1928 presidential election of Liberia, the president, Charles D. B. King, was returned to office with an officially announced majority over his opponent of 234,000 votes. President King thus claimed a "majority" more than 15½ times greater than the entire electorate.

Most Coups

Statisticians contend that Bolivia, since it became a sovereign country in 1825, has had 189 *coups d'état*.

Communist Parties

The largest national Communist party outside the USSR (which had 17 million members in 1981) and Communist states has been the Partito Comunista Italiano (Italian Communist Party), with a membership of 2,300,000 in 1946. The total fell to 1,700,000 by 1976. The membership in mainland China was estimated to be 28 million in 1974.

Voting Ages

The eligibility extremes for voting are 15 years of age in the Philippines and 25 years in Andorra.

2. MILITARY AND DEFENSE
WAR*

Longest War

The longest of history's countless wars was the "Hundred Years' War" between England and France, which lasted from 1338 to 1453 (115 years), although it may be said that the nine Crusades from the First (1096–1104) to the Ninth (1270–91), extending over 195 years, comprised a single Holy War.

Shortest War

The shortest war on record was that between the UK and Zanzibar (now part of Tanzania) from 9:02 to 9:40 a.m. on Aug 27, 1896. The UK battle fleet under Rear-Adm Harry Holdsworth Rawson (1843–1910) delivered an ultimatum to the self-appointed Sultan Sa'id Khalid to evacuate his palace and surrender. This was not forthcoming until after 38 min of bombardment. Admiral Rawson received the Brilliant Star of Zanzibar (first class) from the new Sultan Hamud ibn Muhammad. It was proposed at one time that elements of the local populace should be compelled to defray the cost of the ammunition used.

Bloodiest Wars

By far the most costly war in terms of human life was World War II (1939–45), in which the total number of fatalities, including battle deaths and civilians of all countries, is estimated to have been 54,800,000, assuming 25 million USSR fatalities and 7,800,000 Chinese civilians killed. The country which suffered most was Poland with 6,028,000 or 22.2% of her population of 27,007,000 killed. The total combatant death toll from World War I was only 9,700,000 compared with 15,600,000 in World War II.

In the Paraguayan war of 1864–70 against Brazil, Argentina, and Uruguay, the Paraguayan population was reduced from 1,400,000 to 220,000, of whom only 30,000 were adult males.

The bloodiest civil war in history was the T'ai-p'ing ("Great Peace") rebellion, in which peasant sympathizers of the Southern Ming Dynasty fought the Manchu Government troops in China (1851–64). The rebellion was led by the deranged Hung Hsiu-

---

* See the Guinness Superlatives books (Sterling in US) entitled *History of Land Warfare*, *History of Sea Warfare* and *History of Air Warfare* for further information.

ch'uan (executed) who imagined himself to be a younger brother of Jesus Christ. His force was named *T'ai-p'ing T'ien Kuo* (Heavenly Kingdom of Great Peace). According to the best estimates, the loss of life was between 20 and 30 million including more than 100,000 killed by Government forces in the sack of Nanking July 19-21, 1864.

Most Costly War

The material cost of World War II far transcended that of the rest of history's wars put together and has been estimated at $1.5 trillion. In the case of the UK the cost was over five times as great as that of World War I. The total cost of World War II to the Soviet Union was estimated in May 1959 at $280 billion while a figure of $530 billion has been estimated for the US.

Bloodiest Battle

The battle with the greatest recorded number of casualties was the First Battle of the Somme in France, July 1–Nov 19, 1916, with 1,043,896—Allied 623,907 and 419,989 German. The published German figure of *c.* 670,000 is not now accepted. The gunfire was heard as far away as Hampstead Heath, London. The greatest battle of World War II and the greatest conflict ever of armor was the Battle of Kursk and Oryol which raged for 50 days, July 5–Aug 23, 1943, on the Eastern front, which involved 1,300,000 Red Army troops with 3,600 tanks, 20,000 guns and 3,130 aircraft in repelling a German Army Group which had 2,700 tanks. The final invasion of Berlin by the Red Army, Apr 6–May 2, 1945 is, however, said to have involved 3,500,000 men, 52,000 guns and mortars, 7,750 tanks and 11,000 aircraft on both sides.

Modern historians give no credence, on logistic grounds, to the casualty figures attached to ancient battles, such as the 250,000 reputedly killed at Plataea (Greeks vs. Persians) in 479 BC or the 200,000 allegedly killed in a single day at Châlons-sur-Marne, France in 451 AD.

Greatest Seaborne Invasion

The greatest invasion in military history was the Allied land, air and sea operation against the Normandy coast of France on D-day, June 6, 1944. Thirty-eight convoys of 745 ships moved in on the first three days, supported by 4,066 landing craft, carrying 185,000 men and 20,000 vehicles, and 347 minesweepers. The air assault comprised 18,000 paratroopers from 1,087 aircraft. The 42 available divisions possessed an air support from 13,175 aircraft. Within a month 1,100,000 troops, 200,000 vehicles and 840,000 tons of stores were landed.

The Allied invasion of Sicily, July 10–12, 1943, involved the landing of 181,000 men in 3 days.

Greatest Airborne Invasion

The largest airborne invasion was the Anglo-American assault of three divisions (34,000) men, with 2,800 aircraft and 1,600 gliders, near Arnhem, Netherlands, Sept 17, 1944.

Longest Range Attack

The longest range attack in aviation history was from Ascension Island to Port Stanley, Falkland Islands, by a refueled RAF Vulcan bomber in a round trip of more than 8,000 miles in 1982.

Greatest Evacuation

The greatest evacuation in military history was that carried out by 1,200 Allied naval and civil craft from the beachhead at Dunkerque (Dunkirk), France May 27–June 4, 1940. A total of 338,226 British and French troops were taken off.

Worst Sieges

The worst siege in history was the 880-day siege of Leningrad, USSR by the German Army, Aug 30, 1941–Jan 27, 1944. The best estimate is that between 1.3 and 1.5 million defenders and citizens died.

The longest recorded siege was that of Azotus (now Ashdod), Israel, which, according to Herodotus, was besieged by Psamtik I of Egypt for 29 years in the period 664–610 BC.

ARMED FORCES

Largest Armed Forces

Numerically, the largest regular armed force is 4,750,000 for the People's Republic of China. Her paramilitary forces of armed and unarmed militias have been estimated by the International Institute of Strategic Studies at 12 million plus. Their mid-1981 estimates for the world's two principal military powers are 3,673,000 for the USSR and 2,049,000 for the US.

Defense

The estimated level of spending on armaments throughout the world in 1981 was $640 billion. This represents $140 per person per year, or more than 9% of the world's total production of goods and services. It was estimated in 1981 that there were 23.2 million full-time armed force regulars or conscripts.

The budgeted expenditure on defense by the US government in the year ending June 30, 1982, was $171,023 million or 5.7% of the country's GNP (gross national product). For the financial year 1982 this was raised to $185.8 billion.

The defense burden on the USSR has been variously estimated as a percentage of GNP to be greater than 15% (by China), up to 14% by Britain and up to 13% by the CIA and thus may be nearly three times that of the US.

The best estimates for late 1981 suggest the US has 9,750 nuclear warheads equivalent to 3,400 megatonnes with 1,052 Inter-Continental launchers while the USSR has 8,260 warheads capable of delivering 4,150 megatonnes of TNT equivalent and 1,398 ICBMs.

Largest Navies

The largest navy in terms of manpower is the US Navy, with 528,000 sailors and 188,100 Marines in mid-1981. The active strength in 1981 included 14 aircraft carriers, 79 attack nuclear submarines and 5 diesel attack submarines, 36 strategic missile submarines, 120 guided missile warships (25 cruisers, 82 destroyers, and 13 frigates), and 67 amphibious warfare ships.

The USSR Navy has a larger submarine fleet of 427 boats, with 115 in reserve. Offensive strategic nuclear weapons are carried by 168, of which all but 15 are also nuclear-powered. It has 2 aircraft carriers, 39 cruisers and 73 destroyers.

Greatest Naval Battle

The greatest number of ships and aircraft ever involved in a sea-air action was 231 ships and 1,996 aircraft in the Battle of Leyte Gulf, in the Philippines. It raged from Oct 22–27, 1944, with 166 Allied and 65 Japanese warships engaged, of which 26 Japanese and 6 US ships were sunk. In addition, 1,280 US and 716 Japanese aircraft were engaged.

The greatest naval battle of modern times was the Battle of Jutland on May 31, 1916, in which 151 Royal Navy warships were involved against 101 German warships. The Royal Navy lost 14 ships and

WORST SIEGE: For 880 days, the Germans surrounded Leningrad, USSR, from Aug 1941 to Jan 1944, and 1.3–1.5 million defenders died.

6,097 men and the German fleet 11 ships and 2,545 men.

The greatest of ancient naval battles was the Battle of Salamis, Greece, on Sept 23, 480 BC. There were an estimated 800 vessels in the defeated Persian fleet and 310 in the victorious Greek fleet with a possible involvement of 190,000 men. The death roll at the Battle of Lepanto on Oct 7, 1571, has been estimated at 33,000.

Oldest Army

The oldest army is the 83-strong Swiss Guard in the Vatican City, with a regular foundation dating back to Jan 21, 1506. Its origins, however, extend back before 1400.

Largest Army

Numerically, the world's largest army is that of the People's Republic of China, with a total strength of some 3.6 million in mid-1980. The total size of the USSR's army in mid-1980 was estimated by The International Institute of Strategic Studies at 1,825,000 men.

Oldest Old Soldier

The oldest age to which a veteran soldier has lived is 113 years 1 day by John B. Salling of the Army of the Confederate States of America and the last accepted survivor of the US Civil War (1861–65). He died in Kingsport, Tenn, Mar 16, 1959.

The longest serving US officer was General of the Army Omar Nelson Bradley (1893-1981) who served 69 years in the army.

Youngest Soldiers

President Francisco Macias Nguema of Equatorial Guinea decreed in March 1976 compulsory military service for all boys between 7 and 14. Any parent refusing to hand over his or her son "will be imprisoned or shot." Probably the youngest enlistment in the 20th century was by William Frederick Price (b June 1, 1891) who enlisted in the British Army at Aldershot, May 23, 1903, aged 11 years 356 days.

Tallest Soldier

The tallest soldier of all time was Väinö Myllyrinne (1909–63) who was inducted into the Finnish Army when he was 7 ft 3 in and later grew to 8 ft 1¼ in.

Earliest Tanks*

The first tank was "No. 1 Lincoln," modified to become "Little Willie," built by William Foster & Co Ltd of Lincoln, England. It first ran on Sept 8, 1915. Tanks were first taken into action by the Heavy Section Machine Gun Corps, which later became the Royal Tank Corps, at the battle of Flers-Courcelette, France on Sept 15, 1916. The Mark I Male, which

---

* For further information see *Tank Facts and Feats* by Kenneth Macksey, a Guinness Superlatives Book (Sterling), which deals with all the aspects of the development and history of the tank and other armored fighting vehicles in detail.

FASTEST TANK: The prototype of the XM-1 cost the US Army about $1,800,000, but it can speed at 45 mph.

was armed with a pair of 6-lb guns and 4 machine-guns, weighed 31.4 tons and was driven by a motor developing 105 hp, which gave it a maximum road speed of 3 to 4 mph.

Heaviest and Fastest Tanks

The heaviest tank ever constructed was the German Panzer Kampfwagen Maus II, which weighed 212 tons. By 1945 it had reached only the experimental stage and was not proceeded with.

The heaviest operational tank used by any army was the 91.3-ton 13-man French Char de Rupture 2C bis of 1923. It carried a 155-mm howitzer and had two 250-hp engines giving a maximum speed of 8 mph.

The world's fastest tank is the $1,800,000 XM-1, due for US Army service. The prototype reached 45 mph. The DM 3,600,000 ($1,900,000) German Leopard 2 has the greatest firepower with a 120-mm (4.72-in) gun.

Earliest Guns

Although it cannot be accepted as proved, the best opinion is that the earliest guns were constructed in North Africa, possibly by Arabs, c. 1250. The earliest representation of an English gun is contained in an illustrated manuscript dated 1326 at Oxford. The earliest anti-aircraft gun was an artillery piece on a high-angle mounting used in the Franco-Prussian War of 1870 by the Prussians against French balloons.

Largest Guns

The two most massive guns ever constructed were used by the Germans in the siege of Sevastapol on the Eastern Front in World War II. They were of a caliber of 800 mm (31.5 in) with barrels 94 ft long, and named Dore and Gustav. Their remains were discovered, one near Metzenhof, Bavaria in Aug 1945 and the other in the Soviet zone of Germany. They were built by Krupp as railway guns, carried on 24 cars, two of which had 40 wheels each. The whole assembly of the gun was 141 ft long and weighed 1,482 tons, requiring a crew of 1,500 men. The range for a 9¼-ton projectile was 29 miles.

Greatest Range

The greatest range ever attained by a gun is by the HARP (High Altitude Research Project) consisting of two 16.5-in caliber barrels in tandem, 119.4 ft long and weighing 165 tons, at Yuma, Ariz. On Nov 19, 1966, a 185-lb projectile was fired to an altitude of 111.8 miles (590,550 ft). The static V3 underground firing tubes built by the Germans in 50° shafts at

Mimoyecques, near Calais, France to bombard London were never operative, due to RAF bombing.

The famous long-range gun which shelled Paris in World War I in March 1918 was the *Kaiser Wilhelm Geschütz,* with a caliber of 220 mm (8.66 in), a designed range of 79.5 miles and an achieved range of 76 miles. The "Big Berthas" were mortars of 420-mm (16.53-in) caliber with a range of less than 9 miles.

Largest Cannon

The highest caliber cannon ever constructed is the *Tsar Puchka* (King of Cannons), now housed in the Kremlin, Moscow. It was built in the 16th century with a bore of 922 mm (36¼ in) and a barrel 10 ft 5 in long. It weighs 44 tons.

The Turks fired up to seven shots per day from a bombard 26 ft long, with an internal caliber of 42 in, against the walls of Constantinople (now Istanbul) Apr 12-May 29, 1453. It was dragged by 60 oxen and 200 men and fired a stone cannonball of 1,200 lb.

Mortars

The largest mortars ever constructed were Mallets mortar (Woolwich Arsenal, London, 1857), and the "Little David" of World War II, made in the US. Each had a caliber of 920 mm (36¼ in), but neither was ever used in action.

The heaviest mortar used was the tracked German 600-mm (23.6-in) siege piece known as "Karl" used against Stalingrad.

Largest Catapults

The largest military catapults, or onagers, were capable of throwing a missile weighing 60 lb a distance of 500 yd.

Longest March

The longest march in military history was the famous Long March by the Chinese Communists in 1934-35. In 368 days, of which 268 days were of movement, from Oct to Oct, their force of 90,000 covered 6,000 miles northward from Kiangsi to Yenan in Shensi *via* Yünnan. They crossed 18 mountain ranges and six major rivers and lost all but 22,000 of their force in continual rear-guard actions against Nationalist Kuo-min-tang (KMT) forces.

Most Rapid March

The most rapid recorded march by foot-soldiers was one of 42 miles covered in 11 hours 49 min in a night march by 9 soldiers in full battle dress carrying 40 lb from B Company, 4th Infantry Battalion of the Irish Army, Sept 12–13, 1944.

Earliest Air Force

The earliest autonomous air force is the Royal Air Force of Great Britain, whose origin began with the

Royal Flying Corps (created May 13, 1912); the Air Battalion of the Royal Engineers (Apr 1, 1911) and the Corps of Royal Engineers Balloon Section (1878) which was first operational in Bechuanaland (now Botswana) in 1884. The Prussian Army used a balloon near Strasbourg, France as early as Sept 24, 1870.

Largest Air Force

The greatest air force of all time was the US Army Air Force (now called the US Air Force), which had 79,908 aircraft in July 1944, and 2,411,294 personnel in March 1944. The US Air Force, including strategic air forces, had 555,100 personnel and 3,700 combat aircraft in mid-1980. The USSR Air Force, including Air Defense Forces with about 1,070,000 men in mid-1980, had 5,850 combat aircraft. In addition, the USSR's Offensive Strategic Rocket Forces had about 380,000 operational personnel in mid-1980.

Largest Mutiny

In World War I, 56 French divisions, comprising some 650,000 men and their officers, refused orders on the Western Front sector of General Nivelle in Apr 1917 after the failure of his offensive.

Bombs

The heaviest conventional bomb ever used operationally was the British Royal Air Force's "Grand Slam," weighing 22,000 lb and measuring 25 ft 5 in long, dropped on Bielefeld railway viaduct, Germany, March 14, 1945. In 1949, the US Air Force tested a bomb weighing 42,000 lb at Muroc Dry Lake, Calif.

Atomic Bombs

The two atom bombs dropped on Japan by the US in 1945 each had an explosive power equivalent to that of 20,000 tons (20 kilotons) of trinitrotoluene, called TNT. The one dropped on Hiroshima, code-named "Little Boy," was 10 ft long and weighed 9,000 lb.

The most powerful thermonuclear device so far tested is one with a power equivalent to 57 million tons of TNT, or 57 megatons, detonated by the USSR in the Novaya Zemlya area at 8:33 a.m. GMT on Oct 30, 1961. The shock wave was detected to have circled the world three times, taking 36 hours

27 min for the first circuit. Some estimates put the power of this device at between 62 and 90 megatons. On Aug 9, 1961, Nikita Khrushchev, then the Chairman of the Council of Ministers of the USSR, declared that the Soviet Union was capable of constructing a 100-megaton bomb, and announced the possession of one in East Berlin, Germany, on Jan 16, 1963. Such a device could make a crater in rock 355 ft deep and 1.8 miles wide and a fireball of 46,000 ft, or 8.7 miles, in diameter.

Atom bomb theory began with Albert Einstein's publication of the $E = mc^2$ formula in *Annalen der Physik* in Leipzig on May 14, 1907. It became practical with the mesothorium experiments of Otto Hahn, Fritz Strassman, and Lise Meitner on Dec 17, 1938. Work started in the USSR on atomic bombs in June 1942, although the first chain reaction was not achieved until Dec 1945, by Dr Igor Vasilyevich Kurchatov.

The patent for the fusion or H-bomb was filed in the US on May 26, 1946, by Dr Janos (John) von Neumann (1903–57), a Hungarian-born mathematician, and Dr Klaus Julius Emil Fuchs (b Germany, 1911), the physicist who defected to Russia from England. The largest US H-bomb tested was the 15-megaton "Bravo" at Bikini Atoll, Bahamas, on Mar 1, 1954.

Largest Nuclear Weapons

The most powerful ICBM's are the USSR's SS-18's, each with up to 10 one-megaton MIRV's (multiple independently targetable re-entry vehicles); thus each has power 50 times as great as the Hiroshima bomb. The US Minuteman III has 3 MIRV's, each of 335 kiloton force.

No official estimate has been published of the potential power of the device known as Doomsday, but this far surpasses any tested weapon. If it were practicable to construct, it is speculated that a 50,000-megaton cobalt-salted device could wipe out the entire human race except people who were deep underground and did not emerge for more than five years.

Largest "Conventional" Explosion

The largest use of conventional explosive was for the demolition of the fortifications and U-Boat pens at Heligoland on April 18, 1947. A net charge of 4,253 tons was detonated by Commissioned Gunner E. C. Jellis of the Royal Navy team headed by Lt F. T. Woosnam aboard *HMS Lasso* lying 9 miles out to sea.

Most Bombed Country

The most heavily bombed country has been Laos. It has been estimated that between May 1964 and Feb 26, 1973 some 2½ million tons of bombs of all kinds were dropped along the North to South Ho Chi Minh Trail supply route to South Vietnam.

3. JUDICIAL

LEGISLATION AND LITIGATION

Oldest Statutes

The earliest known judicial code was that of King Ur-Hammu during the Third Dynasty of Ur, Iraq, c. 2145 BC.

Most Inexplicable Statute

Certain passages in several laws have always defied interpretation and the most inexplicable must be a matter of opinion. A judge of the Court of Session of Scotland has sent the editors of this book his candidate which reads, "In the Nuts (unground), (other than ground nuts) Order, the expression nuts shall have reference to such nuts, other than ground nuts, as would but for this amending Order not qualify as nuts (unground) (other than ground nuts) by reason of their being nuts (unground)."

Most Protracted Litigation

The longest contested lawsuit ever recorded ended in Poona, India, Apr 28, 1966, when Balasaheb Patloji Thorat received a favorable judgment on a suit filed by his ancestor Maloji Thorat 761 years earlier in 1205. The points at issue were rights of presiding over public functions and precedences at religious festivals.

Longest Impeachment

The British Parliament's impeachment of Gov Warren Hastings (1732–1818), for maladministration of India, began in 1788 and dragged on for 7 years, until his acquittal Apr 23, 1795. The trial itself lasted only 149 days.

Best-Attended Trial

The greatest attendance at any trial was at that of Major Jesús Sosa Blanco, aged 51, for an alleged 108 murders. At one point in the 12½-hour trial (5:30 p.m. to 6 a.m., Jan 22–23, 1959), 17,000 people were present in the Havana Sports Palace, Cuba.

Largest Award Won Without Attorney

Dr Mark Feldman, a podiatric surgeon of Lauderhill, Fla, became the first litigant in person (without the services of an attorney) to secure 7 figures ($1 million) before a jury in compensatory and punitive damages in Sept 1980. The case concerned conspiracy and fraud alleged against 6 other doctors.

Highest Bail

The highest amount ever demanded as bail was $46,500,000 against Antonio De Angelis in a civil damages suit by the Harbor Tank Storage Co filed in the Superior Court, Jersey City, NJ, Jan 16, 1964, in the Salad Oil Swindle. He was released June 4, 1973.

Abul Hassen Ebtehaj, later Chairman of the Iranian Bank in Teheran, was granted bail in 1977 in excess of $50 million.

Breach of Contract

The greatest damages ever awarded for a breach of contract were £610,392 ($1,709,000), awarded July 16, 1930, to the Bank of Portugal against the printers Waterlow & Sons Ltd of London, arising from their unauthorized printing of 580,000 five-hundred escudo notes in 1925. This award was upheld in the House of Lords on Apr 28, 1932. One of the perpetrators, Arthur Virgilio Alves Reis, served 16 years (1930–46) in jail.

Greatest Personal Injury Damages

The greatest damages for personal injury ever awarded went to Janelle Lynn Stearns, 12, against Park Avenue Hospital Inc and Dr Howard K. Gifford, an anesthetist, in settlement for alleged medical malpractice resulting in severe brain damage following a tonsillectomy at Pomona, Calif in May 1973. If she lives to the average expectation of 63.9 additional years, the payments will total $26,541,832.

The largest single cash payment settlement for a single person has been $6,800,000 to John Coates, 42, a lawyer from Austin, Tex against Remington Arms Co Inc et al, on Oct 2, 1978. The case concerned severe injury from a defectively made hunting rifle.

The highest damages ever quantified have been

$14,387,674 following the crash of a private aircraft at South Lake Tahoe, Calif, on Feb 21, 1967, to the sole survivor Ray Rosendin, 45, by the Santa Clara Superior Court on March 8, 1972. Rosendin was awarded *inter alia* $1,069,374 for the loss of both legs and disabling arm injuries and $1,213,129 for the loss of his wife. Punitive damages against Avco-Lycoming Corp, which allegedly violated Federal regulations when it rebuilt the aircraft engine owned by Rosendin Corp, were originally set at $10½ million but were overturned on appeal.

Defamation Suits

A sum of $16.8 million was awarded to Dr John J. Wild, 58, at the Hennepin District Court of Minnesota on Nov 30, 1972, against the Minnesota Foundation and others for defamation, bad-faith termination of a contract, and interference with professional business relationships, plus $10.8 million in punitive damages. These amounts have not to date been appealed. The $39.6 million awarded in Columbus, O on Mar 1, 1980, to Robert Guccione, publisher of *Penthouse,* for defamation against Larry Flynt, publisher of *Hustler*, was reduced by Judge Craig Wright to $4 million on Apr 17, 1980.

The $500-million libel suit brought by the California resort La Costa against *Penthouse* and its publisher in Mar 1975 reached the court in Dec 1981 by which time the costs exceeded $6 million.

Greatest Compensation for Wrongful Imprisonment

On Aug 12, 1975, William De Palma (b 1938) of Whittier, Calif, agreed to a $750,000 settlement for 16 months' wrongful imprisonment in McNeil Island Federal Prison, Wash. He had been given a 15-year sentence for armed robbery in Buena Park, Calif, on forged fingerprint evidence in 1968.

Alimony

The highest alimony awarded by a court has been $2,261,000 against George Storer Sr, 74, in favor of his third wife Dorothy, 73, in Miami, Fla, on Oct 29, 1974. Mr Storer, a broadcasting executive, was also ordered to pay his ex-wife's attorney $200,000 in fees.

Belgian-born Sheika Dena Al-Fassi, 23, filed the highest ever alimony claim of $3 billion against her former husband Sheik Mohammed Al-Fassi, 28, of the Saudi Arabia royal family, in LA, Calif, in Feb 1982. Explaining the size of the settlement claim,

Marvin Mitchelson alluded to the Sheik's wealth which included 14 homes in Florida alone and numerous private aircraft.

Patent Case

The greatest settlement ever made in a patent-infringement suit is $9,250,000, paid in Apr 1952 by the Ford Motor Co to the Ferguson Tractor Co for a claim filed in Jan 1948.

Greatest Lien

The greatest lien ever imposed by a court is 40 billion lire ($64,800,000) on Apr 9, 1974 in Milan, upon Vittorio and Ida Riva for back taxes allegedly due on a chain of cotton mills around Turin, Italy inherited by their brother Felice (who left for Beirut) in 1960.

Longest Lease

Part of the Cattle Market, Dublin, Ireland was leased by John Jameson to the city's Corporation on a lease for 100,000 years, expiring Jan 21, 101,863 AD.

Most Literal Legal Interpretation

Eugene Schneider of Carteret, NJ, allegedly cut his $80,000 home in half with a chain saw in July 1976 after his wife sued him for divorce, thus fulfilling in his eyes the equal division of property required by NJ law.

Largest Suit for Damages

The highest amount of damages ever sought is $675 trillion (then equivalent to 10 times the US national wealth) in a suit by Mr I. Walton Bader brought in the US District Court, NYC, Apr 14, 1971, against General Motors and others for polluting all 50 states.

Shortest and Longest Wills

The shortest valid will in the world is "Vse zene," the Czech for "All to wife," written and dated Jan 19, 1967, by Herr Karl Tausch of Langen, Hesse, Germany. The shortest will contested but subsequently admitted to probate in English law was the case of *Thorn v. Dickens* in 1906. It consisted of the three words "All for Mother."

The longest will on record was that of Mrs Frederica Cook (US), in the early part of the century. It consisted of four bound volumes containing 95,940 words.

Most Durable Judges

The oldest recorded active judge was Judge Albert R. Alexander (b Nov 8, 1859) of Plattsburg, Mo, magistrate and probate judge of Clinton County. He retired July 9, 1965, at the age of 105 years 8 months and died March 30, 1966. Judge J. Frank Graff (b Dec 28, 1888) was serving as a senior judge at Armstrong County Court House, Pa, since Jan 1, 1923. Judge Vernon D. Hitchings of Norfolk, Va, disposed of his millionth traffic case from Jan 1954 to Jan 19, 1977. Of these, some 965,000 of his verdicts were unappealed or upheld on appeal. In more than 23 years of judgeship to his retirement in Dec 1968, Judge James Hardie Ferguson heard 13,000 cases in the Wilmington Juvenile and Domestic Relations Court, NC, without a single appeal.

Youngest Judges

No collated records on the ages of judicial appointments exist. However, Thomas J. Boynton (b Amherst, Ohio, Aug 31, 1838) is known to have been appointed Federal Judge at Key West, Fla, on Jan 20, 1864, aged 25 years 142 days. Judge Susan I. Broyles (b Alamosa, Colo, June 25, 1949) was appointed County Judge of Conejos County, Colo, on Jan 9, 1973, aged 23 years 198 days.

Most Successful Criminal Lawyer

Sir Lionel Luckhoo, senior partner of Luckhoo and Luckhoo, of Georgetown, Guyana, succeeded in getting his 240th successive murder charge acquittal by Jan 1, 1982.

Deadliest Prosecutor

Joe Freeman Britt, District Attorney in the Sixteenth Judicial District in North Carolina, obtained 23 death verdicts in 28 months to mid-1976, when he had 13 defendants simultaneously on death row.

CRIME AND PUNISHMENT

Mass Killings

The greatest massacre ever imputed by the government of one sovereign nation against a government of another is that of 26,300,000 Chinese killed during the regime of Mao Tse-tung between 1949 and May 1965. This accusation was made by an agency of the USSR government in a radio broadcast Apr 7, 1969. The Walker Report published by the US Senate Committee of the Judiciary in July 1971 placed the total death roll within China since 1949 between 32.25 and 61.7 million.

The death roll in the Great Purge, or *Yezhovshchina,* in the USSR, in 1936–38, has never been published, though evidence of its magnitude may be found in population statistics which show a deficiency of males from *before* the outbreak of the 1941–45 war. On Aug 17, 1942, Stalin indicated to Churchill in Moscow that 10 million *kulaks* (farmers with excessive wealth according to Communist standards) had been liquidated.

At the S.S. (*Schutzstaffel*) extermination camp

WINNINGEST LAWYER: Sir Lionel Luckoo of Guyana has won 240 cases without a loss—all murder charge acquittals.

known as Auschwitz-Birkenau (Oswiecim-Brze-zinka), near Oswiecim, in southern Poland, where a minimum of 920,000 people (Soviet estimate is 4,000,000) were exterminated June 14, 1940–Jan 18, 1945, the greatest number killed in a day was 6,000.

Obersturmbannführer (Lt-Col) Karl Adolf Eichmann (b 1906) of the S.S. was hanged in a small room inside Ramleh Prison, near Tel Aviv, Israel, at just before midnight (local time) on May 31, 1962, for his complicity in the deaths of an indeterminably massive number of Jews during World War II, under the instruction given in Apr 1941 by Adolf Hitler (1889–1945) for the "Final Solution" (*Endlösung*).

Genocide

In Cambodia, according to the Khmer Rouge foreign minister, Ieng Sarg, more than a third of the 8 million Khmers were killed between Apr 17, 1975, and Jan 1979. Under the rule of Pol Pot, towns, money and property were abolished and execution by bayonet and club introduced for such offenses as falling asleep during the day, asking too many questions, playing non-Communist music, being old and feeble, being the offspring of an "undesirable" or being too well educated. Deaths at the Tuol Sleng interrogation center reached 582 in a day.

It has been estimated that 35 million Chinese were wiped out in the Mongolian invasion of 1210–19.

Terrorist Outrages

The greatest death toll from a terrorist bomb was 76 killed and 200 injured at the central railway station, Bologna, Italy, Aug 2, 1980.

Largest Criminal Organization

The largest syndicate of organized crime is the Mafia (derived from an arabic expression connoting beauty, excellence allied with bravery) or La Cosa Nostra ("our thing") which is said to have infiltrated the executive, judiciary and legislative branches of the US Government. It consists of some 3,000 to 5,000 individuals in 24 "families" federated under "The Commission," with an estimated turnover in vice, gambling, protection rackets, cigarettes, bootlegging, hijacking, narcotics, loan-sharking, prostitution and some legitimate business estimated in May 1977 in *Time* magazine at $48,000 million per year, of which some $25,300 million is profit—then 9½ times more than Exxon's profit in 1979.

The biggest Mafia killing was Sept 11–13, 1931,

when the topmost man, Salvatore Maranzano, *Il Capo di Tutti Capi,* and 40 allies were liquidated.

The Mafia is said to have got its start in the US in New Orleans in 1869.

Murder Rates

The country with the highest recorded murder rate is Mexico with 46.3 registered homicides per 100,000 of the population in 1970.

It has been estimated that the total number of murders in Colombia during *La Violencia* (1945–62) was about 300,000, giving a rate over a 17-year period of nearly 48 per day. A total of 592 deaths was attributed to one bandit leader, Teófilo ("Sparks") Rojas, aged 27, between 1948 and his death in an ambush near Armenia on Jan 22, 1963. Some sources attribute 3,500 slayings to him.

The highest homicide rates recorded in NYC have been 58 in a week in July 1972, and 13 in a day in Aug 1972. In 1973, the total for Detroit (population then 1,500,000) was 751.

The country with the lowest officially recorded rate in the world is the Maldives (islands in the Indian Ocean, pop. 100,833 in 1966) with a nil rate among its nationals since its independence in July 1965. In the Indian state of Sikkim, in the Himalayas, murder is practically unknown, while in the Hunza area of Kashmir, in the Karakoram, only one definite case by a Hunzarwal has been recorded since 1900.

Most Prolific Murderers

It was established at the trial of Buhram, the Indian Thug, that he had strangled at least 931 victims with his yellow and white cloth *ruhmal* in the Oudh district between 1790 and 1840. It has been estimated that at least 2 million Indians were strangled by Thugs (*burtotes*) during the reign of the Thugee cult (pronounced "tugee") from 1550 until its final suppression by the British raj in 1853.

The greatest number of victims ascribed to a murderess has been 650 in the case of Countess Erszebet Bathory (1560–1614) of Hungary. At her trial which began Jan 2, 1611, a witness testified to seeing a list of her victims in her own handwriting totaling this number. All were alleged to be young girls from the neighborhood of her castle at Csejthe, where she died on Aug 21, 1614. She was walled up in her room for 3½ years, after being found guilty.

This century's top candidate for most prolific one-at-a-time murderer is Pedro Alonso López (b Co-

lombia, 1949), known as the "Colombian Monster," who was reported captured by the villagers of Ambato, Ecuador in early March 1980. He admitted to more than 300 murders of pre-teen girls in Colombia, Peru and Ecuador since 1973. The remains of 53 victims of the 110 admitted to in Ecuador were rapidly detected after his confession.

In a drunken rampage lasting 8 hours, Apr 26–27, 1982, Policeman Wou Bom-Kon, 27, killed 57 people and wounded 35 with 176 rounds of rifle ammunition and hand grenades in the Kyong Sang-Namdo province of S Korea. He blew himself up with a grenade.

Gang Murders

During the period of open gang warfare in Chicago, the peak year was 1926, when there were 76 unsolved killings. The 1,000th gang murder in Chicago since 1919 occurred on Feb 1, 1967. Only 13 cases have ended in convictions.

Suicide

The estimated daily rate of suicides throughout the world surpassed 1,000 in 1965. The country with the highest recorded suicide rate is Hungary, with 42.6 per 100,000 of the population in 1977. The country with the lowest recorded rate is Jordan, with a single case in 1970 and hence a rate of 0.04 per 100,000.

The final total of the mass cyanide poisoning of the Peoples Temple cult near Port Kaituma, Guyana,

Nov 18, 1978 was 913. The leader was the paranoid "Rev" Jim Jones of San Francisco, who had deposited millions of dollars overseas.

Mass Poisonings

On May 1, 1981, the first victim of the Spanish cooking-oil scandal fell ill. On June 12 it was discovered that his cause of death was the use of "denatured" industrial colza from rape seed. By Feb 1982 the death toll had reached 260 dead with thousands maimed. The manufacturers Ramon and Elias Ferrero await trial in Carabanchel Jail, Madrid.

Last Guillotinings

There were 6 guillotinings in the 1970s.

Largest Hanging

The most people hanged from one gallows was 38 Sioux Indians by William J. Duly outside Mankato, Minn for the murder of unarmed citizens on Dec 26, 1862.

The Nazi Feldkommandant simultaneously hanged 50 Greek resistance fighters as a reprisal in Athens, July 22, 1944.

Death Row

In Oct 1981 there were 180 prisoners in the US on "death row."

Caryl Whittier Chessman, aged 38, convicted of 17 felonies, was executed on May 2, 1960, in the gas chamber at the California State Prison, San Quentin, Calif. In 11 years 10 months and one week on "death row," Chessman had won eight stays of execution.

Samanichi Hirasawa celebrated his 90th birthday on death row in Sendai Risan, northern Japan, on Feb 18, 1982.

Longest Prison Sentences

A 10,000-year sentence was imposed on Dudley Wayne Kyzer, 40, on Dec 4, 1981, in Tuscaloosa, Ala, for a triple murder (includung his mother-in-law) in 1976. A sentence of 384,912 years was *de-*

315

manded at the prosecution of Gabriel March Grandos, 22, at Palma de Mallorca, Spain, March 11, 1972, for failing to deliver 42,768 letters, a sentence of 9 years per letter.

Juan Corona, a Mexican-American, was sentenced on Feb 5, 1973, at Fairfield, Calif, to 25 consecutive life terms for murdering 25 migrant farm workers he had hired, killed and buried in 1970–71 near Feather River, Yuba City, Calif. His 20th century record was surpassed in 1974 by Dean Corll (27 victims) of Houston, Tex, and in 1980 by John Wayne Gacy (33 victims).

Longest Time Served

Paul Geidel (b Apr 21, 1894) was convicted of 2nd degree murder on Sept 5, 1911 as a 17-year-old porter in a NYC hotel. He was released from the Fishkill Correctional Facility, Beacon, NY, aged 85, on May 7, 1980, having served 68 years 8 months 2 days—the longest recorded term in US history. He had first refused parole in 1974.

Most Jailings

There are no collated records on the greatest number of convictions on an individual, but the highest recently reported is 1,433 for the gentlemanly but alcoholic Edward Eugene Ebzery, who died in Brisbane Jail, Queensland, Australia, on Sept 23, 1967.

Greatest Mass Arrest

The greatest mass arrest reported in a democratic country was of more than 13,000 people in an antiwar demonstration designed to block rush-hour traffic in Wash, DC, May 3–5, 1971.

MOST SECURE PRISON: Alcatraz in San Francisco Bay, no longer a prison, was the most secure 1934–63, as no one ever succeeded in escaping, contrary to fictional stories and movies.

Penal Camps

The largest penal camp systems in the world were those near Karaganda and Kolyma, in the USSR, each with a population estimated in 1958 at between 1,200,000 and 1,500,000. The largest labor camp is now said to be the Dubrovlag Complex of 15 camps centered on Pot'ma, Mordovian Republic, USSR. The official NATO estimate for all Soviet camps was "more than one million" in March 1960 compared with a peak of probably 12 million during the Stalinist era.

Most Secure Prison

After it became a maximum security Federal prison in 1934, no convict was known to have lived to tell of a successful escape from the prison on Alcatraz Island in San Francisco Bay. A total of 23 men attempted it, but 12 were recaptured, 5 shot dead, one drowned and 5 presumed drowned. On Dec 16, 1962, three months before the prison was closed, one man reached the mainland alive, only to be recaptured on the spot. John Chase was imprisoned for a record 26 years on Alcatraz.

Most Expensive Prison

Spandau Prison, Berlin, built 100 years ago for 600 prisoners, is now used solely for the person widely and officially purported to be the Nazi war criminal Rudolf Hess (b Apr 26, 1894). The cost of maintenance has been estimated at $415,000 per year for the staff of 105.

Longest Prison Escape

The longest recorded escape by a prisoner who was eventually recaptured was that of Leonard T. Fristoe, 77, who escaped from Nevada State Prison, on Dec 15, 1923, and was turned in by his son on Nov 15, 1969, at Compton, Calif. He had 46 years of freedom under the name Claude R. Willis. He had killed two sheriff's deputies in 1920.

Greatest Jail Break

In Feb 1979, US Army Col Arthur "Bull" Simons (ret) led a band of 14 to break into Gasre prison, Teheran, Iran, to rescue two fellow Americans. Some 11,000 other prisoners took advantage of this and the Islamic revolution in what became history's largest jail break.

In July 1971, Raoul Sendic and 105 other Tupamaro guerrillas escaped from a Uruguayan prison through a tunnel 298 ft long.

Robbery

The greatest robbery on record was of the Reichsbank following Germany's collapse in April and May 1945. The largest haul consisted of negotiable securities valued at $400 million. In Apr 1979, three men were convicted and sentenced to terms of imprisonment at Brantford, Ontario, Canada on a number of conspiracy charges connected with some of these bonds.

Gold bullion, foreign exchange and jewels worth $20 million (worth some $200 million today) were also stolen, allegedly by members of the German and American armies. None of this loot was ever recovered and none of the perpetrators were ever brought to trial.

Art Theft

The greatest recorded robbery by market valuation was the removal of 19 paintings, valued at $19,200,000, from Russborough House, Blessington, Ireland, the home of Sir Alfred and Lady Beit, by 4 men and a woman, Apr 26, 1974. They included the $6.9 million Vermeer *Lady Writing a Letter with her Maid.* The paintings were recovered May 4, 1974, near Glandore, Ireland. Dr Rose Bridgit Dugdale (b 1941) was subsequently convicted.

It is arguable that the value of the *Mona Lisa* at the time of its theft from the Louvre on Aug 21, 1911, was greater than this figure. It was recovered in Italy in 1913 when Vincenzo Perruggia was charged with its theft.

On Sept 1, 1964, antiquities reputedly worth $23 million were recovered from 3 warehouses near the Pyramids in Egypt.

Bank Robbery

During the extreme civil disorder prior to Jan 22, 1976, in Beirut, Lebanon, a guerrilla force blasted the vaults of the British Bank of the Middle East in Bab Idriss and cleared out safe deposit boxes with contents valued by former Finance Minister Lucien Dahadah at $50 million, and by another source at an "absolute minimum" of $20 million.

Jewel Robbery

The greatest recorded theft of jewels was from the bedroom of the "well-guarded" villa of Prince Abdel Aziz Ben Ahmed Al-Thani near Cannes, France, July 24, 1980, valued at $16 million.

Train Robbery

The greatest recorded train robbery occurred between 3:03 a.m. and 3:27 a.m. on Aug 8, 1963, when a General Post Office mail train from Glasgow, Scotland was ambushed at Sears Crossing and robbed at Bridego Bridge near Mentmore, Buckinghamshire, England. The gang escaped with about 120 mailbags containing £2,631,784 ($6,053,103) worth of bank notes being taken to London for pulping. Only £343,448 ($961,654) was recovered.

Largest Object Ever Stolen by a Single Man

On a moonless night at dead calm high water on June 5, 1966, N. William Kennedy, armed with only a sharp axe, slashed free the mooring lines at Wolfe's Cove, St Lawrence Seaway, Quebec, Canada of the 10,639 dwt SS *Orient Trader* owned by Steel Factors Ltd of Ontario. The vessel drifted to a waiting blacked-out tug, thus escaping a ban on any shipping movements during a violent wildcat waterfront strike. She sailed for Spain.

Greatest Kidnapping Ransom

Historically, the greatest ransom paid was that for their chief, Atahualpa, by the Incas to the Spanish conquistador Francisco Pizarro, in 1532–33 at Cajamarca, Peru, which included a hall full of gold and silver worth in modern money some $170 million.

The greatest ransom ever extorted is $60 million for the release of two businessmen, the brothers Jorge Born, 40, and Juan Born, 39, of Argentina, paid to the left-wing urban guerrilla group Montoneros in Buenos Aires, June 20, 1975.

The youngest person ever kidnapped has been Carolyn Wharton, who was born at 12:46 p.m., March 19, 1955, in the Baptist Hospital, Beaumont, Tex, and kidnapped by a woman disguised as a nurse at 1:15 p.m., when the baby was aged 29 min.

Greatest Hijack Ransom

The highest amount ever paid to aircraft hijackers has been $6 million by the Japanese government in the case of a JAL DC-8 held at Dacca airport, Bangladesh on Oct 2, 1977 with 38 hostages. Six convicted criminals were also exchanged. The Bangladesh government had refused to sanction any retaliatory action.

Largest Narcotics Haul

In March 1982, US Customs found, by chance, 22 boxes of highest quality cocaine weighing 3,700 lb from a Medellin, Colombia, flight at Miami International Airport, Fla. The US Drug Enforcement Agency estimated the street value at $950 million.

The bulkiest haul was 3,192 tons of Colombian marijuana in the 14-month-long "Operation Tiburon" concluded by the DEA with the arrest of 495 people and the seizure of 95 vessels, announced on Feb 5, 1982.

The British Home Office disclosed on Dec 23, 1977, that 13 million LSD tablets with a street value approaching $170 million had been destroyed at the conclusion of "Operation Julie."

Greatest Currency Forgery

The greatest recorded forgery was the German Third Reich government's forging operation, code name "Bernhard," engineered by S.S. *Sturmbannführer* Alfred Naujocks in 1940–41. It involved £150 million (now about $300 million) worth of Bank of England £5 notes.

Biggest Bank Fraud

The largest amount of money named in a defalcation case has been a gross £33 million ($75,900,000) at the Lugano, Switzerland, branch of Lloyd's Bank International Ltd Sept 2, 1974. Mark Colombo was arrested pending charges including falsification of foreign currency accounts and suppression of evidence.

Computer Fraud

Between 1964 and 1973, some 64,000 fake insurance policies were created on the computer of the Equity Funding Corporation involving $2,000 million.

Stanley Mark Rifkin (b 1946) was arrested in Carlsbad, Calif by the FBI on Nov 6, 1978, charged with defrauding a Los Angeles bank of $10.2 million by manipulation of a computer system. In June 1980 he was sentenced to 8 years.

Welfare Swindle

The greatest welfare swindle yet worked was that of the gypsy Anthony Moreno, on the French Social Security in Marseilles. By forging birth certificates and school registration forms, he invented 197 fictitious families and 3,000 children on which he claimed benefits from 1960 to mid-1968. Moreno, nicknamed "El Chorro" (the fountain), was later reported free of extradition worries and living in luxury in his native Spain having absquatulated with an estimated $6,440,000.

4. ECONOMIC

MONETARY AND FINANCE

Largest Budget

The greatest annual expenditure budgeted by any country is $769.8 billion by the US Government (federal expenditure) for the fiscal year 1983. The highest budgeted revenue in the US is $665.9 billion for the fiscal year 1981.

In the US, the greatest surplus was $8,419,469,844 in 1947–48, and the greatest budgeted deficit has been $103.9 billion in fiscal year 1983.

Foreign Aid

The total net foreign aid given by the US Government between July 1, 1945, and Jan 1, 1981, was $187,696 million.

The country which received most US aid in 1980 was Israel with $1,849 million. US foreign aid began with $50,000 to Venezuela for earthquake relief in 1812.

Highest Tax Rates

The country with the most confiscatory taxation is Norway where in Jan 1974 the Labor Party and Socialist Alliance abolished the 80% top limit. Some 2,000 citizens were then listed in the *Lignings Boka* as paying more than 100% of their taxable income. The shipping magnate Hilmer Reksten was assessed at 491%.

Highest Tax Demand

The highest recorded tax demand is one for $336 million for 70% of the estate of Howard Hughes.

Least Taxed People

The lowest income tax is paid by the citizens of Bahrain, Kuwait, and Qatar, where the rate, regardless of income, is zero.

Gross National Product

The country with the largest GNP is the US, reaching $3 trillion in 1981.

Poorest Country

The lowest published annual per capita income of any country is Bhutan, with a tentative $80 (1980), but the World Bank has no data for Kampuchea (Cambodia), Laos, Somalia or Vietnam.

National Debt

The largest national debt is that of the US, where the gross Federal public debt surpassed the half-trillion dollar mark in 1975 and reached $1,011,111 million by Oct 1981. This amount in dollar bills would make a pile 52,550 miles high, weighing 736,233 tons.

Foreign Debt

The country most heavily in overseas debt is Brazil with $69 billion.

National Wealth Per Capita

The richest nation, measured by average income per capita of population, is the United Arab Emirates with $30,070 in 1980. The US, which took the lead in 1910, was 14th behind 3 Arab, 9 West European countries and Brunei in 1980.

It has been estimated that the value of all physical assets in the US in 1976 was $6.2 trillion, or $28,800 per person.

Gold Reserves

The country with the greatest monetary gold reserve is the US, whose Treasury had 264.6 million fine oz of the world's 927.02 million fine oz on hand in Jan 1981. Valued at $500 per fine oz, these amounts translate to $132,300 million and $463,510 million respectively. The US Bullion Depository at Fort Knox, 30 miles southwest of Louisville, Ky, has been the principal depository of US gold since 1936. Gold is stored in 446,000 standard mint bars of 400 troy oz (439 oz avoirdupois), measuring $7 \times 3\frac{5}{8} \times 1\frac{5}{8}$ in. On Jan 1, 1981, Fort Knox housed 147,300,000 fine oz or 55.66% of the total US holding.

Worst Inflation

The world's worst inflation occurred in Hungary in June 1946, when the 1931 gold pengö was valued at 130 quintillion (1.3×10^{20}) paper pengös. Notes were issued for szazmillio billion (1 followed by 20 zeros or 10^{20}) pengös on June 3 and withdrawn on July 11, 1946. Notes for 1 sextillion or 10^{21} pengös were printed but not circulated.

In Germany, on Nov 6, 1923, the circulation of Reichsbank marks reached 400,338,326,350,700,000,-000, a level of inflation 755,700 million times the 1913 levels.

Inflation in Israel in 1980 ran at 135% and was thus ahead of Turkey and Argentina.

Currency

Paper money is an invention of the Chinese, first tried in 910 AD and prevalent by 970 AD. The world's earliest bank notes (*banco-sedlar*) were issued in Stockholm, Sweden, in July 1661. The oldest surviving bank note is one for 5 dalers dated Dec 6, 1662.

The largest paper money ever issued was the one kwan note of the Chinese Ming ·dynasty issue of 1368–99, which measured 9×13 in. The smallest note ever issued by a bank was the 10 bani note of the Ministry of Finance of Rumania, issued in 1917. It measured (printed area) 1.09×1.49 in.

Of German *notgeld* (emergency notes) the smallest were the 1-3 pfennig of Passau (1920–21) measuring 0.70×0.72 in.

COINS

Oldest	*c.* 670 BC: electrum staters of King Gyges of Lydia, Turkey[1]
Earliest Dated	MCCXXXIIII (1234): Bishop of Roskilde coins, Denmark (6 known)
Heaviest	43 lb 7¼ oz: Swedish 10 daler copper plate, 1644[2]
Lightest and Smallest	0.002 g or 14,000 to the oz: Nepalese silver ¼ Jawa, *c.* 1740
Most Expensive	$725,000: for the uncirculated Garrett gold Brasher doubloon of 1787, in NYC
Rarest	Many "singletons" known: for example, only 700 Axumite coins are known, of which only one was made of bronze and gold of Kaleb I *c.* 500 AD

[1] Chinese uninscribed "spade" money of the Chou dynasty has been dated to *c.* 770 BC
[2] The largest coin-shaped coin was the 200 Mohur Indian gold coin of 1654, measuring 5⅜ in in diameter and weighing 70 troy oz or 2,177 g

Highest and Lowest Denomination Currency

The highest denomination notes in circulation are US Federal Reserve Bank notes for $10,000. They bear the head of Salmon Portland Chase (1808–73), Secretary of the Treasury during Civil War days. None have been printed since July 1944 and the US Treasury announced in 1969 that no further notes higher than $100 would be issued. Only some 400 $10,000 bills remain in circulation.

The lowest denomination legal tender bank note is the 1 sen (or 1/100th of a rupiah) Indonesian note. Its exchange value in mid-1982 was 648 to the US penny.

Largest Check

The greatest amount paid by a single check in the history of banking was equivalent to $2,046,700,000, handed over by Daniel P. Moynihan, then the US Ambassador to India, in New Delhi, Feb 18, 1974. An internal US Treasury check for $4,176,969,623.57 was drawn on June 30, 1954.

Greatest Coin Collection

The highest price paid for a coin collection has been $7,300,000 by Steven C. Markoff of A-Mark Coin Co Inc of Beverly Hills, Calif, for a hoard of 407,000 US silver dollars from the La Vere Redfield estate in a courtroom auction in Reno, Nev on Jan 27, 1976.

Largest Treasure Trove

The largest hoard ever found was one of about 80,000 aurei in Brescello near Modena, Italy in 1814, said to have been deposited *c.* 37 BC.

The numerically largest hoard ever found was the Brussels hoard of 1908 containing *c.* 150,000 coins.

A hoard of 56,500 Roman coins was found at Cunetio near Marlborough, Wiltshire, England, Oct 15, 1978.

The greatest discovery of treasure is the estimated $2 billion of gold coins and platinum ingots from the sunken Tsarist battleship *Admiral Nakhimov* of 8,524 tons 200 ft down off the Japanese island of Tsushima. She was sunk during the Russo-Japanese War, May 27, 1905.

Largest Mint

The largest mint is the US Mint built in 1965–69 on Independence Mall, Philadelphia, covering 500,000 sq ft (11½ acres) with an annual capacity on a 3-shift 7-day-a-week production of 8,000 million coins. A single stamping machine can produce coins at a rate of 10,000 per hour.

LABOR

Trade Unions

The largest union is Solidarnos (Solidarity) in Poland which by Oct 1980 was reported to have 8 million members. The union with the longest name is probably the International Association of Marble, Slate and Stone Polishers, Rubbers and Sawyers, Tile and Marble Setters' Helpers and Marble Mosaic and Terrazzo Workers' Helpers (Wash DC).

Longest and Shortest Working Weeks

A case of a working week of 142 hours was recorded in June 1980 by Dr Paul Ashton, 32, the an-

EVER SEE A MILLION DOLLARS? In downtown Las Vegas (where else?) the Horseshoe casino has on exhibit 100 $10,000 bills just like the inset.

321

MOST MASSIVE "COINS": One of these holed stone discs (right), used for money in the Yap Islands of the western Pacific, can be traded for one wife or an 18-ft canoe, depending on its size. (Pamela Hollie) Except for the Yap discs, the Swedish copper 10-daler piece of 1644 (below) is the HEAVIEST COIN ever issued. It weighed over 43 lb.

aesthetics registrar at Birkenhead General Hospital, Merseyside, England. This left an average each day of 3 hours 42 min 51 sec for sleep. Some non-consultant doctors are actually contracted to work 110 hours a week or be available for 148 hours.

Some contracts for University lecturers call for a 3-hour week or a 72-hour year spread over 24 weeks.

Labor Disputes

A labor dispute concerning monotony of diet and working conditions was recorded in 1153 BC in Thebes, Egypt. The earliest recorded strike was one by an orchestra leader from Greece named Aristos in Rome c. 309 BC. The cause was meal breaks.

The longest recorded strike ended on Jan 4, 1961, after 33 years. It concerned the employment of barbers' assistants in Copenhagen, Denmark. The longest recorded major strike was one at the plumbing fixtures factory of the Kohler Co in Sheboygan, Wis between Apr 1954 and Oct 1962. The strike is alleged to have cost the United Automobile Workers union about $12 million to sustain.

Lowest Unemployment

In Switzerland in Dec 1973 (population 6,600,000), the total number of unemployed was reported to be 81.

Working Careers

The longest working life has been 98 years by Mr Izumi of Japan (see Chapter 1, *Oldest Living Man*) who started work goading draft animals at a sugar mill at Isen, Tokanushima, Japan in 1872. He became a sugar cane farmer and retired in 1970. Susan O'Hagan (1802–1909) was in domestic service with 3 generations of the Hall family of Lisburn, near Belfast, Northern Ireland, for 97 years from the age of 10 to light duties at 107.

The longest recorded industrial career in one job was that of Miss Polly Gadsby who started at the age of 9 and worked 86 years wrapping elastic for the same company in Leicester, England until she died in 1932 at the age of 95.

FOOD AND DRINK

Calories

Of all countries in the world, based on the latest available data, Belgium and Luxembourg have the largest available total of calories per person. The net supply averaged 3,645 per day in 1974. The lowest *reported* figure is 1,728 calories per day in Upper Volta in 1974. The highest calorific value of any foodstuff is that of pure animal fat, with 930 calories per 100 grams (3.5 oz). Pure alcohol provides 710 calories per 100 grams.

Protein

Australia and New Zealand have the highest recorded consumption of protein per person, an average of 106 grams (3.79 oz) per day in 1969.

Cereals

The greatest consumers of cereal products—flour, milled rice, etc.—are the people of Egypt, with an average of about 500 lb per person annually (600 grams per day) in 1966–67. Figures for 1977 from China suggest a possible consumption (including rice) of 890 grams (31.3 oz).

Sugar

The greatest consumers of sugars are the people of Bulgaria, with an average of 6.26 oz per person per day in 1977.

Meat

The greatest meat eaters in the world—figures include organs and poultry—are the people of the US, with an average consumption of 10.89 oz per person per day in 1977.

Coffee

The world's greatest coffee drinkers are the people of Finland, who consumed 29.2 lb of coffee per person per year in 1980.

The most expensive coffee is Jamaican Blue Mountain, which retails for $15 per lb in NYC, with prices reported as high as $23 per lb elsewhere.

Tea

The world's greatest tea drinkers are the people of Ireland, who consumed 8.21 lb of tea per person per year in 1977.

The most expensive tea marketed is "Oolong Leaf Bud," specially imported by Fortnum and Mason of Piccadilly, London, where in July 1982, it retailed for £19.20 ($33.70) per lb. It is blended from very young

Formosan leaves. Tea bags were invented by Thomas Sullivan of New York in 1904.

Fresh Water

The world's greatest consumers of fresh water are the people and industrial users of the US, whose average consumption was 1,855 gallons per person per day in 1974.

Beer

Of reporting countries, the nation with the highest beer consumption per person is W Germany, with 38.78 gallons per person in 1981. In the Northern Territory of Australia, however, the annual intake has been estimated to be as high as 62.4 gallons per person. A society for the prevention of alcoholism in Darwin had to disband in June 1966, for lack of support.

Wine

The greatest wine drinkers are the French, who consumed 24.2 gallons per person for the year 1980.

Spirits

The greatest consumers of spirits are the people of Poland, who, in 1977, consumed an average of 1.476 gallons per person per year.

Prohibition

The longest-lasting imposition of prohibition against consumption of alcoholic beverages has been 26 years in Iceland (1908–34). Other prohibitions have been in Russia, later the USSR (1914–24), and the US (1920–33). The Faroe Islands have had a public (as opposed to private licensed) prohibition since 1918.

Most Expensive Fruit

The most expensive fruit was 1 lb of strawberries sold at auction by John Synnott of Ashford, Ireland on Apr 5, 1977 in the Dublin Fruit Market to the restaurateur, Mr Leslie Cooke. The "punnet" of 30 berries sold for £530 ($1,260) or $42 a berry. At the Starlight Strawberry Festival in Starlight, Ind, 1 lb (16 berries) of the first-prize berries were bought at auction by Mr Charles Phillips for $950, or almost $60 per berry, on May 30, 1981.

Most Expensive Food

The most expensively priced food (as opposed to spice) is Royal de luxe caviar retailed at £224.50 ($516.35) per 500 grams (17.6 oz) at Fortnum and Mason, London.

Spices

Prices for wild ginseng (root of *Panax quinquefolius*), from the Chan Pak Mt area of China, thought to have aphrodisiacal quality, were reported in Nov 1977 to be as high as $23,000 per oz in Hong Kong. Total shipments from Jilin province do not exceed 141 oz per year. The leading medical journal in the US has likened its effects to "corticosteroid poisoning."

The hottest of all spices is claimed to be Siling labuyo from the Philippines. The most prized condiment is Cà Cuong, a secretion recovered in minute amounts from beetles in N Vietnam. Owing to war conditions, the price rose to $100 per oz before supplies virtually ceased in 1975.

Candy

The top-selling candies are Life Savers, with 29,651,840,000 rolls sold between 1913 and June 30, 1980. A tunnel formed by the holes in the middle placed end-to-end would stretch to the moon and back three times. Paul Shirley, 21, of Sydney, Australia, made one last in his mouth for 4 hours 40 min on Feb 15, 1979, before the hole broke up.

Largest Banquet

The greatest outdoor banquet ever staged was that by President Loubet, President of France, in the gardens of the Tuileries, Paris, Sept 22, 1900. He invited the mayors of France and their deputies, ending up with 22,295 guests. With the Gallic *penchant* for round numbers, the event has always been referred to as "le banquet des 100,000 maires." It was estimated that some 30,000 attended a military feast at Radewitz, Poland, on June 25, 1730, thrown by King August II (1709–1733).

The greatest number of people served indoors at a single sitting was 18,000 municipal leaders at the Palais de l'Industrie, Paris, on Aug 18, 1889.

The menu for the main 5½-hour banquet at the Imperial Iranian 2,500th anniversary gathering at Persepolis in Oct 1971 (see *Party Giving* in Chapter 11), was probably the most expensive ever compiled. It comprised quail eggs stuffed with Iranian caviar, a mousse of crayfish tails in Nantua sauce, stuffed rack of roast lamb, with a main course of roast peacock stuffed with *foie gras,* fig rings, and raspberry sweet champagne sherbet. Wines included *Château Lafite Rothschild* 1945 at $100 per bottle from the cellars of Maxim's, Paris.

Biggest Barbecue

The most monumental barbecue has been one for 10,335 people at the West Pasco Sertoma Club of New Port Richey, Fla, March 28–29, 1981, serving 8,274 lb of meat. The 1981 annual Lancaster Sertoma, Pa, served 22,500 barbecued chickens.

Longest Bread

The longest one-piece loaf ever baked was one of 1,256 ft 2¾ in, created by Bruce Gajewski and baked on the campus of Schenectady County Community College, NY, in an open charcoal oven on May 15, 1982.

Largest Pies

The largest cherry pie weighed 7 tons and contained 4,950 lb of cherries. It measured 14 ft 4 in in diameter, 24 in in depth and was baked on the grounds of the Medusa Cement Corporation, Charlevoix, Mich, May 15, 1976, as part of the town's Bicentennial celebration.

The largest mince pie was one of 2,260 lb, measuring 20 × 5 ft, baked at Ashby-de-la-Zouch, Leicestershire, England, Oct 15, 1932.

The largest meat pie ever baked weighed 6.4 tons, measuring 18 × 6 ft and 18 in deep, in Denby Dale, W Yorkshire, England, baked on Sept 5, 1964. The first was in 1788, baked to celebrate King George III's return to sanity, but the fourth, for Queen Victoria's Jubilee in 1887, went a bit "off" and had to be buried in quicklime.

The largest apple pie ever baked was that in a 16-ft-8-in diameter dish at the Orleans County Fair, NY, Aug 2–3, 1977. Baking time of the 300 bushels of apples and 5,950 lb of sugar was 4 hours 40 min. The total weight was 21,210 lb.

Largest Cakes

The largest cake ever assembled was the Baltimore City Bicentennial Cake of July 4, 1976, with ingredients weighing 69,860 lb. An estimated 10,000 dozen eggs, 21,600 lb of sugar, and a 415-lb pinch of salt were used.

The tallest recorded free-standing wedding cake was one of 50 tiers, 33 ft 9 in tall, baked and constructed by Roy Butterworth and Frank Brennan of Bedford, Nova Scotia, Canada, in Sept 1981.

Largest Chocolate Easter Egg

The largest chocolate Easter egg ever made was one weighing 7,561 lb 13½ oz, measuring 10 ft high, made by Siegfried Berndt at "Macopa" Patisserie, Leicester, England, and completed on Apr 7, 1982.

Largest Hamburger

The largest burger (made of beef) on record is one of 3,020 lb, served in 13,083 portions in City Park, Towner, "Cattle Capitol of North Dakota," on June 19, 1981.

Largest Omelet

The largest omelet ever made was one produced with 20,117 eggs in a pan measuring 30 × 10 ft, cooked by CHQR Radio, Calgary, and the Alberta Egg and Fowl Marketing Board on June 27, 1981, at Calgary's Southcentre Mall, Alberta, Canada.

Mashed Potatoes

A single serving of mashed potatoes weighing 10,286 lb was prepared at the Mantua Potato Festival in Ohio in Sept 1980.

Largest Popsicle®

The largest iced lollipop on a stick was one of 5,750 lb, constructed for the Westside Assembly of God Church, Davenport, Iowa, Sept 7, 1975.

Biggest Salami

The largest salami on record is one 29 ft 2¾ in long with a circumference of 28 in, weighing 734.13 lb, made by Don Smallgoods for Australian Safeway Stores at Broadmeadow, Vic, on Apr 23, 1982.

Longest Sausage

The longest sausage ever made was one of 2.86 miles, weighing 2.17 tons, by Auckland Farmers'

Freezing Cooperative Ltd, New Zealand, on June 26, 1981.

Largest Sundae

The most monstrous ice cream sundae ever concocted is one of 10,808 lb plus 180 lb of strawberries, 100 lb of nuts and 16 gallons of whipped topping, constructed by the Friendly Ice Cream Co and students from the High School at Troy, Ohio, on June 8, 1980.

Longest Banana Split

The longest banana split ever made was 8,006 ft long (over 1½ miles), embracing 11,840 bananas, 865¼ gallons of ice cream, 152½ gallons of topping, 204 lb of nuts and 8,400 cherries by the Selinsgrove High School Band Boosters of Selinsgrove, Pa, on May 1, 1982.

Longest Pastry

The longest cream pastry (known as *mille feuilles* or "a thousand leaves," invented in Florence in the 16th century) ever made was one 1,084 ft long, made by Fritz Strüben-Keller and the Bäckermeister kegel club in Liestal, Switzerland, June 10, 1979.

Largest Pizza

The largest pizza ever baked was one measuring 80 ft 1 in in diameter, 5,037 sq ft in area, and 18,664 lb in weight at the Oma Pizza Restaurant, Glens Falls, NY, owned by Lorenzo Amato, on Oct 8, 1978. It was cut into 60,318 slices.

Largest Dish

The largest single dish is roasted camel, prepared occasionally for Bedouin wedding feasts. Cooked eggs are stuffed in fish, the fish stuffed in cooked chicken, the chickens stuffed into a roasted sheep carcass and the sheep stuffed into a whole camel.

Biggest Round of Drinks

The largest round of drinks ever recorded was one for 1,222 people stood by the *Sunday Sun* and shouted by Jack Amos in Newcastle upon Tyne, England, in Oct 1974, at the conclusion of the Jack o' Clubs road show.

LONGEST BANANA SPLIT: Market St in Selinsgrove, Pa, for 1½ miles was given over to 11,840 bananas with 865¼ gallons of ice cream and all the trimmings on May 1, 1982.

LARGEST PIZZA (above): Measuring more than 80 ft across, this pie, baked in Glens Falls, NY, weighed 18,664 lb and was cut into 60,318 slices.

LONGEST PASTRY (left): In Switzerland a "mille feuilles" 1,084 ft long set a record.

barges) was 73,864 vessels of 420,834,813 tons gross on July 1, 1981. The largest merchant fleet as of mid-1981 was under the flag of Liberia with 2,281 ships of 74,906,390 tons gross.

Largest and Busiest Ports

Physically, the largest port is the Port of NY and NJ. The port has a navigable waterfront of 755 miles (460 miles in NY State and 295 miles in NJ) stretching over 92 sq mi. A total of 261 general cargo berths and 130 other piers give a total berthing capacity of 391 ships at one time. The total warehousing floor space is 18,400,000 sq ft (422.4 acres).

The world's busiest port and largest artificial harbor is the Rotterdam-Europoort in the Netherlands, which covers 38 sq mi. It handled 29,136 seagoing vessels carrying a total of 253 million metric tons of seagoing cargo, and about 180,000 barges, in 1981. It is able to handle 310 seagoing vessels simultaneously, of up to 318,000 metric tons and 68 ft draught.

Airlines

The country with the busiest airlines system is the US, where 200,086,577 revenue passenger miles were flown on scheduled domestic and local services in 1980. This was equivalent to an annual trip of 833 miles for every inhabitant of the US. It was estimated in 1978 that only 37% of adult Americans had never flown in their lives.

ENERGY

To express the various forms of available energy (coal, liquid fuels and water power, etc., but omitting vegetable fuels and peat), it is the practice to convert them all into terms of coal.

The highest consumption is in the US with an average of 29,790 lb per person. With only 5.3% of the world's population, the US consumes 28.6% of the world's gasoline and 32.9% of the world's electric power. For comparison, 14,035 lb was the UK average per person in 1979. The lowest recorded average for 1974 was 28.6 lb per person in Rwanda.

MASS COMMUNICATIONS
AND TRANSPORTATION

Merchant Shipping

The world total of merchant shipping (excluding vessels of less than 100 tons gross, sailing vessels and

FIRST PARKING METERS (and parking tickets) were installed in 1935 in Oklahoma City (above). (© Oklahoma Publishing Co)

CROOKEDEST STREET (left): San Francisco has plenty of steep hills, but none is as crooked *and* steep as Lombard. It has 8 consecutive 90-degree turns of 20-ft radius on the way down. Yes, it's one way.

Railroads

The country with the greatest length of railroad is the US, with 198,963 miles of track on Jan 1, 1980.

Roads and Traffic

The country with the greatest length of road is the US (50 states), with 3,884,732 miles of graded roads on Jan 1, 1979.

The highest traffic volume of any point is at East Los Angeles, where there is an interchange of the Santa Ana, Pomona, Golden State, and Santa Monica Freeways with a 24-hour average on weekdays of 550,300 vehicles in 1981—over 382 per min. The most heavily traveled stretch of road is between 43rd and 47th Sts on the Dan Ryan Expressway in Chicago, with an average daily volume of 254,700 vehicles.

The place with the highest traffic density is Hong Kong. By Jan 1, 1977, there were 191,146 motor ve-

hicles on 678 miles of serviceable roads giving a density of 6.24 yd per vehicle.

Steepest and Crookedest Streets

The steepest streets are Filbert St, Russian Hill and 22nd St, Dolores Heights, San Francisco, with gradients of 31.5% or a rise of 1 ft for every 3.17 ft.

Lombard Street in San Francisco between Hyde and Leavenworth has 8 consecutive 90-degree turns of 20-ft radius as it descends steeply one way.

Widest, Narrowest and Shortest Streets

The widest street is the Monumental Axis, running for 1½ miles from the Municipal Plaza to the Plaza of the Three Powers in Brasilia, the capital of Brazil. The 6-lane boulevard was opened in Apr 1960 and is 273.4 yd wide.

LARGEST SQUARE: Tien An Men Square covering more than 98 acres in Peking, China, contains Chairman Mao's tomb and Memorial Hall.

The Bay Bridge Toll Plaza has 23 lanes (17 westbound) serving San Francisco and Oakland.

The narrowest street is in Port Isaac, Cornwall, England where Temple Bar, at its junction with Dolphin Street, is 19 5/16 in wide at its narrowest point. It is popularly known as "Squeeze-Belly Alley."

The title of "The Shortest Street in the World" has been claimed since 1907 by McKinley St in Bellefontaine, Ohio, which is built of vitrified brick and measures 30 ft in length.

Earliest Parking Meters

The earliest parking meters ever installed were those put in the business district of Oklahoma City, Okla, on July 19, 1935. They were the invention of Carl C. Magee (US).

Earliest Traffic Lights

Semaphore-type traffic *signals* were set up in Parliament Square, London in 1868, with red and green gas lamps for night use. The first traffic light was installed in 1919 in Detroit.

Highest Trail

The highest trail is an 8-mile stretch of the Kangti-suu between Khaleb and Hsin-chi-fu, Tibet, which in two places exceeds 20,000 ft. The highest motor road is one 733.2 miles long between Tibet and southwestern Sinkiang, completed in Oct 1957, which includes passes of an altitude up to 18,480 ft above sea level.

Lowest Road

The lowest road is that along the Israeli shores of the Dead Sea, 1,290 ft below sea level. The lowest pass is the Rock Reef Pass in Everglades National Park, Fla, which is 3 ft above sea level.

Biggest Square

The Tien An Men (Gate of Heavenly Peace) Square in Peking, described as the navel of China, extends over 98 acres.

Longest Highways and Street

The longest motorable road is the Pan-American Highway, which will stretch 17,018 miles from northwest Alaska to southernmost Chile. There remains a gap of 250 miles, known as the Tapon del Darién in Panama, and the Atrato Swamp in Colombia. This was first traversed by the Land-Rover *La Cucaracha Cariñosa* (The Affectionate Cockroach) of the Trans-Darien Expedition (1959–60) crewed by former SAS man Richard E. Bevir (UK) and engineer Terence John Whitfield (Aus). They left Chepo, Panama on Feb 3, 1960 and reached Quibido, Colombia, on June 17, averaging 200 yd per hour of indescribable difficulty. The Range Rover VXC 868 K of the British Trans-America Expedition was the first vehicle to cover the whole route, leaving Alaska on Dec 3, 1971, and arriving in Tierra del Fuego on June 9, 1972.

The $3,500-million Interstate 75, which opened on Dec 21, 1977, now runs 1,564 miles from Sault Ste Marie, Mich, to Tampa, Fla without a traffic light. The Interstate Highway I-80 from NYC to Salt Lake City, Utah is 2,180 miles long.

The longest designated street is Yonge Street, which runs north and west from Toronto, Canada. The first stretch, completed on Feb 16, 1796, ran 34½ miles. Its official length, now extended to Rainy River at the Ontario-Minnesota border, is 1,178.3 miles.

Traffic Jam

The longest traffic jam ever reported was that of Feb 16, 1980 which stretched northward from Lyon, France 109.3 miles towards Paris.

Drivers' Licenses

Regular drivers' licenses are issuable as young as 15 and without a driver education course only in Hawaii and Mississippi. Thirteen US states issue restricted juvenile licenses at 14.

The easiest test for a driver's license is given in Egypt, where the ability to drive 6 meters (19.7 ft) forward and 6 meters in reverse has been deemed sufficient. In 1979 it was reported that accurate reversing between 2 rubber traffic cones had been added, but this soon led to the substitution of white lines when too many cones were destroyed.

Oldest Driver

Roy M. Rawlins (b July 10, 1870) of Stockton, Calif was warned for driving at 95 mph in a 55-mph zone in June 1974. On Aug 25, 1974, he was awarded a Calif State license valid until 1978, but he died on July 9, 1975, one day short of his 105th birthday. Mrs Maude Tull of Inglewood, Calif, who began driving after her husband's death, when she was aged 91, was issued a renewal of her license on Feb 5, 1976, then aged 104.

Walter Herbert Weake of England drove for 75 years without ever having an accident. He began driving in 1894 and drove daily until his death, at age 91, in 1969.

Most Failures on Learner's Test

The record for persistence in taking and failing a test for a driver's license is held by Mrs Miriam Hargrave (b Apr 3, 1908) of Wakefield, Yorkshire, England, who failed her 39th driving test in 8 years on Apr 29, 1970, when she "crashed" through a set of red lights. She finally passed her 40th driving test on Aug 3, 1970. She spent $720 on 212 driving lessons and could no longer afford to buy a car. In 1978, she was reported to dislike right-hand turns.

Mrs Fannie Turner (b 1903) of Little Rock, Ark, passed her *written* test for a driver's license on her 104th attempt in Oct 1978.

Worst Driver

It was reported that a 75-year-old *male* driver received 10 traffic tickets, drove on the wrong side of the road four times, committed four hit-and-run offenses and caused six accidents, all within 20 minutes, in McKinney, Tex, on Oct 15, 1966.

Inland Waterways

The country with the greatest length of inland waterways is Finland. The total length of navigable lakes and rivers is about 31,000 miles.

The longest navigable natural waterway is the Amazon River, which seagoing vessels can ascend as far as Iquitos, in Peru, 2,236 miles from the Atlantic seaboard.

On a National Geographic Society expedition ending on March 10, 1969, Helen and Frank Schreider navigated downstream from San Francisco, Peru, 3,845 miles up the Amazon to Bélem.

Telephones

There were approximately 472,136,789,000 telephones in the world on Jan 1, 1980, it was estimated by the American Telephone and Telegraph Co. The country with the greatest number was the US with 175,505,000 instruments, equivalent to 791 for every 1,000 people or in 97.5 of every 100 households. The territory with fewest is Pitcairn Island with 28 for a population of 63. The country with the lowest proportion is Zaire with less than 1 telephone per 1,000 people.

The greatest total of calls made in any country is in the US, with 245,216 million in 1979 (1,111 calls per person).

The city with most telephones is NYC, which had 5,785,384 (820 per 1,000 people) as of Jan 1, 1980. In 1980, Washington, DC, reached the peak of 1,648 telephones per 1,000 people.

Longest Telephone Cable

The longest submarine telephone cable is the Commonwealth Pacific Cable (COMPAC), which runs for more than 9,000 miles from Australia *via* Auckland, New Zealand, and Hawaii to Port Alberni, Canada. It cost about $98 million and was inaugurated on Dec 2, 1963.

Largest Switchboard

The world's biggest switchboard is that in the Pentagon, Wash, DC, with 25,000 lines and an annual phone bill of $8.7 million.

Telephone Directories

The world's most difficult directory to tear in half is that for Houston, Tx, which runs to 2,889 pages for 939,640 listings. The easiest would be that for Farley, Mo—282 listings on 3 pages.

POSTAGE STAMPS

Earliest Stamp

The earliest adhesive postage stamps ever issued were the "Penny Blacks" of Great Britain, bearing the head of Queen Victoria, placed on sale on May 1 for use on May 6, 1840. A total of 68,158,080 were printed. The British National Postal Museum possesses a unique full proof sheet of 240 stamps printed in Apr 1840 before the corner letters, plate numbers or marginal inscriptions were added.

HIGHEST DENOMINATION STAMP: When this £100 stamp was issued in 1925, the pound sterling was worth $5, so this was a $500 stamp.

MOST VALUABLE ERROR: See the 1918 Jenny biplane printed upside down on this block of 4? That's what made it worth $500,000 in an auction in 1982.

Largest Stamp

The largest stamps ever issued were the special purpose 1913 Express Delivery stamps of China, which measured 9¾ × 2¾ in. The largest standard postage stamp is the Marshall Islands 75-cent stamp issued Oct 30, 1979, which measures 6.3 × 4.33 in.

Smallest Stamp

The smallest stamps ever issued were the 10 cents and 1 peso of the Colombian State of Bolívar, 1863–66. They measured 0.31 × 0.37 in.

Highest and Lowest Denominations

The highest denomination stamp ever issued was a red and black stamp for £100 ($500) with head of George V issued in Kenya 1925–27. Although valid for postage, it was essentially for collection of revenue.

Owing to demonetization and inflation it is difficult to determine the lowest denomination stamp but it was probably the 1946 3000 pengö Hungarian stamp, worth at the time 1.6×10^{-14} parts of a cent.

Highest Price Stamp

The "blue boy" cover, bearing a 5-cent stamp issued by the postmaster at Alexandria, Va, Nov 25, 1946, was purchased for $1 million by Georg Normann, a European collector, *via* David Feldman, dealer, in Geneva, Switzerland, on May 9, 1981.

The highest price ever paid at auction for a stamp was $850,000 ($935,000 with the buyer's premium) for one of the world's rarest stamps, a 1-cent black on magenta British Guiana provisional of 1856, postmarked Apr 4, 1856. It was sold by an Irwin R. Weinberg syndicate, which had bought it in 1970, to an anonymous collector at the Waldorf-Astoria Hotel, NYC on Apr 5, 1980.

High-Priced Error

$500,000 was paid for a 1918 US 24-cent airmail "Princeton" block of 4 of a Jenny biplane with the plane upside down by a Myron Kaller syndicate on July 19, 1979. A single example was purchased for $180,000 at auction in NYC in May 1982.

Rarest Stamps

Unique examples include the British Guiana of 1856 (see above), a Swedish 3-skilling banco yellow color error of 1855, a Gold Coast provisional of 1885, and US Postmaster stamps from Boscowen, New Haven and Lockport, NY.

Largest Philatelic Purchase

The Marc Haas collection of 3,000 postal and pre-postal covers to 1869 was sold for $11 million by Stanley Gibbons International Ltd of London in Aug 1979.

Postal Services

The country with the largest mail is the US, whose people posted 110.1 billion letters and packages in 1981. The US Postal Service then employed 670,239 people with the world's largest vehicle fleet—190,000 cars and trucks. The Direct Mail Marketing Association alleged that 7.5% of US third-class mail, or 2 billion pieces, were "lost" in 1981.

The US also takes first place in the average number of letters which each person mails during one year. The figure was 480 in 1980.

5. EDUCATION

Illiteracy

Literacy is variously defined as "ability to read simple subjects" and "ability to read and write a simple letter." The looseness of definition and the scarcity of data for many countries preclude anything more than approximations, but the extent of illiteracy among adults (15 years old and over) is estimated to have been 34.7% in 1969.

The continent with the greatest proportion of illiterates is Africa, where 81.5% of adults were illiterate. The last published figure for Mali in 1960 showed 97.8% of people over 15 were unable to read.

Universities

Probably the oldest educational institution is the University of Karueein, founded in 859 AD in Fez, Morocco. The University of Bologna (Italy) was founded in 1088.

The university with the greatest enrollment in the world is the State University of New York, which had 348,360 students enrolled in 1981. Its oldest college, at Albany, NY, was founded in 1844.

Bids for building the $3.4-billion University of Riyadh, Saudi Arabia, were accepted in June 1978. The University will house 15,000 families and have its own mass transportation system.

The largest existing university building is the M. V. Lomonosov State University on the Lenin Hills, south of Moscow. It stands 787.4 ft tall, has 32 stories and contains 40,000 rooms. It was constructed in 1949–53.

The most northerly university is Inupiat University of the Arctic at Barrow, Alaska on Lat 71°16′N. Eskimo subjects are featured in the curriculum.

Youngest Professors

The youngest at which anybody has been elected to a chair (full professorship) in a university is 19, in the case of Colin MacLaurin (1698–1746), who was admitted to Marischal College, Aberdeen, Scotland as Professor of Mathematics on Sept 30, 1717. In 1725 he was made Professor of Mathematics at Edinburgh University on the recommendation of Sir Isaac Newton.

In July 1967, Dr Harvey Martin Friedman, PhD (b Sept 23, 1948) was appointed Assistant Professor of Mathematics at Stanford University, Calif, on Sept 1, 1967, just 3 weeks before his 19th birthday.

Most Durable Professors

The longest period for which any professorship has been held is 63 years, in the case of Thomas Martyn (1735–1825), Professor of Botany at Cambridge University from 1762 until his death. His father, John Martyn (1699–1768), had occupied the chair from 1732 to 1762.

LARGEST UNIVERSITY BUILDING is the State University on Lenin Hills south of Moscow. Its 32 stories contain 40,000 rooms.

Dr Joel Hildebrand (b Nov 16, 1881), Professor Emeritus of Physical Chemistry at the University of California, Berkeley, first became an Assistant Professor in 1913, and in 1981 published his 275th research paper.

Youngest Undergraduates

The most extreme recorded case of academic juvenility was that of William Thomson (1824–1907), later Lord Kelvin, who entered Glasgow University aged 10 years 4 months in Oct 1834, and matriculated on Nov 14, 1834.

Jay Luo was reportedly only 12 years old when he received his bachelor of science degree in mathematics from Boise State University, Idaho, in the spring of 1982. Dr Merrill Kenneth Wolf (b Aug 28, 1931) of Cleveland, Ohio, took his B.A. in music from Yale University in Sept 1945, in the month of his 14th birthday.

Largest Schools

At the time of its peak enrollment in 1934, De Witt Clinton High School in the Bronx, NYC had 12,000 students. It was founded in 1897 and now has an enrollment of 4,500.

Most Expensive

L'Institut "Le Rosey" at Rolle, Switzerland, charges annual fees of at least 25,000 Swiss francs (about $12,500).

The most expensive US college is Bennington College, Vermont, at $12,140 for tuition, room and board ($40 per annum more than Harvard) for the school year 1982–83.

Highest Endowment

The greatest single gift in the history of higher education has been the transfer by Robert W. Woodruff of the entire Emily and Ernest Woodruff Trust funds of $105 million to Emory University (founded 1836), Atlanta, Ga, in Nov 1979.

Most Schools Attended

The documented record for the greatest number of schools attended by a pupil is 265 by Wilma Wil-

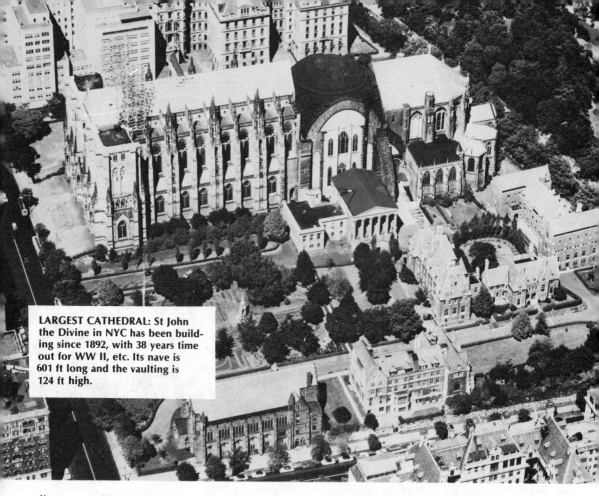

LARGEST CATHEDRAL: St John the Divine in NYC has been building since 1892, with 38 years time out for WW II, etc. Its nave is 601 ft long and the vaulting is 124 ft high.

liams, now Mrs R. J. Horton, from 1933 to 1943 when her parents were in show business in the US.

Lecture Agency

The largest lecture agency is the American Program Bureau of Boston with 400 personalities on 40 major subject areas and a turnover of some $5 million. The top rate in Mar 1981 was $40,000 per speech reportedly commanded by Johnny Carson and Bob Hope.

6. RELIGIONS

Oldest Religion

The oldest major formal religion is Hinduism. Its Vedic precursor was brought to India by Aryans *c.* 1500 BC. The Rig Veda Hindu hymnal was codified *c.* 900 BC or earlier. The Judaic way of life was formulated as early as 2000 BC.

Largest Religious Membership

Religious statistics are necessarily only approximate. The test of adherence to a religion varies widely in rigor, while many individuals, particularly in the East, belong to two or more religions.

Christianity is the leading religion, with some 1.05 billion adherents in 1981. The Vatican statistics office reported that in 1981 there were 749,430,000 Roman Catholics. The largest non-Christian religion is Islam (Muslim) with about 590 million followers.

Largest Clergy

The largest religious organization is the Roman Catholic Church, with 123 cardinals, 411 archbishops, 2,395 bishops, 416,329 priests and 937,600 nuns. There are about 420,000 churches.

World Jewry

The total of world Jewry was estimated to number 14,300,000 in 1980. The highest concentration was in the US, with 5,800,000 of whom 2 million are in the

NY area. The total in Israel is 3,076,000, in Britain 410,000 (of whom 280,000 are in Greater London and 13,000 in Glasgow). The total in Tokyo is only 400.

Earliest Shrine

The earliest known shrine dates from the proto-neolithic Natufian culture in Jericho, where a site on virgin soil has been dated to the 9th millennium BC. A simple rectilinear red-plastered room with a niche housing a stone pillar, believed to be the shrine of a pre-pottery fertility cult dating from *c.* 6500 BC, was also uncovered in Jericho. The oldest surviving Christian church is Qal'at es Salihiye in eastern Syria, dating from 232 AD.

Largest Temple

The largest religious building ever constructed is Angkor Wat (City Temple), covering 402 acres, in Cambodia. It was built to the God Vishnu by the Khmer King Suryavarman II in the period 1113–1150. Its curtain wall measures 1,400 × 1,400 yd and its population, before it was abandoned in 1432, was at times 80,000. The whole complex of 72 major monuments, begun *c.* 900 AD, extends over 15 × 5 miles.

The largest Buddhist temple is Borobudur, near Jogjakarta, Indonesia, built in the 8th century. It is 103 ft tall and 403 ft square.

The largest Mormon temple is in Kensington, Md, dedicated in Nov 1974, with a floor area of 159,000 sq ft.

Largest Synagogue

The largest synagogue is the Temple Emanu-El on Fifth Ave at 65th St, NYC. The temple, completed in Sept 1929, has a frontage of 150 ft on Fifth Ave and 253 ft on 65th St. The sanctuary proper can accommodate 2,500 people, and the adjoining Beth-El Chapel seats 350. When all the facilities are in use, more than 6,000 people can be accommodated.

Largest Mosque

The largest mosque ever built was the now ruined al-Malawiya mosque of al-Mutawakil in Samarra, Iraq, built in 842–852 AD and measuring 401,408 sq ft (9.21 acres) with dimensions of 784 × 512 ft.

The world's largest mosque in use is the Umayyad Mosque in Damascus, Syria, built on a 2,000-year-old religious site measuring 515 × 318 ft, thus covering an area of 3.76 acres.

The largest mosque will be the Merdeka Mosque in Djakarta, Indonesia, which was begun in 1962. The cupola will be 147.6 ft in diameter and the capacity in excess of 50,000 people.

Largest Cathedral

The largest is the cathedral church of the Episcopalian Diocese of NY, St John the Divine, with a floor area of 121,000 sq ft and a volume of 16,822,000 cu ft. The cornerstone was laid on Dec 27, 1892, and work on the Gothic building was stopped in 1941, then restarted in earnest in July 1979. In NY it is referred to as "Saint John the Unfinished." The nave is the longest in the world, 601 ft in length, with a vaulting 124 ft in height.

The cathedral covering the largest area is that of Santa María de la Sede in Seville, Spain. It was built in Spanish Gothic style between 1402 and 1519 and is 414 ft long, 271 ft wide and 100 ft high to the vault of the nave.

Smallest Cathedral

The smallest cathedral is the Cathedral Chapel of St Francis of the American Catholic Church, built in 1933 at Laguna Beach, Calif with an area of 1,008 sq ft and seating for 42 people.

Largest Church

The largest church is the basilica of St Peter, built between 1492 and 1612 in Vatican City, Rome. Its length, measured from the apse, is 611 ft 4 in. Its area is 162,990 sq ft. The inner diameter of the famous dome is 137 ft 9 in and its center is 390 ft 5 in high. The external height is 457 ft 9 in.

The elliptical Basilique de St Pie X at Lourdes, France, completed in 1957 at a cost of $5,600,000, has a capacity of 20,000 under its giant span arches and a length of 656 ft.

The crypt of the underground Civil War Memorial Church in the Guadarrama Mountains, 28 miles from Madrid, Spain, is 853 ft in length. It took 21 years (1937–58) to build, at a reported cost of $392 million and is surmounted by a cross 492 ft tall.

Smallest Church

The smallest is the Union Church at Wiscasset, Maine with a floor area of 31½ sq ft (7 × 4½ ft).

The oldest pagoda in China is Sung-Yo Ssu in Honan, built with 15 12-sided stories in 523 AD.

Most Valuable Sacred Object

The sacred object of the highest intrinsic value is the 15th-century gold Buddha in the Temple of Three Friends in Bangkok, Thailand. It is 10 ft tall and weighs an estimated 6 tons. At $500 per fine ounce, its value has been calculated at $96 million for the gold alone. The gold under the plaster exterior was only found in 1954.

Saints

There are 1,848 "registered" saints (including 60 St Johns), of whom 628 are Italians, 576 French and 271 from the British Isles. The first US-born saint is Mother Elizabeth Ann Bayley Seton (1774–1821) who was canonized Sept 14, 1975. The total includes 15 Popes.

The shortest interval that has elapsed between the death of a saint and his canonization was in the case of St Anthony of Padua, Italy, who died on June 13,

Tallest Spires

The tallest *cathedral* spire is on the Protestant Cathedral of Ulm in Germany. The building is early Gothic and was begun in 1377. The tower, in the center of the west façade, was not finally completed until 1890 and is 528 ft high.

The tallest *church* spire is that of the Chicago Temple of the First Methodist Church on Clark St, Chicago. The building consists of a 22-story skyscraper (erected in 1924) surmounted by a parsonage at 330 ft, a "Sky Chapel" at 400 ft and a steeple cross at 568 ft above street level.

Minarets and Pagodas

The tallest minaret is one of 282 ft at the Sultan Hassan Mosque (founded 1356 AD) in Cairo, Egypt. The tallest free-standing stone tower is the Qutb Minar, south of New Delhi, India, built in 1194 to a height of 238 ft.

The tallest pagoda is the Phra Pathom Chedi at Nakhon Pathom, Thailand, which was built for King Mongkut in 1853–70. It rises to 377 ft.

TALLEST STONE TOWER: Near New Delhi, India, stands the Qutb Minar, built in 1194. It rises 238 ft high.

1231 and was canonized 352 days later on May 30, 1232.

The other extreme is represented by Pope St Leo III who died on June 12, 816, and was made a saint in 1673—857 years later.

Popes

The longest reign of any of the 264 Popes has been that of Pius IX (Giovanni Maria Mastai-Ferretti), who reigned for 31 years 236 days from June 16, 1846 until his death, aged 85, on Feb 7, 1878. Pope Stephen II was elected on March 24, 752, and died two days later.

Oldest Pope

It is recorded that Pope St Agatho (reigned 678–681) was elected at the age of 103 and lived to 106, but recent scholars have expressed doubts. The oldest of recent Pontiffs has been Pope Leo XIII (Gioacchino Pecci), who was born March 2, 1810, elected Pope at the third ballot on Feb 20, 1878, and died on July 20, 1903, aged 93 years 140 days.

Youngest Pope

The youngest of all was Pope Benedict IX (d 1056) (Theophylact), who had three terms as Pope: in 1032–44; Apr to May, 1045; and Nov 8, 1047 to July 17, 1048. It would appear that he was aged only 11 or 12 in 1032, though the Catalogue of the Popes admits only to his "extreme youth."

Slowest and Fastest Election of a Pope

After 31 months without declaring "We have a Pope," the cardinals were subjected to a bread and water diet and the removal of the roof of their conclave by the Mayor of Viterbo before electing Teobaldo Visconti (c. 1210–76), the Archbishop of Liège, as Pope Gregory X at Viterbo, near Rome, on Sept 1, 1271. The papacy was, however, vacant for at least 3 years 214 days in 304–308.

The shortest conclave was that of Oct 21, 1503, for the election of Pope Julius II on the first ballot.

Last Married Pope

The last married Pope was Adrian II (867–872). Rodrigo Borgia was the father of at least six children before being elected Pope Alexander VI in 1492. The first 37 Popes had no specific obligation to celibacy.

YOUNGEST BISHOP: At the tender age of 196 days, this English boy (age 6 in the picture), second son of George III, was appointed bishop of Osnabrück in 1764. He resigned after 39 years. (Spink & Son Ltd)

Pope Hormisdas (514–523) was the father of Pope Silverius (536–537).

Non-Italian Popes

The current Pope John Paul II, elected Oct 16, 1978 (b Karol Wojtyla, May 18, 1920, at Wadowice, near Krakow, Poland) is the first non-Italian Pope since Cardinal Adrian Florenz Boeyens (Pope Adrian VI) of the Netherlands, crowned on Aug 31, 1522.

Stained Glass

The oldest stained glass in the world represents the Prophets in a window of the cathedral of Augsburg, Bavaria, Germany, dating from c. 1050.

The largest stained glass window is the complete mural of The Resurrection Mausoleum, Justice, Ill, measuring 22,381 sq ft, in 2,448 panels completed in 1971.

337

LARGEST FUNERAL: When the President of Egypt, Gamal Abdel Nasser, died in 1970, an estimated 4 million people came out in the streets of Cairo for his funeral.

Largest Funeral

The greatest attendance at any funeral is the estimated 4 million who thronged Cairo, Egypt, for the funeral of President Gamal Abdel Nasser (b Jan 15, 1918) on Oct 1, 1970.

Largest Crowd

The greatest recorded number of human beings assembled with a common purpose was an estimated 12,700,000 at the Hindu feast of Kumbh-Mela, which was held at the confluence of the Yamuna (formerly called the Jumna), the Ganges and the invisible "Sarasvati" at Allahabad, Uttar Pradesh, India, on Jan 19, 1977. The holiest time during this holiest day since 1833 was during the planetary alignment between 9:28 and 9:40 a.m., during which only 200,000 achieved immersion to wash away the sins of a lifetime.

Biggest Demonstrations

A figure of 2,700,000 was published from China for the demonstration against the USSR in Shanghai Apr 3–4, 1969, following border clashes, and one of 10 million for the May Day celebrations of 1963 in Peking.

WORST ACCIDENTS & DISASTERS IN THE WORLD

	Deaths		
Pandemic	75,000,000	Eurasia: The Black Death (bubonic, pneumonic and septicae-mic plague)	1347–51
Genocide	c. 35,000,000	Mongol extermination of Chinese peasantry	1311–40
Influenza	21,640,000	Worldwide: Influenza	Apr–Nov 1918
Famine	c. 20,000,000[1]	Northern China (revealed May 1981)	1969–71
Flood	3,640,000	Yellow (Hwang-ho) River, China	Aug 1931
Circular Storm	1,000,000[2]	Ganges Delta isles, Bangladesh	Nov 12–13, 1970
Earthquake	830,000	Shensi Province, China (2 hours)	Jan 23, 1556
Landslide	180,000	Kansu Province, China	Dec 16, 1920
Atomic Bomb	141,000	Hiroshima, Japan	Aug 6, 1945
Conventional Bombing	c. 50,000[3]	Dresden, Germany	Feb 13–15, 1945
Snow Avalanche	c. 25,000[4]	Yungay, Huascaran, Peru	May 31, 1970
Marine (single ship)	c. 7,700	*Wilhelm Gustloff* (25,484 tons) torpedoed off Danzig by USSR submarine S-13	Jan 30, 1945
Dam Burst	5,000	Manchhu River Dam, Morvi, Gujarat, India	Aug 11, 1979
Panic	c. 4,000[5]	Chungking, China (air raid shelter)	c. June 8, 1941
Tunneling (Silicosis)	c. 2,000	Hawk's Nest hydroelectric tunnel, W Va	1931–35
Explosion	1,963[6]	Halifax, Nova Scotia, Canada	Dec 6, 1917
Fire (single building)	1,670[7]	The Theatre, Canton, China	May 1845
Mining	1,572[8]	Honkeiko Colliery, China (coal dust explosion)	Apr 26, 1942
Riot	c. 1,200	NYC (anticonscription riots)	July 13–16, 1863
Mass Suicide	913	People's Temple Cult by cyanide, Jonestown, Guyana	Nov 18, 1978
Crocodiles (disputed)	c. 900	Japanese soldiers, Ramree Island, Burma	Feb 19–20, 1945

Notes. 1.—In 1770 the great Indian famine carried away a proportion of the population estimated as high as one third, hence a figure of tens of millions. The figure for Bengal alone was probably about 10 million. The loss in the Northern China famine, Feb 1877–Sept 1878, was 9.5 million. It has been estimated that more than 5 million died in the post-World War I famine, in the USSR. The USSR government in July 1923 informed Mr (later President) Herbert Hoover that the ARA (American Relief Administration) had since Aug 1921 saved 20 million lives from famine and famine diseases.

2.—The figure published in 1972 for the Bangladeshi disaster was from Dr Afzal, Principal Scientific Officer of the Atomic Energy Authority Centre, Dacca. One report asserted that less than half of the population of the 4 islands of Bhola, Charjabbar, Hatia and Ramagati (1961 Census 1.4 million) survived. The most damaging hurricane recorded was the billion dollar Betsy (name now retired) in 1965 with an insurance pay-out of $715 million. Hurricane Frederic (Sept 1979) cost insurers $752 million in inflated dollars.

3.—The number of civilians killed by the bombing of Germany has been put variously as 593,000 and "over 635,000." A figure of c. 140,000 deaths in USAF fire raids on Tokyo of March 10, 1945 has been attributed. Total Japanese fatalities were 600,000 (conventional) and 220,000 (nuclear).

4.—A total of 10,000 Austrian and Italian troops is reported to have been lost in the Dolomite valley of Northern Italy on Dec 13, 1916 in more than 100 avalanches. The total is probably exaggerated though bodies were still being found in 1952. 4,000 killed, Santa Valley, below Huascarán, Peru, Jan 10, 1962.

5.—It was estimated that some 5,000 people were trampled to death in the stampede for free beer at the coronation celebration of Czar Nicholas II in Moscow in May 1896.

6.—Some sources maintain that the final death toll was over 3,000 on Dec 6–7. Published estimates of the 11,000 killed at the BASF chemical plant explosion at Oppau, W Germany, on Sept 21, 1921, were exaggerated. The best estimate is 561 killed.

7.—>200,000 killed in the sack of Moscow, freed by Tartars, May 1571. The worst-ever hotel fire killed 162 at the Hotel Daeyungak, Seoul, South Korea, Dec 25, 1971. The worst circus fire killed 168 in Hartford, Conn, on July 6, 1944.

8.—The worst gold mining disaster in South Africa was 152 killed due to flooding in the Witwatersrand Gold Mining Co gold mine in 1909.

WORST ACCIDENTS & DISASTERS IN THE WORLD

(continued)	Deaths		
Fireworks	>800	Dauphine's wedding, Seine, Paris	May 16, 1770
Railroad	>800	Bagmati River, Bihar State, India	June 6, 1981
Tornado	689	South Central States, US (3 hours)	March 18, 1925
Aircraft (Civil)	583	KLM-Pan Am Boeing 747 Ground Crash, Tenerife, Canary Islands	March 27, 1977
Man-Eating Animal	436	Champawat district, India, tigress shot by Col Jim Corbett	1907
Bacteriological and Chemical	c. 300	Novosibirsk B&CW plant, USSR	Apr-May 1979
Hail	246	Moradabad, Uttar Pradesh, India	Apr 20, 1888
Submarine	130	*Le Surcouf* rammed in Caribbean	Feb 18, 1942
Offshore Oil Plant	123	Alexander L. Kielland "Hotel," North Sea	March 27, 1980
Road (single vehicle)	127[9]	Bus plunged into irrigation canal, Sayyoum, Egypt	Aug 9, 1973
Helicopter	54	Israeli military "Sea Stallion," West Bank	May 10, 1977
Ski Lift (Cablecar)	42	Cavalese resort, Northern Italy	March 9, 1976
Mountaineering	40[10]	USSR Expedition on Mt Everest	Dec 1952
Elevator	23	Vaal Reefs Gold Mine lift fell 1.2 miles	May 27, 1980
Lightning	21	Hut in Chinamasa Kraal near Umtali, Rhodesia (single bolt)	Dec 23, 1975
Yacht Racing	9	28th Fastnet Race 23 boats sank or abandoned in Force 11 gale	Aug 13–15, 1979
Space	3	Apollo oxygen fire, Cape Kennedy, Fla	Jan 27, 1967
	3	*Soyuz* II re-entry over USSR	June 29, 1971
Atomic	high but undisclosed	Venting of plutonium waste, Kyshtym, USSR	1957–58

Notes. 9.—The worst year ever for road deaths in the US has been 1969 (56,400). The world's highest death rate is 29 per 100,000 in 1978 in Luxembourg and Portugal. The US's 2 millionth victim since 1899 died in Jan 1973. The global total dead by Sept 1975 was put at 25 million.
10.—According to Polish sources, not confirmed by the USSR. On Mt Fuji, Japan 23 died in blizzard and avalanche on March 20, 1972.

Chapter 11

Human Achievements

1. ENDURANCE AND ENDEAVOR

Travel and Exploration

Lunar Conquest

Neil Alden Armstrong (b Wapakoneta, Ohio, of Scottish-Irish-German ancestry, Aug 5, 1930), command pilot of the *Apollo XI* mission, became the first man to set foot on the moon on the Sea of Tranquillity at 02:56 and 15 sec a.m. GMT on July 21, 1969. He was followed out of the Lunar Module *Eagle* by Col Edwin Eugene Aldrin, Jr (b Glen Ridge, NJ, of Swedish, Dutch and British ancestry, Jan 20, 1930), while the Command Module named *Columbia* piloted by Lt-Col Michael Collins (b Rome, Italy, of Irish and pre-Revolutionary American ancestry, Oct 31, 1930) orbited above.

Eagle landed at 20:17 and 42 sec GMT July 20 and blasted off at 17:54 GMT on July 21, after a stay of 21 hours 36 min. The *Apollo XI* had blasted off from Cape Kennedy, Fla at 13:32 GMT July 16 and was a culmination of the US space program, which, at its peak, employed 376,600 people and attained in the year 1966–67 a peak budget of $5,900 million.

There is evidence that Pavel Belgayev was the cosmonaut selected by the USSR for a manned lunar flight in *Zond 7* on Dec 9, 1968 (219 days before the *Apollo XI* flight), but no launch took place.

First Woman in Space

The first and only woman to orbit the earth was Jr Lt (now Lt-Col) Valentina Vladimirovna Tereshkova-Nikolayev (b March 6, 1937), who was launched in *Vostok VI* from Tyura Tam, USSR, at 9:30 a.m. GMT June 16, 1963, and landed at 8:16 a.m. June 19, after a flight of 2 days 22 hours 42 min, during which she completed over 48 orbits (1,225,000 miles) and came to within 3 miles of *Vostok V*. She was formerly a textile worker. Her mission was variously reported to be punctuated with pleas to be brought back due to giddiness, or to be extended because of her excellent performance.

First "Walk" in Space

The earliest undoubted instance of an astronaut floating free outside a space vehicle was by Astronaut Edward H. White II (killed Jan 27, 1967), for 21 minutes over Hawaii to the US Atlantic coast on June 3, 1965, from *Gemini IV*. Evidence for the earlier claim of Lt-Col Aleksey A. Leonov from *Voskhod 2* on March 18, 1965, is not unreservedly accepted.

Manned Flight Altitude

The greatest altitude attained by man was when the crew of the ill-fated *Apollo XIII* was at apocynthion (*i.e.* their furthest point behind the moon) 158 miles above its surface and 248,665 miles above the earth's surface at 6:21 a.m. EST on Apr 15, 1970. The crew consisted of Capt James Arthur Lovell, Jr, USN (b Cleveland, Ohio, March 25, 1928); John L.

FIRST WOMAN IN SPACE: Valentina Tereshkova (USSR) is also the only woman to orbit the earth. She was in space for almost 3 days and made 48 orbits in 1963, setting a speed record of 17,470 mph.

341

Swigert, Jr (b Denver, Colo, Aug 30, 1931); and Fred Wallace Haise, Jr (b Biloxi, Miss, Nov 14, 1933).

The greatest altitude attained by a woman in flight is 143.5 miles by Valentina Vladimirovna Tereshkova-Nikolayev (previous page) during her 48-orbit flight in *Vostok VI* June 16–19, 1963. The record for a woman in an aircraft is 79,842 ft by Natalia Prokhanova (USSR) (b 1940) in an E-33 jet, May 22, 1965.

Longest Manned Space Flight

The longest time spent in space is 185 days, by the Russians, Valeriy Ryumin, and Leonid Popov on board the Salyut-Soyuz research station *Salyut 6.* They were launched on Apr 8, 1980 in *Soyuz 35* and landed 112 miles southeast of Dzhezkhzgan on Oct 11, 1980.

Oldest and Youngest Astronauts

The oldest of the 107 people of 11 nationalities in space has been Donald Kent ("Deke") Slayton (b Sparta, Wis, Mar 1, 1924) who was aged 51 years 146 days when launched on the *Apollo-Soyuz* mission on July 24, 1975. The youngest was Major (later Col) Gherman Stepanovich Titov (b Sept 11, 1935)

who was 25 years 329 days old when he was launched in *Vostok II* on Aug 6, 1961. The only 5-time spaceman has been Capt John W. Young, USN.

Duration Record on the Moon

The crew of *Apollo XVII* collected a record 253 lb of rock and soil during their 22-hour-5-min "extra-vehicular activity." They were Capt Eugene Andrew Cernan, USN (b Chicago, March 14, 1934) and Dr Harrison H. "Jack" Schmitt (b Santa Rosa, NM, July 3, 1935), who became the 12th man on the moon. The crew were on the lunar surface for a record 74 hours 59½ min Dec 7–19, 1972, during this longest of lunar missions which took 12 days 13 hours 51 min.

Speed in Space

The fastest speed at which humans have traveled is 24,791 mph when the Command Module of *Apollo X* carrying Col (now Brig-Gen) Thomas Patten Stafford, USAF (b Weatherford, Okla, Sept 17, 1930), Cdr (now Capt) Eugene Andrew Cernan and Cdr (now Capt) John Watts Young, USN (b San Francisco, Sept 24, 1930) reached their maximum speed on their trans-earth return flight at an altitude of 400,000 ft on May 26, 1969.

The highest speed ever attained by a woman is 17,470 mph by Valentina Vladimirovna Tereshkova-Nikolayev during her 48-orbit flight in *Vostok VI* June 16–19, 1963.

The highest speed ever achieved by a woman aircraft pilot is 1,669.89 mph by Svetlana Savitskaya (USSR), reported on June 2, 1975.

Speed on Land

The highest speed ever claimed on land is 739.666 mph or Mach 1.0106 in a one-way run by Stan Barrett (US) in the *Budweiser Rocket,* a rocket-engined 3-wheeled car at Edwards Air Force Base, Calif on Dec 17, 1979 (but see also Chapter 8).

The *official* land speed record is 622.287 mph set by Gary Gabelich (b San Pedro, Calif, Aug 29, 1940) on Oct 23, 1970 on the Bonneville Salt Flats, Utah, in the rocket-powered *The Blue Flame,* built by Reaction Dynamics Inc of Milwaukee, Wis.

YOUNGEST MAN IN SPACE (left): Major Titov (USSR) was less than 26 years old in 1961 when he rocketed into space aboard the "Vostok II." (Novasti)

The highest land speed recorded by a woman is 524.016 mph by Mrs Kitty O'Neil Hambleton (US), in the 48,000-hp rocket-powered 3-wheeled S.M.1 *Motivator* over the Alvard Desert, Ore, on Dec 6, 1976. Her official 2-way record was 512.710 mph and she probably touched 600 mph momentarily.

Speed on Water

The highest speed ever achieved on water is an estimated 300 knots (345 mph) by Kenneth Peter Warby (b May 9, 1939) on the Blowering Dam Lake, NSW, Australia Nov 20, 1977, in his unlimited hydroplane *Spirit of Australia*. The official world water speed record is 319.627 mph, set Oct 8, 1978, by Warby on the Blowering Dam Lake.

The record for propeller-driven craft is 202.42 mph by Larry Hill in the supercharged hydroplane *Mr. Ed* at Long Beach, Calif, in Aug 1971. On a one-way run, the *Climax* reached a speed of 205.19 mph.

The fastest woman on water is Mary Rife (US), who has driven a drag boat at more than 190 mph.

Most Traveled Man

The man who visited more countries than anyone else was Jesse Hart Rosdail (1914–77) of Elmhurst, Ill, a teacher of children in the 5th grade. Of the 168 sovereign countries and 47 *de facto* non-sovereign territories (215 in all) listed by the *UN Population Report* of 1982, he visited all, except for N Korea and French Antarctic Territories. He estimated his total mileage as 1,626,605 miles.

Though he has not visited so many currently existing countries, Mehmet S. Ersöz (b 1904, Turkey) has traveled much more widely within some 210 countries. His wife's total was 163 by mid-1978. Fred Specovius (W Germany) has visited every sovereign country except São Tomé and N Korea and every non-sovereign territory except 10, making a total of 209 countries.

LONGEST TIME IN SPACE: Astronaut Ryumin was one of two Russians who spent 185 days on board the "Salyut 6" research station.

343

The most countries visited by a disabled person is 120 sovereign and 63 non-sovereign countries by Prof Daniel J. Crowley of Davis, Calif, who has been confined to a wheelchair since March 1946.

The Methodist preacher Francis Asbury of Birmingham, England, traveled 264,000 miles by horseback in N America from 1771 to 1815, preaching 16,000 sermons.

Most Isolated Human

The farthest any human has been removed from his nearest living fellow man is 2,233.2 miles in the case of the Command Service Module pilot Alfred M. Worden on the US *Apollo XV* lunar mission of July 30–Aug 1, 1971.

Fastest Round-the-World Trip

The fastest time for a round-the-world journey on scheduled flights for a circumnavigation is 44 hours 6 min by David J. Springbett, 41, of Taplow, England from Los Angeles eastward via London, Bahrain, Singapore, Bangkok, Manila, Tokyo and Honolulu Jan 8–10, 1980 over a 23,068-mile route.

The F.A.I. accepts any flight, taking off and landing at the same point, which is as long as the Tropic of Cancer (22,858.754 miles) as a circumnavigational flight.

North Pole Conquests

The claims of both of the two US Arctic explorers, Dr Frederick Albert Cook (1865–1940) and Rear Adm Robert Edwin Peary, USN (1856–1920), in reaching the North Pole are subject to positive proof.

The earliest indisputable attainment of the North Pole over the sea ice was at 3 p.m. (CST) on Apr 19, 1968, by Ralph Plaisted (US) and three companions after a 42-day trek in four snowmobiles. Their arrival was independently verified 18 hours later by a US Air Force weather aircraft. The sea bed is 13,410 ft below the North Pole.

Naomi Uemara (b 1941), the Japanese explorer and mountaineer, became the first person to reach the North Pole in a solo trek across the Arctic ice cap at 04:45 GMT May 1, 1978. He had traveled 450 miles, setting out on March 7 from Cape Edward, Ellesmere Island, in northern Canada. He averaged over 8 miles per day with his sled "Aurora" drawn by 17 huskies (he had hoped to average 10.5 miles per day).

The first woman to set foot on the North Pole was Mrs Fran Phipps, wife of the Canadian bush pilot Weldy Phipps, Apr 5, 1971. Galina Aleksandrovna Lastovskaya (b 1941) and Lilia Vladislavovna Minina (b 1959) were crew members of the USSR atomic icebreaker *Arktika* which reached the Pole on Aug 17, 1977.

The Soviet scientist Dr Pavel A. Gordienko and 3 companions were arguably the first ever to stand on the exact point Lat 90° 00′N (±300 meters) on Apr 23, 1948.

Arctic Crossing

The first crossing of the Arctic sea ice was achieved by the British Trans-Arctic Expedition which left Point Barrow, Alaska, Feb 21, 1968, and arrived at the Seven Island Archipelago northeast of Spitzbergen 464 days later on May 29, 1969, after a haul of 2,920 statute miles and a drift of 700 miles, compared with a straight-line distance of 1,662 miles. The team was Wally Herbert (leader), 34, Maj Ken Hedges, 34, Allan Gill, 38, Dr Roy Koerner, 36 (glaciologist), and 40 huskies. This was the longest sustained (sled) journey ever made on polar pack ice and the first undisputed conquest of the North Pole by sled. Temperatures sank to −47° F during the trek.

South Pole Conquests

The first ships to cross the Antarctic circle (Lat 66° 30′ S) were the 193-crew *Resolution* (462 tons) under Capt James Cook (1728–79), the English navigator, and *Adventure* (336 tons) under Lt T. Furneaux, at 39° E, Jan 17, 1773.

The first person to sight the Antarctic *mainland*— on the best available evidence and against claims made for British and Russian explorers—was Nathaniel Brown Palmer (US) (1799–1877). On Nov 17, 1820, he sighted the Orleans Channel coast of the Palmer Peninsula from his 45-ton sloop *Hero*.

The South Pole (altitude 9,186 ft on ice and 336 ft bed rock) was first reached at 11 a.m. Dec 16, 1911, by a Norwegian party, led by Capt Roald Engebreth Gravning Amundsen (1872–1928), after a 53-day march with dog sleds from the Bay of Whales, to which he had penetrated in the *Fram*. Subsequent calculations showed that Olav Olavson Bjaaland (the last survivor, dying in June 1961, aged 88) and Helmer Hanssen probably passed within 400–600 meters of the exact pole. The other two party members were Sverre H. Hassell and Oskar Wisting.

The first woman to set foot on Antarctica was Mrs Karoline Mikkelsen on Feb 20, 1935. No woman stood on the South Pole until Nov 11, 1969, when Lois Jones, Eileen McSavaney, Jean Pearson, Terry

CONQUEST OF THE NORTH POLE: Admiral Robert E Peary (above) took the photograph (right, above) of his companions after they reached what they believed was the North Pole on Apr 6, 1909. There is considerable doubt about Peary's group's attainment. No doubt though about the CONQUEST OF THE SOUTH POLE by Roald Amundsen who led a Norwegian party, which included Helmer Hanssen (right), in Dec 1911. (Radio Times) THE FIRST ARCTIC SEA CROSSING over the ice was by the British Trans-Arctic Expedition (below) led by Wally Herbert. These 4 men covered 1,662 miles as the crow flies with 40 huskies in temperatures as cold as 47°F below zero.

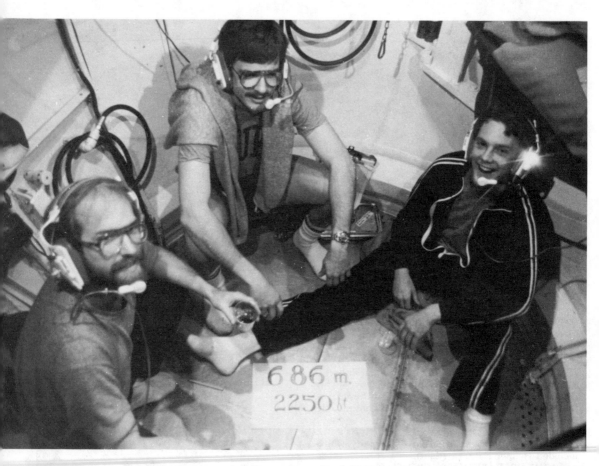

686 m.
2250 ft

RECORD DIVERS (above): These 3 men at Duke University made a simulated dive of 2,250 ft in this dry 8-ft sphere and stayed "underwater" for 43 days in 1981. DEEP SINKER: The descent of 6.78 miles down to the ocean floor by the US Navy manned bathyscaphe "Trieste" (right) set a record in 1960 that has not been exceeded since. The Marianas Trench near Guam in the Pacific was the spot, and the water pressure was 16,883 lb per sq in.

Lee Tickhill (all US), Kay Lindsay (Australia) and Pam Young (New Zealand), arrived by air.

Antarctic Crossing

The first surface crossing of the Antarctic continent was completed at 1:47 p.m. March 2, 1958, after a 2,158-mile trek lasting 99 days from Nov 24, 1957, from Shackleton Base to Scott Base via the Pole. The crossing party of 12 was led by Dr (now Sir) Vivian Ernest Fuchs (b Feb 11, 1908).

The 2,600-mile trans-Antarctic leg of the 1980-82 Trans Globe Expedition was achieved in 66 days on Jan 11, 1981 having passed through the South Pole on Dec 23, 1980. The 3-man party on snowmobiles was led by Sir Ranulph Fiennes (b 1944).

Longest Sled Journey

The longest totally self-supporting polar sled journey ever made was one of 1,080 miles from west to east across Greenland, June 18–Sept 5, 1934 by Capt (now Sir) Martin Lindsay, Lt Arthur Godfrey, Andrew N. C. Croft and 49 dogs.

First on Both North and South Poles

David S. Porter (b 1938) of Hope, NJ, visited the South Pole as a guest of the US Navy Dec 14, 1970 (temperature −38° F) and on Apr 9, 1979 he visited the North Pole where the temperature was −39° F.

Deep Diving Records

The record depth for the extremely dangerous activity of breath-held diving is 282 ft by Jacques Mayol (France) off Elba, Italy on Nov 9, 1973. The pressure on Mayol's thorax was 136.5 lb of force per sq in, and his pulse fell to 36.

Enzo Maiorca (Italy) surfaced unconscious from his dive of 285 ft off Sorrento, Italy, on Sept 27, 1974.

The women's record is 147½ ft by Giuliana Treleani (Italy) off Cuba in Sept 1967.

The record dive with scuba (self-contained underwater breathing apparatus) is 437 ft by John J. Gruener and R. Neal Watson (US) off Freeport, Grand Bahama, on Oct 14, 1968.

The record dive utilizing gas mixtures (nitrogen, oxygen and helium) is a simulated dive of 2,250 ft in a dry chamber by Stephen Porter, Len Whitlock and Erik Kramer at the Duke University Medical Center, Durham, NC, Feb 3, 1981 in a 43-day trial in an 8-ft sphere.

Some divers have survived free swimming for short intervals at depths of 1,400 ft.

Underwater Rescue

The deepest underwater rescue achieved was of the *Pisces III* in which Roger R. Chapman, 28, and Roger Mallinson, 35, were trapped for 76 hours when it sank to 1,575 ft, 150 miles southeast of Cork, Ireland, Aug 29, 1973. She was hauled to the surface by the cable ship *John Cabot* after preliminary work by *Pisces V, Pisces II* and the remote control recovery vessel US CURV, on Sept 1, 1973.

The greatest depth of an actual escape without any equipment has been from 225 ft by Richard A. Slater from the rammed submersible *Nekton Beta* off Catalina Island, Calif on Sept 28, 1970.

Greatest Ocean Descent

The record ocean descent was achieved in the Challenger Deep of the Marianas Trench, 250 miles southwest of Guam, when the Swiss-built US Navy bathyscaphe *Trieste*, manned by Dr Jacques Piccard (b 1914) and Lt Donald Walsh, USN, reached the ocean bed 35,820 ft (6.78 miles) down, at 1:10 p.m. Jan 23, 1960. The pressure of the water was 16,883 lb per sq in (1,215.6 tons per sq ft), and the temperature 37.4° F. The descent required 4 hours 48 min and the ascent 3 hours 17 min.

Deepest Salvage

The greatest depth at which salvage has been achieved is 16,500 ft by the bathyscaphe *Trieste II* (Lt Cdr Mel Bartels, USN) to attach cables to an "electronics package" on the sea bed 400 miles north of Hawaii, May 20, 1972.

Project Jennifer by USS *Glomar Explorer* in June–July 1974, to recover a Golfclass USSR submarine 750 miles northwest of Hawaii cost $550 million but was not successful.

Salvage by Divers

The deepest salvage operation ever achieved with divers was on the wreck of HM Cruiser *Edinburgh* sunk on May 2, 1942, in the Barents Sea off northern Norway inside the Arctic Circle in 803 ft of water. Twelve divers dived on the wreck in pairs using a bell from the *Stephaniturm* (1,423 tons) over 32 days under the direction of former RN officer and project director Michael Steward from Sept 17 to Oct 7, 1981. The 431 gold ingots were divided; $26.3 million to the USSR, $13.15 million to GB and some $32.4 million to the salvage contractors, Jessop Marine Recoveries Ltd (10%) and Wharton Williams Ltd (90%). Keith Cooper, 28, was the first to touch the gold. The longest decompression time was 7 days 10 hours 27 min. The $71.85 million is an all-time record.

Mining Depths

The deepest penetration into the ground by man is in the Western Deep Levels Mine at Carletonville, Transvaal, South Africa, where a record depth of 12,-500 ft (2.36 miles) has been attained. The rock temperature at this depth is 131° F.

The one-month (31-day) record is 1,251 ft for sinking a standard shaft 26 ft in diameter at Buffelsfontein Mine, Transvaal, South Africa, March 1962.

MARRIAGE AND DIVORCE

Longest Marriage

The longest recorded marriage is one of 86 years between Sir Temulji Bhicaji Nariman and Lady Nariman from 1853 to 1940 resulting from a cousin marriage when both were five. Sir Temulji (b Sept 3, 1848) died, aged 91 years 11 months, in Aug 1940 in Bombay.

The only reliable instance of an 83rd anniversary celebrated by a couple marrying at normal ages is that between the late Edd (105) and Margaret (99) Hollen (US) who celebrated their 83rd anniversary on May 7, 1972. They were married in Kentucky on May 7, 1889.

Salus and Minnie Newquist celebrated their 82nd anniversary in Ft Smith, Ark. He was born Mar 5, 1880. They have an 81-year-old "child" and 39 great-great-grandchildren.

Longest Engagement

The longest engagement on record is one of 67 years between Octavio Guillen, 82, and Adriana Martinez, 82. They finally took the plunge in June 1969, in Mexico City.

Most Divorces and Marriages

The greatest number of marriages accumulated in the monogamous world is 25 by the former minister of religion Mr Glynn de Moss Wolfe (US) (b 1908) who married for the 25th time since 1931 his 23rd wife in May 1982. His total number of children is, he says, 41, aged between 56 and 2. He has long kept two wedding dresses (different sizes) in his closet for ready use. He has additionally suffered 19 mothers-in-law.

Mrs Beverly Nina Avery, then aged 48, a barmaid from Los Angeles, set a monogamous world record in Oct 1957 by obtaining her 16th divorce, this one from Gabriel Avery, her 14th husband. She alleged outside the court that 5 of the 14 had broken her nose.

The most often-marrying millionaire, Thomas F. Manville (1894–1967), contracted his 13th marriage to his 11th wife, Christine Erdlen Popa (1940–71) aged 20, in NYC on Jan 11, 1960, when he was 65. His shortest marriage (to his 7th wife) effectively lasted only 7½ hours. His fortune of $20 million came from asbestos, which he unfortunately could not take with him.

Giovanni Vigliotto, 52, was reported to have been arrested in Panama City on Dec 30, 1981, for 82 or 83 polygamous marriages in more than 25 US states. He specialized in "larceny by deception."

Oldest Bride and Bridegroom

Dyura Avramovich, reportedly aged 101, married Yula Zhivich, admitting to 95, in Belgrade, Yugoslavia, in Nov 1963.

Mass Wedding Ceremony

The largest mass wedding ceremony was one of 2,075 couples officiated over by Sun Myung Moon of the Holy Spirit Association for the Unification of World Christianity in Madison Sq Garden, NYC, on July 1, 1982. Moon (who calls himself Rev) was reported to be planning a series of mass ceremonies around the world for other couples of his "church."

Most Expensive Wedding

The most expensive private wedding is reputed to be that of Maria Niarchos, 20, to Alix Chevassus, 36, at her father's estate in Normandy, France on June 16, 1979. Guests consumed an estimated 12,000 bottles of champagne and red wine, the supply of caviar outweighed the demand in four football-field-sized tents. The cost is conservatively estimated at $500,000.

MARINE CIRCUMNAVIGATION RECORDS

(Compiled by Sq Ldr D. H. Clarke)

A true circumnavigation entails passing through two antipodal points (which are at least 12,429 statute miles apart).

CATEGORY	VESSEL	NAME	START PLACE, DATE	FINISH DATE, DURATION
Earliest*	*Vittoria* Expedition of Fernao de Magalhaes (Magellan) (c. 1480–1521)	Juan Sebastion de Elcano or Del Cano (k 1526) and 17 crew	Seville, Spain, Sept 20, 1519	San Lucar, Spain, Sept 6, 1521, 30,700 miles
Earliest Woman	*Etoile*	Crypto-female valet of M de Commerson, named Baré	St Malo, 1766	1769
Earliest Fore-and-Aft Rigged Vessel	*Union,* 98 tons (Sloop)	John Boit Junior (US) and 22 crew	Newport, RI, 1794 (*via* Cape Horn westabout)	Newport, RI, 1796
Earliest Yacht	*Sunbeam,* 170-ft-5.8-in 3-mast topsail schooner	Lord and Lady Brassey (GB), passengers and crew	Cowes, Isle of Wight, 1876	Cowes, Isle of Wight, 1877
Earliest Solo	*Spray,* 36¾-ft gaff yawl	Capt Joshua Slocum, 51 (US) (a non-swimmer)	Newport, RI *via* Magellan Straits, Apr 24, 1895	July 3, 1898, 46,000 miles
Earliest Solo in both directions	*Solitaire,* 34-ft Bermudan sloop	Les Powles (GB)	Falmouth 1975 (westabout *via* Panama)	Lymington, 1978 (unsponsored)
Earliest Motorboat	*Speejacks,* 98 ft	Albert Y. Gowen (US), wife and crew	NYC, 1921	NYC, 1922
Earliest Woman Solo	*Mazurek,* 31-ft-2-in Bermuda sloop	Krystyna Chojnowska-Liskiewicz (Poland)	Las Palmas, Mar 28, 1976 Westward *via* Panama	Tied knot Mar 21, 1978
Earliest Woman Solo *via* Cape Horn	*Express Crusader,* 53-ft Bermuda sloop	Naomi James (NZ/GB)	Dartmouth, England, Sept 9, 1977 (Cape Horn, March 19, 1978)	Dartmouth, June 8, 1978 (266 days 19 hours)
Smallest Boat	*Super Shrimp,* 18-ft-4-in Bermuda sloop	Shane Acton (GB) Iris Derungs (Switz)	Cambridge, England Aug 1972	Cambridge, England Aug 1980
Earliest Submarine	USS *Triton*	Capt Edward L. Beach, USN, plus 182 crew	New London, Conn, Feb 16, 1960	May 10, 1960, 30,708 miles
Fastest Solo (Multihull)	*Manureva,* 70-ft trimaran (ex *Pen Duick IV*)	Alain Colas (France)	St Malo *via* Sydney	March 29, 1974 (167 days)
Fastest Solo (Monohull)	*Cor Caroli,* 29-ft-9-in Bermuda sloop	George Georgier (Bulgaria)	Havana, Cuba Dec 20, 1976	Havana, Dec 20, 1977 201 days 21 hr 36 min
Fastest Time and Fastest Speed (Yacht)	*Flyer,* 76-ft sloop	Cornelis von Rietschoten (Dutch)	Plymouth, Aug 29, 1981	Mar 29, 1982 (220.7 mpd) 120 days 6 hr 35 min
Fastest Solo Speed (Monohull)	*Ocean Bound* 41-ft-8-in Bermuda cutter	David Cowper (GB)	Plymouth, Eng, Aug 1979 (W-E *via* Cape Horn)	224 days 12 hr 28 min (av speed 131.05 mpd)
Fastest (Clipper)	*James Baines* 266 ft	Capt C. McDonald (GB) and crew	Liverpool to Melbourne (58 days) 1854	Melbourne to Liverpool (69 days) 1855
Fastest Solo Westabout *via* Cape Horn	*Ocean Bound,* 41-ft-1-in Bermudan sloop	David Cowper (GB)	Plymouth, Sept 27, 1981	Plymouth, May 17, 1982 (221 sailing days), 31,350 miles (141.85 mpd)
Fastest Ever (Yacht)	*Awahnee II,* 53 ft Bermuda cutter	Bob Griffith (US) and 5 crew	Bluff, NZ, 1970 (eastabout *via* Horn)	Bluff, NZ, 1971 (88 sailing days + 23 days stopovers)
Fastest Ever (Clipper)	*Red Jacket* 260 ft	Capt S. Reid (GB) and crew	From/to Lat 26° 25' W (*via* Horn)	62 days 22 hrs, 1854
Earliest Non-stop Solo (Port-to-Port)	*Suhaili,* 32.4-ft Bermuda ketch	Robin Knox-Johnston (GB) (b 1939)	Falmouth, England, June 14, 1968	Apr 22, 1969 (312 days)
Longest Non-stop Alone at Sea	*Solitaire,* 34-ft Bermudan sloop	Les Powles (GB)	Lymington, July 9, 1980 (eastabout *via* Horn)	Lymington, June 3, 1981, 329 days

* Eduard Roditi, author of *Magellan of the Pacific,* advances the view that Magellan's slave Enrique was the first circumnavigator. He had been purchased in Malacca, but knew the Filipino dialect, Vizayan, when he reached the Philippines from the east in 1521. The first to circumnavigate in both directions was Tobias Furneaux (GB) as 2nd lieutenant aboard the *Dolphin* from/to Plymouth, England east to east, *via* the Magellan Straits, 1766–68, and as captain of the *Adventure* from/to Plymouth west to east *via* Cape Horn in 1772–74.

TRANSATLANTIC MARINE RECORDS

(Compiled by Sq Ldr D. H. Clarke)

CATEGORY	CAPTAIN	VESSEL & SIZE	START	FINISH	DURATION	DATE
Earliest Canoe	"Finn-Man" (Eskimo)	Kayak, 11 ft 10 in	Greenland	Humber, England	Time not known	1613
Earliest Crossing (2 men)	C. R. Webb + 1 crew (US)	*Charter Oak*, 43 ft	New York	Liverpool	35 days 15 hr	1857
Earliest Trimaran (raft)	John Mikes + 2 crew (US)	*Non Pareil*, 25 ft	New York	Southampton, England	51 days	1868
Earliest Solo Sailing (E-W)	Josiah Shackford (US)	15-ton golf sloop	Bordeaux, France	Surinam	35 days	1786
Earliest Solo Sailing (W-E)	Alfred Johnson (US)	*Centennial*, 20 ft	Gloucester, Mass	Wales	46 days	1876
Earliest Woman Sailing (with US husband)	Mrs Joanna Crapo (Scot)	*New Bedford*, 20 ft (Bermudan ketch)	Chatham, Mass	Newlyn, England (earliest with BM rig)	51 days	1877
Earliest Single-handed Race	J. W. Lawlor (US) (winner)	*Sea Serpent*, 15 ft	Boston (June 21)	Coverack, England	45 days	1891
Earliest Rowing	John Brown + 5 British deserters	Ship's boat, *c.* 20 ft	St Helena (June 10)	Belmonte, Brazil (fastest ever row)	28 days (83 mpd)	1799
Earliest Rowing by 2 Men (Northern)	Georg Harboe and Frank Samuelsen (US)	*Fox*, 18⅓ ft	New York (June 6)	Isles of Scilly (Aug 1)	55 days (56 mpd)	1897
Fastest Solo Sailing W-E	J. V. T. McDonald (GB)	*Inverarity*, 38 ft	Nova Scotia	Ireland	16 days (147 mpd)	1922
Earliest Canoe (with sail)	Franz Romer (Germany)	*Deutscher Sport*, 21½ ft	Las Palmas (June 2)	St Thomas, VI	58 days (47 mpd)	1928
Earliest Woman Solo (W-E)	Gladys Gradly (US)	Lugger, 18 ft	Nova Scotia	Hope Cove, Devon, England	60 days	1903
Earliest Woman Solo (E-W)	Mrs Ann Davison (GB)	*Felicity Ann*, 23 ft	Las Palmas, November 20, 1952	Portsmouth, England Dominica	65 days	1952–53
Earliest Woman Solo (Across 2 Oceans)	Anna Woolf (SA)	*Zama Zulu*, 43 ft (Ferroconcrete)	Cape Town	Bowling, Scotland	8,920 miles in 109 days	1976
Fastest Woman Solo	Naomi James (GB)	*Kriterlady*, 53 ft	Plymouth, Eng	Newport, RI	25 days 19 hr 12 min	1980
Fastest 2-woman Crew	Annick Martin (Fr) + Annie Cordelle (Fr)	*Super Marches Bravo*, 45 ft	Plymouth	Newport, RI	21 days 4 hr 28 min	1981
Fastest Crossing Sailing (multihull) (E-W)	Eric Tabarly (France) + 2 crew	*Pen Duick IV*, 67 ft	Tenerife, Canary Is	Martinique	251.4 mpd (10 days 12 hrs)	1968
Fastest Crossing Sailing (monohull) (E-W)	Wilhelm Hirte and crew (Germany)	*Kriter II*, 80 ft	Canary Is	Barbados	13 days 8 hrs	1977
Fastest Crossing (monohul) (W-E)	Wilson Marshall (US) and crew	*Atlantic*, 185 ft	Sandy Hook, NJ	Lizard, Cornwall, Eng (3,054 miles)	12 days 4 hrs (fastest noon to noon 341 miles)	1905
Fastest Crossing Sail (W-E)	A. Eldridge (US) and crew	*Red Jacket* (Clipper) 260 ft	Sandy Hook	Liverpool Bar	12 days, 277.7 mpd	1854
Fastest Solo (E-W) (Northern) (monohull)	Kazimierz Jaworski (Poland)	*Spaniel II*, 56 ft	Plymouth, Eng	Newport, RI	19 days 13 hr 25 min	1980
Fastest E-W (Northern) (monohull)	Bruno Bacilieri (Italy) + Marc Vallin	*Faram Serenissima*, 66½ ft	Plymouth	Newport, RI	16 days 1 hr 25 min	1981
Fastest Solo (E-W) (Northern) (multihull)	Phillip Weld (US)	*Moxie*, 51-ft trimaran	Plymouth, Eng	Newport, RI	17 days 23 hr 12 min	1980
Fastest Solo (E-W) (Southern) (monohull)	Sir Francis Chichester (GB)	*Gipsy Moth V*, 57 ft	Portuguese Guinea	Nicaragua	179.1 mpd (22.4 days)	1970
Fastest Ever Yacht Sail (N. Route) (E-W)	Chay Blyth (GB) + Rob James (GB)	*Brittany Ferries GB*, 65½ ft (Tri)	Plymouth	Newport, RI	14 days 13 hr 54 min (212.1 mpd)	1981

TRANSATLANTIC SAILING: The fastest yacht ever to sail across the Atlantic was "Brittany Ferries" (right) a 65½-ft trimaran piloted by Great Britain's Chay Blyth and Rob James (above). (Intl Sail Inf Svce) They made it in less than 15 days. Sir Francis Chichester set a solo record in 1970 with "Gipsy Moth V" (below left) in 22.4 days. (Photo-Reportage Ltd) The smallest boat to cross either way was Hugo Vilhen's "April Fool," less than 6 ft long (below right). (Associated Newspapers Ltd)

TRANSATLANTIC MARINE RECORDS (continued)

CATEGORY	CAPTAIN	VESSEL & SIZE	START	FINISH	DURATION	DATE
Fastest Solo Rowing (E-W)	Sidney Genders, 51 (GB)	*Khaggavisana*, 19¾ ft	Penzance, Eng	Miami, Fla *via* Antigua	37.3 mpd 162 days 18 hrs	1970
Earliest Solo Rowing (E-W)	John Fairfax (GB)	*Britannia*, 22 ft	Las Palmas, Canary Is (Jan 20)	Ft Lauderdale, Fla (July 19)	180 days	1969
Earliest Solo Rowing (W-E)	Tom McClean (Ireland)	*Super Silver*, 20 ft	St John's, Newfoundland (May 17)	Black Sod Bay, Ireland (July 27)	70.7 days	1969
Smallest (E-W) (Southern)	Hugo S. Vihlen (US)	*The April Fool*, 5 ft 11⅞ in	Casablanca (Mar 29)	Ft Lauderdale, Fla (June 21)	85 days	1968
Smallest (W-E)	Gerry Spiess, 39 (US)	*Yankee Girl*, 10 ft	Norfolk, Va (June 1)	Falmouth, England (July 24)	54 days (3,800 miles)	1979
Smallest (across 2 oceans)	John Riding (GB)	*Sjo Ag*, 12 ft	Plymouth *via* Panama	New Zealand, 1973	Lost in Tasman Sea	1964/1974
Youngest Solo Sailing	David Sandeman, 17½ years	*Sea Raider*, 35 ft	Jersey, CI	Newport, RI	43 days	1976
Oldest Solo Sailing	Monk Farnham (72 years 270 days)	*Seven Bells*, 28 ft	Hampton, Va	Falmouth	40 days (from Bermuda)	1981
Fastest Crossing (W-E) (multihull)	Marc Pajot (Fr) + 3 crew	*Elf Aquitaine*, 61-ft catamaran	Sandy Hook, NJ (July 4)	Lizard, Cornwall (July 14)	9 days 10 hr 6 min (av. 13.3 knots)	1981
Fastest Solo Rowing (W-E)	Gerard d'Aboville (France)	*Captaine Cook* 18 ft 4 in	Chatham, Mass (July 10)	Ushant, France (Sept 20)	71 days 23 hr (44.8 mpd)	1980

TRANSPACIFIC MARINE RECORDS

CATEGORY	CAPTAIN	VESSEL & SIZE	START	FINISH	DURATION	DATE
Fastest (Trans Pac)	Bill Lee (US)	*Merlin* 67 ft	Los Angeles	Honolulu	8 days 11 hrs 1 min	1977
Fastest Yacht (Australia-Horn)	O. K. Pennendreft (Fr) + 13 crew	*Kriter II* 80 ft	Sydney	Cape Horn	21 days (275 mpd)	1975/6
Fastest Clipper (Australia-Horn)	Capt J. N. Forbes (GB) and crew	*Lightning* 244 ft	Melbourne	Cape Horn	19 days 1 hr (315 mpd)	1854
Fastest Solo Monohull (Australia-Horn)	Chris Baranowski (Poland)	*Polonez* 45 ft 3 in	Hobart	Cape Horn	45 days (135 mpd)	1973
Fastest Solo Multihull (Australia-Horn)	Alain Colas (Fr)	*Pen Duick IV* trimaran 70 ft	Sydney	Cape Horn	37 days (160 mpd)	1973/4
Earliest Solo (Woman)	Sharon Sites Adams (US)	*Sea Sharp II*, 31 ft	Yokohama	San Diego	75 days (5,911 miles)	1969
Earliest Rowing	John Fairfax (GB) Sylvia Cook (GB)	*Britannia II* 35 ft	San Francisco Apr 26, 1971	Hayman Is, Australia, Apr 22, 1972	362 days	1971 /1972
Earliest Rowing Solo	Anders Svedlund (Sweden)	*Waka Moana* 24 ft	Chile (June 2)	Samoa	118 days	1974
Smallest Sailing	Gerry Spiess (US)	*Yankee Girl*, 10 ft	Long Beach, Cal	Sydney	105 days	1981

N.B.—The earliest single-handed Pacific crossings were achieved East-West by Bernard Gilboy (US) in 1882 in the 18-ft double-ender *Pacific* and West-East by Fred Rebel (Latvia) in the 18-ft *Elaine* (from Australia), and Edward Miles (US) in the 36¾-ft *Sturdy II* (from Japan), both in 1932.

Oldest Divorce

In March 1980 a divorce was reported in the Los Angeles Superior Court, Calif, between Bernardine and Leopold Delper in which both parties were 88 years old.

Golden Anniversaries

Despite the advent of the computer, records on golden (or 50th) wedding anniversaries remain largely uncollated. Unusual cases reported include that of Mrs Agnes Mary Amy Mynott (b May 25, 1887) who attended the golden anniversary of her daughter Mrs Violet Bangs of St Albans in Dec 20, 1980, some 23 years after her own. The 3 sons and 4 daughters of Mr and Mrs J. Stredwick of East Sussex, England, *all* celebrated their golden anniversaries between May 1971 and Apr 1981. Triplets Lucille (Mrs Vogel), Marie (Mrs McNamara) and Alma (Mrs Prom) Pufpaff all celebrated their golden anniversaries on Apr 12, 1982, having all married in Cleveland, Ohio, in 1932.

Most Married Couple

Jack V. and Edna Moran of Seattle, Wash have married each other 40 times since the original and only really necessary occasion on July 27, 1937 in Seaside, Ore. Subsequent ceremonies have included those at Banff, Canada (1952), Cairo, Egypt (1966) and Westminster Abbey, London (1975).

STUNTS AND MISCELLANEOUS ENDEAVORS

Accordion Playing. Norman English of Fanfare Music, Chorley, England, played an accordion for 82 hours 50 min Apr 6–9, 1981.

Apple Peeling. The longest single unbroken apple peel on record is 172 ft 4 in peeled by Kathy Wafler, 17, of Wolcott, NY, in 11 hours 30 min at the Long Ridge Mall, Rochester, NY, Oct 16, 1976. The apple weighed 20 oz.

Apple Picking. The greatest recorded performance is 365½ US bushels picked in 8 hours by George Adrian, 32, of Indianapolis, on Sept 23, 1980.

APPLE PICKING: In just 8 hours, George Adrian of Indianapolis picked 365½ bushels. (Joe Young)

ACCORDION PLAYING: Norman English of England kept playing for a record 82 hours 50 min for charity.

Baby Carriage Pushing. The greatest distance covered in 24 hours in pushing a perambulator is 345.25 miles by Runner's Factory of Los Gatos, Calif with an all-star team of 57 California runners June 23–24, 1979. A team of 10 students from Sir Joseph Banks and East Hills High Schools with an adult "baby" covered 241.3 miles, Nov 16–17, 1979 at Chipping Norton, NSW, Australia.

Balancing on One Foot. The longest recorded duration for balancing on one foot is 33 hours by V. S. Kumar Anandan of Colombo, Sri Lanka, May 15–17, 1980. The disengaged foot may not be rested on the standing foot nor may any sticks be used for support or balance, but 5-minute rest breaks are allowed after each hour.

Balloon Blowing. In inflating with sheer lung power a standard 1,000-gram meteorological balloon to a diameter of 8 ft, Mel Robson, 40, of Newcastle-upon-Tyne, England, achieved a time of 1 hour 46 min on television in Tokyo on Mar 11, 1982. (This category supplants *Hot Water Bottle Bursting* in this book.)

Balloon Flights. The longest reported toy balloon flight is one of 9,000 miles from Atherton, Calif (released by Jane Dorst) on May 21, 1972 and found on June 10 at Pietermaritzburg, South Africa.

Balloon Release. The largest ever mass balloon release was one of 208,477 at the Sands Hotel re-opening in Las Vegas, Nev, on Jan 15, 1982, arranged by Tommy Walker Spectaculars.

Ball Punching. The duration record is 146 hours 20 min by Pat McEnteggart of Shallon, Julianstown, Ireland, Feb 27–Mar 5, 1981.

Band, One-Man. The greatest number of instruments played in a single tune is 75 in 2 min 11.2 sec by Rory Blackwell at the EMI Bingo and Social Club, Derry's Cross, Plymouth, Devon, England Sept 6, 1977.

Don Davis of Hollywood, Calif was the first one-man band able to play 4 melody and 2 percussion instruments simultaneously without electronics, in 1974. For a rendition of the 4th movement of Beethoven's Fifth Symphony, he utilizes an 8-prong pendular perpendicular piano pounder and a semi-circular chromatic radially operated centrifugally sliding left-handed glockenspiel.

Dave Sheriff of Rugby, England, played his one-man band (at least 3 instruments played simultaneously) for 50 hours 48 sec, Jan 25–27, 1982, at the New Cresta Cabaret Restaurant, Solihull, England. On Feb 8, 1982, Sheriff played 9 instruments (3 melodic and 6 percussion) simultaneously at the BBC studios, Birmingham, England.

Band Marathons. The longest recorded "blow-in" is 100 hours 2 min by the Du Val Senior High School band, Lanham, Md, directed by Lon Scarci, May 13–17, 1977.

Band, Pop. The playing duration record for a 4-man pop group is 144 hours by "Rocking Ricky and the Velvet Collars" at The Talardy Hotel, St Asaph, Wales Nov 12–18, 1976. The group at no time sank below a trio.

Barrel Jumping (on ice skates). The official distance record is 25 ft 5 in over 18 barrels by Yvon Jolin at Terrebonne, Quebec, Canada, in 1981. The feminine record is 20 ft 4½ in over 11 barrels by Janet Hainstock in Mich on Mar 15, 1980.

Barrel Rolling. The record for rolling a full 43.2-gallon metal beer barrel over a measured mile is 8 min 15 sec by a team of 6 from Tinwald Rugby Club, Ashburton, New Zealand, March 3, 1980.

Bathtub Racing. The record for the annual international 36-mile Nanaimo-to-Vancouver, British Columbia, bathtub race is 1 hour 29 min 40 sec by Gary Deathbridge, 25 (Australia) July 30, 1978. Tubs are limited to 75 in and 6-hp motors. The greatest distance for paddling a hand-propelled bathtub in 24 hours is 55 miles 425 yd by a team of 25 from Worcester Canoe Club, England Sept 28–29, 1979.

Baton Twirling. Four members of the Brownhills Majorettes of Walsall, England, twirled for 78 hours 2 min, July 20–23, 1981.

Beard of Bees. The heaviest recorded "beard" of bees was one estimated at not less than 21,000, which swarmed around a queen bee on the chest and throat of Don Cooke of Ohio, June 20, 1980. (Full story of Cooke appears in *Guinness: The Stories Behind the Records.*)

Bedmaking. The record time set under the rigorous rules of the Australian Bedmaking Championships is 28.2 sec by Wendy Wall, 34, of Sydney, NSW, Australia Nov 30, 1978.

BEARD OF BEES (top left and center): Don Cooke gets a big kiss from his wife after donning a full beard 17 in long of 21,000 bees. BATHTUB RACE (above): Every year 6-hp motorized "tubs," of 75 in or less race 36 miles to Vancouver, BC, Canada, from Nanaimo across the strait. (© Stanley C. Dakin, ARPS) ONE-MAN BAND (left, below): Don Davis plays 6 or more instruments at one sitting, including an ooga horn, glockenspiel, kazoo and cymbals, while strumming a banjo and making lights flash. SANDWICH BED OF NAILS (below): Komar holds the ultimate record at 1,642½ lb on top of his chest.

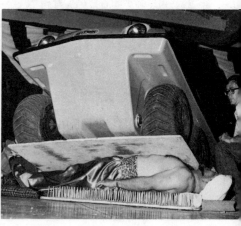

BICYCLE MOUNTING (above): These 13 members of a Japanese uni-cycle club managed to keep their balance for a distance of over 32 ft. WOMAN JUMPS BARRELS (below): Janet Hainstock of Mich jumps more than 20 ft over 11 barrels. BUBBLE GUM CHAMP Susan Montgomery Williams (right) shows that she can blow double bubbles as well as 19¼-in-diameter winners.

Bed of Nails. The duration record for non-stop lying on a bed of nails (sharp 6-in nails 2 in apart) is 102 hours 23½ min by the Rev Ken Owen at the YMCA, Port Talbot, Wales, Sept 29–Oct 3, 1980. Much longer durations are claimed by uninvigilated *fakirs*—the most extreme case being *Silki* who claimed 111 days in São Paulo, Brazil, ending on Aug 24, 1969.

Note that the category of "Iron Maiden" (lying between 2 beds of nails with added weight on top) has been retired with the ultimate record being set at 1642½ lb endured by Komar (Vernon E. Craig) of Wooster, Ohio at Old Chicago Towne March 6, 1977. No further claims for publication will be entertained or published.

Bed Pushing. The longest recorded push of a normally stationary object is 3,233 miles 1,150 yd in the case of a wheeled hospital bed by a team of 9, all employees of Bruntsfield Bedding Centre, Edinburgh, Scotland June 21–July 26, 1979.

Bed Racing. The record time for the annual Knaresborough Bed Race (established 1966) in North Yorkshire, England is 13 min 28 sec for the 2-mile 63-yd course crossing the River Nidd, by the ICI Fibres Flying Fiasco team June 9, 1979.

Beer Mat Flipping. Lack of standardization of the size and weight of beer mats (coasters) has bedeviled the chronicling of records in this international pursuit. A figure of 102 was reported from Stephen Thornton (GB), 22, on Jan 16, 1980.

Beer Stein Carrying. Barmaid Rosie Schedelbauer covered 15 meters (49 ft 2½ in) in 4.0 sec with 5 full steins in each hand in a televised contest in Konigsee, W Germany, June 29, 1981.

Bell Ringing. The longest recorded håndbell ringing recital has been one of 50 hours by the Potomac English Handbell Ringers at Landover Shopping Mall, Maryland, Feb 14–16, 1981.

Bicycle Mounting. On Aug 6, 1981, at Fuchu, Tokyo, Japan, thirteen members of the Mito-Itomi Unicycle Club mounted and rode a single bicycle a distance of 32.8 ft.

Billiard Table Jumping. Joe Darby (1861–1937) cleared a 12-ft billiard table lengthwise, taking off from a running start, using only a 4-in-high solid wooden block, at Wolverhampton, England, Feb 5, 1892.

Boomerang Throwing. The earliest mention of a word similar to "boomerang" is "wo-mur-rang" in Collins' *Account N.S. Wales Vocabulary,* published in 1798. The earliest certain Australian account of a returning boomerang (term established in 1827) was in 1831 by Major (later Sir) Thomas Mitchell. Curved throwing sticks for hunting wild fowl were found in the tomb of Tutankhamen, dating from the mid-14th century BC.

World championships and codified rules were not established until 1970. Jeff Lewry won the world title in 1970-71-72-73, and the Australian title in 1974. The Boomerang Association of Australia's championship record for distance reached before the boomerang returns is 351 ft (diameter) by Bob Burwell in the 1981 championships. The longest unofficial out-and-return on record is one of 370 ft by Al Gerhards at Old Westbury, LI, NY on Oct 20, 1979. Ger Schurink (Netherlands) kept a boomerang aloft for 29.9 sec at Bièvres, France, on Sept 27, 1981.

Brick Carrying. The record for carrying a brick (8 lb 15 oz) in a nominated ungloved hand with the arm extended in an uncradled downward pincer grip is 45 miles by David and Kym Barger of Lamar, Mo on May 21, 1977.

The feminine record of 19.2 miles was set by Cynthia Ann Smolko of Denville, NJ, on May 14, 1977, using a 9-lb-12-oz brick.

For the hod-carrying record, Stan Mallion of Swanley, England, carried bricks totaling 320 lb up the minimum 12-ft ladder Jan 24, 1982, at Dartford. Eric Stenman of Jakobstad, Finland, carried 74 bricks of 8.8 lb each, so totaling 652½ lb in a 8.8-lb hod 16.4 ft on the flat before ascending up a runged ramp to a height of 7 ft on July 25, 1939.

Brick Throwing. The greatest reported distance for throwing a standard 5-lb building brick is 146 ft 1 in by Geoffrey Capes at Braybrook School, Cambridgeshire, England, on July 19, 1978.

Bubble Gum Blowing. The largest bubble blown measured 19¼ in in diameter, created by Mrs Susan Montgomery Williams of Fresno, Calif, in a contest held in Jacksonville, Fla in 1979. Measurement was on a horizontal rather than a vertical basis, to eliminate any elongation due to gravity.

Camping Out. Two brothers Sven and Per and a sister Kari Heistad of Lebanon, NH have never slept indoors since March 1974. The coldest they have experienced has been Christmas morning 1980 with a wind chill temperature of −67° F, which to them is a "three-bag night." Also remarkably the family has no television.

Canal Jumping. In the 1979 Fierljeppen Championship at Winsam, Friesland, Netherlands, Catharinus Hoekstra leapt 57 ft across the water with a pole. A distance of 60 ft 4 in has been attributed to Aarth de Wit.

Card Throwing. Kevin St Onge threw a standard playing card 185 ft 1 in on the Henry Ford Community College campus, Dearborn, Mich, June 12, 1979.

Carriage Driving. The only man to drive 48 horses in a single hitch is Dick Sparrow of Zearing, Iowa, 1972–77. The lead horses were 135 ft away.

Catapulting. The greatest recorded distance for a catapult shot is 1,362 ft by James F. Pfotenhauer, using a patented 16½-ft "Monarch IV Supershot" and a 53-caliber lead shot on Ski Hill, Escanaba, Mich, on Sept 10, 1977.

Champagne Fountain. The tallest successfully filled column of champagne glasses is one 22 high, filled from the top by Carl Groves and Keith Pepper at Melbourne, Victoria, Australia, June 24, 1982. Joseph Achenback, Steven Arnold, Donald Milonowski and Timothy Tweddale of F.E.A.S.T. equaled the world record with 21 on Apr 26, 1981, at the Hilton Hotel, Grand Rapids, Mich.

Clapping. The duration record for continuous clapping (sustaining an average 140 claps per min audible at 100 yd) is 50 hours 17 min by Ashrita Furman of Jamaica, NY, Aug 10–12, 1981.

Club Swinging. Albert Rayner set a world record of 17,512 revolutions (4.9 per sec) in 60 min at Wakefield, England, on July 27, 1981. M. Dobrilla swung continuously for 144 hours at Cobar, NSW, Australia, finishing on Sept 15, 1913.

Coal Bag Carrying. The greatest non-stop bag-carrying feat, carrying 1 cwt (112 lb) of household coal in an open bag, is 23 miles by Alan M. Jones (b Mar 17, 1947) in 5 hours 53 min at the Family Fitness Center, Bellevue, Wash, on May 6, 1981.

Coal Shoveling. The record for filling a 1,120-lb hopper with stove-size pieces of coal is 31.5 sec by Robert Taylor of Dobson, New Zealand, Feb 7, 1981.

Coin Balancing. The greatest recorded feat of coin balancing is the stacking of 170 Canadian coins on top of a Canadian Commemorative penny which was freestanding vertically on another coin by Bruce McConachy (b 1963) of West Vancouver, British Columbia, on Aug 24, 1979.

Coin Snatching. The greatest number of British 10-pence coins caught clean from being flipped from the back of a forearm into the same palm is 62 by Andrew Gleed at the *Evening Star* offices, Ipswich, England, on Sept 22, 1978.

Since it is contended that 100 and more 25-cent US coins are beyond the capacity of the human hand to hold or snatch, claims of this quantity remain under investigation.

Complaining Successfully. Ralph Charell (b Dec 3, 1929), author of *How I Turn Ordinary Complaints into Thousands of Dollars,* between Jan 1963 and June 1977 amassed a total of $80,710.46 ranging between $6.95 and $25,000 in refunds and compensations. A recent complaint was against this publication for failing to list his 51 consecutive profitable transactions in "option trading."

Contest Winnings. The largest recorded individual prize won was $307,500 by Herbert J. Idle, 55, of Chicago in an encyclopedia contest run by Unicorn Press, Inc Aug 20, 1953.

Crawling. The longest continuous voluntary crawl (progression with one or the other knee in unbroken contact with the ground) on record is 26.5 mi by Rod Mahon and Ken Mackenzie of Newtown Abbot, England, on Jan 18, 1982.

The Baptist lay preacher Hans Mullikin, 39, arrived at the White House in Washington, DC on Nov 23, 1978, having crawled all but 8 of the 1,600 miles from Marshall, Tex.

Crochet. Mrs Barbara Jean Sonntag (b 1938) of Craig, Colo, crocheted 330 shells plus 5 stitches (equivalent to 4,412 stitches) in 30 min, at a rate of 147 stitches per min, on Jan 13, 1981. Mrs Sybille Anthony bettered all marathons of this kind in a 120-hour crochet marathon at Toombul Shoppingtown, Queensland, Australia, Oct 3–7, 1977.

Cucumber Slicing. Norman Johnson of the Blackpool College of Art and Technology, England sliced 12 in of a 1½-in-diameter cucumber at 22 slices to the inch (total 244 slices) in 19.11 sec on May 30, 1981.

LEAPING ACT: Marco Canestrelli imitates Superman flying through the air over the backs of 4 elephants in the Ringling Bros and Barnum & Bailey Circus.

DOUBLE FULL-TWISTING SOMERSAULT onto a 2-in-diameter pole: The Robertos show how they toss and catch 11-year-old Roberto Tabak.

CIRCUS ACTS: Tahar Davis is the man who surpasseth all understanders (left). He can't be seen, but he is supporting the 12 other members of the Hassani Troupe in a human pyramid. (© Birmingham Post & Mail) Terry Lemus (above) shows how she performs a triple back somersault on the flying trapeze. Tom Robin Edelston (below) is in the midst of the first-ever triple twisting double somersault on the trapeze at Circus World, Orlando, Fla.

CIRCUS RECORDS

The following represent the greatest feats performed, either for the first time or, if marked with an asterisk, uniquely. A "mechanic" is a safety harness.

Flying Trapeze	Earliest act	Jules Leotard (France)	Circus Napoleon, Paris	1859
	Double back somersault	Eddie Silbon	Paris Hippodrome	1879
	Triple back somersault (female)	Lena Jordan (Latvia) to Lew Jordan (US)	Sydney, Australia	1897
	Triple back somersault (male)	Ernest Clarke to Charles Clarke	Publiones Circus, Cuba	1909
	Triple and a half back somersault	Tony Steel to Lee Strath Marilees	Durango, Mexico	1962
	Triple twisting double somersault	Tom Edelston to John Zimmerman	Circus World, Fla	1981
	Full twisting triple	Miguel Vasquez to Juan Vasquez	Ringling Bros, Barnum & Bailey, Amphitheatre, Chicago	1981
	Quadruple somersault	Miguel Vasquez to Juan Vasquez	Ringling Bros, Barnum & Bailey, Tucson, Ariz	1982
	Double Pass with back somersault	Buster and Anne Melzora with Paul Garee	Latrobe, Pa	1935
	Triple back somersault with 1½ twists	Terry Cavarette Lemus (b Mar 6, 1953)	Circus Circus, Las Vegas	1969
	Head to head stand on swinging bar	* Ed and Ira Millette (né Wolf)	Europe and US	1910–20
	Downward circles or "muscle grinding"	306 by Denise La Grassa (US)	Circus World Museum, Wis	1976
	Single heel hang on swinging bar	Angela Revelle (Angelique)	Australia	1977
Horseback	Running leaps on and off	* 26 by "Poodles" Hanneford	New York City	1915
	Three-high column without "mechanic"	* Willy, Beby and Rene Fredianis	Nouveau Cirque, Paris	1908
	Double back somersault mounted	(John or Charles) Frederick Clarke	Various	c. 1905
	Double back somersault from a 2-high to a trailing horse with "mechanic"	Aleksandr Sergey	Moscow Circus	1956
Fixed Bars	Pass from 1st to 3rd bar with a double back somersault	Phil Shevette, Andres Atayde	Woods Gymnasium, NYC-European tours	1925–27
	Triple flyaway to ground (male)	Phil Shevette	Folies Bergère, Paris	1896
	Triple flyaway to ground (female)	Loretto Twins, Ora and Pauline	Los Angeles	1914
Giant Springboard	Running forward triple back somersault	John Cornish Worland (1855–1933) of the US	St Louis, Mo	1874
Human Juggling	Back somersault feet to feet, a Risley	Richard Risley Carlisle (1814–74) and son	Theatre Royal, Edinburgh	1844
Teeter Board	Quadruple back somersault to a chair	Sylvester Mezzetti (voltigeur) to Butch Mezzetti (catcher)	Kehlavi Troupe at NY Hippodrome	1915–17
	Five-high column	The Yacopis (Argentina)	Ringling Bros, Barnum & Bailey	1941
	Six-man-high perch pyramid	Emilia Ivanova (Bulgaria)	Inglewood, Calif	1976
Aerialist	One-arm swings or planges (no net)	305 by Janet May Klemke (US)	Medina Shrine Circus, Chicago	1938
Low Wire (7 ft)	Feet to feet forward somersault	Con Colleano	Empire Theatre, Johannesburg	1923
High Wire (30–40 ft)	Four-high column (with mechanic)	* The Solokhin Brothers (USSR)	Moscow Circus	1962
	Three-layer, 7-man pyramid	Great Wallendas (Germany)	US	1961
Ground Acrobatics	Stationary double back somersault	François Gouleau (France)		1905
Flexible Pole	Double full-twisting somersault onto a 2-inch-diameter pole	The Robertos, Roberto Tabak (age 11)	Sarasota, Fla	1977
Human Pyramid (or Tuckle)	12 (3 high) (1,700 lb) supported by a single understander	Tahar Davis of the Hassani Troupe	Birmingham, Eng	1979
	Six high (26 ft 3 in high)	Team of 81	Yumenoshima, Tokyo	1981

Dancing. Marathon dancing must be distinguished from dancing mania, which is a pathological condition. The worst outbreak of dancing mania was at Aachen, Germany in July 1374, when hordes of men and women broke into a frenzied dance in the streets which lasted for hours till injury or complete exhaustion ensued.

The most severe marathon dance (staged as a public spectacle in the US) was one by Mike Ritof and Edith Boudreaux, who logged 5,148 hours 28½ min to win $2,000 at Chicago's Merry Garden Ballroom, Belmont and Sheffield, Ill, from Aug 29, 1930, to Apr 1, 1931. Rest periods were progressively cut from 20 to 10 to 5 to nil minutes per hour with 10-in steps and a maximum of 15 sec for closure of eyes.

Largest Dance. The largest dance ever staged was that put on by the Houston Livestock Show at the Astro Hall, Houston, Tex Feb 8, 1969. The attendance was 16,500, with 4,000 turned away.

A total of 18,520 dancers (2,315 squares) took part in the 30th National Square Dance Convention in the Memorial Stadium, Seattle, Wash. The caller was Marv K.

Dancing, Ballet. In the *entrechat* (a vertical spring from the fifth position with the legs extended crisscrossing at the lower calf), the starting and finishing position each count as one, such that in the *entrechat douze* there are *five* crossings and uncrossings. This was performed by Wayne Sleep for the BBC-TV *Record Breakers* program on Jan 7, 1973. He was in the air for 0.71 of a second.

The greatest number of spins called for in classical ballet choreography is the 32 *fouettés rond de jambe en tournant* in "Swan Lake" by Pyotr Ilyich Chaykovskiy (Tchaikovsky) (1840–93). Rowena Jackson (later Chatfield, b Invercargill, New Zealand 1925) achieved 121 such turns at her class in Melbourne, Australia in 1940.

The greatest recorded number of curtain calls ever received by ballet dancers is 89 by Dame Margaret Evelyn Arias, *née* Hookham (b Reigate, Surrey, England May 18, 1919), *alias* Margot Fonteyn, and Rudolf Hametovich Nureyev (born in a train near Irkutsk, USSR March 17, 1938), after a performance of "Swan Lake" at the Vienna Staatsoper, Austria in Oct 1964.

The largest number of ballet dancers used in a production has been 2,000 in the London Coster Ballet of 1962, directed by Lillian Romley at the Royal Albert Hall, London.

Dancing, Ballroom. The individual continuous record is 120 hours 17 min 10 sec by Janab Fareed Nazeer, Feb 27–Mar 4, 1981 at the Open Air Theatre, Jaffna, Sri Lanka. Three girls worked shifts as his partner.

The most successful professional ballroom dancing champions have been Bill Irvine and Bobbie Irvine of London who won 13 world titles, 1960–72.

The oldest competitive ballroom dancer is Albert J. Sylvester (b Nov 24, 1889) of Corsham, Wiltshire, England, who on Apr 26, 1977, won the topmost amateur Alex Moore award for a 10-dance test with his partner, Paula Smith, in Bath, England. By 1981 he had won nearly 50 medals and trophies since he began dancing in 1964.

Dancing, Belly and Charleston. The longest recorded belly dance was one of 100 hours by Sabra Starr of Lansdowne, Pa at Teplitzki's Hotel, Atlantic City, NJ July 4–8, 1977. The Charleston duration record is 110 hours 58 min by the same Sabra Starr Jan 15–20, 1979.

Dancing, Conga. The longest recorded conga line was a "snake" of 8,128 people in Sidmouth, Devon, England Aug 25, 1978.

Dancing, Disco (including Jive, Twist and Go-Go). The longest recorded disco dancing marathon is one of 371 hours by John Sharples of Preston, England, Jan 18–Feb 3, 1982.

Under the strict rules of the European Rock 'n' Roll Association, the duration record for non-stop jiving is 22 hours by Mirco and Manuela Catalano at the Olympia Shopping Centre, Munich, W Germany, Feb 6–7, 1981. However, with a relay of partners, Richard Rimmer of Caterham, Surrey, England, danced jive 97 hours 42 min, Nov 11–16, 1979.

Dancing, Flamenco. The fastest flamenco dancer ever measured is Solero de Jerez, aged 17, who, in Brisbane, Australia in Sept 1967, in an electrifying routine attained 16 heel taps per sec or 1,000 per min.

Dancing, High Kicking. The record for high kicks is 9,100 in 6 hours 51 min by V. S. Kumar Anandan at Galle Face, Colombo, Sri Lanka, Dec 31, 1980–Jan 1, 1981.

Dancing, Limbo. The lowest height for a flaming bar under which a limbo dancer has passed is 6⅛ in off the floor at Port of Spain Pavilion, Toronto, on

LOWEST LIMBO: Marlene Raymond, 15, slithered under a flaming bar 6-⅛ in off the floor without letting any part of her anatomy except her feet touch the floor.

HIGHEST DIVE: Diving head first in a swan dive from a crane 160 ft up in the air, Dana Kunze (inset) set a world record in Japan in 1979.

DOMINO TOPPLING is one of the world's most popular spectator sports, judging by the way people of all ages throng around videotape displays of dominoes racing up and down ramps on the screens at Guinness Museums. In Japan, two Americans toppled 255,389 dominoes on TV under the auspices of the National Hemophilia Foundation. (Right) John Wickham and Erez Klein are scribing circles to be certain the dominoes will fall in perfect concentric circles while the long stretches of the mainstream carry on. It took 5 weeks to set this up and 53 min to tumble.

June 24, 1973, by Marlene Raymond, 15. Strictly no part of the body other than the sole or side of the foot should touch the ground, though brushing the shoulder blade does not in practice usually result in disqualification.

Denise Culp, 8, went under a 5⅞-in bar on roller skates head first at Rock Hill, SC, on July 25, 1981.

Dancing, Tap. The fastest *rate* ever measured for any tap dancer has been 1,440 taps per min (24 per sec) by Roy Castle on the BBC-TV *Record Breakers* program on Jan 14, 1973. The greatest assemblage of tap dancers ever in a single routine is 2,218 choreographed by Betty Laine in a single routine for the BBC TV show *Record Breakers* on Nov 29, 1981, at Eastney Royal Marine Barracks, Portsmouth, England.

Dance Band. The most protracted session is one of 321 hours (13 days 9 hours) by the Black Brothers of Bonn, W Germany ending on Feb 2, 1968. Never less than a quartet were in action during the marathon.

Diving, Highest Shallow. Henri La Mothe (b 1904) set a record by diving 28 ft into 12⅜ inches of water in a child's wading pool on Apr 7, 1979 in Northridge, Calif for a Guinness TV program. He struck the water chest first at a speed of 28.4 mph.

Diving, High. The highest regularly performed head-first dives are those of professional divers from La Quebrada ("the break in the rocks") at Acapulco, Mexico, a height of 118 ft. The leader of the 27 divers in the exclusive Club de Clavadistas is Raul Garcia (b 1928) with more than 35,000 dives. The base rocks are 21 ft out from the takeoff, necessitating a leap 27 ft out. The water is only 12 ft deep.

Dana Kunze (US) dived 160 ft from a crane jib in Tokyo, Japan for Fuji TV on Sept 30, 1979.

On May 8, 1885, Sarah Ann Henley, aged 24, jumped from the Clifton Suspension Bridge across the Avon, England. Her 250-ft fall was slightly cushioned by her voluminous dress and petticoat acting as a parachute. She landed, bruised and bedraggled, in the mud on the Gloucestershire bank and was carried to a hospital by four policemen.

On Feb 11, 1968, Jeffrey Kramer, 24, leaped off the George Washington Bridge 250 ft above the Hudson River, NYC and survived. Of the 696 (to Jan 1, 1980) identified people who have made 240-ft suicide dives from the Golden Gate Bridge, San Francisco since 1937 only 12 survived, and the only one who managed to swim ashore unaided was Todd Sherratt, 17.

Col Harry A. Froboess (Switzerland) jumped 360 ft into the Bodensee from the airship *Graf Hindenburg* June 22, 1936.

The greatest height reported for a dive into a flaming tank is 100 ft into 7½ ft of water by Bill McGuire, 48, at the Holiday Inn in Chicago City Center, Aug 14, 1975.

Kitty O'Neil dived about 180 ft from a helicopter over Northridge, Calif onto an air cushion 30 × 60 ft on Sept 9, 1979 for a TV stunt.

Domino Toppling. The greatest number of dominoes set up single-handed and toppled in a row is 169,713 by Michael Cairney, 23, of London, England at the Mid-Hudson Civic Center, Poughkeepsie, NY June 9, 1979 under the auspices of the National Hemophilia Foundation. The dominoes, stretching 4.3 miles, fell at 2¼ mph, after taking Cairney 13 days to set up.

The record for a team of two setting up is the tumble of 255,389 dominoes in 53 min Aug 24, 1980, at Hakone, Japan. John Wickham and Erez Klein (both US), under the sponsorship of the National Hemophilia Foundation (US), spent 5 weeks setting up the colored dominoes which were toppled not only in long multiple rows, but also in concentric circles and geometric patterns, setting off rockets, releasing eggs that rolled into hot frying pans, and going up ramps. The event appeared on Japanese TV and can be seen on tape at all of the Guinness Museums.

Drumming. The duration drumming record is 738 hours by Boo Boo McAfee of Nashville, Tenn, July 13–Aug 13, 1981.

Ducks and Drakes. The best accepted ducks and drakes (stone-skipping) record is 24 skips (10 plinkers and 14 pitty-pats) by Warren Klope, 20, of Troy, Mich with 14 thin, flat, 4-in limestones, at the annual Mackinac Island, Mich stone-skipping tournament July 5, 1975. This was equaled by John S. Kolar of Birmingham, Mich and Glenn Loy Jr of Flint, Mich on July 4, 1977.

Egg Dropping. The greatest height from which fresh eggs have been dropped to earth and landed intact is 650 ft from a helicopter by David S. Donoghue Oct 2, 1979 over the Tokyo Golf Course.

Egg Hunt. The greatest egg hunt on record involved 28,260 hard-boiled eggs hidden by The North Biloxi Jaycees in a meadow in Harrison County, Miss, for the 17th Annual Harry Fountain Memorial

Easter Egg Hunt on Apr 4, 1982, by 3,800 children aged 1 through 9.

Egg Shelling. Two kitchen hands, Harold Witcomb and Gerald Harding, shelled 1,050 dozen eggs in a 7¼-hour shift at Bowyers, Trowbridge, Wiltshire, England Apr 23, 1971. Both are blind.

Egg and Spoon Racing. Chris Riggio of San Francisco completed a 28½-mile fresh egg and dessert spoon marathon in 4 hours 34 min Oct 7, 1979.

Egg Throwing. The longest recorded distance for throwing a fresh hen's egg and catching it without breaking is 350 ft on their 58th try by William Cole and Jonathan Heller in Central Park, NYC Mar 17, 1979.

Escapology. The most renowned of all escape artists has been Ehrich Weiss, *alias* Harry Houdini (1874–1926), who pioneered underwater escapes from locked, roped and weighted containers while handcuffed and shackled with irons.

One of the major manufacturers of straitjackets acknowledges that an escapologist "skilled in the art of bone and muscle manipulation" could escape from a standard jacket in seconds. The fastest acknowledged claim is 1.68 sec by Bill Shirk in Indianapolis June 19, 1979.

Records claimed for the highest escape from a helicopter or free-fall while handcuffed or hanging suspended upside down from a burning rope have been discontinued.

Family Tree. The farthest back the lineage of any family has been traced is that of K'ung Ch'iu or Confucius (551–479 BC). His great-great-great-great-grandfather is known from the 8th century BC. This man's 84th lineal descendant lives today in Taiwan.

Fashion Show. The longest fashion show ever recorded was one which lasted 48 hours on the Roseland catwalk, Sydney, Australia on June 16–18, 1977, compèred by Patrick Bollen. Lyn Snowdon, Kay Hammond and Virginia Connor all completed 41.4 miles on the catwalk.

Feminine Beauty. Female pulchritude, being qualitative rather than quantitative, does not lend itself to records. It has been suggested that if the face of Helen of Troy (c. 1200 BC) was capable of launching 1,000 ships, then a unit of beauty sufficient to launch one ship should be called a millihelen.

The pioneer beauty contest was staged at Atlantic City, NJ in 1921, and was won by a thin blue-eyed blonde with a 30-in bust, Margaret Gorman.

The world's largest beauty pageant is the annual Miss Universe contest, inaugurated in Long Beach, Calif, in 1952. The most successful country has been the US with 5 winners (1954, 56, 60, 67, 80). The number of countries represented has reached 78.

Ferris Wheel Riding. The endurance record for big wheel riding is 37 days by Rena Clark and Jeff Block at Frontier Village Amusement Park, San Jose, Calif July 1–Aug 7, 1978.

Flute Marathon. The longest recorded time is 48 hours by flautist Joe Silmon on HMS *Grampus* in Gosport, England Feb 19–20, 1977.

Gladiatorial Combat. Emperor Trajan of Rome (98–117 AD) staged a display involving 4,941 pairs of gladiators over 117 days. Publius Ostorius, a freedman, survived 51 combats in Pompeii.

Gold Panning. The fastest time recorded for "panning" 8 planted gold nuggets with a 10-in-diameter pan is 13.4 sec by Dick Huber of Ahwahnee, Calif in the 20th World Gold Panning Championship at Tropico Gold Mine, Rosamond, Calif March 2, 1980. The record for women is 15.27 sec by Mrs Carolyn Box, also of Ahwahnee at the 18th Championship March 4–5, 1978.

Golf Ball Balancing. Lang Martin of Charlotte, NC succeeded on Feb 9, 1980 in balancing 7 new golf balls vertically without using any adhesive, beating his own record of 6 in 1977.

Grape Catching. The longest distance claimed for catching a thrown grape in the mouth is 321 ft 5 in by Paul J. Tavilla. The grape was thrown off the roof of the 31-story Plaza South building, Fla, on May 16, 1982.

Grave Digging. It is recorded that Johann Heinrich Karl Thieme, sexton of Aldenburg, Germany dug 23,311 graves during a 50-year career. In 1826, his understudy dug *his* grave.

Ground Breaking. The highest number of participants in a ground-breaking ceremony is 5,714 for the Owens-Illinois headquarters building at SeaGate, Toledo, Ohio, May 22, 1979.

ESCAPOLOGIST SUPREME: Houdini was best known for his straitjacket escapes. Here he is with feet tied also on the edge of a roof.

HAND-TO-HAND BALANCING: From 1908 to 1917, Harry Berry and Nelson Soule (above) performed this act jumping from a 10-ft-tower onto a trampoline for takeoff. FOOT JUGGLING: Chester Cable (left) balances a 130-lb table on his feet, then twirls it side over side as many as 30 times in 1 min using only his legs.

FEAT OF STRENGTH: A ton of bricks rolls easily off the tongue, but it isn't so easy to move in a wheelbarrow, as Bill Richardson of Yorkshire, England, realizes when he strains his muscles to move the load.

367

HULA-HOOP CHAMP: Chico Johnson (left) broke the old record of 63, by twirling 75 hula hoops at one time in Apr 1982 at Knott's Berry Farm, Calif. The hoops have to gyrate between shoulders and hips.

HUMAN CANNONBALLS (below): Emanuel Zacchini and his daughter Florinda (inset), being of the same caliber, were regularly shot from a cannon distances of up to 175 ft across the arena in the 1930's and 1940's for the Ringling Bros and Barnum & Bailey Circus.

Guitar Playing. The longest recorded solo guitar-playing marathon is one of 230 hours by John D. Marshall of West Bridgford, England, Feb 18–28, 1981, at the Yorker Public House, Nottingham.

Hairdressing. Pierre Ortiz cut, set and styled hair continuously for 342 hours, May 10–26, 1981, in his "New York, New York" salon, Huntington Beach, Calif.

Hair Splitting. The greatest reported achievement in hair splitting has been that of the former champion cyclist and craftsman Alfred West (b London, Apr 14, 1901) who succeeded in splitting a human hair 17 times into 18 parts on 8 occasions. Examples of his work are on permanent display in several Guinness Museums of World Records.

Hammock Swinging. V. Paratore and B. Galvin maintained a hammock in constant swinging motion for 192 hours in San Francisco in April 1979.

Handshaking. The record for handshaking was set by President Theodore Roosevelt (1858–1919), who shook hands with 8,513 people at a New Year's Day White House presentation in Washington, DC Jan 1, 1907. Mayor Joseph Lazarow shook hands with 11,030 people on the Boardwalk, Atlantic City, NJ in 11 hours 5 min on July 3, 1977. *Outside public life this record has become meaningless because aspirants either shake hands with anyone passing by or else shake the same hands repetitively.*

Hand-to-Hand Balancing. The longest horizontal dive achieved in any hand-to-hand balancing act is 22 ft by Harry Berry (top mounter) and the late Nelson Soule (understander) of the Bell-Thazer Brothers from Kentucky, who played at state fairs and in vaudeville 1908–17. Berry used a 10-ft tower and trampoline for impetus.

Handwriting. The longest recorded handwritten letter-writing marathon was one of 505 hours and more than 3,998 letters and their envelopes by Raymond L. Cantwell of Oxford, England (trying to raise money for the Radcliffe Infirmary), Aug 25–Sept 16, 1978.

Hitchhiking. The title of world champion hitchhiker is claimed by Devon Smith who from 1947 to 1971 thumbed lifts totaling 291,000 miles. It was not until his 6,013th hitch that he got a ride in a Rolls-Royce.

Hoop Rolling. In 1968 it was reported that Zolilio Diaz (Spain) had rolled a hoop 600 miles from Mieres to Madrid and back in 18 days.

Hopscotch. The longest recorded hopscotch marathon is one of 90 hours by Steven Couch and Graham Clarke of Chelmsford Fire Station, Chelmsford, England, May 4–8, 1982.

House of Cards. The greatest number of stories achieved in building free-standing houses of standard playing cards without creasing the cards or using any adhesives is 61 in the case of a tower using 3,650 cards by James Warnock at Cantley, Quebec, Canada, on Sept 8, 1978. The height was 11 ft 7 in.

Hula-Hooping. The highest claim for sustaining gyrating hoops between shoulders and hips is 75 by Chico Johnson, 22, on Apr 7, 1982 in Buena Park, Calif. Three complete gyrations are mandatory. The longest recorded marathon for a single hoop is 54 hours by Kym Coberly of Denton, Tex, Oct 7–9, 1978.

Human Cannonball. The record distance for firing a human from a cannon is 175 ft in the case of Emanuel Zacchini in the Ringling Bros and Barnum & Bailey Circus, in 1940. His muzzle velocity was estimated at 54 mph. On his retirement the management was fortunate in finding that his daughter, Florinda, was of the same caliber.

An experiment on Yorkshire TV in England on Aug 17, 1978, showed that when Sue Evans, 17, was fired from a cannon, she was ⅜ in shorter in height on landing.

In the Halifax explosion of Dec 6, 1917 (see *Worst Accidents*), A. B. William Becker (d 1969) was blown some 1,600 yd and found, still breathing, in a tree.

Human Chain. An estimated 17,000 people linked hands in the "Hands Around the Wrekin," a 1,335-ft hill in Shropshire, England, on May 4, 1981. The estimated length of the chain was 3.66 miles. Another chain claimed also to be of 17,000, and measuring 4.78 miles in length, was formed on the frozen Rideau Canal, Ottawa, Canada, at the Winterlude in Feb 1982.

Human Chair (Unsupported Circle). The highest number recorded of people who have demonstrated the physical paradox of all being seated without a chair is an unsupported circle of 5,810 staged by Channel 8 Tokyo, Fuji Telecasting, in Sept 1980.

Human Fly. The greatest climb achieved on the vertical face of a building occurred on May 25, 1981, when Daniel Goodwin ("Spider Man") of Kennebunkport, Maine, climbed up the face of the Sears Tower, Chicago, to a height of 1,454 ft in 40-mph winds in 7½ hours. Goodwin, a professional acrobat and gymnast, used suction cups and T-shaped clamps that had been designed by the previous record holder, George Willig, 27, who had scaled the outside of the World Trade Center, NYC, 1,350 ft up in 3½ hours at the rate of 6.4 ft per min. Like Willig, Goodwin evaded police attempting to stop him as he climbed, and on completing his climb, Goodwin, like Willig, was taken into custody by the police who congratulated him as they handcuffed him, charging him with disorderly conduct. After a night in jail Goodwin was released.

Lead climber Jean-Claude Droyer (b May 8, 1946) of Paris, France, and Pierre Puiseux (b Dec 2, 1953) of Pau, France, climbed up the outside of the Eiffel Tower to a height of 984 ft in 2 hours 18 min on July 21, 1980. They made the climb with no dynamic mechanical assistance.

Jaromir Wagner (b Czechoslovakia 1941) became the first man to fly the Atlantic standing on the wing of an aircraft. He took off from Aberdeen, Scotland, on Sept 28, 1980.

Joke Telling. Dave Van Der Merwe cracked jokes unremittingly for 27 hours 37 min at the Sanlam Centre, Pretoria, Transvaal, S Africa, Nov 27–28, 1981.

The duo duration record is 52 hours by Wayne Malton and Mike Hamilton at the Howard Johnson Motor Hotel, Toronto Airport, Canada, Nov 13–16, 1975.

Juggling. The only juggler in history able to juggle—as opposed to "shower"—10 balls or 8 plates was the Italian Enrico Rastelli, who was born in Samara, Russia, Dec 19, 1896, and died in Bergamo, Italy, on Dec 13, 1931. Here are other juggling records:

16 hoops (hands and feet)	Ala Naite (female, Japan), 1937
7 clubs	Albert Petrovski (USSR), 1963 Sorin Munteanu (Romania), 1975 Jack Bremlov, currently
11 rings	Petrovski, 1963–66 Eugene Belaur Sergei Ignatov (USSR)
Pirouettes with 3 cigar boxes	Kris Kremo (quadruple turn with 3 boxes in midair)
Duration 5 clubs	16 min 20 sec, Ignatov in USSR

Karate Chop. *Note: Claims for breaking bricks and wooden blocks are unsatisfactory because of the lack of any agreed standards upon which comparisons can be made of friability and the spacing of fulcrums.* Karatekas have been measured to exert a force of 3,000 newtons (675 lb of force) and can develop a downward chopping speed of 32.2 mph.

Kissing. The most prolonged osculatory marathon in cinematic history is one of 185 sec by Regis Toomey and Jane Wyman in *You're In the Army Now,* released in 1940.

In a Valentine's Day "Big Kiss-Off" for charity, Debbie Luray and Jim Schuyler kissed for 5 days 12 hours at the Ocean Mall, Singer Island, Fla Feb 14–19, 1980.

The most protracted kiss underwater was one of 2 min 18 sec by Toshiaki Shirai and Yukiko Nagata on Fuji TV in Tokyo, Japan on Apr 2, 1980.

Dave Ward of Piccadilly Radio, Manchester,

JUGGLING 7 CLUBS: Sorin Munteanu of Romania shows how he keeps them flying at the same time.

UPSIDE-DOWN JUGGLER:
Bobby May shows how he can
juggle 5 balls by rebounding
them off a drum on the floor
while he does a headstand on a
table. (Gene S. Jones)

CHEATED DEATH: Roy C. Sullivan (inset on left) is the only
living man to have been struck
by lightning 7 times. Here he
shows where his hat was
burned. Vesna Vulovic (inset
below) is the Yugoslav air hostess who survived without a
parachute when her plane blew
up at 33,330 ft. She was in the
tail unit.

LION TAMER: "Captain" Alfred Schneider, unaided in a cage with 40 lions, mastered and fed them simultaneously in 1925. (Right) Schneider and friend pose motionless for the camera.

"KISS OF LIFE" (below): That's a dummy being kissed. It's practice time for 5 of the Clifton Combined Division of the St John Ambulance force from N Yorkshire, England, who spent 240 hours in one long stretch inflating the dummy and giving it mouth-to-mouth resuscitation.

372

England, kissed 4,079 girls in 8 hours on Feb 13, 1982—a rate of one per 7.06 sec.

Kiss of Life. Five members of the St John Ambulance Clifton Combined Division, N Yorkshire, England, maintained a "Kiss of Life" (mouth-to-mouth resuscitation) for 240 hours with 224,029 inflations July 26–Aug 5, 1981. The "patient" was a dummy.

Kite Flying. The longest recorded flight is one of 169 hours by The Sunrise Inn team, Fort Lauderdale, Fla managed by Will Yolen, Apr 30–May 7, 1977.

A claim for an altitude record of 37,908 ft (by triangulation) by Steven W. Flack over Boonville, NY, on Sept 9, 1978, is not unreservedly accepted by *Kitelines* magazine of Baltimore, Md. The kite was not recovered. The classic record is 31,955 ft up by a chain of 8 kites over Lindenberg, (now East) Germany, on Aug 1, 1919.

The most kites flown on a single line is 4,128 by Kazuhiko Asaba, 55, at Kamakura, Japan Sept 21, 1978.

The largest kite ever flown was Gerard van der Loo's 507-lb nylon kite measuring 53.4 × 105 × 116 ft, with an area of 19,528 sq ft. It was launched by a team of 70 at Scheveningen, Netherlands, on Aug 8, 1981, and flew above 131 ft for 37 min.

Knitting. The most prolific hand-knitter has been Mrs Gwen Matthewman (b 1927) of Featherstone, W Yorkshire, England, who in 1979 knitted 915 garments involving 11,012 oz of wool (equivalent to the fleece of 89 sheep). She has been timed to average 111 stitches per min in a 30-min test. Her technique has been filmed by the world's only Professor of Knitting—a Japanese.

Knot Tying. The fastest recorded time for tying the six Boy Scout Handbook knots (square knot, sheet bend, sheep shank, clove hitch, round turn and two half hitches and bowline) on individual ropes is 8.1 sec by Clinton R. Bailey Sr, 52, of Pacific City, Ore on Apr 13, 1977.

Leap Frogging. Fourteen members of Phi Gamma Delta fraternity at the University of Seattle, Wash, covered 602 miles in 126 hours 46 min, March 20–25, 1981.

Life Saving. In Nov 1974, the City of Galveston, Tex and the Noon Optimist Club unveiled a plaque to the deaf-mute lifeguard Leroy Colombo (1905–74), who saved 907 people from drowning in the waters around Galveston Island, 1917–1974.

Lightning-Struck. The only living man in the world to be struck by lightning 7 times is former Shenandoah Park Ranger Roy C. Sullivan (US), the human lightning-conductor of Virginia. His attraction for lightning began in 1942 (lost big toenail) and was resumed in July 1969 (lost eyebrows), in July 1970 (left shoulder seared), on Apr 16, 1972 (hair set on fire) and, *finally*, he hoped, on Aug 7, 1973: as he was driving along a bolt came out of a small, low-lying cloud, hit him on the head through his hat, set his hair on fire again, knocked him 10 ft out of his car, went through both legs, and knocked his left shoe off. He had to pour a pail of water over his head to cool off. Then, on June 5, 1976, he was struck again for the sixth time, his ankle injured. When he was struck for the *seventh* time on June 25, 1977, while fishing, he was sent to Waynesboro Hospital with chest and stomach burns. He can offer no explanation for his magnetism, but he has donated his lightning-burnt Ranger hats to some of the Guinness World Records Exhibit Halls.

Lion Taming. The greatest number of lions mastered and fed in a cage simultaneously by an unaided lion-tamer was 40, by "Captain" Alfred Schneider in 1925.

Clyde (Raymond) Beatty (b Bainbridge, Ohio, June 10, 1903, d Ventura, Calif, July 19, 1965) likewise handled more than 40 "cats" (mixed lions and tigers) simultaneously. Beatty, top of the bill for 40 years, insisted on being called a lion-trainer. More than 20 lion-tamers have died of injuries since 1900.

Log Rolling. The record number of International Championships is 10 by Jubiel Wickheim (of Shawnigan Lake, BC, Canada) between 1956 and 1969. At Albany, Ore, on July 4, 1956, Wickheim rolled on a 14-in log against Chuck Harris of Kelso, Wash for 2 hours 40 min before losing.

Merry-Go-Round. The longest marathon ride on record is one of 312 hours 43 min by Gary Mandau, Chris Lyons and Dana Dover in Portland, Ore, Aug 20–Sept 2, 1976.

Message in a Bottle. The longest recorded interval between drop and pick-up is 64 years, between Aug 7, 1910 ("please write to Miss Gladys Potter") in Grand Lake, and Aug 1974 from Lake Huron. Miss Potter was traced and found to be Mrs Oliver Scheid, 76, of Columbus, Ohio.

A bottle apparently bearing a message written on Nov 19, 1899, by Capt Charles Weieerishen of the SS *Crown Princess Cecilia* off Varberg, Sweden, was reportedly picked up on the coast of Victoria, BC, Canada, on Dec 9, 1936.

Milk Bottle Balancing. The greatest distance walked by a person continuously balancing a full pint milk bottle on his head is 18 miles 880 yd by Willie Hollingsworth of Freeport, NY, March 24, 1979.

Modeling. The largest reported contract in the history of modeling is $1,500,000 for 5 years' rights to the face, eyes and lips of Cheryl Tiegs, paid by the cosmetic group Noxell in Dec 1979. *Fortune* says her legs are still "up for grabs."

Morse Code. The highest recorded speed at which anyone has received Morse code is 75.2 wpm—over 17 symbols per sec. This was achieved by Ted R. McElroy (US) in a tournament at Asheville, NC, July 2, 1939. The highest speed recorded for hand key transmitting is 175 symbols per min by Harry A. Turner of the US Army Signal Corps at Camp Crowder, Mo, Nov 9, 1942.

Motorcycle Stunting. The longest distance ever achieved for motorcycle long jumping is 212 ft by Alain Jean Prieur (b July 4, 1939) of France at Montlhéry near Paris, over 16 buses on Feb 6, 1977.

The pioneer of this form of exhibition—Evel Knievel (Robert Craig Knievel) (b Oct 17, 1938, in Butte, Mont) had suffered 433 bone fractures by his 1975 season.

The greatest endurance feat on a "wall of death" was 6 hours 7 min 38 sec by Hugo Dabbert (b Hildesheim, Sept 24, 1938) at Russelheim, W Germany, Aug 4, 1980. He rode 6,841 laps on the 32.8-ft-diameter wall on a Honda CM 400 averaging 21.8 mph for the 133.4 miles.

The category of ramp jumping with a car has been discontinued.

Musical Chairs. The largest game on record was one starting with 4,514 participants and ending with Scott Ritter, 18, on the last chair at Ohio State University in Columbus, Apr 25, 1982.

Needle Threading. The record number of strands of cotton threaded through a number 13 needle (eye ½ × 1/16 in) in 2 hours is 3,795 by Brenda Robinson of the College of Further Education, Chippenham, Wiltshire, England, on March 20, 1971.

Noodle Making. Mark Pi of the China Gate Restaurant, Toledo, O, made 1,024 noodle strips (exceeding 5 ft each in length) in 60 sec on WDHO-TV Mar 4, 1981.

Omelet Making. Howard Helmer of NYC cooked 217 two-egg omelets in 30 min at Disneyland, Anaheim, Calif, on July 14, 1978.

Onion Peeling. The record for onion peeling is 50 lb (52 onions) in 5 min 23 sec by Alfonso Salvo of York, Pa, on Oct 28, 1980. Before the current requirement of having at least 50 onions in the 50 lb, a record of 3 min 18 sec was set by Alain St John of Plainfield, Conn on July 6, 1980.

Organ Marathons. The longest church organ recital ever sustained was one of 92 hours by Robert A Hawkins of New Longton, Preston, England, June 15–19, 1981.

The longest recorded electric organ marathon is 411 hours by Vince Bull at the Comet Hotel, Scunthorpe, England June 2–19, 1977.

Paddle Boating. The longest recorded voyage in a paddle boat is 2,226 mi in 103 days by the foot power of Mick Sigrist and Brad Rud down the Mississippi from the headwaters in Minn to the Gulf of Mexico, Aug 4–Nov 11, 1979.

Party Giving. The most expensive private party ever thrown was that of Mr and Mrs Bradley Martin of Troy, NY. It was staged at the Waldorf-Astoria Hotel, NYC in Feb 1897. The cost to the host and hostess was estimated to be $369,200 in the days when dollars were made of gold.

The "International Year of the Child" children's party in Hyde Park, London was attended by the Royal Family and 160,000 children, May 30–31, 1979. The longest street party ever staged was for 5,500 children by the Oxford Street Association (to celebrate the Royal Wedding) on July 25, 1981, along the entire length from Park Street to St Giles Circus, London, England.

The largest Christmas Party ever staged was that thrown by the Boeing Co in the 65,000-seat Kingdome, Seattle in two shows before an audience of 103,152 people on Dec 15, 1979. It was managed by general chairman John Mathiasen and produced by Greg Thompson with a cast of 2,506. The floor was decorated with 1,000 Christmas trees, each with 100 lights; 150,000 snow-white balloons; and 3 ice ponds.

MODELING QUEEN: Cheryl Tiegs shows why she can obtain $1½ million for the rights to use her face, eyes and lips for 5 years in cosmetic ads. Her legs are "up for grabs," "Fortune" magazine wrote.

MILK BOTTLE BALANCER: Willie Hollingsworth (left) of Freeport, NY, walked 18½ miles without dropping the full bottle from his head.

RIDING IN ARMOR: With a weight of 112 lb on his back, Dick Brown (right) rode 167 miles in 3 days in Scotland.

MOST NORTHERLY PARACHUTE JUMP: Dr Jack Wheeler (left) exited a DeHavilland Twin Otter piloted by Capt Rocky Parsons on Apr 15, 1981 at 8:30 AM from an altitude of 8,000 ft at a temperature of −25°F. He fell to 3,000 ft before displaying his canopy and landed at a latitude of exactly 90° N. Wheeler has a history of daredevil experiences. "WALL OF DEATH" (above): This motorcycle stunt involves riding halfway up a 32.8-ft-diameter wall for as many laps as you can. Hugo Dabbert (shown here) rode more than 6 hours at an average speed of 21.8 mph for 6,841 laps (133.4 mi) without stop. NOODLE MAKING (below): Mark Pi of Toledo, O, makes noodles the Chinese way by twirling and cutting a long roll of dough. In one minute, he made 1,024 strips 5 ft or more in length.

PARACHUTING RECORDS

First from Tower	Louis-Sébastian Lenormand (1757–1839)	quasi-parachute	Montpellier, France	1783
First from Balloon	André-Jacques Garnerin (1769–1823)	2,230 ft	Monçeau Park, Paris	Oct 22, 1797
First from Aircraft (man)	"Capt" Albert Berry	aerial exhibitionist	St Louis	Mar 1, 1912
(woman)	Mrs Georgina "Tiny" Broadwick		Griffith Park, Los Angeles	June 21, 1913
First Free Fall	Mrs Georgina "Tiny" Broadwick	pilot, Glenn L. Martin	North Island, San Diego	Sept 13, 1914
Lowest Escape	Squad Leader T. Spencer, RAF	30–40 ft	Wismar Bay, Baltic Sea	Apr 19, 1945
Longest Duration Fall	Lt Col Wm. H. Rankin, USMC	40 min, due to thermals	North Carolina	July 26, 1956
Highest Escape	Flt Lt J. de Salis and Fg Off P. Lowe, RAF	56,000 ft	Monyash, Derby, Eng	Apr 9, 1958
Longest Delayed Drop (man)	Capt Joseph W. Kittinger[1]	84,700 ft (16.04 miles) from balloon at 102,800 ft	Tularosa, NM	Aug 16, 1960
(woman)	O. Kommissarova (USSR)	46,250 ft	over USSR	Sept 21, 1965
(civilian)	R. W. K. Beckett (GB)	30,000 ft from 32,000 ft	D. F. Malan Airport, Capetown, So Africa	Nov 23, 1969
	Harry Ferguson (GB)			
Most Southerly	T/Sgt Richard J. Patton (d 1973)	Operation Deep Freeze	South Pole	Nov 25, 1956
Most Northerly	Dr Jack Wheeler (US)	Pilot, Capt Rocky Parsons (−25 °F)	In Lat 90° 00′ N	Apr 15, 1981
Career Total (man)	Yuri Baranov (USSR) and Anatolyi Osipov (USSR)	10,000	over USSR	to Sept 1980
(woman)	Valentina Zakoretskaya (USSR)	8,000	over USSR	Sept 1969–Sept 1980
Highest Landing	Ten USSR parachutists[2]	23,405 ft	Lenina Peak	May 1969
Heaviest Load	US Space Shuttle *Columbia* (external rocket retrieval)	80 ton capacity triple array each 120 ft dia	Atlantic, off Cape Canaveral, Fla	Apr 12, 1981
Highest from Bridge	Donald R. Boyles	1,053 ft	Royal Gorge, Colo	Sept 7, 1970
Highest Tower Jump	Herbert Leo Schmidtz (US)	KTUL-TV Mast 1,984 ft	Tulsa, Okla	Oct 4, 1970
Connected Free Fall	60-man team	Formation held 5 sec (FAI rules)	Zephyrhills, Fla	Apr 18, 1981
Highest Column	8-member Enquirer team	170 ft	Livermore, Calif	Oct 23, 1977
Most Traveled	Kevin Seaman from a Cessna Skylane (pilot, Charles Merritt)	12,186 miles	Jumps in all 50 US states	July 26–Oct 15, 1972
Oldest Man	Edwin C. Townsend	85 years 1 day	Riverview, Fla	Feb 6, 1982
Oldest Woman	Mrs Ardeth Shuler Evitt (US)	first jump at 74 years 6 months	Mooresville, Ind	Aug 6, 1978
24-Hour Total	D. Bruce MacLaughlin (US)	235 (120 at night)	E Taunton, Mass	Sept 17–18, 1981

[1] Maximum speed in rarefied air was 825.2 mph at 90,000 ft—marginally supersonic. [2] Four were killed.

Parachute, Longest Fall Without Parachute. The greatest altitude from which anyone has bailed out without a parachute and survived is 21,980 ft. This occurred in Jan 1942 when Lt (now Lt-Col) I. M. Chisov (USSR) fell from an Ilyushin 4 which had been severely damaged. He struck the ground a glancing blow on the edge of a snow-covered ravine and slid to the bottom. He suffered a fractured pelvis and severe spinal damage. It is estimated that the human body reaches 99% of its low-level terminal velocity after falling 1,880 ft, which takes 13–14 sec. This is 117–125 mph at normal atmospheric pressure in a random posture, but up to 185 mph in a head-down position.

Vesna Vulovic, 23, a Jugoslavenski Aerotransport hostess, survived when her DC-9 blew up at 33,330 ft over the Czechoslovak village of Serbska Kamenice on Jan 26, 1972. She was hospitalized for 16 months after emerging from a 27-day coma, having broken many bones. She is now Mrs Breka.

Piano Playing. The longest piano-playing marathon has been one of 1,172 hours 27 min (48 days 20 hours 27 min) playing 22 hours every day (with 5-min intervals each playing hour) from Jan 6 to Feb 24, 1978, by Roger Lavern at the Osborne Tavern, London.

The women's record is 133 hours non-stop (5 days 13 hours) by 280-lb Mrs Marie Ashton, aged 40, in a theatre at Blyth, Northumberland, England, Aug 18–23, 1958. Her last piece was "Five Minutes More." *This category has since been discontinued.*

Piano Tuning. The record time for pitch raising (one semi-tone or 100 cents) and then returning a piano to a musically acceptable quality is 4 min 20 sec by Steve Fairchild at the Piano Technicians Guild contest at the Dante Piano Co factory, NY, Feb 5, 1980.

Pipe Smoking. The duration record for keeping a pipe (0.1 oz of tobacco) continuously alight with only an initial match under IAPSC (International Association of Pipe Smokers Clubs) rules is 126 min 39 sec by 4-time champion William Vargo of Swartz Creek, Mich, at the 27th World Championships in 1975. The only 5-time champion is Paul T. Spaniola (US) 1951–66–70–73–77. Longer durations have been recorded in less rigorously invigilated contests in which the foul practices of "tamping" and "gardening" were not unknown.

Plate Spinning. The greatest number of plates spun simultaneously is 72 by Shukuni Sasaki of Takamatsu, Japan, Nio Town Taiyo Exhibition, Kagawa, on July 16, 1981.

Pogo Stick Jumping. The greatest number of jumps achieved on a pogo stick is 120,715 by Jeff Kane in 16 hours 12 min in Oak Lawn, Ill, June 9–10, 1980.

Pole Sitting. There being no international rules, the "standards of living" atop poles vary widely. The record squat is 399 days by Frank Perkins from June 1, 1975, to July 4, 1976, in an 8 × 8 ft box atop a 50-ft telegraph pole in San Jose, Calif.

Modern records do not, however, compare with that of St Simeon the Younger (*c.* 521–597 AD), called Stylites (Greek, *stylos* = pillar), a monk who spent his last 45 years on a stone pillar on the Hill of Wonders, Syria. This is probably the earliest example of record setting.

Potato Peeling. The greatest amount of potatoes peeled by 5 people to an institutional cookery standard with regular kitchen knives in 45 min is 587 lb 8 oz by J. Mills, M. McDonald, P. Jennings, E. Gardiner and V. McNulty at Bourke Street Hall, Melbourne, Australia, on Mar 17, 1981.

Psychiatrist, Fastest. The world's fastest "psychiatrist" was Dr Albert L. Weiner of Erlton, NJ, who dealt with up to 50 patients a day in 4 treatment rooms. He relied heavily on narcoanalysis, muscle relaxants and electro-shock treatments. In Dec 1961, he was found guilty on 12 counts of manslaughter from using unsterilized needles. He had been trained in osteopathy, which includes all varieties of medicine, but had no specialization in psychiatry.

Quoit Throwing. The world's record for rope quoit throwing is an unbroken sequence of 4,002 pegs by Bill Irby, Sr of Australia in 1968.

Longest on a Raft. The longest recorded survival alone on a raft is 133 days (4½ months) by Second Steward Poon Lim (b Hong Kong) of the UK Merchant Navy, whose ship, the SS *Ben Lomond,* was torpedoed in the Atlantic 565 miles west of St Paul's Rocks at Lat 00° 30′ N and Long 38° 45′ W at 11:45 a.m. on Nov 23, 1942. He was picked up by a Brazilian fishing boat off Salinópolis, Brazil, Apr 5, 1943, and was able to walk ashore. In July 1943 he was awarded the British Empire Medal, and now lives in NYC.

Maurice and Maralyn Bailey survived 118⅓ days in an inflatable dinghy 4½ ft in diameter in the northeast Pacific from March 4 to June 30, 1973.

Riding in Armor. The longest recorded ride in full armor weighing 112 lb is one of 167 miles from Edinburgh to Dumfries, Scotland, in 3 days (riding time 28½ hours) by Dick Brown, 48, June 13–15, 1979.

Riveting. The record for riveting is 11,209 in 9 hours by J. Moir at the Workman Clark Ltd shipyard, Belfast, N Ireland in June 1918. His peak hour was his seventh with 1,409, an average of nearly 23½ per min.

Rocking Chair. The longest recorded duration of a "Rockathon" is 432 hours by Mrs Maureen Weston of Petreburgh Athletics Club, Peterborough, Cambridge, England Apr 14–May 2, 1977.

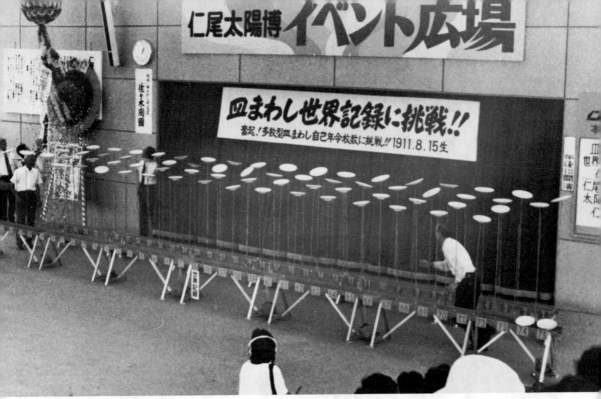

皿まわし世界記録に挑戦!!
奮起!多数型皿まわし自己年令枚数に挑戦!!1911.8.15生

仁尾太陽博 イベント広場

PLATE SPINNER Shukuni Sasaki (above) of Takamatsu, Japan, has been setting records since 1980, when he had 55 plates going at the same time. His current record (1982) is 72 as seen here in a 75-plate try. He has to move quickly back and forth as the plates wobble when they lose speed. ROLLER COASTER RIDING: Jim King of Panama City, Fla (left and below) beat his own endurance record by 200 hours when he stayed on for 368 hours (more than 15 days) through sun and storm.

SOLO SINGING MARATHON WIN-
NER: Pat Power of Ireland (top left)
sang continuously for 171 hours 15 min
in 1981. STRONG TEETH enables John
Massis of Belgium (above) to perform
such stunts as holding down a helicopter with a 375-lb upward pull using
only a mouth harness, for a Guinness
TV show. SMOKING 135 cigarettes at a
time is not so much a smoking art as a
mouth-opening stunt. Jim Purol and
Mike Papa (left) hold the record for 27
cigars each also.

Roller Coasting. The endurance record for riding on a roller coaster is 368 hours by Jim King at the Miracle Strip Amusement Park, Panama City, Fla, June 22–July 7, 1980. He covered a distance of 10,425 miles to average 28.3 mph. The minimum qualifying average speed required for this event is 25 mph.

Rolling Pin. The record distance for a woman to throw a 2-lb rolling pin is 175 ft 5 in by Lori La Deane Adams, 21, at the Iowa State Fair, Aug 21, 1979.

Rummage Sale. The largest known rummage sale or "white elephant sale" was held at the Cleveland, O, Convention Center on Oct 28 and 29, 1981. On the first day $274,909.76 was collected, and for the two days, a total of $382,270.19 was raised for the non-profit Garden Center.

See-Saw. The most protracted session for see-sawing indoors is one of 1,101 hours 40 min on an indoor suspension see-saw by George Partridge and Tamara Marquez of Auburn High School, Auburn, Wash, March 28–May 13, 1977.

Georgia Chaffin and Tammy Adams of Goodhope Junior High School, Cullman, Ala, completed 730½ hours outdoors, June 25–July 25, 1975.

Search, Longest. Walter Edwin Percy Zillwood (b Deptford, London, Dec 1900) traced his missing sister Lena (Mrs Elizabeth Eleanor Allen, b Nov 1897, d Jan 1982) after 79 years with the help of the Salvation Army on May 3, 1980.

Sermon. The longest sermon on record was delivered by the Rev Donald Thomas of Brooklyn, NY, for 93 hours, Sept 18–22, 1978.

From May 31 to June 10, 1969, the 14th Dalai Lama (b July 6, 1935, as Tenzin Gyalto), the exiled ruler of Tibet, preached a sermon on Tantric Buddhism for 5 to 7 hours per day to total 60 hours, in India.

Shaving. The fastest demon barber on record is Gerry Harley, who shaved 845 men in 60 min with a cut-throat razor at the Army and Navy Pub, Gillingham, England, on Sept 16, 1981, taking a perfunctory 4¼ sec per volunteer.

Sheaf Tossing. The best performance for tossing an 8-lb sheaf for height is 64.86 ft by Trond Ulleberg of Skolleborg, Norway, on Nov 11, 1978. Such pitchfork contests date from 1914.

Shoe Shining. In this category (limited to teams of 4 teenagers, an 8-hour time limit, and all shoes "on

the hoof") the record is 6,780 pairs by the Sheffield (England) Citadel Band of the Salvation Army on Feb 27, 1982.

Shorthand, Fastest. The highest recorded speeds ever attained under championship conditions are: 300 words per minute (99.64% accuracy) for 5 minutes and 350 wpm (99.72% accuracy, that is, two insignificant errors) for 2 minutes by Nathan Behrin (US), in NYC in Dec 1922. Behrin (b 1887) used the Pitman system invented in 1837. Morris I. Kligman, official court reporter at the US Court House, NYC has taken 50,000 words in 5 hours (a sustained rate of 166.6 wpm). Rates are dependent upon the nature, complexity, and syllabic density of the material.

G. W. Bunbury of Dublin, Ireland, held the unique distinction of writing at 250 wpm for 10 minutes on Jan 23, 1894.

Showering. The most prolonged continuous shower bath on record is one of 336 hours by Arron Marshall of Rockingham Park, W Australia, July 29–Aug 12, 1978.

The feminine record is 121 hours 1 min by Lisa D'Amato, Nov 5–10, 1981, at Harper College, Binghamton, NY.

Desquamation can be a positive danger.

Singing. The longest recorded solo singing marathon is one of 171 hours 15 min by Pat Power at the Blue Anchor Lounge, Bellurgan, Co Louth, Ireland, July 24–Aug 1, 1981. The marathon record for a choir is 72 hours 2 min by the combined choir of Girls High School and Prince Edward School, Salisbury, Zimbabwe, Sept 7–10, 1979.

Acharya Prem Bhikuji started chanting the Akhand Ram Dhum in 1964 and devotees took this up in rotation completing their devotions 13 years later on July 31, 1977 at Jamnagar, India.

Slinging. The greatest distance recorded for a slingshot is 1,434 ft 2 in, using a 51-in-long sling and a 2-oz stone, by Lawrence L. Bray at Loa, Utah, on Aug 21, 1981.

Smoke-Ring Blowing. The highest recorded number of smoke rings formed with the lips from a single pull of a cigarette with cheek tapping disallowed, is 355 by Jan van Deurs Formann of Copenhagen, Denmark, achieved in Switzerland in Aug 1979.

Smokers, Most Voracious. Jim Purol and Mike Papa each smoked 135 cigarettes simultaneously for 5 min on Oct 5, 1978, at Ramey's Lounge, Detroit,

Mich. On Sept 3, 1979, at the same venue, they each smoked 27 cigars simultaneously for 5 min.

Snowshoe Travel. The fastest officially recorded time for covering a mile is 6 min 23.8 sec by Richard Lemay (Frontenac Club of Quebec) at Manchester, NH, in 1973.

Speech-Listening. The Guild of Professional Toastmasters (founded 1962) has only 12 members. Its founder, Ivor Spencer, listened to a speech in excess of 2 hours by the maudlin guest of honor of a retirement luncheon. The Guild also elects the most boring speaker of the year, but for professional reasons will not publicize the winners' names until a decent interval has elapsed.

Spinning. The duration record for spinning a clock balance wheel by hand is 5 min 26.8 sec by Philip Ashley, aged 16, of Leigh, Greater Manchester, England, May 20, 1968.

Spitting. The greatest distance achieved at the annual (July) tobacco-spitting classic (instituted 1955) at Raleigh, Miss is 33 ft 7½ in by Jeff Barker on July 25, 1981. (In 1980 he reached 45 ft at Fulton, Miss.) In the 3rd International Spittin', Belchin' and Cussin' Triathlon, Harold Fielden reached 34 ft ¼ in at Central City, Colo, July 13, 1973. Distance is dependent on the quality of salivation, absence of cross wind, two-finger pucker and the coordination of the back arch and neck snap. Sprays or wads smaller than a dime are not measured.

Randy Ober of Bentonville, Ark, spat a tobacco wad 44 ft 6 in at the Calico 3rd Annual Tobacco Chewing and Spitting Championships north of Barstow, Calif, Mar 30, 1980.

The record for projecting a melon seed under WCWSSA (World Championship Watermelon Seed Spitting Association) rules is 65 ft 4 in by John Wilkinson in Luling, Tex, on June 28, 1980. The greatest reported distance for a cherrystone is 65 ft 2 in by Rick Krause, at Eau Claire, Mich on July 5, 1980. Spitters who care about their image wear 12-in block-ended boots so practice spits can be measured without a tape.

Stair Climbing. The 100-story record for stair climbing was set by Dennis W. Martz in the Detroit Plaza Hotel, Detroit, Mich on June 26, 1978, at 11 min 23.8 sec.

The record for running a vertical mile in continuous action is 1 hour 25 min 6 sec in ascent and 44 min 39 sec in descent, set by Richard Black, 44, president of the Maremont Corp, in 9 round trips up and down the stairs of Lake Point Tower, Chicago, on July 13, 1978. *These records can only be attempted in buildings with a minimum of 70 stories.*

Pete Squires raced up the 1,575 steps of the Empire State Building, NYC, in 10 min 59 sec on Feb 12, 1981. Mary Beth Evans set the women's record for the event when she scaled the 1,050 vertical ft in 13 min 34 sec on Feb 11, 1982.

The record for the 1,760 steps in the world's tallest free-standing structure, Toronto's CN Tower, is 10 min 16 sec by Michael Round.

In the line of duty, Bill Stevenson has mounted 334 of the 364 steps of the tower in the Houses of Parliament, England, 3,756 times in 14 years (1968–82)—equivalent to 23.39 ascents of Mt Everest.

Standing Up. The longest period on record that anyone has stood up continuously is more than 17 years, from 1955 to Nov 1973, in the case of Swami Maujgiri Maharij while performing the *Tapasya* or penance in Shahjahanpur, Uttar Pradesh, India. When sleeping he would lean against a plank. He died aged 85 in Sept 1980.

Stilt Walking. Even with a safety wire, very high stilts are extremely dangerous—25 steps are deemed to constitute "mastery." Eddy Wolf (also known as Steady Eddy) of Loyal, Wis, mastered stilts measuring 40 ft 2 in from ground to ankle over a distance of 31 steps without touching his safety handrail wire, in Hollywood, Calif, on Dec 4, 1981.

Hop pickers use stilts up to 15 ft. In 1892 M. Garisoain of Bayonne, France stilt-walked 4.97 miles into Biarritz in 42 min to average 7.10 mph.

In 1891 Sylvain Dornon stilt-walked from Paris to Moscow *via* Vilno in 50 stages for the 1,830 miles. Another source gives his time as 58 days.

The endurance record is 3,008 miles by Joe Bowen from Los Angeles to Bowen, Ky, Feb 20–July 26, 1980.

Masahami Tatsushiko (Japan), 28, ran 100 meters on 1-ft-high stilts in 14.5 sec in Tokyo on March 30, 1980.

Stowaway. The most rugged stowaway was Socarras Ramirez, who escaped from Cuba June 4, 1969, by stowing away in an unpressurized wheel well in the starboard wing of a Douglas DC-8 in a 5,600-mile Iberian Airlines flight from Havana to Madrid. He survived 8 hours at 30,000 ft where temperatures were −8°F.

STAIRS AND STILTS: Racing up the 86 floors (1,575 steps) of the Empire State Building has become an annual event. (Top left): Peter Squire is here setting a record on Feb 12, 1981. (Jerry Soalt) The record for running a vertical mile is still held by a businessman, Richard Black (left), who made 9 round trips up and down a Chicago tower in 1978. STILT WALKING records have passed back and forth between three competitors for several years. The latest is held by "Steady Eddy" Wolf (above), who took 31 steps with 40-ft-2-in-high stilts in Dec 1981.

ROPE-WALKING MARVEL: Charles Blondin (left) was such an intrepid tightrope artist that he crossed Niagara Falls nine times in 1859–60. One time he stopped in the middle, lay down on his back, and raised himself back on one leg. After a few crossings he carried his 145-lb friend and agent, Harry Colcord, on his back (shown left) three times. Colcord had to get down onto the rope several times during the trip which took as long as 50 minutes. (Francis Petrie)

SWINGER: Mollie Jackson (above) set the record at 185 hours without stop. **STRING BALL:** Francis A. Johnson (left) of Darwin, Minn, has been adding to this ball until now, 40 ft around, it needs its own house. (MInneapolis Star Tribune)

WORLD'S LARGEST TWINE BALL
GUINNESS BOOK OF WORLD RECORDS

FRANCIS A. JOHNSON
DARWIN, MINN.

Stretcher Bearing. The longest recorded carry of a stretcher case with a 140-lb "body" is 127 miles in 45 hours 45 min by two 4-man teams from the Sri Chinmoy marathon team of Jamaica, NY, Apr 17–19, 1981.

String Ball. The largest ball of string on record is one of 12 ft 9 in in diameter, 40 ft in circumference and weighing 10 tons, amassed by Francis A. Johnson of Darwin, Minn, between 1950 and 1978.

Submergence. The longest submergence under water (excluding the use of diving bells) is 147 hours 15 min established by Robert Ingolia in tests in which the US Navy received all the data in 1961.

The continuous duration record (i.e. no rest breaks) for scuba (self-contained underwater breathing apparatus) without surface air hoses, is 69 hours 1 min by Robert Newton at the Holiday Inn, Leicester, England, May 21–24, 1982. Measures have to be taken to reduce the risk of severe desquamation.

Suggestion Box. The most prolific suggestion box stuffer on record is John Drayton (b Sept 18, 1907) of Newport, Gwent, Wales, who has plied British Rail and the companies from which it was formed with a total of 29,809 suggestions from 1924 to Jan 4, 1982. One out of every seven was accepted.

Swinging. The record duration for continuous swinging is 185 hours by Mollie Jackson at Marymount College, Tarrytown, NY, March 25–Apr 1, 1979.

Tailoring. The highest speed in making a 3-piece wool suit, starting with shearing the sheep and ending with a finished article, is 1 hour 34 min 33.42 sec by 65 members of the Melbourne College of Textiles, Pascoe Vale, Australia, on June 24, 1982. The catching and fleecing took 2 min 21 sec; the carding, spinning, weaving and tailoring occupied the remaining time.

Talking. The record for non-stop talking is 159 hours by Kapila Kumarasinghe, 16, on Buddhist culture in Colombo, Sri Lanka, June 18–24, 1981.

The longest continuous political speech on record was one of 37 hours 45 min by K. H. Neville Ajith in Colombo, Sri Lanka, Oct 30–31, 1981.

The women's non-stop talking record was set by Mrs Mary E. Davis, who, Sept 2–7, 1958, started talking at a radio station in Buffalo, NY, and did not draw breath until 110 hours 30 min 5 sec later in Tulsa, Okla.

The longest recorded lecture was one of 59½ hours by James Gray of Evergreen Valley College, San Jose, Calif, Apr 11–14, 1980. The title of the lecture was "Everything You Ever Wanted to Know about Sociology and People."

Historically the longest after-dinner speech with unsuspecting victims was 3 hours, delivered by the Rev Henry Whitehead (d March 1896) at the Rainbow Tavern, Fleet St, London, on Jan 16, 1874. Both Nicholas Parsons and the well-known writer, Gyles Brandreth of London, spoke for 12 hours 40 min, Apr 3–4, 1982, in support of the National Playing Fields Association to beat the record for the longest after-dinner speech.

Pulling with Teeth. The "strongest teeth in the world" belong to John "Hercules" Massis (b Wilfried Oscar Morbée, June 4, 1940) of Oostakker, Belgium, who at Evrey, France on March 19, 1977, raised a weight of 513⅝ lb to a height of 6 in from the ground with a bit in his teeth. Massis prevented a helicopter from taking off using only a mouth harness in Los Angeles Apr 7, 1979, for the "Guinness Spectacular" ABC-TV show.

Throwing. The greatest distance any inert object heavier than air has been thrown is 857 ft 8 in, in the case of a plastic "Skyro" by Tom McRann, 30, in Golden Gate Park, San Francisco, June 9, 1980.

Tightrope and Wire Walking. The greatest 19th century tightrope walker was Jean François Gravelet, *alias* Charles Blondin (1824–1897), of France, who made the earliest crossing of Niagara Falls on a 3-in rope 1,100 ft long, 160 ft above the Falls June 30, 1859. He also made a crossing with Harry Colcord pickaback on Sept 15, 1860. Though other artists still find it difficult to believe, Colcord was his agent.

The greatest height above street level in a high-wire performance was when Philippe Petit, 24, of Nemours, France crossed on a wire 1,350 ft above the street in NYC between the newly constructed twin towers of the World Trade Center on Aug 7, 1974. He shot the 140-ft-long wire across by bow and arrow. He was charged with criminal trespass after a 75-min display of at least 7 crossings. The police psychiatrist's verdict was, "Anyone who does this 110 stories up can't be entirely right."

The oldest wire walker was "Professor" William Ivy Baldwin (1866–1953) who crossed South Boulder Canyon, Colo on a 320-ft wire with a 125-ft drop, on his 82nd birthday, July 31, 1948.

The tightrope endurance record is 185 days by Henri Rochetain (b 1926) of France on a wire 394 ft long, 82 ft above a supermarket in St Etienne, France, March 28–Sept 29, 1973. His ability to sleep on the wire has left doctors puzzled. During this time, he walked some 310 miles on the wire to keep fit.

The longest tightrope walk by any funambulist was achieved by Rochetain on a wire 3,790 yd long slung across a gorge at Clermont-Ferrand, France, July 13, 1969. He required 3 hr 20 min to negotiate the crossing.

Steven McPeak (b Apr 21, 1945) performed the highest high-wire act by crossing on a thin wire he had rigged between two peaks of the Zugspitze on the W German-Austrian border on June 25, 1981, at a height of 3,150 ft above the ground below, and 9,718 ft above sea level. He needed 181 steps to cross the snow-covered gorge.

On the same day he finished the longest wire walk, beating his previous record set in Rio de Janeiro, Brazil, by walking on a 46.5-cm diameter cable up the Zugspitze cable car lift in 3 stints aggregating 5 hours 4 min for a total of 7,485 ft, with a one-day walk of 3,117 ft. The gradient was above 30°. At his highest, McPeak was 2,313 ft higher than at the cable car base.

Farrell Hettig of Sarasota, Fla beat Steve McPeak by 5 sec when they raced up a wire ascending to 57 ft at an angle of 39° in Los Angeles, on "Guinness Spectacular I" ABC-TV show in Apr 1979. McPeak ascended a wire to 45 ft at an angle of 40° in 71 sec in Los Angeles Aug 10, 1979.

McPeak has also successfully ridden a 41-ft-tall unicycle across a high wire which was itself suspended 40 ft above the ground, and rolled on a 100-ft-high unicycle in front of the Hilton Hotel in Las Vegas, Nev.

Tire Supporting. The greatest number of car tires supported in a free-standing "lift" at one time is 80 by Gary Windebank of Romsey, England Sept 27, 1980. The total weight was 1,182 lb. The tires were Michelin XZX 155 × 13.

Treasure Finding. The most successful treasure hunter has been C. Fred Ahrendt of Dayton, Ohio, who, by Aug 1976, had found with his metal detector 175 class rings (earliest, 1890) and 179 wedding rings of 14 or more carats. Employees of crematoria are officially excluded from the competition.

Tree Climbing. The fastest climb up a 100-ft fir spar pole and return to the ground is one of 27.93 sec by Clarence Bartow of Grant's Pass, Ore on July 27, 1980. The fastest time up a 29.5-ft coconut tree bare-

foot is 4.88 sec by Fuatai Solo, 17, in Sukuna Park, Fiji, Aug 22, 1980.

Tree Sitting. The duration record for sitting in a tree is 182 days 2 min by Glen T. Woodrich, 23, at Golf N' Stuff Amusement Park, Norwalk, Calif, Jan 1–July 2, 1978.

Typing, Fastest. The highest recorded speeds attained with a ten-word penalty per error on a manual machine are:

One Minute: 170 words, Margaret Owen (US) (Underwood Standard), NYC, Oct 21, 1918.

One Hour: 147 words (net rate per min), Albert Tangora (US) (Underwood Standard), Oct 22, 1923.

The official hour record on an electric machine is 9,316 words (40 errors) on an IBM machine, giving a net rate of 149 wpm by Margaret Hamma, now Mrs Dilmore (US), in Brooklyn, NYC June 20, 1941. Mrs Barbara Blackburn of Everett, Wash can maintain 150 wpm for 50 min (37,500 key strokes) and attains a speed of 170 wpm using the Dvorak Simplified Keyboard (DSK) system.

In an official test in 1946, Stella Pajunas, now Mrs Garnard, attained a speed of 216 words in a minute on an IBM machine.

Typing, Longest. The duration record for typing on an electric typewriter is 214 hours by Violet Gibson Burns in Cremorne, NSW, Australia Feb 18–27, 1980.

Mrs Marva Drew, 51, of Waterloo, Iowa, between 1968 and Nov 30, 1974, typed the numbers 1 to 1,000,000 on a manual typewriter. She used 2,473 pages. When asked why, she replied, "But I love to type."

The longest duration typing marathon on a manual machine is 120 hours 15 min by Mike Howell, a 23-year-old blind office worker from Greenfield, Oldham, Greater Manchester, England, Nov 25–30, 1969, on an Olympia manual typewriter in Liverpool. In aggregating 561,006 strokes he performed a weight movement of 2,780 tons plus a further 174 tons in moving the carriage on line spacing.

Waiters' Marathon. Beverly Hills restaurateur Roger Bourban (b May 10, 1948) ran a full marathon of 26 mi 385 yards in full uniform in London, England, May 9, 1982, carrying a free-standing open bottle on a tray (gross weight 3 lb 2 oz) in 2 hours 42 min, using the same hand the whole way.

Walking-on-Hands. The duration record for walking-on-hands is 871 miles by Johann Hurlinger of

2

1

3

4

**TIGHTROPE AND WIRE WALKING SPE-
CIALIST** is Steve McPeak of Las Vegas who
holds more records in the Guinness Book
than anyone else, and who is probably the
world's most sure-footed and best balanced
human. 1. Climbing at an angle of 37° at
Santa Cruz, Calif, Amusement Park. 2. Crossing the 800-ft-long wire at Anaheim Stadium
as 55,000 watch. 3. Hanging from a trapeze
attached to a helicopter above Chicago.
4. Walking up a cable from Rio de Janeiro to
Sugar Loaf Mt, 2,400 ft. 5. On a 40-ft-tall
unicycle he built riding on a 40-ft-high wire
in Las Vegas. 6. Walking up a cable 3,117 ft
long at a 30° grade to the peak of the Zugspitze in the W German-Austrian Alps.
7. Close-up of Steve McPeak. (Franklin Berger
and David A. Boehm)

5

6

7

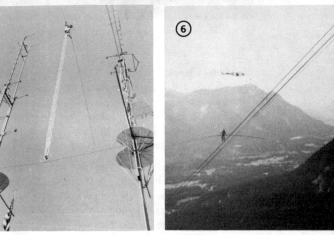

WALKING ON HANDS (above): Thomas P. Hunt is in the process of setting a speed record of 18.4 sec for the 50-meter inverted sprint for a Japanese TV audience in 1979. RUNNING WITH A BOTTLE ON A TRAY (above, right): Roger Bourban won the full marathon of 26 mi 385 yards in London, after winning all the waiters' marathons in Beverly Hills, Calif. The bottle was open, didn't spill, and he ran the entire way in waiter's uniform, holding the tray in the same hand. BIGGEST YO-YO (right): Dr Tom Kuhn of San Francisco constructed this 256-lb spool. It was test-launched from a crane 150 ft high in 1979.

Austria, who, in 55 daily 10-hour stints, averaged 1.58 mph from Vienna to Paris in 1900.

Thomas P. Hunt of the USAF Academy, Colorado Springs, completed a 50-meter inverted sprint in 18.4 sec in Tokyo, Japan on Sept 22, 1979.

Wheelbarrow Racing. The fastest time reached for a 1-mile wheelbarrow race is 5 min 1.59 sec by Bryan Zellweger ("charger") and Jack Zellweger ("rider") at the Ladner Centennial Sports Festival, Delta, BC, Canada, July 1, 1979.

Whip Cracking. The longest stock whip ever "cracked" (*i.e.* the end made to travel above the speed of sound—760 mph) is one of 104 ft 5 in (excluding the handle), wielded by Noel Harris at Sunbury, Melbourne, Australia, June 24, 1982.

Window Cleaning. The fastest time in the annual Ettore Challenge Cup in England has been 24 sec plus ten ½-sec smear penalties to equal 29 sec by Nicholas Woolman in Birmingham Apr 29, 1980, for 3 standard 40.94 × 45.39-in office windows with an 11.8-in-long squeegee and 15.83 pints of water.

Wire Slide. The greatest distance recorded in a wire slide is from a height of 175 ft over a distance of 300 ft by Grant Page with Bob Woodham over his shoulder across the Australian landmark known as "The Gap" for the filmed episode in "The Stunt Men" in 1972.

Wood Cutting. The earliest competitions date from Tasmania in 1874. The records set at the Lumberjack World Championships at Hayward, Wis (founded 1960), are:

Power Saw   11.16 sec
   by Ron Johnson (US)   1980
One-Man Bucking   22.83 sec.
   by Ron Hartill (Can)   1976
Standing Block Chop   26.9 sec.
   by Ron Wilson (Aust)   1973
Underhand Block Chop   20.3 sec.
   by Jim Alexander (Aust)   1973
Two-Man Bucking   9.98 sec.
   by Merv Jensen (NZ) and Cliff Hughes (NZ)   1980

White pine logs 14 in in diameter are used for chopping and 20 in for sawing.

Writing Small. In 1926 an account was published of Alfred McEwen's pantograph record in which the 56-word version of the Lord's Prayer was written by diamond point on glass in the space of 0.0016 × 0.0008 in.

Frank C. Watts of Felmingham, Norfolk, England, demonstrated for photographers, on Jan 24, 1968, the ability, without mechanical or optical aids, to write the Lord's Prayer 34 times (9,452 letters) within the size of a definitive postage stamp (0.84 × 0.71 in).

Writing under Handicap. The ultimate feat in "funny writing" would appear to be the ability to write extemporaneously and decipherably backwards, upside down, laterally inverted (mirror-style) while blindfolded, with both hands simultaneously. Three claims to this ability with both hands and feet simultaneously are under investigation.

Yodeling. The most protracted yodel on record was that of Errol Bird for 10 hours 15 min in Lisburn, N Ireland, Oct 6, 1979.

Yo-Yo. The yo-yo originates from a Filipino jungle fighting weapon recorded in the 16th century weighing 4 lb with a 20-ft thong. The word means "come-come." Though illustrated in a book in 1891 as a bandalore, the yo-yo did not become a craze until it was marketed by Donald F. Duncan of Chicago in 1926. The most difficult modern yo-yo trick is the "Whirlwind," incorporating both inside and outside horizontal loop-the-loops.

The individual continuous endurance record is 120 hours by John Winslow of Gloucester, Va, Nov 23–28, 1977.

Dr Allen Bussey in Waco, Tex on Apr 23, 1977 completed 20,302 loops in 3 hours (including 6,886 in a single 60-min period). He used a Duncan Imperial with a 34½-in nylon string.

The largest yo-yo ever constructed was one by Dr Tom Kuhn weighing 256 lb, test-launched from a 150-ft crane in San Francisco on Oct 13, 1979.

EATING RECORDS

While no healthy person has been reported to have succumbed in any contest for eating non-toxic food or drinking non-alcoholic drinks, such attempts, from a medical point of view, must be regarded as *extremely* inadvisable, particularly among young people. Gastronomic record attempts should aim at improving the *rate* of consumption, rather than the volume. *Guinness* will not list any records involving the consumption of more than 2 liters (approximately 2 quarts) of beer or any at all involving liquor. Nor will this book list records for potentially dangerous categories such as consuming live ants, goldfish, quantities of chewing gum or marshmallows, or raw eggs in shells. The ultimate in stupidity—the eating of a bicycle—has, however, been recorded since it is unlikely to attract competition.

Records for eating and drinking by trenchermen do not match those suffering from the rare disease of bulimia (morbid desire to eat) and polydipsia (pathological thirst). Some bulimia patients have to spend 115 hours a day eating, with an extreme consumption of 384 lb 2 oz of food in 6 days by Matthew Daking, aged 12, in 1743 (known as Mortimer's case). Fannie Meyer of Johannesburg, after a skull fracture, was stated in 1974 to be unsatisfied by less than 192 pints of water a day. By Oct 1978, she was down to 62 pints. Miss Helge Andersson (b 1908) of Lindesberg, Sweden, was reported in Jan 1971 to have been drinking 48 pints of water a day since 1922—a total of 105,120 gallons.

The world's greatest trencherman has been Edward Abraham ("Bozo") Miller (b 1909) of Oakland, Calif. He consumed up to 25,000 calories per day, or more than 11 times that recommended. He stands 5 ft 7½ in tall but weighs from 280 to 300 lb with a 57-in waist. He has been undefeated in eating contests since 1931 (see next page).

The bargees (barge sailors) on the Rhine are reputed to be the world's heaviest eaters, with 5,200 calories per day. However, the New Zealand Sports

Federation of Medicine reported in Dec 1972 that a long-distance road runner consumed 14,321 calories in 24 hours.

Specific records have been claimed as follows:

Baked Beans. 2,780 cold beans one by one, with a cocktail stick, in 30 min by Karen Stevenson of Merseyside, Eng, Apr 4, 1981.

Bananas. 17 (edible weight min 4½ oz each) in 2 min by Dr Ronald L. Alkana at the University of California, Irvine on Dec 7, 1973.

Beer. Steven Petrosino drank one liter of beer in 1.3 sec on June 22, 1977, at "The Gingerbreadman," in Carlisle, Pa.

Peter G. Dowdeswell (b London, July 29, 1940) of Earls Barton, Northants, Eng, drank 2 liters in 6 sec on Feb 7, 1975. He also holds the speed record for consuming 2 Imperial pints, in 2.3 sec, on June 11, 1975.

Bicycle. 15 days by Monsieur "Mangetout" (M. Lotito), in the form of stewed tires and metal filings, at Evrey, France, March 17–Apr 2, 1977. No further entries in this category will be accepted.

Champagne. 1,000 bottles per year by Bobby Acland of the "Black Raven," Bishopsgate, London, England.

Cheese. 16 oz of hard English cheddar in 1 min 13 sec by Peter Dowdeswell (see *Beer*) in Earls Barton, England, on July 14, 1978.

Chicken. 27 (2-lb pullets) by "Bozo" Miller (see previous page) at a sitting at Trader Vic's, San Francisco in 1963.

Clams. 424 Little Necks in 8 min by Dave Barnes at Port Townsend Bay, Wash, on May 3, 1975.

Doughnuts. 12¾ (weighing 51 oz) in 5 min 46 sec by James Wirth, and 13 (52 oz) in 6 min 1.5 sec by John Haight, both at the Sheraton Inn, Canandaigua, NY, Mar 3, 1981.

Eels. 1 lb of elvers (1,300) in 13.7 sec by Peter Dowdeswell (see *Beer*) at Reeves Club, Bristol, England, on Oct 20, 1978.

Eggs. (Hard-boiled) 14 in 58 sec by Peter Dowdeswell (see above) in Corby, England, on Feb 18, 1977. (Soft-boiled) 32 in 78 sec by Peter Dowdeswell in

Northampton, England, on Apr 8, 1978. (Raw, without shells) 13 in 2.2 sec by Peter Dowdeswell in Norwich, England, on Jan 26, 1978.

Frankfurters. 23 (2-oz) in 3 min 10 sec by Linda Kuerth, 21, at Veterans Stadium, Philadelphia, on July 12, 1977.

Gherkins. 1 lb in 43.6 sec by Rex Barker of Elkhorn, Neb, on Oct 30, 1975.

Grapes. 3 lb 1 oz in 34.6 sec by Jim Ellis of Montrose, Mich, on May 30, 1976.

Hamburgers. 20¾ hamburgers (weighing 3½ oz each or 4½ lb of meat) and buns in 30 min by Alan Peterson at Longview, Wash on Feb 8, 1979.

Ice Cream. 3 lb 6 oz of unmelted ice cream in 90 sec by Bennett D'Angelo at Dean Dairy, Waltham, Mass on Aug 7, 1977.

Lemons. 12 quarters (3 lemons) whole (including skin and seeds) in 15.3 sec by Bobby Kempf of Roanoke, Va on May 2, 1979.

Meat. One whole roast ox in 42 days by Johann Ketzler of Munich, Germany, in 1880.

Milk. One Imperial quart (1.2 US quarts) in 3.2 sec by Peter Dowdeswell (see above) at Dudley Top Rank Club, West Midlands, England on May 31, 1975.

Oysters. 250 (total weight 4 lb 13 oz out of the shell) in 2 min 52.33 sec by Ron Hansen of Sydney at the Packer's Arms, Queenstown, South Island, New Zealand, on June 30, 1982.

The record for opening oysters is 100 in 3 min 1 sec by Douglas Brown (b 1944) at Christchurch, New Zealand, on Apr 29, 1975.

Pancakes. 62 (each 6 in in diameter, buttered and with syrup) in 6 min 58.5 sec by Peter Dowdeswell (see above) in Northampton, England on Feb 9, 1977.

Peanuts. 100 (whole, out of the shell) singly in 46 sec by Jim Kornitzer at Brighton, England on Aug 1, 1979.

Pickled Onions. 91 (total weight 30 oz) in 1 min 8 sec by Pat Donahue in Victoria, BC, Canada, on March 9, 1978.

QUEEN OF THE FRANKFURTERS: At a contest in Veterans Stadium, Philadelphia, Linda Kuerth, 21 (left) won by swallowing 23 hot dogs without rolls in 3 min 10 sec. (Neil Benson) Eating BAKED BEANS one by one with a pointed stick isn't easy in any event, but eating 2,780 in 30 min is a record Karen Stevenson (above) of England can be proud of. ICE CREAM may seem easy to eat, but champion Bennett D'Angelo (left, below) of Waltham, Mass, who downed 3 lb 6 oz of unmelted 12° ice cream in 90 sec in 1977, says it causes a headache and pounding of the nerves in the temple and forehead. He likes banana splits too, but eaten leisurely. (Geri Martin)

SPAGHETTI EATING CHAMPION (below): Consuming 100 yds of spaghetti in 27.75 sec enabled Donna Maiello of the Bronx, NY, to win a contest as well as set a world record. She raised her head from the plate (lower corner) long enough to be interviewed by Channel 7, NYC, and to be photographed. HAMBURGERS BY THE DOZEN: Alan Peterson of Longview, Wash (right) ate 4½ lb of meat with buns (20¾ in all) in 30 min. Washing it down is allowed. TREE EATER: Jay Gwaltney (right, below) eating an 11-ft-tall birch sapling. He ate branches, leaves and the 4.7 in-diameter trunk over a period of 89 hours to win $10,000 as first prize in a WKQX-Chicago radio station contest called "What's the Most Outrageous Thing You Would Do?"

Potatoes. 3 lb in 1 min 22 sec by Peter Dowdeswell in Earls Barton, England on Aug 25, 1978.

Potato Chips. 30 2-oz bags in 24 min 33.6 sec, without a drink, by Paul G. Tully of Brisbane University, Australia, in May 1969. (Charles Chip Inc of Mountville, Pa produced chips 4 × 7 in from outsize potatoes in Feb 1977.)

Prunes. 144 in 53.5 sec by Peter Dowdeswell in Paris, July 21, 1980.

Ravioli. 250 pieces (average of each piece ⅓ oz) in 66 min by John Keogh of Manchester, Eng, Feb 16, 1981.

Sandwiches. 40 (jam and butter, 6 × 3¾ × ½ in) in 17 min 53.9 sec by Peter Dowdeswell (see above) on Oct 17, 1977, at the Donut Shop, Reedley, Calif.

Sausages. 96 1-oz sausages in 6 min by Steve Meltzer of Brooklyn, NY, on Oct 14, 1974.

Shellfish. 82 (unshelled) whelks in 5 min 26 sec by John Fletcher at the Castle Inn, Dover, Eng, July 27, 1980.

Shrimps. 3 lb in 4 min 8 sec by Peter Dowdeswell (see above) at Earls Barton, England, on May 25, 1978.

Snails. 350 in 8 min 29 sec by Thomas Green of La Plata, Md, in Dominique's Restaurant, Wash, DC, on July 14, 1981.

Spaghetti. 100 yd in 27.75 sec by Donna Maiello at Ann and Tony's Restaurant, Bronx, NYC, on May 22, 1982.

Tortillas. 74 (total weight 4 lb 1½ oz) in 30 min by Tom Nall in the 2nd World Championship at Mariano's Mexican Restaurant, Dallas, Tex on Oct 16, 1973.

Tree. 11-ft birch (4.7-in diameter trunk) in 89 hours by Jay Gwaltney, 19, on WKQX's Outrageous Contest, Chicago, Sept 11–15, 1980. As he finished, he said, about the taste, "as far as trees go, it's not bad."

WEALTH AND POVERTY

The comparison and estimation of extreme personal wealth are beset with intractable difficulties. Quite apart from reticence and the element of approximation in estimating the valuation of assets, as Jean Paul Getty (1892–1976) once said: "If you can count your millions, you are not a billionaire." The term "millionaire" was invented *c.* 1740 and "billionaire" in 1861.

The earliest dollar billionaires were John Davison Rockefeller (1839–1937); Henry Ford (1863–1947); and Andrew William Mellon (1855–1937). In 1937, the last year in which all 3 were alive, a billion dollars was worth about 11 times as much in purchasing power as it is today.

Richest Men

The fortune of Daniel K. Ludwig (b South Haven, Mich, June 1897) was estimated as high as $3,000 million in 1977. It is believed that his wood pulp investment in 4,000,000 acres of Amazonian jungle around Jari, Brazil, in 1967 for $3 million had led to a drain of more than $1 billion by Apr 1981 by which time he was described by *Fortune Magazine* as an "ex-billionaire." The only other living US businessman to have experienced the problems of a ninth nought is (Henry) Ross Perot (b Texarkana, Tex June 27, 1930) who was, in Dec 1969, worth in excess of a billion dollars on paper before the slump in Electronic Data Systems shares.

The richest man in the US at the mid-year 1981 is believed to be Forrest E. Mars, Senior (b 1907) of Las Vegas, whose worth is nearing $1 billion.

Highest Income

The greatest incomes derive from the collection of royalties per barrel by rulers of oil-rich sheikdoms who have not abrogated personal entitlement. Shaikh Zayid ibn Sultan an-Nuhayan (b 1918), head of state of the United Arab Emirates, arguably has title to some $9 billion of the country's annual gross national product.

The highest gross income ever achieved in a single year by a private citizen is an estimated $105 million in 1927 by the Neapolitan-born gangster Alphonse ("Scarface Al") Capone (1899–1947). This was derived from illegal liquor trading and alky-cookers (illicit stills), gambling establishments, dog tracks, dance halls, "protection" rackets and vice. On his

MILLIONAIRE AND MIL-LIONAIRESS: In 1937 when John D. Rockefeller (above) died, Shirley Temple (right) was just making her first million in the movies at age 9. Dollars in that era were worth 10.97 times as much as in 1981. The dimes that Rockefeller gave away would be worth dollars today. The full story of how Shirley flunked an "Our Gang" film test is told in the book, "Guinness: The Stories Behind the Records."

MOST MISERLY MISER: Hettie Green in the early 1900's kept more than $31 million in the bank, but she was so stingy that she would not pay for a doctor for her son, searched for a free clinic, and wasted so much time her son had to have his leg amputated. She lived on cold oatmeal, and left $95 million when she died in 1916.

business card, Capone described himself as a "Second Hand Furniture Dealer."

Paul McCartney reputedly earned in excess of £25 million ($57.5 million) in 1979–80 for the highest gross income in a year by a Briton.

Youngest Millionaire and Millionairess

The youngest person ever to accumulate $1 million dollars was the child film actor Jackie Coogan (b Los Angeles, Oct 26, 1914), co-star with (Sir) Charles Chaplin (1889–1977) in "The Kid," made in 1920.

Shirley Temple (b Apr 23, 1928, Santa Monica, Calif), formerly Mrs John Agar, Jr, now Mrs Charles Black, accumulated wealth in excess of $1 million before she was 10 years old. Her child actress career spanned the years 1934–39.

Millionairesses

The world's wealthiest woman was probably Princess Wilhelmina Helena Pauline Maria of Orange-Nassau (1880–1962), formerly Queen of the Netherlands (from 1890 to her abdication, Sept 4, 1948), with a fortune which was estimated at over $550 million.

The cosmetician Madame Charles Joseph Walker (née Sarah Breedlove, b Louisiana Delta, Dec 23, 1867), a black woman, is reputed to have become the first self-made millionairess. She was an uneducated orphan whose fortune was founded on a hair straightener. She had been a scrubwoman and a laundress.

It was estimated by the United States Trust Co in 1980 that over half of the US' 574,342 millionaires are in fact millionairesses, with the highest density in Idaho (264.6 per 10,000) and the lowest in Wyoming. NY State (56,096) leads Calif (38,691) in number of millionaires.

Greatest Miser

If meanness is measurable as a ratio between expendable assets and expenditure then Henrietta

(Hetty) Howland Green (*née* Robinson) (1835–1916), who kept a balance of over $31,400,000 in one bank alone, was the all-time world champion. She was so stingy that her son had to have his leg amputated because of the delays in finding a *free* medical clinic. She herself lived off cold oatmeal because she was too thrifty to heat it. Her estate proved to be worth $95 million.

Richest Families

It has been tentatively estimated that the combined value of the assets nominally controlled by the Du Pont family of some 1,600 members may be on the order of $150 billion. The family arrived from France on Jan 1, 1800. Capital from Pierre Du Pont (1730–1817) enabled his son Eleuthère Irénée Du Pont to start his explosives company (E. I. Du Pont) in the US.

Biggest Dowry

The largest recorded dowry was that of Elena Patiño, daughter of Don Simón Iturbi Patiño (1861–1947), the Bolivian tin millionaire, who in 1929 bestowed $22,400,000 from a fortune at one time estimated to be worth $350 million.

Highest Earnings

The highest remuneration reported for any US business executive in 1981 was $5,658,000 in salary, bonus, stock awards and other benefits received by Mr Roland Genin, executive vice-president of the NY oil-field-equipment manufacturer Schlumberger. The highest amount in pure salary was $640,000 by C. C. Garvin, Jr, chairman of Exxon.

Highest Fee

The highest paid investment consultant in the world is Dr Harry D. Schultz, who operates in Western Europe. His standard consultation fee for 60 min is $2,000 on weekdays and $3,000 on weekends. His quarterly retainer permitting companies to call him on a daily basis is $28,125. He writes and edits an information-packed International Newsletter instituted in 1964, now sold at $25 per copy.

Lowest Incomes

The poorest people in the world are the Tasaday tribe of cave-dwellers of central Mindanao, the Philippines, who were "discovered" in 1971 and live without any domesticated animals, agriculture, pottery, wheels or clothes.

Return of Cash

Jim Priceman, 44, assistant cashier at Doft & Co Inc, returned an envelope containing $37.1 million in *negotiable* bearer certificates found outside 110 Wall Street to A G Becker Inc, NYC on Apr 6, 1982. In announcing a reward of $250, Becker was acclaimed as "being all heart."

Greatest Bequests

The greatest bequests in a lifetime of a millionaire were those of the late John Davison Rockefeller (1839–1937), who gave away sums totaling $750 million.

The Scottish-born US citizen Andrew Carnegie (1835–1919) is estimated to have made benefactions totaling $350 million in the last 18 years of his life. These included 7,689 church organs and 2,811 libraries. He had started in a bobbin factory at $1.20 a week.

The largest bequest made in the history of philanthropy was the $500 million gift, announced on Dec 12, 1955, to 4,157 educational and other institutions by the Ford Foundation (established 1936) of NYC.

2. HONORS, DECORATIONS AND AWARDS

Eponymous Record

The largest object to which a human name is attached is the universe itself—in the case of the "standard" cosmological model devised in 1922 by the Russian mathematician Aleksandr Aleksandrovich Friedman (1888–1925) and known as Friedman's Universe. The model was undermined in Jan 1980 by the quadruple or isotrophy theory, which denies the Friedmanian model. The new model may eventually be named after F. Melchiori of the University of Florence.

Highest US Decoration

The highest US military decoration is the Congressional Medal of Honor. Five marines received both the Army and Navy Medals of Honor for the same acts in 1918, and 14 officers and men from 1863 to 1915 have received the medal on two occasions.

Top Jet Ace

The greatest number of kills in jet-to-jet battles is 16 by Capt Joseph Christopher McConnell (USAF) in the Korean War (1950–53). He was killed on Aug 25, 1954. It is possible that an Israeli ace may have surpassed this total in the period 1967–70, but the identity of pilots is subject to strict security.

Top Woman Ace

The record score for any woman fighter pilot is 12 by Jr Lt Lydia Litvak (USSR) in the Eastern Front campaign of 1941–43. She was killed in action on Aug 1, 1943.

Submarine Warfare

The largest target ever sunk by a submarine was the Japanese aircraft carrier *Shinano* (59,000 tons) by the *USS Archerfish* (Commander Joseph F. Enright, USN) Nov 29, 1944.

Most Decorated Soldier

Audie Murphy (1924–71) was the most decorated soldier in World War II, receiving the Medal of Honor, the Silver Star with 2 oak leaf clusters, the Bronze Star with an oak leaf cluster, the Distinguished Service Cross, the French Croix de Guerre, the Legion of Merit, the Purple Heart with 2 oak leaf clusters, and the French Légion d'Honneur.

Most Statues

The record for raising statues to oneself was set by Generalissimo Dr Rafael Leónidas Trujillo y Molina (1891–1961), a former President of the Dominican Republic. In March 1960 a count showed that there were "over 2,000." The country's highest mountain was named Pico Trujillo (now Pico Duarte). One province was called Trujillo and another Trujillo Valdez. The capital was named Ciudad Trujillo (Trujillo City) in 1936, but reverted to its old name of Santo Domingo on Nov 23, 1961. Trujillo was assas-

TOP SCORING AIR ACES

The "scores" of air aces in both wars are still hotly disputed. The highest figures officially attributed have been:

Country	World War I 1914–1918	World War II 1939–1945
World	80 Rittm Manfred Freiherr (Baron) von Richthofen (Germany)*	352 Major Erich Hartmann (Germany)
US	26 Capt Edward Vernon Rickenbacker, M.H., D.S.C. (7 o.l.c.), L. d'H., C. de G.	40 Major Richard I. Bong, M.H., D.S.C., S.S., D.F.C. (6 o.l.c.), A.M. (11 o.l.c.).
Canada	72 Lt-Col William Avery Bishop, V.C., C.B., D.S.O. and bar, M.C., D.F.C., L. d'H., C. de G.	31½ Sq-Ldr George F. Beurling, D.S.O., D.F.C., D.F.M. and bar.

* Fewer than 60 of this total could subsequently be verified from German records. The official score of Col Rene Paul Fonck (Belgium) was 75, but unofficially as high as 126.

MOST CLUSTERS AND GOLD STARS

Navy Cross	4 gold stars	Brig Gen Lewis B. Puller, USMC
		Cdr Roy M. Davenport, USN
Distinguished Service Cross	7 clusters	Capt Edward Rickenbacker (d 1973)
Silver Star	8 clusters	Col David H. Hackworth, USA
	2 gold stars	Lt-Col Raymond L. Murray, USMC
Distinguished Flying Cross	11 clusters	Col Francis S. Gabreski, USAF
	8 gold stars	Capt Howard J. Finn, USMC
Distinguished Service Medal (Army)	4 clusters	Gen of the Army Douglas MacArthur (also one Naval award)
		Gen of the Army Dwight D. Eisenhower
Distinguished Service Medal (Navy)	3 gold stars	Fleet Adm William F. Halsey
Legion of Merit	5 clusters	Maj Gen Richard Steinbach
	4 gold stars	Lt Gen Claire E. Hutchin
Purple Heart	9 clusters	Sgt Raymond E. Tirva

sinated in a car ambush on May 30, 1961, and May 30 is now celebrated annually as a public holiday.

The man to whom most statues have been raised is undoubtedly Vladimir Ilyich Ulyanov, *alias* Lenin (1870–1924), busts of whom have been mass-produced. Busts of Mao Tse-tung (1893–1976) and Ho Chi Minh (1890–1969) have also been mass-produced.

MOST DECORATED SOLDIER: Audie Murphy (left), who died in 1971 after a post-World War II career in the movies, received 8 major medals and honors, including the US Medal of Honor and the French Legion of Honor. (US Army) The TOP NAVY AWARD, the Navy Cross with 4 gold stars, went to Commander (later Rear Admiral) Roy M. Davenport (right). In World War II, under his command, 22 ships were sunk and 5 damaged, including a battleship.

Most Honorary Degrees

The greatest number of honorary degrees awarded to any individual is 90, given to Rev Father Theodore M. Hesburgh (b 1918), president of the University of Notre Dame, South Bend, Ind. These were accumulated from 1954 through June 1982.

Most Valuable Annual Award

The highest valued annual award is the Templeton Foundation Prize for Progress in Religion inaugurated in 1972 by John M. Templeton of England. The award was increased to £100,000 (about $175,000) for 1982 and was won by the preacher Billy Graham (b Nov 7, 1918).

Nobel Prizes

The Nobel Foundation of $8,960,000 was set up under the will of Alfred Bernhard Nobel (1833–96), the unmarried Swedish chemist and chemical engineer who invented dynamite in 1866. The Nobel Prizes are presented annually on Dec 10, the anniversary of Nobel's death and the festival day of the Foundation. Since the first Prizes were awarded in 1901, the highest cash value of the award, in each of the six fields of Physics, Chemistry, Medicine and Physiology, Literature, Peace and Economics was $177,000 (approx) in 1980.

Individual Nobel Prize Winners

Individually, the only person to have won two Prizes outright is Dr Linus Carl Pauling (b Feb 28, 1901), Prof of Chemistry since 1931 at the Calif Institute of Technology, Pasadena, Calif. He was awarded the Chemistry Prize for 1954 and the Peace Prize for 1962. Only two others have won two Prizes. One was Madame Marie Curie (1867–1934), born in Poland as Marja Sklodowska, who shared the 1903 Physics Prize with her husband, Pierre Curie (1859–1906), and Antoine Henri Becquerel

397

(1852–1908), and won the 1911 Chemistry Prize outright. The other was Prof John Bardeen (b May 23, 1908), who shared the Physics Prize in 1956 and 1972. The Peace Prize has been awarded three times to the International Committee of the Red Cross (founded Oct 29, 1863), of Geneva, Switzerland, namely in 1917, 1944 and in 1963, when it was shared with the International League of Red Cross Societies. Prof Frederick Sanger (UK) (b Aug 13, 1918) twice shared the Chemistry Prize (1958 and 1980).

Most Nobel Prizes by Countries

US citizens have won outright or shared in the greatest number of awards (including those made in 1981) with a total of 156 made up of 43 for Physics, 23 for Chemistry, 55 for Medicine-Physiology, 9 for Literature, 17 for Peace and 9 for Economics.

By classes, the US holds the records for Medicine-Physiology, Physics, Peace, Economics, and Chemistry. France has the record for Literature with 12.

Oldest and Youngest Nobel Prize Winners

The oldest prizeman was Prof Francis Peyton Rous (b Baltimore, 1879–1970), who worked at the Rockefeller Institute, NYC. He shared the Medicine Prize in 1966, at the age of 87.

The youngest laureate has been Prof Sir William Lawrence Bragg (b Adelaide, South Australia, 1890, d 1971), of the UK, who, at the age of 25, shared the 1915 Physics Prize with his father, Sir William Henry Bragg (1862–1942), for work on X-rays and crystal structures. Bragg and also Theodore William Richards (1868–1928) (US) who won the 1914 Chemistry Prize, carried out their prize work when aged 23. The youngest Literature prizeman was (Joseph) Rudyard Kipling (UK) (1865–1936) at the age of 41, in 1907. The youngest Peace Prize winner was the Rev Dr Martin Luther King, Jr (b Jan 15, 1929, assassinated Apr 4, 1968), of the US, in 1964 at the age of 35.

Who's Who

The longest entry of the 66,000 entries in *Who's Who in America* is that of Dr Glenn T. Seaborg (b Apr 19, 1912), whose all-time record listing of 100 lines compares with the 9-line sketch of President Reagan.

In the British *Who's Who,* the longest entry was that of Winston Churchill, who appeared in 67 editions from 1899 (18 lines) and had 211 lines by the 1965 edition. When he died he was replaced by the romantic novelist, Barbara Cartland, who has 119 lines. The youngest entry of those who qualify without hereditary title is Yehudi Menuhin (b NYC, Apr 22, 1916), the concert violinist now living in England, who first appeared in the 1932 edition, aged 15.

Chapter 12

Sports, Games and Pastimes

Many more sports, records and details can be found in the "Guinness Book of Sports Records, Winners and Champions" published in 1982 by Sterling.

Earliest

The origins of sport stem from the time when self-preservation ceased to be the all-consuming human preoccupation. Archery was a hunting skill in Mesolithic times (by *c.* 8000 BC), but did not become an organized sport until later, certainly by about 300 AD, among the Genoese and possibly as early as the 12th century BC, as an archery competition is described in Homer's *Iliad*. The earliest dated evidence for sport is *c.* 2750–2600 BC for wrestling. Ball games by girls, depicted on Middle Kingdom murals at Beni Hasan, Egypt, have been dated to *c.* 2050 BC.

Fastest

The highest speed reached in a non-mechanical sport is in sky-diving, in which a speed of 185 mph is attained in a head-down free-falling position, even in the lower atmosphere. In delayed drops, a speed of 625 mph has been recorded at high rarefied altitudes. The highest projectile speed in any moving ball game is *c.* 188 mph in pelota (jai-alai). This compares with 170 mph (electronically timed) for a golf ball driven off a tee.

Slowest

In amateur wrestling, before the rules were modified toward "brighter wrestling," contestants could be locked in holds for so long that a single bout once lasted for 11 hours 40 min. In the extreme case of the 2-hour 41-min pull in the regimental tug o'war in Jubbulpore, India, Aug 12, 1889, the winning team moved a net distance of 12 ft at an average speed of 0.00084 mph.

Longest

The most protracted sporting contest was an automobile duration test of 222,612 miles (equivalent to 8.93 times around the equator) by Appaurchaux and others in a Ford Taunus at Miranas, France. This was contested over 142 days (July–Nov) in 1963.

The most protracted non-mechanical sporting event is the *Tour de France* cycling race. In 1926 this was over 3,569 miles, lasting 29 days, but is now reduced to 23 days.

USED CAR: With chains to keep it more or less in one piece, this Ford Taunus was driven 222,612 miles in 142 days for an automobile endurance record in the longest sporting event ever staged. (Ford Motor Co)

Largest Field

The largest field for any ball game is that for polo with 12.4 acres, or a maximum length of 300 yd and a width, without side-boards, of 200 yd (with boards the width is 160 yd). Twice a year in the parish of St Columb Major, Cornwall, England, a game called hurling (not to be confused with the Irish game) is played on a "field" which consists of the entire parish, approximately 25 square miles.

Biggest Sports Contract

In March 1982 the National Football League concluded a deal worth $2 billion for 5 years coverage of their games by the 3 major TV networks (ABC, CBS and NBC). This represents $14.2 million for each team in the league.

Most Expensive Sport

The most expensive of all sports is the racing of large yachts—"J" type boats and International 12-m boats. The owning and racing of these is beyond the means of individual millionaires and is confined to multi-millionaires or syndicates.

Largest Crowd

The greatest number of live spectators for any sporting spectacle is the estimated 2,500,000 who annually line the route of the New York Marathon. However, spread over 23 days, it is estimated that more than 10 million see the annual *Tour de France* along the route.

FOOTBALL SCORES: The NFL will receive $2 billion from the 3 major US networks for the rights to televise football for 5 years. As a result, NBC announced a record advertising rate—$400,000 for 30 sec—for Super Bowl XVII.

The largest crowd traveling to any single sporting event is "more than 400,000" for the annual *Grand Prix d'Endurance* motor race on the Sarthe circuit near Le Mans, France. The record stadium crowd was one of 199,854 for the Brazil vs Uruguay soccer match in the Maracaña Municipal Stadium, Rio de Janeiro, Brazil, July 16, 1950.

The largest television audience for a single sporting event (excluding Olympic events) was the estimated 1.5 billion who watched the final of the 1982 World Cup soccer competition.

Most Participants

The *Round the Bays* 6.5-mile run in Auckland, NZ attracted an estimated 70,000 runners on March 28, 1981. The most runners in a marathon were the 16,350 in the London Marathon on May 9, 1982, of whom 15,758 finished.

In May 1971, the "Ramblin' Raft Race" on the Chattahoochee River at Atlanta, Ga, attracted 37,683 competitors on 8,304 rafts.

According to a report issued in 1978, 55 million people are actively involved in sports in the USSR, using 3,282 stadiums, 1,435 swimming pools and over 66,000 indoor gymnasiums. It is estimated that some 29% of the East German population participates in sport regularly.

Most Officials

Tennis is the sport with the highest ratio of officials to participants. For a singles match there should be 13—ten line, one net-cord and one foot-fault judge, in addition to the umpire.

Worst Disasters

The worst disaster in recent history was when an estimated 604 were killed after some stands at the Hong Kong Jockey Club race course collapsed and caught fire on Feb 26, 1918. During the reign of Antoninus Pius (138–161 AD) the upper wooden tiers in the Circus Maximus, Rome, collapsed during a gladiatorial combat, killing 1,112 spectators.

Greatest Earnings

The greatest fortune amassed by an individual in sport is an estimated $69 million by the boxer Muhammad Ali Haj to the end of 1981.

The highest-paid woman athlete is tennis player Martina Navratilova (b Prague, Czechoslovakia, Oct 18, 1956) with official earnings of $865,437 in 1981.

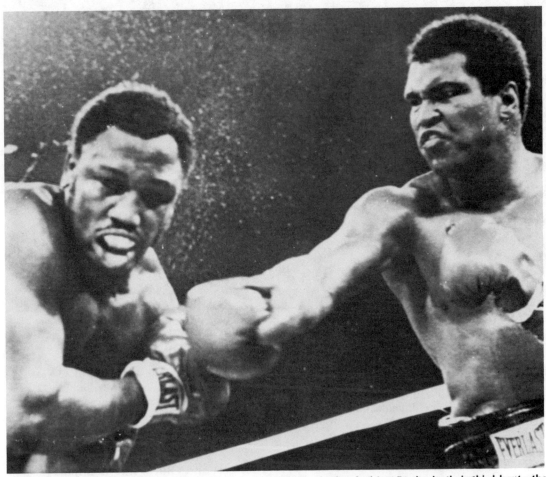

FOR FISTFULS OF DOLLARS: Muhammad Ali slams a right to the head of Joe Frazier in their third bout—the "Thrilla' in Manila." Ali's great gate appeal was worth some $69 million for 61 fights during his 21-year career. (AP)

Most Versatile Athletes

Charlotte "Lottie" Dod (1871–1960) won the Wimbledon singles title (1887 to 1893) 5 times, the British Ladies Golf Championship in 1904, an Olympic silver medal for archery in 1908, and represented England at hockey in 1899. She also excelled at skating and tobogganing.

Mildred (Babe) Didrikson Zaharias (US) was an All-American basketball player, took the silver medal in the high jump, and gold medals in the javelin throw and hurdles in the 1932 Olympics. Turning professional, she first trained as a boxer, and then, switching to golf, eventually won 19 championships, including the US Women's Open and All-American Open. She holds the women's world record also for longest throw of a baseball—296 ft.

Most Prolific Recordbreaker

Between Jan 24, 1970, and Nov 1, 1977, Vasili Alexeyev (USSR) (b Jan 7, 1942) broke 80 official world records in weight lifting.

Shortest Reign

Olga Rukavishnikova (USSR) (b Mar 13, 1955) held the pentathlon world record for only 0.4 sec at Moscow on July 24, 1980. That is the difference between her second place time of 2 min 04.8 sec in the final 800m event of the Olympic five-event competition, and that of the third-placed Nadezda Tkachenko (USSR), whose overall points came to more than Rukavishnikova's total—5,083 points to 4,937 points.

PACE SETTER: By shooting the highest score ever made in competition for a world title (2,571 of a possible 2,880) Darrell Pace (US) earned the Olympic gold medal in Montreal in 1976. (Don Morley/All-Sport)

Longest Reign

The longest reign as a world champion is 33 years (1829–62) by Jacques Edmond Barre (France, 1802–73) at real (royal) tennis.

Youngest and Oldest Recordbreakers

The youngest age at which any person has broken a non-mechanical world record is 12 years 298 days for Gertrude Caroline Ederle (b Oct 23, 1906) of the US, who broke the women's 880-yd freestyle swimming world record with 13 min 19.0 sec at Indianapolis, Ind, Aug 17, 1919.

The oldest person to break a world record is Irishborn John J. Flanagan (1868–1938), triple Olympic hammer throw champion for the US, 1900–1908, who set his last world record of 184 ft 4 in at New Haven, Conn, July 24, 1909, aged 41 years 196 days.

Youngest and Oldest Champions

The youngest person to have successfully participated in a world title event was a French boy, whose name is not recorded, who coxed the winning Netherlands pair at Paris on Aug 26, 1900. He was not more than 10 and may have been as young as 7. The youngest individual Olympic winner was Marjorie Gestring (US) (b Nov 18, 1922), who took the springboard diving title at the age of 13 years 268 days at the Olympic Games in Berlin, Aug 12, 1936. Oscar G. Swahn (see below) was aged 65 years 258 days when he won the gold medal in the 1912 Olympic Running Deer team shooting competition.

Youngest and Oldest Internationals

The youngest age at which any person has won international honors is 8 years in the case of Joy Foster, the Jamaican singles and mixed doubles table tennis champion in 1958. It would appear that the greatest age at which anyone has actively competed for his country is 72 years 280 days in the case of Oscar Gomer Swahn (Sweden) (1847–1927), who won a silver medal for shooting in the Olympic Games at Antwerp on July 26, 1920. He qualified for the 1924 Games, but was unable to participate because of illness.

Heaviest Sportsmen

The heaviest sportsman of all time was the wrestler William J. Cobb of Macon, Ga, who in 1962 was billed as the 802-lb "Happy Humphrey." The heaviest player of a ball game was Bob Pointer, the 487-lb tackle on the 1967 Santa Barbara High School football team.

AEROBATICS

Earliest

The first aerobatic maneuver is generally considered the sustained inverted flight in a Blériot of Célestin-Adolphe Pégoud (1889–1915) at Buc, France, Sept 21, 1913, but Lieut Peter Nikolayevich Nesterov (1887–1914), of the Imperial Russian Air Service, performed a loop in a Nieuport Type IV monoplane at Kiev, USSR, Aug 27, 1913.

World Championships

Held biennially since 1960 (excepting 1974), scoring is based on the system devised by Col José Aresti of Spain. The competitions consist of two compulsory and two free programs. Team competition has been won on 4 occasions by the USSR. No individual has won more than one title, the most successful competitor being Igor Egorov (USSR) who won in 1970, was second in 1976, fifth in 1972 and eleventh in 1968. The most successful in the women's competition has been Lidia Leonova (USSR) with first place in 1976, second in 1978, third in 1972 and fifth in 1970. The US had a clean sweep of all the medals in 1980.

Inverted Flight

The duration record for inverted flight is 4 hours 9 min 5 sec by John "Hal" McClain in a Swick Taylorcraft on Aug 23, 1980 over Houston Raceways, Tex.

Loops

On June 21, 1980, R. Steven Powell performed 2,315⅔ inside loops in a Bellanca Decathalon over Almont, Mich. John McClain achieved 180 outside loops in a Bellanca Super Decathalon on Sept 2, 1978, over Houston, Tex.

ARCHERY

Earliest References

Though the earliest evidence of the existence of bows is seen in the Mesolithic cave paintings in Spain, archery as an organized sport appears to have developed in the 3rd century AD. Competitive archery may, however, date back to the 12th century BC. The world governing body is the *Fédération Internationale de Tir à l'Arc* (FITA), founded in 1931.

Highest Championship Scores

The highest scores achieved in either a world or Olympic championship for Double FITA rounds are: men, 2,571 points (possible 2,880) by Darrell Pace (US) posted at the 1976 Olympics at Montreal, July 27–30, 1976; women, 2,515 by Luann Ryon (US) at Canberra, Australia, Feb 11–12, 1977.

Most Titles

The greatest number of world titles (instituted 1931) ever won by a man is 4 by Hans Deutgen

ARCHERY WORLD RECORDS

WOMEN

Event	Name	Record/Maximum	Year
FITA	Natalia Butuzova (USSR)	1324/1440	1982
70 m.	Natalia Butuzova (USSR)	328/360	1979
60 m.	Ho Jin Kim (S Kor)	336/360	1980
50 m.	Paivi Meriduoto (Fin)	331/360	1982
30 m.	Valentina Rodionova (USSR)	353/360	1981
Team	USSR	3878/4320	1979
	(Natalia Butuzova, Keto Lossaberidze, Olga Rogova)		

MEN

Event	Name	Record/Maximum	Year
FITA	Darrell Pace (US)	1341/1440	1979
90 m.	Vladimir Esheyev (USSR)	322/360	1980
70 m.	Sante Spigarelli (Italy)	338/360	1978
50 m.	Sante Spigarelli (Italy)	340/360	1976
30 m.	Darrell Pace (US)	356/360	1978
Team	USSR	3887/4320	1981
	(Vladimir Esheyev, Stanislav Zabrodsky, Alexander Gabelkov)		

is 1,113 yd 30 in by Arlyne Rhode (b May 4, 1936) at Wendover, Utah, on Sept 10, 1978. Don Brown (b Nov 13, 1945) (US) set the flight record for the handbow with 1,227 yd 11 in on Oct 5, 1980, and April Moon (US) set a women's record of 1,039 yd 13 in on Sept 13, 1981, both at Ivanpah Dry Lake.

Greatest Pull

Gary Sentman of Roseburg, Ore, drew a longbow weighing a record 176 lb to the maximum draw on the arrow (28¼ in) at Forksville, Pa, Sept 20, 1975.

Highest 24-Hour Scores

The record score at target archery over 24 hours by a pair of archers is 51,633 during 48 Portsmouth Rounds (60 arrows at 20 yd with a 2-in diameter 10 ring) shot by Jimmy Watt and Gordon Danby at the Epsom Showgrounds, Auckland, NZ, Nov 18–19, 1977.

The highest recorded score at field archery over 24 hours by a team of four is 32,682 by Bill Chambers, Ben Gramero, Jim Ruffley and Bill Hands of Holland Moss Field Archery Club at Skelmersdale, England, July 18–19, 1981.

LONG SHOT: April Moon broke her own women's handbow flight shooting record in 1981 with a shot of 1,039 yd 13 in at Ivanpah Dry Lake, Calif.

(b Feb 28, 1917) (Sweden), 1947–50. The greatest number won by a woman is 7 by Mrs Janina Spychajowa-Kurkowska (b Feb 8, 1901) (Poland), 1931–34, 36, 39 and 47.

Oscar Kessels (Belgium) participated in 21 world championships.

Olympic Medals

Hubert van Innis (Belgium) (1866–1961) won 6 gold and 3 silver medals in archery events at the 1900 and 1920 Olympic Games.

Flight Shooting

The longest flight shooting records are achieved in the footbow class. In the unlimited footbow division, Harry Drake (b May 7, 1915) of Lakeside, Calif, holds the record at 1 mile 268 yd, shot at Ivanpah Dry Lake, Calif, Oct 24, 1971. The crossbow record is 1,359 yd 29 in, held by Drake and set at the same venue, Oct 14–15, 1967. The female footbow record

AUTO RACING*

Earliest Races

There are various conflicting claims, but the first automobile race was the 201-mile Green Bay-to-Madison, Wis, run in 1878, won by an Oshkosh steamer.

In 1887, Count Jules Felix Philippe Albert de Dion de Malfiance (1856–1946) won the *La Velocipede* 19.3-mile race in Paris in a De Dion steam quadricycle in which he is reputed to have exceeded 37 mph.

The first "real" race was from Paris to Bordeaux and back (732 miles) June 11–13, 1895. The winner was Emile Levassor (1844–97) (France) driving a Panhard-Levassor two-seater with a 1.2-liter Daimler engine developing 3½ hp. His time was 48 hours 47 min (average speed 15.01 mph). The first closed-circuit race was held over 5 laps of a mile dirt track at Narragansett Park, Cranston, RI on Sept 7, 1896. It was won by A. H. Whiting, who drove a Riker electric.

---

* For more detailed information about auto racing, see *The Guinness Guide to Grand Prix Motor Racing*, available from Sterling.

The oldest auto race in the world still being regularly run is the R.A.C. Tourist Trophy, first staged on the Isle of Man on Sept 14, 1905. The oldest continental race is the French Grand Prix first held June 26–27, 1906. The Coppo Florio, in Sicily, has been irregularly held since 1900.

Fastest Circuits

The highest average lap speed attained on any closed circuit is 250.958 mph in a trial by Dr Hans Liebold (b Oct 12, 1926) (Germany) who lapped the 7.85-mile high-speed track at Nardo, Italy, in 1 min 52.67 sec in a Mercedes-Benz C111-IV experimental coupé on May 5, 1979. It was powered by a V8 engine with two KKK turbochargers with an output of 500 hp at 6,200 rpm.

The highest average race lap speed for a closed circuit is 214.158 mph by Mario Gabriele Andretti (US) (b Trieste, Italy, Feb 28, 1940) driving a 2.6-liter turbocharged Viceroy Parnelli-Offenhauser on the 2-mile 22-degree banked oval at Texas World Speedway, College Station, Tex, Oct 6, 1973.

The fastest road circuit was the Francorchamps circuit near Spa, Belgium, then 14.10 km (8 miles 1,340 yd) in length. It was lapped in 3 min 13.4 sec (average speed of 163.086 mph) on May 6, 1973, by Henri Pescarolo (b Paris, France, Sept 25, 1942) driving a 2,933-cc V12 Matra-Simca MS 670 Group 5 sports car. The race lap average speed record at Berlin's AVUS track was 171.75 mph by Bernd Rosemeyer (Germany) (1909–38) in a 6-liter V16 Auto Union in 1937.

The fastest world championship Grand Prix circuit in current use is the 2.932-mile course at Silverstone, Northamptonshire, England (opened 1948). The race lap record is 1 min 14.40 sec (average speed 141.87 mph) by Gianclaudio (Clay) Regazzoni (Switzerland) (b Sept 5, 1939) driving a Saudia-Williams FW07 on July 14, 1979. The practice lap record is 1 min 11.88 sec (146.84 mph) by Alan Jones (Australia) (b Nov 2, 1946) in a Saudia-Williams on July 12, 1979. A test run of 1 min 10.8 sec (average speed 149.08 mph) was recorded by Nelson Piquet Soutomaior (Brazil) in a Brabham-Cosworth BT48 on June 17, 1980.

The Motor Industry Research Association (MIRA) High Speed Circuit (2.82-mile lap with 33-degree banking on the bends) at Lindley, Warwickshire, England, was lapped in 1 min 2.8 sec (average speed 161.655 mph) by David Wishart Hobbs (b Leamington, England, June 9, 1939) driving a 4,994-cc V12 Jaguar XJ13 Group 6 prototype sports car in Apr 1967.

Fastest Races

The fastest race in the world is the NASCAR Busch Clash, a 125-mile event on the 2½-mile 31-degree banked tri-oval at Daytona International Speedway, Daytona Beach, Fla. In the 1979 event, Elzie Wylie "Buddy" Baker (b Jan 25, 1941) of Charlotte, NC, averaged 194.384 mph in an Oldsmobile.

The fastest road race was the 1,000-km (621-mile) sports car race held on the Francorchamps circuit. The record time for this 71-lap (622.055-mile) race was 4 hours 1 min 9.7 sec (average speed 154.765 mph) by Pedro Rodriguez (1940–71) of Mexico and Keith Jack "Jackie" Oliver (b Chadwell Heath, Essex, England, Aug 14, 1942), driving a 4,998-cc flat-12 Porsche 917K Group 5 sports car on May 9, 1971.

The fastest average speed for a Grand Prix race is 138.80 mph for a time of 1 hour 26 min 11.17 sec in the British Grand Prix by Clay Regazzoni (Switzerland) driving a Saudia-Williams FW07 over 68 laps (199.37 miles) at Silverstone on July 14, 1979.

Toughest Circuits

The Targa Florio (first run May 9, 1906) was widely acknowledged to be the most arduous race in the world. Held on the Piccolo Madonie Circuit in Sicily, it covered 11 laps (492.126 miles) and involved the negotiation of 9,350 corners over severe mountain gradients and narrow rough roads.

The record time was 6 hours 27 min 48.0 sec (average speed 76.141 mph) by Arturo Francesco Merzario (b Civenna, Italy, March 11, 1943) and Sandro Munari (b Venice, Italy, 1940) driving a 2,998.5-cc flat-12 Ferrari 312 P Group 5 sports car in the 56th race on May 21, 1972. The lap record was 33 min 36.0 sec (average speed 79.890 mph) by Leo Juhani Kinnunen (b Tampere, Finland, Aug 5, 1943) on lap 11 of the 54th race in a 2,997-cc flat-8 Porsche 908/3 Spyder Group 6 prototype sports car on May 3, 1970.

The most grueling and slowest Grand Prix circuit is that for the Monaco Grand Prix (first run Apr 14, 1929), run through the streets and around the harbor of Monte Carlo. It is 3.312 km (2.058 miles) in length and has 11 pronounced corners and several sharp changes of gradient. The race is run over 76 laps (156.4 miles) and involves on average about 1,600 gear changes.

The record for the race is 1 hour 54 min 11.259 sec (average speed 82.21 mph) by Riccardo Patrese (b Italy, Apr 17, 1954) in a Brabham-Ford, May 23, 1982. The race lap record is 1 min 26.35 sec (average speed 85.79 mph) by Patrese in 1980. The practice lap record is 1 min 23.28 sec (average speed 88.96 mph) by Rene Arnoux in a Renault Elf Turbo on May 22, 1982.

Le Mans

The greatest distance ever covered in the 24-hour *Grand Prix d'Endurance* (first held May 26–27, 1923) on the old Sarthe circuit (8 miles 650 yd) at Le Mans, France, is 3,314.222 miles by Dr Helmut Marko (b Graz, Austria, Apr 27, 1943) and Jonkheer Gijs van Lennep (b Bloemendaal, Netherlands, March 16, 1942) driving a 4,907-cc flat-12 Porsche 917K Group 5 sports car June 12–13, 1971. The record for the current circuit is 3,134.56 miles by Didier Pironi (b March 26, 1952) and Jean-Pierre Jaussaud (b June 3, 1937) (average speed 130.60 mph) in an Alpine Renault, June 10–11, 1978. The race lap record (8.475-mile lap) is 3 min 34.2 sec (average speed 142.44 mph) by Jean Pierre Jabouille (b France, Oct 1, 1942) driving an Alpine Renault on June 11, 1978. The practice lap record is 3 min 27.6 sec (average speed 146.97 mph) by Jacques-Bernard "Jacky" Ickx (b Belgium, Jan 1, 1945) in a turbocharged 2.1-liter Porsche 936/78 on June 7, 1978.

The race has been won by Ferrari cars nine times, in 1949, 54, 58 and 60–65. The most wins by one man is 6 by Jacky Ickx (Belgium), who won in 1969, 75–77 and 81–82.

Most Successful Drivers

Based on the World Drivers' Championships, inaugurated in 1950, the most successful driver is Juan-Manuel Fangio (b Balcarce, Argentina, June 24, 1911), who won five times in 1951, 54–57. He retired in 1958, after having won 24 Grand Prix races (2 shared).

The most successful driver in terms of race wins is Richard Lee Petty (b Randleman, NC, July 2, 1937) with 195 NASCAR Grand National wins, 1967–81. (See also *Stock Car Racing.*)

The most Grand Prix victories is 27 by Jackie Stewart (b June 11, 1939) of Scotland between Sept 12, 1965 and Aug 5, 1973. Jim Clark (1936–1968) of Scotland holds the record of Grand Prix victories in one year with 7 in 1963. He won 61 Formula One and Formula Libre races between 1959 and 1968. The most Grand Prix starts is 176 (out of a possible 184) between May 18, 1958, and Jan 26, 1975, by (Norman) Graham Hill (1929–1975). He took part in 90 *consecutive* Grands Prix between Nov 20, 1960 and Oct 5, 1969.

Indianapolis 500

The Indianapolis 500-mile race (200 laps) was inaugurated on May 30, 1911. The most successful driver has been Anthony Joseph "A. J." Foyt, Jr (b Houston, Tex, Jan 16, 1945), who won in 1961, 64, 67 and 77.

The record time is 3 hours 4 min 5.54 sec (average speed 162.962 mph) by Mark Donohue (b NJ, March 18, 1937, d 1975), driving a 2,595-cc 900-bhp turbocharged Sunoco McLaren M16B-Offenhauser on May 27, 1972.

The race lap record is 46.41 sec (average speed 193.924 mph) by Mario Andretti (b Trieste, Feb 28, 1940) (US), driving a Penske-Cosworth PC6 in 1978. The qualifying lap record speed is 208.7 mph by Rick Mears (US) driving a Penske-Cosworth on May 21, 1982.

The record prize fund was $2,067,475 for the 66th race on May 31, 1982. The individual prize record is $318,819 by Johnny Rutherford on May 25, 1980.

Fastest Pit Stop

Bobby Unser (US) took 4 sec to take on fuel on lap 10 of the Indianapolis 500 on May 30, 1976.

Closest Finishes

The closest finish to a World Championship race was in the Italian Grand Prix at Monza on Sept 5, 1971. Just 0.61 sec separated winner Peter Gethin (GB) from the fifth placer.

The closest finish in the Indianapolis 500 was in the 1982 race when the winner, Gordon Johncock, crossed the finish line just 0.16 sec before runner-up Rick Mears.

Oldest and Youngest World Champions

The oldest was Juan-Manuel Fangio, who won his last World Championship Aug 18, 1957, aged 46 years 55 days. The youngest was Emerson Fittipaldi (b São Paulo, Brazil, Dec 12, 1946) who won his first World Championship Sept 10, 1972, aged 25 years 273 days.

Oldest and Youngest Grand Prix Winners and Drivers

The youngest Grand Prix winner was Bruce Leslie McLaren (1937–70) of New Zealand, who won the US Grand Prix at Sebring, Fla, on Dec 12, 1959, aged 22 years 104 days. The oldest Grand Prix win-

THE MAN AT LE MANS: With over 400,000 spectators each year, the Le Mans 24-hour race attracts the largest crowd to travel to any sporting event, and Jacky Ickx, with 6 victories, has the most wins in the grueling contest. (Keystone)

ner was Tazio Giorgio Nuvolari (1892–1953) of Italy, who won the Albi Grand Prix at Albi, France, on July 14, 1946, aged 53 years 240 days.

The oldest Grand Prix driver was Louis Alexandre Chiron (Monaco, 1899–1979), who finished 6th in the Monaco Grand Prix on May 22, 1955, aged 55 years 292 days. The youngest Grand Prix driver was Michael Christopher Thackwell (b New Zealand, March 30, 1961) who took part in the Canadian Grand Prix in Sept 28, 1980, aged 19 years 182 days.

Land Speed Records

For details of the land speed record see chapters 8 and 11.

The most successful land speed record breaker was Major Sir Malcolm Campbell (1885–1948) (UK). He broke the official record nine times between Sept 25, 1924, with 146.157 mph in a Sunbeam, and Sept 3, 1935, when he achieved 301.129 mph in the Rolls-Royce-engined *Bluebird*.

The world speed record for compression-ignition-engined cars is 190.344 mph (average of two runs over measured mile) by Robert Havemann of Eureka, Calif, driving his *Corsair* streamliner, powered by a turbocharged 6,981-cc 6-cylinder GMC 6-71 diesel engine developing 746 bhp, at Bonneville Salt Flats, Utah, in Aug 1971. The faster run was made at 210 mph.

Rocket or Jet-Engined Dragsters

The highest terminal velocity recorded by any dragster is 392.54 mph by Kitty O'Neil (US) at El Mirage Dry Lake, Calif, on July 7, 1977. The lowest elapsed time was 3.72 sec also by Kitty O'Neil on the same occasion.

Terminal velocity is the speed attained at the end of a 440-yd run made from a standing start, and elapsed time is the time taken for the run.

Piston-Engined Dragsters

The lowest elapsed time recorded by a piston-engined dragster is 5.637 sec by Donald Glenn "Big Daddy" Garlits (b 1932) of Seffner, Fla, driving his rear-engined AA-F dragster, powered by a 7,948-cc supercharged Dodge V8 engine, during the National Hot Rod Association's Supernationals at Ontario Motor Speedway, Calif, Oct 11, 1975.

The highest terminal velocity recorded is 255.58 mph by Shirley Muldowney (US) at Pomona, Calif, in Jan 1979.

The world record for two runs in opposite directions over 440 yd from a standing start is 6.70 sec by Dennis Victor Priddle (b 1945) of Yeovil, Somerset, England, driving his 6,424-cc supercharged Chrysler dragster, developing 1,700 bhp using nitromethane and methanol, at Elvington Airfield, England, Oct 7, 1972. The faster run took 6.65 sec.

Stock Car Racing

Richard Petty of Randleman, NC, was the first stock car driver to attain $1 million lifetime earnings on Aug 1, 1971. His earnings through 1981 were $4,396,808. Petty also holds several NASCAR records, including: most races won (194), most victories in a single season (27 in 1967), most consecutive wins (10 in 1967) and most victories in the Daytona 500 (7).

Earliest Rally

The earliest long rally was promoted by the Parisian daily *Le Matin* in 1907 from Peking to Paris, over about 7,500 miles on June 10. The winner,

RALLY KILLER: Shekhar Mehta of Uganda on his way to his record fifth win in the Safari Rally, the longest annual automobile rally, in 1982 in his Nissan-Datsun Violet GTS car. (All-Sport)

Prince Scipione Borghese (1871–1927), arrived in Paris on Aug 10, 1907 in his 40-hp Itala accompanied by his chauffeur, Ettore, and Luigi Barzini.

Longest Rallies

The longest ever rally was the *Singapore Airlines* London-Sydney Rally over 19,329 miles, from Covent Garden, London, on Aug 14, 1977, to the Sydney Opera House, won Sept 28, 1977, by Andrew Cowan, Colin Malkin and Michael Broad in a Mercedes 280E.

The longest rally held annually is the Safari Rally (first run 1953 through Kenya, Tanzania and Uganda), which is up to 3,874 miles long, as in the 17th Safari held Apr 8–12, 1971. It has been won a record 5 times by Shekhar Mehta (Uganda) in 1973, 79–82.

Monte Carlo

The Monte Carlo Rally (first run 1911) has been won a record 4 times by Sandro Munari (Italy) in 1972, 75–77. The smallest car to win was an 851-cc Saab driven by Erik Carlsson (b Sweden, March 5, 1929) and Gunnar Häggbom of Sweden, in 1962, and by Carlsson and Gunnar Palm in 1963.

Pikes Peak Race

The Pikes Peak Auto Hill Climb, Colorado (instituted 1916) has been won by Bobby Unser 13 times between 1956 and 1974 (10 championship, 2 stock and 1 sports car title). On June 30, 1968, in the 46th race, he set an absolute record of 11 min 54.9 sec in his 5,506-cc Chevrolet championship car over the 12.42-mile course, rising from 9,402 to 14,110 ft through 157 curves.

Duration Record

The greatest distance ever covered in one year is 400,000 km (248,548.5 miles) by François Lecot (1879–1949), an innkeeper from Rochetaillée, France, in a 1,900-cc 66-bhp Citroën 11 sedan mainly between Paris and Monte Carlo, from July 22, 1935 to July 26, 1936. He drove on 363 of the 370 days allowed.

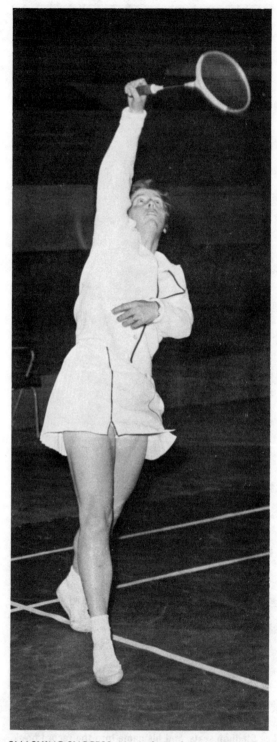

BADMINTON

Origins

A game similar to badminton was played in China in the 2nd millennium BC. The modern game may have evolved c. 1870 at Badminton Hall in Avon, England, the seat of the Dukes of Beaufort, or from a game played in India. The first modern rules were codified in Poona in 1876. The oldest club is the Newcastle Badminton Club, England, formed as the Armstrong College Club, Jan 24, 1900.

International Championships

The International Championship or Thomas Cup (instituted 1948) has been won 7 times by Indonesia, in 1958, 61, 64, 70, 73, 76 and 79.

The Ladies International Championship or Uber Cup (instituted 1956) has been won 5 times by Japan (1966, 69, 72, 78 and 81).

Most Titles

The record number of All-England Championship (instituted 1899) titles won is 21 by Sir George Thomas (1881–1972) between 1903 and 1928. The record for men's singles is 8 by Rudy Hartono Kurniawan (b Aug 18, 1948) of Indonesia (1968–74, 76). The most, including doubles, by women is 17, a record shared by Muriel Lucas (1899–1910) and Mrs G. C. K. Hashman (*née* Judy Devlin) (US) (b Oct 22, 1935), whose wins came from 1954 to 1967, including a record 10 singles titles.

Shortest Game

In the 1969 Uber Cup in Djakarta, Indonesia, Noriko Takagi (later Mrs Nakayama) (Japan) beat Poppy Tumengkol (Indonesia) in 9 min.

Marathons

The longest singles match is 74 hours 41 min by Mike Watts and Bryan Garnham at Llansamlet Parish Hall, Swansea, Wales, Oct 15–18, 1981.

SMASHING SUCCESS: Mrs Judy Hashman makes a fine overhead smash on her way to the ninth (in 1966) of her record ten All-England singles titles. Including doubles, she won 17 titles in all. (AP)

Longest Hit

Frank Rugani drove a shuttlecock 79 ft 8½ in in indoor tests at San Jose, Calif, Feb 29, 1964.

61 in 1961: Roger Maris watches the ball fly into the Yankee Stadium seats, and his name into the record book, with his 60th home run. On the last day of the 1961 season he hit number 61. (NY Yankees)

BASEBALL

Earliest Games

The Reverend Thomas Wilson, of Maidstone, Kent, England, wrote disapprovingly, in 1700, of baseball being played on Sundays. The earliest game on record under the Cartwright (Alexander Joy Cartwright, Jr, 1820–92) rules was on June 19, 1846, in Hoboken, NJ, where the "New York Nine" defeated the Knickerbockers 23 to 1 in 4 innings. The earliest all-professional team was the Cincinnati Red Stockings in 1869, who had 56 wins and 1 tie that season.

Home Runs

Henry L. (Hank) Aaron broke the major league record set by George H. (Babe) Ruth of 714 home runs in a lifetime when he hit No. 715 on Apr 8, 1974. Between 1954 and 1974 he hit 733 home runs for the Milwaukee and Atlanta Braves in the National League. In 1975, he switched to the Milwaukee Brewers in the American League and in that year and 1976, when he finally retired, he hit 22 more, bringing his lifetime total to 755, the major league record.

The Japanese slugger Sadaharu Oh (b May 20, 1940), of the Yomiuri Giants, hit 868 career home runs before retiring at the end of the 1980 season.

An all-league record of almost 800 in a lifetime has been claimed for Josh Gibson (1911–47) mostly for the Homestead Grays of the Negro National League, who was elected in 1972 to the Baseball Hall of Fame in Cooperstown, NY. Gibson is said to have hit 75 round-trippers in one season, in 1931, but no official records were kept.

The most officially recorded home runs hit by a professional player in the US in one season is 72, by Joe Bauman, of the Rosewell, NM team, a minor league club, in 1954. The major league record is 61 by Roger Maris, of the NY Yankees, in 1961.

The most home runs in a professional game is 8, by Justin Clarke of the Corsicana, Tex, minor league team, on June 15, 1902. The major league record is 4, by 10 players.

Frank Robinson (b Aug 31, 1935) hit home runs in the most major league ballparks—at least one in 32 different stadiums during regular season games from 1956–1977.

The longest home run ever measured was one of 618 ft by Roy Edward "Dizzy" Carlyle (1900–56) in a minor league game at Emeryville Ball Park, Calif, July 4, 1929. Babe Ruth hit a 587-ft homer for the Boston Red Sox vs NY Giants in an exhibition game

HOMERS OF THE BRAVES: Hank Aaron follows through on his swing for his 700th home run, hit on July 21, 1973, in Atlanta. Although best known for his career record 755 round trippers, Aaron also set major league career marks by appearing in 3,298 games, driving in 2,297 runs and hitting for 6,856 total bases. (Atlanta Braves)

at Tampa, Fla, in 1919. The longest measured home run in a regular-season major league game is 565 ft by Mickey Mantle (b Oct 20, 1931) for the NY Yankees vs Washington Senators on Apr 17, 1953, at Griffith Stadium, Wash DC.

Fastest Pitcher

The fastest pitcher in the world is L. Nolan Ryan (now with the Houston Astros) who, on Aug 20, 1974, in Anaheim Stadium, Calif, was electronically clocked at a speed of 100.9 mph.

Longest Throw

The longest throw of a 5-5¼-oz (regulation) baseball is 445 ft 10 in by Glen Gorbous (b Canada) Aug 1, 1957. Mildred "Babe" Didrikson (later Mrs George Zaharias) (1914–56) threw a ball 296 ft at Jersey City, NJ, July 25, 1931.

Fastest Base Runner

Ernest Evar Swanson (1902–73) took only 13.3 sec to circle the bases at Columbus, Ohio, in 1932, averaging 18.45 mph.

Hit by Pitch

Ron Hunt, an infielder who played with various National League teams from 1963 to 1974, led the league in getting hit by pitched balls for a record 7 consecutive years. His career total is 243, also a major league record.

Youngest and Oldest Players

The youngest major league player of all time was the Cincinnati pitcher Joe Nuxhall, who started his career in June 1944, aged 15 years 10 months 11 days.

Leroy Satchel Paige (1906?–82) pitched three scoreless innings for the Kansas City Athletics at age 59 in 1965. Baseball's color barrier had kept him out of the major leagues until 1948, when he was a 42-year-old "rookie," and his record of 6 wins and 1 loss helped the Cleveland Indians win the pennant. His birthday is listed as July 7, 1906, but many believe he was born earlier. The Atlanta Braves carried Paige on their roster in 1968 to allow him to qualify for a pension.

Shortest and Tallest Players

The shortest major league player was surely Eddie Gaedel, a 3-ft-7-in, 65-lb midget, who pinch hit for the St Louis Browns vs the Detroit Tigers on Aug 19, 1951. Wearing number ⅛, the batter with the smallest ever major league strike zone walked on four pitches. Following the game, major league rules were hastily rewritten to prevent the recurrence of such an affair.

SHORT CAREER: Eddie Gaedel, at 43 in tall, made only one plate appearance in the major leagues, leading off the bottom of the first inning as a pinch hitter. After walking on four pitches, the smallest ever major leaguer was replaced by a pinch runner. The affair was the brainchild of Bill Veeck, who claims his epitaph will read, "He helped the little man." (UPI)

OLD-TIMER'S DAY: After a legendary career in the Negro leagues, Satchel Paige made it to the majors as a rookie when he was 42 years old or older. Paige enjoyed contributing to the confusion that surrounded his birth date. In his last major league appearance, he was 59—or was he? (UPI)

Fastball pitcher James Rodney Richard (b March 7, 1950) of the Houston Astros is probably the tallest ever major league ballplayer at 6 ft 8½ in, a measurement confirmed by the Astro's front office despite Richard's official listing as 6 ft 8 in.

Do-Nothing Record

Toby Harrah of the Texas Rangers (AL) played an entire doubleheader at shortstop on June 26, 1976, without having a chance to make any fielding plays, assists or putouts.

Do-Everything Record

Two major league ballplayers, Bert Campaneris (b Mar 12, 1942) and Cesar Tovar (b July 3, 1940), have the distinction of playing each of the nine field positions in a single major league game. Campaneris did it first, on Sept 8, 1965, when his team, the Kansas City Athletics, announced he would. He played

one inning at each position, including the full eighth inning as a pitcher and gave up just one run. Tovar duplicated the feat on Sept 22, 1968, when he played for the Minnesota Twins. He pitched a scoreless first inning and retired the first batter, none other than Campaneris.

Tale of Two Cities Record

Joel Youngblood (b Aug 28, 1951) started a day game at Wrigley Field in Chicago on Aug 4, 1982, as a NY Met, hit a single in the 3rd inning, left the game when he received word that he had been traded to the Montreal Expos, and immediately made plane reservations to Philadelphia where the Expos were playing a night game. He had dinner on the plane, took a taxi from the airport, arrived at the field in the 3rd inning, was substituted for the Expos' right fielder in the 6th inning, and got a single in his one time at bat. His record: playing (and getting a hit) for two different teams in two different cities in the same day. Other major leaguers have played for two teams in one day, but in only one city as they were swapped between games of a doubleheader.

Longest and Shortest Games

The longest professional game was a minor league contest of 33 innings, finally won by the Pawtucket Red Sox, 3–2, over the Rochester Red Wings. The game began at 8 p.m. on Apr 18, 1981 and was suspended, tied at 2–2, at 4:07 a.m. after 32 innings. The game was completed in just 18 min on June 23, 1981, for a total playing time of 8 hours 25 min. The 19 spectators remaining at McCoy Stadium, Pawtucket, RI, at the end of the 32nd inning were given season passes.

In the major leagues the Brooklyn Dodgers and Boston Braves played to a 1–1 tie after 26 innings on May 1, 1920. The SF Giants beat the NY Mets, 8–6, in 23 innings in a game that lasted 7 hours 23 min and was the second game of a doubleheader on May 31, 1964. The NY Giants needed only 51 min to beat the Philadelphia Phillies, 6–1, in 9 innings on Sept 28, 1919.

Managers

Connie Mack (1892–1956) managed in the major leagues for 53 seasons—3 with Pittsburgh (NL), 1894–96, and 50 with the Philadelphia Athletics (AL), the team he owned, 1901–50. He amassed a record 3,776 regular-season victories (952 victories ahead of John McGraw). Eddie Stanky managed the Texas Rangers (AL) for one day (June 23, 1977) before deciding he did not want the job—even though his team beat Minnesota, 10–8. It is believed to be the shortest term for anyone who signed a managerial contract (that is, excluding interim managers).

Charles D. "Casey" Stengel (1890–1975) set records by managing the NY Yankees (AL) in 10 World Series and winning 7 of them, including 5 in a row (1949–53).

Most Intensive Spectating

Bill Rattray and Joe Hoban of Houston and Miles Berry of LA watched all 26 major league teams in one week, Apr 9–15, in 13 cities in the US and Canada, a round trip of 14,153 miles.

World Series Attendance

The World Series record attendance is 420,784 (6 games with total gate receipts of $2,626,973.44) when the Los Angeles Dodgers beat the Chicago White Sox 4 games to 2, Oct 1–8, 1959.

The single game record is 92,706 for the fifth game (gate receipts $552,774.77) at the Memorial Coliseum (no longer used for baseball), LA, Oct 6, 1959.

ROOTING AROUND: Despite the cold and snow that bedeviled the opening of the 1982 season, these 3 fans (left to right: Joe Hoban, Miles Berry and Bill Rattray), here with friends in St Louis, saw all 26 major league teams in only 7 days.

MAJOR LEAGUE ALL-TIME RECORDS

(including 1981 season)

Individual Batting

Highest percentage, lifetime (5,000 at-bats)
.367 Tyrus R. Cobb, Det AL, 1905–26; Phil AL, 1927–28

Highest percentage, season (500 at-bats) (Leader in each league)
.438 Hugh Duffy, Bos NL, 1894
.422 Napoleon Lajoie, Phil AL, 1901

Most consecutive games played
2,130 Henry Louis Gehrig, NY AL, June 1, 1925 through Apr 30, 1939

Most runs batted in, season
190 Lewis R. (Hack) Wilson, Chi NL, 155 games, 1930

Most runs batted in, game
12 James L. Bottomley, St L NL, Sept 16, 1924

Most runs batted in, inning
7 Edward Cartwright, St L AA, Sept 23, 1890

Most runs batted in, lifetime
2,297 Henry L. Aaron, Mil NL, 1954–65, Atl NL, 1966–74; Mil AL, 1975–76

Most base hits, season
257 George H. Sisler, St L AL, 154 games, 1920

Most hits in succession
12 M. Frank (Pinky) Higgins, Bos AL, June 19–21 (4 games), 1938
Walter Dropo, Det AL, July 14, July 15, 2 games, 1952

Most base hits, consecutive, game
7 Wilbert Robinson, Balt NL, June 10, 1892, 1st game (7-ab), 6-1b, 1-2b
Renaldo Stennett, Pitt NL, Sept 16, 1975 (7-ab), 4-1b, 2-2b, 1-3b
Cesar Gutierrez, Det AL, June 21, 1970, 2nd game (7-ab) 6-1b, 1-2b (extra-inning game)

Most consecutive games batted safely, season
56 Joseph P. DiMaggio, NY AL (91 hits—16-2b, 4-3b, 15 hr), May 15 to July 16, 1941

Most total bases, lifetime
6,856 Henry L. Aaron, Mil NL, 1954–65, Atl NL, 1966–74; Mil AL, 1975–76

Most total bases, season
457 George H. (Babe) Ruth, NY AL, 152 gs (85 on 1b, 88 on 2b, 48 on 3b, 236 on hr), 1921

Most total bases, game
18 Joseph W. Adcock, Mil NL (1-2b, 4-hr), July 31, 1954

Most one-base hits (singles), season
202 William H. Keeler, Balt NL, 128 games, 1898

Most two-base hits, season
67 Earl W. Webb, Bos AL, 151 games, 1931

Most three-base hits, season
36 J. Owen Wilson, Pitts NL, 152 games, 1912

Most home runs, season
61 Roger E. Maris, NY AL (162-game schedule) (30 home, 31 away), 161 gs, 1961

60 George H. (Babe) Ruth, NY AL (154-game schedule) (28 home, 32 away), 151 gs, 1927

Most base hits
4,191 Tyrus R. Cobb, Det AL, 1905–26; Phil AL, 1927–28; 24 years

Most home runs, lifetime
755 Henry L. Aaron, Mil NL, 1954 (13), 1955 (27), 1956 (26), 1957 (44), 1958 (30), 1959 (39), 1960 (40), 1961 (34), 1962 (45), 1963 (44), 1964 (24), 1965 (32); Atl NL, 1966 (44), 1967 (39), 1968 (29), 1969 (44), 1970 (38), 1971 (47), 1972 (34), 1973 (40), 1974 (20); Mil AL, 1975 (12), 1976 (10)

Most home runs, bases filled, lifetime
23 Henry Louis Gehrig, NY AL, 1927–1938

Most home runs with bases filled, season
5 Ernest Banks, Chi NL, May 11, 19, July 17 (1st game), Aug 2, Sept 19, 1955
James E. Gentile, Balt AL, May 9 (2), July 2, 7, Sept 22, 1961

Most home runs, with bases filled, same game
2 Anthony M. Lazzeri, NY AL, May 24, 1936
James R. Tabor, Bos AL (2nd game), July 4, 1939
Rudolph York, Bos AL, July 27, 1946
James E. Gentile, Balt AL, May 9, 1961 (consecutive at-bats)
Tony L. Cloninger, Atl NL, July 3, 1966
James T. Northrup Det AL, June 24, 1968 (consecutive at-bats)
Frank Robinson, Balt AL, June 26, 1970 (consecutive at-bats)

Most consecutive games hitting home runs
8 R. Dale Long, Pitt NL, May 19–28, 1956

Most home runs, one doubleheader
5 Stanley F. Musial, St L NL, 1st game (3), 2nd game (2), May 2, 1954
Nathan Colbert, SD NL, 1st game (2), 2nd game (3), Aug 1, 1972

Most bases on balls, game
6 James E. Foxx, Bos AL, June 16, 1938

Most bases on balls, season
170 George H. (Babe) Ruth, NY AL, 152 games, 1923

Most hits, pinch-hitter, lifetime
150 Manuel R. Mota, SF NL, 1962; Pitt NL, 1963–1968; Mont NL, 1969; LA NL, 1969–1980

Most consecutive pinch hits, lifetime
9 David E. Philley, Phil NL, Sept 9, 11, 12, 13, 19, 20, 27, 28, 1958; Apr 16, 1959

Most consecutive home runs, pinch-hitter
3 Del Unser, Phil NL, June 30, July 5, 10, 1979
Lee Lacy, LA NL, May 2, 6, 17, 1978 (one walk in between)

Base Running

Most stolen bases, lifetime
938 Louis C. Brock, Chi-St L NL, 1961–79

Most stolen bases, season since 1900
118* Louis C. Brock, St L NL, 153 games, 1974

Most stolen bases, game
7 George F. (Piano Legs) Gore, Chi NL, June 25, 1881
William R. (Sliding Billy) Hamilton, Phil NL, 2nd game, 8 inn, Aug 31, 1894

---

* As of Aug 9, 1982, Ricky Henderson of Oakland had 105 stolen bases—a record pace.

LUCKY CARDS: Stan "The Man" Musial had a good day on May 2, 1954—he hit 5 homers in a doubleheader. In his first 6 seasons with the St Louis Cardinals, Musial helped lead them to 4 pennants and 3 World Series titles. Using an odd, peek-a-boo batting stance, he amassed 3,630 hits in the majors for a .331 lifetime batting average. (St Louis Cardinals)

Base Running (continued)

Most times stealing home, lifetime
  35 Tyrus R. Cobb, Det-Phil AL, 1905–28

Fewest times caught stealing, season (50+ attempts)
  2 Max Carey, Pitt NL, 1922 (53 atts)

Pitching

Most games, lifetime
  1,070 J. Hoyt Wilhelm, NY-St L-Atl-Chi-LA (448) NL, 1952–57, 69–72; Clev-Balt-Chi-Cal (622) AL, 1957–69

Most games, season
  106 Mike Marshall, LA NL, 1974

Most complete games, lifetime
  751 Denton T. (Cy) Young, Clev-St L-Bos NL (428); Bos-Clev AL (323), 1890–1911

Most complete games, season
  74 William H. White, Cin NL, 1879

Most innings pitched, game
  26 Leon J. Cadore, Bklyn NL, May 1, 1920
      Joseph Oeschger, Bos NL, May 1, 1920

Lowest earned run average, season
  0.90 Ferdinand M. Schupp, NY NL, 1916 (140 inn)
  1.01 Hubert B. (Dutch) Leonard, Bos AL, 1914 (222 inn)
  1.12 Robert Gibson, St L NL, 1968 (305 inn)

Most games won, lifetime
  511 Denton T. (Cy) Young, Clev NL (239) 1890–98; St L NL (46) 1899–1900; Bos AL (193) 1901–08; Clev AL (29) 1909–11; Bos NL (4) 1911

Most games won, season
  60 Charles Radbourn, Providence NL, 1884

Most consecutive games won, lifetime
  24 Carl O. Hubbell, NY NL, 1936 (16); 1937 (8)

Most consecutive games won, season
  19 Timothy J. Keefe, NY NL, 1888
      Richard W. Marquard, NY NL, 1912

Most shutout games, season
  16 George W. Bradley, St L NL, 1876
      Grover C. Alexander, Phil NL, 1916

Most shutout games, lifetime
  113 Walter P. Johnson, Wash AL, 21 years, 1907–27

Most consecutive shutout games, season
  6 Donald S. Drysdale, LA NL, May 14, 18, 22, 26, 31, June 4, 1968

Most consecutive shutout innings
  58 Donald S. Drysdale, LA NL, May 14-June 8, 1968

Perfect game—9 innings
  1880 John Lee Richmond, Worcester vs Clev NL, June 12   1–0
        John M. Ward, Prov vs Buff NL, June 17 AM   5–0
  1904 Denton T. (Cy) Young, Bos vs Phil AL, May 5   3–0
  1908 Adrian C. Joss, Clev vs Chi AL, Oct 2   1–0
  †1917 Ernest G. Shore, Bos vs Wash AL, June 23 (1st g)   4–0
  1922 C. C. Robertson, Chi vs Det AL, Apr 30   2–0
  *1956 Donald J. Larsen, NY AL vs Bklyn NL, Oct 8   2–0
  1964 James P. Bunning, Phil NL vs NY, June 21 (1st g)   6–0
  1965 Sanford Koufax, LA NL vs Chi, Sept 9   1–0
  1968 James A. Hunter, Oak AL vs Minn, May 8   4–0
  1981 Leonard H. Barker II, Cleve AL vs Tor, May 15   3–0
Special mention
  1959 Harvey Haddix, Jr, Pitt vs Mil NL, May 26, pitched 12 perfect innings, allowed hit in 13th and lost.

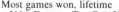

A TRAIN TO CATCH: Walter "Big Train" Johnson's career record of 3,508 strikeouts has stood since 1927, but now 4 major league pitchers are threatening to surpass it (strikeout totals to end of 1981): Gaylord Perry (3,336), Nolan Ryan (3,249), Steve Carlton (3,148), and Tom Seaver (3,075). No one, however, is close to matching Johnson's record 113 shutouts. (UPI)

---

†Starting pitcher, "Babe" Ruth, was banished from game by Umpire Owens after giving first batter, Morgan, a base on balls. Shore relieved and while he pitched to second batter, Morgan was caught stealing. Shore then retired next 26 batters to complete "perfect" game.
*World Series game.

PERFECT PITCH: The scoreboard tells the story as Don Larsen's 97th (and final) pitch flies toward home plate (it was a called third strike) to complete the only perfect game in World Series play. The Yankee second baseman in the photo is Billy Martin, the always fiery (and sometimes fired) big-league manager. (UPI)

Most strikeouts, lifetime
3,508 Walter P. Johnson, Wash AL, 1907–27

Most strikeouts, season
505 Matthew Kilroy, Balt AA, 1886 (Distance 50 ft)

383 L. Nolan Ryan, Cal AL, 1973 (Distance 60 ft 6 in)

Most strikeouts, game (9 inn) since 1900
19 Steven N. Carlton, St L NL vs NY, Sept 15, 1969 (lost)
G. Thomas Seaver, NY NL vs SD, Apr 22, 1970
L. Nolan Ryan, Cal AL, vs Bos, Aug 12, 1974

Most strikeouts, extra-inning game
21 Thomas E. Cheney, Wash AL vs Balt (16 inns), Sept 12, 1962 (night)

Most no-hit games, lifetime
5 L. Nolan Ryan, Cal AL, 1973 (2)–74–75; Hou NL, 1981

Most consecutive no-hit games
2 John S. Vander Meer, Cin NL, June 11–15, 1938

World Series Records

Most series played
14 Lawrence P. (Yogi) Berra, NY, AL, 1947, 49–53, 55–58, 60–63

Highest batting percentage (20 g min.), total series
.391 Louis C. Brock, St L NL, 1964, 67–68 (g-21, ab-87, h-34)

Highest batting percentage, 4 or more games, one series
.625 4-game series, George H. (Babe) Ruth, NY AL, 1928

Most runs, total series
42 Mickey C. Mantle, NY AL, 1951–53, 55–58, 60–64

Most runs, one series
10 Reginald M. Jackson, NY AL, 1977

Most runs batted in, total series
40 Mickey C. Mantle, NY, AL, 1951–53, 55–58, 60–64

Most runs batted in, game
6 Robert C. Richardson, NY AL, (4) 1st inn, (2) 4th inn, Oct 8, 1960

Most runs batted in, consecutive times at bat
7 James L. (Dusty) Rhodes, NY NL, first 4 times at bat, 1954

Most base hits, total series
71 Lawrence P. (Yogi) Berra, NY AL, 1947, 49–53, 55–58, 60–61

Most home runs, total series
18 Mickey C. Mantle, NY AL, 1952 (2), 53 (2), 55, 56 (3), 57, 58 (2), 60 (3), 63, 64 (3)

Most home runs, one series
5 Reginald M. Jackson, NY AL, 1977

Most home runs, game
3 George H. (Babe) Ruth, NY AL, Oct 6, 1926; Oct 9, 1928
Reginald M. Jackson, NY AL, Oct 18, 1977

Pitching in most series
11 Edward C. (Whitey) Ford, NY AL, 1950, 53, 55–58, 60–64

Most victories, total series
10 Edward C. (Whitey) Ford, NY AL, 1950 (1), 55 (2), 56 (1), 57 (1), 60 (2), 61 (2), 62 (1)

Most victories, no defeats
6 Vernon L. (Lefty) Gomez, NY AL, 1932 (1), 36 (2), 37 (2), 38 (1)

Most games won, one series
3 games in 5-game series
Christy Mathewson, NY NL, 1905
J. W. Coombs, Phil AL, 1910
Many others won 3 games in series of more games.

Most shutout games, total series
4 Christy Mathewson, NY NL 1905 (3), 1913

Most shutout games, one series
3 Christy Mathewson, NY NL 1905

Most strikeouts, one pitcher, total series
94 Edward C. (Whitey) Ford, NY AL, 1950, 53, 55–58, 60–64

Most strikeouts, one series
23 in 4 games
Sanford Koufax, LA NL, 1963
18 in 5 games
Christy Mathewson, NY NL, 1905
20 in 6 games
C. A. (Chief) Bender, Phil AL, 1911
35 in 7 games
Robert Gibson, St L NL, 1968
28 in 8 games
W. H. Dinneen, Bos AL, 1903

Most strikeouts, one pitcher, game
17 Robert Gibson, St L NL, Oct 2, 1968

Most Series Won
22 New York AL, 1923, 1927, 1928, 1932, 1936–39, 1941, 1943, 1947, 1949–53, 1956, 1958, 1961, 1962, 1977, 1978

BASKETBALL

Origins

Ollamalitzli was a 16th century Aztec precursor of basketball played in Mexico. If the solid rubber ball was put through a fixed stone ring placed high on one side of the stadium, the player was entitled to the clothing of all the spectators. The captain of the losing team often lost his head (by execution). Another game played much earlier, in the 10th century BC by the Olmecs in Mexico, called *Pok-ta-Pok,* also resembled basketball in its concept of a ring through which a round object was passed.

Modern basketball (which may have been based on the German game of *Korbball*) was devised by the Canadian-born Dr James A. Naismith (1861–1939) at the Training School of the International YMCA College at Springfield, Mass, in Dec 1891. The first game played under modified rules was on Jan 20, 1892. The first public contest was on March 11, 1892.

The International Amateur Basketball Federation (FIBA) was founded in 1932.

Most Accurate Shooting

The greatest goal-shooting demonstration was made by a professional, Ted St. Martin, now of Jacksonville, Fla, who, on June 25, 1977, scored 2,036 consecutive free throws.

Using 2 basketballs and 2 rebounders, Robert Kyle, 26, made 240 free throws (of 317 attempts) in 10 min on May 19, 1982, in Mecca, Ind.

In a 24-hour period, May 31–June 1, 1975, Fred L. Newman of San Jose, Calif, scored 12,874 baskets out of 13,116 attempts (98.15%). Newman has also made 88 consecutive free throws while blindfolded at the Central YMCA, San Jose, Calif, Feb 5, 1978.

The longest reported string of consecutive free throws made at any level of organized game competition is 126 by Daryl Moreau over 2 seasons (Jan 17, 1978–Jan 9, 1979) of high school play for De La Salle in New Orleans, La.

Longest Field Goal

The longest *measured* field goal in a college game was made from a measured distance of 89 ft 3 in by Les Henson for Virginia Tech vs Florida State, Jan 21, 1980. In an AAU game at Pacific Lutheran University on Jan 16, 1970, Steve Myers sank a shot while standing out of bounds at the other end of the court. Though the basket was illegal, the officials gave in to crowd sentiment and allowed the points to count. The distance is claimed to be 92 ft 3½ in from measurements made 10 years later.

Individual Scoring

Marie Boyd (now Eichler) scored 156 points in a girls' high school basketball game for Central HS, Lonaconing, Md, in a 163–3 victory over Ursaline Academy, on Feb 25, 1924. The boys' high school record is 135 points by Danny Heater of Burnsville, W Va, on Jan 26, 1960.

In college play, Clarence (Bevo) Francis of Rio Grande College, Ohio, scored 113 points against Hillsdale on Feb 2, 1954. One year earlier, Francis scored 116 points in a game, but the record was disallowed because the competition was with a two-year school.

Wilton Norman (Wilt) Chamberlain (b Aug 21, 1936) holds the professional record with 100 points for the Philadelphia Warriors vs NY Knicks, scored

THROUGH THE HOOP: Bevo Francis helped rescue tiny Rio Grande College when his scoring feats attracted large paying crowds around the country. In 1953–54, Francis averaged 46.5 points per game, including his record 113-point performance. (UPI)

on March 2, 1962. During the same season, Wilt set the record for points in a season (4,029) and he also holds the career record (31,419).

Pearl Moore of Francis Marion College, Florence, SC, scored a record 4,061 points during her college career, 1975–79. The men's college career scoring record is 4,045 points by Travis Grant for Kentucky State, 1969–72.

Mats Wermelin (Sweden), 13, scored all 272 points in a 272–0 win in a regional boys' tournament in Stockholm, Sweden, on Feb 5, 1974.

Tallest Players

The tallest player of all time is reputed to be Suleiman Ali Nashnush (b 1943) who played for the Libyan team in 1962 when he measured 8 ft tall. Aleksandr Sizonenko of Kuibyshev Stroitel and USSR is 7 ft 10 in tall. The tallest woman player is Iuliana Semenova (USSR) who is reputed to stand 7 ft 2 in tall and weigh 281 lb.

Youngest and Oldest

Bill Willoughby (b May 20, 1957) made his NBA debut for the Atlanta Hawks on Oct 23, 1975, when he was 18 years 5 months 3 days old. The oldest NBA player was Bob Cousy (b Aug 9, 1928), who was 41 years 6 months 2 days old when he appeared in the last of seven games he played for the team he was coaching (Cincinnati Royals) during 1969–70.

NBA Championships

The most National Basketball Association titles (instituted 1947) have been won by the Boston Celtics with 14 championships between 1957 and 1981. The Celtics also hold the record for consecutive championships with 8 (1959–66).

Olympic Champions

The US won all 7 Olympic titles from the time the sport was introduced to the Games in 1936 until 1968, without losing a single contest. In 1972, in Munich, their run of 63 consecutive victories was broken when they lost, 51–50, to the USSR in a much-disputed final game. They regained the Olympic title in Montreal in 1976, again without losing a game.

World Champions

Brazil, the USSR and Yugoslavia are the only countries to win the World Men's Championship

WHEN IN ROME: Although best remembered as an NBA star, Oscar Robertson also won an Olympic gold medal in Rome in 1960, playing on a US squad that also included Jerry West, Terry Dischinger, Walt Bellamy, Jerry Lucas, Darrell Imhoff, Bob Boozer, Adrian Smith and others. Some consider that team to be the best amateur squad ever assembled.

(instituted 1950) on more than one occasion. Brazil won in 1959 and 1963; the USSR in 1967 and 1974; Yugoslavia in 1970 and 1978.

In 1975, the USSR won the women's championship (instituted 1953) for the fifth consecutive time since 1959.

Marathon

The longest game is 90 hours 2 min by two teams of five at Jordanhill College of Education, Glasgow, Scotland, Mar 23–27, 1981.

Greatest Attendances

The Harlem Globetrotters played an exhibition to 75,000 in the Olympic Stadium, West Berlin, Germany, in 1951. The largest indoor basketball crowd was at the Superdome, New Orleans, La, where admissions of 61,612 were recorded for both the semifinal doubleheader (Mar 27, 1982) and final game (UNC vs Georgetown, Mar 29, 1982) of the 1982 NCAA Division One Tournament.

NBA REGULAR SEASON RECORDS (INCLUDING 1981–82)

The National Basketball Association's Championship series was established in 1947. Prior to 1949, when it joined with the National Basketball League, the professional circuit was known as the Basketball Association of America.

SERVICE

Most Games, Lifetime
1,270 John Havlicek, Bos 1963–78

Most Games, Consecutive, Lifetime
844 John Kerr, Syr-Phil-Balt Oct 31, 1954–Nov 4, 1965

Most Complete Games, Season
79 Wilt Chamberlain, Phil 1962

Most Minutes, Lifetime
47,859 Wilt Chamberlain, Phil-SF-LA 1960–73

Most Minutes, Season
3,882 Wilt Chamberlain, Phil 1962

SCORING

Most Seasons Leading League
7 Wilt Chamberlain, Phil 1960–62; SF 1963–64; SF-Phil 1965; Phil 1966

Most Points, Lifetime
31,419 Wilt Chamberlain, Phil-SF-LA 1960–73

Most Points, Season
4,029 Wilt Chamberlain, Phil 1962

Most Points, Game
100 Wilt Chamberlain, Phil vs NY, Mar 2, 1962

Most Points, Half
59 Wilt Chamberlain, Phil vs NY, Mar 2, 1962

Most Points, Quarter
33 George Gervin, SA vs NO, Apr 9, 1978

Most Points, Overtime Period
13 Earl Monroe, Balt vs Det, Feb 6, 1970
Joe Caldwell, Atl vs Cin, Feb 18, 1970

Highest Scoring Average, Lifetime (400+ games)
30.1 Wilt Chamberlain, Phil-SF-LA 1960–73

Highest Scoring Average, Season
50.4 Wilt Chamberlain, Phil 1962

Field Goals Made

Most Field Goals, Lifetime
12,681 Wilt Chamberlain, Phil-SF-LA 1960–73

Most Field Goals, Season
1,597 Wilt Chamberlain, Phil 1962

Most Field Goals, Game
36 Wilt Chamberlain, Phil vs NY, Mar 2, 1962

Most Field Goals, Half
22 Wilt Chamberlain, Phil vs NY, Mar 2, 1962

Most Field Goals, Quarter
13 David Thompson, Den vs Det, Apr 9, 1978

Most 3-Point Field Goals, Game
8 Rick Barry, Hou vs Utah, Feb 9, 1980
John Roche, Den vs Sea, Jan 9, 1982

Most 3-Point Field Goals, Season
73 Don Buse, Ind 1982

Field Goal Percentage

Most Seasons Leading League
9 Wilt Chamberlain, Phil 1961; SF 1963; SF-Phil 1965; Phil 1966–68; LA 1969, 72–73

Highest Percentage, Lifetime
.588 Artis Gilmore, Chi 1977–82

BULLS' EYE: After 5 seasons with the Chicago Bulls, Artis Gilmore leads the NBA with his .588 lifetime field goal percentage, up .011 after the 1981–82 season. Despite this NBA record, the Bulls traded away the 7-ft-2-in center after the 1982 playoffs had ended. (Chicago Bulls)

MURPHY'S LAW: It didn't pay to foul Calvin Murphy (#23 in white) during the 1980–81 season. That season the 5-ft-10-guard made 95.7% of his free throws, including 78 straight without a miss. (Houston Rockets)

Most Rebounds, Quarter
18 Nate Thurmond, SF vs Balt, Feb 28, 1965

Highest Average (per game), Lifetime
22.9 Wilt Chamberlain, Phil-SF-LA 1960–73

Highest Average (per game), Season
27.2 Wilt Chamberlain, Phil 1961

ASSISTS

Most Seasons Leading League
8 Bob Cousy, Bos 1953–60

Most Assists, Lifetime
9,887 Oscar Robertson, Cin-Mil 1961–74

Most Assists, Season
1,099 Kevin Porter, Det 1979

Most Assists, Game
29 Kevin Porter, NJ vs Hou Feb 24, 1978

Most Assists, Half
19 Bob Cousy, Bos vs Minn, Feb 27, 1959

Most Assists, Quarter
12 Bob Cousy, Bos vs Minn, Feb 27, 1959
John Lucas, Hou vs Mil, Oct 27, 1977

Highest Average (per game), Lifetime
9.5 Oscar Robertson, Cin-Mil 1961–74

Highest Average (per game), Season
13.4 Kevin Porter, Det 1979

PERSONAL FOULS

Most Personal Fouls, Lifetime
3,855 Hal Greer, Syr-Phil 1959–73

Most Personal Fouls, Season
372 Steve Johnson, KC 1982

Most Personal Fouls, Game
8 Don Otten, TC vs Sheb, Nov 24, 1949

DISQUALIFICATIONS
(Fouling Out of Game)

Most Disqualifications, Lifetime
127 Vern Mikkelsen, Minn, 1950–59

Most Disqualifications, Season
26 Don Meineke, Ft W 1953

Most Games, No Disqualifications, Lifetime
1,045 Wilt Chamberlain, Phil-SF-LA 1960–73 (Entire Career)

Highest Percentage, Season
.727 Wilt Chamberlain, LA 1973

Free Throws Made

Most Free Throws Made, Lifetime
7,694 Oscar Robertson, Cin-Mil 1961–74

Most Free Throws Made, Season
840 Jerry West, LA 1966

Most Free Throws Made, Consecutive, Season
78 Calvin Murphy, Hou Dec 27, 1980–Feb 28, 1981

Most Free Throws Made, Game
28 Wilt Chamberlain, Phil vs NY, Mar 2, 1962
Bill Cartwright, NY vs KC, Nov 17, 1982

Most Free Throws Made (No Misses), Game
19 Bob Pettit, St L vs Bos, Nov 22, 1961

Most Free Throws Made, Half
19 Oscar Robertson, Cin vs Balt, Dec 27, 1964

Most Free Throws Made, Quarter
14 Rick Barry, SF vs NY, Dec 6, 1966

Free Throw Percentage

Most Seasons Leading League
7 Bill Sharman, Bos 1953–57, 59, 61

Highest Percentage, Lifetime
.900 Rick Barry, SF-GS-Hou 1966–67, 73–80

Highest Percentage, Season
.957 Calvin Murphy, Hou 1981

REBOUNDS

Most Seasons Leading League
11 Wilt Chamberlain, Phil 1960–62; SF 1963; Phil 1966–68; LA 1969, 71–73

Most Rebounds, Lifetime
23,924 Wilt Chamberlain, Phil-SF-LA 1960–73

Most Rebounds, Season
2,149 Wilt Chamberlain, Phil 1961

Most Rebounds, Game
55 Wilt Chamberlain, Phil vs Bos, Nov 24, 1960

Most Rebounds, Half
32 Bill Russell, Bos vs Phil, Nov 16, 1957

BOBSLEDDING AND TOBOGGANING

Origins

The oldest known sled is dated *c.* 6500 BC and came from Heinola, Finland. The first known bobsled race took place at Davos, Switzerland, in 1889. The International Federation of Bobsleigh and Tobogganing was formed in 1923, followed by the International Bobsleigh Federation in 1957.

Olympic and World Titles

The Olympic 4-man bob title (instituted 1924) has been won 4 times by Switzerland (1924, 36, 56, 72). The US (1932, 36), Switzerland (1948, 80), Italy (1956, 68) and W Germany (1952, 72) have won the Olympic boblet event (instituted 1932) twice. The most gold medals won by an individual is 3 by Meinhard Nehmer (b June 13, 1941) (E Germany) and Bernhard Germeshausen (b Aug 21, 1951) (E Germany) in the 1976 two-man, 1976 and 1980 four-man events. The most medals won is 6 (2 gold, 2 silver, 2 bronze) by Eugenio Monti (Italy) (b Jan 23, 1928) from 1956 to 1968.

The world 4-man bob has been won 13 times by Switzerland (1924, 36, 39, 47, 54–57, 71–73, 75, 82). Italy won the 2-man title 14 times (1954, 56–63, 66, 68–69, 71, 75). Eugenio Monti has been a member of 11 world championship crews, 8 two-man and 3 four-man.

Tobogganing

The word toboggan comes from the Micmac American Indian word *tobaakan.* The oldest tobogganing club in the world, founded in 1887, is at St Moritz, Switzerland, home of the Cresta Run, which dates from 1884, and site of the introduction of the skeleton one-man racing toboggan.

On the Cresta Run, the record from the Junction (2,913 ft) is 42.96 sec (average 63.08 mph) by Poldi Berchtold of Switzerland on Feb 22, 1975. The record from the top (3,977 ft long with a drop of 514 ft) is 53.24 sec (average speed 50.92 mph), also by Berchtold on Feb 9, 1975. Speeds of 90 mph are occasionally attained.

The greatest number of wins in the Grand National (instituted 1885) is eight by the 1948 Olympic champion Nino Bibbia (Italy) (b Sept 9, 1924) in 1960–64, 66, 68, 73. The greatest number of wins in the Curzon Cup (instituted in 1910) is eight by Bib-

bia in 1950, 57–58, 60, 62–64, 69, who hence won the double in 1960, 62–64.

Lugeing

In lugeing the rider adopts a sitting, as opposed to a prone position. Official international competition began at Klosters, Switzerland, in 1881. The first European championships were at Reichenberg (now East) Germany, in 1914 and the first world championships at Oslo, Norway, in 1953. The International Luge Federation was formed in 1957. Lugeing became an Olympic sport in 1964.

Most Luge World Titles

The most successful rider in the world championships is Thomas Köhler (E Germany) (b June 25, 1940), who won the single-seater title in 1962, 64 (Olympic), 66, and 67, and shared in the two-seater title in 1967 and 68 (Olympic). Margit Schumann (E Germany) (b Sept 14, 1952) has won the women's championship 5 times—in 1973, 74, 75, 76 (Olympic) and 77.

Highest Luge Speed

The highest recorded photo-timed speed is 85.38 mph by Asle Strand (Norway) at Tandådalens Linbane, Sälen, Sweden, on May 1, 1982.

BOWLING

Origins

Bowling can be traced to articles found in the tomb of an Egyptian child of 5200 BC where there were nine pieces of stone to be set up as pins at which a stone "ball" was rolled. The ball first had to roll through an archway made of three pieces of marble. There is also resemblance to a Polynesian game called *ula maika* which utilized pins and balls of stone. The stones were rolled a distance of 60 ft. In the Italian Alps about 2,000 years ago, the underhand tossing of stones at an object is believed the beginnings of *bocci,* a game still widely played in Italy and similar to bowling. The ancient Germans played a game of nine-pins called *Heidenwerfen*—knock down pagans. Martin Luther is credited with the statement that nine was the ideal number of pins. In the British Isles, lawn bowls was preferred to bowling at pins. In the 16th century, bowling at pins was the national sport in Scotland. How bowling at pins came to the US is a matter of controversy. Early British settlers probably brought lawn bowls and set up what is known as Bowling Green at the tip of Manhattan Island in NY but perhaps the Dutch under Henry Hudson were the ones to be credited. Some historians say that in Connecticut the tenth pin was added to evade a legal ban against the nine-pin game in 1845 but others say that tenpins was played in NYC before this and point to Washington Irving's "Rip Van Winkle," written about 1818, as evidence.

Lanes

In the US there were 8,591 bowling establishments with 154,412 lanes in 1980 and about 65 million bowlers.

The world's largest bowling center (now closed) was the Tokyo World Lanes Center, Japan, with 252 lanes. Currently the largest center is the Willow Grove Park Lanes, Philadelphia, which has 116 lanes.

Organizations

The American Bowling Congress (ABC), established in NY on Sept 9, 1895, was the first body to standardize rules, and the organization now comprises 4,800,000 men who bowl in leagues and tournaments. The Women's International Bowling Congress (WIBC) has a membership of 4,200,000. The Professional Bowlers Association (PBA), formed in 1958, comprises nearly 2,200 of the world's best bowlers.

World Championships

The Fédération Internationale des Quilleurs world championships were instituted in 1954. The highest pinfall in the individual men's event is 5,963 for 28 games by Ed Luther (US) at Milwaukee, Wis on Aug 28, 1971.

In the women's event (instituted 1963) the record is 4,720 in 24 games by Bong Coo (Philippines) at Manila, Philippines, Dec 1979.

Marathons

John Francis Damiani bowled for 155 hours 4 min at the Lancaster Lanes, NY, Aug 15–21, 1980.

ABC LEAGUE RECORDS

Highest Scores

The highest individual score for three games is 886 by Allie Brandt of Lockport, NY, on Oct 25, 1939. Glenn Allison, 54, rolled a perfect 900 in a 3-game series in league play on July 1, 1982, at La Habra, Calif, but the ABC refused to recognize the record when an ABC inspector examined the lanes and determined they had been illegally oiled (for other 900 series see *Most Perfect Scores,* below). Highest team score is 3,858 by Budweisers of St Louis on March 12, 1958.

The highest season average attained in sanctioned competition is 240 by John Johns of Canton, Ohio, in 99 games in a 5-man league in 1978–79.

Consecutive Strikes

The record for consecutive strikes in sanctioned match play is 33 by John Pezzin (b 1930) at Toledo, Ohio, on March 4, 1976.

Most Perfect Scores

The highest number of sanctioned 300 games is 27 (through 1980) by Elvin Mesger of Sullivan, Mo. The maximum 900 for a three-game series has been recorded four times in unsanctioned games—by Leo Bentley at Lorain, Ohio, on March 26, 1931; by Joe Sargent at Rochester, NY, in 1934; by Jim Murgie in Philadelphia, on Feb 4, 1937; and by Bob Brown at Roseville Bowl, Calif, on Apr 12, 1980.

ABC TOURNAMENT RECORDS

Highest Individual

Highest three-game series in singles is 801 by Mickey Higham of Kansas City, Mo, in 1977. Best three-game total in any ABC event is 804 by Lou Veit of Milwaukee, Wis, in team in 1977. Jim Godman of Lorain, Ohio, holds the record for a nine-game All-Events total with 2,184 (731–749–704) set in Indianapolis, Ind, in 1974. ABC Hall of Famers Fred Bujack of Detroit, Bill Lillard of Houston, and Nelson Burton Jr of St Louis, have won the most championships with 8 each. Bujack shared in 3 team and 4 team All-Events titles between 1949 and 1955, and also won the individual All-Events title in 1955. Lillard bowled on Regular and team All-Events champions in 1955 and 1956, the Classic team champions in 1962 and 1971, and won regular doubles and All-Events titles in 1956. Burton shared in 3 Classic team titles, 2 Classic doubles titles and has won Classic singles twice and Classic All-Events.

Highest Doubles

The ABC record of 558 was set in 1976 by Les Zikes of Chicago and Tommy Hudson of Akron, Ohio. The record score in a doubles series is 1,453, set in 1952 by John Klares (755) and Steve Nagy (698) of Cleveland.

Perfect Scores

Les Schissler of Denver scored 300 in the Classic team event in 1967, and Ray Williams of Detroit scored 300 in Regular team play in 1974. In all, there have been only thirty-eight 300 games in the ABC tournament through 1980. There have been 20 perfect games in singles, 14 in doubles, and four in team play.

Best Finishes in One Tournament

Les Schissler of Denver won the singles, All-Events, and was on the winning team in 1966 to tie Ed Lubanski of Detroit and Bill Lillard of Houston as the only men to win three ABC crowns in one year. The best four finishes in one ABC tournament were third in singles, second in doubles, third in team and first in All-Events by Bob Strampe, Detroit, in 1967, and first in singles, third in team and doubles and second in All-Events by Paul Kulbaga, Cleveland, in 1960.

Most Tournament Appearances

Bill Doehrman of Fort Wayne, Ind, has competed in 71 consecutive ABC tournaments, beginning in 1908. (No tournaments were held 1943–45.)

Youngest and Oldest Winners

The youngest champion was Ronnie Knapp of New London, Ohio, who was a member of the 1963 Booster team champions when he was 16 years old. The oldest champion was Joe Detloff of Chicago, Ill, who, at the age of 72, was a winner in the 1965 Booster team event. The oldest doubles team in ABC competition totaled 165 years in 1955: Jerry Ameling (83) and Joseph Lehnbeutter (82), both from St Louis.

KEEPS ON ROLLING: Bill Doehrman first entered the ABC Tournament in 1908 and hasn't missed one since. (ABC)

Strikes and Spares in a Row

In the greatest finish to win an ABC title, Ed Shay set a record of 12 strikes in a row in 1958, when he scored a perfect game for a total of 733 in the series.

The most spares in a row is 23, a record set by Lt Hazen Sweet of Battle Creek, Mich, in 1950.

Attendance

Largest attendance on one day for an ABC Tournament was 5,257 in Milwaukee in 1952. The total attendance record was set at Reno, Nev, in 1977 with 174,953 in 89 days.

WIBC RECORDS

Highest Scores

The highest individual score for three games is 853 by Sherrie Langford, 25, in the Clearwater Classic Tournament, Clearwater, Fla, on Feb 19, 1982. Patty Ann of Arlington Heights, Ill, had a record 227 average in league play in the 1979–80 season. The highest 5-woman team score for a 3-game series is 3,379 by Freeway Washer of Cleveland in 1960.

Perfect Games

The most 300 games rolled in a career is 6 by Donna Adamek of Duarte, Calif. The oldest woman to bowl a perfect game was Helen Duval of Berkeley, Calif, at age 66 in 1982. Of all the women who rolled a perfect game, the one with the lowest average was Diane Ponza of Santa Cruz, Calif, who had a 112 average in the 1977–78 season.

Consecutive Strikes, Spares and Splits

The record for most consecutive strikes is shared by three women: Betsy Corrigan of Xenia, Ohio; Sharon Graff of Cleburne, Tex; and Patty Ann of Arlington Heights, Ill. Joan Taylor of Syracuse, NY,

made 27 consecutive spares. Shirley Tophigh of Las Vegas, Nev, holds the unenviable record of rolling 14 consecutive splits.

Championship Tournament

The highest score for a 3-game series in the annual WIBC Championship Tournament is 737 by D. D. Jacobson in the 1972 singles competition. The record for one game is 300 (the only perfect game) by Lori Gensch in the 1979 doubles event.

The most championships won by an individual is 10 by Dorothy Miller of Chicago, Ill, over a 20-year span, 1928–48.

Myrtle Schulte of St Louis has participated in 54 tournaments through 1982. The oldest participant was Ethel Brunnick of Santa Monica, Calif, at age 94 in 1981. Mary Ann Keiper of St Louis was only 5 years old when she participated in the 1952 tournament. The youngest champion was Leila Wagner of Seattle, Wash, who was 18 when she was a member of the championship 5-woman team in 1979.

PBA RECORDS

Most Titles

Earl Anthony of Dublin, Calif, has won a lifetime total of 39 PBA titles through Aug 1982. The record number of titles won in one PBA season is 8, by Mark Roth of North Arlington, NJ, in 1978.

Consecutive Titles

Only three bowlers have ever won three consecutive professional tournaments—Dick Weber in 1961, Johnny Petraglia in 1971, and Mark Roth in 1977.

Highest Earnings

The greatest lifetime earnings on the Professional Bowlers Association circuit have been won by Earl Anthony who has taken home $1,068,156 through Aug 1982. Anthony also holds the season earnings record with $164,735 in 1981.

Perfect Games

A total of 119 perfect (300-point) games were bowled in PBA tournaments in 1979. Dick Weber rolled 3 perfect games in one tournament (Houston) in 1965, as did Billy Hardwick of Louisville, Ky (in the Japan Gold Cup competition) in 1968, Roy

BOWLED THEM OVER: In 20 years of the WIBC Championship Tournament, 1928–48, Dorothy Miller of Chicago earned a record 10 titles. (WIBC)

425

Buckley of Columbus, Ohio (at Chagrin Falls, Ohio) in 1971, John Wilcox (at Detroit), and Norm Meyers of St Louis (at Peoria, Ill) in 1979.

Don Johnson of Las Vegas, Nev, bowled at least one perfect game in 11 consecutive seasons (1965–1975). Guppy Troup, of Savannah, Ga, rolled 6 perfect games on the 1979 tour.

BOXING

Boxing with gloves was depicted on a fresco from the Isle of Thera, Greece, which has been dated to 1520 BC. The earliest prize-ring code of rules was formulated in England, Aug 16, 1743, by the champion pugilist Jack Broughton (1704–89), who reigned from 1729 to 1750. Boxing, which had in 1867 come under the Queensberry Rules, formulated for John Sholto Douglas, 9th Marquess of Queensberry, was not established as a legal sport in Britain until after a ruling of Mr Justice Grantham following the death of Billy Smith (Murray Livingstone) due to a fight on Apr 24, 1901, at Covent Garden, London.

Longest Fight

The longest recorded fight with gloves was between Andy Bowen of New Orleans and Jack Burke in New Orleans, Apr 6–7, 1893. The fight lasted 110 rounds (7 hours 19 min from 9:15 p.m. to 4:34 a.m.) but was declared no contest (later changed to a draw) when both men were unable to continue. The longest recorded bare knuckle fight was one of 6 hours 15 min between James Kelly and Jack Smith at Fiery Creek, Dalesford, Australia, Dec 3, 1855. The greatest recorded number of rounds is 276 in 4 hours 30 min, when Jack Jones beat Patsy Tunney in Cheshire, England, in 1825.

Shortest Fight

There is a distinction between the quickest knockout and the shortest fight. A knockout in 10½ sec (including a 10-sec count) occurred on Sept 26, 1946, when Al Couture struck Ralph Walton while the latter was adjusting his mouthpiece in his corner at Lewiston, Me. If the time was accurately taken it is clear that Couture must have been more than halfway across the ring from his own corner at the opening bell.

The shortest fight on record appears to be one in a Golden Gloves tournament in Minneapolis, Minn,

Nov 4, 1947, when Mike Collins floored Pat Brownson with his first punch and the contest was stopped, without a count, 4 sec after the bell.

The shortest world heavyweight title fight occurred when Tommy Burns (1881–1955) (né Noah Brusso) of Canada knocked out Jem Roche in 1 min 28 sec in Dublin, Ireland, March 17, 1908. The duration of the Clay vs Liston fight at Lewiston, Me, May 25, 1965, was 1 min 52 sec (including the count) as timed from the video tape recordings despite a ringside announcement giving a time of 1 min. The shortest world title fight was when Al McCoy knocked out George Chip in 45 sec for the middleweight crown in NYC, Apr 7, 1914.

Tallest

The tallest boxer to fight professionally was Gogea Mitu (b 1914) of Rumania in 1935. He was 7 ft 4 in and weighed 327 lb. John Rankin, who won a fight in New Orleans, in Nov 1967, also claimed 7 ft 4 in.

WORLD HEAVYWEIGHT CHAMPIONS

Longest and Shortest Reigns

The longest reign of any world heavyweight champion is 11 years 8 months and 7 days by Joe Louis (b Joseph Louis Barrow, 1914–81), from June 22, 1937, when he knocked out James J. Braddock in the 8th round at Chicago until announcing his retirement on March 1, 1949. During his reign Louis made a record 25 defenses of his title. The shortest reign was by Leon Spinks (US) (b July 11, 1953) for 212 days, Feb 15–Sept 15, 1978. Ken Norton (US) (b Aug 6, 1945) was recognized by the WBC as champion for 83 days, March 18–June 9, 1978.

Heaviest and Lightest

The heaviest world champion was Primo Carnera (Italy) (1906–67), the "Ambling Alp," who won the title from Jack Sharkey in 6 rounds in NYC, on June 29, 1933. He scaled 267 lb for this fight but his peak weight was 270 lb. He had the longest reach at 85½ in (fingertip to fingertip) and an expanded chest measurement of 53 in. Charles "Sonny" Liston had the largest fists, with a 15-in circumference. The lightest world champion was Robert James Fitzsimmons (1863–1917), (b Helston, Cornwall, England) who, at a weight of 167 lb, won the title by knocking out James J. Corbett in 14 rounds at Carson City, Nev, March 17, 1897.

TITLE DEEDS

JOE LOUIS (near right) kept the heavyweight title for over 11 years, the longest reign at any weight class. Known as "The Brown Bomber," Louis successfully defended his title a record 25 times. Louis' largest purse, earned in his 8th-round KO of Billy Conn in 1946, was $625,916—a far cry from today's high-priced bouts. Ringside seats cost a then-record $100.

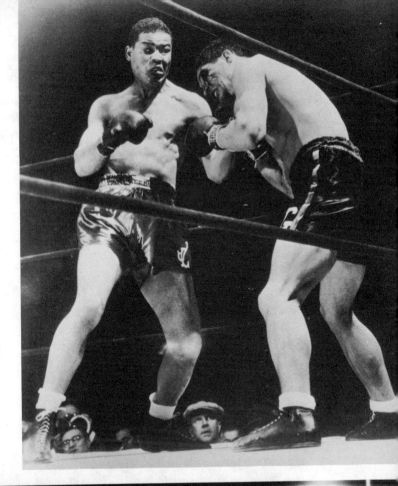

JERSEY JOE WALCOTT (bottom left) holds the upper hand as Ezzard Charles covers up in their title bout in Pittsburgh in 1951. Charles, who had won the heavyweight title vacated by Joe Louis in 1949, was dethroned by Walcott, who, at age 37, became the oldest man to win the heavyweight championship. Walcott is now the boxing commissioner in New Jersey. (AP)

LORDS OF THE RING

SUGAR RAY LEONARD (above left) and Thomas Hearns fought to unite the WBA and WBC welterweight titles in a fight that had a total purse for both fighters of $17.1 million, the largest ever, of which Leonard earned a record share with an estimated $12 million (more than three times greater than Joe Louis' lifetime earnings of $3.8 million for 71 fights). The discovery of a detached retina in his left eye put Leonard's boxing future in jeopardy. (All-Sport)

ARCHIE MOORE (left) scored 143 knockouts in his 28-year career. Moore held the light-heavyweight title until 1962, when he was either 45 or 48 years old (his year of birth is uncertain). Either way, it was the greatest age for a world champion. Known as a thinking man's fighter, Moore twice fought unsuccessfully for the heavyweight title, losing to Rocky Marciano in 1955 and to Floyd Patterson in 1956. (Radio Times Hulton Picture Library)

The greatest differential in a world title fight was 86 lb between Carnera (270 lb) and Tommy Loughran (184 lb) of the US, when the former won on points at Miami, Fla, March 1, 1934.

Tallest and Shortest

The tallest world champion was Primo Carnera, who was measured at 6 ft 5.4 in by the Physical Education Director at the Hemingway Gymnasium of Harvard, although he was widely reported and believed in 1933 to be 6 ft 8½ in tall. Jess Willard (1881–1968), who won the title in 1915, was often described as being 6 ft 6¼ in tall, but was in fact 6 ft 5¼ in. The shortest was Tommy Burns (1881–1955) of Canada, world champion from Feb 23, 1906, to Dec 26, 1908, who stood 5 ft 7 in and weighed 179 lb.

Oldest and Youngest

The oldest man to win the heavyweight crown was Jersey Joe Walcott (b Arnold Raymond Cream, Jan 31, 1914, at Merchantville, NJ), who knocked out Ezzard Charles on July 18, 1951, in Pittsburgh, when aged 37 years 5 months 18 days. Walcott was the oldest title holder at 38 years 7 months 23 days when he lost to Rocky Marciano on Sept 23, 1952. The youngest age at which the world title has been won is 21 years 331 days by Floyd Patterson (b Waco, NC, Jan 4, 1935), who won the vacant title by beating Archie Moore in 5 rounds in Chicago on Nov 30, 1956.

Undefeated

Rocky Marciano (b Rocco Francis Marchegiano) (1923–69) is the only heavyweight champion to have been undefeated in his entire professional career (1947–1956). His record was 49 wins (43 by KO) and no losses or draws. (It should be noted that Larry Holmes' successful defense of his WBC heavyweight title against Gerry Cooney on June 11, 1982, was his 40th professional victory against no losses or draws.)

Most Recaptures

Muhammad Ali Haj (b Cassius Marcellus Clay, in Louisville, Ky, Jan 17, 1942) is the only man to regain the heavyweight title twice. Ali first won the title on Feb 25, 1964, defeating Sonny Liston. He defeated George Foreman on Oct 30, 1974, having been stripped of his title by the world boxing authorities on Apr 28, 1967. He lost his title to Leon Spinks on Feb 15, 1978, but regained it on Sept 15, 1978 by defeating Spinks in New Orleans.

Earliest Title Fight

The first world heavyweight title fight, with gloves and 3-minute rounds, was between John L. Sullivan (1858–1918) and "Gentleman" James J. Corbett (1866–1933) in New Orleans, Sept 7, 1892. Corbett won in 21 rounds.

WORLD CHAMPIONS (ANY WEIGHT)

Longest and Shortest Reign

Joe Louis's heavyweight duration record stands for all divisions. The shortest reign has been 33 days by Tony Canzoneri (US) (1908–59) who was junior welterweight champion from May 21 to June 23, 1933.

Youngest and Oldest

The youngest at which any world championship has been won is 17 years 176 days by Wilfred Benitez (b Sept 12, 1958) of Puerto Rico, who won the WBA light-welterweight title in San Juan, March 6, 1976.

The oldest world champion was Archie Moore (b Archibald Lee Wright, Collinsville, Ill , Dec 13, 1913 or 1916), who was recognized as a light-heavyweight champion up to Feb 10, 1962, when his title was removed. He was then between 45 and 48. Bob Fitzsimmons (1863–1917) had the longest career of any official world titleholder with over 32 years from 1882 to 1914. He won his last world title aged 40 years 183 days in San Francisco on Nov 25, 1903. He was an amateur from 1880 to 1882.

Greatest "Tonnage"

The greatest "tonnage" in a world title fight was 488¾ lb when Primo Carnera (259¼ lb) fought Paolino Uzcudun (229½ lb) of Spain, in Rome, Italy, Oct 22, 1933.

The greatest "tonnage" recorded in any fight is 700 lb, when Claude "Humphrey" McBride of Okla at 340 lb knocked out Jimmy Black of Houston at 360 lb in the 3rd round at Oklahoma City, June 1, 1971.

Smallest Champions

The smallest man to win any world title has been Netranoi Vorasingh (b Apr 22, 1959) (Thailand), WBC light-flyweight champion from May to Sept 1978, at 4 ft 11 in tall. Jimmy Wilde (b Merthyr Tydfil, 1892, d 1969, UK), who held the flyweight title from 1916 to 1923, was reputed never to have fought above 108 lb.

Longest Fight

The longest world title fight (under Queensberry Rules) was between the lightweights Joe Gans (1874–1910), of the US, and Oscar "Battling" Nelson (1882–1954), the "Durable Dane," at Goldfield, Nev, Sept 3, 1906. It was terminated in the 42nd round when Gans was declared the winner on a foul.

Most Recaptures

The only boxer to win a world title five times at one weight is Sugar Ray Robinson (b Walker Smith, Jr, in Detroit, May 3, 1920) who beat Carmen Basilio (US) in the Chicago Stadium on March 25, 1958, to regain the world middleweight title for the fourth time. The other title wins were over Jake LaMotta (US) in Chicago on Feb 14, 1951; Randy Turpin (UK) in NYC on Sept 12, 1951; Carl "Bobo" Olson (US) in Chicago on Dec 9, 1955; and Gene Fullmer (US) in Chicago on May 1, 1957. The record number of title bouts in a career is 33 or 34 (at bantam and featherweight) by George Dixon (1870–1909), *alias* "Little Chocolate," of Canada, between 1890 and 1901.

Most Titles Simultaneously

The only man to hold world titles at three weights simultaneously was "Hammerin'" Henry Armstrong (b Dec 12, 1912), now the Rev Henry Jackson, of the US, at featherweight, lightweight and welterweight from Aug to Dec 1938.

Most Knockdowns in Title Fights

Vic Toweel (South Africa) knocked down Danny O'Sullivan of London 14 times in 10 rounds in their world bantamweight fight at Johannesburg, Dec 2, 1950, before the latter retired.

ALL FIGHTS

Largest Purse

The greatest purse received is an estimated $12 million by Sugar Ray Leonard (US) (b May 17, 1956) when he beat Thomas Hearns (US) for the undisputed world welterweight title at Las Vegas, Nev, on Sept 16, 1981. The total purse for both fighters was a record $17.1 million.

The largest stake ever fought for in the bare-knuckle era was $22,500 in a 27-round fight when

Jack Cooper beat Wolf Bendoff at Port Elizabeth, South Africa, July 26, 1889.

Highest and Lowest Attendances

The greatest paid attendance at any boxing fight has been 120,757 (with a ringside price of $27.50) for the Tunney vs Dempsey world heavyweight title fight at the Sesquicentennial Stadium, Philadelphia, Sept 23, 1926. The indoor record is 63,360 for the Spinks vs Ali world heavyweight title fight at the Louisiana Superdome in New Orleans, Sept 15, 1978. The record for live gate receipts is $7,293,600 for the Larry Holmes vs Gerry Cooney WBC heavyweight title bout in Las Vegas, Nev, on June 11, 1982. The highest non-paying attendance is 135,132 at the Tony Zale vs Billy Pryor fight at Juneau Park, Milwaukee, Wis, Aug 18, 1941.

The smallest attendance at a world heavyweight title fight was 2,434 at the Clay vs Liston fight at Lewiston, Me, May 25, 1965.

Highest Earnings in Career

The largest known fortune ever made in a fighting career (or any sports career) is an estimated $69 million (including exhibitions) amassed by Muhammad Ali from Oct 1960 to Dec 1981, in 61 fights comprising 549 rounds.

Most Knockouts

The greatest number of knockouts in a career is 143 by Archie Moore (1936 to 1963). The record for consecutive KO's is 44, set by Lamar Clark of Utah at Las Vegas, Nev, Jan 11, 1960. He knocked out 6 in one night (5 in the first round) in Bingham, Utah, on Dec 1, 1958.

Most Fights

The greatest recorded number of fights in a career is 1,024 by Bobby Dobbs (US) (1858–1930), who is reported to have fought from 1875 to 1914, a period of 39 years. Abraham Hollandersky, *alias* Abe the Newsboy (US), is reputed to have had 1,309 fights in the 14 years from 1905 to 1918, but many of them were exhibition bouts.

Most Fights Without Loss

Hal Bagwell, a lightweight, from Gloucester, England, was reputedly undefeated in 180 consecutive fights, of which only 5 were draws, between Aug

WEIGHTING AROUND: Hammerin' Henry Armstrong held 3 world titles at the same time (1938), the only man to do so. Current rules require a fighter to surrender one title when he acquires another. (Radio Times Hulton Picture Library)

15, 1938, and Nov 29, 1948. His record of fights in the wartime period (1939–46) is very sketchy, however. Of boxers with complete records, Packey McFarland (1888–1936) (US) went undefeated in 97 fights from 1905 to 1915. Pedro Carrasco (b Huelva, Spain, Nov 7, 1943) won 83 consecutive fights between Apr 1964 and Nov 1970, and in all had 90 wins and one draw.

Olympic Gold Medals

Only two boxers have won three Olympic gold medals: southpaw László Papp (b 1926, Hungary), who took the middleweight (1948) and the light-middleweight titles (1952 and 56), and Cuban heavyweight Teofilo Stevenson (b Mar 23, 1952), who won the gold medal in his division for three successive Games (1972, 76 and 80). The only man to win two titles in one meeting was Oliver L. Kirk (US), who took both the bantam and featherweight titles at St Louis, Mo, in 1904, when the US won all the titles. Harry W. Mallin (GB) was in 1924 the first boxer ever to defend an Olympic title successfully when he retained the middleweight crown.

The oldest man to win an Olympic gold medal in boxing was Richard K. Gunn (b 1870) (GB), who won the featherweight title on Oct 27, 1908, in London, aged 38.

Amateur World Championships

Two boxers have won two world championships (instituted 1974): Teofilo Stevenson (Cuba), heavyweight 1974 and 1978, and Angel Herrera (b Aug 2, 1952), featherweight 1978 and lightweight 1982.

BULLFIGHTING

Earliest

In the latter half of the second millennium BC, bull leaping was practiced in Crete. Bullfighting in Spain was first reported by the Romans in Baetica (Andalusia) in the third century BC.

The first renowned professional *espada* (bullfighter) was Francisco Romero of Ronda, in Andalusia, Spain, who introduced the *estoque* and the red *muleta* c. 1700. Spain now has some 190 active matadors. Since 1700, 42 major matadors have died in the ring.

Largest Stadiums

The world's largest bullfighting ring, the Plaza, Mexico City, with a capacity of 48,000, was closed in March 1976. The largest of Spain's 312 bullrings is Las Ventas, Madrid, with a capacity of 24,000.

Most Successful Matadors

The most successful matador measured by bulls killed was Lagartijo (1841–1900), born Rafael Molina, whose lifetime total was 4,867.

In 1884, Romano set a record by killing 18 bulls in a day in Seville, and in 1949 El Litri (Miguel Báes) set a Spanish record with 114 *novilladas* in a season.

The longest career of any full matador was that of Bienvenida (1922–75) (*né* Antonio Mejías) from 1942 to 1974. (Recent Spanish law requires compulsory retirement at age 55.)

Highest Paid Matadors

The highest-paid bullfighter in history is El Cordobés (b Manuel Benitex Pérez, probably on May 4, 1936, in Palma del Rio, Spain), who became a multimillionaire in 1965, during which year he fought 111 *corridas* up to Oct 4, receiving over $15,000 for each half hour in the ring. In 1970, he received an estimated $1,800,000 for 121 fights.

Paco Camino (b Dec 19, 1941) received $27,200 (2,000,000 *pesetas*) for a *corrida*. He retired in 1977.

CANOEING

Origins

The acknowledged pioneer of canoeing as a modern sport was John Macgregor (1825–92), a British barrister, in 1865. The Canoe Club was formed on July 26, 1866.

Olympic and World Titles

Gert Fredriksson (b Nov 21, 1919) of Sweden has won the most Olympic gold medals with 6 (1948, 52, 56, 60). The most by a woman is 3 by Ludmila Pinayeva (née Khvedosyuk, b Jan 14, 1936) (USSR) in the 500-m K.1 in 1964 and 1968, and the 500-m K.2 in 1972. The most gold medals at one Games is 3 by Vladimir Parfenovich (b Dec 2, 1958) (USSR) in 1980.

Yuri Lobanov (USSR) (b Sept 29, 1952) has won a record 11 titles from 1972 to 1979. Ludmila Pinayeva added 6 other world titles to her 3 Olympic golds, from 1966 to 1973, for a female record.

Highest Speed

The Olympic 1,000-m best performance of 3 min 02.70 sec by the 1980 USSR K4 on July 31, 1980, represents a speed of 12.24 mph. They achieved 13.14 mph over the first quarter of the course.

Longest Journey

The longest canoe journey in history was one of 8,880 miles from New Orleans by paddle and portage *via* the Mississippi River, Prescott, Minnesota, Grand Portage, Lake Superior and across Canada to the Bering Sea and Nome, Alaska, by Jerry Robert Pushcar (b Nov 26, 1949), accompanied only by a Samoyed dog, from Jan 10, 1975, to Nov 12, 1977.

The longest journey without portage or aid of any kind is one of 6,102 miles by Richard H. Grant and Ernest "Moose" Lassey circumnavigating the eastern US from Chicago to New Orleans to Miami to NYC, returning back to Chicago *via* the Great Lakes, from Sept 22, 1930, to Aug 15, 1931.

Highest Altitude

In Sept 1976 Dr Michael Jones (1951–78) and Michael Hopkinson of the British Everest Canoe Expedition canoed down the Dudh Kosi River in Nepal from an altitude of 17,500 ft.

Eskimo Rolls

The record for Eskimo rolls is 1,000 in 53 min 5.7 sec by Terry Russell (b 1956) at Swanley, Kent, England, on Apr 20, 1980. A "hand-rolling" record of 100 rolls in 3 min 23 sec was set in the Crystal Palace Pool, London, on Feb 25, 1980, by John Bouteloup (21).

Longest Open Sea Voyage

Beatrice and John Dowd, Ken Beard and Steve Benson (Richard Gillett replaced him mid-journey) paddled 2,170 miles out of a total journey of 2,192 miles from Venezuela to Miami, Fla, via the West Indies from Aug 11, 1977, to Apr 29, 1978, in two Klepper Aerius 20 kayaks.

Longest Race

The longest regularly held canoe race in the US is the Texas Water Safari (instituted 1963) which covers the 419 miles from San Marcos to Seadrift, Tex, on the San Marcos and Guadalupe rivers. Robert Chatham and Butch Hodges set the record of 37 hours 18 min, June 5–6, 1976.

CROSS-COUNTRY RUNNING

International Championships

The earliest international cross-country race was run between England and France on a course 9 miles 18 yd long from Ville d'Avray, outside Paris, on March 20, 1898 (England won by 21 points to 69). The inaugural International Cross-Country Championships took place at the Hamilton Park Racecourse, Scotland, on March 28, 1903. Since 1973 the race has been run under the auspices of the International Amateur Athletic Federation.

The greatest margin of victory in the International Cross-Country Championships has been 56 sec, or 390 yd, by Jack T. Holden (England) at Ayr Racecourse, Scotland, March 24, 1934. The narrowest win was that of Jean-Claude Fayolle (France) at Ostend, Belgium, on March 20, 1965, when the timekeepers were unable to separate his time from that of Melvyn Richard Batty (England).

The greatest men's team wins have been those of England, with a minimum of 21 points (the first six runners to finish) on two occasions, 1924 and 1932.

COUNTRY MILES: French runner Alain Mimoun (#1) streaks to one of his four world titles, a record he shares with Jack Holden and Gaston Roelants. (H. W. Neale)

Most Appearances

The runner with the largest number of international championship appearances is Marcel Van de Wattyne of Belgium, who participated in 20 competitions in the years 1946–65. Two women have competed in 14 of the 15 races held: Margaret Coomber (*née* MacSherry) (b June 13, 1950) (Scotland), 1967–80; and Jean Lochhead (b Dec 24, 1946) (Wales), 1967–79, 81.

Most Wins

The greatest number of men's individual victories is 4 by Jack Holden (England) in 1933–35, and 39; by Alain Mimoun-o-Kacha (b Jan 1, 1921) (France) in 1949, 52, 54 and 56; and Gaston Roelants (b Feb 5, 1937) (Belgium) in 1962, 67, 69 and 72. Doris Brown-Heritage (US) (b Sept 17, 1942) won the women's race 5 times, 1967–71.

The greatest number of team victories has been by England with 45 for men, 11 for junior men and 6 for women.

Largest Field

The largest recorded field in any cross-country race was 10,055 starters in the 18.6-mile Lidingöloppet, near Stockholm, Sweden, on Oct 4, 1981. There were 9,650 finishers.

CURLING

Origins

Although a 15th century bronze figure in the Florence Museum appears to be holding a curling stone, the earliest illustration of the sport was in one of the winter scenes by the Flemish painter Pieter Brueghel, *c.* 1560. The game was introduced into Canada in 1759. Organized administration began in 1838 with the formation of the Grand (later Royal) Caledonian Curling Club, the international legislative body until the foundation of the International Curling Federation in 1966. The first indoor ice rink to introduce curling was in Montreal in 1807.

433

1973. Andrew McQuistin, of Stranraer, Scotland, skipped a Scotland rink (team) to a 1–0 victory over Switzerland, scoring in the tenth end after nine consecutive blank ends, in the Uniroyal World Junior Championships at Kitchener-Waterloo, Ontario, Canada on March 16, 1980.

Marathon

The longest recorded curling match is one of 67 hours 32 min by eight members of the Edinburgh Young Curlers at Murrayfield, Sept 10–13, 1981. The duration record for 2 curlers is 38 hours by Jim Paul and Chris McCrady at the Brockville Country Club, Ontario, Canada, Mar 26–28, 1982.

Largest Bonspiel

The largest bonspiel in the world is the Manitoba Bonspiel held in Winnipeg, Canada. There were 736 teams, or rinks, of 4 players in the Jan 1981 tournament.

Largest Rink

The world's largest curling rink is the Big Four Curling Rink, Calgary, Alberta, Canada, opened in 1959. Each of its two floors has 24 sheets of ice, the total accommodating 96 teams and 384 players.

STONED AGAIN: Jim Paul (in action) and Chris McCrady threw a total of 65,600 lb of curling stones in 205 ends in their 38-hour marathon. (Recorder & Times, Brockville, Ontario)

The US won the first Gordon International Medal series of matches, between Canada and the US, at Montreal in 1884. Although demonstrated at the Winter Olympics of 1924, 1932 and 1964, curling has never been included in the official Olympic program.

Most Titles

The record for world championships for the Air Canada Silver Broom (instituted 1959) is 14 wins by Canada, in 1959–64, 66, 68–72, 80, 82. The most Strathcona Cup (instituted 1903) wins is seven by Canada (1903, 09, 12, 23, 38, 57, 65) against Scotland. A women's world championship was instituted in 1979 and the title has been won by Switzerland, Canada, Sweden and Denmark.

"Perfect" Games

Stu Beagle, of Calgary, Canada, played a perfect game (48 points) against Nova Scotia in the Canadian championships (Brier) at Ft William (now Thunder Bay), Ontario, on March 8, 1960. Bernice Fekete of Edmonton, Alberta, Canada, skipped her rink to two consecutive eight-enders on the same ice at the Derrick Club, Edmonton, on Jan 10 and Feb 6,

CYCLING

Earliest Race

The earliest recorded bicycle race was a velocipede race over 2 km (1.24 miles) at the Parc de St Cloud, Paris, on May 31, 1868, won by Dr James Moore (GB) (1847–1935).

Highest Speed

The highest speed ever achieved on a bicycle is 140.5 mph by Dr Allan V. Abbott, 29, of San Bernardino, Calif, behind a windshield mounted on a 1955 Chevrolet over ¾ of a mile at Bonneville Salt Flats, Utah, Aug 25, 1973. His speed over a mile was 138.674 mph. Considerable help is provided by the slipstreaming effect of the lead vehicle.

Fred Markham recorded an official unpaced 8.80 sec for 200 m (50.84 mph) on a streamlined bicycle at Ontario, Calif, May 6, 1979.

The greatest distance ever covered in one hour is 76 miles 504 yd by Leon Vanderstuyft (Belgium) on the Montlhéry Motor Circuit, France, Sept 30, 1928. This was achieved from a standing start paced by a motorcycle. The 24-hour record behind pace is 860 miles 367 yd by Hubert Opperman in Melbourne, Australia on May 23, 1932.

The greatest distance covered in 60 min unpaced is 30 miles 1,258 yd by Eddy Merckx at Mexico City, on Oct 25, 1972. The 24-hour record on the road is 515.8 miles by Teuvo Louhivouri of Finland on Sept 10, 1974.

Tour de France

The greatest number of wins in the Tour de France (inaugurated 1903) is 5 by Jacques Anquetil (b Jan 8, 1934) (France), who won in 1957, 1961–64; and Eddy Merckx (b June 17, 1945) (Belgium) who won five titles (1969–72, 1974).

The closest race ever was in 1968 when after 2,898.7 miles over 25 days (June 27–July 21) Jan Jannssen (Netherlands) (b May 19, 1940) beat Herman van Springel (Belgium) in Paris by 38 sec. The

BIG WHEEL: Bernard Hinault of France averaged 23.51 mph in winning the 1981 Tour de France. By earning his fourth win in 1982, Hinault is only one victory shy of the record shared by Eddie Merckx and Jacques Anquetil. (All-Sport)

longest course was 3,569 miles on June 20 to July 18, 1926. The length of the course is usually about 3,000 miles, but varies from year to year.

The fastest average speed was 23.51 mph by Bernard Hinault (b Nov 14, 1954) (France) in 1981. The greatest number of participants was in 1982, when 170 started.

Six-Day Races

The greatest number of wins in six-day races is by Patrick Sercu (b June 27, 1944), of Belgium, who, by Apr 1982, had taken his total number of victories to 84 in 18 years.

Most Olympic Titles

The greatest number of gold medals ever won is 3 by Paul Masson (France) in 1896, Francisco Verri (Italy) in 1906 and Robert Charpentier (France) in 1936. Daniel Morelon (France) won two in 1968 and a third in 1972. He also won a bronze medal in 1964. Marcus Hurley (US) (1884–1950) won 4 events in the "unofficial" cycling competition in the 1904 Games.

World Titles

The only 4 male cyclists to have won 7 world titles in any single world championship event are Leon Meredith (GB) who won the Amateur 100-km paced event, 1904–05, 07–09, 11, 13; Jeff Scherens (Belgium) who won the Professional sprint title in 1932–37 and 47; Antonio Maspes (Italy) who won the Professional sprint title in 1955–56, 59–62, 64; and Daniel Morelon (France) who won the Amateur sprint title in 1966–67, 69–71, 73, 75.

Yvonne Reynders (Belgium) won a total of 7 titles in women's events: the pursuits in 1961, 64–65 and the road title in 1959, 61, 63 and 66. Beryl Burton (GB) equaled this total by winning the pursuits title in 1959–60, 62–63, 66 and the road title in 1960 and 67.

Longest One-Day Race

The longest single-day "massed start" road race is the Bordeaux-to-Paris, France, event of 342 to 385 miles. Paced over all or part of the route, the highest average speed was in 1979 with 29.24 mph by André Chalmel (France). The longest unpaced single-day race is the Bristol-to-Bradford, England, 245-mile event.

435

ITINERANT PEDALER: Repairing over 1,000 flat tires was one aspect of Walter Stolle's 18-year bicycle tour. He logged over 402,000 miles in visiting 159 countries, 1959–76.

Touring

The greatest number of participants in a bicycle tour is 17,344 in the 36-mile Citibank—AYH Five Borough Tour of NYC on Apr 25, 1982.

The longest cycle tour on record is the more than 402,000 miles amassed by Walter Stolle (b Sudetenland, 1926), an itinerant lecturer. From Jan 24, 1959 to Dec 12, 1976, he covered 159 countries, had 5 bicycles stolen and suffered 231 other robberies, along with over 1,000 flat tires. From 1922 to Dec 25, 1973, Tommy Chambers (b 1903) of Glasgow, Scotland, had ridden a verified total of 799,405 miles. On Christmas Day he was badly injured and has not ridden since.

John Hathaway of Vancouver, Canada, covered 50,600 miles, visiting every continent from Nov 10, 1974 to Oct 6, 1976.

Veronica and Colin Scargill, of Bedford, England, traveled 18,020 miles around the world, on a tandem, Feb 25, 1974–Aug 27, 1975.

Endurance

Tommy Godwin (1912–75) (GB) in the 365 days of 1939 covered 75,065 miles or an average of 205.65 miles per day. He then completed 100,000 miles in 500 days to May 14, 1940.

Nicholas Mark Sanders (b Nov 26, 1957) of Glossop, England, circumnavigated the world (13,609 road miles) between Feb 7 and July 5 (138 days), 1981.

Lon Haldeman rode from Santa Monica, Calif, to NYC (2,976 miles) in a record 9 days 20 hours 2 min in 1982. Susan Notorangelo set the women's trans-America cycling record when she completed the 2,932-mile journey from Santa Monica to NYC in 11

days 16 hours 15 minutes, July 1–13, 1982. Gerry and Ted Milner rode across Canada from Vancouver, BC, to Halifax, Nova Scotia, on a tandem, covering the 3,800 miles in 15 days 15 hours 4 min, June 5–21, 1981.

Johnny J. Colson, 24, from Warner Robins, Ga, bicycled around the perimeter of the continental US in 146 days, beginning in Savannah, Ga, on Mar 3, 1981, and returning to Savannah on July 26, 1981. His 12,670-mile continuous journey was accomplished without resorting to other means of transportation at any point. (*As it was not the editors' intention to make a time trial of this cycling tour, this category will be deleted in future editions. No further claims will be entertained or published.*)

Vivekananda Selva Kumar Anandan of Sri Lanka cycled for 187 hours 28 min non-stop around Vihara Maha Devi Park, Colombo, Sri Lanka, May 2–10, 1979. The distance covered was 1,476.8 miles and he was moving 99.6% of the time.

Roller Cycling

The four-man 12-hour record is 717.9 miles by a Northampton team at the Guildhall, Northampton, England, on Jan 28, 1978. The 24-hour solo record is 792.7 miles by Bruce W. Hall at San Diego University, Calif, Jan 22–23, 1977. Paul Swinnerton (GB) achieved a record 102 mph for 200 meters on rollers on Feb 12, 1982, at Stoke-on-Trent, England.

Stationary Cycling

David Steed of Tucson, Ariz, stayed stationary without support for 9 hours 15 min on Nov 25, 1977.

EQUESTRIAN SPORTS*

Origin

Evidence of horse riding dates from a Persian engraving dated *c.* 3000 BC. Pignatelli's academy of horsemanship at Naples dates from the 16th century. The earliest jumping competition was at the Agricultural Hall, London, in 1869. Equestrian events have been included in the Olympic Games since 1912.

Most Olympic Medals

The greatest number of Olympic gold medals is 5 by Hans-Günter Winkler (b July 24, 1926) (W Germany), who won 4 team gold medals as captain in 1956, 60, 64 and 72, and won the individual Grand Prix in 1956. The most team wins in the Prix des Nations is 5 by Germany in 1936, 56, 60, 64, and 1972.

The lowest score obtained by a winner was no faults, by Frantisek Ventura (Czechoslovakia) on "Eliot" in 1928, and by Alwin Schockemöhle (W Germany) on "Warwick Rex" in 1976. Pierre Jonqueres d'Oriola (France) is the only two-time winner of the individual gold medal, in 1952 and 1964.

World Titles

The men's world championship (instituted 1953) has been won twice by Hans-Günter Winkler of W Germany in 1954 and 1955, and Raimondo d'Inzeo

* For more detailed information about equestrian sports, see *The Guinness Guide to Equestrianism*, available from Sterling.

of Italy in 1956 and 1960. The women's title (1965–74) was won twice by Jane "Janou" Tissot (*née* Lefebvre) of France on "Rocket" in 1970 and 1974.

Jumping Records

The official *Fédération Equestre Internationale* high jump record is 8 ft 1¼ in by "Huaso," ridden by Capt A. Larraguibel Morales (Chile) at Santiago, Chile, on Feb 5, 1949, and 27 ft 6¾ in for a long jump over water by "Something," ridden by André Ferreira (S Africa) at Johannesburg on Apr 26, 1975.

The greatest recorded height reached bareback is 6 ft 7 in by "Silver Wood" at Heidelberg, Victoria, Australia, Dec 10, 1938.

Longest Ride

Thomas L. Gaddie (US) rode 11,217.2 miles from Dallas, Tex, to Fairbanks, Alaska, and back in 295 days, Feb 12–Dec 2, 1980, with seven horses.

The Bicentennial "Great American Horse Race," begun on May 31, 1976, from Saratoga Springs, NY, to Sacramento, Calif (3,500 miles) was won by Virl Norton on "Lord Fauntleroy"—a mule—in 98 days. His actual riding time was 315.47 hours.

Marathon

Eric Reynders of Belgium rode at all paces (including jumping) for 64 hours 45 min at Zutendaal, Belgium, Mar 2–5, 1982.

HORSING AROUND: Thomas L. Gaddie aboard "Little Doc," a quarter-horse, in Yukon, Canada, during his 10-month, 11,217.2-mile ride from Texas to Alaska and back. Gaddie spent a total of 1,340 hours 44 min in the saddle, spreading the work among seven horses. (Rocky L. Gaddie)

FENCING

Origins

Fencing (fighting with single sticks) was practiced as a sport, or as part of a religious ceremony, in Egypt as early as *c.* 1360 BC. The first governing body for fencing in Britain was the Corporation of Masters of Defence founded by Henry VIII before 1540, and fencing was practiced as sport, notably in prize fights, since that time. The foil was the practice weapon for the short court sword from the 17th century. The épée was established in the mid-19th century and the light sabre was introduced by the Italians in the late 19th century.

Most Olympic Titles

The greatest number of individual Olympic gold medals won is 3 by Ramón Fonst (Cuba) (1883–1959) in 1900 and 1904 (2) and Nedo Nadi (Italy) (1894–1952) in 1912 and 1920 (2). Nadi also won 3 team gold medals in 1920 making a then unprecedented total of 5 gold medals at one Olympic meet.

Edoardo Mangiarotti (Italy) (b Apr 7, 1919) holds the record of 13 Olympic medals (6 gold, 5 silver, 2 bronze), won in the foil and épée competitions from 1936 to 1960.

FOILED AGAIN: Helene Mayer of Germany captured 3 women's world foil titles. Mayer also won the Olympic gold medal in Los Angeles in 1932. (Mary Evans)

MOST OLYMPIC AND WORLD FENCING TITLES

Event	Olympic Gold Medals	World Championships (not held in Olympic years)
Men's Foil, Individual	2 Christian d'Oriola (France) (b Oct 3, 1928) 1952, 56	4 Christian d'Oriola (France) 1947, 49, 53, 54
	2 Nedo Nadi (Italy) (1894–1952) 1912, 20	
Men's Foil, Team	6 France 1924, 32, 48, 52, 68, 80	12 Italy 1929–31, 33–35, 37, 38, 49, 50, 54, 55
Men's Epée, Individual	2 Ramón Fonst (Cuba) (1883–1959) 1900, 04	3 Georges Buchard (France) (b Dec 21, 1893) 1927, 31, 33
		3 Aleksey Nikanchikov (USSR) (b July 30, 1940) 1966, 67, 70
Men's Epée, Team	6 Italy 1920, 28, 36, 52, 56, 60	10 Italy 1931, 33, 37, 49, 50, 53, 55, 57, 58
Men's Sabre, Individual	2 Jean Georgiadis (Greece) (b 1874) 1896, 1906	3 Aladar Gerevich (Hungary) (b March 16, 1910) 1935, 51, 55
	2 Dr Jenö Fuchs (Hungary) (b Oct 29, 1882) 1908, 12	3 Jerzy Pawlowski (Poland) (b Oct 25, 1932) 1957, 65, 66
	2 Rudolf Kárpáti (Hungary) (b July 17, 1920) 1956, 60	3 Yacov Rylsky (USSR) (b Oct 25, 1932) 1958, 61, 63
	2 Viktor Krovopouskov (USSR) (b Sept 29, 1948) 1976, 80	
Men's Sabre, Team	9 Hungary 1908, 12, 28, 32, 36, 48, 52, 56, 60	16 Hungary 1930, 31, 33–35, 37, 51, 53–55, 57, 58, 66, 73, 78, 81
Women's Foil, Individual	2 Ilona Schacherer-Elek (Hungary) (b May 17, 1907) 1936, 48	3 Helene Mayer (Germany) (1910–53) 1929, 31, 37
		3 Ilona Schacherer-Elek (Hungary) 1934, 35, 51
		3 Ellen Müller-Preiss (Austria) (b May 6, 1912) 1947, 49, 50 (shared)
Women's Foil, Team	4 USSR 1960, 68, 72, 76	13 USSR 1956, 58, 61, 63, 65–66, 70–71, 74–75, 77–79

The most gold medals won by a woman is four (one individual, three team) by Elena Novikova-Belova (USSR) (b July 28, 1947) from 1968 to 1976, and the record for all medals is 7 (2 gold, 3 silver, 2 bronze), by Ildikó Sagi-Retjö (formerly Ujlaki-Retjö) (Hungary) (b May 11, 1937) from 1960 to 1976.

Most World Titles

The greatest number of individual world titles won is 4 by Christian d'Oriola (see adjacent table), but note that d'Oriola also won 2 individual Olympic titles. Likewise, of the 3 women foilists with 3 world titles (Helene Mayer, Ellen Müller-Preiss and Ilona Schacherer-Elek) only Elek also won 2 individual Olympic titles.

FIELD HOCKEY

Origin

A representation of two players with curved snagging sticks apparently in an orthodox "bully" position was found in Tomb No. 17 at Beni Hasan, Egypt, and has been dated to *c*. 2050 BC. There is a reference to the game in Lincolnshire, England, in 1277. The *Fédération Internationale de Hockey* was formed on Jan 7, 1924. The first IFWHA (International Federation of Women's Hockey Associations) Championship Tournament of 21 nations was at Edinburgh, Scotland, in 1975, when England won the Silver Quaich.

Earliest International

The first international match was the Wales vs Ireland match on Jan 26, 1895. Ireland won 3–0.

The first women's international match was an England vs Ireland game in Dublin in 1896. Ireland won 2–0.

Highest International Score

The highest score in international field hockey was when India defeated the US 24–1 at Los Angeles, in the 1932 Olympic Games.

The highest score in a women's international match occurred when England defeated France 23–0 at Merton, Surrey, on Feb 3, 1923.

Most Olympic Medals

The Indians were Olympic Champions from the re-inception of Olympic hockey in 1928 until 1960, when Pakistan beat them 1–0 at Rome. They had their eighth win in 1980. Of the 6 Indians who have won 3 Olympic gold medals, two have also won a silver medal—Leslie Claudius in 1948, 52, 56 and 60 (silver), and Udham Singh in 1952, 56, 60 (silver) and 64.

The inaugural women's Olympic competition was won by Zimbabwe in 1980.

Most International Appearances

Avtar Singh Sohal (b Mar 22, 1938) represented Kenya 167 times between 1957 and 1972.

Greatest Scoring Feats

The greatest number of goals scored in international field hockey is 150 by Paul Litjiens (b Nov 9, 1947) (Netherlands) in 112 games to April 1979. The fastest goal in an international match was in 7 sec by John French for England vs W Germany at Nottingham, England, on Apr 25, 1971.

Greatest Goalkeeping

Richard James Allen (b June 4, 1902) (India) did not concede a goal during the 1928 Olympic Tournament and only a total of 3 in the following two Olympics of 1932 and 1936. In these three games India scored a total of 102 goals.

Longest Game

The longest international game on record was one of 145 min (into the sixth period of extra time), when Netherlands beat Spain 1–0 in the Olympic Tournament at Mexico City on Oct 25, 1968.

Highest Attendance

The highest attendance at a women's hockey match was 65,165 for the match between England and the US at the Empire Stadium, Wembley, London, on Mar 11, 1978.

Marathon

Two teams of eleven from Epsom Girls Grammar School, Auckland, NZ played for 35 hours 3 min 50 sec, Apr 21–22, 1980.

FISHING

Largest Catches

The largest fish ever caught on a rod is an officially ratified man-eating great white shark (*Carcharodon carcharias*) weighing 2,664 lb, and measuring 16 ft 10 in long, caught by Alf Dean at Denial Bay, near Ceduna, South Australia, on Apr 21, 1959. In June 1978 a great white shark measuring 29 ft 6 in in length and weighing over 10,000 lb was harpooned and landed by fishermen in the harbor of San Miguel, Azores.

A white pointer shark weighing 3,388 lb was caught on a rod by Clive Green off Albany, W Australia, on Apr 26, 1976, but this will remain unratified as whale meat was used as bait.

The largest marine animal ever killed by *hand* harpoon was a blue whale 97 ft in length by Archer Davidson in Twofold Bay, NSW, Australia, in 1910. Its tail flukes measured 20 ft across and its jaw bone 23 ft 4 in.

Smallest Catch

The smallest fish ever to win a competition was a smelt weighing 1/16 of an oz, caught by Peter Christian at Buckenham Ferry, Norfolk, England, on Jan 9, 1977. This beat 107 other competitors.

Freshwater Casting

The longest freshwater cast ratified under ICF (International Casting Federation) rules is 574 ft 2 in by

---

FISHING WORLD RECORDS

Selected Sea and Freshwater fish records taken by tackle as ratified by the International Game Fish Association to Jan 1982. For a more complete listing of IGFA all-tackle records, see the *Guinness Book of Sports Records, Winners & Champions* (Sterling), published in 1982.

Species	Weight in lb	oz	Name of Angler	Location	Date
Amberjack	155	10	Joseph Dawson	Challenger Bank, Bermuda	June 24, 1981
Barracuda††	83	0	K. J. W. Hackett §§	Lagos, Nigeria	Jan 13, 1952
Bass (Giant Sea)	563	8	James D. McAdam, Jr	Anacapa Island, Calif	Aug 20, 1968
Black Runner (Cobia)	110	5	Eric Tinworth	Off Mombasa, Kenya	Sept 8, 1964
Carp†	55	5	Frank J. Ledwein	Clearwater Lake, Minn	July 10, 1952
Cod	98	12	Alphonse J. Bielevich	Isle of Shoals, NH	June 8, 1969
Marlin (Black)	1,560	0	Alfred C. Glassell, Jr	Cabo Blanco, Peru	Aug 4, 1953
Marlin (Atlantic Blue)	1,282	0	Larry Martin	St Thomas, US VI	Aug 6, 1977
Marlin (Pacific Blue)	1,153	0	Greg D. Perez	Ritidian Point, Guam	Aug 21, 1969
Marlin (Striped)	417	8	Phillip Bryers	Cavalli Isles, New Zealand	Jan 14, 1977
Marlin (White)	181	14	Evando Luiz Coser	Vitoria, Brazil	1980
Pike (Northern)	62	8	Jurg Nötzli	Reuss-Weiher, Rickenbach, Switz	June 15, 1979
Sailfish (Atlantic)	128	1	Harm Steyn	Luanda, Angola	March 27, 1974
Sailfish (Pacific)	221	0	C. W. Stewart	Santa Cruz I, Galapagos Is	Feb 12, 1947
Salmon (Chinook)§	93	0	Howard C. Rider	Kelp Bay, Alaska	June 24, 1977
Shark (Blue)	437	0	Peter Hyde	Catherine Bay, NSW, Australia	Oct 2, 1976
Shark (Mako)**	1,080	0	James L. Melanson	Montauk, NY	Aug 26, 1979
Shark (White or Man-eating)	2,664	0	Alfred Dean	Ceduna, South Australia	Apr 21, 1959
Shark (Porbeagle)	465	0	Jorge Potier	Cornwall, England	July 23, 1976
Shark (Thresher)‡	802	0	Dianne North	Tutukaka, New Zealand	Feb 8, 1981
Shark (Tiger)	1,780	0	Walter Maxwell	Cherry Grove, SC	June 14, 1964
Sturgeon‡‡	407	0	Raymond Pittenger	Sacramento River, Calif	May 10, 1979
Swordfish	1,182	0	L. E. Marron	Iquique, Chile	May 7, 1953
Tarpon	283	0	M. Salazar	Lago de Maracaibo, Venezuela	March 19, 1965
Trout (Lake)¶	65	0	Larry Daunis	Great Bear Lake, Northwest Terr, Canada	Aug 8, 1970
Tuna (Allison or Yellowfin)	388	12	Curt Wiesenhutter	San Benedicto Islands, Mexico	Apr 1, 1977
Tuna (Atlantic Big-eyed)	375	8	Cecil Browne	Ocean City, Md	Aug 26, 1977
Tuna (Pacific Big-eyed)	435	0	Dr Russel V. A. Lee	Cabo Blanco, Peru	Apr 17, 1957
Tuna (Bluefin)	1,496	0	Ken Fraser	Aulds Cove, Nova Scotia, Canada	Oct 26, 1979
Wahoo	149	0	John Pirovano	Cat Cay, Bahamas	June 15, 1962

†† A barracuda weighing 103 lb 4 oz was caught on an untested line by Chester Benet at West End, Bahamas, on Aug 11, 1932. Another weighing 48 lb 6 oz was caught barehanded by Thomas B. Pace at Panama City Beach, Fla, on Apr 19, 1974. §§ Hackett was only 11 years 137 days old at the time. † A carp weighing 83 lb 8 oz was taken (not by rod) near Pretoria, South Africa. A 60-lb specimen was taken by bow and arrow by Ben A. Topham in Wythe Co, Va, on July 5, 1970. § A salmon weighing 126 lb 8 oz was taken (not by rod) near Petersburg, Alaska. ** A 1,295-lb specimen was taken by two anglers off Natal, South Africa, on March 17, 1939, and a 1,500-lb specimen harpooned inside Durban Harbour, South Africa, in 1933. ‡ W. W. Dowding caught a 922-lb thresher shark in 1937 on an untested line. ‡‡ An 834-lb sturgeon was landed (not by a rod) by Garry Oling at Albion, BC, Canada, from the Fraser River on Aug 11, 1981. ¶ A 102-lb trout was taken from Lake Athabasca, northern Saskatchewan, Canada, on Aug 8, 1961.

Walter Kummerow (W Germany), for the Bait Distance Double-Handed 30-g event held at Lenzerheide, Switzerland, in the 1968 Championships.

The longest Fly Distance Double-Handed cast is 257 ft 2 in by S. Sheen of Norway, also set at Lenzerheide in Sept 1968.

Longest Fight

The longest recorded fight between a fisherman and a fish is 32 hours 5 min by Donal Heatley (NZ) (b 1938) with a black marlin (estimated length 20 ft and weight 1,500 lb) off Mayor Island off Tauranga, New Zealand, Jan 21–22, 1968. It towed the 12-ton launch 50 miles before breaking the line.

Spear-fishing

The largest fish ever taken underwater was an 804-lb giant black grouper by Don Pinder of the Miami Triton Club, Fla, in 1955.

FISH SCALES: Ken Fraser poses with the 1,496-lb bluefin tuna he landed after a 45-min fight off Nova Scotia, Canada, for an all-tackle record.

World Championships

The *Confédération Internationale de la Pêche Sportive* championships were inaugurated as European championships in 1953. They were recognized as World Championships in 1957. France won 12 times between 1956 and 1981 and Robert Tesse (France) took the individual title uniquely three times, 1959–60, 65. The record weight (team) is 76 lb 8 oz in 3 hours by W Germany in the Neckar at Mannheim, W Germany on Sept 21, 1980. The individual record is 37 lb 7 oz by Wolf-Rüdiger Kremkus (W Germany) at Mannheim on Sept 20, 1980. The most fish caught is 652 by Jacques Isenbaert (Belgium) at Dunajvaros, Yugoslavia on Aug 27, 1967.

FOOTBALL

Origins

The origin of modern football stems from the "Boston Game" as played at Harvard. Harvard declined to participate in the inaugural meeting of the Intercollegiate Football Association in NYC in Oct 1873, on the grounds that the proposed rules were based on the non-handling "Association" code of English football. Instead, Harvard accepted a proposal from McGill University of Montreal, who played the more closely akin English Rugby Football. The first football match under the Harvard Rules was thus played against McGill at Cambridge, Mass, in May 1874. Most sports historians point to a contest between Rutgers and Princeton at New Brunswick, NJ, on Nov 6, 1869, as the first football game, but many American soccer historians regard this contest as the first intercollegiate *soccer* game. (Rutgers won the game, 6 goals to 4, and there were 25 players to a side.) In Nov 1876, a new Intercollegiate Football Association, with a pioneer membership of 5 colleges, was inaugurated at Springfield, Mass, to reconcile the conflicting versions of the sport. It was not until 1880 that the game, because of the organizational genius of Walter Camp of Yale, began to take its modern form. Among other things, he reduced the number of players on a side to 11, which it is today (and defined their positions), and also replaced the scrum with the line of scrimmage.

Professional football dates from the Latrobe, Pa vs Jeannette, Pa match at Latrobe, in Aug 1895. The National Football League was founded in Canton, Ohio, in 1920, although it did not adopt its present name until 1922. The year 1969 was the final year in

STAGG HUNT: Alabama coach Bear Bryant (left) made news in 1981 when his 315th victory made him the winningest college coach. After 37 seasons, Bryant's record stood at 315 wins, 81 losses and 17 ties. Amos Alonzo Stagg (right), now second-best with 314 victories, played or coached football for 74 of his 102 years, including a record 57 seasons as a head coach. Stagg first introduced many features of today's game. (Stagg photo courtesy University of Chicago)

MODERN MAJOR-COLLEGE INDIVIDUAL RECORDS
(Through 1981 Season)

Points			
Most in a Game	43	Jim Brown (Syracuse)	1956
Most in a Season	174	Lydell Mitchell (Penn State)	1971
Most in a Career	356	Tony Dorsett (Pittsburgh)	1973–76
Touchdowns			
Most in a Game	7	Arnold Boykin (Mississippi)	1951
Most in a Season	29	Lydell Mitchell (Penn State)	1971
Most in a Career	59	Glenn Davis (Army)	1943–46
	59	Tony Dorsett (Pittsburgh)	1973–76
Field Goals			
Most in a Game	6	Frank Nester (West Virginia)	1972
	6	Charlie Gogolak (Princeton)	1965
	6	Vince Fusco (Duke)	1976
Most in a Season	23	Obed Ariri (Clemson)	1980
Most in a Career	60	Obed Ariri (Clemson)	1977–80
Other Season Records			
Yards Gained Rushing	2,342 yd	Marcus Allen (So Cal)	1981
Highest Average Gain per Rush	9.35 yd	Greg Pruitt (Oklahoma)	1971
Most Passes Attempted	509	Bill Anderson (Tulsa)	1965
Most Passes Completed	296	Bill Anderson (Tulsa)	1965
Most Touchdown Passes	47	Jim McMahon (Brigham Young)	1980
Most Yards Gained Passing	4,571 yd	Jim McMahon (Brigham Young)	1980
Most Passes Caught	134	Howard Twilley (Tulsa)	1965
Most Yards Gained on Catches	1,779 yd	Howard Twilley (Tulsa)	1965
Most Touchdown Passes Caught	18	Tom Reynolds (San Diego St)	1969
Most Passes Intercepted by	14	Al Worley (Washington)	1968
Highest Punting Average	49.8 yd	Reggie Roby (Iowa)	1981

which professional football was divided into separate National and American Leagues, for record purposes.

College Series Records

The oldest collegiate series still contested is that between Yale and Princeton dating from 1873, or 3 years before the passing of the Springfield rules, with 104 games played through 1981. The most regularly contested series is between Lafayette and Lehigh, who have met 117 times between 1884 and the end of 1981.

Yale University became the only college to win more than 700 games when they finished the 1979 season with a total of 701 victories in 107 seasons. Yale has 718 wins in 109 seasons to the end of 1981.

Coaching Records

The longest serving head coach was Amos Alonzo Stagg (1862–1965), who served Springfield in 1890–91, Chicago from 1892 to 1932 and College of the Pacific from 1933 to 1946, making a total of 57 years. He later served as an assistant coach to his son. Paul "Bear" Bryant (b Sept 11, 1913) is the winningest college coach with 315 victories from 1945 through 1981. Bryant has been head coach at Maryland (1945), Kentucky (1946–1953), Texas A&M (1954–1957), and Alabama (1958 to the present).

The record for most victories by a professional coach is 325, by George Halas (b Feb 2, 1895), who coached the Chicago Bears, 1920–29, 33–42, 46–55, 58–67.

NFL Champions

The Green Bay Packers have won a record 11 NFL titles from 1929 through 1967. The Packers also won the first two Super Bowls (instituted Jan 1967), when the games were a competition between NFL and AFL champions. The Pittsburgh Steelers have the most Super Bowl victories with 4 (1975–76, 79–80). The 1972 Miami Dolphins had the best record for one season, including playoffs and Super Bowl (played Jan 1973), with 17 wins and no losses or ties.

Highest Score

The most points ever scored (by one team and both teams) in a college football game was 222 by Georgia Tech, Atlanta, Ga, against Cumberland University of Lebanon, Tenn on Oct 7, 1916. Tech

also set records for the most points scored in one quarter (63), most touchdowns (32) and points after touchdown (30) in a game, and the largest victory margin (Cumberland did not score).

Longest Streaks

The longest collegiate winning streak is 47 straight by Oklahoma. The longest unbeaten streak is 63 games (59 won, 4 tied) by Washington from 1907 to 1917. Macalaster University of St Paul, Minn, ended a record 50-game losing streak when, with 11 sec remaining in the game, a 23-yd field goal beat Mount Senario, 17–14, on Sept 6, 1980. It was Macalaster's first victory since Oct 11, 1974.

All-America Selections

The earliest All-America selections were made in 1889 by Caspar Whitney of *The Week's Sport* and later of *Harper's Weekly*.

FOOT SOLDIERS: Glenn Davis (#41), known as Mr Outside, scored 59 career td's for the West Point Army team, rushing for a record 8.26 yd per carry. He won the Heisman Trophy in 1946, one year after his teammate Doc Blanchard (#35), a.k.a. Mr Inside. (USMA)

ALL-TIME US PROFESSIONAL RECORDS
(Through 1981 Season)

SERVICE

Most Seasons, Active Player
26 George Blanda, Chi Bears, 1949–58; Balt, 1950; AFL: Hou, 1960–66; Oak, 1967–75

Most Games Played, Lifetime
340 George Blanda, Chi Bears, 1949–58; Balt, 1950; AFL: Hou, 1960–66; Oak, 1967–75

Most Consecutive Games Played, Lifetime
282 Jim Marshall, Cleve, 1960; Minn, 1961–79

Most Seasons, Head Coach
40 George Halas, Chi Bears, 1920–29, 33–42, 46–55, 58–67

SCORING

Most Seasons Leading League
5 Don Hutson, GB, 1940–44
Gino Cappelletti, Bos, 1961, 63–66 (AFL)

Most Points, Lifetime
2,002 George Blanda, Chi Bears, 1949–58; Balt, 1950; AFL: Hou, 1960–66; Oak, 1967–75 (9-td, 943-pat, 335-fg)

Most Points, Season
176 Paul Hornung, GB, 1960 (15-td, 41-pat, 15-fg)

Most Points, Rookie Season
132 Gale Sayers, Chi, 1965 (22-td)

Most Points, Game
40 Ernie Nevers, Chi Cards vs Chi Bears, Nov 28, 1929 (6-td, 4-pat)

Most Points, One Quarter
29 Don Hutson, GB vs Det, Oct 7, 1945 (4-td, 5-pat) 2nd Quarter

Touchdowns
Most Seasons Leading League
8 Don Hutson, GB, 1935–38, 41–44

Most Touchdowns, Lifetime
126 Jim Brown, Cleve, 1957–65 (106-r, 20-p)

Most Touchdowns, Season
23 O. J. Simpson, Buff, 1975 (16-r, 7-p)

Most Touchdowns, Rookie Season
22 Gale Sayers, Chi, 1965 (14-r, 6-p, 1-prb, 1-krb)

Most Consecutive Games Scoring Touchdowns
18 Lenny Moore, Balt, 1963–65

Most Touchdowns, Game
6 Ernie Nevers, Chi Cards vs Chi Bears, Nov 28, 1929 (6-r)
William (Dub) Jones, Cleve vs Chi Bears, Nov 25, 1951 (4-r, 2-p)
Gale Sayers, Chi vs SF, Dec 12, 1965 (4-r, 1-p, 1-prb)

Points After Touchdown
Most Seasons Leading League
8 George Blanda, Chi Bears, 1956; AFL: Hou, 1961–62; Oak, 1967–69, 72, 74

Most Points After Touchdown, Lifetime
943 George Blanda, Chi Bears, 1949–58; Balt, 1950; AFL: Hou, 1960–66; Oak, 1967–75

Most Points After Touchdown, Season
64 George Blanda, Hou, 1961 (AFL)

Most Points After Touchdown, Game
9 Marlin (Pat) Harder, Chi Cards vs NY, Oct 17, 1948
Bob Waterfield, LA vs Balt, Oct 22, 1950
Charlie Gogolak, Wash vs NY, Nov 27, 1966

Most Consecutive Points After Touchdown
234 Tommy Davis, SF, 1959–65

Most Points After Touchdown (no misses), Game
9 Marlin (Pat) Harder, Chi Cards vs NY, Oct 17, 1948
Bob Waterfield, LA vs Balt, Oct 22, 1950

Field Goals
Most Seasons Leading League
5 Lou Groza, Cleve, 1950, 52–54, 57

Most Field Goals, Lifetime
335 George Blanda, Chi Bears, 1949–58; Balt, 1950; AFL: Hou, 1960–66; Oak, 1967–75

Most Field Goals, Season
34 Jim Turner, NY, 1968 (AFL)

Most Field Goals, Game
7 Jim Bakken, St L vs Pitt, Sept 24, 1967

Most Consecutive Games, Field Goals
31 Fred Cox, Minn, 1968–70

Most Consecutive Field Goals
20 Garo Yepremian, Mia, 1978; NO, 1979

Longest Field Goal
63 yd Tom Dempsey, NO vs Det, Nov 8, 1970

RUSHING

Most Seasons Leading League
8 Jim Brown, Cleve, 1957–61, 63–65

Most Yards Gained, Lifetime
12,312 Jim Brown, Cleve, 1957–65

Most Yards Gained, Season
2,003 O. J. Simpson, Buff, 1973

Most Yards Gained, Game
275 Walter Payton, Chi vs Minn, Nov 20, 1977

Longest Run from Scrimmage
97 yd Andy Uram, GB vs Chi Cards, Oct 8, 1939 (td)
Bob Gage, Pitt vs Chi Bears, Dec 4, 1949 (td)

Highest Average Gain, Lifetime (799 att)
5.2 Jim Brown, Cleve, 1957–65 (2,359–12,312)

Highest Average Gain, Game (10 att)
17.1 Marion Motley, Cleve vs Pitt, Oct 29, 1950 (11–188)

Most Touchdowns Rushing, Lifetime
106 Jim Brown, Cleve, 1957–65

Most Touchdowns Rushing, Season
19 Jim Taylor, GB, 1962
Earl Campbell, Hou, 1979
Chuck Muncie, SD, 1981

Most Touchdowns Rushing, Game
6 Ernie Nevers, Chi Cards vs Chi Bears, Nov 28, 1929

PASSING

Most Seasons Leading League
6 Sammy Baugh, Wash, 1937, 40, 43, 45, 47, 49

Most Passes Attempted, Lifetime
6,467 Fran Tarkenton, Minn, 1961–66, 72–78; NY Giants, 1967–71 (3,686 completions)

Most Passes Attempted, Season
609 Dan Fouts, SD, 1981 (360 completions)

Most Passes Attempted, Game
68 George Blanda, Hou vs Buff, Nov 1, 1964 (AFL) (37 completions)

Most Passes Completed, Lifetime
3,686 Fran Tarkenton, Minn, 1961–66, 72–78; NY Giants, 1967–71 (6,467 attempts)

Most Passes Completed, Season
360 Dan Fouts, SD, 1981 (609 attempts)

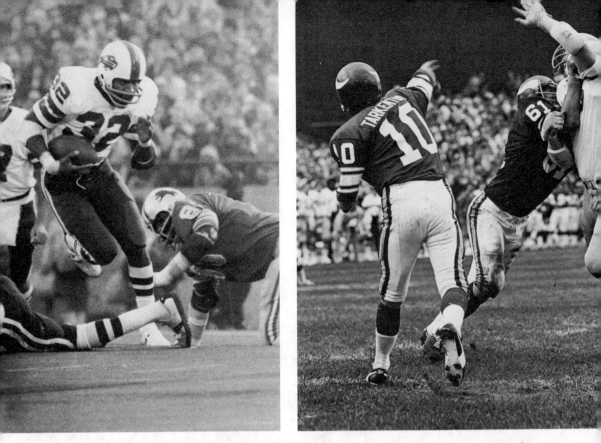

BY THE YARD: O. J. Simpson (#32, left) rushed for a record 2,003 yd in the 1973 season. Two years later he set a season td mark by reaching the end zone 23 times. Simpson rushed for a then-record 273 yd in the game shown in this photo, in 1976, but Walter Payton eclipsed that record with 275 yd in 1977. Fran Tarkenton (#10, right) set several significant career passing marks in his 18-year career. He threw 6,467 passes—more than anyone else—and completed a record 3,686 of them, for an unequaled total of 47,003 yd. Tarkenton could put points on the scoreboard, too—he threw a record 342 td passes. He'd probably be the first to tell you, "That's incredible!" (Simpson photo courtesy Robert L. Smith/Buffalo Bills; Tarkenton photo courtesy Minnesota Vikings)

FULL GAINER: Jim Brown (#32) dives into the end zone to score against the Colts in the 1964 NFL Championship Playoff. Brown scored 126 td's in his career (not including playoff scores), 106 of which came on running plays. With an astounding 5.2 yd per carry lifetime average, Brown rushed for 12,312 yd in his career. (Pro Football Hall of Fame)

PUTTING THE FOOT IN FOOTBALL: Steve O'Neal (#20) of the NY Jets follows through on his punt from the end zone in Denver's Mile High Stadium. The line of scrimmage (from which punts are measured) had been the 1-yd line. The ball, which sailed well over the receiver's head, bounced and rolled to the Denver 1-yd line—a 98-yd punt! (Pro Football Hall of Fame)

Passing (continued)

Most Passes Completed, Game
   42   Richard Todd, NY Jets vs SF, Sept 21, 1980 (59 attempts)

Most Consecutive Passes Completed
   17   Bert Jones, Balt vs NY Jets, Dec 15, 1974

Longest Pass Completion (all tds)
   99   Frank Filchock (to Farkas), Wash vs Pitt, Oct 15, 1939
         George Izo (to Mitchell), Wash vs Cleve, Sept 15, 1963
         Karl Sweetan (to Studstill), Det vs Balt, Oct 16, 1966
         C. A. Jurgensen (to Allen), Wash vs Chi, Sept 15, 1968

Most Yards Gained Passing, Lifetime
47,003 Fran   Tarkenton, Minn, 1961–66, 72–78; NY Giants, 1967–71

Most Yards Gained Passing, Season
 4,802 Dan Fouts, SD, 1981

Most Yards Gained Passing, Game
  554 Norm Van Brocklin, LA vs NY Yanks, Sept 28, 1951 (41–27)

Most Touchdown Passes, Lifetime
  342 Fran   Tarkenton,   Minn, 1961–66, 72–78; NY Giants, 1967–71

Most Touchdown Passes, Season
   36 George Blanda, Hou, 1961 (AFL)
        Y. A. Tittle, NY, 1963

Most Touchdown Passes, Game
    7 Sid Luckman, Chi Bears vs NY, Nov 14, 1943
      Adrian Burk, Phil vs Wash, Oct 17, 1954
      George Blanda, Hou vs NY, Nov 19, 1961 (AFL)
      Y. A. Tittle, NY vs Wash, Oct 28, 1962
      Joe Kapp, Minn vs Balt, Sept 28, 1969

Most Consecutive Games, Touchdown Passes
   47 John Unitas, Balt, 1956–60

Passing Efficiency, Lifetime (1,500 att)
  60.3 Ken Stabler, Oak, 1970–79; Hou, 1980–81 (3,223–1,944)

Passing Efficiency, Season (100 att)
  70.3 Sammy Baugh, Wash, 1945 (182–128)

Passing Efficiency, Game (20 att)
  90.9 Ken Anderson, Cin vs Pitt, Nov 10, 1974 (22–20)

Passes Had Intercepted

Most Passes Intercepted, Game
    8 Jim Hardy, Chi Cards vs Phil, Sept 24, 1950 (39 attempts)

Most Consecutive Passes Attempted, None Intercepted
  294 Bryan (Bart) Starr, GB, 1964–65

Fewest Passes Intercepted, Season (Qualifiers)
   1 Joe Ferguson, Buff, 1976 (151 attempts)

Lowest Percentage Passes Intercepted, Lifetime (1,500 att)
   3.3 Roman Gabriel, LA, 1962–72; Phil, 1973–77 (4,498–149)

Lowest Percentage Passes Intercepted, Season (Qualifiers)
   0.66 Joe Ferguson, Buff, 1976 (151–1)

PASS RECEPTIONS

Most Seasons Leading League
   8 Don Hutson, GB, 1936–37, 39, 41–45

Most Pass Receptions, Lifetime
   649 Charley Taylor, Wash, 1964–75, 77

Most Pass Receptions, Season
   101 Charley Hennigan, Hou, 1964 (AFL)

Most Pass Receptions, Game
   18 Tom Fears, LA vs GB, Dec 3, 1950 (189 yd)

Most Pass Receptions by a Running Back, Game
   17 Clark Gaines, NY Jets vs SF, Sept 21, 1980

Most Yards Gained Pass Receptions, Game
   303 Jim Benton, Cleve vs Det, Nov 22, 1945

Longest Pass Reception (all tds)
   99 Andy Farkas (Filchock), Wash vs Pitt, Oct 15, 1939
      Bobby Mitchell (Izo), Wash vs Cleve, Sept 15, 1963
      Pat Studstill (Sweetan), Det vs Balt, Oct 16, 1966
      Gerry Allen (Jurgensen), Wash vs Chi, Sept 15, 1968

Most Consecutive Games, Pass Receptions
   127 Harold Carmichael, Phil, 1972–1980

Touchdowns Receiving

Most Touchdown Passes, Lifetime
   99 Don Hutson, GB, 1935–45

Most Touchdown Passes, Season
   17 Don Hutson, GB, 1942
      Elroy (Crazy Legs) Hirsch, LA, 1951
      Bill Groman, Hou, 1961 (AFL)

Most Touchdown Passes, Game
   5 Bob Shaw, Chi Cards vs Balt, Oct 2, 1950
      Kellen Winslow, SD vs Oak, Nov 22, 1981

Most Consecutive Games, Touchdown Passes
   11 Elroy (Crazy Legs) Hirsch, LA, 1950–51
      Gilbert (Buddy) Dial, Pitt, 1959–60

PASS INTERCEPTIONS

Most Interceptions by, Lifetime
   81 Paul Krause, Wash (28), 1964–67; Minn (53), 1968–79

Most Interceptions by, Season
   14 Richard (Night Train) Lane, LA, 1952

Most Interceptions by, Game
   4 By many players, twice by Jerry Norton St L vs Wash, Nov 20, 1960; St L vs Pitt, Nov 26, 1961

Most Touchdowns Interception Returns, Lifetime
   9 Ken Houston, Hou 1967–79; Wash 1973–80

PUNTING

Most Seasons Leading League
   4 Sammy Baugh, Wash, 1940–43
      Jerrel Wilson, AFL: KC, 1965, 68; NFL: KC, 1972–73

Most Punts, Lifetime
   1,072 Jerrel Wilson, AFL: KC, 1963–69; NFL: KC, 1970–77; NE, 1978

Most Punts, Season
   114 Bob Parsons, Chi, 1981

Most Punts, Game
   14 Dick Nesbitt, Chi Cards vs Chi Bears, Nov 30, 1933
      Keith Molesworth, Chi Bears vs GB, Dec 10, 1933
      Sammy Baugh, Wash vs Phil, Nov 5, 1939
      John Kinscherf, NY vs Det, Nov 7, 1943
      George Taliaferro, NY Yanks vs LA, Sept 28, 1951

Longest Punt
   98 yd Steve O'Neal, NY Jets vs Den, Sept 21, 1969 (AFL)

Average Yardage Punting

Highest Punting Average, Lifetime (300 punts)
   45.1 yd Sammy Baugh, Wash, 1937–52 (338)

Highest Punting Average, Season (20 punts)
   51.4 yd Sammy Baugh, Wash, 1940 (35)

Highest Punting Average, Game (4 punts)
   61.8 yd Bob Cifers, Det vs Chi Bears, Nov 24, 1946

PUNT RETURNS

Yardage Returning Punts

Most Yards Gained, Lifetime
   2,714 Rick Upchurch, Den, 1975–81

Most Yards Gained, Season
   655 Neal Colzie, Oak, 1975

Most Yards Gained, Game
   205 George Atkinson, Oak vs Buff, Sept 15, 1968

Longest Punt Return (all tds)
   98 Gil LeFebvre, Cin vs Brk, Dec 3, 1933
      Charlie West, Minn vs Wash, Nov 3, 1968
      Dennis Morgan, Dall vs St L, Oct 13, 1974

Average Yardage Returning Punts

Highest Average, Lifetime (75 returns)
   13.2 Billy (White Shoes) Johnson, Hou, 1974–79

Highest Average, Season (Qualifiers)
   23.0 Herb Rich, Balt, 1950

Highest Average, Game (3 returns)
   47.7 Chuck Latourette, St L vs NO, Sept 29, 1968

Touchdowns Returning Punts

Most Touchdowns, Lifetime
   8 Jack Christiansen, Det, 1951–58

Most Touchdowns, Season
   4 Jack Christiansen, Det, 1951
      Rick Upchurch, Den, 1976

Most Touchdowns, Game
   2 Jack Christiansen, Det vs LA, Oct 14, 1951; vs GB, Nov 22, 1951
      Dick Christy, NY Titans vs Den, Sept 24, 1961
      Rick Upchurch, Den vs Cleve, Sept 26, 1976
      Leroy Irvin, LA vs Atl, Oct 11, 1981

KICKOFF RETURNS

Yardage Returning Kickoffs

Most Yards Gained, Lifetime
   6,922 Ron Smith, Chi, 1965, 70–72; Atl, 1966–67; LA, 1968–69; SD, 1973; Oak, 1974

Most Yards Gained, Season
   1,317 Bobby Jancik, Hou, 1963 (AFL)

PURPLE PEOPLE-EATER: Jim Marshall (dark uniform) played in 282 consecutive regular-season NFL games, to the consternation of quarterbacks around the league. Marshall scooped up a record 29 opponents' fumbles, the most famous of which he "returned" in the wrong direction. (Minnesota Vikings)

Touchdowns Returning Kickoffs

Most Touchdowns, Lifetime
6   Ollie Matson, Chi Cards, 1952 (2), 54, 56, 58 (2)
Gale Sayers, Chi, 1965, 66 (2), 67 (3)
Travis Williams, GB, 1967 (4), 69, 71

Most Touchdowns, Season
4   Travis Williams, GB, 1967
Cecil Turner, Chi, 1970

Most Touchdowns, Game
2   Thomas (Tim) Brown, Phil vs Dall, Nov 6, 1966
Travis Williams, GB vs Cleve, Nov 12, 1967

FUMBLES

Most Fumbles, Lifetime
105   Roman Gabriel, LA, 1962–72; Phil, 1973–77

Most Fumbles, Season
17   Dan Pastorini, Hou, 1973

Most Fumbles, Game
7   Len Dawson, KC vs SD, Nov 15, 1964 (AFL)

Longest Fumble Run
104   Jack Tatum, Oak vs GB, Sept 24, 1972

Most Opponents' Fumbles Recovered, Lifetime
29   Jim Marshall, Cleve, 1960; Minn, 1961–79

Most Opponents' Fumbles Recovered, Season
9   Don Hultz, Minn, 1963

Most Opponents' Fumbles Recovered, Game
3   Corwin Clatt, Chi Cards vs Det, Nov 6, 1949
Vic Sears, Phil vs GB, Nov 2, 1952
Ed Beatty, SF vs LA, Oct 7, 1956
Ron Carroll, Hou vs Cin, Oct 27, 1974
Maurice Spencer, NO vs Atl, Oct 10, 1976
Steve Nelson, NE vs Phil, Oct 8, 1978
Charles Jackson, KC vs Pitt, Sept 6, 1981
Willie Buchanon, SD vs Den, Sept 27, 1981

Kickoff Returns (continued)

Most Yards Gained, Game
294   Wally Triplett, Det vs LA, Oct 29, 1950 (4)

Longest Kickoff Return for Touchdown
106   Al Carmichael, GB vs Chi Bears, Oct 7, 1956
Noland Smith, KC vs Den, Dec 17, 1967 (AFL)
Roy Green, St L vs Dall, Oct 21, 1979

Average Yardage Returning Kickoffs

Highest Average, Lifetime (75 returns)
30.6   Gale Sayers, Chi, 1965–71

Highest Average, Season (15 returns)
41.1   Travis Williams, GB, 1967 (18)

Highest Average, Game (3 returns)
73.5   Wally Triplett, Det vs LA, Oct 29, 1950 (4–294)

GAMBLING

World's Biggest Win

The world's biggest gambling win is $5.5 million in the Pennsylvania weekly Lotto game by an unnamed player on June 19, 1982.

World's Biggest Loss

An unnamed Italian industrialist was reported to have lost $1,920,000 in five hours at roulette in Monte Carlo, Monaco, on March 6, 1974. A Saudi Arabian prince was reported to have lost more than $1 million in a single session at the Metro Club, Las Vegas, Nev, in Dec 1974.

Largest Casino

The largest casino in the world is the Resorts International Casino, Atlantic City, NJ, with an annual win in 1979 of $232,945,748. The Casino comprises 60,000 sq ft, containing 127 gaming tables and 1,640 slot machines. Attendances total over 35,000 daily at peak weekends.

BIG DEAL: Earl Arnall dealt blackjack for nearly 8 full days in Las Vegas in 1977.

BINGO

Origins

Bingo is a lottery game which, as keno, was developed in the 1880's from lotto, whose origin is thought to be the 17th century Italian game *tumbule*. It has long been known in the British Army (as Housey-Housey) and the Royal Navy (as Tombola). The winner was the first to complete a random selection of numbers from 1–90. The US version of Bingo differs in that the selection is from 1–75.

Largest House

The largest "house" in Bingo sessions was at the Empire Pool, Wembley, London, on Apr 25, 1965, when 10,000 attended.

Bingo-Calling Marathon

A session of 265 hours 1 min was held at the Excess Sports and Social Club, Worthing, England, in Sept, 1981, with Alan Beech and Jeff McGee calling.

BLACKJACK

Marathon

Earl Arnall, a dealer at the King 8 Casino in Las Vegas, Nev, spent 190 hours at the blackjack table, June 22–30, 1977. Ardeth Hardy set the women's mark of 169 hours 47 min of continuous dealing during the same period. Both took 5-min rest breaks within each hour.

HORSE RACING

Topmost Tipster

The only recorded instance of a racing correspondent forecasting ten out of ten winners on a race card was at Delaware Park, Wilmington, Del, on July 28, 1974, by Charles Lamb of the *Baltimore News American*.

Greatest Pay-Out

A sum of $382,344 ($305,876.80 after witholding tax) was won by an unnamed bettor from a $2 ticket for the "Pick Six" selection of six winners at Hialeah Race Track, Fla, on Jan 25, 1982. On Dec 12, 1976 Mr Lim Chooi Seng won Malaysian $1,112,400 (now

FEELS LIKE A MILLION BUCKS: Jeff Randolph (center) was playing a slot machine at Caesars Tahoe Casino in July 1981 when he hit the jackpot. The machine awarded him $992,012.15 and the casino management threw in nearly $8,000 to bring the winnings to $1 million. (Caesars Tahoe)

about $440,000) on "Freedom Fighter" in the sixth race at Penang.

Largest Bookmaker

The world's largest bookmaker is Ladbrokes of London, with a turnover from gambling in 1981 of £552 million ($993.6 million).

See also *Harness Racing* and *Horse Racing*.

ROULETTE

Longest Run

The longest run in an ungaffed (*i.e.* true) wheel reliably recorded is six successive coups (in No. 10) at El San Juan Hotel, Puerto Rico, July 9, 1959. The odds with a double zero were 1 in 38^6, or 3,010,936,383, to 1. The longest "marathon" on record is one of 31

days from Apr 10 to May 11, 1970, at The Casino de Macao, to test the validity or invalidity of certain contentions in 20,000 spins.

SLOT MACHINES

Largest

The world's biggest slot machine (or one-armed bandit) is Super Bertha (555 cu ft) installed by Si Redd at the Four Queens Casino, Las Vegas, Nev, in Sept 1973. Once in every 25 billion plays it may yield $1 million for a $10 investment.

Biggest Win

The biggest beating handed to a "one-armed bandit" was $992,012.15, rounded up by the management to "an even million dollars," by Jeff Randolph of Delano, Calif, at Caesars Tahoe Casino, South Lake Tahoe, Nev, on July 17, 1981.

GAMES AND PASTIMES

BACKGAMMON

Forerunners of the game have been traced back to a dice and a board game found in excavations at Ur, dated to 3000 BC. Later the Romans played a game remarkably similar to the modern one. The name "Backgammon" is variously ascribed to Welsh ("little battle"), or Saxon ("back game"). Modern variations include the American Acey Deucey.

At present there are no world championships held, but a points rating system may soon be introduced internationally, thereby enabling players to be ranked.

Marathon

Dick Newcomb and Greg Peterson of Rockford, Ill, played backgammon for 151 hours 11 min, June 30–July 6, 1978.

BRIDGE (CONTRACT)

Bridge (corruption of Biritch) is thought to be either of Levantine origin, similar games having been played there in the early 1870's, or to have come from the East—probably India.

Auction bridge (highest bidder names trump) was invented c. 1902. The contract principle, present in several games (notably the French game *Plafond, c.* 1917), was introduced to bridge by Harold S. Vanderbilt (US) on Nov 1, 1925, during a Caribbean voyage aboard the SS *Finland.* The new version became a world-wide craze after the US vs GB challenge match between Rumanian-born Ely Culbertson (1891–1955) and Lt-Col Walter Thomas More Buller (1887–1938) at Almack's Club, London, Sept 1930. The US won the 200-hand match by 4,845 points.

Most World Titles

The World Championship (Bermuda Bowl) has been won most often by Italy's Blue Team (*Squadra Azzura*), 1957–9, 61–3, 65–7, 69, 73–5, whose team also won the Olympiad in 1964, 68 and 72. Giorgio Belladonna (b 1923) was in all these winning teams.

Most Master Points

In the latest ranking list based on Master Points awarded by the World Bridge Federation, the leading male player in the world was Giorgio Belladonna, a member of Italy's Blue Team, with 1,766¼ points, followed by four more Italians. The world's leading woman player is Dorothy Hayden Truscott (US) with 322¼ points.

Marathon

The longest recorded session is one of 180 hours by four students at Edinburgh University, Scotland, Apr 21–28, 1972.

Perfect Deals

The mathematical odds against dealing 13 cards of one suit are 158,753,389,899 to 1, while the odds against receiving a "perfect hand" consisting of all 13 spades are 635,013,559,596 to 1. The odds against each of the 4 players receiving a complete suit (a "perfect deal") are 2,235,197,406,895,366,368,301,559,999 to 1.

MASTERMIND: Dorothy Hayden Truscott leads all women with 322¼ World Bridge Federation master points.

CHECKMATES: Nona Gaprindashvili (left) here unsuccessfully challenges Elizaveta Bykova for the women's world chess title. Gaprindashvili later captured the title and held on to it for over 16 years.

CHECKERS

Checkers, also known as draughts, has origins earlier than chess. It was played in Egypt in the second millennium BC. The earliest book on the game was by Antonio Torquemada of Valencia, Spain in 1547. There have been three US vs GB international matches (crossboard) in 1905, 27 and 73, two won by the US and one by GB.

Walter Hellman (1916–75) (US) won a record 6 world championships, 1948–67.

Most Opponents

Newell W. Banks (b Detroit, Mich, Oct 10, 1887) played 140 games simultaneously, winning 133 and drawing 7, in Chicago in 1933. His playing time was 145 min, so averaging about one move per sec. In 1947 he played blindfolded for 4 hours per day for 45 consecutive days, winning 1,331 games, drawing 54 and losing only 2, while playing six games at a time. Patrick Moore (b Mar 4, 1923) (GB) played 149 games simultaneously, at Twickenham, Greater London, on May 30, 1981, winning 118, losing 27 and drawing 4.

Longest and Shortest Games

In competition the prescribed rate of play is not less than 30 moves per hour with the average game lasting about 90 min. In 1958 a match between Dr Marion Tinsley (US) and Derek Oldbury (GB) lasted 7 hours 30 min. The shortest possible game is one of 20 moves, composed by Alan M. Beckerson (GB) on Nov 2, 1977.

CHESS

The game originated in ancient India under the name Chaturanga (literally "four-corps")— an army game. The name chess is derived from the Persian word *shah*. The earliest reference is from the Middle Persian Karnamak (*c.* 590–628), though there are grounds for believing its origins are from the 2nd century, owing to the discovery, announced in Dec 1972, of two ivory chessmen in the Uzbek Soviet Republic, datable to that century. The *Fédération Internationale des Echecs* was established in 1924. There were an estimated 7 million registered players in the USSR in 1973.

Longest Games

The master game with the most moves on record was when Yedael Stepak (b Aug 21, 1940) (Israel) beat Yaakov Mashian (b Dec 17, 1943) (Iran, later Israel) in 193 moves in Tel Aviv, Israel, March 23–Apr 16, 1980. The total playing time was 24½ hours.

The slowest reported move (before modern rules) in an official event is reputed to have been played by Louis Paulsen (1833–91) (Germany) against Paul Charles Morphy (1837–84) (US) on Oct 29, 1857.

The game ended in a draw on move 56 after 15 hours of play, of which Paulsen used most of the allotted time. Grandmaster Friedrich Sämisch (1896–1975) (Germany) ran out of the allotted time (2½ hours for 45 moves) after only 12 moves, in Prague, Czechoslovakia, in 1938.

World Champions

World champions have been generally recognized since 1886. The longest undisputed tenure was 27 years by Dr Emanuel Lasker (1868–1941) of Germany, from 1894 to 1921. Robert J. (Bobby) Fischer (b Chicago, March 9, 1943) is reckoned on the officially adopted Elo system to be the greatest Grandmaster of all time, with a 2,785 rating.

The women's world championship was held by Vera Menchik-Stevenson (1906–44) (GB) from 1927 till her death, and was successfully defended a record 7 times. Nona Gaprindashvili (USSR) (b May 3, 1941) held the title from 1962 to 1978, and defended successfully 4 times.

The USSR has won the men's team title a record 13 times and the women's title 8 times.

The youngest world champion was Mikhail Nekhemevich Tal (USSR) (b Nov 9, 1936) when he took the title on May 7, 1960, aged 23 years 180 days. The oldest was Wilhelm Steinitz (1836–1900) who was 58 years old when he lost his title to Lasker in 1894.

José Raúl Capablanca (1888–1942) (Cuba) lost only 34 games in his adult career, 1909–39, for the fewest games lost by a world champion. He was unbeaten from Feb 10, 1916, to Mar 21, 1924, and was world champion from 1921 to 1927.

Marathon

The longest recorded session is one of 168 hours by Stan Zygmunt and Ilya Schwartzman at the 45th Avenue Shopping Center, Munster, Ind, Dec 28, 1979–Jan 4, 1980.

Most Opponents

Vlastimil Hort (b Jan 12, 1944) (Czechoslovakia), in Seltjarnes, Iceland, Apr 23–24, 1977, played 550 opponents, including a record 201 simultaneously. He only lost ten games.

The record for most consecutive games played is held by Branimir Brebrich (Canada), who played 575 games (533 wins, 27 draws, 15 losses) in Edmonton, Canada, Jan 27–28, 1978, during 28 hours of play.

Georges Koltanowski (Belgium, later of US) tackled 56 opponents "blindfold" and won 50, drew 6, lost 0 in 9¾ hours at the Fairmont Hotel, San Francisco, on Dec 13, 1960.

CRIBBAGE

The invention of the game (once called Cribbidge) is credited to the English dramatist Sir John Suckling (1609–42). It is estimated that some ten million people play in the US alone.

Rare Hands

F. Art Skinner, of Alberta, Canada, is reported to have had three maximum 29-point hands. Paul Nault of Athol, Mass, had two such hands within eight games in a tournament on March 19, 1977. Derek Hearne dealt two hands of six clubs with the turn-up card the remaining club on Feb 8, 1976, in Blackpool, Lancashire, England. Bill Rogers of Burnaby, BC, Canada scored 29 in the crib in 1975.

Marathon

Geoff Lee, Ken Whyatt, Ray Charles and Paul Branson played for 120 hours at the RAOB Club, Mapperley, England, Mar 16–21, 1982.

DARTS*

The origins of darts date from the use by archers of heavily weighted 10-in throwing arrows for self-defense in close quarters fighting. The "dartes" were used in Ireland in the 16th century and darts was played on the *Mayflower* by the Plymouth pilgrims in 1620. The modern game dates from at least 1896 when Brian Gamlin of Bury, Lancashire, England, is credited with inventing the present numbering system on the board. The first recorded score of 180 (three triple 20's) was by John Reader at the Highbury Tavern in Sussex, England, in 1902. Today there are an estimated 6 million dart players in the British Isles.

Most Titles

Eric Bristow (b Apr 25, 1957) (GB) has the most wins in the World Masters Championships (instituted 1974) with 3, in 1977, 79 and 81. He has also

---

* For more detailed information about darts, see *The Guinness Book of Darts*, available from Sterling.

THE ARTFUL DARTER: Eric Bristow with the Winmau World Masters trophy that he won for the third time when he beat John Lowe in the 1981 final. (Colorsport)

won the World Professional Championship (instituted 1978) twice, 1980–81. John Lowe (b July 21, 1945) (GB) is the only man to have won each of the four major world titles: World Masters (1976 and 80), World Professional (1979), World Cup Singles (1981), and *News of the World* (1981).

Fastest Match

The fastest time taken for a match of three games of 301 is 1 min 58 sec by Ricky Fusco (GB) at the Perivale Residents Association Club, Middlesex, England, on Dec 30, 1976.

Fastest "Round the Board"

The record time for going round the board clockwise in "doubles" at arms length is 9.2 sec by Dennis Gower at the Millers Arms, Hastings, England on Oct 12, 1975 and 14.5 sec in numerical order by Jim Pike (1903–60) at the Craven Club, Newmarket, England in March 1944. The record for this feat at the 9-ft throwing distance, retrieving own darts, is 2 min 13 sec by Bill Duddy (b Sept 29, 1932) at

The Plough, Harringey, London, England on Oct 29, 1972.

Lowest Possible Scores

Scores of 201 in four darts, 301 in six darts, 401 in seven darts and 501 in nine darts, have been achieved on various occasions. The lowest number of darts thrown for a score of 1,001 is 19 by Cliff Inglis (b 1935) (160, 180, 140, 180, 121, 180, 40) at the Bromfield Men's Club, Devon, England on Nov 11, 1975. A score of 2,001 in 52 darts was achieved by Alan Evans (b 1949) at Ferndale, Glamorgan on Sept 3, 1976. A score of 3,001 in 79 darts was thrown by Charlie Ellix (b 1941) at The Victoria Hotel, Tottenham, London on Apr 29, 1977.

24-Hour Scores

Eight players from the Royal Hotel, Newsome, England, scored, on one board, 1,358,731 in 24 hours, May 26–27, 1981.

Million-and-One

Eight players from The Sir John Barleycorn, Bitterne, England scored 1,000,001 with 39,566 darts in one session, Apr 4–6, 1980.

Marathon

John Hedley and David Robson played for 120 hours 10 min at the Royal Oak Inn, Hirst Courtney, Selby, England, Mar 19–23, 1982.

FRISBEE®

Competitive play began in 1957, and championships are supervised by the International Frisbee disc Association.

Distance

The world record for outdoor distance is 500 ft on a throw by Tetsuro Arita of Tokyo, Japan on May 4, 1980. The indoor distance record is held by Joseph Youngman of L'Anse, Mich, with a 363.5-ft toss at Cedar Falls, Iowa, Apr 26, 1981.

Liz Reeves holds the women's outdoor distance record (401.5 ft, set in Surrey, England, June 14, 1980), while the women's indoor distance record belongs to Suzanne Fields, of Boston, who threw 229.6 ft in Cedar Falls, Iowa, Apr 26, 1981.

The 24-hour group distance record is 428.02 miles set in Vernon, Conn, by the South Windsor Ultimate Frisbee disc Team, July 8–9, 1977. Dan Roddick and Alan Bonopane of Pasadena, Calif, hold the world record for 24-hour pair distance with 250.02 miles, Dec 30–31, 1979.

Skills

Mark Vinchesi set the record for maximum time aloft by keeping a Frisbee disc in the air for 15.2 sec in Amherst, Mass, on Aug 20, 1978. For women, the time-aloft record is 11.47 sec, set in Sonoma, Calif, by Denise Garfield on Oct 5, 1980.

The greatest distance achieved for throwing a Frisbee disc, running, and catching it is 271.2 ft by Tom Monroe of Huntsville, Ala, on Aug 24, 1979, in Irvine, Calif.

Fastest Guts Catch

Alan Bonopane threw a professional model Frisbee disc at a speed of 74 mph and his teammate Tom Selinske made a clean catch of the throw on Aug 25, 1980 in San Marino, Calif.

Marathons

The Alhambra Frisbee disc Club of Alhambra, Calif, set the group marathon mark with 1,001 hours, May 7–June 18, 1978. The two-person marathon record is held by Duncan Urquhart and John Keenan, who played 102 hours in Tarrytown, NY, Aug 22–26, 1979.

MONOPOLY®

The patentee of Monopoly, the world's most popular proprietary board game of which Parker Brothers has sold in excess of 80 million copies, was Charles Darrow (1889–1967). He invented the patented version of the game in 1933, while an unemployed heating engineer, using the street names of Atlantic City, NJ, where he spent his vacations.

Marathon

The longest game by four players ratified by Parker Brothers is 408 hours by Peter Callon, Paul Taplin, John Cresswell and Lesley De Wahl of Shanklin, Isle of Wight, England, Feb 5–22, 1981.

POOL AND BILLIARDS

Pool

Pool or championship pocket billiards with numbered balls began to become standardized *c.* 1890. The greatest exponents were Ralph Greenleaf (US) (1899–1950), who won the "world" professional title

BANK SHOT: The $500 bills in this photo may be only play money, but the money that Parker Brothers has made from sales of Monopoly is real. In the 50 years since the game was patented, over 80 million games have been sold. (Parker Bros, Inc.)

19 times (1919–1937), and William Mosconi (US), who dominated the game from 1941 to 1957.

Michael Eufemia holds the record for the greatest continuous run in a straight pool match, pocketing 625 balls without a miss on Feb 2, 1960 before a large crowd at Logan's Billiard Academy, Brooklyn, New York.

The greatest number of balls to be pocketed in 24 hours is 13,437 by Patrick Young at the Lord Stanleyk Plaistow, London, England, July 20–21, 1981.

The longest game is 218 hours 30 min by Lance Deek and David Williams at Bogey's Club, Cardiff, Wales, June 19–28, 1981.

3-Cushion Billiards

This pocketless variation dates back to 1878. The world governing body, *Union Mondiale de Billiard*, was formed in 1928. The most successful exponent, 1906–52, was William F. Hoppe (b Oct 11, 1887, Cornwall-on-Hudson, NY; d Feb 1, 1959) who won 51 billiards championships in all forms. The most UMB titles have been won by Raymond Ceulemans (Belgium) (b 1937) with 16 (1963–66, 1968–73, 1975–80), with a peak average of 1.679 in 1978.

SCRABBLE® CROSSWORD GAME

The crossword game was invented by Alfred M. Butts in 1931 and was developed, refined and trademarked as Scrabble Crossword Game by James Brunot in 1948. He sold the North American rights to Selchow & Richter Company, NY, the European rights to J. W. Spears & Sons, London, and the Australian rights to Murfett Pty Ltd, Melbourne.

Marathon

The longest Scrabble Crossword Game is 129 hours 42 min by Marie Warrell and Carol Brockie at The Cock Inn, Sarratt, England, Aug 27–Sept 1, 1981.

SKATEBOARDING

The highest recorded speed on a skateboard under US Skateboard Association (now disbanded) rules is 71.79 mph on a course at Mt Baldy, Calif, in a prone position, by Richard K. Brown, age 33, on June 17, 1979. The stand-up record is 53.45 mph by John Hutson, 23, at Signal Hill, Long Beach, Calif, June 11, 1978. The high jump record is 5 ft 4 in by Trevor Baxter of Burgess Hill, Sussex, England, on July 26, 1981.

At the 4th US Skateboard Association championships at Signal Hill on Sept 25, 1977, Tony Alva, 19, of Santa Monica, Calif, took off from a moving skateboard, jumped over 17 barrels (12-in diameters) and landed on another skateboard.

Mike Kinney won a marathon contest at Reseda, Calif, on May 26, 1979, with 217.3 miles in 30 hours 35 min.

TABLE FOOTBALL

Marathon

Sean and Roger Connolly played for 42 hours 38 min at Warrenpoint, County Down, Ireland, Apr 24–26, 1981.

GETTING WORDS IN EDGEWISE: Marie Warrell (left) and Carol Brockie must have sat for a long spell when they played Scrabble for almost 5½ days in 1981.

GLIDING

Emanuel Swedenborg (1688–1772) of Sweden made sketches of gliders *c.* 1714. The earliest man-carrying glider was designed by Sir George Cayley (1773–1857) and carried his coachman (possibly John Appleby) about 500 yd across a valley in Brompton Dale, Yorkshire, England, in the summer of 1853. Gliders now attain speeds claimed at over 200 mph.

Most World Titles

The most world individual championships (instituted 1948) won is 3 by Helmut Reichmann (b 1942) (W Germany) in 1970, 74 and 78; and Douglas George Lee (b Nov 7, 1945) (GB) in 1976, 78 and 81.

Hang Gliding

In the 11th century, the monk Eilmer is reported to have flown from the 60-ft-tall tower of Malmesbury Abbey, Wiltshire, England. The earliest modern pioneer was Otto Lilienthal (1848–96) of Germany who made about 2,500 flights in gliders of his own construction between 1891 and 1896. Professor Francis Rogallo of the US National Space Agency developed a flexible "wing" in the 1950's from his research into space capsule re-entries.

The official FAI record for the farthest distance covered is 118.7 miles by Helmut Denz (W Germany) in a Comet 165 from Hippach to Rottenmann, Austria, on May 20, 1981. Jim Lee (US) claimed 168 miles in California in 1981.

SOAR HEAD: Paul Bikle experienced −65°C temperatures in reaching an altitude of 46,266 ft in his glider.

The official FAI height gain record is 4,175.76 meters (13,699.8 ft) by Ian Kibblewhite (NZ) at Owens Valley, Calif, on July 22, 1981.

Championships

The World Team Championships, held in 1978, 1979 and 1981, were won by Great Britain.

SELECTED GLIDING WORLD RECORDS (SINGLE-SEATERS)

DISTANCE
907.7 miles — Hans-Werner Grosse (W Germany) in an ASW-12 on Apr 25, 1972, from Lübeck to Biarritz.

DECLARED GOAL FLIGHT
779.4 miles — Bruce Drake, David Speight. S. H. "Dick" Georgeson (all NZ) all in Nimbus 2s, from Te Anau to Te Araroa, Jan 14, 1978.

ABSOLUTE ALTITUDE
46,266 ft — Paul F. Bikle, Jr (US) in a Schweizer SGS 1-23E over Mojave, Calif (released at 3,963 feet) on Feb 25, 1961 (also record altitude gain—42,303 ft).

GOAL AND RETURN
1,015.7 miles — Karl H. Striedieck (US) in an ASW-17 from Lock Haven, Pa to Tenn on May 9, 1977.

SPEED OVER TRIANGULAR COURSE

100 km	102.74 mph	Ross Briegleb (US) in a Kestrel 17 over the US on July 18, 1974.
300 km	98.59 mph	Hans-Werner Grosse (W Germany) in an ASW-17 over Australia on Dec 24, 1980.
500 km	94.00 mph	Georg Eckle (W Germany) in an ASW-17 over South Africa on Dec 10, 1979.
750 km	89.5 mph	Hans-Werner Grosse (W Germany) in an ASW-17 over Australia on Jan 6, 1982.
1,000 km	90.29 mph	Hans-Werner Grosse (W Germany) in an ASW-17 over Australia, on Jan 3, 1979.
1,250 km	82.79 mph	Hans-Werner Grosse (W Germany) in an ASW-17 over Australia on Dec 9, 1980.

GOLF*

Origins

Although a stained glass window in Gloucester Cathedral, dating from 1350, portrays a golfer-like figure, the earliest mention of golf occurs in a prohibiting law passed by the Scottish Parliament in March 1457, under which "golff be utterly cryit doune and not usit." The Romans had a cognate game called *paganica*, which may have been carried to Britain before 400 AD. The Chinese National Golf Association claims the game is of Chinese origin ("*Ch'ui Wan*—the ball-hitting game") from the 3rd or 2nd century BC. There were official ordinances prohibiting a ball game with clubs in Belgium and Holland from 1360. Gutta-percha balls succeeded feather balls in 1848, and were in turn succeeded in 1902 by rubber-cored balls, invented in 1899 by Coburn Haskell (US). Steel shafts were authorized in the US in 1925.

Oldest Clubs

The oldest club of which there is written evidence is the Gentleman Golfers (now the Honourable Company of Edinburgh Golfers) formed in March 1744—10 years prior to the institution of the Royal and Ancient Club of St Andrews, Fife,

* For more detailed information about golf, see *Golf Facts and Feats* (Sterling).

WELL ROUNDED: In the 1981 Nigerian Open, Peter Tupling played four rounds of golf (72 holes) in 255 strokes, averaging 63.75 per round and ending up 29 under par. (Steve Powell, All-Sport)

WATCH THE BIRDIES: All eyes follow Sam Snead's drive in Canada Cup play. Snead carded a 59 for 18 holes in the 1959 Greenbrier Open, later renamed the Sam Snead Festival. "Slammin' Sam" won a record 84 US PGA tournaments in his career. (Radio Times Hulton Picture Library)

Scotland. The oldest existing club in North America is the Royal Montreal Club (Nov 1873) and the oldest in the US is St Andrews, Westchester County, NY (1888). An older claim is by the Foxbury Country Club, Clarion County, Pa (1887).

Highest and Lowest Courses

The highest golf course in the world is the Tuctu Golf Club in Morococha, Peru, which is 14,335 ft above sea level at its lowest point. Golf has, however, been played in Tibet at an altitude of over 16,000 ft.

The lowest golf course in the world was that of the now defunct Sodom and Gomorrah Golfing Society at Kallia (Qulya), on the northern shores of the Dead Sea, 1,250 ft below sea level. Currently the lowest is the par-70 Furnace Creek Golf Course, Death Valley, Calif, at an average 220 ft below sea level.

Longest Course

The world's longest course is the par-77, 8,325-yd International GC, Bolton, Mass, from the "Tiger" tees, remodeled in 1969 by Robert Trent Jones.

Longest Hole

The longest hole in the world is the 7th hole (par 7) of 909 yd at the Sano Course, Satsuki GC, Japan. In Aug 1927, the 6th hole at Prescott Country Club in Arkansas measured 838 yd.

Largest Green

Probably the largest green in the world is that of the par-6, 695-yd 5th hole at International GC, Bolton, Mass, with an area greater than 28,000 sq ft.

Biggest Bunker

The world's biggest trap is Hell's Half Acre on the 585-yd 7th hole of the Pine Valley course, Clementon, NJ, built in 1912 and generally regarded as the world's most trying course.

Lowest Scores for 9 and 18 Holes

At least four players are recorded to have played a long course (over 6,000 yd) in a score of 58, most recently by Monte Carlo Money (b Dec 3, 1954) (US) on the par-72, 6,607-yd Las Vegas Municipal GC, Nev, on Mar 11, 1981.

Alfred Edward Smith (b 1903), the English professional at Woolacombe, achieved an 18-hole score of 55 (15 under bogey 70) on his home course on Jan 1, 1936. The course measured 4,248 yd. The detail was 4, 2, 3, 4, 2, 4, 3, 4, 3=29 out, and 2, 3, 3, 3, 3, 2, 5, 4, 1=26 in.

Nine holes in 25 (4, 3, 3, 2, 3, 3, 1, 4, 2) was recorded by A. J. "Bill" Burke in a round of 57 (32 + 25) on the 6,389-yd par 71 Normandie course in St Louis on May 20, 1970. The tournament record is 27 by Mike Souchak (US) (b May 1927) for the second nine (par 35) first round of the 1955 Texas Open; Andy North (US) (b Mar 9, 1950) second nine (par 34), first round, 1975 BC Open at En-Joie GC, Endicott, NY; and Jose Maria Canizares (Spain) (b Feb 18, 1947), first nine, third round, in the 1978 Swiss Open on the 6,811-yd Crans-Sur course.

The US PGA tournament record for 18 holes is 59 (30 + 29) by Al Geiberger (b Sept 1, 1937) in the second round of the Danny Thomas Classic, on the 72-par, 7,249-yd Colonial CC course, Memphis, Tenn, June 10, 1977.

In non-PGA tournaments, Sam Snead had 59 in the Greenbrier Open (now called the Sam Snead Festival), at White Sulphur Springs, W Va, on May 16, 1959; Gary Player (South Africa) (b Nov 1, 1935) carded 59 in the second round of the Brazilian Open in Rio de Janeiro on Nov 29, 1974; and David Jagger (GB) also had 59 in a Pro-Am tournament prior to the 1973 Nigerian Open at Ikoyi Golf Club, Lagos.

The lowest recorded score on an 18-hole course (over 6,000 yd) for a woman is 62 (30 + 32) by Mary (Mickey) Kathryn Wright (b Feb 14, 1935), of Dallas, on the Hogan Park Course (6,286 yd) at Midland, Tex, in Nov 1964.

Wanda Morgan (b March 22, 1910) recorded a score of 60 (31 + 29) on the Westgate and Birchington Golf Club course, Kent, England, over 18 holes (5,002 yd) on July 11, 1929.

Lowest Scores for 36 Holes

The record for 36 holes is 122 (59 + 63) by Sam Snead in the 1959 Greenbrier Open (now called the Sam Snead Festival) (non-PGA) (see above), May 16–17, 1959. Horton Smith (see below) scored 121 (63 + 58) on a short course on Dec 21, 1928.

Lowest Scores for 72 Holes

The lowest recorded score on a first-class course is 255 (29 under par) by Leonard Peter Tupling (b Apr 6, 1950) (GB) in the Nigerian Open at Ikoyi Golf Club, Lagos, in Feb 1981, made up of 63, 66, 62 and 64 (average 63.75 per round). Horton Smith (1908–63), twice US Masters Champion, scored 245

(63, 58, 61 and 63) for 72 holes on the 4,700-yd course (par 64) at Catalina Country Club, Calif, to win the Catalina Open, Dec 21–23, 1928.

The lowest 72 holes in a US professional event is 257 (60, 68, 64 and 65) by Mike Souchak in the 1955 Texas Open at San Antonio.

The lowest 72 holes in an Open championship in Europe is 262 by Percy Alliss (1897–1975) of Britain, with 67, 66, 66 and 63 in the Italian Open Championship at San Remo in 1932, and by Lu Liang Huan (b Dec 10, 1935) (Taiwan) in the 1971 French Open at Biarritz. Kelvin D. G. Nagle (b Dec 21, 1920) of Australia shot 261 in the Hong Kong Open in 1961.

Longest Drive

In long-driving contests 330 yd is rarely surpassed at sea level.

In officially regulated long-driving contests over level ground the greatest distance recorded is 392 yd by Tommie Campbell (b July 24, 1927) (Foxrock Golf Club), a member of the Irish PGA, made at Dun Laoghaire, Co Dublin, in July 1964.

The USPGA record is 341 yd by Jack William Nicklaus (b Columbus, Ohio, Jan 21, 1940), then weighing 206 lb, in July 1963.

Valetin Barrios (Spain) drove a Slazenger B51 ball 568½ yd on an airport runway at Palma, Majorca, on March 7, 1977.

The longest on an ordinary course is 515 yd by Michael Hoke Austin (b Feb 17, 1910) of Los Angeles, in the US National Seniors Open Championship at Las Vegas, Nev, Sept 25, 1974. Aided by an estimated 35-mph tailwind, the 6-ft-2-in 210-lb golfer drove the ball on the fly to within a yard of the green on the par-4, 450-yd 5th hole of the Winterwood Course. The ball rolled 65 yd past the hole.

Arthur Lynskey claimed a drive of 200 yd out and 2 miles down off Pikes Peak, Colo, June 28, 1968.

A drive of 2,640 yd (1½ miles) across ice was achieved by an Australian meteorologist named Nils Lied at Mawson Base, Antarctica, in 1962. On the moon, the energy expended on a mundane 300-yd drive would achieve, craters permitting, a distance of a mile.

Longest Hitter

The golfer regarded as the longest consistent hitter the game has ever known is the 6-ft-5-in-tall, 230-lb George Bayer (US) (b Sept 17, 1925), the 1957 Canadian Open Champion. His longest measured drive was one of 420 yd at the fourth in the Las Vegas Invitational in 1953. It was measured as a precaution

THE ONE THAT GOT AWAY was, according to Mike Souchak, a putt "that short" in a qualifying round for the 1956 British Open. One year earlier, the 210-lb golfer set a US pro record with a 257 for 72 holes in the Texas Open. (AP)

against litigation since the ball struck a spectator. Bayer also drove a ball pin high on a 426-yd hole in Tucson, Ariz. Radar measurements show that an 87-mph impact velocity for a golf ball falls to 46 mph in 3.0 sec.

Longest Putt

The longest recorded holed putt in a major tournament was one of 86 ft on the vast 13th green at the Augusta National, Ga, by Cary Middlecoff (b Jan 1921) in the 1955 Masters Tournament.

Bobby Jones was reputed to have holed a putt in excess of 100 ft on the 5th green in the first round of the 1927 British Open at St Andrews, Scotland.

Most Rounds in a Day

The greatest number of rounds played on foot in 24 hours is 22 rounds plus 5 holes (401 holes) by Ian Colston, 35, at Bendigo GC, Victoria, Australia (6,061 yd), Nov 27–28, 1971. He covered more than 100 miles.

MOST WINS IN MAJOR TOURNAMENTS

US Open	Willie Anderson (1880–1910)	4	1901–03–04–05
	Robert Tyre Jones, Jr (1902–71)	4	1923–26–29–30
	W. Ben Hogan (b Aug 13, 1912)	4	1948–50–51–53
	Jack William Nicklaus (b Jan 21, 1940)	4	1962–67–72–80
US Amateur	R. T. Jones, Jr	5	1924–25–27–28–30
British Open	Harry Vardon (1870–1937)	6	1896–98–99, 1903–11–14
British Amateur	John Ball (1861–1940)	8	1888–90–92–94–99, 1907–10–12
PGA Championship (US)	Walter C. Hagen (1892–1969)	5	1921–24–25–26–27
	Jack W. Nicklaus	5	1963–71–73–75–80
Masters Championship (US)	Jack W. Nicklaus	5	1963–65–66–72–75
US Women's Open	Elizabeth (Betsy) Earle-Rawls (b May 4, 1928)	4	1951–53–57–60
	"Mickey" Wright (b Feb 14, 1935)	4	1958–59–61–64
US Women's Amateur	Mrs Glenna Vare (*née* Collett) (b June 20, 1903)	6	1922–25–28–29–30–35

ON COURSE: It took some 21 years, but Kathy Whitworth finally surpassed Mickey Wright as the winningest player in the LPGA when she earned her 83rd tournament victory in June 1982. (LPGA)

The most holes played on foot in a week (168 hours) is 1,128 by Steve Hylton at the Mason Rudolph Golf Club (6,060 yd), Clarksville, Tenn, Aug 25–31, 1980.

Fastest Rounds

With such variations in lengths of courses, speed records, even for rounds under par, are of little comparative value. Rick Baker completed 18 holes (6,142 yd) in 26 min 20.55 sec at the Metropolitan Golf Club, Melbourne, Australia, on Feb 14, 1981, during the Victorian Open, but this test permitted striking the ball while it was still moving. The record for a still ball is 28.09 min by Gary Wright (b Nov 27, 1946) at Tewantin-Noosa Golf Club, Queensland, Australia (18 holes, 6,039 yd), on Dec 9, 1980.

Eighty-three players completed the 18-hole 6,412-yd Prince George Golf and Country Club course, BC, Canada, in 12 min 14.5 sec in 1973, using only one ball.

Most Tournament Wins

The record for winning tournaments in a single season is 18 (plus one unofficial), including a record 11 consecutively, by Byron Nelson (b Feb 4, 1912) (US), March 8–Aug 4, 1945.

Sam Snead has won 84 official USPGA tour events to Dec 1979, and has been credited with a total 134 tournament victories since 1934.

Kathy Whitworth (b Sept 27, 1939) (US) has won 83 professional tournaments from 1962 to June 1982. Mickey Wright (US) won a record 13 tournaments in 1963.

Jack Nicklaus (US) is the only golfer who has won all five major titles (British Open, US Open, Masters, PGA and US Amateur) twice, while setting a record total of 19 major tournament victories (1959–80). His

FOR THE GREEN: Jack Nicklaus' career earnings reached nearly $4 million by July 4, 1982. Nicklaus has slammed to 19 major tournament victories in both the PGA and Masters. A consistent long hitter, the "Golden Bear" holds tournament scoring records for the Masters and US Open, the latter set in 1980 after many observers suspected he had passed his prime. Here he blasts out of a bunker off the 18th green on the way to winning the 1970 World Match Play Tournament. (E. D. Lacey)

remarkable record in the US Open is 4 firsts, 8 seconds and 2 thirds.

In 1930 Bobby Jones achieved a unique "Grand Slam" of the US and British Open and Amateur titles.

US Open

This championship was inaugurated in 1894. The lowest 72-hole aggregate is 272 (63, 71, 70, 68) by Jack Nicklaus on the Lower Course (7,015 yd) at Baltusrol Golf Club, Springfield, NJ, June 12–15, 1980. The lowest score for 18 holes is 63 by Johnny Miller (b Apr 29, 1947) of Calif on the 6,921-yd, par-71 Oakmont (Pa) course on June 17, 1973, and Jack Nicklaus and Tom Weiskopf (b Nov 9, 1942), both on June 12, 1980.

The longest delayed result in any national open championship occurred in the 1931 US Open at Toledo, Ohio. George von Elm (1901–61) and Billy Burke (1902–72) tied at 292, then tied the first replay at 149. Burke won the second replay by a single stroke after 72 extra holes.

US Masters

The lowest score in the US Masters (instituted at the 6,980-yd Augusta National Golf Course, Ga, in 1934) was 271 by Jack Nicklaus in 1965 and Raymond Floyd (b 1942) in 1976. The lowest rounds have been 64 by Lloyd Mangrum (1914–74) (1st round, 1940), Jack Nicklaus (3rd round, 1965), Maurice Bembridge (GB) (b Feb 21, 1945) (4th round, 1974), Hale Irwin (b June 3, 1945) (4th round,

1975), Gary Player (S Africa) (4th round, 1978), and Miller Barber (b March 31, 1931) (2nd round, 1979).

US Amateur

This championship was inaugurated in 1893. The lowest score for 9 holes is 30 by Francis D. Ouimet (1893–1967) in 1932.

British Open

The Open Championship was inaugurated in 1860 at Prestwick, Strathclyde, Scotland. The lowest score for 9 holes is 29 by Tom Haliburton (Wentworth) and Peter W. Thomson (Australia), at Royal Lytham and St Anne's, Lancashire, England, on July 10, 1963; by Tony Jacklin (GB, b July 1944) in the 1970 Open at St Andrews, Scotland; and by Bill Longmuir (b June 10, 1953) on the Royal Lytham and St Anne's course on July 18, 1979.

The lowest scoring round in the Open itself is 63 by Mark Hayes (US, b July 12, 1949) at Turnberry, Strathclyde, Scotland, in the second round on July 7, 1977, and by Isao Aoki (b Aug 31, 1942) (Japan) in the third round in Muirfield, July 19, 1980. Henry Cotton (GB) at Royal St George's, Sandwich, Kent, England, completed the first 36 holes in 132 (67 + 65) on June 27, 1934.

The lowest 72-hole aggregate is 268 (68, 70, 65, 65) by Tom Watson (US) (b Sept 4, 1949) at Turnberry, Scotland, ending on July 9, 1977.

British Amateur

The lowest score for nine holes in the British Championship (inaugurated in 1885) is 29 by Richard Davol Chapman (1911–78) of the US at Royal St George's, Sandwich, Kent (par 70, 6,633 yd) on May 27, 1948.

World Cup (formerly Canada Cup)

The World Cup (instituted 1953) has been won most often by the US with 15 victories between 1955 and 1979. The only men on six winning teams have been Arnold Palmer (b Sept 10, 1929) (1960, 62–64, 66–67) and Jack Nicklaus (1963–64, 66–67, 71, 73). The only man to take the individual title three times is Jack Nicklaus (US) in 1963–64, 1971. The lowest aggregate score for 144 holes is 545 by Australia (Bruce Devlin and David Graham) at San Isidro, Buenos Aires, Argentina, Nov 12–15, 1970, and the lowest score by an individual winner was 269 by Roberto de Vicenzo, 47, on the same occasion.

Ryder Trophy

The biennial Ryder Cup (instituted 1927) professional match between the US and GB (Europe in 1979) has been won by the US 20½–3½. William Earl "Billy" Casper (b San Diego, Calif, June 24, 1931) has the record of winning most matches, with 20 won (1961–75). Christy O'Connor Sr (b Dec 21, 1924) (GB) played in 10 matches to 1973.

Walker Cup

The US versus Great Britain–Ireland series instituted in 1921 (for the Walker Cup since 1922), now biennial, has been won by the US 25½–2½ to date. Joe Carr (GB–I) played in 10 contests (1947–67).

Biggest Victory Margin

The greatest margin of victory in a major tournament is 21 strokes by Jerry Pate (b Sept 16, 1953) (US) in the Colombian Open with 262, Dec 10–13, 1981.

Highest Earnings

The greatest amount ever won in official USPGA golf prizes is $3,972,446 by Jack Nicklaus to July 4, 1982.

The record for a year is $530,808 by Tom Watson (US) in 1980.

The highest LPGA career earnings by a woman is $1,205,132 by JoAnne Carner to July 1, 1982.

Beth Daniel (b Oct 14, 1956) earned a record $231,000 in 1980.

Youngest and Oldest Champions

The youngest winner of the British Open was Tom Morris, Jr (1851–75) at Prestwick, Ayrshire, Scotland, in 1868, aged 17 years 249 days. The oldest British Open champion was "Old Tom" Morris (1821–1908) who was aged 46 years 99 days when he won in 1867. In modern times, the 1967 champion Roberto de Vicenzo (b Buenos Aires, Argentina, Apr 14, 1923) was aged 44 years 93 days. The oldest US Amateur Champion was Jack Westland (b Dec 14, 1904) at Seattle, Wash, on Aug 23, 1952, aged 47 years 253 days.

Longest Span

Jacqueline Ann Mercer (*née* Smith) (b Apr 5, 1929) won her first South African title at Humewood

GC, Port Elizabeth, in 1948, and her fourth title at Port Elizabeth GC on May 4, 1979, 31 years later.

Richest Prize

The greatest first-place prize money was $500,000 (total purse $1.1 million) won by Johnny Miller (US) (b Apr 29, 1947) at Sun City, Bophuthatswana, S Africa, Dec 31, 1981–Jan 3, 1982. After 72-hole scores of 277, Miller beat Severiano Ballesteros (who won $160,000 for second place) in a playoff.

Probably the greatest prize for one shot was the £50,000 ($110,000) won by Isao Aoki (Japan) by acing the 155-yd second hole in the World Match Play Championship at Wentworth on Oct 12, 1979.

HOLES-IN-ONE

In 1981, *Golf Digest* was notified of 35,757 holes-in-one, so averaging over 90 per day.

Longest

The longest straight hole shot in one is the 10th hole (447 yd) at Miracle Hills GC, Omaha, Neb. Robert Mitera achieved a hole-in-one there on Oct 7, 1965. Mitera, aged 21 and 5 ft 6 in tall, weighed 165 lb. A two-handicap player, he normally drove 245 yd. A 50-mph gust carried his shot over a 290-yd drop-off. The group in front testified to the remaining distance.

The longest dogleg achieved in one is the 480-yd 5th hole at Hope CC, Ark, by L. Bruce on Nov 15, 1962.

The women's record is 393 yd by Marie Robie of Wollaston, Mass, on the first hole of the Furnace Brook GC, Sept 4, 1949.

Most

The greatest number of holes-in-one in a career is 61 by Harry Lee Bonner from 1967 to 1982, most at his home 9-hole course of Las Gallina, San Rafael, Calif. The most holes-in-one by a professional golfer is 42 by Mancil Davis, who is only 28 years old.

Douglas Porteous, 28, aced 4 holes over 39 consecutive holes—the 3rd and 6th on Sept 26, and the 5th on Sept 28 at Ruchill GC, Glasgow, Scotland, and the 6th at the Clydebank and District GC Course on Sept 30, 1974. Robert Taylor holed the 188-yd 16th hole at Hunstanton, Norfolk, England, on three successive days—May 31, June 1 and 2, 1974. Joseph F. Vitullo (b Apr 1, 1916) aced the 130-yd 16th hole at

DOLLAR DRIVE: John Miller went to Sun City, Bophuthatswana, and came home $500,000 richer when, after a playoff, he won a golf tournament there. (Steve Powell, All-Sport)

the Hubbard GC, Ohio, for the tenth time on June 26, 1979.

Consecutive

There is no recorded instance of a golfer performing three consecutive holes-in-one, but there are at least 15 cases of "aces" being achieved in two consecutive holes, of which the greatest was Norman L. Manley's unique "double albatross" on two par-4 holes (330-yd 7th and 290-yd 8th) on the Del Valle CC course, Saugus, Calif, on Sept 2, 1964.

The only woman ever to card consecutive aces is Sue Prell, on the 13th and 14th holes at Chatswood GC, Sydney, Australia, on May 29, 1977.

The closest recorded instances of a golfer getting 3 consecutive holes-in-one were by the Rev Harold Snider (b July 4, 1900) who aced the 8th, 13th and 14th holes of the par-3 Ironwood course in Phoenix, Ariz, on June 9, 1976, and the late Dr Joseph Boydstone on the 3rd, 4th and 9th at Bakersfield GC, Calif on Oct 10, 1962.

Youngest and Oldest

The youngest golfer recorded to have shot a hole-in-one was Coby Orr (aged 5) of Littleton, Colo, on the 103-yd fifth hole at the Riverside GC, San Antonio, Tex, in 1975.

The oldest golfers to have performed the feat are George Miller, 93, at the 11th (116 yd) at Anaheim GC, Calif, on Dec 4, 1970; Charles Youngman, 93, at the Tam O'Shanter Club, Toronto, in 1971; and William H. Diddel, 93, on the 142-yd 8th at the Royal Poinciana GC, Naples, Fla, on Jan 1, 1978. Maude Hutton became the oldest woman to make a hole-in-one when, at age 86, she aced the 102-yd 14th hole at Kings Inn Golf and Country Club, Sun City Center, Fla, on Aug 7, 1978.

GREYHOUND RACING

Earliest Meeting

In Sept 1876, a greyhound meeting was staged at Hendon, North London, England, with a railed hare operated by a windlass. Modern greyhound racing originated with the perfecting of the mechanical hare by Owen P. Smith at Emeryville, Calif, in 1919.

Fastest Dog

The highest speed at which any greyhound has been timed is 41.72 mph (410 yd in 20.1 sec) by "The Shoe" for a track record at Richmond, NSW, Australia, on Apr 25, 1968. It is estimated that he covered the last 100 yd in 4.5 sec or at 45.45 mph.

Winning Streak

An American greyhound, "Joe Dump," won a world record 31 consecutive victories from Nov 18, 1978 to June 1, 1979.

GYMNASTICS

Earliest References

A primitive form of gymnastics was practiced in ancient Greece and Rome during the period of the ancient Olympic Games (776 BC to 393 AD), but Johann Friedrich Simon was the first teacher of modern gymnastics, at Basedow's School, Dessau, Germany, in 1776.

World Championships

The greatest number of individual titles won by a man in the World Championships is 10 by Boris Shakhlin (USSR) between 1954 and 1964. He was also on three winning teams. The women's record is 10 individual wins and 5 team titles by Larissa Semyonovna Latynina (b Dec 27, 1934, retired 1966) of the USSR, between 1956 and 1964.

Japan has won the men's team title a record 5 times (1962, 66, 70, 74, 78) and the USSR has won the women's title on 7 occasions (1954, 58, 62, 70, 74, 78, 81).

The most overall titles in modern rhythmic gymnastics is 3 by Maria Gigova (Bulgaria) in 1969, 71 and 73 (shared). Galina Shugurova (USSR) won 8 apparatus titles from 1969 to 1977.

Olympic Games

Japan has won the most men's titles with 5 victories (1960, 64, 68, 72, 76). The USSR has won 8 women's team titles (1952–80).

The only men to win 6 individual gold medals are Boris Shakhlin (b Jan 21, 1932) (USSR), with one in

ROUTINE VICTORIES: Boris Shakhlin earned 6 individual gold medals in Olympic competition, a feat that was matched by Nikolai Andrianov. Shakhlin also won 10 individual titles in the World Championships, a feat that is unmatched. (World Sports)

1956, 4 (2 shared) in 1960 and one in 1964; and Nikolai Andrianov (b Oct 14, 1952) (USSR) with one in 1972, 4 in 1976 and one in 1980.

The most successful woman has been Vera Caslavska-Odlozil (b May 3, 1942) (Czechoslovakia), with 7 individual gold medals, 3 in 1964 and 4 (one shared) in 1968. Larissa Latynina of the USSR won 6 individual and 3 team gold medals for a total of 9. She also won 5 silver and 4 bronze for an all-time record total of 18 Olympic medals.

The most medals for a male gymnast is 15 by Nikolai Andrianov (USSR), 7 gold, 5 silver and 3 bronze, 1972–80. Alexander Ditiatin (USSR) (b Aug 7, 1957) is the only man to win a medal in all eight categories in the same Games, with 3 gold, 4 silver and 1 bronze at Moscow in 1980.

Nadia Comaneci (b Nov 12, 1961) (Rumania) was the first gymnast to be awarded a perfect score of 10.00 in the Olympic Games, in the 1976 Montreal Olympics. She ended the competition with a total of 7 such marks (4 on the uneven parallel bars, 3 on the balance beam).

Youngest International Competitor

Anita Jokiel (Poland) was aged 11 years 2 days when she competed at Brighton, East Sussex, England, on Dec 6, 1977.

World Cup

In the first World Cup Competition in London in 1975, Ludmilla Tourisheva (now Mrs Valery Borzov) (b Oct 7, 1952) of the USSR won all 5 available gold medals.

Chinning the Bar

The record for 2-arm chins from a dead hang position is 135 by Joe Hernandez (b 1961) at Dysart Junior HS, Cashion, Ariz, on May 22, 1980. William Aaron Vaught (b 1959) did 20 one-arm chin-ups at Finch's Gymnasium, Houston, Tex, on Jan 3, 1976.

Francis Lewis (b 1896) of Beatrice, Neb, in May 1914, achieved 7 consecutive chins using only the middle finger of his left hand. His body weight was 158 lb.

Sit-Ups

The greatest recorded number of consecutive sit-ups on a hard surface without feet pinned or knees bent is 27,051 by L/Cpl Michael Tyne (b May 28, 1962) at Minley Manor, Hampshire, England, June 5–6, 1982.

ON THE BEAM: Larissa Latynina earned 18 Olympic medals—the record for either sex in any sport. Nine were gold. Latynina also won 10 individual and 5 team titles in the World Championships.

Rope Climbing

The US Amateur Athletic Union (AAU) records are tantamount to world records: 20 ft (hands alone) 2.8 sec, by Don Perry, at Champaign, Ill, on Apr 3, 1954; 25 ft (hands alone), 4.7 sec, by Garvin S. Smith at Los Angeles, on Apr 19, 1947.

Parallel Bar Dips

Thomas Gildert performed a record 533 consecutive parallel bar dips on July 1, 1980, at the Colorall Leisure Center, Nelson, England. Jack LaLanne (b 1914) is reported to have done 1,000 in Oakland, Calif, in 1945.

ROPE JUMPING

The longest recorded non-stop rope-jumping marathon was one of 12 hours 8 min by Frank P. Oliveri (estimated 120,744 turns) at Great Lakes Training Center, Chicago, Ill, on June 13, 1981.

Other rope-jumping records made without a break:

Most quintuple turns	5 Katsumi Suzuki	Saitama, Japan	May 29, 1975
Most turns in 1 minute	330 Brian D. Christensen	Ridgewood Shopping Center, Tenn	Sept 1, 1979
Most turns in 10 seconds	108 Albert Rayner	Wakefield, Eng	June 28, 1978
Most doubles (with cross)	691 Frank P. Olivieri	Henrietta, NY	Nov 6, 1980
Double turns	10,133 Katsumi Suzuki (Japan)	Saitama	Sept 29, 1979
Treble turns	381 Katsumi Suzuki (Japan)	Saitama	May 29, 1975
Quadruple turns	51 Katsumi Suzuki (Japan)	Saitama	May 29, 1975
Duration	1,264 miles Tom Morris (Aust)	Brisbane-Cairns	1963
Most on a single rope (50m-rope)	88 (32 turns)	Todoroki Ground, Kanagawa, Japan	Oct 24, 1980
On a tightrope (consecutive)	55 Bryan Andrew(*né* Dewhurst)	BBC TV Centre, London	May 5, 1980

Vertical Jump

The greatest height reached in a vertical jump (the difference between standing and jumping fingertip reach) is 48 in by Darrell Griffith (US) of the University of Louisville in 1976. Olympic Pentathlon champion Mary E. Peters (GB) reportedly jumped 30 in in Calif in 1972.

Push-Ups

Tommy Gildert (b 1944) did 9,105 consecutive push-ups at the Burnley Boys Club, Lancashire, England, on July 1, 1979.

Noel Barry Mason did 267 fingertip push-ups on June 10, 1979. Paul Henry Allen Lynch, 27, performed 760 one-armed push-ups in 46 min 12 sec at the YMCA, Wimbledon, Greater London, on June 10, 1982. Fred Kueffer did 265 consecutive handstand push-ups at Kellogg HS, Little Canada, Minn, where he is gymnastic coach, on Nov 10, 1981.

Jumping Jacks

The greatest number of consecutive side-straddle hops is 30,000 by Steven Sokol, 25, at Oakridge Mall, San Jose, Calif, on May 8, 1982. He took 7 hours 25 min 23 sec.

Somersaults

Ashrita Furman performed 6,773 forward rolls over 10 miles in Central Park, NYC, on Nov 19, 1980.

Corporal Wayne Wright (GB) of the Royal Engineers, made a successful dive and tucked somersault over 37 men at Old Park Barracks, Dover, Kent, England on July 30, 1980.

Shigeru Iwasaki (b 1960) backwards somersaulted over 50 m (54.68 yd) in 10.8 sec in Tokyo, March 30, 1980.

HANDS-DOWN RECORD: Fred Kueffer, 32, displays perfect form on his way to 265 consecutive handstand push-ups. He warmed up, immediately prior to the record, by running 6 miles.

HANDBALL (COURT)

Origin

Handball is a game of ancient Celtic origin. In the early 19th century only a front wall was used, but later side and back walls were added. The court is now standardized 60 ft by 30 ft in Ireland, Ghana and Australia, and 40 ft by 20 ft in Canada, Mexico and the US. The game is played with both a hard and soft ball in Ireland, and a soft ball only elsewhere.

The earliest international contest was in NYC in 1887, between the champions of the US and Ireland.

World Championships

World championships were inaugurated in NY in Oct 1964 with competitors from Australia, Canada, Ireland, Mexico and the US. The US has the most wins with two, 1964 and 1967 (shared with Canada).

Most Titles

The most successful player in the USHA National Four-Wall Championships has been James Jacobs (US), who won a record 6 singles titles (1955–56, 57, 60, 64–65) and shared in 6 doubles titles (1960, 62–63, 65, 67–68). Martin Decatur has shared in 8 doubles titles (1962–63, 65, 67–68, 75, 78–79), 5 of these with Jacobs as his partner. Fred Lewis also won 6 singles titles (1972, 74–76, 78, 81).

HARNESS RACING

Origins

Trotting races were held in Valkenburg, Netherlands, in 1554. In England the trotting gait (the simultaneous use of the diagonally opposite legs) was known in the 16th century. The sulky first appeared in harness racing in 1829. Pacers thrust out their fore and hind legs simultaneously on one side.

Greatest Winnings

The greatest amount won by a trotting horse is $1,960,986 by "Ideal du Gazeau" (France) to the end of 1981. The record for a pacing horse is $2,019,213 by "Niatross" (US) in just 2 years, 1979 and 1980.

The greatest award won by a harness horse in a single season is $1,414,313 by "Niatross" during 1980.

The largest ever purse was $2,011,000 for the Woodrow Wilson 2-year-olds race at Meadowlands, NJ, on Aug 6, 1980, of which a record $1,005,000 went to the winner "Land Grants" driven by Del Insko.

Highest Price

The highest price paid for a trotter is $5.25 million for "Mystic Park" by Lana Lobell Farms from Allen, Gerald and Irving Wechter of NY and Robert Lester of Florida, announced on July 13, 1982. The highest

IN HARNESS: The pacer "Niatross" earned over $2 million in his 2-year career, winning 37 of 39 starts. He shattered the mile time-trial record by nearly 3 sec.

TROTTING

Time Trial (mile track)	1:54.8	"Nevele Pride" (driver, Stanley Dancer) (US), at Indianapolis	Aug 31, 1969
	1:54.8	"Lindy's Crown" (driver, Howard Beissinger) (US) at Du Quoin, Ill	Aug 30, 1980
Race Record (mile)	1:54.8	"Lindy's Crown" (driver, Howard Beissinger) (US) at Du Quoin, Ill	Aug 30, 1980

PACING

Time Trial (mile track)	1:49.2	"Niatross" (driver, Clint Galbraith) (US) at Lexington, Ky	Oct 1, 1980
Race Record (mile)	1:51.8	"Genghis Khan" (driver, Bill O'Donnell) at E Rutherford, NJ	Aug 13, 1982

price ever paid for a pacer is $8.25 million for "Merger" by Finder/Guida of NY from John Campbell, David Morisey and Peter Oud of Canada in 1982.

Most Successful Driver

The most successful sulky driver in North America has been Herve Filion (Canada) (b Quebec, Feb 1, 1940) who reached a record of 7,956 wins and $35.9 million in purse money by the end of the 1981 season, after a record 637 victories in the 1974 season. Filion won the North American championship for the eleventh time in 1980. The greatest earnings in a year is $4,065,608 by William O'Donnell in 1981.

HOCKEY

Origins

There is pictorial evidence of a hockey-like game (Kalv) being played on ice in the Netherlands in the early 16th century. The game probably was first played in North America on Dec 25, 1855, at Kingston, Ontario, Canada, but Halifax also lays claim to priority.

The International Ice Hockey Federation was founded in 1908. The National Hockey League was inaugurated in 1917. The World Hockey Association was formed in 1971 and disbanded in 1979 when 4 of its teams joined the NHL.

Olympic Games

Canada has won the Olympic title six times (1920, 24, 28, 32, 48, 52) and the world title 19 times, the last being at Geneva in 1961. The longest Olympic career is that of Richard Torriani (Switzerland) from 1928 to 1948. The most gold medals won by any player is 3; this was achieved by 4 USSR players in the 1964, 68 and 72 Games—Vitaliy Davidov, Aleksandr Ragulin, Anatoliy Firssov and Viktor Kuzkin.

Stanley Cup

This cup, presented by the Governor-General Lord Stanley (original cost $48.67), became emblematic of world professional team supremacy 33 years after the first contest at Montreal in 1893. It has been won most often by the Montreal Canadiens, with 22 wins in 1916, 24, 30–31, 44, 46, 53, 56–60 (a record 5 straight), 65–66, 68–69, 71, 73, 76–79. Henri Richard played in his eleventh finals in 1973.

Longest Game

The longest game was 2 hours 56 min 30 sec (playing time) when the Detroit Red Wings eventually beat the Montreal Maroons 1-0 in the 17th minute of the sixth period of overtime at the Forum, Montreal, at 2:25 a.m. on March 25, 1936, 5 hours 51 min after the opening faceoff. Norm Smith, goaltender for the Red Wings, turned aside 92 shots in registering the NHL's longest single shutout.

Longest Career

Gordie Howe (b March 31, 1928, Floral, Saskatchewan, Canada) skated 25 years for the Detroit Red Wings from 1946–47 through the 1970–71 season, playing in a total of 1,687 NHL regular-season games. During that time he also set records for most career goals, assists, and scoring points; was selected as an all-star a record 21 times; and collected 500 stitches in his face (see also *Individual Scoring*).

After leaving the Red Wings, he ended a 2-year retirement to skate with his two sons as teammates and played for 6 more seasons with the Houston Aeros and the New England Whalers of the World Hockey Association, participating in 497 games.

With the incorporation of the (now Hartford) Whalers into the NHL for the 1979–80 season, Gordie Howe skated in all 80 regular season games (for a record total of 1,767) in his record 26th year in that league, and the remarkable 52-year-old grandfather was again selected as an NHL all-star, a record 22nd

GOAL ORIENTED: Wayne Gretzky, who surprised NHL fans when he set assist and point records in the 1980–81 season, showed he was no flash in the pan when, in 1981–82, he broke those records and also set a goal-scoring record by netting 92 goals, including a record 10 hat-tricks. He helped the Edmonton Oilers to team records for goals, assists and points. (Edmonton Oilers)

time. Including Howe's 157 NHL playoff appearances, he skated in 2,421 "major league" games.

Most Consecutive Games

Garry Unger, playing for Toronto, Detroit, St Louis, and Atlanta, skated in 914 consecutive NHL games without a miss during 13 seasons from Feb 24, 1968, to Dec 21, 1979, when a torn shoulder muscle kept him on the bench.

The most consecutive complete games by a goaltender is 502, set by Glenn Hall (Detroit, Chicago), beginning in 1955 and ending when he suffered a back injury in a game against Boston on Nov 7, 1962.

Longest Season

The only man ever to play 82 games in a 78-game season is Ross Lonsberry. He began the 1971–72 season with the Los Angeles Kings where he played 50 games. Then, in January, he was traded to the Philadelphia Flyers (who had played only 46 games at the

time) where he finished out the season (32 more games).

Dennis Owchar (with Pittsburgh and Colorado) and Jerry Butler (with St Louis and Toronto) played 82 games in an 80-game season in 1977–78; and Mike O'Connell (with Boston and Chicago) matched this feat in 1980–81.

Longest Streaks

In the 1981–82 season, the NY Islanders won 15 consecutive games, Jan 21–Feb 20, 1982. The longest a team has ever gone without a defeat is 35 games, set by the Philadelphia Flyers with 25 wins and 10 ties from Oct 14, 1979, to Jan 6, 1980.

Team Scoring

The greatest number of goals recorded in a World Championship match has been 47-0 when Canada beat Denmark on Feb 12, 1949.

The Edmonton Oilers set NHL records of 417 goals, 706 assists and 1,123 points in the 1981–82 season.

The NHL record for both teams is 21 goals, scored when the Montreal Canadiens beat the Toronto St Patricks at Montreal 14-7 on Jan 10, 1920. The most goals ever scored by one team in a single game was set by the Canadiens, when they defeated the Quebec Bulldogs on March 3, 1920 by a score of 16-3.

The most goals in a period is 9 by the Buffalo Sabres in the second period of their 14-4 victory over Toronto on March 19, 1981.

The Detroit Red Wings scored 15 consecutive goals without an answering tally when they defeated the NY Rangers 15-0 on Jan 23, 1944.

Fastest Scoring

Toronto scored 8 goals against the NY Americans in 4 min 52 sec on March 19, 1938.

The fastest goals that have ever been scored from the opening whistle both came at 6 sec of the first period: by Henry Boucha of the Detroit Red Wings on Jan 28, 1973, against Montreal; and by Jean Pronovost of the Pittsburgh Penguins on March 25, 1976, against St Louis. Claude Provost of the Canadiens scored a goal against Boston after 4 sec of the opening of the second period on Nov 9, 1957.

The fastest scoring record is held by Bill Mosienko (Chicago) who scored 3 goals in 21 sec against the NY Rangers on March 23, 1952.

Gus Bodnar (Toronto Maple Leafs) scored a goal against the NY Rangers at 15 sec of the first period of *his first NHL game* on Oct 30, 1943. Later in his career, while with Chicago, Bodnar again entered the record book when he assisted on all 3 of Bill Mosienko's quick goals.

Several fast scoring feats have been reported from non-NHL competition: Kim D. Miles scored in 3 sec for Univ of Guelph vs Univ of W Ontario on Feb 11, 1975; Steve D'Innocenzo scored 3 goals in 12 sec for Holliston vs Westwood in a high school game in Mass on Jan 9, 1982; Clifford "Fido" Purpur, 38, scored 4 goals in 25 sec for the Grand Forks AMerks vs Winnipeg All Stars in Grand Forks, ND, on Jan 29, 1950. In team play, the Skara Ishockeyclubb, Sweden, scored 3 goals in 11 sec against Orebro IK at Skara on Oct 18, 1981; the Vernon Cougars scored 5 goals in 56 sec against Salmon Arm Aces at Vernon, BC, Canada, on Aug 6, 1982; the Kamloops Knights of Columbus scored 7 goals in 2 min 22 sec vs Prince George Vikings on Jan 25, 1980.

Individual Scoring

The career record in the NHL for regular season goals is 801 by Gordie Howe of the Detroit Red Wings and Hartford Whalers. Howe has scored 1,850 points in his NHL career, with 1,049 assists. With 68 goals, 92 assists, and 160 points in Stanley Cup competition; and 202 goals, 377 assists, and 579 points in WHA season and playoff games, Howe's unequaled professional career scoring totals are 1,071 goals and 1,518 assists, for 2,589 points.

Wayne Gretzky (b Jan 26, 1961) of the Edmonton Oilers shattered the NHL season records for goals, assists and points when he netted 92 goals and made 120 assists for a total of 212 points in the 1981–82 season. He scored an additional 12 points (5 goals, 7 assists) in the Stanley Cup playoffs.

Guy Lafleur (b Sept 20, 1951), of the Montreal Canadiens, scored both 50 or more goals and 100 or more points for 6 consecutive seasons, from 1974–75 through 1979–80. Bobby Orr (b Parry Sound, Ontario, Canada, March 20, 1948) had 6 consecutive 100-or-more-point seasons from 1969–70 to 1974–75. Phil Esposito (b Feb 20, 1942) (Boston) and Marcel Dionne (b Aug 3, 1951) (Detroit, LA) both scored 100 or more points in 6 seasons, but not consecutively.

The most goals ever scored in one game is 7 by Joe Malone of the Quebec Bulldogs against the Toronto St Patricks on Jan 31, 1920. Malone, playing for the Montreal Canadiens in 1917–18, had a season record 2.2 goals-per-game average (44 goals in 20 games). Six different men have scored 4 goals in one period—Harvey Jackson (Toronto), Max Bentley (Chi-

cago), Clint Smith (Chicago), Red Berenson (St Louis), Grant Mulvey (Chicago), and Bryan Trottier (NY Islanders).

The most points scored in one NHL game is 10, a record set by Darryl Sittler of the Toronto Maple Leafs, on Feb 7, 1976, against the Boston Bruins. He had 6 goals and 4 assists.

Charlie Simmer of the LA Kings had 56 goals on 171 shots in the 1980–81 season to record the best shooting percentage—32.7%.

In 1921–22, Harry (Punch) Broadbent of the Ottawa Senators scored 25 goals in 16 consecutive games to set an all-time "consecutive game goal-scoring streak" record.

The most assists recorded in an NHL game is 7 by Billy Taylor of Detroit on March 16, 1947 against Chicago (Detroit won 10-6); and by Wayne Gretzky for Edmonton vs Washington, Feb 15, 1980.

Most 3-Goal Games

In his 18-year NHL career, Phil Esposito of Chicago, Boston and the NY Rangers, scored 3 or more goals in 32 games. Five of these were 4-goal efforts.

CENTER OF ATTENTION: Phil Esposito became the NHL's career hat-trick leader with 32 3-or-more-goal games. The high-scoring center was runner-up to Gordie Howe with 717 career NHL goals. (Al Ruelle/Boston Bruins)

Wayne Gretzky (Edmonton) scored 3 or more goals in 10 games during the 1981–82 season. The term "hat-trick" properly applies when 3 goals are scored consecutively by one player in a game without interruption by either an answering score by the other team or a goal by any other player on his own team. In general usage, a "hat-trick" is any 3-goal effort by a player in one game.

Goaltending

The longest any goalie has gone without a defeat is 33 games, a record set by Gerry Cheevers of Boston in 1971–72. The longest a goalie has ever kept successive opponents scoreless is 461 min 29 sec by Alex Connell of the Ottawa Senators in 1927–28. He registered 6 consecutive shutouts in this time.

The most shutouts ever recorded in one season is 22 by George Hainsworth of Montreal in 1928–29 (this is also a team record). This feat is even more remarkable considering that the season was only 44 games long at that time, compared to the 80-game season currently used.

Terry Sawchuk registered a record 103 career shutouts in his 20 seasons in the NHL. He played for Detroit, Boston, Toronto, Los Angeles, and the NY Rangers during that time. He also appeared in a record 971 games.

The only goaltender to score a goal in an NHL game is Bill Smith (NY Islanders), against the Colorado Rockies in Denver, Nov 28, 1979. After the Rockies had removed their goaltender in favor of an extra skater during a delayed penalty, a Colorado defenseman's errant centering pass sent the puck skidding nearly the full length of the ice and into his own untended goal. Goalie Smith was the last Islander to touch the puck and was credited with the goal even though he did not take the actual "shot."

Penalties

The most any team has been penalized in one season is the 2,621 min assessed against the Philadelphia Flyers in 1980–81. The most penalty-filled game was a contest between Boston and Minnesota in Boston on Feb 26, 1981, with a total of 84 penalties (42 by each team) for 406 min (211 min by Minnesota).

David "Tiger" Williams (Toronto, Vancouver) has amassed 2,435 penalty min over 8 seasons, 1974–75 to 1981–82. Dave Schultz (Philadelphia) earned 472 min of penalties in the 1974–75 season. Randy Holt (LA) was assessed 67 penalty min in a game against Philadelphia on Mar 11, 1979.

Fastest Player

The highest speed measured for any player is 29.7 mph (without the puck) for Bobby Hull (then of the Chicago Black Hawks) (b Jan 3, 1939). The highest puck speed is also attributed to Hull, whose left-handed slap shot has been measured at 118.3 mph. Also known as the "Golden Jet," Hull is the only player beside Gordie Howe to score over 1,000 goals in NHL and WHA play.

HORSE RACING

Origins

Horsemanship was an important part of the Hittite culture of Anatolia, Turkey, dating from about 1400 BC. The 33rd ancient Olympic Games of 648 BC featured horse racing. The earliest horse race recorded in England was one held *c.* 210 AD at Netherby, Cumbria, among Arabians brought to Britain by Lucius Septimius Severus (146–211 AD), Emperor of Rome. Organized horse racing began in New York State at least as early as March 1668.

Longest Race

The longest recorded horse race was one of 1,200 miles in Portugal, won by "Emir," a horse bred from Egyptian-bred Blunt Arab stock. The holder of the world record for long distance racing and speed is "Champion Crabbet," who covered 300 miles in 52 hours 33 min, carrying 245 lb, in 1920.

Victories

The horse with the best win-loss record was "Kincsem," a Hungarian mare foaled in 1874, who was unbeaten in 54 races (1876–79), including the English Goodwood Cup of 1878.

"Camarero," foaled in 1951, won his first 56 races, 1953–55, and had 73 wins in 77 starts altogether.

Most Valuable Horse

The most expensive horse ever is the 1982 Belmont Stakes winner "Conquistador Cielo." It was reported in Aug 1982 that he had been syndicated for $36.4 million, in 40 shares of $910,000 each.

The highest price for a yearling is $4.25 million for a colt by "Nijinsky II"—"Spearfish" bought on July 19, 1982, at Keeneland, Ky, by Robert Sangster (GB).

THE PUCK STOPS HERE: Gerry Cheevers (left), who drew stitch marks on his mask whenever it protected him from injury, went 33 straight games without a loss for the Bruins. Terry Sawchuk (above) notched a record 103 shutouts in a 971-game career. (Cheevers photo courtesy Boston Bruins; Sawchuk photo courtesy NY Rangers)

THE PUCK STARTS HERE: (Left) Bobby Hull's slap shot went screaming at goaltenders at 118.3 mph. Hull, the only player besides Gordie Howe to score 1,000 NHL and WHA goals, was also, at 29.7 mph, the fastest skater. Bill Smith (below), thanks to a fluke play, is the only NHL goalie to be credited with scoring a goal. (Smith photo courtesy NY Islanders)

HORSE CENTS: "John Henry" (#1A, above foreground), with Willie Shoemaker up, is first to the wire for the $600,000 first prize in the 1½-mile Arlington Million. The first horse ever to pass $3 million in purses, "John Henry" was purchased as a yearling for only $1,100 and changed hands seven times before Sam Rubin bought him for $25,000 in 1978. Willie Shoemaker is the all-time winningest jockey, with 8,136 winners and nearly $88 million in purses to June 6, 1982. The late Red Smith, in his last column, called Shoemaker one of the best all-around athletes he had known. According to Smith, the 4-ft-11½-in jockey would find a way to win, whatever the game. (UPI)

CROWN JEWEL: No horse had won the Triple Crown for 25 years until "Secretariat" thundered home with a spectacular 31-length win in the 1973 Belmont Stakes. Ron Turcotte was in the saddle when the 2-time Horse of the Year put on this extraordinary show of strength. (AP)

HORSES' SPEED RECORDS

Distance	Time mph	Name	Course	Date
¼ mile	20.8s. 43.26	*Big Racket* (Mex)	Mexico City, Mex	Feb 5, 1945
½ mile	44.4s. 40.54	*Sonido* (Ven)	‡Caracas, Ven	June 28, 1970
	44.4s. 40.54	*Western Romance* (Can)	Calgary, Canada	Apr 19, 1980
⅝ mile	53.6s. 41.98†	*Indigenous* (GB)	‡*Epsom, England	June 2, 1960
	53.89s. 41.75††	*Raffingora* (GB)	‡*Epsom, England	June 5, 1970
	55.4s. 40.61	*Zip Pocket* (US)	Phoenix, Ariz	Apr 22, 1967
	55.4s. 40.61	*Big Volume* (US)	Fresno, Calif	Oct 15, 1977
¾ mile	1m. 06.2s. 40.78	*Broken Tendril* (GB)	*Brighton, England	Aug 6, 1929
	1m. 07.2s. 40.18	*Grey Papa* (US)	Longacres, Wash	Sept 4, 1972
Mile	1m. 31.8s. 39.21	*Soueida* (GB)	*Brighton, England	Sept 19, 1963
	1m. 31.8s. 39.21	*Loose Cover* (GB)	*Brighton, England	June 9, 1966
	1m. 32.2s. 39.04	*Dr. Fager* (US)	Arlington, Ill	Aug 24, 1968
1¼ miles	1m. 57.4s. 38.33	*Double Discount* (US)	Arcadia, Calif	Oct 9, 1977
1½ miles	2m. 23.0s. 37.76	*Fiddle Isle* (US)	Arcadia, Calif	Mar 21, 1970
		John Henry (US)	Arcadia, Calif	Mar 16, 1980
2 miles**	3m. 15.0s. 36.93	*Polazel* (GB)	Salisbury, England	July 8, 1924
2½ miles	4m. 14.6s. 35.35	*Miss Grillo* (US)	Pimlico, Md	Nov 12, 1948
3 miles	5m. 15.0s. 34.29	*Farragut* (Mex)	Aguascalientes, Mex	Mar 9, 1941

* Course downhill for ¼ of a mile.
** A more reliable modern record is 3 min 16.75 sec by *Il Tempo* (NZ) at Trentham, Wellington, New Zealand, on Jan 17, 1970.
† Hand-timed.   †† Electrically timed.   ‡ Straight courses.

Greatest Winnings

The greatest amount ever won by a horse is $3,371,610 by the gelding "John Henry" (foaled 1975) from 1977 to June 1982.

The most won by a mare is $1,535,443 by "Dahlia," from 1972 to 1976.

The most won in a year is $1,798,030 by "John Henry" in 1981.

Triple Crown

Eleven horses have won all three races in one season which constitute the American Triple Crown (Kentucky Derby, Preakness Stakes and the Belmont Stakes). This feat was first achieved by "Sir Barton" in 1919, and most recently by "Seattle Slew" in 1977 and "Affirmed" in 1978.

The only Triple Crown winner to sire another winner was "Gallant Fox," the 1930 winner, who sired "Omaha," who won in 1935.

Dead Heats

There is no recorded case in turf history of a quintuple dead heat. The nearest approach was in the Astley Stakes, at Lewes, England, on Aug 6, 1880, when "Mazurka," "Wandering Nun" and "Scobell" triple dead-heated for first place, just ahead of "Cumberland" and "Thora," who dead-heated for fourth place. Each of the five jockeys thought he had won. The only three known examples of a quadruple dead heat were between "Honest Harry," "Miss Decoy," "Young Daffodil" and "Peteria" at Bogside, England, on June 7, 1808; between "Defaulter," "The Squire of Malton," "Reindeer" and "Pulcherrima" in the Omnibus Stakes at The Hoo, England, on Apr 26, 1851; and between "Overreach," "Lady Go-Lightly," "Gamester" and "The Unexpected" at Newmarket, England, on Oct 22, 1855.

Since the introduction of the photo-finish, the highest number of horses in a dead heat has been three, on several occasions.

Jockeys

The most successful jockey of all time is Willie Shoemaker (b weighing 2½ lb on Aug 19, 1931) now weighing 98 lb and standing 4 ft 11½ in, who beat Johnny Longden's lifetime record of 6,032 winners on Sept 7, 1970. From March 1949 to June 6, 1982, he rode 8,136 winners from 35,369 mounts, earning $87,951,800.

Chris McCarron (US), 19, won a total of 546 races in 1974.

The greatest amount ever won by any jockey in a year is $8,398,604 by Chris McCarron (b 1955) in 1981.

The most winners ridden on one card is 8 by Hubert S. Jones, 17, out of 13 mounts at Caliente, Calif, on June 11, 1944 (of which 5 were photo-finishes); by Oscar Barattuci at Rosario City, Argentina, on Dec 15, 1957; and by Dave Gall from 10 mounts at Cahokia Downs, East St Louis, Ill, on Oct 18, 1978.

The longest winning streak is 12 races by Sir Gordon Richards (GB) who won the last race at Nottingham, Eng, on Oct 3, 1933, 6 out of 6 at Chepstow on Oct 4, and the first 5 races the next day at Chepstow.

The oldest jockey was Levi Burlingame (US), who rode his last race at Stafford, Kan, in 1932, aged 80. The youngest jockey was Frank Wootton (1893–1940) (English Champion jockey 1909–12), who rode his first winner in South Africa aged 9 years 10 months. The lightest recorded jockey was Kitchener (d 1872), who won the Chester Cup in England on "Red Deer" in 1844 at 49 lb. He was said to have weighed only 40 lb in 1840.

Trainers

The greatest number of wins by a trainer in one year is 494 by Jack Van Berg in 1976. The greatest amount won in a year is $3,953,906 by Charles Wittingham (US) in 1981.

Owners

The most winners by an owner in one year is 494 by Dan R. Lasater (US) in 1974, when he also won a record $3,022,960 in prize money.

ICE SKATING

Origins

The earliest reference to ice skating is in Scandinavian literature of the 2nd century, although its origins are believed, on archeological evidence, to be 10 centuries earlier still. The earliest known illustration is a Dutch woodcut of 1498. The earliest skating club was the Edinburgh Skating Club, Scotland, formed c. 1742. The first recorded race was from Wisbech to Whittlesea, East Anglia, in 1763. The earliest artificial ice rink in the world was opened at the Baker Street Bazaar, Portman Square, London, on Dec 7, 1842. The International Skating Union was founded at Scheveningen, Netherlands in 1892.

Longest Race

The longest race regularly held was the "Elfstedentocht" ("Tour of the Eleven Towns") in the Netherlands, covering 200 km (124 miles 483 yd). The fastest time was 7 hours 35 min by Jeen van den Berg (b Jan 8, 1928) on Feb 3, 1954. The race has now been transferred to Lake Vesivärji near Lahti, Finland.

Largest Rink

The world's largest indoor artificial ice rink is in the Moscow Olympic indoor arena which has an ice area of 86,800 sq ft.

Marathon

The longest recorded skating marathon is 109 hours 5 min by Austin McKinley of Christchurch, NZ, June 21–25, 1977.

FIGURE SKATING

Most Difficult Jump

The first ever triple Axel performed in competition was by Vern Taylor (b 1958) (Canada) in the World Championships at Ottawa on March 10, 1978.

A quadruple twist lift has been performed by only one pair, Sergei Shakrai (b June 28, 1958) and Marina Tcherkasova (b Nov 17, 1964) of the USSR, in an international championship at Helsinki, Finland, on Jan 26, 1977. They were also the first skaters to accomplish simultaneous triple jumps at that level, at Strasbourg, France, on Feb 1, 1978.

Highest Marks

The highest number of maximum 6 marks awarded for one performance in an international championship was 12 to Aleksandr Zaitsev and Irina Rodnina (USSR) in the European pairs competition in Cologne, W Germany on Feb 7, 1978.

The highest score from a single set of marks in any figure skating competition was gained by Jayne Torvill (b Oct 7, 1957) and Christopher Dean (b July 27, 1958) of Great Britain when awarded maximum sixes for presentation from 8 of the 9 judges in the ice dance event of the European championships at Lyon, France, on Feb 5, 1982. They received a further 3 sixes for technical merit for a total of 11, the highest for ice dancing.

Donald Jackson (Canada) was awarded 7 "sixes" (the most by a soloist) in the world men's championship at Prague, Czechoslovakia, in 1962.

World Titles

The greatest number of individual world men's figure skating titles (instituted 1896) is 10 by Ulrich Salchow (1877–1949), of Sweden, in 1901–05, 07–11. The women's record (instituted 1906) is also 10 indi-

Olympic Titles

The most Olympic gold medals won by a figure skater is 3 by Gillis Grafstrüm (1893–1938), of Sweden, in 1920, 24 and 28 (also silver medal in 1932); by Sonja Henie (see above) in 1928, 32 and 36; and by Irina Rodnina (see above) in the pairs event in 1972, 76 and 80.

SPEED SKATING

World Titles

The greatest number of world overall titles (instituted 1893) won by any skater is 5 by Oscar Mathisen (Norway) (1888–1954) in 1908–09, 12–14, and Clas Thunberg (b Apr 5, 1893) of Finland, in 1923, 25, 28–29 and 31. The most titles won by a woman is 4 by Mrs Inga Voronina, *née* Artomonova (1936–66) of Moscow, USSR, in 1957–58, 62 and 65, and Mrs Atje Keulen-Deelstra of the Netherlands (b Dec 31, 1938) in 1970, 72–74.

The record score achieved in the world overall title is 162.973 points by Eric Heiden (US) at Oslo, Norway, Feb 10–11, 1979.

Olympic Titles

The most Olympic gold medals won in speed skating is 6 by Lidia Skoblikova (b March 8, 1939), of Chelyabinsk, USSR, in 1960 (2) and 1964 (4). The male record is held by Clas Thunberg (see above) with 5 gold (including 1 tied gold) and also 1 silver and 1 tied bronze in 1924–28; and by Eric Heiden (US) (b June 14, 1958) who won 5 gold medals, all at Lake Placid, NY, in 1980.

PEACH OF A PAIR: Irina Rodnina and her husband, Aleksandr Zaitsev, skate to the 1976 Olympic pairs gold medal. Rodnina, who replaced an earlier partner with Zaitsev, has earned a total of 3 Olympic golds and 10 world titles. (Tony Duffy, All-Sport)

vidual titles, by Sonja Henie (Apr 8, 1912–Oct 12, 1969), of Norway, between 1927 and 1936. Irina Rodnina (b Sept 12, 1949), of the USSR, has won 10 pairs titles (instituted 1908)—four with Aleksiy Ulanov (1969–72) and six with her husband Aleksandr Zaitsev (1973–77). The most ice dance titles (instituted 1950) won is 6 by Aleksandr Gorshkov (b Dec 8, 1946) and Ludmilla Pakhomova (b Dec 31, 1946), both of the USSR, in 1970–74 and 76.

WORLD SPEED SKATING RECORDS
(Ratified by the I.S.U.)

Distance	min:sec	Name and Nationality	Place	Date
MEN				
500 m	36.91*	Evgeni Kulikov (USSR)	Medeo, USSR	Mar 28, 1981
1,000 m	1:13.39	Gaetan Boucher (Canada)	Davos, Switz	Jan 31, 1981
1,500 m	1:54.79	Eric Heiden (US)	Davos, Switz	Jan 19, 1980
3,000 m	4:04.06	Dmitri Ogloblin (USSR)	Medeo, USSR	Mar 28, 1979
5,000 m	6:54.66	Aleksandr Baranov (USSR)	Medeo, USSR	Mar 18, 1982
10,000 m	14:23.59	Tomas Gustafson (Sweden)	Oslo, Norway	Jan 31, 1982
WOMEN				
500 m	40.18	Christa Rothenburger (E Ger)	Medeo, USSR	Mar 28, 1981
1,000 m	1:20.81	Natalia Petruseva (USSR)	Medeo, USSR	Mar 28, 1981
1,500 m	2:05.39	Natalia Petruseva (USSR)	Medeo, USSR	Mar 27, 1981
3,000 m	4:21.70	Gaby Schonbrunn (E Ger)	Medeo, USSR	Mar 28, 1981

* This represents an average speed of 30.30 mph.

ICE AND SAND YACHTING

Origins

The sport originated in the Low Countries from the year 1600 (earliest patent granted) and along the Baltic coast. The earliest authentic record is Dutch, dating from 1768. Land or sand yachts of Dutch construction were first reported on beaches (now in Belgium) in 1595. The earliest international championship was staged in 1914.

Largest Ice Yacht

The largest known ice yacht was *Icicle,* built for Commodore John E. Roosevelt for racing on the Hudson River, NY in 1869. It was 68 ft 11 in long and carried 1,070 sq ft of canvas.

Highest Speeds

The highest speed officially recorded by an ice yacht is 143 mph by John D. Buckstaff in a Class A stern-steerer on Lake Winnebago, Wis in 1938. Such a speed is possible in a wind of 72 mph.

The official world record for a sand yacht is 66.48 mph by Christian Yves Nau (France) in *Mobil* at Le Touquet, France on March 22, 1981. A speed of 88.4 mph was attained by Nord Embroden (US) in *Midnight at the Oasis* at Superior Dry Lake, Calif on Apr 15, 1976.

HIGH FIVE: András Balczó leads all pentathletes with 3 Olympic golds, 2 silvers, and an additional 5 world titles.

LACROSSE

Origin

The game is of American Indian origin, derived from the inter-tribal game *baggataway,* and was played by Iroquois Indians in lower Ontario, Canada, and upper New York State, before 1492. The French named it after their game of *Chouler à la crosse,* known in 1381. The game was included in the Olympic Games of 1908, and featured as an exhibition sport in the 1928 and 1948 Games.

World Championship

The US won three of the four World Championships in 1967, 74 and 82. Canada won the other in 1978, beating the US 17–16 in overtime—this was the first drawn international match.

Highest Score

The highest score in any international match was US over Canada, 28–4, at Stockport, England, on July 3, 1978.

MODERN PENTATHLON

The Modern Pentathlon (Riding, Fencing, Shooting, Swimming and Running) was inaugurated into the Olympic Games at Stockholm in 1912.

Most World Titles

The record number of world titles won is 6 by András Balczó (Hungary) in 1963, 65–67 and 69, and the Olympic title in 1972, which also rates as a world title.

Olympic Titles

The greatest number of Olympic gold medals won is three by Balczó, a member of Hungary's winning team in 1960 and 68, and the 1972 individual champion. Lars Hall (Sweden) uniquely has won two individual championships (1952 and 56). Balczó has won a record number of five medals (3 gold and 2 silver).

Probably the greatest margin of victory was by William Oscar Guernsey Grut (b Sept 17, 1914) (Sweden) in the 1948 Games in London, when he won three events and placed fifth and eighth in the other two events.

Highest Scores

Point scores in riding, fencing, cross-country and hence overall scores have no comparative value between one competition and another. In shooting and swimming (300 m), where measurements are absolute, the point scores are of record significance.

Three athletes have had perfect rounds in the shooting competition (200/200), for 1,132 points: Charles Leonard (US) in Berlin on Aug 3, 1936 (no points were given in the 1936 Olympics); Danieli Massala (Italy) at Jonkoping, Sweden on Aug 21, 1978; and George Horvath (Sweden) at the Moscow Olympics on July 22, 1980. The fastest time for the 300-m swimming competition is 3 min 10.856 sec for 1,348 points by Ivar Sisniega (Mexico) at the Moscow Olympics on July 23, 1980.

MOTORCYCLING*

Earliest Races

The first motorcycle race was held on an oval track at Sheen House, Richmond, Surrey, England, on Nov 29, 1897, won by Charles Jarrott (1877–1944) on a Fournier. The oldest motorcycle races in the world are the Auto-Cycle Union Tourist Trophy (TT) series, first held on the 15.81-mile "Peel" ("St John's") course on the Isle of Man on May 28, 1907, and still run on the island, on the "Mountain" circuit (37.73 miles).

Longest Circuits

The 37.73-mile "Mountain" circuit, over which the two main TT races have been run since 1911, has 264 curves and corners and is the longest used for any motorcycle race.

Fastest Circuits

The highest average lap speed attained on any closed circuit is 160.288 mph by Yvon du Hamel (Canada) (b 1941) on a modified 903-cc four-cylinder Kawasaki Z1 on the 31-degree banked 2.5-mile Daytona International Speedway, Fla, in March 1973. His lap time was 56.149 sec.

The fastest road circuit is the Francorchamps circuit near Spa, Belgium. It is 14.12 km (8 miles 1,340

yd) in length and was lapped in 3 min 50.3 sec (average speed of 137.150 mph) by Barry S. F. Sheene (b Holborn, London, England, Sept 11, 1950) on a 495-cc four-cylinder Suzuki during the Belgian Grand Prix on July 3, 1977.

Fastest Race

The fastest track race in the world was held at Grenzlandring, W Germany, in 1939. It was won by Georg Meier (b Germany Nov 9, 1910) at an average speed of 134 mph on a supercharged 495-cc flat-twin BMW.

The fastest road race is the 500-cc Belgian Grand Prix on the Francorchamps circuit (see above). The record time for this 10-lap 87.74-mile race is 38 min 58.5 sec (average speed of 135.068 mph) by Barry Sheene (UK) on a 495-cc four-cylinder Suzuki on July 3, 1977.

Longest Race

The longest race is the Liège 24 Hours. The greatest distance ever covered is 2,761.9 miles (average speed 115.08 mph) by Jean-Claude Chemarin and Christian Leon of France on a 941-cc four-cylinder Honda on the Francorchamps circuit (8 miles 1,340 yd) near Spa, Belgium, Aug 14–15, 1976.

World Championships

Most world championship titles (instituted by the *Fédération Internationale Motocycliste* in 1949) won are 15 by Giacomo Agostini (Italy) in the 350-cc class 1968–74 and in the 500-cc class 1966–72 and 75. Agostini (b Lovere, Italy, June 16, 1942) is the only man to win two world championships in five consecutive years. Agostini won 122 races in the world championship series between Apr 24, 1965, and Aug 29, 1976, including a record 19 in 1970, also achieved by Stanley Michael Bailey "Mike" Hailwood, (b Oxford, England, Apr 2, 1940) in 1966.

Klaus Enders (Germany) (b 1937) won 6 world side-car titles, 1967, 69–70, 72–74.

Joël Robert (b Chatelet, Belgium, Nov 11, 1943) has won six 250-cc moto-cross (also known as "scrambles") world championships (1964, 68–72). Between Apr 25, 1964, and June 18, 1972, he won a record fifty 250-cc Grands Prix. He became the youngest moto-cross world champion on July 12, 1964, when he won the 250-cc championship aged 20 years 8 months.

Alberto "Johnny" Cecotto (b Caracas, Venezuela, Jan 1956) was the youngest person to win a world

---

* For more detailed information about motorcycling, see *The Guinness Book of Motorcycling Facts and Feats,* available from Sterling.

and FIM absolute records with an overall average of 318.598 mph and had a fastest run at an average of 318.66 mph.

The world record average speed for two runs over 1 km (1,093.6 yd) from a standing start is 16.68 sec by Henk Vink (b July 24, 1939) (Netherlands) on his supercharged 984-cc 4-cylinder Kawasaki, at Elvington Airfield, Yorkshire, England, on July 24, 1977. The faster run was made in 16.09 sec.

The world record for two runs over 440 yd from a standing start is 8.805 sec by Henk Vink on his supercharged 1,132-cc 4-cylinder Kawasaki, at Elvington Airfield, Yorkshire, England, on July 23, 1977. The faster run was made in 8.55 sec.

The fastest time for a single run over 440 yd from a standing start is 7.08 sec by Bo O'Brechta (US) riding a supercharged 1,200-cc Kawasaki-based machine at Ontario, Calif, in 1980. The highest terminal velocity recorded at the end of a 440-yd run from a standing start is 199.55 mph by Russ Collins at Ontario, Calif, on Oct 7, 1978.

CC RIDER: Riding his nitro-burning 2,000-cc 8-cylinder Honda, "Sorcerer," Russ Collins reached 199.55 mph at the end of a ¼-mile run from a standing start.

championship. He was aged 19 years 211 days when he won the 350-cc title on Aug 24, 1975. The oldest was Hermann-Peter Müller (1909–76) of W Germany, who won the 250-cc title in 1955, aged 46.

Most Successful Machines

Italian MV-Agusta motorcycles won 37 world championships between 1952 and 1973 and 276 world championship races between 1952 and 1976. Japanese Honda machines won 29 world championship races and 5 world championships in 1966. In the 7 years Honda contested the championship (1961–67) its annual average was 20 race wins.

Speed Records

Official world speed records must be set with two runs over a measured distance within a time limit (one hour for FIM records, two hours for AMA records).

Donald Vesco (b Loma Linda, Calif, Apr 8, 1939) riding his 21-ft-long *Lightning Bolt* streamliner, powered by two 1,016-cc Kawasaki engines on Bonneville Salt Flats, Utah, on Aug 28, 1978, set AMA

MOUNTAINEERING

Origins

Although bronze-age artifacts have been found on the summit (9,605 ft) of the Riffelhorn, Switzerland, mountaineering, as a sport, has a continuous history dating back only to 1854. Isolated instances of climbing for its own sake exist back to the 13th century. The Atacamenans built sacrificial platforms near the summit of Llullaillaco in South America (22,058 ft) in late pre-Columbian times, c. 1490.

Greatest Wall

The highest final stage in any wall climb is that on the south face of Annapurna I (26,545 ft). It was climbed by the British expedition led by Christian Bonington Apr 2–May 27, 1970, when Donald Whillans, 36, and Dougal Haston, 27, scaled to the summit. They used 18,000 ft of rope.

The longest wall climb is on the Rupal-Flank from the base camp at 11,680 ft to the South Point (26,384 ft) of Nanga Parbat—a vertical ascent of 14,704 ft. This was scaled by the Austro-Germano-Italian Expedition led by Dr Karl Maria Herrligkoffer in Apr 1970.

The most demanding free climbs are those rated at 5.13, the premier location for these being in the Yosemite Valley, Calif.

PARTNERS IN CLIMB: Tenzing Norgay stood atop Mt Everest as Edmund Hillary took this historic photograph after the two men became the first to successfully climb the 29,028-ft mountain. In the 30 years since that first ascent, 120 other climbers have reached the top, including 6 who have done it twice.

Mount Everest

Mount Everest (29,028 ft) was first climbed at 11:30 a.m. on May 29, 1953, when the summit was reached by Edmund Percival Hillary (b July 20, 1919), of New Zealand, and the Sherpa, Tenzing Norgay (b as Namgyal Wangdi, in Nepal in 1914, formerly called Tenzing Khumjung Bhutia). The successful expedition was led by Col (later Hon Brigadier) Henry Cecil John Hunt (b June 22, 1910).

A total of 122 climbers have succeeded to June 1982, including six who have done it twice. Franz Oppurg (1948–81) (Austria) was the first to make the final ascent solo, on May 14, 1978, while Reinhold Messner (Italy) was the first to make the entire climb solo on Aug 20, 1980. Messner and Peter Habeler (b July 22, 1942) (Austria) made the first entirely oxygen-less ascent on May 8, 1978. Four women have reached the summit, the first being Junko Tabei (b Sept 22, 1939) (Japan) on May 16, 1975. The oldest person was Dr Gerhard Schmatz (W Germany) (b June 5, 1929) aged 50 years 88 days on Oct 1, 1979.

Reinhold Messner, with his ascent of Kangchenjunga in 1982, became the first person to climb the world's three highest mountains, having earlier reached the summits of Everest and K2. He has successfully scaled a record 7 of the world's 14 main summits of over 8,000 m (26,250 ft).

Highest Bivouac

Douglas Scott and Dougal Haston (both GB) bivouacked in a snow hole at 28,700 ft on the South Summit of Everest on the night of Sept 24, 1975.

OLYMPIC GAMES

Note: These records include the un-numbered Games held at Athens in 1906.

Origins

The earliest celebration of the ancient Olympic Games of which there is a certain record is that of July 776 BC (when Coroibos, a cook from Elis, won a foot race), though their origin probably dates from perhaps as early as *c.* 1370 BC. The ancient Games were terminated by an order issued in Milan in 393 AD by Theodosius I, "the Great" (*c.* 346–95), Emperor of Rome. At the instigation of Pierre de Fredi, Baron de Coubertin (1863–1937), the Olympic Games of the modern era were inaugurated in Athens on Apr 6, 1896.

LEGATOR: Baron Pierre de Coubertin was the main force behind reviving the Olympic Games after a 1,503-year hiatus. Now, not even 100 years after the first modern Olympics, politics, nationalism, drug abuse and uncertain standards of amateurism threaten to end the Baron's dream of competition open to athletes of all nations.

Most Medals

In the ancient Olympic Games, victors were given a chaplet (head garland) of olive leaves. Leonidas of Rhodos won 12 running titles from 164 to 152 BC.

The most individual gold medals won by a male competitor in the modern Games is 10 by Raymond Clarence Ewry (US) (b Oct 14, 1874, at Lafayette, Ind; d Sept 27, 1937), a jumper (see *Track and Field*). The female record is seven by Vera Caslavska-Odlozil (b May 3, 1942) of Czechoslovakia (also see *Gymnastics*).

The only Olympian to win 4 consecutive individual titles in the same event has been Alfred A. Oerter (b Sept 19, 1936, NYC) who won the discus title in 1956, 60, 64 and 68.

The only man to win a gold medal in both the Summer and Winter Games is Edward F. Eagan (US) (1898–1967) who won the 1920 light-heavy-weight boxing title and was a member of the winning four-man bob in 1932.

Gymnast Larissa Latynina (b Dec 27, 1934) (USSR) won a record 18 medals (see *Gymnastics*). The record at one celebration is 8 medals by gymnast Aleksandr Ditiatin (b Aug 7, 1957) (USSR) in 1980.

Most Olympic Gold Medals at One Games

Mark Spitz (US), the swimmer, won a record 7 gold medals at one celebration (4 individual and 3 relay) at Munich in 1972.

The most gold medals won in individual events at one celebration is 5 by speed skater Eric Heiden (b June 14, 1958) (US) at Lake Placid, NY in 1980.

Youngest and Oldest Gold Medalists

The youngest woman to win a gold medal is Marjorie Gestring (US) (b Nov 18, 1922) aged 13 years 9 months, in the 1936 women's springboard event. The youngest winner ever was a French boy (whose name is not recorded) who coxed the Netherlands coxed pair in 1900. He was not more than 10 and may have been as young as 7. He substituted for Dr Hermanus Brockmann, who coxed in the heats but proved too heavy. Oscar G. Swahn was a member of the winning Running Deer shooting team in 1912, aged 65 years 258 days.

Longest Span

The longest competitive span of any Olympic competitor is 40 years by Dr Ivan Osiier (Denmark) (1888–1965), in fencing, 1908–32 and 48, and by Magnus Konow (Norway) (1887–1972) in yachting, 1908–20 and 36–48. The longest span for a woman is 24 years (1932–56) by the Austrian fencer Ellen Müller-Preiss. Raimondo d'Inzeo (b Feb 8, 1925) competed for Italy in equestrian events in a record 8 celebrations (1948–76), gaining one gold medal, 2 silver and 3 bronze medals. Janice Lee York Romary (b Aug 6, 1928), the US fencer, competed in all 6 Games from 1948 to 1968, and Lia Manoliu (Rumania) (b Apr 25, 1932) competed 1952–72, winning the discus title in 1968.

Largest Crowd

The largest crowd at any Olympic site was 150,000 at the 1952 ski-jumping at the Holmenkollen, outside Oslo, Norway. Estimates of the number of spectators of the marathon race through Tokyo on Oct 21, 1964, have ranged from 500,000 to 1,500,000.

Most and Fewest Competitors

The greatest number of competitors in any summer Olympic Games has been 7,147 at Munich in 1972. A record 122 countries competed in the 1972 Munich Games. The fewest was 311 competitors from 13 countries in 1896. In 1904 only 12 countries participated. The largest team was 880 men and 4 women from France at the 1900 Games in Paris.

Most Participations

Four countries have never failed to be represented at the 20 celebrations of the Summer Games: Australia, Greece, Great Britain and Switzerland. Of these, only Great Britain has been present at all Winter celebrations as well.

National Medals

The total figures for most medals and most gold medals for all Olympic events (including those now discontinued) for the Summer (1896–1980) and Winter Games (1924–1980) are:

	Gold	Silver	Bronze	Total
1. US*	660†	511	444	1,615
2. USSR (formerly Russia)	402	330	296	1,028
3. GB (including Ireland to 1920)*	169	205	186	560

* Excludes medals won in official art competitions, 1912–48.

† The AAU (US) reinstated James F. Thorpe (1888–1953), the disqualified high scorer in the 1912 decathlon and pentathlon events on Oct 12, 1973, but no issue of medals has yet been authorized by the International Olympic Committee. If allowed, this would give the US 2 more gold medals.

MEDAL CRAFT

VERA CASLAVSKA-ODLOZIL (above), a Russian gymnast, leads all women athletes with 7 gold medals, 3 in 1964 and 4 in 1968. (Tony Duffy, All-Sport)

ERIC HEIDEN (top left) swept all 5 speed skating events in the 1980 Winter Olympics to set a mark for the most individual golds won at one Games. (UPI)

AL OERTER (lower left) became the only Olympic athlete to win a gold medal in the same event in 4 consecutive Games when he captured the discus throw in 1956, 60, 64 and 68. (All-Sport)

ALEKSANDR DITIATIN (below) set a record for the most medals won at one Games when he earned 8 medals in the 1980 gymnastics competition in Moscow. With 3 golds, 4 silvers and 1 bronze, he won a medal in all 8 events. (Tony Duffy, All-Sport)

SKIMS THE SURFACE: Tony Williams traveled at 137.96 mph on Lake Windermere in Oct 1981 to set the speed record for Class OZ powerboats. Two of the best-known powerboaters, Bill Muncey and Dean Chenoweth, have died recently in this dangerous sport where any disturbance in the water can cause the driver to lose control. (Sporting Pictures Ltd)

NIGHT AND DAY: Phil Munden (below left) of the US Army parachute team, the Golden Knights, shares a record with teammate Bill Wenger for nighttime dead center landings with 43. Jacqueline Smith (below right) landed a world accuracy record under pressure when she achieved 10 consecutive dead center strikes in the 1978 World Championships in Yugoslavia. (Munden photo courtesy US Army)

PARACHUTING

Origins

Parachuting became a regulated sport with the institution of world championships in 1951. A team title was introduced in 1954, and women's events were included in 1956.

Most Titles

The USSR won the men's team titles in 1954, 58, 60, 66, 72, 76 and 80 and the women's team titles in 1956, 58, 66, 68, 72 and 76. Nikolai Ushamyev (USSR) has won the individual title twice, 1974 and 80.

Greatest Accuracy

Jacqueline Smith (GB) (b March 29, 1951) scored 10 consecutive dead center strikes (4-in disk) in the World Championships at Zagreb, Yugoslavia, Sept 1, 1978. At Yuma, Ariz, in March 1978, Dwight Reynolds scored a record 105 daytime dead centers, and Bill Wenger and Phil Munden tied with 43 nighttime DCs, competing as members of the US Army team, the Golden Knights. With electronic measuring the official FAI record is 50 DCs by Alexander Aasmiae (USSR) at Ferghana, USSR, Oct 1979.

POLO

Earliest Games

Polo is usually regarded as being of Persian origin, having been played as *Pulu c.* 525 BC. Other claims have come from Tibet and the Tang dynasty of China 250 AD.

The earliest club of modern times was the Kachar Club (founded in 1859) in Assam, India. The game was introduced into England from India in 1869 by the 10th Hussars at Aldershot, Hampshire, and the earliest match was one between the 9th Lancers and the 10th Hussars on Hounslow Heath, west of London, in July 1871. The earliest international match between England and the US was in 1886.

Highest Score

The highest aggregate number of goals scored in an international match is 30, when Argentina beat the US 21–9 at Meadowbrook, LI, NY, in Sept 1936.

Most Olympic Medals

Polo has been part of the Olympic program on five occasions: 1900, 08, 20, 24 and 36. Of the 21 gold medalists, a 1920 winner, John Wodehouse, the 3rd Earl of Kimberley (1883–1941) uniquely also won a silver medal (1908).

Highest Handicap

The highest handicap based on eight 7½-min "chukkas" is 10 goals, introduced in the US in 1891 and in the UK and Argentina in 1910. The latest of the 39 players to have received 10-goal handicaps are Alberto Heguy and Alfredo Harriot of Argentina, and in England, Eduardo Moore (Argentina). A match of two 40-goal handicap teams was staged for the first time ever at Palermo, Buenos Aires, Argentina, in 1975.

Largest Crowd

Crowds of more than 50,000 have watched floodlit matches at the Sydney, Australia, Agricultural Shows.

A crowd of 40,000 watched a game played at Jaipur, India, in 1976, when elephants were used instead of ponies. The length of the polo sticks used has not been ascertained.

POWERBOAT RACING*

Origins

The earliest application of the gasoline engine to a boat was by Jean Joseph Etienne Lenoir (1822–1900) on the River Seine, Paris, in 1865. The sport was given impetus by the presentation of a championship cup by Sir Alfred Harmsworth of England in 1903, which was also the year of the first offshore race from Calais to Dover.

Highest Speeds

The fastest offshore record, as recognized by the Union Internationale Motonautique, is 97.39 mph by Ted Toleman's Class I Cougar *Slick 50* on the Solent on Sept 25, 1981.

The recognized speed record for Class OZ, a circuit boat, is 137.96 mph by Tony Williams on Lake Windermere, England, on Oct 14, 1981.

---

* For more details about powerboat racing, see *The Guinness Book of Motorboating Facts and Feats,* available from Sterling.

RIDING THE AIRWAVES: From a takeoff speed of 55 mph, Peter Horak jumped a powerboat 120 ft through the air for a television documentary. (Greg Meny)

The fastest UIM inboard engine category for circuit racing is R4 at 131.12 mph by F. Forstei (Italy).

Harmsworth Trophy

Of the 25 international contests from 1903 to 1961, the US won the most with 16. The greatest number of wins was achieved by Garfield A. Wood (US) with 8 (1920–21, 26, 28–30, 32–33). The only boat to win three times is *Miss Supertest III,* owned by James G. Thompson (Canada), driven by Bob Hayward (Canada), in 1959–61. This boat also achieved the record speed of 119.27 mph at Picton, Ontario, Canada, in 1961.

In 1980 competition for the Trophy was revived as an invitation match race awarded on points scored in certain specified offshore races. The winner in 1980 was Bill Elsworth (US) and in 1981 Paul Clauser (US).

Gold Cup

The Gold Cup (instituted 1903) was won 8 times by Bill Muncey (1929–81) (US) (1956–57, 61–62, 72,

77–79). The record speed attained is 128.338 mph for a 2½-mile lap by the unlimited hydroplane *Atlas Van Lines,* driven by Bill Muncey in a qualifying round on the Columbia River, Wash, in July 1977, and again in July 1978.

Cowes International Offshore Powerboat Classic

The record average for this international offshore race (instituted 1961) is 79.64 mph by *Satisfaction* driven by Bill Elswick (US) over the 213.75 nautical mile (246.13 miles) course in 3 hours 4 min 35 sec on Aug 23, 1980. The only three-time winner has been Tommy Sopwith (b Nov 15, 1932) (GB) on 1961, 68 and 70.

Longest Race

The longest race has been the Port Richborough (London) to Monte Carlo Marathon Offshore International event. The race extended over 2,947 miles in 14 stages, June 10–25, 1972. It was won by *H.T.S.* (GB), driven by Mike Bellamy, Eddie Chater and

Jim Brooks in 71 hours 35 min 56 sec (average speed 41.15 mph).

Dragsters

Eddie Hill (US) recorded 220.76 mph in his blown fuel hydro drag boat *The Texan*, as recognized by the Southern Drag Boat Association, at San Antonio, Tex, on Aug 29, 1981.

Longest Jump

The longest jump achieved by a powerboat has been 120 ft by Peter Horak (b May 7, 1943) (US) in a Glastron Carlson CVX 20 Jet Deluxe with a 460 Ford V8 engine (takeoff speed 55 mph) for a documentary TV film "The Man Who Fell from the Sky," at Salton Sea, Calif, on Apr 26, 1980.

RODEO

Origins

Rodeo, which developed from 18th century *fiestas*, came into being with the early days of the North American cattle industry. The sport originated in Mexico and spread from there into the cattle regions of the US. Steer wrestling began with Bill Pickett (Tex) in 1900. The other events are calf roping, bull riding, saddle and bareback bronc riding.

The largest rodeo in the world is the Calgary Exhibition and Stampede at Calgary, Alberta, Canada. The record attendance has been 1,069,830, July 8–17, 1977. The record for one day is 148,486 on July 7, 1979. The oldest continuously-held rodeo is that at Payson, Ariz, first held in Aug 1887.

Most World Titles

The record number of all-round titles is 6 by Tom Ferguson (b Dec 20, 1950) consecutively, 1974–79, and by Larry Mahan (b Nov 21, 1943) (1966–70 and 73). Jim Shoulders (b 1928) of Henryetta, Okla, won a record 16 world championships between 1949 and 1959.

Time Records

Records for timed events, such as calf roping and steer wrestling, are not always comparable, because of the widely varying conditions due to the size of arenas and amount of start given the stock. The fastest time recently recorded for roping a calf is 5.7 sec

by Lee Phillips in Assiniboia, Saskatchewan, Canada, in 1978, and the fastest time for overcoming a steer is 2.4 sec by James Bynum at Marietta, Okla, in 1955; by Carl Deaton at Tulsa, Okla, in 1976; and by Gene Melton at Pecatonica, Ill, in 1979.

The standard required time to stay on in bareback, saddle bronc and bull riding events is 8 sec. In the now discontinued ride-to-a-finish events, rodeo riders have been recorded to have survived 90 min or more, until the mount had not a buck left in it.

The highest score in bull riding was 98 points by Denny Flynn on "Red Lightning" at Palestine, Ill, in 1979.

Highest Earnings

The record figure for prize money in a single season is $105,862 by Jimmie Cooper (US) in 1981. The greatest earnings in a rodeo career is $738,862 by Tom Ferguson to Aug 1, 1982. Ferguson also holds the record for the most money won at one rodeo with $17,225 earned at Houston, Tex, in 1982.

Youngest Champion

The youngest winner of a world title is Metha Brorsen of Okla, who was only 11 years old when she won the International Rodeo Association Cowgirls barrel racing event in 1975.

Champion Bull

The top bucking bull was probably "Honky Tonk," an 11-year-old Brahma, who unseated 187 riders in an undefeated eight-year career to his retirement in Sept 1978.

Champion Bronc

Traditionally a bronc called "Midnight" owned by Jim McNab of Alberta, Canada, was never ridden in 12 appearances at the Calgary Stampede.

ROLLER SKATING

Origin

The first roller skate was devised by Jean Joseph Merlin (1735–1803) of Huy, Belgium, in 1760, and was first worn by him in public in London. James L. Plimpton of NYC produced the present four-wheeled type and patented it in Jan 1863. The first indoor rink was opened in the Haymarket, London, in about 1824. The great boom periods were 1870–75, 1908–12, 1948–54 and 1978–81, each originating in the US.

Largest Rink

The largest indoor rink ever to operate was located in the Grand Hall, Olympia, London, England. It had an actual skating area of 68,000 sq ft. It first opened in 1890 for one season, then again from 1909 to 1912.

The largest rink now in operation is the Fireside Roll-Arena in Hoffman Estates, Ill, which has a total skating surface of 29,859 sq ft.

Roller Hockey

Roller hockey was first introduced in England as Rink Polo, at the old Lava rink, Denmark Hill, London, in the late 1870's. The Amateur Rink Hockey Association was formed in 1905, and in 1913 became the National Rink Hockey (now Roller Hockey) Association. Britain won the inaugural World Championship in 1936, and since then Portugal has won the most with 12 titles from 1947 to 1982.

Most Titles

Most world speed titles have been won by Alberta Vianello (Italy) with 16 between 1953 and 1965. The records for figure titles are 5 by Karl Heinz Losch in 1958–59, 61–62, 66, and 4 by Astrid Bader, also of W Germany, in 1965–68. Most world pair titles have been taken by Dieter Fingerle (W Germany) with 4 in 1959, 65–67.

Speed Records

The fastest speed (official world's record) is 25.78 mph by Giuseppe Cantarella (Italy) who recorded 34.9 sec for 440 yd on a road at Catania, Italy, on Sept 28, 1963. The mile record on a rink is 2 min 25.1 sec by Gianni Ferretti (Italy). The greatest distance skated in one hour on a rink by a woman is 21.995 miles by Marisa Danesi at Inzell, W Germany, on Sept 28, 1968. The men's record on a track is 23.133 miles by Alberto Civolani (Italy) at Inzell, W Germany, on Sept 28, 1968. He went on to skate 50 miles in 2 hours 20 min 33.1 sec.

Marathon

The longest recorded continuous roller skating marathon was one of 337 hours 20 min by Robert Zorn, Ken Morris and Cary Cube at Roller World, Santee, Calif, Aug 19–Sept 2, 1981.

Endurance

Theodore J. Coombs (b 1954) of Hermosa Beach, Calif, skated 5,193 miles from Los Angeles to NYC and back to Yates Center, Kan, from May 30 to Sept 14, 1979.

ROWING

Oldest Race

The Sphinx stela of Amenhotep II (1450–1425 BC) records that he *stroked* a boat for some three miles.

WORLD ROWING RECORDS

MEN—Fastest times over 2,000 m course (still water)

	min:sec	Country	Place	Date
Single Sculls	6:49.68	Nikolai Dougan (USSR)	Amsterdam	Aug 26, 1978
Double Sculls	6:12.48	Norway	Montreal	July 23, 1976
Coxed Pairs	6:56.94	E Germany	Copenhagen	Aug — 1971
Coxless Pairs	6:33.02	E Germany	Montreal	July 23, 1976
Coxed Fours	6:09.17	E Germany	Amsterdam	June 30, 1979
Coxless Fours	5:53.65	E Germany	Montreal	July 23, 1976
Quadruple Sculls	5:47.38	W Germany	Lucerne	June 4, 1980
Eights	5:32.17	E Germany	Montreal	July 18, 1976

WOMEN—Fastest times over 1,000 m course (still water)

	min:sec	Country	Place	Date
Single Sculls	3:34.31	Christine Scheiblich (E Germany)	Amsterdam	Aug 21, 1977
Double Sculls	3:16.27	USSR	Moscow	July 16, 1980
Coxless Pairs	3:26.32	E Germany	Amsterdam	Aug 21, 1977
Coxed Fours	3:14.03	E Germany	Lucerne	June 15, 1976
Quadruple Sculls	3:08.49	E Germany	Montreal	July 19, 1976
Eights	2:57.38	E Germany	Lucerne	June 15, 1980

The earliest established sculling race is the Doggett's Coat and Badge, first rowed on Aug 1, 1716, from London Bridge to Chelsea, and still contested annually. Although rowing regattas were held in Venice in 1300, the first English regatta probably took place on the Thames by the Ranelagh Gardens near Putney, London, in 1775. Boating began at Eton, England, in 1793. The oldest club, the Leander Club, was formed *c.* 1818.

Olympic Games

Five oarsmen have won 3 gold medals: John B. Kelly (US) (1889–1960), father of Princess Grace of Monaco, in the sculls (1920) and double sculls (1920 and 24); his cousin Paul V. Costello (US) (b Dec 27, 1899) in the double sculls (1920, 24 and 28); Jack Beresford, Jr (GB) (1899–1977) in the sculls (1924), coxless fours (1932) and double sculls (1936); Vyacheslav Ivanov (USSR) (b July 30, 1938) in the sculls (1956, 60 and 64); and Siegfried Brietzke in the coxless pairs (1972) and the coxless fours (1976 and 80).

Highest Speed

Speeds in tidal or flowing water are of no comparative value. The highest recorded speed for 2,000 m on non-tidal water by an eight is 5 min 32.17 sec (13.46 mph) by E Germany at the Montreal Olympics on July 18, 1976. A team from the Penn AC (US) was timed in 5 min 18.8 sec (14.03 mph) in the FISA Championships on the Meuse River, Liège, Belgium, on Aug 17, 1930.

Longest Race

The longest annual rowing race is the annual Tour du Lac Leman, Geneva, Switzerland for coxed fours (the five-man team taking turns as cox) over 99 miles. The record winning time is 13 hours 26 min 30 sec by Utrechtse Roeivereniging Viking, Netherlands, Sept 12–13, 1981.

Sculling

The record number of world professional sculling titles (instituted 1831) won is 7 by William Beach (Australia) between 1884 and 1887.

Cross-Channel Row

The fastest row across the English Channel is 3 hours 50 min by the Rev Sidney Swann (1862–1942) on Sept 12, 1911.

SCULL SESSIONS: Vyacheslav Ivanov won the Olympic gold medal for the sculls in three successive games. Four other rowers have also won three golds.

SHOOTING

Earliest Club

The Lucerne Shooting Guild (Switzerland) was formed *c.* 1466, and the first recorded shooting match was held at Zurich in 1472.

Olympic Games

The record number of medals won is 11 by Carl Townsend Osburn (US) (1884–1966) in 1912, 1920 and 1924, consisting of 5 gold, 4 silver and 2 bronze. Six other marksmen have won 5 gold medals. The only marksman to win 3 individual gold medals has been Gudbrand Gudbrandsönn Skatteboe (Norway) (1875–1965) in 1906.

Trick Shooting

The greatest rapid-fire feat was by Ed McGivern (US), who twice fired from 15 ft in 0.45 sec 5 shots which could be covered by a silver half-dollar piece

INDIVIDUAL WORLD SHOOTING RECORDS
(as ratified by the International Shooting Union—UIT)

			Max-Score		
Free Rifle	300m	3 × 40 shots	1200–1160	Lones W. Wigger (US)	Seoul, 1978
			1160	Lones W. Wigger (US)	Rio de Janeiro, 1981
		60 shots prone	600–592	Gennadi Lushikov (USSR)	Oulu, Finland, 1981
			592	Alexander Mastrianin (USSR)	Oulu, Finland, 1981
			592	Lones W. Wigger (US)	Rio de Janeiro, 1981
			592	Philip Whitworth (US)	Rio de Janeiro, 1981
Standard Rifle	300m	3 × 20 shots	600–580	Lones W. Wigger (US)	Rio de Janeiro, 1981
Small-Bore Rifle	50m	3 × 40 shots	1200–1173	Viktor Vlasov (USSR)	Moscow, 1980
	50m	60 shots prone	600–600	Alistair Allan (GB)	Titograd, Yugo, 1981
			600	E. Van de Sande (US)	Rio de Janeiro, 1981
Free Pistol	50m	60 shots	600–581	Aleksandr Melentev (USSR)	Moscow, 1980
Rapid-Fire Pistol	25m	60 shots	600–599	Igor Puzyrev (USSR)	Titograd, Yugo, 1981
Center-Fire Pistol	25m	60 shots	600–597	Thomas D. Smith (US)	São Paulo, Brazil, 1963
Standard Pistol	25m	60 shots	600–583	Ragnar Skanaker (Sweden)	Seoul, 1978
Running Target	50m	60 shots "normal runs"	600–595	Igor Sokolov (USSR)	Miskulc, Hungary, 1981
Trap	—	200 birds	200–199	Angelo Scalzone (Italy)	Munich, 1972
			199	Michel Carrega (France)	Thun, Switz, 1974
Skeet	—	200 birds	200–200	Matthew Dryke (US)	São Paulo, Brazil, 1981
Air Rifle	10m	60 shots	600–590	Harald Stanvaag (Norway)	The Hague, Neth, 1982
Air Pistol	10m	60 shots	600–587	Valdas Tourla (USSR)	The Hague, Neth, 1982

---

at the Lead Club Range, SD, on Aug 20, 1932.

McGivern also, on Sept 13, 1932, at Lewiston, Mont, fired 10 shots in 1.2 sec from two guns at the same time double action (no draw), all 10 shots hitting two 2¼ × 3½ in playing cards at 15 ft.

The most renowned trick shot of all time was Annie Oakley (née Mozee) (1860–1926). She demonstrated the ability to shoot 100 of 100 in trap shooting for 35 years, aged between 27 and 62. At 30 paces she could split a playing card end-on, hit a dime in mid-air or shoot a cigarette from the lips of her husband—one Frank Butler.

Bench Rest Shooting

The smallest group on record at 1,000 yd is 5.093 in by Rick Taylor with a 300 Weatherby at Williamsport, Pa, on Aug 24, 1980.

Clay Pigeon Shooting

The record number of clay birds shot in an hour is 1,905 by Terry Harper (b Jan 10, 1943) at Beverley, England, on a skeet range, on May 19, 1982. Graham Douglas Geater (b July 21, 1947) shot 2,264 targets in

BENCHMARK: Rick Taylor set the mark for bench rest shooting when he grouped his shots within just over 5 in at 1,000 yd.

an hour on a trap-shooting range at the NILO Gun Club, Papamoa, NZ on Jan 17, 1981.

Most world titles have been won by Susan Nattrass (Canada) with 6, 1974–5, 77–9, 81.

Small-Bore Rifle Shooting

Richard Hansen shot 5,000 bull's-eyes in 24 hours at Fresno, Calif, on June 13, 1929.

Highest Score in 24 Hours

The Central Lancashire Rifle Club team of John Jepson, Graham Sharples, Derek Byron and Joseph Graham, scored 85,752 points (averaging 94.03 per card), Nov 26–27, 1976.

GAME SHOOTING

Record Heads

The world's finest head is the 23-pointer stag head in the Maritzburg collection, E Germany. The outside span is 75½ in, the length 47½ in and the weight 41½ lb. The greatest number of points is probably 33 (plus 29) on the stag shot in 1696 by Frederick III (1657–1713), the Elector of Brandenburg, later King Frederick I of Prussia.

Largest Shoulder Guns

The largest bore shoulder guns made were 2-bore. Less than a dozen of these were made by two English wildfowl gunmakers *c.* 1885. Normally the largest guns made are double-barrelled 4-bore weighing up to 26 lb which can be handled only by men of exceptional physique. Larger smooth-bore guns have been made, but these are for use as punt-guns.

Biggest Bag

The largest animal ever shot by any big game hunter was a bull African elephant (*Loxodonta africana africana*) shot by E. M. Nielsen of Columbus, Neb, 25 miles north-northeast of Mucusso, Angola, on Nov 7, 1974. The animal, brought down by a Westley Richards 0.425, stood 13 ft 8 in tall at the shoulder.

In Nov 1965, Simon Fletcher, 28, a Kenyan farmer, claims to have killed two elephants with one 0.458 bullet.

The greatest recorded lifetime bag is 556,000 birds, including 241,000 pheasants, by the 2nd Marquess of

HOTSHOT: Graham Geater hit 2,264 targets in one hour at a trap-shooting range in New Zealand in 1981.

Ripon (1852–1923) of England. He himself dropped dead on a grouse moor after shooting his 52nd bird on the morning of Sept 22, 1923.

SKIING

Origins

The most ancient ski in existence was found well preserved in a peat bog at Höting, Sweden, dating from *c.* 2500 BC. The earliest recorded military use was at the Battle of Isen, near Oslo, Norway. The Trysil Shooting and Skiing Club (founded 1861), in Norway, claims to be the world's oldest. The oldest ski competitions are the Holmenkollen Nordic events which were first held in 1866. The first downhill was staged in Australia in the 1850's. The first Slalom event was run at Mürren, Switzerland, on Jan 21, 1922. The International Ski Federation (FIS) was founded on Feb 2, 1924. The Winter Olympics were inaugurated on Jan 25, 1924. The FIS recognizes both the Winter Olympics and the separate World Ski Championships as world championships.

Most Alpine World Titles

The World Alpine Championships were inaugurated at Mürren, Switzerland, in 1931. The greatest number of titles won has been by Christel Cranz (b July 1, 1914), of Germany, with 7 individual—4 Slalom (1934, 37–39) and 3 Downhill (1935, 37, 39); and 5 Combined (1934–35, 37–39). She also won the gold medal for the Combined in the 1936 Olympics. The most titles won by a man is 7 by Anton "Toni" Sailer (b Nov 17, 1935), of Austria, who won all 4 in 1956 (Giant Slalom, Slalom, Downhill and the non-Olympic Alpine Combination) and the Downhill, Giant Slalom and Combined in 1958.

Most Nordic World Titles

The first world Nordic championships were those of the 1924 Winter Olympics at Chamonix, France. The greatest number of titles won is 9 by Galina Koulakova (b Apr 29, 1942) (USSR), 1968–78. She also won 4 silver and 4 bronze medals for a record total of 17. The most won by a man is 8, including relays, by Sixten Jernberg (b Feb 6, 1929) (Sweden),

1956–64. Johan Grottumsbraaten (1899–1942), of Norway, won 6 individual titles (2 at 18 km and 4 Combined) in 1926–32. The record for a jumper is 5 by Birger Ruud (b Aug 23, 1911), of Norway, in 1931–32 and 1935–37. Ruud is the only person to win Olympic titles in each of the dissimilar Alpine and Nordic disciplines. In 1936 he won the ski-jumping and the Alpine downhill.

World Cup

The Alpine World Cup, instituted in 1967, has been won 4 times by Gustavo Thoeni (Italy) (b Feb 28, 1951) in 1971–73, and 75. The women's cup has been won 6 times by the 5-ft-6-in 150-lb Annemarie Moser (née Pröll) (Austria) in 1971–75 and 79. From Dec 1972 to Jan 1974 she completed a record sequence of 11 consecutive downhill victories. She holds the women's record of 62 individual event wins (1970–79). The most by a man is 66 by Ingemar Stenmark (b Mar 18, 1956) (Sweden), 1974–82, including a record 14 in one season in 1979.

The Nordic World Cup, instituted in 1979, was first won by Oddvar Braa (Norway) with the women's title won by Galina Koulakova (USSR).

Most Olympic Victories

The most Olympic gold medals won by an individual for skiing is 4 by Sixten Jernberg (b Feb 6, 1929), of Sweden, in 1956–64 (including one for a relay); and by Aleksandr Tikhonov (b Jan 2, 1947) (USSR) who won all 4 as a member of the winning team in the 4 × 7.5-km biathlon relay, 1968–80. In addition, Jernberg has won 3 silver and 2 bronze medals for a record 9 Olympic medals. The only woman to win 4 gold medals is Galina Koulakova (b Apr 29, 1942) of USSR who won the 5 km and 10 km (1972) and was a member of the winning 3 × 5-km relay team in 1972 and the 4 × 5-km team in 1976. Koulakova also has won 2 silver and 2 bronze medals, 1968–80.

The most Olympic gold medals won in men's Alpine skiing is 3, by Anton "Toni" Sailer in 1956 and Jean-Claude Killy in 1968.

Highest Speed

The highest speed ever claimed for any skier is 126.24 mph by Franz Weber (Austria). The fastest by a woman is 111.29 mph by Marty Martin-Kunz (US). Both were achieved at Silverton, Colo, on Apr 24, 1982.

The highest average race speed in the Olympic downhill was in 1976 by Franz Klammer (b Dec 3,

GOING DOWNHILL: The most successful skier in the world championships, Christel Cranz won 12 titles—7 individual and 5 combined, 1934–39. (Popperfoto)

SNOWBIRD: In a sport that may be humankind's closest approach to unaided flight, Armin Kogler of Austria soared to the official world record with a jump of 180 meters (590½ ft) in Feb 1981. (Don Morley, All-Sport)

1953) of Austria on the Patscherkofel course, Innsbruck, Austria, with 63.894 mph on Feb 5, 1976.

Closest Verdict

The narrowest winning margin in a championship ski race was one hundredth of a second by Thomas Wassberg (Sweden) (b March 23, 1956) over Juha Mieto (Finland) in the Olympic 15 km cross-country race at Lake Placid, NY on Feb 17, 1980. His winning time was 41 min 57.63 sec.

Longest Jump

The longest ski jump ever recorded is one of 181 m (593 ft 10 in) by Bogdan Norcic (Yugoslavia) (b Sept 19, 1953) who fell on landing at Planica, Yugoslavia, in Feb 1977.

The official record is 180 m (590 ft 6 in) by Armin Kogler (Austria) (b Sept 4, 1959) at Oberstdorf, W Germany, on Feb 26, 1981. The longest jump on a 90 m hill is 128.5 m (421 ft 6 in) by Steve Collins (b 1936) at Thunder Bay, Canada, on Dec 15, 1980.

The women's record is 98 m (321 ft 6 in) by Anita Wold of Norway, at Okura, Sapporo, Japan, on Jan 14, 1975.

The longest jump achieved in the Olympics is 117 m (384 ft) by Juoko Tormanen (Finland) (b Apr 10, 1954) at Lake Placid, NY, on Feb 23, 1980.

The longest dry ski jump is 92 m (301 ft 10 in) by Hubert Schwarz (W Germany) at Berchtesgarten, W Germany, on June 30, 1981.

Longest Races

The world's longest ski races are the Grenader, run just north of Oslo, Norway, and the Konig Ludwig Lauf in Oberammergau, W Germany. Both are 90 km (55.9 miles). The Canadian Ski Marathon at 120 km (74.6 miles) is longer, but is run in two parts on consecutive days.

The world's greatest Nordic ski race is the Vasaloppet, which commemorates an event in 1521 when Gustavus Vasa (1496–1560), later King of Sweden, fled 85.8 km (53.3 miles) from Mora to Sälen, Sweden. He was overtaken by loyal, speedy scouts on skis, who persuaded him to return eastwards to Mora

493

to lead a rebellion and become the king of Sweden. The re-enactment of this journey is an annual event, with a record 12,000 entrants (including 188 women) in 1981. The record time is 4 hours 5 min 58 sec by Ola Hassis (Sweden) on March 4, 1979.

The Vasaloppet is now the longest of 10 long distance races, constituting the world loppet, staged in 10 countries.

The longest downhill race is the *Inferno* in Switzerland, 8.7 miles from the top of the Schilthorn to Lauterbrunnen. In 1981 there was a record entry of 1,401, with Heinz Fringen (Switzerland) winning in a record 15 min 44.57 sec.

Steepest Descent

Sylvain Saudan (b Lausanne, Switzerland, Sept 23, 1936) achieved a descent of Mt Blanc on the northeast side down the Couloir Gervasutti from 13,937 ft on Oct 17, 1967, skiing gradients in excess of 60 degrees.

Greatest Descent

The greatest reported aggregate elevation descended in 12 hours is 416,000 ft by Sarah Ludwig, Scott Ludwig, and Timothy B. Gaffney, at Mt Brighton, Mich on Feb 16, 1974.

Highest Altitude

Yuichiro Miura (Japan) skied 1.6 miles down Mt Everest on May 6, 1970, starting from 26,574 ft.

Longest Run

The longest all-downhill ski run in the world is the Weissfluhjoch-Küblis Parsenn course (7.6 miles long), near Davos, Switzerland. The run from the Aiguille du Midi top of the Chamonix lift (vertical lift 8,176 ft) across the Vallée Blanche is 13 miles.

Backflip on Skis

The greatest number of skiers to perform a back layout flip while holding hands is 28 at Bromont, Quebec, Canada, on Feb 10, 1982, for the "That's Incredible" TV show.

Duration

The longest non-stop Nordic skiing marathon was one that lasted 48 hours by Onni Savi, aged 35, of Padasjoki, Finland, who covered 305.9 km (190.1

miles) between noon on Apr 19 and noon on Apr 21, 1966.

Dan Quinlan (b Nov 12, 1960) (US) covered 180.7 miles in 24 hours at Williston, Vt, Feb 17–18, 1982.

Pat Purcell and John McGlynn (US) completed 81 hours 12 min of Alpine skiing at Holiday Mountain, Monticello, NY, Feb 1–4, 1979.

Longest Lift

The longest chair lift in the world is the Alpine Way to Kosciusko Châlet lift above Thredbo, near the Snowy Mountains, NSW, Australia. It takes from 45 to 75 min to ascend the 3.5 miles, according to the weather. The highest is at Chacaltaya, Bolivia, rising to 16,500 ft. The longest gondola ski lift, at Killington, Vt, is 3.4 miles long.

Ski Parachuting

The greatest recorded vertical descent in parachute ski-jumping is 3,300 ft by Rick Sylvester (b Apr 3, 1942) (US), who on July 28, 1976, skied off the 6,600-ft summit of Mt Asgard in Auyuittuq National Park, Baffin Island, Canada, landing on the Turner Glacier. The jump was made for a sequence in the James Bond film *The Spy Who Loved Me*.

Snowmobiling

The record speed for a snowmobile is 148.6 mph, set by Tom Earhart (US) in a Budweiser-Polaris snowmobile designed and owned by Bob Gaudreau, at Lake Mille Lacs, Minn, on Feb 25, 1982.

Richard and Raymond Moore and Loren Matthews drove their snowmobile 5,876 miles from Fairbanks, Alaska, to Fenton, Mich, in 39 days, from Feb 3 to Mar 13, 1980.

SOCCER

Origins

A game with some similarities termed *Tsu-chu* was played in China in the 3rd and 4th centuries BC. One of the earliest references to the game in England is a Royal Proclamation by Edward II in 1314 banning the game in the City of London. The earliest clear representation of the game is in a print from Edinburgh, Scotland, dated 1672–73. The game became standardized with the formation of the Football Association in England on Oct 26, 1863. The world's oldest club is Sheffield FC of England, formed on

Oct 24, 1857. Eleven players on a side was standardized in 1870.

Highest Team Scores

The highest score recorded in any first-class match is 36. This occurred in the Scottish Cup match between Arbroath and Bon Accord on Sept 5, 1885, when Arbroath won 36–0 on their home ground. But for the lack of nets and the consequent waste of retrieval time, the score might have been even higher.

The highest goal margin recorded in any international match is 17, when England beat Australia 17–0 at Sydney on June 30, 1951. This match is not listed by England as a *full* international.

Individual Scoring

The most goals scored by one player in a first-class match is 16 by Stephan Stanis (*né* Stanikowski, b Poland, July 15, 1913) for Racing Club de Lens vs Aubry-Asturies, in Lens, France, on Dec 13, 1942.

The record number of goals scored by one player in an international match is 10 by Gottfried Fuchs for Germany, which beat Russia 16–0 in the 1912 Olympic tournament (consolation event) in Sweden.

Artur Friedenreich (1892–1969) (Brazil) scored an undocumented 1,329 goals in a 43-year first-class football career. The most goals scored in a specified period is 1,216 by Edson Arantes do Nascimento (b Baurú, Brazil, Oct 23, 1940), known as Pelé, the Brazilian inside left, from Sept 7, 1956, to Oct 2, 1974 (1,254 games). His best year was 1958 with 139. His *milesimo* (1,000th) came in a penalty for his club, Santos, in the Maracaña Stadium, Rio de Janeiro, on Nov 19, 1969, when he was playing in his 909th first-class match. He came out of retirement in 1975 to add to his total with the New York Cosmos of the North American Soccer League. By his retirement on Oct 1, 1977 his total had reached 1,281 in 1,363 games. He added 2 more goals later in special appearances. Franz ("Bimbo") Binder (b 1911) scored 1,006 goals in 756 games in Austria and Germany between 1930 and 1950.

Fastest Goals

The record for an international match is 3 goals in 3½ min by Willie Hall (Tottenham Hotspur) for England against Ireland on Nov 16, 1938, at Old Trafford, Manchester, England.

In amateur soccer, wind-aided goals in 3 sec after kickoff have been scored by a number of players.

ATHLETE'S FEAT: Although some may consider the award premature, Pelé, who scored 1,281 goals in the world's most popular sport, was named "Athlete of the Century" by the French sports magazine "L'Equipe" after polling 20 international newspapers. Jesse Owens was runner-up. (Steve Hasel)

Tony Bacon, of Schalmont HS, scored three goals vs Ichabod Crane HS in 63 sec at Schenectady, NY on Oct 8, 1975.

Goalkeeping

The longest that any goalkeeper has succeeded in preventing any goals being scored past him in international matches is 1,142 min for Dino Zoff (Italy) from Sept 1972 to June 1974.

The biggest goalie on record was Willie J. ("Fatty") Foulke of England (1874–1916) who stood 6 ft 3 in and weighed 311 lb. By the time he died, he tipped the scales at 364 lb. He once stopped a game by snapping the cross bar.

Most Internationals

The greatest number of appearances for a national team is 150 by Hector Chumpitaz (b Apr 12, 1943) (Peru) from 1963 to 1982. This includes all matches played by the national team. The record for full internationals against other national teams is 115 by Bjorn Nordqvist (b Oct 6, 1942) (Sweden) from 1963 to 1978.

Most Successful National Coach

Helmut Schoen (b Sept 15, 1915) of W Germany coached his teams to victory in the 1972 European championship and the 1974 World Cup, as well as finishing second in the 1966 World Cup and 1976 European championships, and third in the 1970 World Cup. George Raynor's Swedish teams won the 1948 Olympic competition and were second in the 1958 World Cup and third in both the 1950 World Cup and the 1952 Olympic competition.

Longest Match

The world duration record for a first-class match was set in the Copa Libertadores championship in Santos, Brazil, Aug 2–3, 1962, when Santos drew 3–3 with Penarol FC of Montevideo, Uruguay. The game lasted 3½ hours (with interruptions), from 9:30 p.m. to 1 a.m.

A match between the Simon Fraser University Clansmen and the Quincy College Hawks lasted 4 hours 25 min (221 min 43 sec playing time) at Pasadena, Calif, in Nov 1976.

The Scottish Cup match between Inverness Thistle and Falkirk during the winter of 1978–79 was postponed a record 29 times due to weather conditions. Finally Falkirk won the game, 4–0.

Crowds

The greatest recorded crowd at any football match was 205,000 (199,854 paid) for the Brazil vs Uruguay World Cup final in Rio de Janeiro, Brazil, on July 16, 1950.

The highest attendance at any amateur match is 120,000 at Senayan Stadium, Djakarta, Indonesia, on Feb 26, 1976, for the Pre-Olympic Group II Final between North Korea and Indonesia.

World Cup

The *Fédération Internationale de Football Association* (FIFA) was founded in Paris on May 21, 1904, and instituted the World Cup Competition in 1930, in Montevideo, Uruguay.

The only countries to win three times have been Brazil (1958, 62, 70) and Italy (1934, 38, 82). Brazil was also third in 1938 and 1978, and second in 1950, and is the only one of the 47 participating countries to have played in all 12 competitions.

Antonio Carbajal (b 1923) played for Mexico in goal in the competitions of 1950, 54, 58, 62 and 66.

The record goal scorer has been Just Fontaine

HOT FOOT: A tired but triumphant Geoff Hurst raises the World Cup trophy he helped England win by scoring a record 3 goals in the 1966 final game. (Topix)

(France) with 13 goals in 6 games in the final stages of the 1958 competition. The most goals scored in the final game is 3 by Geoffrey Hurst (West Ham United) for England vs W Germany on July 30, 1966. Gerd Müller (W Germany) scored 14 goals in two World Cup finals (1970 and 74).

The highest score in a World Cup match is New Zealand's 13–0 defeat of Fiji in a qualifying match at Auckland on Aug 16, 1981. The highest score in the Finals Tournament is Hungary's 10–1 win over El Salvador at Elche, Spain, on June 15, 1982.

The fastest goal scored in World Cup competition was one in 27 sec by Bryan Robson for England vs France in Bilbao, Spain, on June 16, 1982.

NASL Records

The North American Soccer League was created in 1968 through the merger of the two competing professional soccer leagues: the United Soccer Association and the National Professional Soccer League.

The NY Cosmos have won a record 4 NASL championships, 1972, 77–78 and 80.

Giorgio Chinaglia (b Jan 24, 1947) of the NY Cosmos scored a record 34 goals during the 1978 season. He also set the record for points that season with 79. (The NASL awards 2 points for a goal and 1 point for an assist.) Through 1981, Chinaglia had scored a league-record 155 goals in 164 regular-season games. Alan Hinton (Vancouver) had the most assists in a season with 30 in 1978.

Giorgio Chinaglia (NY) scored 7 goals in one playoff game against the Tulsa Roughnecks on Aug 31, 1980. He also added an assist, and his total points for a single game (15) is also a league record.

Steve Davis (LA) scored goals in 10 consecutive games in 1977, and Mike Stojanovic (San Diego) matched this feat in 1981.

Derek Smethurst (Seattle) scored the fastest goal, at 11 seconds against Minnesota on May 2, 1979.

Goalkeeper Lincoln Phillips (Washington) went 528 consecutive minutes without allowing a goal in 1970. The fewest goals allowed in a season is 8 by Bob Rigby (Philadelphia) in 1973. The record for most saves in a game is 22, by Mike Winter (St Louis) vs Rochester, May 27, 1973.

The greatest crowd to see a soccer game in the US and Canada was the 77,691 spectators at Giants Sta-

HEAD TO HEAD: Although the soccer ball juggling record he set here has since been surpassed, Mikael Palmqvist has retained the heading mark by extending his own record from 2 hours 20 min to 3 hours.

dium, NJ, who watched an NASL playoff game between the NY Cosmos and Ft Lauderdale Strikers on Aug 14, 1977.

Most Olympic Wins

The only country to have won the Olympic football title three times is Hungary in 1952, 1964 and 1968. The UK won in 1908 and 1912 and also the unofficial tournament of 1900. The highest Olympic score is Denmark 17 vs France "A" 1 in 1908.

Ball Control

Alan Nyanjong Abuto (21) of Kenya juggled a regulation soccer ball for 11 hours 36 min 19 sec non-stop at Manhattanville College, NY, on Feb 7, 1982. He did 85,295 repetitions with feet, legs and head without the ball ever touching the ground.

Mikael Palmqvist headed a regulation soccer ball non-stop for 3 hours (27,193 repetitions) at Bromölla Sporting Hall, Sweden, on Aug 15, 1981.

COSMOS' TOPPER: Giorgio Chinaglia (in white) of the NY Cosmos holds NASL goal-scoring records for a career (155 through 1981), season (34) and game (7). (NY Cosmos)

Marathons

The longest recorded 11-a-side soccer marathon is 65 hours 1 min by Callinafercy Soccer Club, Co Kerry, Ireland, Aug 1–3, 1980.

The longest recorded authenticated 5-a-side games have been (outdoors) 73 hours by two teams (no substitutes) from Three Medical Troop, Commando Logistic Regiment, Royal Marines at Arbroath, Scotland, Oct 24–26, 1980, and (indoors) 100 hours 10 min by two teams (no substitutes) representing Bogarts Club and Spenders Disco at the Deeside Leisure Centre, Clwyd, Wales, Apr 8–12, 1982.

SOFTBALL

Origins

Softball, as an indoor derivative of baseball, was invented by George Hancock at the Farragut Boat Club of Chicago, in 1887. Rules were first codified in Minneapolis in 1895 as Kitten Ball. The name Softball was introduced by Walter Hakanson at a meeting of the National Recreation Congress in 1926. The name was adopted throughout the US in 1930. Rules were formalized in 1933 by the International Joint Rules Committee for Softball and adopted by the Amateur Softball Association of America. The International Softball Federation was formed in 1950 as governing body for both fast pitch and slow pitch.

World Championships

The US has won the men's world championship (instituted in 1966) four times, 1966, 68, 76 (shared) and 80. The US has also won the women's title (instituted in 1965) twice, in 1974 and 78.

Marathons

The longest fast pitch marathon is 56 hours 10 min by two teams of nine (no substitutes) at Gardner, Mass, Sept 5–7, 1981. The longest for slow pitch is 90 hours 3 min by two teams of ten players at Marshfield, Mass, Sept 2–6, 1981.

SQUASH

Earliest Champion

Although racquets with a soft ball was played in 1817 at Harrow School (England), there was no recognized champion of any country until J. A. Miskey of Philadelphia won the American Amateur Singles Championship in 1907.

World Amateur Title

Australia has won the team title 4 times. Geoffrey B. Hunt (b March 11, 1947) (Australia) took the individual title in 1967, 69 and 71.

WORLD CHAMPIONSHIP SOFTBALL RECORDS

MEN

Most runs	12	Generoso Lopez (Venezuela)	1966
Most home runs	4	Robert "Bob" Burrows (Canada)	1976
Most hits	17	Basil McLean (New Zealand)	1976
RBIs	14	Chuck Teuscher (US)	1966
	14	Robert "Bob" Burrows (Canada)	1976
Highest average	.556	Seiichi Tanaka (Japan)	1980
Most wins	6	Owen Walford (NZ)	1976
	6	Owen Walford (US)	1980
Most innings pitched	59	Ty Stofflet (US)	1976
Most strikeouts	98	Ty Stofflet (US)	1976
Most perfect games	1	Joe Lynch (US); Chuck Richard (US);	1976
		Dave Ruthowsky (Canada)	1968

WOMEN

Most runs	13	Kathy Elliott (US)	1974
Most hits	17	Miyoko Naruse (Japan)	1974
RBIs	11	Miyoko Naruse (Japan); Keiko Usul (Japan); Kathy Elliott (US)	1974
Highest average	.550	Tamara Bryce (Panama)	1978
Most wins	6	Lorraine Wooley (Australia)	1965
	6	Nancy Welborn (US)	1970
Most innings pitched	50	Nancy Welborn (US)	1970
Most strikeouts	76	Joan Joyce (US)	1974
Most perfect games	2	Joan Joyce (US)	1974

JOAN JOYCE struck out 76 batters and pitched 2 perfect games in 1974. Now she's a pro golfer with the LPGA.

OFF THE WALL: Geoff Hunt has dominated men's squash with 4 World Open titles, 3 World Amateur titles and 8 titles in the British Open Championship. (All-Sport)

World Open Title

The World Open championship, instituted in 1976, has been won 4 times by Geoffrey B. Hunt (Australia), in 1976, 77, 79 and 80.

British Open Championship

The most wins in the Open Championship (amateur or professional), held annually in Britain, is 8 by Geoffrey Hunt in 1969, 74, and 76–81. Hashim Khan (b 1915) (Pakistan) won 7 times and has also won the Vintage title 5 times, 1978–82.

The most wins in the Women's Squash Rackets Championship is 16 by Heather McKay (née Blundell) (b July 31, 1941) of Australia, 1961 to 1977. She also won the World Open title in 1976 and 79. In her career from 1959 to 1980 she lost only two games.

British Amateur Championship

The most wins in the Amateur Championship is 6 by Abdel Fattah Amr Bey (Egypt), later appointed Ambassador in London, who won in 1931–33 and 1935–37.

Longest and Shortest Championship Matches

The longest recorded match was one of 2 hours 35 min in the British Amateur Championships at Wembley, England, on Dec 12, 1976, when Murray Lilley (New Zealand) beat Barry O'Connor (GB) 9–3, 10–8, 2–9, 7–9, 10–8. The second game lasted 58 min and there were a total of 98 lets called in the match.

Deanna Murray beat Christine Rees in only 9½ min in a Ladies Welsh title match at Rhos-on-Sea, Clwyd, Wales, on Oct 21, 1979.

Marathon Record

The longest squash marathon has been 120 hours 51 min by Peter Fairlie at the Bridge of Allan Sports Club, Stirling, Scotland, June 30–July 5, 1979. (*This category will be confined to two players only.*)

SWIMMING

Earliest References

Swimming in schools in Japan was ordered by Imperial edict of Emperor Go-Yozei (1586–1611) as early as 1603, but competition was known from 36 BC. Sea water bathing was fashionable at Scarborough, New Yorkshire, England, as early as 1660.

Largest Pools

The largest swimming pool in the world is the salt-water Orthlieb Pool in Casablanca, Morocco. It is 480 m (1,574 ft) long, 75 m (246 ft) wide, and has an area of 8.9 acres.

The largest land-locked swimming pool with heated water was the Fleishhacker Pool on Sloat Boulevard, near Great Highway, San Francisco. It measures 1,000 ft by 150 ft (3.44 acres), is up to 14 ft deep, and can contain 7,500,000 gallons of water. It was opened on May 2, 1925, but has now been abandoned.

The world's largest competition pool is at Osaka, Japan. It accommodates 13,614 spectators.

Fastest Swimmers

The fastest 50 m in a 50-m pool is 22.54 sec by Robin Leamy (b Apr 1, 1961) (US), averaging 4.96 mph, at Milwaukee, Wis, on Aug 15, 1981.

DIFFERENT STROKES: Jill Sterkel (above), winner of the Broderick Award as the outstanding female collegiate athlete in 1980–81, swam a 50-meter pool in 25.79 sec—the fastest by a woman. Sterkel was a member of the US gold medal 4 × 100 freestyle relay team in 1976. Mark Spitz (right) waves to the crowd while wearing his record seventh gold medal won at the 1972 Olympics. He won titles in the freestyle, butterfly and 4-stroke medley. Spitz set 26 world records, the most by any swimmer under modern conditions. (Sterkel photo courtesy Univ of Texas; Spitz photo by AP)

The fastest by a woman is 25.79 sec by Jill Sterkel (b 1961) (US), averaging 4.34 mph, at Austin, Tex, on Apr 3, 1981.

Most World Records

Men: 32, Arne Borg (Sweden) (b 1901), 1921–29. Women: 42, Ragnhild Hveger (Denmark) (b Dec 10, 1920), 1936–42. Under modern conditions (only metric distances in 50-meter pools) the most is 26 by Mark Spitz (US), 1967–72, and 23 by Kornelia Ender (E Germany), 1973–6.

World Titles

In the world swimming championships (instituted in 1973), the greatest number of medals won is 10 by Kornelia Ender of E Germany (8 gold, 2 silver). The most by a man is 7 (6 gold, 1 bronze) by James Montgomery (US).

The most medals in a single championship is 6 by Tracy Caulkins (US) (b Jan 11, 1963) in 1978 with 5 gold and a silver.

Most Olympic Gold Medals

The greatest number of Olympic gold medals won is 9 by Mark Andrew Spitz (US) (b Feb 10, 1950), as follows:

100 m freestyle	1972
200 m freestyle	1972
100 m butterfly	1972
200 m butterfly	1972
4 × 100 m freestyle relay	1968 and 1972
4 × 200 m freestyle relay	1968 and 1972
4 × 100 m medley relay	1972

All but one of these performances (the 4 × 200 m relay of 1968) were also world records at the time.

The record number of gold medals won by a woman is 4 shared by Mrs Patricia McCormick (*née* Keller) (US) (b May 12, 1930) with the High and Springboard Diving double in 1952 and 1956 (also the women's record for individual golds); by Dawn Fraser (Australia) (b Sept 4, 1937) with the 100 m freestyle (1956, 60, 64) and the 4 × 100 m freestyle relay (1956); and by Kornelia Ender (now Matthes) (E Germany) (b Plauen, E Germany, Oct 25, 1958) with the 100 and 200 m freestyle (1976), the 100 m butterfly (1976) and the 4 × 100 m medley relay (1976). Dawn Fraser is the only swimmer to win the same event on three successive occasions.

Most Individual Gold Medals

The record number of individual gold medals won is 4 shared by four swimmers: Charles M. Daniels (US) (1884–1973) (100 m freestyle 1906 and 1908, 220 yd freestyle 1904, 440 yd freestyle 1904); Roland Matthes (E Germany) (b Nov 17, 1950) with 100 m and 200 m backstroke 1968 and 1972, and Spitz and McCormick (see above).

Most Olympic Medals

The most medals won is 11 by Spitz, who in addition to his 9 golds (see above), won a silver (100 m butterfly) and a bronze (100 m freestyle), both in 1968.

The most medals won by a woman is 8 by Dawn Fraser, who in addition to her 4 golds (see above) won 4 silvers (400 m freestyle 1956, 4 × 100 m freestyle relay 1960 and 1964, 4 × 100 m medley relay 1960); by Shirley Babashoff (US) who won 2 golds (4 × 100 m freestyle relay 1972 and 1976) and 6 silvers (100 m freestyle 1972, 200 m freestyle 1972 and 1976, 400 m and 800 m freestyle 1976, and 400 m medley 1976); and by Kornelia Ender (E Germany) who, in addition to her 4 golds (see above), won 4 silvers (200 m individual medley 1972, 4 × 100 m medley 1972, 4 × 100 m freestyle 1972 and 1976).

Closest Verdict

The closest victory in the Olympic Games was in the Munich 400 m individual medley final on Aug 30, 1972, when Gunnar Larsson (Sweden) won by 2/1,000ths of a sec in 4 min 31.981 sec over Tim McKee (US)—a margin of less than ⅛ in, or the length grown by a fingernail in 3 weeks. This led to a change in international rules with timings and places decided only to hundredths.

HAUL OF FAME: Tracy Caulkins, here wearing her record 6 medals (5 gold, 1 silver) from the 1978 World Championships, eclipsed Johnny (Tarzan) Weissmuller's 54-year-old record as winner of the most US national titles when she reached 39 with 4 wins in the US Short Course Championships in April 1982. (Tony Duffy, All-Sport)

WATERMARKS: Craig Beardsley (far left) with Mike Bruner, whose 200 m butterfly record he broke in 1980. Beardsley lowered his own record in 1981. Vladimir Salnikov (right), holder of 3 long-distance freestyle records, here rejoices after becoming the first swimmer to break 15 min for the 1,500 m freestyle—a performance that earned the Olympic gold medal at Moscow. He also later bettered his own time. (Both photos by All-Sport)

SWIMMING WORLD RECORDS

At distances recognized by the Fédération Internationale de Natation Amateur as of Aug 16, 1982. FINA no longer recognizes any records made for non-metric distances. Only performances in 50-m pools are recognized as World Records.

MEN

Distance	min:sec	Name and Nationality	Place	Date
		FREESTYLE		
100 m	49.36	Ambrose (Rowdy) Gaines (US)	Austin, Tex	Apr 3, 1981
200 m	1:48.93	Ambrose (Rowdy) Gaines (US)	Mission Viejo, Calif	July 20, 1982
400 m	3:49.57	Vladimir Salnikov (USSR)	Moscow	Mar 12, 1982
	3:49.57	Vladimir Salnikov (USSR)	Kiev, USSR	July 14, 1982
800 m	7:52.83	Vladimir Salnikov (USSR)	Moscow	Feb 14, 1982
1,500 m	14:56.35	Vladimir Salnikov (USSR)	Moscow	Mar 13, 1982
4 × 100 Relay	3:19.74	US National Team (Jack Babashoff, Ambrose Gaines, David McCagg, James Montgomery)	W Berlin	Aug 22, 1978
4 × 200 Relay	7:20.82	US National Team (Bruce Furniss, William Forrester, Bobby Hackett, Ambrose Gaines)	W Berlin	Aug 24, 1978
		BREASTSTROKE		
100 m	1:02.62	Steven Lundquist (US)	Mission Viejo, Calif	July 20, 1982
200 m	2:14.77	Victor Davis (Canada)	Guayaquil, Ecuador	Aug 6, 1982
		BUTTERFLY STROKE		
100 m	53.81	William Paulus (US)	Austin, Tex	Apr 3, 1981
200 m	1:58.01	Craig Beardsley (US)	Kiev, USSR	Aug 22, 1981
		BACKSTROKE		
100 m	55.49	John Naber (US)	Montreal	July 19, 1976
200 m	1:59.19	John Naber (US)	Montreal	July 24, 1976
		INDIVIDUAL MEDLEY		
200 m	2:02.78	Alex Baumann (Canada)	Heidelberg, W Ger	July 29, 1981
400 m	4:19.78	Riccardo Prado (Brazil)	Guayaquil, Ecuador	Aug 3, 1982
		MEDLEY RELAY (Backstroke, Breaststroke, Butterfly Stroke, Freestyle)		
4 × 100 m	3:40.34	US National Team (Richard Carey, Steven Lundquist, Matthew Gribble, Ambrose "Rowdy" Gaines)	Guayaquil, Ecuador	Aug 8, 1982

WOMEN

Distance	min:sec	Name and Nationality	Place	Date
		FREESTYLE		
100 m	54.79	Barbara Krause (E Germany)	Moscow	July 21, 1980
200 m	1:58.23	Cynthia Woodhead (US)	Tokyo	Sept 3, 1979
400 m	4:06.28	Tracey Wickham (Australia)	W Berlin	Aug 24, 1978
800 m	8:24.62	Tracey Wickham (Australia)	Edmonton, Canada	Aug 5, 1978
1,500 m	16:04.49	Kim Linehan (US)	Ft Lauderdale	Aug 19, 1979
4 × 100 Relay	3:42.71	E Germany (Barbara Krause, Caren Metschuck, Ines Diers, Sarina Hulsenbeck)	Moscow	July 27, 1980
4 × 200 Relay	8:07.44	Mission Viejo (US)	Milwaukee	Aug 14, 1981
		BREASTSTROKE		
100 m	1:08.60	Ute Geweniger (E Germany)	Split, Yugo	Sept 8, 1981
200 m	2:28.36	Lina Kachushite (USSR)	Potsdam, E Germany	Apr 6, 1979
		BUTTERFLY STROKE		
100 m	57.93	Mary Meagher (US)	Milwaukee	Aug 16, 1981
200 m	2:05.96	Mary Meagher (US)	Milwaukee	Aug 13, 1981
		BACKSTROKE		
100 m	1:00.86	Rica Reinisch (E Germany)	Moscow	July 23, 1980
200 m	2:09.91	Kornelia Sirch (E Germany)	Guayaquil, Ecuador	Aug 8, 1982
		INDIVIDUAL MEDLEY		
200 m	2:11.73	Ute Geweniger (E Germany)	E Berlin	July 4, 1981
400 m	4:36.10	Petra Schneider (E Germany)	Guayaquil, Ecuador	Aug 2, 1982
		MEDLEY RELAY (Backstroke, Breaststroke, Butterfly Stroke, Freestyle)		
4 × 100 m	4:05.88	E German National Team (Kristin Otto, Ute Geweniger, Ines Geissler, Birgit Meinecke)	Guayaquil, Ecuador	Aug 8, 1982

GOLD WATER: Ute Geweniger (left) won the Olympic 100 m breaststroke title in 1980 and went on to break the world record for that event 3 times in 1981. Barbara Krause (right) picked up 3 gold medals in the Moscow Olympics, winning the 100 m freestyle in world record time. (Both photos by All-Sport)

Olympic Medals for Diving

Klaus Dibiasi (Italy) won a total of 5 diving medals (3 gold, 2 silver) in 4 Games from 1964 to 1976. He is also the only diver to win the same event (highboard) at 3 successive Games (1968, 72 and 76). Pat McCormick (see above) won 4 gold medals.

World Diving Titles

Two divers have won 3 gold medals: Phil Boggs (US) in 1973, 75 and 78; and Greg Louganis (US) in 1978 and 82 (2). Klaus Dibiasi of Italy won 4 medals (2 gold and 2 silver) in 1973 and 1975. Trina Kalinina (USSR) (b Feb 8, 1959) won 5 medals (3 gold, 1 silver, 1 bronze) in 1973, 75 and 78.

Perfect Dive

In the 1972 US Olympic Trials, held in Chicago, Michael Finneran (b Sept 21, 1948) was awarded a score of 10 by all seven judges for a backward 1½ somersault 2½ twist free dive from the 10-m board, an achievement without precedent.

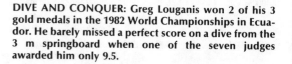

DIVE AND CONQUER: Greg Louganis won 2 of his 3 gold medals in the 1982 World Championships in Ecuador. He barely missed a perfect score on a dive from the 3 m springboard when one of the seven judges awarded him only 9.5.

Long Distance Swimming

A unique achievement in long distance swimming was established in 1966 by Mihir Sen of Calcutta, India. He swam the Palk Strait from Sri Lanka to India (in 25 hours 36 min, Apr 5–6); the Straits of Gibraltar (Europe to Africa in 8 hours 1 min on Aug 24); the Dardanelles (Gallipoli, Europe, to Sedulbahir, Asia Minor, in 13 hours 55 min on Sept 12); the Bosphorus (in 4 hours on Sept 21) and the entire length of the Panama Canal (in 34 hours 15 min, Oct 29–31). He had earlier swum the English Channel in 14 hours 45 min on Sept 27, 1958.

The longest ocean swim claimed is one of 128.8 miles by Walter Poenisch (US) (b 1914), who started from Havana, Cuba, and arrived at Little Duck Key, Fla (in a shark cage and wearing flippers) 34 hours 15 min later, July 11–13, 1978.

The greatest recorded distance ever swum is 1,826 miles down the Mississippi from Ford Dam, near Minneapolis, to Carrollton Avenue, New Orleans, July 6 to Dec 29, 1930, by Fred P. Newton, then 27, of Clinton, Okla. He was in the water a total of 742 hours, and the water temperature fell as low as 47° F. He protected himself with petroleum jelly.

The longest swim using the highly exhausting butterfly stroke exclusively was an officially measured 10 miles by twins James and Jonathan di Donato (b Oct 24, 1953) (US) off Ft Lauderdale, Fla, Aug 27, 1980.

The longest duration swim ever achieved was one of 168 continuous hours, ending on Feb 24, 1941, by the legless Charles Zibbelman, *alias* Zimmy (b 1894), of the US, in a pool in Honolulu, Hawaii.

The longest duration swim by a woman was 87 hours 27 min in a salt water pool at Raven Hall, Coney Island, NY by Mrs Myrtle Huddleston of NYC, in 1931.

The greatest distance covered in a continuous swim is 299 miles by Ricardo Hoffmann (b Oct 5, 1941) from Corrientes to Santa Elena, Argentina, in the River Parana in 84 hours 37 min, Mar 3–6, 1981.

J. Hestoy (Faroe Islands) was reported to have swum 55.41 miles in a pool in 1982.

The greatest lifetime distance by a swimmer is 36,748 miles recorded by Gustave Brickner (b Feb 10, 1912) of Charleroi, Pa, in 54 years to Oct 1981.

Earliest Channel Swimmers

The first to swim the English Channel (without a life jacket) was the merchant navy captain Matthew Webb (1848–83) (GB), who swam breaststroke from Dover, England, to Calais Sands, France, in 21 hours 45 min, Aug 24–25, 1875. Webb swam an estimated 38 miles to make the 21-mile crossing. Paul Boyton (US) had swum from Cap Gris Nez to the South Foreland in his patent lifesaving suit in 23 hours 30 min, May 28–29, 1875. There is good evidence that Jean-Marie Saletti, a French soldier, escaped from a British prison hulk off Dover by swimming to Boulogne in July or Aug 1815. The first crossing from France to England was made by Enrico Tiraboschi, a wealthy Italian living in Argentina, who crossed in 16 hours 33 min on Aug 12, 1923, to win a $5,000 prize. By the end of 1981 the English Channel had been swum by 228 persons on 366 occasions.

The first woman to succeed was Gertrude Ederle (b Oct 23, 1906) (US) who swam from Cap Gris Nez, France, to Deal, England, on Aug 6, 1926, in the then record time of 14 hours 39 min. The first woman to swim from England to France was Florence Chadwick of California, in 16 hours 19 min on Sept 11, 1951.

Youngest and Oldest Channel Swimmers

The youngest conqueror is Marcus Hooper (b June 14, 1967) of Eltham, England, who swam from Dover to Sangatte, France, in 14 hours 37 min, when he was aged 12 years 53 days. The youngest woman was Abla Adel Khairi (b Egypt, Sept 26, 1960), aged 13 years 326 days when she swam from England to France in 12 hours 30 min on Aug 17, 1974.

The oldest conqueror of the 21-mile crossing has been James Edward "Doc" Counsilman (b Dec 28, 1920), head coach of the 1976 US Olympic Swim team, who was 58 years 260 days when he swam from Dover to Cap Gris Nez on Sept 14, 1979. The oldest woman to conquer the Channel was Stella Taylor (b Bristol, Avon, England, Dec 20, 1929), aged 45 years 350 days when she swam it in 18 hours 15 min on Aug 26, 1975.

Most Conquests of the English Channel

The greatest number of Channel conquests is 24 by Michael Read (GB), to July 19, 1982, including a record 6 in one year. Cindy Nicholas made her first crossing of the Channel on July 29, 1975, and her fifteenth on Aug 24, 1981.

Fastest Channel Crossings

The official Channel Swimming Association record is 7 hours 40 min by Penny Dean (b March 21, 1955) of California, who swam from Shakespeare Beach, Dover, England to Cap Gris Nez, France on July 29, 1978.

The fastest crossing by a relay team is 7 hours 22 min by 6 British swimmers from England to France on Aug 9, 1981.

Double Crossings of the Channel

Antonio Abertondo (Argentina), aged 42, swam from England to France in 18 hours 50 min (8:35 a.m. on Sept 20 to 3:25 a.m. on Sept 21, 1961) and after about 4 minutes' rest returned to England in 24 hours 16 min, landing at St Margaret's Bay at 3:45 a.m. on Sept 22, 1961, to complete the first "double crossing" in 43 hours 10 min.

Cynthia Nicholas, a 19-year-old from Canada, became the first woman to complete a double crossing of the English Channel, Sept 7–8, 1977. Her astonishing time of 19 hours 55 min was more than 10 hours faster than the previous mark. She achieved a still faster time of 19 hours 12 min, Aug 4–5, 1979.

The relay record is 16 hours 5½ min by 6 Saudi Arabian men on Aug 11, 1977.

Triple Crossing of the Channel

The first triple crossing of the English Channel was by Jon Erikson (b Sept 6, 1954) (US) in 38 hours 27 min, Aug 11–12, 1981.

Underwater Channel Swim

The first underwater cross-Channel swim was achieved by Fred Baldasare (US), aged 38, who completed a 42-mile swim from France to England with scuba in 18 hours 1 min, July 10–11, 1962.

CHANNEL ENERGY: Jon Erikson (right), the first swimmer to make a triple crossing of the English Channel, relaxes here with his father, Ted. Both had held records for the fastest double crossing.

Relay Records

The longest recorded mileage in a 24-hour relay swim (team of 5) is 89 miles 1,455.3 yd by a team from Loughborough University, Leicestershire, England, May 13–14, 1980.

The fastest time recorded for 100 miles in a pool by a team of 20 swimmers is 21 hours 41 min 4 sec by the Dropped Sports Swim Club of Indiana State University at Terre Haute, Ind, Mar 12–13, 1982. Four swimmers from the Darien YMCA, Conn, covered 300 miles in relay in 122 hours 59 min 40 sec, Nov 25–30, 1980.

Peter Saville, John Mason, Robert Mortimer and Duncan Moulder, of Stratford upon Avon Sub Aqua Club, swam an underwater relay of 279.099 miles in 168 hours at the Holiday Inn, Birmingham, England, June 30–July 7, 1979.

Treading Water

The duration record for treading water (vertical posture in an 8-ft square without touching the lane markers) is 80 hours by V. S. Kumar Anandan at Anna Swimming Pool, Madras, India, June 28–July 2, 1981.

TABLE TENNIS

Earliest Reference

The earliest evidence relating to a game resembling table tennis has been found in the catalogues of London sporting goods manufacturers in the 1880's. The old Ping-Pong Association was formed there in 1902, but the game proved only a temporary craze until resuscitated in 1921.

World Championships

Instituted in 1927, the world championships were held annually until 1957, when the competitions became biennial (rendering most of the following personal records virtually unbreakable). G. Viktor Barna (1911–72) (Hungary) won 5 men's singles titles (1930, 32–35) and 8 men's doubles titles (1929–35, 39). Including his 2 mixed doubles titles, Barna won a total of 15 personal world championships. The most wins in the women's singles is 6 by Angelica Rozeanu (b Oct 15, 1921) (Rumania), 1950–55. Maria Mednyanszky (1901–79) (Hungary) won 7 women's doubles titles (1928, 1930–35) and 6 mixed doubles titles (1927–28, 1930–31, 1933–34). Including

her 5 wins in women's singles, Mednyanszky won 18 personal titles in the world championships.

The most victories in the men's team championships (Swaythling Cup) is 12 by Hungary from 1927 through 1979. The women's team title (Marcel Corbillon Cup, instituted in 1934) has been won most often by Japan, with 8 victories from 1952 through 1971.

Longest Rally

In a Swaythling Cup match in Prague on March 14, 1936, between Alex Ehrlich (Poland) and Paneth Farcas (Rumania), the opening rally lasted for 1 hour 58 min.

Robert Siegel and Donald Peters of Stamford, Conn, staged a rally lasting 8 hours 33 min on July 30, 1978.

Fastest Rallying

The record number of hits in 60 sec is 162 by Nicky Jarvis and Desmond Douglas in London, England, on Dec 1, 1976. This was equaled by Douglas and Paul Day at Blackpool, England, on March 21, 1977. The most by women is 148 by Linda Howard and Melodi Ludi at Blackpool, Lancashire, England, on Oct 11, 1977.

With a paddle in each hand, Gary D. Fisher of Olympia, Wash, completed 5,000 consecutive volleys over the net in 44 min 28 sec on June 25, 1979.

Longest Match

In the Swaythling Cup final match between Austria and Rumania in Prague, Czechoslovakia, in 1936, the play lasted for 11 hours, beginning Sunday, March 15, and completed the following Wednesday.

Marathon

The longest recorded time for a marathon singles match by two players is 132 hours 31 min by Danny Price and Randy Nunes in Cherry Hill, NJ, Aug 20–26, 1978.

The longest doubles marathon by 4 players is 101 hours 1 min 11 sec by Lance, Phil and Mark Warren and Bill Weir at Sacramento, Calif, Apr 9–13, 1979.

Highest Speed

No conclusive measurements have been published, but in a lecture M. Sklorz (W Germany) stated that a smashed ball had been measured at speeds up to 105.6 mph.

Youngest International

The youngest international (in any sport) was Joy Foster, aged 8, when she represented Jamaica in the West Indies Championships at Port of Spain, Trinidad, in Aug 1958.

TENNIS

Origins

The modern game of lawn tennis is generally agreed to have evolved as an outdoor form of Royal Tennis. "Field Tennis" was mentioned in an English magazine (*Sporting Magazine*) on Sept 29, 1793. The earliest club for such a game, variously called Pelota or Lawn Rackets, was the Leamington Club, founded in 1872 by Major Harry Gem. In Feb 1874, Major Walter Clopton Wingfield of England (1833–1912) patented a form called "sphairistike," but the game soon became known as lawn tennis.

Amateurs were permitted to play with and against professionals in Open tournaments starting in 1968.

Davis Cup

The most wins in the Davis Cup (instituted 1900), the men's international team championship, have been (inclusive of 1981) by the US with 27.

Roy Emerson (b Nov 3, 1936) (Australia) played on 8 Cup-winning teams, 1959–62, 1964–67.

Nicola Pietrangeli (Italy) (b Sept 11, 1933) played a record 164 rubbers, 1954 to 1972, winning 120. He played 110 singles (winning 78) and 54 doubles (winning 42). He took part in 66 ties.

Federation Cup

The most wins in the Federation Cup (instituted 1963), the women's international team championship, is 11 by the US. Virginia Wade (GB) played each year from 1967 to 1982, in a record 54 ties, playing 97 rubbers, including 53 singles (winning 34) and 44 doubles (winning 30). Christine Evert Lloyd (b Dec 21, 1954) (US) won all of her 28 singles matches, 1977–82.

Wightman Cup

The most wins in the Wightman Cup, contested annually by women's teams from the US and GB (instituted 1923) have been 44 by the US through

MANY RETURNS: Durable Virginia Wade has been the mainstay of Britain's teams in international competition, playing in 54 Federation Cup ties since 1967 and every Wightman Cup competition since 1965. (Leon Serchuk)

1981. Virginia Wade (b July 10, 1945) (GB) played in a record 17 ties and 15 rubbers between 1965 and 1981.

Greatest Domination

The "grand slam" is to hold at the same time all four of the world's major championship titles: Wimbledon, the US Open, Australian and French championships. The first time this occurred was in 1935 when Frederick John Perry (GB) (b 1909) won the French title, having won Wimbledon (1934), the US title (1933–34) and the Australian title (1934).

The first player to hold all four titles simultaneously was J. Donald Budge (US) (b June 13, 1915), who won the championships of Wimbledon (1937), the US (1937), Australia (1938), and France (1938). He subsequently retained Wimbledon (1938) and the US (1938). Rodney George Laver (Australia) (b Aug 9, 1938) achieved this grand slam in 1962 as an amateur and repeated as a professional in 1969 to become the first two-time grand slammer.

Two women players also have won all these four titles in the same tennis year. The first was Maureen Catherine Connolly (US). She won the US title in

1951, Wimbledon in 1952, retained the US title in 1952, won the Australian in 1953, the French in 1953, and Wimbledon again in 1953. She won her third US title in 1953, her second French title in 1954, and her third Wimbledon title in 1954. Miss Connolly (later Mrs Norman Brinker) was seriously injured in a riding accident shortly before the 1954 US championships; she died in June 1969, aged only 34.

The second woman to win the "grand slam" was Margaret Smith Court (Australia) (b July 16, 1942) in 1970.

Greatest Crowd

The greatest crowd at a tennis match was the 30,472 who came to the Houston Astrodome in Houston, Tex, on Sept 20, 1973, to watch Billie Jean King beat Bobby Riggs, over 25 years her senior, in straight sets in the so-called "Tennis Match of the Century."

The record for an orthodox match is 25,578 at Sydney, Australia, on Dec 27, 1954, in the Davis Cup Challenge Round vs the US (1st day).

Highest Earnings

The greatest reward for playing a single match is the $500,000 won by Jimmy Connors (US) (b Sept 2, 1952) when he beat John Newcombe (Australia) (b May 23, 1944) in a challenge match at Caesar's Palace Hotel, Las Vegas, Nev, Apr 26, 1975.

The record winnings for a year, not including special restricted events and team tennis salaries, is $1,019,345 in 1979 by Bjorn Borg (b June 6, 1956) (Sweden). The women's record is $865,437 in 1981 by Martina Navratilova (b Prague, Oct 18, 1956).

The highest total prize money is $680,000 for the Dubai Golden Tournament in Nov 1980.

Fastest Service

The fastest service ever *measured* was one of 163.6 mph by William Tatem Tilden (1893–1953) (US) in 1931. The American professional Scott Carnahan, 22, was electronically clocked at 137 mph at Pauley Pavilion in Los Angeles during the third annual "Cannonball Classic" sponsored by *Tennis* magazine, and reported in the fall of 1976.

Tennis Marathons

The longest recorded tennis singles match is one of 105 hours by Ricky Tolston and Jeff Sutton at Bill Faye Park, Kinston, NC, May 7–11, 1979.

HOLDING COURT: Billie Jean King is the Queen of Wimbledon, with a record 20 titles in that famous tournament. A great contributor to the advancement of women's sports, she made news at Wimbledon in 1982 by reaching the semi-finals at age 38. (Leon Serchuk)

The duration record for doubles is 84 hours 7 min by Daryl Murray, Richard Monao, Stephen Duerden and Stephen Foord at the Racquet Centre, Silverwater, NSW, Australia, Jan 7–10, 1980.

Longest Game

The longest known singles game was one of 37 deuces (80 points) between Anthony Fawcett (Rhodesia) and Keith Glass (GB) in the first round of the Surrey championships at Surbiton, Surrey, England, on May 26, 1975. It lasted 31 min.

Longest Career

The championship career of C. Alphonso Smith (b March 18, 1909) of Charlottesville, Va, extended from winning the US National Boy's title at Chicago on Aug 14, 1924, to winning the National 70-and-over title at Santa Barbara, Calif, in Aug 1979. Smith has won 31 US National titles in all.

WIMBLEDON RECORDS

The first Championship was in 1877. Professionals first played in 1968. From 1971 the tie-break system was introduced, which effectually prevents sets proceeding beyond a 17th game, i.e., 9–8.

Most Appearances

Arthur W. Gore (1868–1928) (GB) made 36 appearances between 1888 and 1927, and was in 1909 at 41 years the oldest singles winner ever. In 1964 Jean Borotra (b Aug 13, 1898) of France made his 35th appearance since 1922. In 1977 he appeared in the Veterans' Doubles, aged 78.

Most Wins

Six-time singles champion Billie Jean King (*née* Moffitt) has also won 10 women's doubles and 4 mixed doubles during the period 1961 to 1979, to total a record 20 titles.

The greatest number of singles wins was 8 by Helen N. Moody (*née* Wills) (b Oct 6, 1905) (US), who won in 1927–30, 32–33, 35 and 38.

The greatest number of singles wins by a man since the Challenge Round (wherein the defending champion was given a bye until the final round) was abolished in 1922 is 5 consecutively by Bjorn Borg (Sweden) in 1976–80. The all-time men's record was seven by William C. Renshaw, 1881–6 and 89.

The greatest number of doubles wins by men was 8 by the brothers Doherty (GB)—Reginald Frank (1872–1910) and Hugh Lawrence (1875–1919). They won each year from 1897 to 1905 except for 1902. Hugh Doherty also won 5 singles titles (1902–06) and holds the record for most men's titles with 13.

The most wins in women's doubles was 12 by Elizabeth "Bunny" Ryan (US) (1894–1979). The greatest number of mixed doubles wins was 7 by Elizabeth Ryan, giving her a record total of 19 doubles wins.

The men's mixed doubles record is 4 wins: by Elias Victor Seixas (b Aug 30, 1923) (US) in 1953–56; by Kenneth N. Fletcher (b June 15, 1940) (Australia) in 1963, 65–66 and 68; and by Owen Keir Davidson (Australia) (b Oct 4, 1943) in 1967, 71 and 73–74.

Youngest Champions

The youngest champion ever at Wimbledon was Charlotte (Lottie) Dod (1871–1960), who was 15 years 285 days old when she won in 1887.

The youngest male singles champion was Wilfred Baddeley (b Jan 11, 1872), who won the Wimbledon title in 1891 at the age of 19 years 175 days.

Richard Dennis Ralston (b July 27, 1942) (US) was 17 years 341 days old when he won the men's doubles with Rafael H. Osuna (1938–69), of Mexico, in 1960.

The youngest-ever player at Wimbledon is reputedly Miss Mita Klima (Austria), who was 13 years old in the 1907 singles competition. The youngest player to win a match at Wimbledon is Kathy Rinaldi (b March 24, 1967) (US), who was 14 years 91 days old on June 23, 1981.

Oldest Champions

The oldest champion was Margaret Evelyn du Pont (*née* Osborne) (b Mar 4, 1918) (US) when she won the mixed doubles in 1962 with Neale Fraser (Aus). The oldest singles champion was Arthur Gore (GB) at 41 years 6 months in 1909.

Greatest Attendance

The record crowd for one day at Wimbledon is 38,291 on June 27, 1979. The total attendance record was set at the 1981 Championships with 358,250.

SWEDE SUCCESS: Bjorn Borg made news in the 1982 Wimbledon Championships with his absence. The 5-time singles champion refused to compete after officials would not let him skip the qualifying rounds. (All-Sport)

NET RESULTS: Bill Tilden, whose serve was measured at 163.6 mph, won 16 titles—a men's record—in the US Championships (now US Open), including 7 singles, in the 1920's.

US CHAMPIONSHIPS

Most Wins

Margaret Evelyn du Pont (*née* Osborne) won a record 24 titles between 1941 and 1960. She won a record 13 women's doubles (12 with Althea Louise Brough), 8 mixed doubles and 3 singles. The men's record is 16 by William Tatem Tilden, including 7 men's singles, 1920–25, 1929—a record for singles shared with Richard Dudley Sears (1861–1943), 1881–87; William A Larned (1872–1926), 1901–02, 1907–11, and at women's singles by Molla Mallory (*née* Bjurstedt) (1892–1959), 1915–16, 1918, 1920–22, 1926 and Helen Moody (*née* Wills), 1923–25, 1927–29, 1931.

Youngest and Oldest

The youngest champion was Vincent Richards (1903–59) who was 15 years 139 days when he won the doubles with Bill Tilden in 1918. The youngest singles champion was Tracy Ann Austin (b Dec 12, 1962) who was 16 years 271 days when she won the women's singles in 1979.

The oldest champion was Margaret du Pont who won the mixed doubles at 42 years 166 days in 1960. The oldest singles champion was William Larned at 38 years 242 days in 1911.

TRACK AND FIELD

Earliest References

Track and field athletics date from the ancient Olympic Games. The earliest accurately known Olympiad dates from July 776 BC, at which celebration Coroibos won the foot race. The oldest surviving measurements are a long jump of 23 ft 1½ in by Chionis of Sparta *c.* 656 BC, and a discus throw of 100 cubits (*c.* 152 ft) by Protesilaus.

Oldest Race

The oldest continuously held foot race is the "Red Hose Race" held at Carnwath, Scotland, since 1507. First prize is a pair of hand-knitted knee-length red stockings. Michael Glen, of Bathgate, won a record 14 times, 1951–66.

Earliest Landmarks

The first time 10 sec ("even time") was bettered for 100 yd under championship conditions was when John Owen, then 30 years old, recorded 9 4/5 sec in the AAU Championships at Analostan Island, Wash, DC, on Oct 11, 1890. The first recorded instance of 6 ft being cleared in the high jump was when Marshall Jones Brooks (1855–1944) jumped 6 ft 0⅛ in at Marston, near Oxford, England, on March 17, 1876. The breaking of the "4-minute barrier" in the one mile was first achieved by Dr Roger Gilbert Bannister (b Harrow, England, March 23, 1929), when he recorded 3 min 59.4 sec on the Iffley Road track, Oxford, at 6:10 p.m. on May 6, 1954.

Most Records in a Day

The only athlete to have his name entered in the record book 6 times in one day was J. C. "Jesse" Owens (US) (1913–80) who at Ann Arbor, Mich, on May 25, 1935, equaled the 100-yd running record with 9.4 sec at 3:15 p.m.; long-jumped 26 ft 8¼ in at 3:25 p.m.; ran 220 yd (straight away) in 20.3 sec at 3:45 p.m.; and 220 yd over low hurdles in 22.6 sec at 4 p.m. The two 220-yd runs were also ratified as 200-m world records.

Fastest Runners

Robert Lee Hayes (b Dec 20, 1942), of Jacksonville, Fla, may have reached a speed of about 27 mph at St Louis, on June 21, 1963, in his then world record 9.1 sec for 100 yd. Marlies Göhr (*née* Oelsner) (b E Germany, March 21, 1958) reached a speed of over 24 mph in her world record 100 m in 10.88 sec at Dresden, E Germany, on July 1, 1977.

Oldest and Youngest Record Breakers

The greatest age at which anyone has broken a standard world record is 41 years 196 days in the case of John J. Flanagan (1868–1938), who set a world record in the hammer throw on July 24, 1909. The female record is 35 years 255 days for Dana Zátopkova (*née* Ingrova) (b Sept 19, 1922) of Czechoslovakia, who broke the women's javelin record with 182 ft 10 in at Prague, Czechoslovakia, on June 1, 1958.

The youngest individual record breaker is Carolina Gisolf (b July 13, 1913) (Netherlands) who set a women's high jump mark with 5 ft 3⅜ in at Maastricht, Netherlands, on July 18, 1925, aged 15 years 5 days. The male record is 17 years 198 days by Thomas Ray (1862–1904) when he pole vaulted 11 ft 2¼ in on Sept 19, 1879.

Highest Jumper

The greatest height cleared above an athlete's own head is 23¼ in by Franklin Jacobs (US), who cleared 7 ft 7¼ in despite a physical height of only 5 ft 8 in, at NY on Jan 28, 1978.

The greatest height cleared by a woman above her own head is 12 in by Cindy John Holmes (b Aug 29, 1960) (US), 5 ft tall, who jumped 6 ft at Provo, Utah, on June 1, 1982.

Most Olympic Gold Medals

The most Olympic gold medals won is 10 (an absolute Olympic record) by Ray C. Ewry (US) (b Oct 14, 1873, d Sept 29, 1937) with:

Standing High Jump	1900, 1904, 1906, 1908
Standing Long Jump	1900, 1904, 1906, 1908
Standing Triple Jump	1900, 1904

The most gold medals won by a woman is 4, a record shared by Francina E. Blankers-Koen (Netherlands) (b Apr 26, 1918) with 100 m, 200 m, 80 m hurdles and 4 × 100 m relay (1948); Betty Cuthbert (Australia) (b Apr 20, 1938) with 100 m, 200 m, 4 × 100 m relay (1956) and 400 m (1964); and Barbel Wöckel (*née* Eckert) (b March 21, 1955) (E Germany) with 200 m and 4 × 100 m relay in 1976 and 1980.

Most Olympic Medals

The most medals won is 12 (9 gold and 3 silver) by Paavo Johannes Nurmi (Finland) (1897–1973) with:

1920   Gold: 10,000 m; Cross-Country, Individual and Team; silver: 5,000 m
1924   Gold: 1,500 m; 5,000 m; 3,000 m Team; Cross-Country, Individual and Team.
1928   Gold: 10,000 m; silver: 5,000 m; 3,000 m steeplechase.

The most medals won by a woman athlete is 7 by Shirley de la Hunty (*née* Strickland) (b July 18, 1925) (Australia) with 3 gold, 1 silver and 3 bronze in the 1948, 1952 and 1956 Games. A recently discovered photofinish indicates that she finished third, not fourth, in the 1948 200 m event, thus unofficially increasing her total to 8. Irena Szewinska (*née* Kirszenstein) of Poland has also won 7 medals (3 gold, 2 silver, 2 bronze) in 1964, 1968, 1972 and 1976. She is the only woman ever to win Olympic medals in track and field in 4 successive Games.

OVER HIS HEAD: Franklin Jacobs cleared a bar 23¼ in above his own head. Since Jacobs is short for a high jumper (5 ft 8 in), the height he cleared was not a world record. Still, he served as inspiration for 5-ft-tall Cindy Holmes, who set a women's record by clearing a bar 10 in over her head. (Fairleigh Dickinson Univ)

WORLD TRACK AND FIELD RECORDS

World Records for the 32 men's events (excluding the walking records, see under Walking) scheduled by the International Amateur Athletic Federation as of Aug 19, 1982. Note: On July 27, 1976, IAAF eliminated all records for races measured in yards, except for the mile (for sentimental reasons). All distances up to (and including) 400 m must be electrically timed to be records. When a time is given to one-hundredth of a second, it represents the official electrically-timed record. In one case, a professional performance has bettered or equaled the IAAF mark, but the same highly rigorous rules as to timing, measuring and weighing are not necessarily applied.

MEN

RUNNING

Event	min:sec	Name and Nationality	Place	Date
100 m	9.95	James Ray Hines (US)	Mexico City	Oct 14, 1968
200 m (turn)	19.72	Pietro Mennea (Italy)	Mexico City	Sept 12, 1979
400 m	43.86	Lee Edward Evans (US)	Mexico City	Oct 18, 1968
800 m	1:41.72	Sebastian Coe (GB)	Florence, Italy	June 10, 1981
1,000 m	2:12.18	Sebastian Coe (GB)	Oslo	July 11, 1981
1,500 m	3:31.36	Steven Ovett (GB)	Coblenz, W Ger	Aug 27, 1980
1 mile	3:47.33	Sebastian Coe (GB)	Brussels	Aug 28, 1981
2,000 m	4:51.4	John Walker (NZ)	Oslo	June 30, 1976
3,000 m	7:32.1	Henry Rono (Kenya)	Oslo	June 27, 1978
5,000 m	13:00.42	David Moorcroft (GB & NI)	Oslo	July 7, 1982
10,000 m	27:22.4	Henry Rono (Kenya)	Vienna	June 11, 1978
20,000 m	57:24.2	Jos Hermens (Neth)	Papendal, Neth	May 1, 1976
25,000 m	1 hr. 13:55.8	Toshihiko Seko (Japan)	Christchurch, NZ	Mar 22, 1981
30,000 m	1 hr. 29:18.8	Toshihiko Seko (Japan)	Christchurch, NZ	Mar 22, 1981
1 hour	13 miles 24⅔ yd	Jos Hermens (Neth)	Papendal, Neth	May 1, 1976

FIELD EVENTS

Event	ft	in	Name and Nationality	Place	Date
High Jump	7	8¾	Gerd Wessig (E Ger)	Moscow	Aug 1, 1980
Pole Vault	19	0¾	Vladimir Poliakov (USSR)	Tbilisi, USSR	June 26, 1981
Long Jump	29	2½	Robert Beamon (US)	Mexico City	Oct 18, 1968
Triple Jump	58	8½	Joao de Oliveira (Brazil)	Mexico City	Oct 15, 1975
Shot Put	72	8	Udo Beyer (E Ger)	Gothenburg, Sweden	July 6, 1978
Discus Throw	233	5‡	Wolfgang Schmidt (E Ger)	E Berlin	Aug 9, 1978
Hammer Throw	275	6	Sergey Litvinov (USSR)	Moscow	June 3, 1982
Javelin Throw	317	4	Ferenc Paragi (Hungary)	Tata, Hungary	Apr 23, 1980

‡ Ben Plucknett (US) threw 237 ft 4 in at Stockholm on July 7, 1981 but was subsequently disqualified from competition.

Note: One professional performance which was equal or superior to the IAAF marks, but where the same highly rigorous rules as to timing, measuring and weighing were not necessarily applied, was the Shot Put of 75 ft by Brian Ray Oldfield (US), at El Paso, Tex, on May 10, 1975.

FOR THE RECORD: A moment of reflection helped Ferenc Paragi (left) hurl the javelin a record 317 ft 4 in. Ed Moses (above, #943 in the lead) earned an Olympic gold with the first of his three 400 m hurdles world records. Moses amassed an unbeaten string of over 70 races with his ability to maintain 13 strides between hurdles while his competitors would tire and increase their number of steps. (Paragi photo from John Topham Picture Library; Moses photo by Tony Duffy, All-Sport)

STARTING BLOCKS: Renaldo "Skeets" Nehemiah set 11 world indoor sprint hurdles records, 1978–82, and was the first to break 13 sec for the 110 m high hurdles, with a hand-timed 12.8 in 1979. Here he sets the current official world record of 12.93 at Zurich in 1981. In 1982 his new "starting blocks" will be from defensive backs because he joined the NFL's SF 49ers. (Steve Powell, All-Sport)

HURDLING

Event	min:sec	Team	Place	Date
110 m (3'6")	12.93	Renaldo Nehemiah (US)	Zurich	Aug 19, 1981
400 m (3'0")	47.13	Edwin Corley Moses (US)	Milan	July 3, 1980
3,000 m Steeplechase	8:05.4	Henry Rono (Kenya)	Seattle, Wash	May 13, 1978

RELAYS

4 × 100 m	38.03	US Team (William Collins, Steven Earl Riddick, Clifford Wiley, Steven Williams)	Düsseldorf, W Ger	Sept 3, 1977
4 × 200 m	1:20.26†	University of Southern California (US) (Joel Andrews, James Sanford, William Mullins, Clancy Edwards)	Tempe, Ariz	May 27, 1978
4 × 400 m	2:56.16	US Olympic Team (Vincent Matthews, Ronald Freeman, G. Lawrence James, Lee Edward Evans)	Mexico City	Oct 20, 1968
4 × 800 m	7:08.1	USSR Team (Vladimir Podoliakov, Nikolai Kirov, Vladimir Malosemlin, Anatoli Reschetniak)	Podolsk, USSR	Aug 12, 1978
4 × 1,500 m	14:38.8	W German Team (Thomas Wessinghage, Harald Hudak, Michael Lederer, Karl Fleschen)	Cologne, W Ger	Aug 17, 1977

† The time of 1:20.2 achieved by the Tobias Striders at Tempe, Ariz on May 27, 1978 was not ratified as the team was composed of varied nationalities.

DECATHLON

8,723 points	Juergen Hingsen (W Ger)	Ulm, W Ger	Aug 14–15, 1982

(First day: 100 m 10.74 sec, long jump 25 ft 9 in, shot put 52 ft 6 in, high jump 7 ft 0¾ in, 400 m 47.65 sec; second day: 110 m hurdles 14.64 sec, discus 147 ft 4½ in, pole vault 15 ft 1½ in, javelin 207 ft 0¼ in, 1,500 m 4 min 15.14 sec.)

ON THE RIGHT TRACK: Mary Decker Tabb (left), here breaking her own 880-yd indoor record in 1980, has again bounced back from injuries (her career has been plagued by them since her track debut as a young teenager) to set 3 world records in 1982. Tatyana Kazankina (#340) crosses the finish line for a world record and gold medal at 800 m in the 1976 Olympics. Though this record was surpassed, Kazankina later set a world record at 1,500 m in 1980—after winning the gold medal for that event in Moscow. (Decker Tabb photo by UPI; Kazankina photo by Tony Duffy, All-Sport)

WORLD TRACK AND FIELD RECORDS (Continued)

WOMEN

RUNNING

Event	min:sec	Name and Nationality	Place	Date
100 m	10.88	Marlies Oelsner (now Göhr) (E Ger)	Dresden	July 1, 1977
	10.88	Marlies Göhr (E Ger)	Karl Marx Stadt, E Ger	July 9, 1982
200 m (turn)	21.71	Marita Koch (E Ger)	Karl Marx Stadt, E Ger	June 10, 1979
400 m	48.60	Marita Koch (E Ger)	Turin, Italy	Aug 4, 1979
800 m	1:53.43	Nadyezda Olizarenko (née Mushta) (USSR)	Moscow	July 27, 1980
1,500 m	3:52.47	Tatyana Kazankina (USSR)	Zurich, Switz	Aug 13, 1980
1 mile	4:18.08††	Mary Decker Tabb (US)	Paris	July 9, 1982
3,000 m	8:26.78	Svyetlana Ulmosova (USSR)	Moscow	July 25, 1982
5,000 m	15:08.26	Mary Decker Tabb (US)	Eugene, Ore	June 5, 1982
10,000 m	31:35.3	Mary Decker Tabb (US)	Eugene, Ore	July 18, 1982

HURDLES

100 m (2'9")	12.36	Grazyna Rabsztyn (Poland)	Warsaw	June 13, 1980
400 m (2'6")	54.28	Karin Rossley (E Ger)	Jena, E Ger	May 17, 1980

FIELD EVENTS

Event	ft	in	Name and Nationality	Place	Date
High Jump	6	7	Sara Simeoni (Italy)	Brescia, Italy	Aug 4, 1978
Long Jump	23	7½	Valeria Ionescu (Rumania)	Bucharest	July 31, 1982
Shot Put	73	8†	Ilona Slupianek (née Schoknecht) (E Ger)	Potsdam	May 11, 1980
Discus Throw	235	7	Marica Petkova (née Vergova) (Bulgaria)	Sofia	July 13, 1980
Javelin Throw	237	6	Tiina Lillak (Finland)	Helsinki	July 29, 1982

† Helena Fibingerova (Czech) set an indoor record of 73 ft 10 in at Jablonec, Czechoslovakia, on Feb 19, 1977.
†† Decker ran an indoor mile in 4:17.55 in Houston, Feb 16, 1980. No official record was set as the track was "oversize."

HEPTATHLON

6,772 points   Ramona Neubert (E Ger)   Halle, E Ger   June 19–20, 1982
(100 m hurdles 13.59 sec, shot put 49 ft 6½ in, high jump 6 ft 0 in, 200 m 23.14 sec, long jump 22 ft 5¼ in, javelin 139 ft 7 in, 800 m 2 min 06.20 sec.)

BAR BELLE: Italy's Sara Simeoni cleared 6 ft 5½ in in the Olympic high jump in Moscow in 1980. It wasn't good enough to break her own world record set 2 years earlier, but it was good enough for a gold medal and an Olympic record.

RELAYS

Event	min:sec	Team	Place	Date
4 × 100 m	41.60	E Germany (Romy Müller, Barbel Wöckel, Marlies Göhr, Ingrid Auerswold)	Moscow	Aug 1, 1980
4 × 200 m	1:28.15	E Germany (Marlies Göhr, Romy Müller, Barbel Wöckel, Marita Koch)	Jena, E Ger	Aug 10, 1980
4 × 400 m	3:19.23	E Germany (Doris Maletzski, Brigitte Rohde, Ellen Streidt, Christina Brehmer)	Montreal	July 31, 1976
4 × 800 m	7:52.3	USSR (Tatyana Providokhina, Valentina Gerasimova, Svetlana Styrkina, Tatyana Kazankina)	Podolsk, USSR	Aug 16, 1976

IN ANY EVENT: Ramona Neubert (left) has added 560 points to the heptathlon record by breaking it 3 times. Two great sprinters: Irena Szewinska (above left) earned 7 Olympic medals over 4 Games; Marita Koch (above right) holds 3 world records, including one as part of a 4 x 200 relay team. (Photos by Tony Duffy, All-Sport)

Most Wins at One Games

The most gold medals at one Olympic celebration is 5 by Nurmi in 1924 (see above) and the most individual is 4 by Alvin C. Kraenzlein (US) (1876–1928) in 1900 with 60 m, 110 m hurdles, 200 m hurdles and long jump.

Oldest and Youngest Olympic Champions

The oldest athlete to win an Olympic title was Irish-born Patrick J. "Babe" McDonald (US) (1878–1954) who was aged 42 years 26 days when he won the 56-lb weight throw at Antwerp, Belgium, on Aug 21, 1920. The oldest female champion was Lia Manoliu (Rumania) (b Apr 25, 1932) aged 36 years 176 days when she won the discus at Mexico City on Oct 18, 1968.

The youngest gold medalist was Barbara Jones (US) (b March 26, 1937) who was a member of the winning 4 × 100 m relay team, aged 15 years 123 days, at Helsinki, Finland, on July 27, 1952. The youngest male champion was Robert Bruce Mathias (US) (b Nov 17, 1930) aged 17 years 263 days when he won the decathlon at London, Aug 5–6, 1948.

The oldest Olympic medalist was Tebbs Lloyd Johnson (b Apr 7, 1900), aged 48 years 115 days when he was third in the 1948 50,000 m walk. The oldest woman medalist was Dana Zatopkova aged 37 years 248 days when she was second in the javelin in 1960.

Standing High Jump

The best high jump is 6 ft 2¾ in by Rune Almen (b Oct 20, 1952) (Sweden) at Karlstad, Sweden, on May 30, 1980. The best high jump by a woman is 4 ft 11 in by Grete Bjørdalsbakke (b June 23, 1960) (Norway) at Orsta, Norway on Dec 12, 1979.

One-Legged High Jump

Arnie Boldt (b 1958), of Saskatchewan, Canada, cleared a height of 6 ft 8¼ in in Rome, Italy, on Apr 3, 1981, in spite of the fact that he has only one leg.

Standing Long Jump

Joe Darby (1861–1937), the famous Victorian professional jumper from Dudley, Worcestershire, England, jumped a measured 12 ft 1½ in *without* weights at Dudley Castle, on May 28, 1890. Johan Christian Evandt (Norway) achieved 11 ft 11¾ in as an amateur in Reykjavik, Iceland, on March 11,

1962. The best long jump by a woman is 9 ft 7 in by Annelin Mannes (Norway) at Flisa, Norway on March 7, 1981.

Running Backwards

The fastest time recorded for running 100 yd backwards is 13.1 sec by Paul Wilson (NZ) in Tokyo, Sept 22, 1979. He ran 100 m in 14.4 sec.

Three-Legged Race

The fastest recorded time for a 100-yd three-legged race is 11.0 sec by Olympic medalists Harry L. Hillman (1881–1945) and Lawson Robertson (1883–1951) in Brooklyn, NYC, on Apr 24, 1909.

Ambidextrous Shot Put

Allan Feuerbach (US) has put a 16-lb shot a total of 121 ft 6¾ in (51 ft 5 in with his left hand and 70 ft 1¾ in with his right) at Malmö, Sweden, on Aug 24, 1974.

Blind 100 Meters

The fastest time recorded for 100 m by a blind man is 11.4 sec by Graham Henry Salmon (b Sept 5, 1952) of Loughton, Essex, England, at Grangemouth, Scotland, on Sept 2, 1978.

Longest Career

Duncan McLean (1884–1980) of Scotland set a world age—92—record of 100 m in 21.7 sec in Aug 1977, over 73 years after his best ever sprint of 100 yd in 9.9 sec in South Africa in Feb 1904.

Dimitrion Yordanidis completed a marathon race in 7 hours 33 min at the age of 98 in Athens, Greece, on Oct 10, 1976.

Endurance

Ernst Mensen (1799–1846) (Norway), a former seaman in the British Navy, is reputed to have run from Istanbul, Turkey, to Calcutta, in West Bengal, India, and back in 59 days in 1836, so averaging an improbable 92.4 miles per day.

Max Telford (b Hawick, Scotland, Feb 2, 1935) of New Zealand ran 5,110 miles from Anchorage, Alaska, to Halifax, Nova Scotia, in 106 days 18 hours 45 min from July 25 to Nov 9, 1977.

The greatest non-stop run recorded is 352.9 miles in 121 hours 54 min by Bertil Järlåker (Sweden) at

Longest Race

The longest races ever staged were the 1928 (3,422 miles) and 1929 (3,665 miles) transcontinental races from NYC to Los Angeles. The Finnish-born Johnny Salo (1893–1931) was the winner in 1929 in 79 days, from March 31 to June 18. His elapsed time of 525 hours 57 min 20 sec gave a running average of 6.97 mph. His margin of victory was only 2 min 47 sec.

24-Hour Record

The greatest distance run on a standard track in 24 hours is 170 miles 974 yd by Dave Dowdle (b Nov 7, 1954) (Gloucester AC) at Blackbridge, Gloucester, England, May 22–23, 1982. The best by a woman is 133 miles 939 yd by Lynn Fitzgerald (b Sept 9, 1947) (Highgate Harriers) in the same race.

Fastest 100 Miles

The fastest recorded time for 100 miles is 11 hours 30 min 51 sec by Donald Ritchie (b July 6, 1944) at Crystal Palace, London, on Oct 15, 1977. The best by a woman is 15 hours 44 min 27 sec by Marcy Schwam (US) at Greenwich, Conn, Nov 1–2, 1980.

Fastest 100 Kilometers

Donald Ritchie ran 100 km in a record 6 hours 10 min 20 sec at Crystal Palace, London, on Oct 28, 1978. The women's best, run on the road, is 7 hours 27 min 22 sec by Chantal Langlace (b Jan 6, 1955) (France) at Amiens, France on Sept 6, 1980.

Six-Day Race

The greatest distance covered by a man in six days (*i.e.* the 144 permissible hours between Sundays in Victorian times) was 623¾ miles by George Littlewood (England), who required only 141 hours 57½ min for this feat on Dec 3–8, 1888, at the old Madison Square Garden, NYC.

Pancake Race Record

The annual "Housewives" Pancake Race at Olney, Buckinghamshire, England, was first mentioned in 1445. The record for the winding 415-yd course (three tosses mandatory) is 61.0 sec, set by Sally Ann Faulkner, 16, on Feb 26, 1974. The record for the counterpart race at Liberal, Kansas, is 58.5 sec by Sheila Turner (b July 9, 1953) in 1975.

MARATHON MAN: Alberto Salazar crashes the tape at the finish line of the 1981 NYC Marathon as the official clock overhead reveals the world record time. Salazar timed 20.6 sec off the 12-year-old mark. In the same race, Allison Roe became the new women's record holder as an injury forced 3-time champion Grete Waitz to drop out of the race. (UPI)

Norrköping, Sweden, May 26–31, 1980. He was moving 95.04% of the time.

Terry Fox (1958–81), a Canadian with an artificial leg, ran 3,339 miles from St John's, Newfoundland to Thunder Bay, Ontario, in 143 days, Apr 12–Sept 2, 1980, raising nearly $10 million for cancer research.

The Marathon

There is no official marathon record because of the varying severity of courses. The best time over 26 miles 385 yd is 2 hours 8 min 13.0 sec (average 12.26 mph) by Alberto Salazar (b Cuba, Aug 7, 1958) (US) in the NYC Marathon on Oct 25, 1981. The fastest time by a woman is 2 hours 25 min 28.74 sec (average 10.81 mph) by Allison Roe (b May 30, 1956) (NZ) in the NYC Marathon on Oct 25, 1981.

NO TURN LEFT UNSTONED: Italian-born Tina Stone loves to run. Now living in California, she logged a total of 14,005.5 miles in 1981.

10 hours 47 min 9.3 sec by a team from the San Francisco Dolphins Southend Running Club, on Apr 3, 1977.

The best time for a 100 × 400 m relay is 1 hour 29 min 11.8 sec (average 53.5 sec) by the Physical Training Institute, Leuven, Belgium, on Apr 19, 1978. The best women's club time for 100 × 100 meters relay is 23 min 28 sec by Amsterdanse dames athletievereniging, on Sept 26, 1981, in Amsterdam, Netherlands.

Twelve runners from the Rochester Institute of Technology, NY, ran 2,846.5 miles in relay from Will Rogers State Beach Park, Santa Monica, Calif to Chesapeake Bay, at Annapolis, Md, in 14 days 4 hours 8 min from Nov 22 to Dec 6, 1979. Thirteen runners from the Melbourne Fire Brigade, Australia, ran 3,908 miles in relay from Darwin to Melbourne in 18 days 20 hours 25 min, May 25–June 13, 1979.

The longest relay ever run was of 7,100 miles (5,504 laps of 1.29 miles) by about 200 students from the Liverpool University Derby Hall of Residence, Jan 16–Feb 22, 1980. The most participants is 4,550 (182 teams of 25) in the Batavierenrace, 99.85 miles from Nijmegan to Enschede, Netherlands, won by the University of Wales in 9 hours 24 min 44 sec on Apr 24, 1982.

Trans-America

The fastest time for the cross-America run is 46 days, 8 hours 36 min by Frank Giannino Jr (b 1952) (US) for the 3,100 miles from San Francisco to NYC, Sept 1–Oct 17, 1980.

Greatest Mileage

Jay F. Helgerson (b Feb 3, 1955) of Foster City, Calif, ran a certified marathon (26 miles 385 yd) or longer, each week for 52 weeks from Jan 28, 1979 to Jan 19, 1980, totalling 1,418 racing miles.

The greatest distance run in one year is 14,005.5 miles by Tina Maria Stone (b Naples, Italy, Apr 5, 1934) of Irvine, Calif, in 1981.

Douglas Alistair Gordon Pirie (b Feb 10, 1931) (GB), who set 5 world records in the 1950s, estimated that he had run a total distance of 216,000 miles in 40 years to 1981.

Mass Relay Record

The record for 100 miles by 100 runners belonging to one club is 7 hours 56 min 55.6 sec by Shore AC of New Jersey, on June 5, 1977. The women's mark is

TRAMPOLINING

Origin

The sport of trampolining (from the Spanish word *trampolin,* a springboard) dates from 1936, when the prototype "T" model trampoline was developed by George Nissen (US). Trampolines were used in show business at least as early as "The Walloons" of the period, 1910–12.

Marathon Record

The longest recorded trampoline bouncing marathon is one of 1,248 hours (52 days) set by a team of 6 in Phoenix, Ariz, from June 24 to Aug 15, 1974. The solo record is 166 hours 9 min by Jeff Schwartz, 19, at Glenview, Ill, Aug 14–25, 1981.

Most Titles

Four men have won a world title (instituted 1964) twice: Dave Jacobs (US) in 1967–68, Wayne Miller (US) in 1966 and 70, Richard Tison (France) in 1974 and 76, and Evgeni Janes (USSR), 1976 (shared) and 1978. Judy Wills won the first 5 women's titles (1964–68).

VOLLEYBALL

Origin

The game was invented as Minnonette in 1895 by William G. Morgan at the YMCA gymnasium at Holyoke, Mass. The International Volleyball Association was formed in Paris in Apr 1947. The ball travels at a speed of up to 70 mph when smashed over the net, which stands 7 ft 11½ in high. In the women's game it is 7 ft 4¼ in high.

World Titles

World Championships were instituted in 1949. The USSR has won 5 men's titles (1949, 52, 60, 62 and 78). The USSR won the women's championship in 1952, 56, 60 and 70. The record crowd is 60,000 for the 1952 world title matches in Moscow, USSR.

Most Olympic Medals

The sport was introduced to the Olympic Games for both men and women in 1964. The only volleyball player to win four medals is Inna Ryskal (USSR) (b June 15, 1944), who won a silver medal in 1964 and 76 and golds in 1968 and 72.

The record for medals for men is held by Yuriy Poyarkov (USSR), who won gold medals in 1964 and 68, and a bronze in 1972.

Marathon

The longest recorded volleyball marathon by two teams of six is 75 hours 30 min by 12 players from Kinston, NC, Jan 31–Feb 3, 1980.

WALKING

Longest Race

The Paris-Colmar event (until 1980 it was the Strasbourg-Paris event, instituted in 1926 in the reverse direction), now 319 miles, is the world's longest annual walk event. Gilbert Roger (France) has won 6 times (1949, 53–54, 56–58). The fastest performance is by Roger Pietquin (b 1938) (Belgium) who walked 315 miles in the 1980 race in 60 hours 1 min 10 sec (deducting 4 hours of compulsory stops), averaging 5.25 mph.

Dimitru Dan (1890–1978) of Rumania was the only man of 200 entrants to succeed in walking 100,-000 km (62,137 miles), in a contest organized by the Touring Club de France on Apr 1, 1910. By March 24, 1916, he had covered 96,000 km (59,651 miles), averaging 27.24 miles per day.

Longest in 24 Hours

The best official performance on a track is 133 miles 21 yd by Huw Neilson (GB) at Walton-on-Thames, Surrey, England, Oct 14–15, 1960. The best by a woman is 122.5 miles by Annie van den Meer (Netherlands) at Rouen, France, May 2–3, 1981, over a 1.185-km-lap road course.

Most Olympic Medals

Walking races have been included in the Olympic schedule since 1906, but walking matches have been known since 1589. The only walker to win 3 gold medals has been Ugo Frigerio (Italy) (1901–68) with the 3,000 m and 10,000 m in 1920 and the 10,000 m in 1924. He also holds the record of most medals with 4 (having additionally won the bronze medal in the 50,000 m in 1932), which total is shared with Vladimir Golubnitschiy (USSR) (b June 2, 1936), who won gold medals for the 10,000 m in 1960 and 1968, the silver in 1972 and the bronze in 1964.

Walking Backwards

The greatest exponent of reverse pedestrianism has been Plennie L. Wingo (b Jan 24, 1895) then of Abilene, Tex, who started on his 8,000-mile transcontinental walk on Apr 15, 1931, from Santa Monica, Calif, to Istanbul, Turkey, and arrived on Oct 24, 1932. He celebrated the walk's 45th anniversary by covering the 452 miles from Santa Monica to San Francisco, Calif, backwards, in 85 days, aged 81 years.

The longest distance recorded for walking backwards in 24 hours is 80.5 miles by Veikko Matias (b Apr 23, 1941) of Kangasala, Finland, at Kankaapää Airfield, Niinisalo, Finland, Oct 7–8, 1978.

"Non-Stop" Walking

Tom Benson, 49, walked 357.78 miles in 6 days 3 hours 1 min at Preston, England, May 29–June 4,

TRACK WALKING—WORLD RECORDS

The International Amateur Athletic Federation recognizes men's records at 20km, 30km, 50km and 2 hours. This table also includes world bests for other standard distances.

MEN

Event	Time hr	min	sec	Name and Country	Place	Date
3 km		10	54.61	Carlo Mattioli (Italy)	Milan, Italy	Feb 6, 1980
10 km		38	31.41	Werner Heyer (E Ger)	E Berlin (indoors)	Jan 12, 1980
20 km	1	20	06.8	Daniel Bautista (Mexico)	Montreal	Oct 17, 1979
30 km	2	06	54.0	Ralf Kowalsky (E Ger)	E Berlin, E Ger	Mar 28, 1982
50 km	3	41	39.0	Raul Gonzalez (Mexico)	Fana, Norway	May 25, 1979
1 hr		15121	meters	Daniel Bautista (Mexico)	Monterrey, Mexico	Mar 26, 1980
2 hr		28358	meters	Ralf Kowalsky (E Ger)	E Berlin, E Ger	Mar 28, 1982

WOMEN

Event	Time hr	min	sec	Name and Country	Place	Date
3 km		13	02.17	Sally Pierson (Australia)	Melbourne, Australia	Feb 21, 1982
5 km		22	14.0	Aleksandra Derevinskaya (USSR)	Orel, USSR	July 11, 1982
10 km		46	42.6	Susan Cook (Australia)	Adelaide, Australia	May 23, 1982

1982. He was not permitted any stops for rest and was moving 98.16% of the time.

Most Titles

Four-time Olympian Ronald Owen Laird (b May 31, 1938) of the NYAC, won a total of 65 US National titles from 1958 to 1976, plus 4 Canadian championships.

Walking Around the World

The first person reported to have "walked around the world" is George M. Schilling (US), Aug 3, 1897–1904, but the first verified achievement was by David Kunst (b 1939), who started with his brother John from Waseca, Minn, on June 10, 1970. John was killed by Afghani bandits in 1972. David arrived home, after walking 14,500 miles, on Oct 5, 1974.

Tomas Carlos Pereira (b Argentina, Nov 16, 1942) spent 10 years, Apr 6, 1968, through Apr 8, 1978, walking 29,825 miles around all 5 continents.

Walking Across North America

John Lees, 27, of Brighton, England, Apr 11–June 3, 1972, walked 2,876 miles across the US from City Hall, Los Angeles, to City Hall, NYC, in 53 days 12 hours 15 min (53.746 miles per day).

Sean Eugene Maguire (b Sept 15, 1956) (US) walked 7,327 miles from the Yukon River, north of Livengood, Alaska, to Key West, Fla, in 307 days, from June 6, 1978 to Apr 9, 1979.

The record for the trans-Canada (Halifax to Vancouver) walk of 3,764 miles is 96 days by Clyde McRae, 23, from May 1 to Aug 4, 1973.

WATER POLO

Origins

Water polo was developed in England as "Water Soccer" in 1869 and was first included in the Olympic Games in Paris in 1900.

ROAD WALKING—WORLD BEST PERFORMANCES

It should be noted that severity of road race courses and the accuracy of their measurement may vary, sometimes making comparisons of times unreliable.

MEN

Event	hr	min	sec	Name and Country	Place	Date
20 km	1	18	49	Daniel Bautista (Mexico)	Eschborn, W Ger	Sept 29, 1979
30 km	2	03	06	Daniel Bautista (Mexico)	Cherkassy, USSR	Apr 27, 1980
50 km	3	37	36*	Yevgeniy Ivchenko (USSR)	Moscow	May 23, 1980
	3	37	36*	Boris Yakovlyev (USSR)	Moscow	May 23, 1980
	3	41	19	Raul Gonzalez (Mexico)	Prague-Podebrady, Czech	June 11, 1978

WOMEN

Event	hr	min	sec	Name and Country	Place	Date
10 km		46	48	Susan Cook (Australia)	Moss, Australia	Feb 11, 1980
20 km	1	39	31	Susan Cook (Australia)	Melbourne, Australia	Dec 20, 1981
50 km	5	09	41	Lillian Millen (GB)	Sleaford, GB	July 18, 1981

* questionable distance

Olympic Victories

Hungary has won the Olympic tournament most often with 6 wins, in 1932, 36, 52, 56, 64 and 76. Five players share the record of 3 gold medals: George Wilkinson (1879–1946) in 1900, 08 and 12; Paulo (Paul) Radmilovic (1886–1968) and Charles Sidney Smith (1879–1951) in 1908, 12 and 20—all GB; and the Hungarians Deszö Gyarmati (b Oct 23, 1927) and György Kárpáti (b June 23, 1935) in 1952, 56 and 64.

Radmilovic also won a gold medal for the 4 × 200 m freestyle relay in 1908.

Marathon

Two teams of seven from the Manly-Warringah Amateur Water Polo Club played for 24 hours 10 min at the Aquatic Centre, French's Forest, NSW, Australia, Oct 3–4, 1980.

PRETTY TRICKY: Ana Maria Carrasco of Venezuela set the women's record for tricks with 6,970 points at Berkeley, Calif. (Steve Powell, All-Sport)

WATER SKIING

Origins

The origins of water skiing lie in plank gliding or aquaplaning. A 19th century treatise on sorcerers refers to Eliseo of Tarentum who, in the 14th century, "walks and dances" on the water. The first report of aquaplaning was from the Pacific coast of the US in the early 1900's. A photograph exists of a "plank-riding" contest in a regatta won by a Mr H. Storry at Scarborough, Yorkshire, England, on July 15, 1914. Competitors were towed on a *single* plank by a motor launch.

The present-day sport of water skiing was pioneered by Ralph W. Samuelson on Lake Pepin, Minn, on two curved pine boards in the summer of 1922, though claims have been made for the birth of the sport on Lake Annecy (Haute Savoie), France, in 1920. The first World Water Ski Organization was formed in Geneva, Switzerland, on July 27, 1946.

Slalom

The world record for slalom is 3 buoys on a 35-ft-3-in line at 36 mph by Bob LaPoint (US) at McCormick Lake, Seffner, Fla on Sept 21, 1980.

The women's record is 1½ buoys on a 37-ft line by Sue Fieldhouse (Australia) at Thorpe, England, on Sept 5, 1981.

Tricks

The tricks record is 9,250 points by Cory Pickos (b 1964) (US) at Kroonstad, S Africa, on Mar 27, 1982, and at Seffner, Fla, on Apr 24, 1982. The women's record is 6,970 points by Ana Maria Carrasco (Venezuela) at Berkeley, Calif, on July 25, 1981.

Longest Run

The greatest distance traveled is 1,190 miles by Helge Johansen (22) and Trond Georg Larsen (23) of Narvik, Norway, in the harbor, Aug 14–16, 1980.

Most Titles

World overall championships (instituted 1949) have been twice won by Alfredo Mendoza (US) in 1953 and 55, Mike Suyderhoud (US) in 1967 and 69, and George Athans (Canada) in 1971 and 73, and three times by Mrs Willa McGuire (*née* Worthington) of the US, in 1949–50 and 55, and Elizabeth

Allan-Shetter (US) in 1965, 69, and 75. Allan-Shetter has also won a record 8 individual championship events. The US has won the team championship on 13 successive occasions, 1957–81.

Jumps

The first recorded jump on water skis was by Ralph W. Samuelson, off a greased ramp at Lake Pepin in 1925. The longest jump recorded is one of 196 ft 10 in by Michael Hazelwood (GB) at Kirtons Farm, Reading, England, on Aug 2, 1981. The women's record is 148 ft 6 in by Kathy Hulmes (GB) at Kirtons Farm on Aug 1, 1982.

Barefoot

The first person to waterski barefoot is reported to be Dick Pope, Jr, at Lake Eloise, Fla, on March 6, 1947. The barefoot duration record is 2 hours 42 min 39 sec by Billy Nichols (US) (b 1964) on Lake Weir, Fla, on Nov 19, 1978. The backwards barefoot record is 39 min by Paul McManus (Australia). The best officially recorded barefoot jump is 56 ft 5 in by Peter Lindenberg (So Africa) in Natal, on Apr 27, 1980. The official barefoot speed record (two runs) is 110.02 mph by Lee Kirk (US) at Firebird Lake, Phoenix, Ariz, on June 11, 1977. His fastest run was 113.67 mph. The fastest by a woman is 68.18 mph by Lorraine Dee Nelson (b Jan 23, 1959) (US) at Long Beach, Calif, on Aug 24, 1980.

Highest Speed

The fastest water skiing speed recorded is 136.36 mph by Grant Michael Torrens (b 1957) (Australia) on the Hawkesbury River, Windsor, NSW, Australia, on Mar 7, 1982. His drag boat driver was Wayne John Jones. Donna Patterson Brice (b 1953) set a feminine record of 111.11 mph at Long Beach, Calif, on Aug 21, 1977.

WEIGHT LIFTING

Origins

Amateur weight lifting is of comparatively modern origin, and the first "world" championship was staged at the Café Monico, Piccadilly, London, on March 28, 1891. Prior to that time, weight lifting consisted of professional exhibitions in which some of the advertised poundages were open to doubt. The first to raise 400 lb was Karl Swoboda (1882–1933) (Austria) in Vienna, with 401¼ lb in 1910, using the continental clean and jerk style.

Greatest Lift

The greatest weight ever raised by a human being is 6,270 lb in a back lift (weight raised off trestles) by the 364-lb Paul Anderson (US) (b Oct 17, 1932), the

522

1956 Olympic heavyweight champion, at Toccoa, Ga, on June 12, 1957. The greatest by a woman is 3,564 lb with a hip and harness lift by Mrs Josephine Blatt (*née* Schauer) (US) (1869–1923) at the Bijou Theatre, Hoboken, NJ, on Apr 15, 1895.

The greatest overhead lifts made from the ground are the clean and jerks achieved by super-heavyweights.

The greatest overhead lift ever made by a woman is 286 lb in a continental jerk by Katie Sandwina, *née* Brummbach (Germany) (b Jan 21, 1884, d as Mrs Max Heymann in NYC, in 1952) *c.* 1911. She stood 5 ft 11 in tall, weighed 210 lb, and is reputed to have unofficially lifted 312½ lb and to have once shouldered a 1,200-lb cannon taken from the tailboard of a Barnum & Bailey circus wagon.

Power Lifts

Paul Anderson as a professional has bench-pressed 627 lb, achieved 1,200 lb in a squat, and deadlifted 820 lb, making a career aggregate of 2,647 lb.

Precious McKenzie (b June 6, 1936) was the first man to total 11 times his body weight (121 lb) with 1,339 lb at Honolulu, Hawaii on May 5, 1979. Lamar Grant (US) deadlifted five times his body weight (123¼ lb) with 617 lb at Dayton, Ohio on Nov 2, 1979. Mike Bridges (US) is the first to hold the total records in three classes simultaneously, on Nov 8, 1980.

The newly instituted two-man dead lift record was raised to 1,448 lb by Clay and Doug Patterson in Arlington, Tex, on Dec 15, 1979.

Hermann Görner (Germany) performed a one-handed dead lift of 734½ lb in Dresden on July 20, 1920. He once raised 24 men weighing 4,123 lb on a plank with the soles of his feet, in London on Oct 12, 1927, and also carried on his back a 1,444-lb piano for a distance of 52½ ft on June 3, 1921.

Peter B. Cortese (US) achieved a one-arm dead lift of 370 lb—22 lb over triple his body weight—at York, Pa, on Sept 4, 1954.

The greatest power lift by a woman is a squat of 545½ lb by Jan Suffolk Todd (b May 22, 1952) (US)

GETS A RAISE: Powerful Paul Anderson once raised 6,270 lb in a back lift from trestles. A gold medalist in the 1956 Olympics, he later turned professional, switching from weight lifting to powerlifting, where he once succeeded with a squat lift of 1,200 lb.

OFFICIAL WORLD WEIGHT LIFTING RECORDS
(As of Aug 14, 1982)

Bodyweight Class and Lift	kg	lb	Name and Country	Place	Date
Flyweight					
(52 kg—114½ lb)					
Snatch	114	251¼	Bronislaw Ryzhik (USSR)	USSR	May 18, 1982
Jerk	142	313	Aleksandr Senyshin (USSR)	USSR	May 18, 1982
Total	252.5	556½	Lubomir Khadjiev (Bulgaria)	Hungary	June 1, 1982
Bantamweight					
(56 kg—123¼ lb)					
Snatch	126.5	278¾	Wu Shu-teh (China)	Japan	Aug 16, 1981
Jerk	158	348¼	Oksen Mirzoyan (USSR)	USSR	Oct 28, 1981
Total	277.5	611¾	Andreas Letz (E Ger)	E Germany	Apr 10, 1981
Featherweight					
(60 kg—132¼ lb)					
Snatch	136	299½	Daniel Nunez (Cuba)	Cuba	Aug 13, 1982
Jerk	170.5	374¾	Redzheb Redzheboy (Bulgaria)	USSR	Mar 5, 1982
Total	302.5	666¾	Beloslav Manolov (Bulgaria)	France	Sept 14, 1981
	302.5	666¾	Daniel Nunez (Cuba)	France	Sept 14, 1981
Welterweight					
(67.5 kg—148¾ lb)					
Snatch	152.5	336	Joachim Kunz (E Ger)	E Germany	Apr 2, 1982
Jerk	196	432	Joachim Kunz (E Ger)	E Germany	June 2, 1981
Total	345	760½	Joachim Kunz (E Ger)	E Germany	June 2, 1981
Middleweight					
(75 kg—165¼ lb)					
Snatch	162.5	358	Viktor Doumev (USSR)	USSR	July 25, 1982
Jerk	206.5	455¼	Yanko Rusev (Bulgaria)	Bulgaria	May 8, 1982
Total	360	793½	Asen Zlatev (Bulgaria)	USSR	July 24, 1980
	360	793½	Yanko Rusev (Bulgaria)	France	Sept 16, 1981
Light-Heavyweight					
(82.5 kg—181¾ lb)					
Snatch	179	394½	Ismail Arsamakov (USSR)	USSR	May 21, 1982
Jerk	223.5	492½	Aleksandr Pervi (USSR)	USSR	Mar 5, 1982
Total	400	881¾	Yurik Vardanyan (USSR)	USSR	July 26, 1980
Middle-Heavyweight					
(90 kg—198¼ lb)					
Snatch	190	418¾	Yurik Vardanyan (USSR)	USSR	May 21, 1982
Jerk	228	502½	Yurik Vardanyan (USSR)	USSR	May 21, 1982
Total	415	914¾	Yurik Vardanyan (USSR)	USSR	May 21, 1982
(100 kg—220½ lb)					
Snatch	195	429¾	Yuri Zakharevich (USSR)	USSR	May 22, 1982
Jerk	237.5	523½	Viktor Sots (USSR)	USSR	May 22, 1982
Total	430	947¾	Yuri Zakharevich (USSR)	USSR	May 22, 1982
Heavyweight					
(110 kg—242½ lb)					
Snatch	193	425	Leonid Taranenko (USSR)	USSR	Dec 22, 1981
Jerk	241	531¼	Aleksandr Borissenok (USSR)	USSR	May 23, 1982
Total	427.5	942¼	Leonid Taranenko (USSR)	USSR	Dec 22, 1981
Super-Heavyweight					
(Over 110 kg—242½ lb)					
Snatch	202.5	446¼	Anatoli Pisarenko (USSR)	USSR	May 23, 1982
Jerk	258.5	569¼	Anatoli Pisarenko (USSR)	USSR	May 23, 1982
Total	457.5	1,008½	Anatoli Pisarenko (USSR)	USSR	May 23, 1982

PICKUP: Anatoli Pisarenko has emerged as the successor to Vasili Alexeyev as the dominating lifter in the super-heavyweight class. Pisarenko has, for the first time, brought the record for the total over 1,000 lb. (All-Sport)

(weighing 195 lb) at Columbus, Ga, in Jan 1981. The official record for the three-lift total is 1,267 lb by Bev Francis (b Feb 15, 1955) (Australia) at Honolulu, Hawaii, on May 12, 1981.

A dead lift record of 4,702,646.25 lb in 24 hours was set by a team of ten at the Darwin Weightlifting Club, Darwin, England, Aug 14–15, 1981.

Most Olympic Medals

Winner of most Olympic medals is Norbert Schemansky (US) with 4: gold, middle-heavyweight 1952; silver, heavyweight 1948; bronze, heavyweight 1960 and 1964.

Most World Titles

The most world title wins, including Olympic Games, is 8 by John Davis (US) (b Jan 12, 1921) in 1938, 46–52; by Tommy Kono (US) (b June 27, 1930) in 1952-9; and by Vasili Alexeyev (USSR) (b Jan 7, 1942) 1970-7.

WRESTLING

Earliest References

The earliest depictions of wrestling holds and falls on wall plaques and a statue indicate that organized wrestling dates from *c.* 2750–2600 BC. It was the most popular sport in the ancient Olympic Games and victors were recorded from 708 BC. The Greco-Roman style is of French origin and arose about 1860. The International Amateur Wrestling Federation (FILA) was founded in 1912.

Best Records

In international competition, Osamu Watanabe (b Oct 21, 1940) (Japan), the 1964 Olympic freestyle featherweight champion, was unbeaten and unscored-upon in 187 consecutive matches.

Wade Schalles (US) has won 668 bouts from 1964 to 1980.

Most World Championships

The greatest number of world championships won by a wrestler is 10 by the freestyler Aleksandr Medved (USSR), with the light-heavyweight titles in 1964 (Olympic) and 66, the heavyweight 1967 and 68 (Olympic), and the super-heavyweight title 1969, 70, 71 and 72 (Olympic). The only wrestler to win the same title in 7 successive years has been Valeriy Rezantsev (b Feb 2, 1947) (USSR) in the Greco-Roman light-heavyweight class, 1970–76, including the Olympic Games of 1972 and 1976.

Most Olympic Titles

Three wrestlers have won three Olympic titles. They are: Carl Westergren (1895–1958) (Sweden) in 1920, 24 and 32; Ivar Johansson (1903–79) (Sweden) in 1932 (two) and 36; and Aleksandr Medved (b Sept 16, 1937) (USSR) in 1964, 68 and 72.

The only wrestler with more medals is Imre Polyak (b Apr 16, 1932) (Hungary) who won the silver medal for the Greco-Roman featherweight in 1952, 56 and 60, and the gold in 1964.

Longest Bout

The longest recorded bout was one of 11 hours 40 min between Martin Klein (Estonia, representing Russia) and Alpo Asikáinen (Finland) in the Greco-Roman middleweight "A" event for the silver medal in the 1912 Olympic Games in Stockholm, Sweden. Klein won.

Heaviest Heavyweight

The heaviest wrestler in Olympic history is Chris Taylor (1950–79), bronze medallist in the super-heavyweight class in 1972, who stood 6 ft 5 in tall and weighed over 420 lb.

Sumo Wrestling

The sport's origins in Japan certainly date from *c.* 23 BC. The heaviest ever *sumotori* is Kazuhisa Shiki, *alias* Genkaiho (now named Rinho), who in 1981, at a height of 5 ft 9½ in, attained 447.6 lb. Weight is amassed by overeating a high protein stew called *chankonabe.*

The most successful wrestlers have been Koki Naya (b 1940), *alias* Taiho ("Great Bird"), who won 32 Emperor's Cups until his retirement in 1971; Sa-daji Akiyoshi (b 1912), *alias* Futabayama, who won 69 consecutive bouts in the 1930's; and the *ozeki* Torokichi, *alias* Raiden, who in 21 years (1789–1810) won 240 bouts and lost only 10 for the highest ever winning percentage of .962.

BIG FIGHTS: Hawaiian-born Jesse Kuhaulua, the first non-Japanese to win an official sumo wrestling tournament, here takes on two US Marines in a charity exhibition. (John Topham Picture Library)

The youngest of the 58 men to attain the rank of *Yokozuna* (Grand Champion) was Toshimitsu Obata, *alias* Kitanoumi, in July 1974, aged 21 years 2 months. He set a record in 1978 winning 82 of the 90 bouts that top *rikishi* fight annually. Hawaiian-born Jesse Kuhaulua (b June 16, 1944), now a Japanese citizen named Daigoro Watanabe, *alias* Taka-miyama, was the first non-Japanese to win an official tournament in July 1972 and in 1981 set a record of 1,232 consecutive top division bouts.

YACHTING

Origin

Yachting in England dates from the £100 stake race between King Charles II of England and his brother, James, Duke of York, on the Thames River, on Sept 1, 1661, over 23 miles, from Greenwich to Gravesend. The earliest club is the Royal Cork Yacht Club (formerly the Cork Harbour Water Club), established in Ireland in 1720. The word "yacht" is from the Dutch, meaning to hunt or chase.

Highest Speed

The official world sailing speed record is 36.04 knots (41.50 mph) achieved by the 73½-ft *Crossbow II* over a 500-m (547-yd) course off Portland Harbor, Dorset, England, on Nov 17, 1980. The vessel, which had a sail area of 1,400 sq ft, was designed by Rod McAlpine-Downie and owned and steered by Timothy Colman. In an unsuccessful attempt on the record in Oct 1978, *Crossbow II* is reported to have momentarily attained a speed of 45 knots (51 mph).

The fastest 24-hour single-handed run by a sailing yacht was recorded by Nick Keig (b June 13, 1936), of the Isle of Man, who covered 340 nautical miles in a 37½-ft trimaran, *Three Legs of Mann I,* during the Falmouth to Punta, Azores, race, June 9–10, 1975, averaging 14.16 knots (16.30 mph). The fastest bursts of speed reached were about 25 knots (28.78 mph).

Longest Race

The longest regular sailing race is the quadrennial Whitbread Round the World race (instituted Aug 1973) organized by the Royal Naval Sailing Association. The distance is 26,180 nautical miles from Portsmouth, England, and return with stops and re-starts at Cape Town, Auckland and Mar del Plata. The record (sailing) time is 120 days 6 hours 35 min by *Flyer* crewed by Cornelius van Rietschoten (Netherlands), finishing on Mar 29, 1982.

Most Competitors

1,261 sailing boats started the 233-mile Round Zealand (Denmark) race in June 1976 over a course of 233 miles.

Most Successful

The most successful racing yacht in history was the British Royal Yacht *Britannia* (1893–1935), owned by King Edward VII while Prince of Wales, and subsequently by King George V, which won 231 races in 625 starts.

America's Cup

The America's Cup was originally won as an outright prize by the schooner *America* on Aug 22, 1851, at Cowes, England, but was later offered by the NY Yacht Club as a challenge trophy. On Aug 8, 1870, J. Ashbury's *Cambria* (GB) failed to capture the trophy from the *Magic*, owned by F. Osgood (US). Since then the Cup has been challenged by GB in 16 contests, by Canada in 2 contests, and by Australia 6 times, but the US holders have never been defeated, winning 77 races and losing only 8. The closest race ever was the fourth race of the 1962 series, when the 12-m sloop *Weatherly* beat her Australian challenger *Gretel* by about 3½ lengths (75 yd), a margin of only 26 sec, on Sept 22, 1962. The fastest time ever recorded by a 12-m boat for the triangular course of 24 miles is 2 hours 46 min 58 sec by *Gretel* in 1962.

Olympic Victories

The first sportsman ever to win individual gold medals in four successive Olympic Games was Paul B. Elvström (b Feb 24, 1928) (Denmark) in the Firefly class in 1948 and the Finn class in 1952, 56 and 60. He has also won 8 other world titles in a total of 6 classes.

The lowest number of penalty points by the winner of any class in an Olympic regatta is 3 points (6 wins [1 disqualified] and 1 second in 7 starts) by *Superdocious* of the Flying Dutchman class sailed by Lt Rodney Stuart Pattison (b Aug 5, 1943), British Royal Navy, and Ian Somerled Macdonald-Smith (b July 3, 1945), in Acapulco Bay, Mexico, in Oct 1968.

WIND BAG: The coveted America's Cup trophy has never been captured by a non-US boat in the best-of-seven series off of Newport, RI. (AP)

Admiral's Cup

The ocean racing series to have attracted the largest number of participating nations (three boats allowed to each nation) is the Admiral's Cup held by the Royal Ocean Racing Club in the English Channel in alternate years. Up to 1981, Britain had won 8 times. A record 19 nations competed in the 1975, 77 and 79 competitions.

Largest Marina

The largest marina in the world is that of Marina Del Rey, Los Angeles, Calif, which has 7,500 berths.

Boardsailing (Windsurfing)

The record speed for boardsailing, often termed windsurfing, is 24.63 knots (28.36 mph) by Jaap van der Rest (Netherlands) at Maalaea Bay, Maui, Hawaii on July 18, 1980.

NEWLY VERIFIED RECORDS

The following pages include records which were received and verified too late to be included in the main sections of this book.

Oldest Man (p 16). China solemnly announced on July 29, 1982 that census takers had unearthed a Lan Buping in Guangxi Region, whose birthdate was said to be Apr 13, 1848.

Oldest Quadruplets (p 21). The Ottman quads of Munich, W Germany, born on May 5, 1912, were still alive in Aug 1982.

Heaviest Baby (p 23). Tying the record, a boy was delivered by Caesarean section weighing 22 lb 8 oz on May 24, 1982, at Sipetu Hospital, Transkei, S Africa.

Motionlessness (p 40). William A. Fuqua of Corpus Christi, Tex, before a crowd of 4,000 in the Gallery and Mall, Glendale, Calif, remained motionless for 8 hours 35 min, and then after a 4-min rest break remained motionless for a further 1 hour 31 min.

g Forces (p 40). A land diver of Pentecost Island, New Hebrides, dived from a platform 81 ft 3 in up on May 15, 1982. The body speed was 50 ft/sec, and the force was in excess of 110 g.

Rarest Dog (p 61). "Iskut" died on Apr 20, 1982, and 2 of the bitches have been put to sleep.

Most Valuable Dogs (p 62). A Belfast bookmaker, Alf McLean, reportedly paid more than £40,000 ($72,000) for "Indian Joe," winner of the 50th Greyhound Derby, whelped in Sept 1977.

Heaviest Cat (p 65). A weight of 45 lb 10 oz was recorded on June 23, 1982, for a 6-year-old male tabby named "Himmy," owned by Thomas Vyse of Cairns, Australia. His measurements are neck 15 in, waist 32 in, length 38 in.

Smallest Starfish (p 84). The recently described *Asterina phylactica* found in the Adriatic and Mediterranean, does not exceed 0.58 in in diameter.

Dahlia (p 101). An 11-ft-10-in example was grown by F. Wentzel of Fort Victoria, Zimbabwe in 1982.

Zucchini (p 101). M.M. Ricci of Montreal, Canada, grew a zucchini that weighed 36 lb 3 oz and was 29½ in long.

Champagne Cork Flight (p 146). A distance of 105 ft 9 in was achieved by Peter Kirby at Idlewild Park, Reno, Nev on July 4, 1981.

Most Expensive Photograph (p 153). Ansel Adams' *Moonrise*, taken in New Mexico in 1944, was sold for $71,500 at auction in Feb 1981.

Rubik's Cubism (p 155). Minh Thai, 16, a Vietnamese refugee won the world championship held in Budapest, Hungary, on June 5, 1982, with a winning time of 22.95 sec from a standardized dislocation.

Largest Poster (p 162). A poster 929 ft 7½ in long and 1 meter (39.37 in) tall was exhibited at the University of Lund (Sweden) Carnival, May 21–23, 1982.

Largest Mural (p 165). A ground painting covering an area of 142,000 sq ft was completed by the Ottawa High School Art Dept, at the Hillcrest Drive-In Theatre, Ottawa, Canada, on Mar 27, 1982.

Longest Palindrome (p 168). Edward Benbow has now extended his palindrome to 44,444 words.

Smallest Violin (photo on p 182). Michael Roman of Somerset, Pa, in 1981, at age 65, made a 1-in-long violin that is playable and can be heard by the human ear without amplification. He had to make 7 hollow shapes before he had one that resounded, 27 pegs to get 4 good ones, and 7 tails to get one.

Highest TV Ad (p 202). The rate for 30 sec on Super Bowl XVII will be $400,000, it was announced by NBC.

Highest Box Office Gross (p 205). *Star Trek II* grossed $14,347,221 in 1,621 theatres on its opening weekend, June 4–6, 1982. The greatest opening month (25 days starting June 11, 1982) was $86.9 million for Steven Spielberg's *E.T.* in 1,323 theatres in the US.

Most Expensive Homes (p 219). Kenstead Hall, London, the residence of the late king of Saudi Arabia has been put on the market for £16 million ($28,800,000).

Largest Car (p 246). Of "altered" cars, the longest is a 6-wheeled 1927 Cadillac chassis 41 ft 7 in long.

Largest Airliners (p 258). A Boeing 747 flew from Hong Kong to Oakland, Calif on Feb 27, 1982 with 610 passengers.

Autogyros (p 264). Wallis reached a new record altitude of 18,253 ft in his WA-121 on Aug 3, 1982.

Computers (p 271). In a demonstration run at Control Data Corp's Cybernet Center, Arden Hills, Minn on June 3, 1982, the Cyber 205 attained 397,950,224 calculations in one sec.

NY Stock Exchange Sales (p 280). A record number of shares, 137,330,000, were traded on Aug 26, 1982. The Dow-Jones Index climbed a record 38.81 points on Aug 17, 1982.

Thinnest TV Set (p 282). Screen is 1.9 in, not 0.19.

Largest Hamburger

Cigarette Cards (p 284). A Honus Wagner American Tobacco Co card was sold for $25,000 in Dec 1981 in NYC.

Most Densely Populated (p 296). Monaco's latest figures (mid-1981) are a population of 27,000 in 470 acres, giving a density of 36,765 per sq mi.

Longest Reigns (p 301). King Sobhuza II of Swaziland died on Aug 21, 1982, ending his reign of 82 years.

Defamation Suit (p 312). *Penthouse* was cleared of libel in May 1982, but later the judge demanded a new verdict for part of the case.

Most Durable Judge (p 313). Judge J. Frank Graff died on Nov 2, 1981, after 58 years 10 months 1 day continuous service on the bench.

Biggest Barbecue (p 325). 46,000 chicken halves were barbecued for 19,000 people by Ernie Morgado at Iolani School, Honolulu, Hawaii, on Jan 31, 1981.

Largest Hamburger (p 325). A weight of 3,591 lb was registered for a hamburger 16 ft in diameter and 2½ in thick, made by the Community Club of Rutland, ND.

Biggest Round of Drinks (p 326). Paul Deer of U-Zoo & Co., Atlanta, Ga, treated 1,501 customers to a free round of drinks on July 14, 1982.

Longest Pastry (p 326). A flaky pastry filled with almond paste, called a "Dutch Letter," 1,233 ft in length was baked by Jaarsma Bakery, Pella, Iowa, July 2, 1981.

Round-the-World N-S (p 344). The first to go via both poles, a British expedition of two, Sir Ranulph Twisleton-Wykeham Fiennes and Charles Burton (GB), made the journey of 35,000 mi in just under 3 years. They crossed the Antarctic in open snowmobiles and were the first to cross the 9,000-ft-high Scott Glacier.

Most Expensive Wedding (p 348). In Haiti, the wedding reception of Jean-Claude Duvalier and Michele Bennet at the Croix de Banquets Presidential Ranch on May 27, 1980 is reported to have cost the Haiti National Treasury more than US $1 million.

Transatlantic Crossing W-E (p 352). Twice between Aug 12 and Aug 29, 1982, a boat of less than 10 ft set a record. Tom McClean (Ireland) first made the crossing in a 9-ft-9-in boat in 50 days, then Bill

Dunlop (US) sailed his 9-ft-1-in boat across in 78 days.

Bell Ringing (p 357). The 12 Handbell Ringers of Ecclesfield School, Sheffield, England, completed a marathon of 52 hours 9 min July 17–19, 1982.

Boomerang Throwing (p 357). Peter Ruhf, under US rules, set an out-and-return record of 375 ft at Randwick, Sydney, Australia, on June 28, 1982.

Dancing, Disco (p 362). John Sharples of Preston, England, danced 371 hours Jan 18–Feb 3, 1982.

Karate (p 370). Fifteen members of the Black Leopard Karate School demolished a 7-room wooden farmhouse in Alberta, Canada, in 3 hours 18 min by foot and empty hand on June 13, 1982.

Piano Playing (p 378). David Scott played 1,218 hours (50 days 18 hours) May 7–June 27, 1982, at Wagga Wagga Leagues Football Club, Australia.

Pogo Stick Jumping

Pogo Stick Jumping (p 378). Michael Barban of St Louis, Mo, jumped 122,171 times in 15 hours 26 min on Feb 13, 1982.

Talking (p 385). Gyles Brandreth broke his own record for a marathon after-dinner speech by talking for 12 hours 40 min on Apr 3–4, 1982 at the London Embassy Hotel, England.

Whistling Loudest (new category). Stephen West achieved 117 decibels at Blues Point, Sydney, Australia on June 26, 1982.

Auto Racing: Pike's Peak Race (p 408). In the

1979 race Dick Dodge set a record time of 11 min 54.18 sec in a Chevrolet-powered Wells Coyote.

Baseball: Base Running (p 415). By Aug 29, 1982, Rickey Henderson had stolen 122 bases—already a major league record for one season—with 31 games remaining in the season.

Bowling: Largest Bowling Center (p 423). Fukuyana Bowl, Osaka, Japan, with 144 lanes.

Canoeing: Olympic and World Titles (p 432). Vladimir Parfenovich (USSR) won 11 world titles from 1979 to 1982, including his 3 Olympic wins.

Gymnastics: Push-Ups (p 467). Colin Hewick, 23, did 10,029 consecutive push-ups at the South Holderness Sports Centre, Humberside, England, on July 18, 1982.

Powerboat Racing: Longest Jump (p 487). The longest boat jump on to land is 172 ft by Norm Bagvie (NZ) from the Shotover River on July 1, 1982, in the 1½-ton jetboat *Valvdene*.

Skiing Endurance (p 494). Two claims are awaiting verification—one for 102 hours by **Rob Smith** and **Harry Slutter** and the other for 121 hours.

Swimming: Men's World Records (p 502). Steve Lundquist (US) broke his own record in the 100-meter breaststroke with a time of 1 min 2.53 sec at Indianapolis on Aug 21, 1982.

Talking

INDEX

Chevrotain 55, 57
Chickens 71, ranch 291, plucking 293, eating 390
Children, see Motherhood
Chimneys 212, demolished 230
Chimpanzees 53
Chinning the bar 466
Chocolate, factory 275, Easter egg 325
Choirs 184, 381
Chorus line 196
Christianity, see Religions
Christian names 170, 171
Christmas, tree 104, cards 180, party 374
Churches 335
Cigarettes 284, plant 279, cards, lighter 284
Cigars 284
Cinema, see Motion pictures
Circle, unsupported 369
Circuits, motorcycle 479
Circulation, newspaper, periodical 179
Circumnavigation, automobile, truck 246, amphibious vehicle 248, flight 256, 257, 260, 344, marine 349
Circum-polar flight 258
Circuses 219, 359–61, fire toll 339
Cities 297, 298, 299
Civil war 305
Clams 44, 90, 92, eating 390
Clapping 358
Clay pigeon shooting 490
Clergy 334
Cliffs 124
Climate, see Weather
Climbing, cat 66, stairs 382, 383, trees 386, rope 466, mountain 480–81
Clocks 270–71
Closest victories, Olympic Games 493, 501
Cloth 285
Clouds 127
Clover 101
Club swinging 358
Clydesdale horses 60, 61
Coaches, football 442, 443, soccer 496
Coal, mine 236, bag carrying, shoveling 358
Coasters, beer 283
Coastline 295
Cobra 76
Cockatoo 68
Codifier, boxing rules 426
Coffee 323
Coffin, gold 286
Coincidental birth dates 24
Coins 320, 322, balancing, snatching 358
Cold 126, 127, 155
Collard 98
Collections, teeth 31, bottles, liquors 145–46, beer cans and coasters 283, cigar bands, cigarettes, cigarette cards 284, cigarette packets, credit cards, 285, matchbox labels 287, post cards 288, coins 320, stamps 331–32
Colleges 333
Collision, ship 240
Colony 295
Color, sensitivity 31, blindness 31
Columns 228–29, cave 123, monumental 230
Coma 35

Comets 130, 132, 134
Comic strips 177
Commerce 272–81
Commercials 201; see also Advertising
Communications 330–31, 332
Communist parties 304
Community garden 292
Companies, see Commerce
Compensation, legal 312
Competitors, Olympic 482
Complaints, successful 358
Composers 186, 187, popular 189–90, hymnists 191
Computers 271, human 28, 29, company 275, fraud 318
Concerts 184
Conchs 90, 92
Concrete structure 225
Condors 67, 68, 69
Conga dancing 362
Consecutive, holes-in-one 464, hockey games 470, Olympic titles 482, 483
Consonants 167
Constellations 137
Contest winnings 358
Continents 115
Contracts, television 201, breach of 311, sports 400
Contrived names 171
Conveyor belt 268
Cooling tower 212
Copper mines 235
Cork flight, champagne 146
Corn 292, 293
Coronation robe 285
Corporations, see Commerce
Correspondence 178
Countries 295–96, 298, 299, 311, 319, in 24 hours 252
Couples 9, 14, married 353
Coups d'état 304
Court trials 311–12
Covered bridge 224
Cow 294
Coypu 54
Crabs 86
Cranes (mechanical) 268
Craters 109, 130, 131, 133
Crawling 358
Credit cards 285
Crematorium 228
Cribbage 453
Crime and punishment 313–18
Criminal, lawyer 313, organization 314
Criticism, theatre 195
Crocodiles 73, 339, prehistoric 96
Crop yields 292
Cross-country running 432–33
Crossword, puzzles 180, game (Scrabble) 456
Crowded cities 296, 299
Crowds 338, sports 400, 482, 485, 496, 508
Crustaceans 86
Cucumber 98, 99, slicing 358
Curling 433–34
Currency 319–20, 321, forgery 318
Currents 113, electric 156
Curtain calls 362
Curtains 285
Cut, canal 225
Cut, finest 158
Cycling 250–51, 399, 434–36

Dahlia 101
Daisy chain 102
Damages 311–12
Dams 225–26, 339
Dance band 365
Dancing 362, 363, 365
Darts 453–54
Davis Cup 507
Day's run under sail 238
Dead heats (horse racing) 475
Dead Sea Scrolls 176
Death, leading cause 34, alcoholic poisoning 35, snakebite 76, earthquake 108, space flight 140, rate, infant 300, row 315, accidents and disasters 339–40
Debt, national, foreign 319
Decorations 305, 396–97
Deer 54–57, 55
Defamation suits 312
Defense spending 306
Degrees, honorary 397
Delta 119
Deltiology 288
Demolitions 230
Demonstrations 338
Density 150, population 296, 297, 298, 299
Dentists 31, 301
Dentition 31
Department stores 275–76
Deposits, bank 281
Depressions 118
Depth, whales 45, pinnipeds 50, bird 68, fish 83, 84, crustacean 86, sponge 93, roots 102, ocean 111, 112, depression 118, lake 120, 121, caves, canyons 123, drilling 234, 348, mining 235, 348, submarines 239, subway, 253, diving 346, 347, salvage 347
Descendants 19
Descent, whales 45, pinnipeds 50, diving 346, 347, ocean 346, 347, parachute 376, 377, skiing 494
Desert 123–24
Destroyer 239
Detectable sound 32
Diamonds 149, 150, 151
Diary 178
Dictionaries 176
Diesel-engined car 242
Dik-dik 54
Dinosaurs 93–94, 95
Director, movie 206
Directories, tearing telephone 331
Disasters 339–40, sports 400
Disco dancing 362
Discs, see Records
Diseases 32, 34
Disguises 196
Dish, food 326
Dish telescopes 146
Distance, frisbee throwing 454–55, 24-hour run 517, lifetime running 518, water skiing 521
Distilleries 276
Diving, animal 45, 50, bird 68, depth 346, 347, salvage by 347, high 363, 365, shallow 365; see also Swimming
Divorces 300, 312, 348, 353
Doctors 301
Document 172
Dogs 61–65, 66, 290
Dolls 285

534

Foods and drinks 323–27, abstinence from 39, consumption 323–27, 389–90
Football 441–48, stadium 219
Foot races 510–18, 519–20
Footstep, moon 131
Foreign aid 318
Forest 97
Forgery, currency 318
Forging 269
Forts 215
Fossils, animal 93–96, plant 97
Fountain 229, champagne 358
Fowl, see Birds
Frankfurters, eating 390, 391
Frauds 318
Free throw ace 421
Freight train 252
Frequency 156
Fresh water 324
Freshwater casting 440–41
Friction 156
Frisbee 454–55
Frogs 78, 79, 80
Frontiers 295–96
Fruits, 98, 99, 324
Fuel economy, cars 244, 245
Fumble recovery 448
Funeral 338, dog 65
Fungi 106
Furnace, blast 267
Furniture 286
Furs 58

Gaining weight 13
Galaxies 137–38
Galleries 162
Gambling 449–50
Game preserve 107
Games and pastimes 451–56
Gang murders 315
Garages 212
Garbage dump 230
Garden, community 292
Garlic 98
Gas, flare, tank 234, deposits 235, pipeline 269
Gasoline consumption, car 244, 245
Gastropods 90, 92
Gauges, railroad 252
Geckos 75
Geese 72
Gems 149–52
Generators 266
Genocide 314, 339
Gerbils 66, 67
Gestation period, animal 44, mammal 49, literary 176; see also Incubation
Geysers 111
g forces 40, 41, animal 45, bird 67
Gherkins, eating 390
Giantesses 8, 9, 23
Giants 5–9
Ginseng 324
Giraffe 42, 43
Glaciers 119
Gladiatorial combat 366
Gladiolus 101
Glass 286, stained 337
Gliding 457
Globe, revolving 230
Goalkeeping, field hockey 439, soccer 495, 497
Goal-scoring goalie 472

Goaltending, ice hockey 469, 472, 473
Goat 44, 290
Gobies 80
Gold, nuggets 150, mines 235, auction price 286, reserves 319, panning 366
Gold Cup 486
Golden records 208, platinum 207
Goldfish 83
Golf 399, 458–65, shoes 288
Golf ball balancing 366
Googol 154
Goose egg 292
Gorges 123
Gorillas 52, 53
Gourd 98, 99
Government 301–04
Grade, railroad 252
Graham's number 154
Grain elevator 215
Grand Canyon, 123
Grandparents, multiple great- 20
Grand-slam home runs 415
Grand slams, golf 462, tennis 507–08
Grapefruit 98
Grapes, vine 101, vineyard 279, 291, catching 366, eating 390
Grass 105
Grave, site 279, digging 366
Green, golf 459
Greyhound racing 465, valuable dog 62
Grocery stores 277
Gross national product 319
Ground, figures 165, breaking 366
Growth, animal 44, plant 97, tree 104, bamboo, grass 105
Guide dog 62
Guillotinings 315
Guinea pig, 66, 67
Guitars 182, 183, playing 369
Gulf 112
Guns 286, 308–09, 491
Gusher, oil 234
Guts catch 455
Gymnastics 465–67
Gyroplanes 255, 264

Hailstones 126, 128, 340
Hair 30, 31, splitting 369
Hairdressing 369
Halites 118
Hamburgers 325, eating 390, 392
Hammock swinging 369
Hamsters 44, 66
Handball (court) 468
Handicaps, polo 485
Handpumped railcars 253
Hands, hand-to-hand balancing 367, 369, shaking 369, walking on 386, 388
Hand span 187
Handwriting 369
Hangars 212
Hang-gliding 457
Hangings 315
Harbor, artificial 327
Hardness 149
Hares 46, 66
Harmonica 182
Harmsworth Trophy 485, 486
Harness racing 468–69
Hat 286
Hat-trick 471–72
Heads, stag 491
Hearing, human 32, bat, dolphin 54

Heart, stoppages 36, 37, 40, transplants 36, 37
Heat, see Temperature
Heavyweight champ, undefeated 429
Heavyweight title fight, first 429
Hedgehog-tenrecs 44, 57
Hedges 101
Height, human 5–13, animal 42, 43, horse 60, 61
Helicopters 263–64, fatalities 340, stunts 387
Helipad 264
Herds 49
Hiccoughing 35
Hieroglyphs 166
High diving 363, 365
High kicking 362
High scorers, basketball 418–19
Highways 328, 329–30
High wire walking 361, 385–86, 387
Hijacking 318
Hill 118, figure 165
Himalayan ibex 59
Hit by pitches 412
Hitchhiking 369
Hitting streak, consecutive games 414
Hockey 469–72, career 469, roller 488
Holes 159, golf 459
Holes-in-one 464–65
Hollyhock 101
Holoalphabetic sentence 169
Home runs 410, 411, 415, 417
Homicides 314–15
Homophones 169
Honey 89
Honorary degrees 397
Honors 395–98
Hoop rolling 369
Hop field 291
Hopscotch 369
Horns, animal 57
Horseback acrobatics 361
Horse racing 472, 474–76, gambling on 449–50; see also Equestrian sports, Harness racing
Horses 58–61, 290, 294, race 43, 58, 59, 472, 474, 475, carriage driving 358, most valuable 472; see also Horse racing
Hospitals 301
Hotels 215–16, 217, 230, 231, 277, fire toll 339
Hotshot 490–91
House of cards 369
Houses 216, 218, 219
Housing 300
Hovercraft 254, 265
Hula hooping 368, 369
Human, computer 28, 29, isolation 40, 344, -powered ships 237, -powered vehicles 250, 253, -powered flight 264, achievements 341–98, pyramid 360, 361, cannonball 368, 369, chain, chair 369, fly 370
Humidity 124
Hummingbirds 70, 71
Hunger strike 39
Hunting bags 491
Hurricanes 339
Hydroelectric tunnel 227
Hydrofoils 239
Hydroplane 343
Hymns 190–91
Hyperventilation 36

Manuscript 171–72
Maps 180
Marathons, model train 254, band 354, crocheting 358, dance 362, flute 366, guitar, letter-writing, hopscotch, hula hooping 369, kissing 370, merry-go-round ride 373, organ playing 374, piano playing 378, singing 380, 381, typing 386, waiters' 386, 388, badminton 409, basketball 419, bowling 423, curling 434, equestrian 437, field hockey 439, bingo-calling, blackjack play and dealing 449, roulette 450, backgammon, bridge 451, chess, cribbage 453, darts 454, frisbee, Monopoly 455, Scrabble, skateboarding, table football 456, rope jumping 467, ice skating 476, roller skating 488, ski 493, soccer, softball 498, squash 499, table tennis 506, tennis 508, foot racing 516, 517, 518, trampolining 518, volleyball, walking 519, water polo 521
Marble 150
Marches, military 309
Marching band 184, 185
Marina 527
Marine circumnavigation 349
Marine disaster 339
Marine records, circumnavigation 349, transatlantic 350–52, transpacific 352
Market 278
Marlin 82
Marmoset 53
Marriage 348, 353, ages 300, 348
Marsupials 58, 59
Maser beams 159
Mashed potatoes 325
Massacres 313–14
Mass arrest 316
Mass killings 313, poisonings 315
Mass relays 518
Mass suicide 339
Mast, radio, 222
Master Points (bridge) 451
Matadors 431
Matchbox labels 287
Mathematics, human ability at 28, 29
Matter 143
Maze 230
Meanings, word 168
Measurement, time 270
Measures, weight, length 154, time 155, balance 156
Meat 323, eating 390
Mechanic, racing 249
Mechanical world 237–71
Medals, Olympic 402, 404, 419, 422, 431, 432, 435, 437, 438–39, 465–66, 469, 477, 478, 482, 483, 485, 489, 492, 500, 501, 502, 503, 504, 511, 512, 514, 515, 516, 519, 521 523, 525, 527, national distribution 482
Medical insurance 277
Medicine, pill taking, injections 36
Meeting attendance 272
Melons 98, 99
Membership, religious 334
Memory, human 28
Menhir 230
Merchandise, see Stores
Merchandise market 278
Merchant shipping 327
Merger 272

Merry-go-round ride 373
Message in a bottle 373–74
Meteorites 129–30
Meteorological records, see Weather
Meteors 129
Microphone 197
Microscope 158
Midgets 10, 11
Migration, bird 67
Mileage, gasoline 244, 245, car 246, 24-hour run 517, lifetime running 518
Military and defense 305–11
Military awards 396, 397
Milk, yields 292, drinking 390
Milk bottle balancing 374, 375
Milking 292
Millionaires 348, 393–94
Millionairesses 394–95
Millipedes 89
Minaret 336
Mineral water 277
Mines 235–36, 348, disaster 339
Mint 320
Mirages 127
Miser 394–95
Misprints 180
Moats 215
Mobile 164, 165
Model, railways 254, aircraft 265
Modeling 374, 375
Modern pentathlon 478–79
Mollusks 90–92
Monarchs 301–02, 303, 304
Money and finance 318–20
Monkeys 52, 53
Monoliths 115
Monopoly (game) 455
Monorail 254
Monuments 230
Moon 130, 131, 133, landings 131, 133, 140, conquest 341, stay on 342
Moose 54, 55
Morse code 374
Mortality 34, infant 300
Mortars 309
Mortician 279
Mosaic 164, 165
Mosques 335
Mosses 105
Motherhood 19–23
Moths 45, 88, 89
Motionlessness 40, 41
Motion pictures 202–06
Motorcycles 249–50, jumping 374
Motorcycling 479–80
Motor trip 247
Mountaineering 480–81, disaster 340
Mountains 116–18, submarine 112, moon 133
Mount Everest 116, 481
Mouse 49, 54, 66, 67, marsupial 58
Moustaches 30, 31
Movies, see Motion pictures
Movie theatres 202–05
Moving sidewalks 268
Multiple births (livestock) 291
Mummies 19
Muntjac 57
Murals 165
Murder 314–15
Muscles 26, 27
Museums 162, 164

Mushrooms 98, 106, farm 292
Music 180–91; see also Records
Musical chairs 374
Musical instruments 180–84
Musical notes, human voice 31–32, electronic 156, orchestral 184
Musicians 182, 183, 184, 185, 186, 187
Mutiny 310

Nails, bed of 355, 357
Nails, finger 28, 29
Names 118, 137, 169, 170–71
Narcotics hauls 318
NASL records 496–97
National, anthems 190, debt, wealth per capita 319
Natural bridge 120, 122, 123
Natural world 108–28
Naturist resort 231
Navies 306
NBA championships 419
Necks, human 28, 29
Needle threading 374
Neon sign 227
Nerve gas 144
Nests 68
Net, fish 276
Newspapers 179
Newts 79
NFL champions 443
Night clubs 219–20
Nobel Prizes 397–98
No-hit games 417
Noise 156; see also Sound
Non-stop walking 519
Noodle making 374, 376
Northern Lights 130
North Pole conquests 344, 345, 347
Notation, musical 180
Notes, see Musical notes
Novels 172, 174, 175, 176
Nuclear, particles 143, cooling tower, power plant 212, arsenal 306, 310
Nudist camp 231
Nuggets, gold 150
Numbers, see Numeration
Numeration 154–55
Nutria 54
Nuts, see Peanuts
Nuts (mechanical) 269
Nylon 287

Obelisks 231
Observatories 146, 147, 148
Oceanaria 107
Oceans 111–15, descent 347
Octopus 90, 91
Office, term of 303
Office buildings 212
Officials, sports 400
Offshore oil plant disaster 340
Oil, fields, gusher, spill, platforms 234, tanks 269, company, refinery 277
Oil plant disaster, offshore 340
Okra 98
Olympic Games 401, 402, 403, 404, 419, 422, 431, 432, 434, 435, 437, 438–39, 465–66, 469, 472, 477, 478, 479, 481–83, 485, 489, 492, 493, 497, 500, 501, 502, 503, 504, 511, 512, 514, 515, 516, 519, 521, 523, 525, 527
Olympic medals, see Medals
Olympic titles, consecutive 482, 483
Omelets 325, making 374

One-man band 354, 355
One-man concerts, attendance 184, 185,
  price 185, 188
One-man shows 193, 195
Onions 98, peeling 374, eating pickled
  390
Opal 150
Open pit 236
Opera 188, houses 186, 188
Operations 36, 39
Opossums 49
Orange 98
Orangutan 52, 53
Orbit, moon 130, earth, solar system
  133, planets 134–35, satellites, man
  140–41, woman 341, 342
Orbiter, space shuttle 260
Orchestras 184
Orchids 100, 105
Organized crime 314
Organs 183, playing 374
Organ transplants, see Transplants
Origins of man 15–16
Oryx 44, 54
Oscars 203, 204, 206
Ostriches 67, 68, 70, 71, 72
Otters, sea 46, 58
Overdue book 179
Ox, eating whole 390
Oysters, eating, opening 390

Pacers, see Harness racing
Pacific crossings, see Transpacific
  crossings
Paddle boating 374
Pagodas 336
Painite 150, 152
Paintbrush 162
Painters, see Artists
Paintings 160–62
Palaces 214, 215
Palindromes 168
Pancakes, eating 390, race 517
Panda 42, 43
Pandemic 339
Panic deaths 339
Paper, airplane 265–66, mill 277, writ-
  ing 290
Paperweight 288
Parachute, falls without 377
Parachuting 376, 377, 484, 485, ski 494
Parallel bar dips 466
Park 107
Parking, lot 212, tickets 328, meters 328,
  329
Parkinson's disease 34
Parliament 302
Parrots 68, 72
Parsnip 98
Participants, sports 400, 433, 436, 482
Particle accelerators 159
Particles, sub-nuclear 143
Party giving 374
Passenger liners 238
Passengers, air 262
Passers 444, 445, 446
Passes 329
Pass receivers 447
Pastry 326, 327
Patent, radio 197, television 198, "per-
  petual motion" 267, case 312
Patient, cancer 34, coma 35, iron lung
  36

Pay-out, horse-race 449, slot-machine
  450
Payroll 272
Peanuts 98, 99, eating 390
Pear 98
Pearls 150, 152
Peeling, apple 353, onion 374, potato
  378
Pelota (jai-alai) 399
Pelota (tennis) 507
Penal camps 316
Penalties, hockey 472
Penguins 68
Peninsula 115
Penknife 287
Pen pals 178
Pens 288
Pentathlon, see Modern pentathlon
Penthouse 219
Pepper 98, 99
Per capita income 319
Perfect deals (bridge) 451
Perfect development 26, 27
Perfect dive 504
Perfect games, World Series 416, 417,
  curling 434, softball 498
Perfect numbers 154
Perfect scores (bowling) 423, 424,
  425–26
Performers 193, 194, 195, 196, 200
Perfume 143
Periodicals 179
Permafrost 127
Personal injury damages 311
Personal names 170–71
Petrels 71
Petunia 101
Pharmaceutical company 277
Phillumenist 287
Philodendron 101
Phonograph 207–10
Photographic store 277
Photography 153
Physical extremes 155–59
Physicians 301
Physiology, human 25–41
Pi 154, memorizing 28
Pianists 186, 187
Piano 180, 181, composition 187, play-
  ing, tuning 378
Pickles, eating gherkins, eating pickled
  onions 390
Pier 231, pleasure 220
Pies 325
Piggery 292
Pigs 290, 294
Pikes Peak auto race 408
Pill taking 36
Pilots 262
Pineapple 98
Ping Pong, see Table tennis
Pinnipeds 50, 51
Pipe 288, smoking 378
Pipelines 269
Pistols 288
Piston engines, car 245, 407, aircraft
  261
Pit, open 235, 236
Pitch 32, 54
Pitcher 412
Pit stop 406
Pizza 326, 327
Place names 118, 170
Plague 34, deaths 339

Planetaria 147
Planets 134–36, stellar 137
Plants 97–102
Plateau 118
Plate spinning 378, 379
Platforms, oil 234, railroad 253
Platinum, discs 207, mine 236
Playing cards 288
Playing field 400
Plays 192, 195, 196
Poems 178
Poets laureate 177–78
Pogo stick jumping 378
Poisoning, alcoholic 35, mass 315
Poisons, animal 76, 79, 83, 84, 93, toad-
  stool 106, organism 144
Polar conquests 344, 345, 347
Polar lights 130
Polder 226
Poles, flag 229, totem 233
Pole sitting 378
Police dogs 62
Political and social records 295–304
Political division 295
Polo 485, field 400, water 520–21
Polydipsia 389
Pony 58
Pool (game) 455–56
Pools, swimming 499
Popcorn plant 278
Popes 337
Pop festival 184
Pop group 210
Popsicle 325
Population 296, 297, 298, 299, 300
Porcelain 288
Porcupine 54
Portraits 161, 162, painter 162
Ports 327
Postage stamps 331–32
Postal services 332
Post cards 172, 173, 288
Poster 162, 163
Potato chips, eating 393
Potatoes 98, 292, mashed 325, peeling
  378, eating 393
Pothole, glacial 119
Pot lid 288
Poverty 395, national 319
Power, producers 266–67, lines 270
Powerboat racing 485–87
Power-driven vessels 237
Power plant, solar 267
Precious stones 149–52
Precipitation, see Rainfall
Pregnancies 24
Prehistoric, animals 93–96, rocks 115,
  monuments 230
Press, forging 269
Pressure, barometric 125, 128, physical
  155–56
Primates 15, 52, 53
Prime ministers 303
Prime numbers 154
Printed work 171
Printers 176–77
Printing 171, 172, 175, 176–77, machine
  269, error 331, 332
Prisons 316, sentences 315–16, escapes
  317
Prison term 316
Private houses 216, 218, 219
Prizes, TV 201, contest 358, valuable
  397, Nobel 397–98, golf 464

Second 155
Seeds 100, 102, 105, 144, spitting 382
See-saw 381
Seller, slowest 176
Sentences 169–70
Sermons 381
Service, tennis 508, 510
Sewage, works 215, sewerage tunnel 227
Sex, size difference between sexes 14, 44, ratio 300
Shakespeare's plays 195, TV production 199, 201
Sharks 44, 45, 80, 81, 82, 440, prehistoric 96
Sharpness 158
Shaving 381
Sheaf tossing 381
Sheep 290, 294, wild (Bharal) 46, station 291, shearing 294
Sheet music 189–90
Shellbacks 241
Shellfish, eating 393
Shelling, egg 366
Shells 90, 92
Shipbuilding 278
Shipping, line 278, merchant 327
Ships 237–41, 317
Shipwrecks 237, 241, 339, 340
Shipwreck survival 378
Shock, electric 41
Shoes 288, 289
Shoe shining 381
Shooting 402, 479, 489–91
Shopping centers 278
Shorthand 381
Shot put 512, 513, ambidextrous 516
Shouting 32
Shoveling, coal 358
Showering 381
Shrews 47, 53, 57
Shrimps, eating 393
Shrine 335
Shutouts, baseball 416, hockey 469, 472, 473
Siamese twins 20
Sidewalks, moving 268
Sieges 306, 307
Sight, human 31, bird 68, lines of 118; see also Eye
Signatures, see Autographs
Signs, advertising 227–28
Silence 156, 157, musical 187
Silver 150, mine 235, auction price 289
Simultaneous games, checkers 452, chess 453
Simultaneous titles (boxing) 430, 431
Singers 31–32, 33, 184, 185, 186, 187–88, 207–08, 209, 210; see also Records
Singing, voice range 31–32, 33, marathon 380, 381; see also Songs
Sire, dog 62
Sitting, in unsupported circle 369, pole 378, tree 386
Sit-ups 466
Six-day racer, bicycle 435, on foot 517
Size differences between sexes 14, 44
Skateboarding 456
Skating, ice, figure, speed 476–77, roller 487–88
Skid marks 249
Skiing 491–94; see also Water skiing
Ski lifts 494, disaster 340
Skull 28

Sky-diving 399
Slalom, snow 491, 492, water 521
Sled journey 347
Sleeplessness 40
Slide 220, 221
Slide rule 154, 155
Slimming 14
Slinging (slingshot) 381
Slooow-seller (book) 176
Sloth 46, 47
Slot machines 450
Smell, sense of 45, smelliest substance 143
Smoke-ring blowing 381
Smokers 284, voracious 380, 381
Smokestack demolition 230
Smoking, pipe 378
Snails 46, 90, 92, eating 393
Snakes 75–77, prehistoric 96
Sneezing 35
Snore 36
Snow avalanche 339
Snow construction 232
Snowfall 127
Snowmobiling 494
Snowshoe travel 382
Snow Train, Arctic 246, 247
Snuff box 289
Soccer 400, 494–98, stadium 219
Sofa 286
Softball 498
Soft drinks 279
Solar, eruption 132, telescope 147, 148
Solar-powered airplane 258, 259
Solar power plant 267
Soldiers 307, decorations 396, 397
Somersaults 359, 360, 361, 467, 494
Songs 189–90, 207–10
Song writers 189–90; see also Composers
Sound 32, pitch 32, 65, insects 88, highest note 156, of pop group 210
Sound movie 202
Sounds, speech 167
Southernmost voyage 241
South Pole conquests 344, 345
Space 129–41
Space flight 140–41, 341–42, fatalities 340
Space shuttle 260
Space "walk" 341
Spaghetti, eating 392, 393
Span, hand 187, bridge 222, 223, power line 270
Spas 216
Spear-fishing 441
Special cars 245
Spectating, intensive 414
Speeches 302, 385, listening 382
Speed, talking 32, 33, birds 44, 67, mammal 46, 47, pinniped 50, bat 50–53, tortoise 74, snake, reptile 74, 75, 76, fish 82, 83, spider 85, insect 88, centipede 89, snail 90, protozoan, bacteria 106, glacier 119, jet stream 124, lightning 127, light 129, moon 130, comets 134, planet 135, space vehicle 140, camera 153, solid visible object 159, destroyer 239, land 242, 243, 342–43, 407, reverse driving 248–49, cycle 250, 434–35, rail 251, 254, monorail 254, aircraft 257, 258, 259, 260, 261, 263, 264, in space 342,

(Speed, continued)
water 343, karate chop 370, sky-diving, pelota (jai-alai ball) 399, golf ball 399, 460, tobogganing, lugeing 422, canoeing 432, cycling 434, frisbee 455, gliding 457, greyhound 465, hockey player, hockey puck 472, 473, horses 475, ice skating, ice yachting, sand yachting 478, motorcycle 480, powerboats 485–86, roller skating 488, rowing 488, 489, skiing 492, snowmobile 494, swimming 499–500, 502, 503, table tennis ball 506, tennis ball 508, running humans 511, 512, 514, volley ball 519, water skiing 522, yachts 526, 527
Speed skating (ice) 477
Spellings 170
Spending, defense 306
Spices 324
Spiders 84–85
Spinning 382, plates 378, 379
Spiral staircase 232
Spires 336
Spirits, see Alcoholic beverages
Spitting 382
Spoil dump 236
Sponges 93
Spoon 289
Sports 399–448, 457–528
Sports careers 402, 463–64, 469, 482, 508, 516
Sports competitors, international 402, 495, 507
Sports field 400
Sportsmen 402
Spreading plant 101
Springbok 49
Sprinters, women 514, 515
Square 329
Squash 98
Squash (sport) 498–99
Squid 45, 90, 91
Stadiums 212, 213, 219, 431
Stage 192
Stained glass 337
Stairs 232, climbing 382, 383
Stalactite 123
Stalagmite 123
Stamps, postage 331–32
Standards of living 300–01
Standing up 382
Stanley Cup 469
Starfishes 84, 116
Stars 129, 136–37
Stationary cycling 436
Stations, railroad 253
Statues 232, 396
Stature, variable 10; see also Height
Statutes 311
Steam engines, ship 237, car 241, train 251–52
Steel company 279
Steepness 117
Stellar planets 137
Stibiotantalite 150
Stilt walking 382, 383
Stock car racing 407
Stock exchanges 280, 281
Stockings, nylon 287
Stocks 280, 281
Stones, precious 149–52
Stone-skipping 365

Stores, department 275–76, chain 275, 276, 277, drug 276, grocery 277, photographic 277
Stork 68
Storm toll 339
Stowaway 382
Straits 114–15
Strawberries 98, 324
Streets 328–29, 330
Strength, primate 53, horses 61, dogs 62
Stretcher bearing 385
Strikeouts 416, 417
Strikes 323, hunger 39
Strikes, consecutive (bowling) 423, 424
String ball 384, 385
Stringed instruments 183
Structures 211–36, tallest 222, strongest 226
Students 332, 333
Studio, movie 206
Stuffed bird 283
Stunts and miscellaneous endeavors 353–89
Sturgeon 80, 83
Submarine canyon 123
Submarine depression 118
Submarine drilling 234
Submarine mountain 112
Submarine pipeline 269
Submarine river 119
Submarines 239, fatalities 340, target 396
Submarine tunnels 227
Submergence, unaided 36, 37, bird 68, violin and organ playing 182, 183, longest duration 346, 347, 385
Sub-nuclear particles 143
Subterranean, river 119, lake 120, 121
Subways 253–54, tunnel 227
Sugar 323, beet 101, 292
Sugar mill 279
Suggestion box 385
Suicide 315, mass 339
Suite, hotel 216
Sumo wrestling 526
Sun 133–34, approach to 141
Sundae 326
Sundial 271
Sunfish 80, 84
Sunflower 100, 101
Sunken treasure 320
Sunshine 127
Sunspots 133–34
Super-novae 137
Supersonic flight 258, 259
Surgery 36, 39
Survival, cancer patient 34, in iron lung 36, on raft 378
Suspension bridges 223
Swallowing 36
Swamp 124
Swans 67, 68, 71
Swarm, locust 87, 88
Sweetness 144
Swifts 44, 68
Swimming, birds 68, fish 82, 83, human sport 479, 499–506
Swimming pools 499
Swindle, welfare 318
Swinging 384, 385
Switchboard 331
Sword 289
Swordfish 83

Sword swallowing 36, 37
Symphonies 186, 187
Synagogue 335
Synchrotrons 159

Table 289
Tablecloth 289
Table football 456
Table tennis 402, 506–07
Tailoring 385
Takeoffs, airplane 262
Takeoff weight 258
Take-over 272
Talkative bird 72
Talking 32, 33, 385
Tandem bicycle 250, 251, journey 436
Tanker 240
Tanks, gas 234, oil 269
Tanks (military) 307–08
Tap dancing 365
Tapes, pre-recorded 207
Tapestries 289
Tasmanian wolf 58, 59
Tattoos 38, 39
Taxation 319
Taxi, fleet, fare 248
Tea 323
Teeth 31, decay 34, pulling with 380, 385
Tektites 130
Telephones 330–31
Telescopes 146–48
Telethon 200, 201
Television 198–202
Temperature, 124, 125, 126, 127, human body 35, endured 40–41, mammal 42, 44, bird 44, sea 112, 347, atmosphere, equable, ranges 124, land 125, 127, moon, sun 133, planets 135, man-made, terrestrial 155, flame 156
Temples 335
Temple tower 234
Tennis 507–10, real (royal) 402, 507
Tenrecs 44, 47, 49, 57
Tent 232
Termites 88
Term of office 303
Terrorist killing 314
Test tube baby 24, 25
Text 171
Theatre 191–96
Theatregoers 195
Thefts 317
Thimble 289
Three-legged race 516
Throwing, egg 366, inert object 385, baseball 412
Thunder 128
Thylacine 58
Tickets, parking 328
Tidal power station 266
Tidal river barrier 232
Tidal wave 114
Tides 112–13
Tigers 44, 48, 49, man-eating 340
Tightrope walking 361, 384, 385–86, 387
Time, scale of 15, measure 155, measurer 270, capsule 289, in space 342, 343, on moon 342
Tin mining 236
Tipster, horse-racing 449
Tires 247
Tire supporting 386
Title recaptures (boxing) 429, 430

Toads 78, 79
Toadstool 106
Tobacco company 279
Tobacco spitting 382
Tobogganing 422
Toes 28
Tomato 101
Tomb 233
Tongue-twister 169
"Tonnage" 429
Topaz 150
Tornado toll 340
Tortillas, eating 393
Tortoises 43, 46, 74, prehistoric 96
Totem pole 233
Touchdown, Mr 444, 445
Touch sensitivity 28
Tour de France 399, 400, 435
Touring, cycle 436
Towers 222, free-standing 336
Towing, automobile 249
Towns 299
Toys, manufacturer, store 279
Toy soldier 290
Track and field 510–18
Tracking, dog 65
Tractor 248
Trade unions 320
Traffic 328, 330, lights 329, jam 330
Trail 329
Trailer tour 247
Trainers, dog 65, horse 476
Train robbery 317
Trampolining 518
Trams 254
Trans-America, run 518, walk 520
Transatlantic crossings, radio transmission 197, television 198, ships 238, amphibious vehicle 248, flight 256, 257, 258–61, balloon 264, marine records 350, 351, 352, on airplane wing 370
Trans-Canada, unicycle ride 250, walk 520
Transformer 270
Transmission lines 270
Transpacific crossings, ships 238, 239, amphibious vehicle 248, flight 257, balloon 264, marine records 352
Transplants, heart 36, 37, kidney 39
Transportation 327–30
Trapeze, flying 360, 361
Trap-shooting 490–91
Travel, motor trip 247, countries in 24 hours, rail journey 252, canoe 432
Traveled men 343–44
Treading water 506
Treasure 320, hunter 386
Treaty 303
Tree frogs 79
Trees 102–04, climbing, sitting 386, eating 392, 393
Trencherman 389
Trial 311
Tribes, tallest 10, shortest 13
Tributaries 118, 119
Tricks, water skiing 521
Trick shooting 489–90
Trip, see **Travel**
Triplane 256
Triple Channel crossing 505
Triple Crown 474, 475
Triplets 21, 23
Trotters, see **Harness racing**

Index compiled by Henry W. Engel

GUINNESS
WORLD RECORDS
EXHIBIT HALL

EMPIRE STATE OBSERVATORY tickets are also on sale at the Guinness ticket booth along with EXHIBIT HALL tickets.

A ROYAL VISIT TO NEW YORK'S GUINNESS EXHIBIT HALL: Queen Sofia of Spain (right) and Prince Felipe are watching dominoes tumble on the video screen. The man in the middle is Marvin Reiter, managing director of the Guinness Museums.

ADMISSION
$3.00 general admission
$2.00 for age 12 or under
Family rate—$7.50 for 2 adults and 1 child
$1.50 each additional child
Group rate—Special rates for groups of 10 or more
HOURS: Open daily 9:30 A.M.–6:00 P.M. (July and August to 8:00 P.M.)

543

GUINNESS
Museums
Around
the World

GUINNESS MUSEUMS AROUND THE WORLD

- **Empire State Building**
  New York City
- **Ocean Boulevard**
  Myrtle Beach, S.C.
- **Clifton Hill**
  Niagara Falls, Canada
- **Parkway**
  Gatlinburg, Tenn.
- **Lake of the Ozarks**
  Missouri
- **Fisherman's Wharf**
  San Francisco
- **Tivoli**
  Stockholm, Sweden
- **Fuji Safari Park**
  Gotemba, Japan
- **Linnonmake (Borgbackem)**
  Helsinki, Finland